Civil Society and Democracy

Themes in Politics Series

Themes in Politics series presents essays on important issues in the study of political science and Indian politics. Each volume in the series brings together the most significant articles and debates on an issue, and contains a substantive introduction and bibliography.

Civil Society and Democracy
A Reader

Edited by

CAROLYN M. ELLIOTT

OXFORD
UNIVERSITY PRESS

OXFORD
UNIVERSITY PRESS

YMCA Library Building, Jai Singh Road, New Delhi 110 001

Oxford University Press is a department of the University of Oxford. It furthers the
University's objective of excellence in research, scholarship, and education
by publishing worldwide in

Oxford   New York

Auckland   Bangkok   Buenos Aires   Cape Town   Chennai
Dar es Salaam   Delhi   Hong Kong   Istanbul   Karachi   Kolkata
Kuala Lumpur   Madrid   Melbourne   Mexico City   Mumbai   Nairobi
São Paulo   Shanghai   Taipei   Tokyo   Toronto

Oxford is a registered trade mark of Oxford University Press
in the UK and in certain other countries

Published in India
By Oxford University Press, New Delhi

ISBN 019 566196 6

Typeset by Excellent Laser Typesetters in Garamond (10.5/12)
Printed by Roopak Printers, Delhi 110032
Published by Manzar Khan, Oxford University Press
YMCA Library Building, Jai Singh Road, New Delhi 110 001

PREFACE

This volume seeks to make accessible in India a selection of the best pieces written about civil society published in India and elsewhere. It also makes available selected papers from a conference on Voluntary Action and Civil Society convened by the Indo-American Centre for International Studies (then ASRC) in Hyderabad in December 1998.

The conference drew together two groups of participants who do not often meet in the Indian context—academics and staff of voluntary agencies. Their discussions served to identify themes of particular interest within India and guided the selection of pieces for this volume. Participants queried whether a concept first articulated in the western tradition of political philosophy had relevance to India. Should civil society be understood as including only western-style voluntary associations, or the larger array of groupings in the Indian social environment? Further, does civil society include only the groupings that serve progressive purposes, or should it be understood to include various kinds of non-democratic groupings? That is, how does one think about a civil society that is uncivil?

A second major concern was the relationship between civil society and the state. Since India is in the midst of controversies regarding privatizing some state functions, there was a concern about the politics of the civil society discourse. Is it part of the neo-liberal politics of globalization? Is it necessarily anti-state?

These discussions provided a backdrop for a number of more concrete discussions about the functioning of voluntary associations. With one excellent exception, these concerns are not represented in this volume because they tap into a universe of international literature too vast to represent adequately in combination with the academic literature on civil society.

A major purpose of the volume is to bring together theoretical and empirical materials. While theoretical examination of the concepts of civil society are rich, critical and varied, empirical investigations are only beginning. The materials herein draw from the traditions of both historical analysis and empirical field research. They show that the empirical realities in the west, which is the setting for most of the theorizing about civil society, did not fit the theories any more than realities outside the west fit western-based theory. They suggest that the dynamic question is not differences between east and west, but between theory and experience.

Another purpose of the volume is to place Indian debates on civil society in the perspective of issues arising in other non-western countries. These provide both useful models of analysis and benchmarks for India's political development.

The previously published materials in the volume are drawn largely from refereed academic journals published in the US, Europe, and Australia. Several pieces were published originally in the *Economic and Political Weekly* in India. Wherever an author has published in both a book and a journal, the journal article has been selected. A few materials appeared only as chapters in a book. For reasons of space, all pieces have been edited to consolidate the argument.

I wish to express many thanks to Vijay Mahajan of BASIX in Hyderabad, whose astute advice provided purpose and shape to the conference, and to Rajesh Tandon of PRIA in Delhi for his enthusiastic support of the project.

This volume is dedicated to the memory of Cassie Pyle, long-time director of the Council for the International Exchange of Scholars in Washington, DC which administered the senior Fulbright programme. She was a distinguished creator and leader of international education programmes and a dear friend. This is a tribute to her life's work that fostered civil societies around the globe.

June 2003   CAROLYN M. ELLIOTT

CONTENTS

CONTRIBUTORS

ANDRÉ BÉTEILLE, Professor (retired), Department of Sociology, Delhi School of Economics and Corresponding Fellow of the British Academy, UK.

HANS BLOMKVIST, Associate Professor, Department of Government, University of Uppsala, Sweden.

NEERA CHANDHOKE, Professor, Department of Political Science, Delhi University, India.

PARTHA CHATTERJEE, Director, Centre for the Study of Social Sciences, Kolkata, India.

CAROLYN M. ELLIOTT, Professor Emerita, Department of Political Science, University of Vermont, USA.

NANCY FRASER, Professor, Department of Political Science, New School for Social Research, USA.

DIPANKAR GUPTA, Professor, Centre for the Study of Social Systems, Jawaharlal Nehru University, India.

ROBERT HEFNER, Associate Director, Institute for the Study of Economic Culture, Boston University, USA.

JUDE HOWELL, Fellow, Institute of Development Studies, University of Sussex, UK.

MEHRAN KAMRAVA, Assistant Professor, Department of Political Science, California State University at Northridge, USA.

GURPREET MAHAJAN, Professor, Centre for Political Studies, Jawaharlal Nehru University, India.

FRANK O MORA, Associate Professor, Department of International Studies, Rhodes College, USA.

MARK ROBINSON, Fellow, Institute of Development Studies, University of Sussex, UK.

GARRY RODAN, Associate Professor, School of Politics and International Studies, Murdoch University, Australia.

NANCY ROSENBLUM, Professor, Department of Government; Harvard University, USA.

LLOYD RUDOLPH, Professor Emeritus, Department of Political Science, University of Chicago, USA.

SUSANNE HOEBER RUDOLPH, Professor Emerita, Department of Political Science, University of Chicago, USA.

CHARLES TAYLOR, Professor, Department of Philosophy, McGill University, Montreal, Canada.

ASHUTOSH VARSHNEY, Professor, Department of Political Science, Centre for South Asian Studies, University of Michigan, USA.

MICHAEL WALZER, Professor, School of Social Science, Institute for Advanced Study, Princeton, USA.

GORDON WHITE, Professor (deceased), Institute of Development Studies, University of Sussex, UK.

LAURENCE WHITEHEAD, Official Fellow in Politics, Nuffield College, Oxford, UK.

SHANG XIAOYUAN, Research Fellow, Social Policy Research Centre, University of New South Wales, Australia.

ACKNOWLEDGEMENTS TO THE PUBLISHERS

The publishers wish to thank the following for permission to include articles/extracts in this volume:

Duke University Press for Charles Taylor, 'Modes of Civil Society', *Public Culture*, 3: 1 (1990), pp. 95-7, 99-118.

Dissent magazine and Michael Walzer for 'The Idea of Civil Society', *Dissent*, 38: 2 (1991).

Economic and Political Weekly for Partha Chatterjee, 'Beyond the Nation? or Within?' (4-11 January 1997), pp. 30-4 and for Gurpreet Mahajan, 'Civil Society and its Avatars' (15 May 1999), pp. 1188-96.

MIT Press for Nancy Fraser, 'Rethinking the Public Sphere: A Contribution to the Critique of Actually Existing Democracy', in Craig Calhoun (ed.), *Habermas and the Public Sphere* (1992), pp. 109-42.

Frank Cass Publishers for Lawrence Whitehead, 'Bowling in the Bronx: The Uncivil Interstices Between Civil and Political Society', from Robert Fine and Shirin Rai (eds), *Civil Society* (1997) and for Neera Chandhoke, 'The Civil and Political Society,' from *Democratization*, 8: 2 (2001), pp. 1-24.

Johns Hopkins University Press for Ashutosh Varshney, 'Ethnic Conflict and Civil Society: India and Beyond,' *World Politics*, 53: 3 (2001), pp. 362-98, © Center for International Studies, Princeton University.

Journal of Contemporary Asia for Garry Rodan, 'Civil Society and Other Political Possibilities in Southeast Asia,' 27: 2 (1997).

Social Research for Nancy Rosenblum, 'Civil Societies: Liberalism and the Moral Uses of Pluralism,' 61: 3 (1994), pp. 539-61.

Taylor and Francis for Mehran Kamrava and Frank O. Mora, 'Civil Society and Democratization in Comparative Perspective: Latin America and the Middle East,' in *Third World Quarterly*, 19: 5, pp. 893-916.

Transaction Publishers for Robert Hefner, 'Civil Society: Cultural Possibility of a Modern Ideal in Society,' in *Society*, 34: 2 (1998) pp. 16-28.

1

CIVIL SOCIETY AND DEMOCRACY
A Comparative Review Essay

Carolyn M. Elliott

The Mythic Dimension of Civil Society[1]

The language of 'civil society' burst on the contemporary political scene with the rise of the Solidarity movement in Poland. First articulated by liberals during the transformation of eighteenth-century Europe, the phrase had fallen into disuse during the nine-teenth-century's fascination with the state. In the 1970s, as the communist states began to disintegrate, intellectuals and political activists throughout Eastern Europe invoked the image of civil society to mobilize citizens against repressive states and reclaim a sphere of privacy in social life.[2] In historic liberal terms, dissident leaders asserted their rights to free speech and free association to carve out a social space for their activities. In their enthusiasm for getting the

---

1 John L. and Jean Comaroff, *Civil Society and the Political Imagination in Africa: Critical Perspectives* (Chicago: University of Chicago Press, 1999), p. 4.

2 B. Geremak, 'Civil Society Then and Now,' *Journal of Democracy*, 3 (2), 1992, pp. 3–12. According to Gideon Baker, the movement in its early stage had a much broader conception which included workers' self-management and radical local democracy, not simply a minimal, parliamentary state. Jude Howell and Jenny Pearce (ed.), *Civil Society and Development* (Boulder: Lynn Rienner, 2001), p. 55.

state out of their lives, some called for the virtual uncoupling of society from the state.[3]

The language of civil society was picked up by western intellectuals of various political persuasions to articulate their discomforts with modern society and government. In Western Europe, civil society was conceptualized in opposition to neo-corporatist arrangements that had brought organized labour and its parties into institutionalized patterns of governance but afforded little access to other constituencies.[4] The greens led efforts to open public spaces for new social and cultural organizations. Many were critical of representative democracy itself and suggested civil society as an alternative way of accomplishing collective goals.

Proponents of free market economies saw in civil society a way of arguing for the downsizing of government. They emphasized the capacity of social groups to regulate themselves and care for their own, enabling the return of crucial functions to the private sector.[5] At the margins, neo-liberals portrayed government and society as a zero-sum game, and blamed government interference for disorganizing society. They attributed family disintegration, divorce, and teenage pregnancy to the welfare state.

For communitarians of both the left and the right, civil society enabled articulation of their concerns about community life. Communitarians in western societies are critical of the sole emphasis on individual rights in classical liberalism and look for a political philosophy emphasizing personal responsibility and commitment to the collective good. Citing declining rates of voting and participation in public-spirited work, as well as social disorganization, they worried about lack of civic engagement, declining faith in public institutions, estrangement among citizens, and over-emphasis on the market in social life.[6]

The language of civil society was picked up by people's movements in large parts of the world. Beginning perhaps among the Chinese students in Tienanmen Square, civil society became a kind of

[3] Krishan Kumar, 'Civil Society: An Inquiry into the Usefulness of a Historical Term,' *British Journal of Sociology*, 44, 1993, p. 386.

[4] Bob Edwards and Michael Foley, 'Civil Society and Social Capital Beyond Putnam,' *American Behavioral Scientist*, 42(1), September 1998, p. 125.

[5] For example, Vanourek, Hamilton and Finn, *Is There Life After Big Government: The Potential of Civil Society* (Indianapolis, Ind.: Hudson Institute, 1996).

[6] Jean Elshtain, *Democracy on Trial* (New York: Basic Books, 1995).

'aspirational shorthand' for ideas of equity, participation, and public fairness.[7] In Southeast Asia it has been used by advocates of democracy and civil rights, in Latin America by social movements seeking transformation into a new egalitarian and participatory socio-political order, and in the Middle East by intellectuals opposing repressive regimes. In Africa analysts have noted the capacity of peasants to subvert or defy the predatory state through diverse ways of 'invisible government' embedded in kinship, ritual, and magic.[8] Global society theorists have expressed their frustrations with governments throughout the world by adopting people-centred development as their answer to the state's failure to bring about social and economic transformation.[9]

The image of civil society has had strong resonance among reformers in India. Critics of the developmental state argue for decentralization to local communities or voluntary development groups to serve peoples' needs better. Others, however, are more critical of civil society in India and call for transformation. Alarmed at the rise of fundamentalist Hindu groups and caste-based *senas*, they seek construction of a new civil society based on equality and individual rights.[10] Fundamental to each of these persuasions is belief in the significance of civil society to democratic governance.

While enthusiasm for civil society is not universal in either the west or the third world, the dominant discourses are enamoured with civil society. It has assumed mythic proportions as a tool of the social imagination, an ideological construct for a good society.[11] Its

---

[7] Robert Hefner, 'On the History and Cross-Cultural Possibility of a Democratic Ideal,' in Hefner (ed.), *Democratic Civility* (New Brunswick NJ: Transaction Publisher, 1999), p. 23. Earlier version in this volume.

[8] There are many sources, among them on the Middle East, A. R. Norton (ed.), *Civil Society in the Middle East*, Vols 1 and 2 (Leiden: EF Brill, 1995). On Latin America, Arturo Escobar and Sonia Alvarez (eds), *The Making of Social Movements in Latin America* (Boulder: Westview Press, 1992). On Africa, Robert Fatton, *Predatory Rule: State and Civil Society in Africa* (Boulder: Lynne Rienner, 1992). On Asia, Garry Rodan, 'Civil Society and Other Political Possibilities in Southeast Asia,' *Journal of Contemporary Asia*, 27(2), 1997, pp. 156–8, 60–76. In this volume.

[9] Rajni Kothari, *State Against Democracy: In Search of Humane Governance* (Delhi: Ajanta Publishers, 1988).

[10] Neera Chandhoke, *State and Civil Society* (Delhi: Sage, 1995), pp. 241–8.

[11] Comaroff and Comaroff, p. 24.

proponents see all kinds of benefits, from preserving privacy, empowering citizens for problem-solving and counterbalancing the state to training citizens, deepening participation, and increasing the effectiveness of government. Civil society is an answer to civic estrangement and an emblem of modernization, the new magic bullet for development and democracy.

A concept that promises so much to such widely differing constituencies risks meaning nothing at all. Post-modern observers John and Jean Comaroff suggest civil society's inchoate and polymorphous character is precisely what makes it appealing, but as social ideology, not social analysis.[12] We agree that the concept of civil society has assumed a multitude of different meanings, thus complicating social analysis. The goal of this essay is to reassess the foundations of the concept of civil society and thereby examine its potential for democratizing societies.

We shall begin with a consideration of how the concept of civil society developed in the western tradition of political thought, leading to three different lines of political analysis. We shall then explore its meanings among current political observers and test these out against empirical investigations of civil society. In conclusion, we shall consider guidance offered by these materials for strengthening democratic civil society in India.

The argument we will build is that the relationship between civil society and democracy is inherently political, inseparable from the nature of the state and the political forces arising from society. Further, as in all politics, the relationship is context-specific.[13] It is difficult to identify any general principles that remain viable across all countries, for each case reveals the significance of balances, intersections, and trade-offs. Indeed, we shall find that the questions asked about civil society differ according to the politics of each region, such that American scholars, Europeans, and Indians are framing the issues differently. For American scholars civil society is projected as an answer to anomie, for Europeans as an answer to interventionist government, and India as a possible avenue toward pluralist democracy. Thirdly, contrary to those who see civil society as only a

---

12 Comaroff and Comaroff, p. 8.

13 Sudipta Kaviraj emphasizes the specificity of types of both civil societies and states in his 'In Search of Civil Society,' Kaviraj and Khilnani, *Civil Society* (Cambridge: Cambridge University Press, 2001), p. 318.

western-based concept, we shall find that the cultural resources and historical memories for articulating a conception of civil society are available across the globe. But the development and sustaining of democratic governance based in civil society depends on the contemporary array of values, organizations, and political institutions.[14]

CIVIL SOCIETY IN THE WESTERN TRADITION

Since the concept of civil society was first articulated in the western political theory of liberalism, it is useful to begin by probing its meanings in that literature. Charles Taylor identifies two major traditions, one deriving from John Locke and the other from Montesquieu. Both were looking for ways to limit the potential for despotism of an absolutist state. In John Locke's metaphor, society exists before government. Humans live in a pre-political community under natural law. For the most part they cooperate and respect each other's rights, but they do perceive the need for a common judge and government to protect against troublemakers jeopardizing life and property. Therefore they contract among themselves to establish a government accountable to them, retaining rights to change the government if it steps out of line. From this metaphor come the conceptions of a self-directing society, a limited state and civil society as a source of resistance to the state.[15]

A second lineage is from the eighteenth-century French thinkers, Montesquieu and his disciple Alexis de Tocqueville, the great French observer of early America. Their answer to the problem of limiting the absolutist state was to have a constitution defined in law and protected by a counterbalancing force of independent bodies. For Montesquieu these were the towns and estates of medieval Europe that were wealthy centres of independent activity holding extensive rights. For de Tocqueville they were local associations of citizens 'acting together in the affairs of daily life.'[16] He noted that to sustain limited government in a country such as America, without aristocrats heading compulsory associations of their dependents, citizens had to

14 Hefner, p. 145.

15 Charles Taylor, 'Modes of Civil Society,' *Public Culture*, 3(1), 1990, pp. 95–118. In this volume.

16 Alexis de Tocqueville, *Democracy in America* (New York: Harper and Row, 1969), Vol. II, Part II, ch. 7, p. 521.

come together voluntarily in associations. For de Tocqueville as for Mon-tesquieu, these intermediary associations play a dual role. They have a life in society outside the political structure, but they are also important constituents of the political system, dispersing power and providing a basis for representation of social diversity.

The tension between these two streams of thought provides some of the ambiguity in the current conceptions of civil society and their dangers. From the Lockean tradition comes the emphasis on self-regulation, which at the extreme becomes a dream of eliminating politics. Among the legacies of this tradition are not only limited government, but also notions of either pre-political solidarity, as in the claims of ethnic nationalism, or abandonment of public policy to the invisible hand of the market. From the Montesquieu tradition comes the conception of civil society engaged with politics, educating citizens, facilitating communication, and making government more effective. At the extension of this tradition are the risks of too tight a collaboration between state and privileged associations within civil society, as in corporatism, or protecting associational autonomy at the expense of democracy.[17] The two faces of civil society—self-regulation and providing a counterweight to the state—are present in both traditions, but with different emphases.[18]

Subsequent theorists confronting the problems of capitalist economy developed a third tradition of civil society thought that is critical of liberal formulations.[19] Hegel enlarged the notion of civil society from the liberal emphasis on the market to include social practices distinct from economic life. As the terrain where individuals seek their particular interests, Hegel's civil society is egoist, selfish and fragmented. The interdependence of individuals in modern society carries the seeds of community, as expressed in the range of intermediary associations arising in civil society. Hegel was sceptical, however, about the capacity of individuals to overcome self-serving interests. Lest social life disintegrate into a mere accumulation of private actions,

[17] Dipankar Gupta, 'Civil Society or the State: What Happened to Citizenship?' in Ramachandra Guha and Jonathan Parry (eds), *Institutions and Inequalities* (Delhi: Oxford, 1999). (In this volume).

[18] Michael Foley and Bob Edwards, 'The Paradox of Civil Society,' *Journal of Democracy*, 38(2), 1996, pp. 38–52. Similarly, Chandhoke refers to civil society as 'Janus-Faced.' 'The "Civil" and the "Political" in Civil Society,' *Democratization*, 8(2), Summer 2001. (In this volume, p. 261).

[19] Chandhoke, *State and Civil Society*, ibid., and Kumar, ibid.

he emphasized the need for organizations, law, and an overarching state to integrate individuals into the needs of the community and provide a sphere of freedom within which they could pursue particular interests.

Modern theorist Jurgen Habermas elucidated the critical role of communication in this process of integration. He formulated civil society as a site where public opinion is formed through discourse in which private individuals forge a common understanding about public goals and exercise scrutiny over the state. For this discourse to produce freedom, it must be a deliberative exchange of reasoned arguments, not assertion of inherited ideas or identities, nor assertion of selfish interests. To emphasize this critical distinction, Habermas limited the label of public sphere to that of reason-based solidarity.[20]

Marx and Gramsci reversed Hegel's celebration of the state and saw it instead as an instrument of domination linked in an unholy alliance with bourgeois elements in civil society seeking to protect propertied interests. Marx made a trenchant critique of the illusion of freedom created by the distinction between civil and political society. Gramsci extended understanding of the modes of domination in modern societies by showing how intellectual and cultural organizations create non-violent modes of hegemony. He proposed, however, that civil society could also provide the possibility of liberation, as a terrain where rising social groups may challenge the power of the state and the dominating classes associated with it.

Throughout this tradition, civil society is seen to involve modes of education and negotiation, attitudes of tolerance and other-regarding, patterns of discourse and vehicles of association. Its potential for elitist hegemony or contestation and liberation has divided historical observers, as it divides contemporary commentators. Current commentators assessing the political import of civil society have drawn from the tradition four different conceptions of civil society.

CIVIL SOCIETY AS A SECTOR OF ASSOCIATIONS

Currently the most commonly used definition of civil society is a space between the family and the state where people associate across

[20] Craig Calhoun, 'Civil Society and the Public Sphere,' *Public Culture*, 5, 1993, pp. 267–80.

ties of kinship, aside from the market, and independent of the state.[21] It includes both relatively formal organizations and the informal array of friendships and networks of social life outside the family. It is the arena of community meetings and street corner activity, clubs and churches, *sabha*s and *samaj*s, professional associations and unions, social movements and community action groups. It is both a collection of organizations and the relatively protected space which they occupy.

Purposely missing from this definition is any statement about the purposes or organizational nature of these groups, or how they get along together. One does not assume the groups are concerned with public purposes nor that they are democratically organized. It is not necessarily harmonious, as Marc Robinson argues, and is often a sphere of ideological conflict among groups or against the state.[22]

How is civil society different from society itself? Most modern analysts emphasize the intentional nature of associations. These are not families of birth nor the segmentary communities of medieval society. Medieval communities superimposed political, economic, ritual and other obligations on each other, and allowed neither exit nor other memberships. Ernest Gellner labelled this state of unfreedom a 'tyranny of the cousins.'[23] In this light, traditionally organized tribal groups in the Middle East and Africa cannot be considered participants in a civil society, despite their use of modern modes of communication and economic life.[24] Also excluded are local oligarchies in Central America founded on inherited structures of social exclusivity, despite their rhetoric of market democracy.[25]

[21] This differs from the well-known definition by Cohen and Arato by excluding the family. Jean Cohen and Andrew Arato, *Political Theory and Civil Society* (Cambridge: MIT Press, 1992), p. 18. Others argue the market must be included in conceptions of civil society in order to discern how capitalism shapes the voluntary sector. See Howell and Pearce, p. 80.

[22] Mark Robinson, 'Civil Society and Ideological Contestation,' 2000, in this volume. See also Chandhoke in this volume.

[23] Ernest Gellner, 'The Importance of Being Modular,' John Hall (ed.), *Civil Society: Theory, History, Comparison* (Cambridge UK: Polity Press, 1995), p. 35.

[24] Mustapha Kamel al-Sayyid, 'The Concept of Civil Society and the Arab World,' in Brynen, Korany and Noble (eds), *Political Liberalization in the Arab World*, (1) (Boulder: Lynne Rienner, 1995), p. 137.

[25] Carlos Vilas, 'Prospects for Democratization in a Post-Revolutionary Setting,' *Journal of Latin American Studies*, 28(2), 1996, pp. 474–5.

Since most of the civil society literature has come out of the west, class cleavages are often taken as the model for contestation within civil society, particularly by scholars like Gramsci who are grounded in the Marxist tradition. As Mark Robinson argues, this is not easily transferred to the non-western context where capitalism is not ascendant nor is class the basis of identity.[26] Susanne Rudolph and Lloyd Rudolph argue that caste associations in India are substantially similar to the norms of intentional association featured in civil society analysis. Though membership is limited by caste, the identification of who constitute the caste, and even its name, have changed historically as members mobilized for social and political goals.[27] Caste associations challenge the common sociological distinction between inherited and chosen identities.[28] On the other hand, the apparently voluntary nature of many associations in western experience also carries an inherited dimension. Robert Hefner points out that the associations which form the social pillars of democracy in The Netherlands, a widely appreciated model of civil society pluralism, are religious groups in a society where religious affiliation is largely inherited.[29] On the ground, western society is less secular, less individualistic, and less different from so-called traditional societies than in theoretical models.

A related issue is the inclusion of informal interactions. Western theorists working from modern urban society emphasized the difference between life-sustaining daily interaction and the kinds of public-regarding activities made possible by the organization of formal associations. Ashutosh Varshney points out, however, that in villages of the developing world few such associations exist. The history of popular struggles in the west as well shows that lower class and other marginalized groups not admitted to formal civic space had to form other modes of interaction to exchange views on matters of public concern. He argues that what is crucial to the notion of civil society is that families and individuals connect with other families and

26 Robinson, in this volume.

27 Susanne Hoeber Rudolph, 'Civil Society and the Realm of Freedom,' *Economic and Political Weekly*, 13 May 2000, p. 1767.

28 This distinction was made in Ferdinand Tonnies' concept of gemeinschaft and gesellshaft. See Sudipta Kaviraj's critique of this distinction in relation to India 'In Search of Civil Society,' in Kaviraj and Khilnani (eds), *Civil Society: History and Possibilities* (Cambridge: Cambridge University Press, 2001), p. 304.

29 Hefner, p. 34.

individuals to talk about matters of public relevance without interference of the state.[30]

Whether civil society should be limited to non-state associations
is another definitional issue. Seeking to distinguish civil from political
associations, some have argued that the goal of organizations in civil
society should be seen as the generation of influence, not the conquest
of power.[31] Yet, as Mark Robinson argues, it is frequently difficult
to distinguish between civil and political organizations because the
same or related organizations are active in both sectors. His account
of Hindu politics in India shows how militant nationalists are seeking
to create an ideological hegemony through such civil society institutions as the media, research institutes, youth organizations, and
religious bodies, while also pursuing power through a cadre-based
political party.[32]

Furthermore, in many settings local government displays more of
the qualities of a voluntary association than of the state. While
generally endowed with some measure of authority, local governments often function primarily as lobbies for local interests confronting a hierarchical bureaucracy or vehicles for eliciting voluntary
participation by citizens in collective projects.[33] Similarly, opposition
political parties in systems where they have no hope of gaining power
function more like interest groups than contenders for power. And
on the other hand, as Charles Taylor points out, trade unions and
employers associations in western states often work so closely with
government that distinguishing between government and society no

[30] Ashutosh Varshney, 'Ethnic Conflict and Civil Society,' *World Politics*,
53(3), 2001, p. 362. (In this volume).

[31] Laurence Whitehead, 'Bowling in the Bronx,' Robert Fine and Shirin Rai
(eds), *Civil Society* (London: Frank Cass, 1997), p. 100. (In this volume).

[32] Robinson, in this volume. See also Katzenstein and Kothari's analysis of
the dual strategies of social movements, acting as lobbies and litigants in a civil
society mode versus seeking electoral support in political arenas. Mary Katzenstein,
Smita Kothari, Uday Mehta, 'Social Movement and Politics in India: Institutions,
Interests and Identities in Kohli (ed.) *The Success of India's Democracy* (Cambridge:
Cambridge University Press, 2001), pp. 242–69. Rob Jenkins discusses the
capacities of Indian party leaders to draw on non-party networks for policy
reform in his *Democratic Politics and Economic Reform in India* (Cambridge:
Cambridge University Press, 1999).

[33] James Manor and Richard C. Crook, *Democracy and Decentralization in
South Asia and West Africa* (New York: Cambridge University Press, 1998).

longer describes the dynamics of policy-making.[34] Again, as observed above, the line between state and society is blurry in both west and east. Nonetheless, some measure of autonomy from the center of state authority is a widely accepted criterion of civil society.

A firmer distinction is civil society's relationship to the law. While the impulse of civil society is inclusion, the notion of 'civil' excludes those that act primarily outside the law. Mafia organizations and criminal gangs, guerrilla movements and terrorist cells cannot be considered members of civil society. Not only do they implicitly or explicitly challenge accepted rules that protect civil society space, their use of violence denies the efficacy of discourse that connects civil society associations with each other and the state. Their operations are very different from those of civil disobedience that explicitly reaffirm the need for law while challenging particular laws. Practitioners of civil disobedience make extensive use of discourse to explain what and why they are acting.[35]

Circumstances of severe inequality, however, throw up questions about this distinction. Partha Chatterjee poses the example of squatter communities in Calcutta that live outside the law but conduct their internal affairs almost as models of civil society.[36] These settlements occupy land illegally, receive no police protection, and have no access to city services. Yet they have internally respected mechanisms for solving collective problems and integrating a great diversity of residents. They also have a great need for organizing to make representations to the state, for protection against eviction as well as to secure subsidies and services they formulate as a matter of right. In a society with unequal access to the law and little provision for the poor, emphasizing legality as the baseline criterion of civil society has permitted government on occasion to engage in most uncivil behaviour, such as forcible clearance of slums.

Clearly, as one adapts a concept that arose in one context, the modernizing west, to a much broader array of settings, emphasis should be on what the concept seeks to capture about social reality, not on exact forms. The associational conception of civil society is most useful as referring to the dense array of self-generated, relatively

[34] Taylor, in this volume, p. 44.

[35] Joan Bondurant, *The Conquest of Violence: The Gandhian Philosophy of Conflict* (Berkeley: University of California Press, 1965).

[36] Partha Chatterjee, 'Community in the East,' *Economic and Political Weekly*, 33(6), 1998, p. 277.

sustained patterns of interaction connecting individuals and families, facilitating the articulation of values and advancement of interests.[37]

Benefits of Associational Life

Basically a structural perspective on civil society, the associational analysis envisions no particular teleology, toward development, democracy *or* any other goal.[38] A number of authors believe the very density of associations, apart from their purposes, carries intrinsic benefits for society. Market-oriented analysts have argued that trade unions and co-determination agreements between workers and capitalists draw on the solidarities within civil society to facilitate bargaining and implementation. Francis Fukuyama goes further to argue that civil society is critical in enabling societies to grow firms large enough for competition in global markets. Citing the greater success of Germany and the United States compared to India and China, he argues that the patterns of extra-familial trust (which he calls 'generalized trust') built up in civil society enable capitalist firms to expand beyond the limitations of family ownership.[39]

The benefits of associations for democratic development have attracted the most attention. Looking at American society from the perspective of de Tocqueville, Robert Putnam develops the analysis as follows: associations in civil society allow individuals to express their interests and amplify voices that might not be heard. They provide forums where citizens get information and engage in deliberation over public issues, making their representations more reasoned

[37] Varshney, in this volume, p. 433. There is a lively literature in anthropology contesting the western-based conception of civil society, some arguing that civil society appears in other forms in places such as Africa while others argue the concept is not helpful in understanding many non-western societies. See Chris Hann and Elizabeth Dunn, *Civil Society: Challenging Western Models* (London: Routledge, 1996). Partha Chatterjee argues for preserving the bourgeois conception of civil society drawn from western history, in order to highlight the conflicting desires of modernity animating cultural debates in India. Chatterjee, 'Two Poets and Death,' in Timothy Mitchell (ed.), *Questions of Modernity* (Minneapolis: University of Minnesota Press, 2000).

[38] Jean-Francois Bayart, 'Civil Society in Africa,' in Patrick Chabal (ed.), *Political Domination in Africa* (Cambridge: Cambridge University Press, 1986), p. 118.

[39] Francis Fukuyama, *Trust: The Social Virtues and the Creation of Prosperity* (London: Penguin, 1995).

and useful to government. They strengthen democratic institutions and government accountability by monitoring performance, insisting on proper procedures, and pursuing civil rights.[40]

Finally, Putnam argues that associations create social capital. This enables government to get citizen cooperation more easily, enhancing its effectiveness and therefore its legitimacy. Named for its analogy to physical and human capital, social capital refers to features of social organization that facilitate coordination and cooperation for mutual benefit.[41] Like other kinds of capital, social capital can be accumulated and reinvested. The bonds built within associations foster norms of reciprocity and make it less costly for members to cooperate for new purposes. They broaden the participants' sense of self and encourage formation of a collective consciousness. Putnam has argued that patterns of trust developed within associations provide the basis for 'generalized trust' throughout the society, building a basis for civic engagement, public spiritedness, and effective government.[42]

Putnam recognizes that some associations are more productive of values supporting good government than others. Specifically, associations that are built on horizontal bonds are better than those based on hierarchy, and face-to-face associations have a more powerful impact on members than larger ones. Associational bonds cutting across social groups are better than those limited to within groups because they nourish wider cooperation, while dense but segregated networks may become the basis for civil strife. These caveats are a minor chord, however, in his major argument which, following de Tocqueville, celebrates the positive contribution of associations to democracy because of the social capital they produce. In his view these contributions may arise from purely social groups or sports clubs as well as from those with a community orientation.

Eastern Europe and parts of the third world see the benefits of associations more from the Lockean perspective. Reacting to interventionist states, theorists there view the state and civil society in opposition. Civil society fosters democracy by limiting the state, providing space for protest groups, generating demands, monitoring excess, confronting powerholders, and sustaining a balance of power

[40] Robert Putnam, *Bowling Alone* (New York: Simon and Schuster, 2000).

[41] Robert Putnam, 'Bowling Alone: America's Declining Social Capital,' *Journal of Democracy*, 6, 1995, p. 67.

[42] Putnam, ibid., pp. 167–75.

between state and society.[43] Drawing also on the theories of Gramsci, they see civil society as a possible site for confronting the cultural hegemony of the state by offering alternative conceptions of politics.

American political philosopher Michael Walzer suggests a more modest consequence for democratic governance.[44] From the non-Marxist left, he finds that civil society provides a way forward from disillusionment with the universal claims of socialism. He notes that all the comprehensive answers to the problems of modern society proposed by the great intellectual movements of the twentieth century have proved tragically wrong. Citizens do not have time for full engagement with politics, as communitarians require, nor did socialism succeed in eliminating the state. Capitalism cannot dispense with the state either, but has no way of explaining why people should think of themselves as citizens sharing a common fate instead of as mere consumers or taxpayers. Finally, nationalism as a basis for providing community solidarity risks exclusivity and racism. To Walzer, the virtue of civil society is that it makes no such high-minded claims. Its pluralist competition between voluntary groups and their differing views of the good life leaves it flexible, contingent on changing circumstances, and inherently responsive to local needs. In contrast to the large-scale state of either socialism or welfare state bureaucracy, he envisions a politics for ordinary people in people-size arenas.

Also a minimalist, philosopher Nancy Rosenblum contemplates how associational memberships may benefit individual citizens. She argues that belonging to even the most non-democratic organizations may serve moral purposes for individuals.[45] People join associations for private reasons that are often quite different from the explicit purposes of the organization. Even mean-spirited associations can have a salutary effect on their members by providing sociability, respect, or non-destructive outlets for aggression. Therefore she examines not the content of individual experiences, which is varied and unpredictable, but the benefits of holding a number of different memberships. A plurality of associational experiences, she argues, gives members practice in differentiating among spheres and

[43] Gordon White, 'Civil Society, Democratization and Development (I)' Democratization, 1(3), Autumn 1994, pp. 382 ff. See Also Bayart, p. 125.

[44] Michael Walzer, 'The Idea of Civil Society,' Dissent, 38(2), 1991, pp. 293–304. (In this volume).

[45] Nancy Rosenblum, 'Civil Societies: Liberalism and the Moral Uses of Pluralism,' Social Research, 61(3), 1994, pp. 539–61. (In this Volume).

adjusting their conduct to each. Should they be subject to arbitrariness in one sphere, they may find tolerance in another, thereby enlarging their personal capacity for self-reflection and freedom. Further, changing associational memberships enables individuals to experiment with different identities and therefore not be trapped into a single representation of self. In these analyses, what is needed for associations to prepare citizens for democracy is not their values, but a plurality of available associations with permeable boundaries, most importantly allowing exit.

Critical Perspectives

Experience raises many questions about these views. European historians have criticized the selective reading of history propelling accounts of civil society in the west. Northern Italy, celebrated in Robert Putnam's analysis of civil society, was home to fascism in the mid-twentieth century, despite its long tradition of citizen participation and historic experience with republican governance.[46] Even more compelling is Sheri Berman's account of the fall of German democracy to Nazism, which she attributes to too much civil society rather than too little.[47] In the context of ineffectual political parties, Weimar citizens turned instead to the vigorous but exclusivist associations of civil society, exacerbating tensions between social groups and increasing dissatisfaction with the regime. These associations provided a crucial training ground for Nazi cadres who came not from alienated, apolitical Germans, but from activists trained in civil society organizations. Berman sees Putnam's analysis of Italy as arising from a quintessentially American perspective born out of a national history of social harmony where the state played a minimal role.[48]

In contemporary Eastern Europe, the coalitions of activist groups in civil society collapsed into conflict over post-revolution goals. Xenophobia and national separatism, searches for scapegoats, and

[46] For the most authoritative review, see Sidney Tarrow, 'Making Social Science Work Across Space and Time: A Critical Reflection on Robert Putnam's Making Democracy Work,' *American Political Science Review*, 90(2), June 1996, pp. 389–97.

[47] Sheri Berman, 'Civil Society and the Collapse of the Weimar Republic,' *World Politics* 49, April 1997, pp. 401–29.

[48] Sheri Berman, 'Civil Society and Political Institutionalization,' *American Behavioral Scientist*, 40(5), March/April 1997, pp. 62–74.

animosity toward minorities are rising with the loss of stability and order. In retrospect civil society may have been a chimera, unable to substitute for the slow task of building a political culture of tolerance and negotiation to sustain democratic institutions. Krishan Kumar argues that this fascination with civil society has had the negative consequence of deflecting attention from the critical tasks of building the institutional supports for democracy. He finds that 'the theory of the state in post-communist societies is in total disarry'.[49]

A similar concern emerges from the post-authoritarian states of Latin America. Omar Encarnacion reports that in Brazil, the vigour of associational activity has deflected attention from the hard task of building political parties to work with the newly democratic government.[50] Therefore government is without negotiating partners to craft compromises needed for implementation of wrenching but necessary economic reforms. In such acute situations, one cannot expect the culture or good will of autonomous organizations in civil society to substitute for political bargaining backed up by state authority.

From the Indian perspective, Gurpreet Mahajan is also critical of Putnam's lack of historical awareness. She points out that his appreciation of voluntary associations has a different meaning in the west where associational ties have already been modernized. In India many associations are hierarchical and based on ascriptive ties, giving them a very different moral weight.[51] She fears that moving to an associative concept of democracy before rights are firmly established means leaving intact the social structures of inequality. Further, as Sudipta Kaviraj points out, when such associations are based in religious or communal majorities, they may demand a totalist commitment inimicable to any concept of individual rights.[52] The pluralism endorsed by theorists like Nancy Rosenblum may be a conservative force in a country like India.

These critiques point to an important lacuna in the associational view of civil society: its avoidance of politics. Associational life may support democratic institutions, as Putnam argues, but when these institutions are absent or ineffective, as in Weimar Germany or the

[49] Kumar, p. 389.

[50] Omar Encarnacion, 'Tocqueville's Missionaries,' *World Policy Journal*, 17(1), Spring 2000, p. 9.

[51] Gurpreet Mahajan, 'Civil Society and its Avtars,' *Economic and Political Weekly*, 15 May 1999, pp. 1188–96. (In this volume).

[52] Kaviraj, p. 320.

states now moving from authoritarian rule, civil society can detract from democracy. From her study of Nazi Germany, Sheri Berman observes that 'even the most seemingly harmless civil organizations can, under certain circumstances, be turned to antidemocratic purposes.'[53] Whether civil society activity has positive or negative consequences for democratic development depends in large part on the response of political institutions.

At issue is not only the capacity of political institutions to respond to group interests or to implement policy effectively, but also to deal with conflicting ideological conceptions arising from civil society. As Mark Robinson shows, public life in India is now engaged in a multifaceted challenge to the secular character of the Indian state that was nurtured in Hindu organizations of civil society.[54] Treating all associational life as fundamentally similar and benign tends to devalue political ends in favour of an emphasis on policy outcomes. It is more concerned with how policies are implemented, not with why they were adopted and what ends they serve.[55]

CIVIL SOCIETY AS NORMS AND VALUES

The second approach to civil society is normative. As Augustus Norton writes in his critique of civil society in the Middle East, 'Civil society is more than an admixture of various forms of association, it also refers to a quality—civility—without which the milieu consists of feuding factions, cliques, and cabals. Civility implies tolerance, the willingness of individuals to accept disparate political views and social attitudes. It is a cast of mind.'[56] Theorists of deliberative democracy following Habermas add to these values the significance of reasoned discourse as the mode through which civil society formulates its sense of the public interest.

Observers drawing from the major traditions of political philosophy emphasize different values within civil society discourse. Those working from the western liberal tradition tend to emphasize individual rights as among its core values. Thus Mahajan argues 'to secure

[53] Berman, p. 567.

[54] Robinson, in this volume.

[55] Foley, Edwards and Diani, p. 27. Also Howell and Pearce, p. 43, and Rob Jenkins, 'Mistaking "Governance" for "Politics"; Foreign Aid, Democracy, and the Construction of Civil Society' in Kaviraj and Khilnani, p. 268.

[56] Norton, p. 214.

individual liberty along with social equality…it is necessary to go back in history and retrieve a rights-based conception of civility.'[57] She points out that the first theorists of civil society were primarily concerned with establishing the rights of individuals in order to challenge prevailing forms of inequality, and only after they were firmly accepted did the rights-based conception change to an associative one, emphasizing self-management and direct participation. Theorists from the European philosophic tradition, on the other hand, are more likely to emphasize the collective dimension that sustains ties across all the groupings in society. Thus Jeffrey Alexander conceives of it as a realm of solidarity that 'simultaneously affirms the sanctity of the individual and these individuals' obligations to the collectivity.'[58]

The normative view of civil society is especially important to democratic theorists critical of procedural views of democracy. They observe that democracy is a matter of culture as well as organization, and caution that over-emphasis on procedure—laws, elections, etc.— impoverishes understanding of the requirements of democracy. Civil society is the source of the virtues that sustain democratic interactions, trust, tolerance, cooperation, and equality.[59] Though none argues that civility is sufficient for democracy, they see it providing the indispensable spirit that enables societies to be largely self-governing within a limited state.

For societies to sustain these values, the educative functions of civil society are critically important. Recognizing that citizenship skills must be developed and citizens motivated for engagement with public causes, they follow de Tocqueville in looking to associations in civil society as its 'schools of virtue.'[60] Therefore many of the normative

[57] Gurpreet Mahajan, in this volume.

[58] Jeffrey Alexander, 'The Paradoxes of Civil Society,' *International Sociology*, 12(2), June 1997, p. 115.

[59] Edward Shils, 'The Virtue of Civil Society,' *Government and Opposition* 26(1), Winter 1991, pp. 3–20.

[60] Rosenblum, in this volume. Partha Chatterjee describes how Rabindranath Tagore similarly perceived the need to educate people to become a public where they would assume responsibilities for the larger good. (Partha Chatterjee, 'Two Poets and Death', p. 37). Susanne and Lloyd Rudolph discuss Gandhi's perception of the educative functions of civil society, notably in his ashram. His goal was inner transformation to prepare for public life, not the more limited rational project of learning democratic procedures. Rudolph and Rudolph, in this volume.

civil society persuasion argue that the associations of civil society should be democratically structured so members internalize democratic values. Only those organizations that exhibit these values may be considered members of civil society.

Critical Perspectives

While these various values are widely accepted as ideals, placing them among the criteria for identifying civil society invites both analytic and strategic problems. If one defines civil society as including only those groups that are democratically inclined, the argument connecting civil society and democracy becomes circular.[61] It also invites interventions in civil society organizations to make them more democratic. In a justly celebrated review of strategies for building civil society, Axel Hadenius suggests that governments should seek to ensure in some manner that organizations function internally in a democratic manner.[62] But Nancy Rosenblum contemplates whether congruence between liberal-democratic norms and internal group organization should be enforced by law. At risk is the autonomy of groups, one of the defining characteristics of civil society.[63] She finds that some proposals for democratizing civil society would make its associations virtual artifacts of government.

Furthermore, an overemphasis on the values of civil society may make democratic politics more difficult. Stepan and Linz caution that the principled purposes and styles of organization common in civil society organizations can make them overly critical of patterns of negotiation and compromise needed for coalition-building in political arenas.[64] They point out that the tasks of political parties—aggregating and representing differences, routinizing procedures for regulating conflict, structuring compromises—are legitimate and necessary for governance. The moral posture of civil society organizations renews and holds accountable democratic politics, but may also engender a

[61] Michael Foley and Bob Edwards, 'The Paradox of Civil Society,' *Journal of Democracy*, 7(3), July 1996, pp. 38–53.

[62] Axel Hadenius and Fredrik Uggla, 'Making Civil Society Work, Promoting Democratic Development: What Can States and Donors Do?' *World Development*, 24(10), 1996, p. 1636.

[63] Rosenblum, in this volume.

[64] Juan Linz and Alfred Stepan, *Problems of Democratic Transition and Consolidation* (Baltimore: The Johns Hopkins University Press, 1996), p. 10.

dangerous cynicism among persons who fail to see the differing roles of civil society and political society.

The normative emphasis on rational discussion risks excluding discourses that would seem to be significant communications of a civil society. Nancy Fraser points out that actors communicate in different ways depending on their gender, class, ethnicity, and other social backgrounds. The capacity to participate in the type of debate envisioned by Habermas is not equally available to all, so that speakers 'lacking the legitimate competence are de facto excluded from the social domains in which this is required, or are condemned to silence.'[65] Neera Chandhoke considers the incommensurability between the languages of Indian tribals and officials of the democratic state, exacerbated by the severe differential in power. She argues that power so structures the very conceptualizations of negotiation, mediation, and challenge in the dominant civil society discourse that these modes of exchange are inaccessible to the speakers of the tribal language.[66] Similarly, the slum-dwellers of Chatterjee's concern draw on a range of tactics from mendicancy to violence while reasoned speech is unavailable to them.[67]

Susanne Rudolph and Lloyd Rudolph demonstrate how Gandhi adapted the language of civil society to communicate with a rural, religious, and predominantly illiterate audience. Using travelling theatre, oral tales, prayer meetings, and other kinds of performances, he created a 'public' focused on matters of common concern embued with the values of tolerance and civility.[68] Where no such language is created, the modes of discourse of modern democracy render impossible both deliberation and citizenship.

Overemphasis on the values of civil society may also deflect from inquiry into the systems and relationships that constitute it.[69] Patterns

65 Nancy Fraser, 'Rethinking the Public Sphere,' in Craig Calhoun (ed.), *Habermas and the Public Sphere* (Cambridge and London: MIT Press, 1992), pp. 109–42. (In this volume).

66 Neera Chandhoke, 'Languages of Civil Society; Translations, Slippages, and Domination,' ms. 2000.

67 Kaviraj, p. 317.

68 Susanne H. Rudolph and Lloyd I. Rudolph, 'The Coffee House and the Ashram: Gandhi, Civil Society and Public Spheres,' 2000. In this volume.

69 Howell and Pearce criticize civil society as a concept that is intrinsically appealing to international development donors who fail to do rigorous analysis of the structural factors underpinning poverty and underdevelopment, ibid., p. 29.

of associational life and social communication differentiate between privileged insiders and marginalized outsiders. Indeed, the possibility of excluding unwanted participants is often one of the attractions of associational membership. Since the capacity to build associations is unevenly distributed in any society, and generally favours those groups less dependent on clientilist ties for subsistence, civil society is often based in the middle to upper classes.[70] Groups enjoying already established understandings about the sharing of power more easily sustain the values of respect and tolerance. Yet, as John Comaroff and Jean Comaroff point out, the civilized society of bourgeois Europe rested on a series of contradictions built on inequality. While promising equality it separated citizens from colonial subjects, nationals from immigrants, the propertied from the unpropertied, the law abiding from the criminal.[71]

These several considerations have led many scholars to reject the concept of civil society as an ideological mask of conservatism and/ or western cultural hegemony expressed through modernization theory.[72] They perceive that the emphasis on values obscures structural underpinnings and holds out modern western society as the model of civility. Thus Comaroff and Comaroff see the communitarian ideals of the current civil society debate as exercises in nostalgia that mask how capitalist development erodes the institutions and mechanisms that made these ideals conceivable. Similarly, Shelly Feldman argues in aid-dominated Bangladesh, the commitment of internationally funded NGOs to market operation contradicts the values of reciprocity and solidarity needed for collective action to challenge social hierarchy.[73]

Michael Edwards questions the emphasis on trust in situations of marked inequality. He argues that the values of trust and partnership put forward by civil society proponents offer a false promise to the poor. Their confidence in others is easily abused by unscrupulous

[70] David Blaney and Mustapha Kamal Pasha, 'Civil Society and Democracy in the Third World,' *Studies in Comparative International Development* (Spring 1993), 28(1), p. 9.

[71] Comaroff and Comaroff, p. 23.

[72] al-Sayyid, pp. 132–3.

[73] Shelly Feldman, 'NGOs and Civil Society: (Un)stated Contradictions, *Annals of the American Academy of Political and Social Science* (1997), 554, pp. 46–55.

persons placed to take unfair advantage of them.[74] Such critiques reveal the need for placing a discussion of civil society values in the larger context of social and political forces.

Finally, one must question the role of political culture in determining political events. One might find, for example, that sustaining of democracy, at least in the early years of a democratic transition, depends more on compromise agreements and a balance of power among warring parties than on a political culture of trust. Many observers of Arab politics emphasize the contingent nature of democracy there.[75] More important than cultural support by the population, they suggest, is an agreement among elites to share power. Thus, as with the associational conception, we are driven to a political formulation to provide a context for the normative analysis.

CIVIL SOCIETY, POLITICAL SOCIETY, AND CITIZENSHIP

Whereas the interest of civil society in the United States has been animated by worry about lack of civic engagement and in Eastern Europe by resistance to interventionist states, Indian discussion flows from concerns about the extension of democracy to previously subordinated groups, so-called 'democratic deepening.' The question is how to make citizenship meaningful, and with what effect on civil society and established institutions of governance.

For this discussion, theorists have found it useful to distinguish between civil society and political society and to examine their different trajectories. Civil society refers to self-organized associations and social movements that may (or may not) attempt to influence power-holders, while political society comprises parties and other contestants for power in political institutions. Civil society grows at a different pace and through different means from political society. While political society can be created from the outside by extension

[74] Michael Edwards, 'Enthusiasts, Tacticians and Sceptics: The World Bank, Civil Society and Social Capital,' http://www.worldbank.org/poverty/scapital/library/Edwards.pdf. Accessed 30 July 2002. This is the gist of the debate between Gandhi and Ambedkar over the concept of trusteeship.

[75] Rex Brynen, Bahgat Korany and Paul Noble, 'Introduction: Theoretical Perspectives on Arab Liberalization and Democratization,' Rex Brynen (ed.), *Political Liberalization and Democratization in the Arab World*, Vol. I (Boulder: Lynne Rienner, 1999), p. 12. See discussion of pacts in Latin America by Terry Lynn Karl,' Dilemmas of Democratization in Latin America,' *Comparative Politics* (October 1990), p. 1–21.

of citizenship rights, civil society grows organically and incrementally. The result may be a gap in the mapping of civil society organizations against the inclusive boundaries of democratic government. Thus Laurence Whitehead asks, 'How are the associative and communicative practices of "civil society" related to the aspirational or juridical fictions of political society in new democracies?'[76]

Civil society may become more liberal but not more democratic. Some of the organizations seeking expansion of the space for autonomous organizations in Southeast and East Asia base their claims on elitist notions such as meritocracy. They seek organizational autonomy and influence on public policy only for particular kinds of associations, largely those representing business and professionals. Whether these elites will support further democratization to include such groups as labour, or become frightened of labour militancy and urge a return to authoritarian controls, is yet to be seen.[77] Similarly, critics of the civil society movement in the Middle East point out that while there is an impressive growth of professional associations, seminars, and even political satire, many of the associations have very particular interests that do not extend beyond protecting certain rights and privileges from the state.[78] This kind of civil society, Whitehead argues, has little moral significance despite its adept use of the modern language of civil society.

Political society poses threats to civil society in different contexts. Whitehead identifies three major ones: traditional family and particularist loyalties jeopardizing impersonal civic rights, interventionist states denying autonomy to civil society associations, and the 'majoritarian incivility' characterizing many sectors of modern societies.[79]

[76] Laurence Whitehead, 'Bowling in the Bronx: The Uncivil Interstices between Civil and Political Society,' Robert Fine and Shirin Rai (eds), *Civil Society* (London: Frank Cass, 1997), pp. 94–114. (In this volume).

[77] Gordon White, 'Civil Society, Democratization and Development (II)' *Democratization*, 2(2), Summer 1995, p. 63. Kaviraj points out that the contribution of the bourgeoisie to democratization is historically specific to the west, not a universal tendency of the class. Kaviraj in Kaviraj, p. 297.

[78] Mehran Kamrava and Frank Mora, 'Civil Society and Democratization in Comparative Perspective: Latin America and the Middle East' *Third World Quarterly*, 19(5), 1998. (In this volume, p. 344).

[79] Whitehead, in this volume, p. 130. Whitehead fails to recognize, however, that most of the so-called primordial loyalties are modern constructions crafted for modern purposes. On the transformation of Hinduism see Hansen, ibid.

The last refers to such phenomena as irresponsible media, organized crime, speculative financial markets, and apathetic electorates. In established democracies these phenomena may be attributed to the atomization of modern society, highlighted in the communitarian critiques of Elshtain and Putnam, while in the new democracies of Eastern Europe they are part of the 'uncivil inheritances' left in the wake of authoritarian regimes.

In the third world, many fear that political democracy will empower social forces with no interest in the practices or culture of democracy. In Algeria and Egypt, Islamist movements have generated impressive social service organizations within civil society, but these same movements contain factions that have assassinated prominent intellectuals to prevent disagreement with their views on Islamic society. Democratic procedures could enable such movements to come to power only to disestablish any space for autonomous organizations.[80]

Where democratic procedures are in place, political society may be dangerous for associational life. The practices of democracy—elections, parties, campaigning politicians—often disrupt previous patterns of collaboration among social groups. Reports of communal clashes in India frequently argue that neighbours of different communities lived together peacefully, with local mechanisms for settling the occasional incident, until outside politicians arrived looking for issues on which to mobilize partisan support.[81] Similarly, Susanne Rudolph reports studies of how community-based initiatives for forest conservation in Himalayan villages have been disrupted by electoral competition. She concludes the 'causal arrows in the relationship between democracy and associationalism sometimes run in the reverse direction, and the effect is negative, not positive.'[82]

[80] al-Sayyid, p. 145. Ibrahim argues, on the other hand that including these movements in electoral politics would 'tame' them. Saad Eddin Ibrahim, 'Religion and Democracy: The Case of Islam, Civil Society and Democracy,' Inogushi, Newman and Keane (eds), *Changing Nature of Democracy* (Tokyo: UN Press, 1998), pp. 221–2.

[81] Varshney in this volume, p. 436. Thomas Blom Hansen argues, however, that the model of communal clashes being caused by demonic outsiders, with no basis in localized violence and antagonism is mistaken. *The Saffron Wave* (Princeton: Princeton University Press, 1999), p. 203.

[82] Susanne Rudolph, 'Civil Society and the Realm of Freedom,' *Economic and Political Weekly* (13 May 2001), p. 1764. From her studies of the democratic

Still Partha Chatterjee opts for political society over civil society as the site of post-modern creativity. Identifying political society with democracy, and civil society with modernization, he argues that the parties and protest groups making up political society have greater capacity for bringing forward the concerns of marginalized peoples than modernized civil society.[83] He forecasts an emerging opposition between modernity and democracy, i.e. between civil society and political society, as new groups claim entitlements that directly contradict the universalist 'modern' conventions of civil society. As these groups become more successful politically, he sees Indian democracy moving from a basis in individual rights to collective rights, challenging civic regulation.

Chatterjee's argument has generated lively debate about the difference between commitments to democratic inclusion and to civil society values. Distressed by the rise of caste-based parties, Andre Beteille warns that these parties have engendered a 'competitive populism' that casts all secular mediating institutions as elitist and opens up politics to the intrusion of caste.[84] He argues that civil society depends on the strength of autonomous mediating institutions open to all categories of citizens, such as schools, newspapers, professional associations, and banks. These institutions are needed to inculcate the secular, inclusive values of liberal democracy and protect individuals from exclusionary policies based on social group memberships. The Indian state, he believes, has given into mass pressures and failed to protect modern institutions from sectarian forces.

Beteille's critics argue that in seeking to protect the autonomy of intermediate institutions, he prizes institutions over citizenship.

---

transition in Africa, however, Tripp argues that the problem is not the effect of electoral democracy but that historic patterns of neo-patrimonial rule, personal rule, and state-based clientelism have remained intact and are manifesting themselves in the democratic context. Aili Mari Tripp, 'Political Reform in Tanzania: The Struggle for Associational Autonomy,' *Comparative Politics* (January 2000), p. 212.

83 Partha Chatterjee, 'Beyond the Nation? or Within?' *Economic and Political Weekly* (4–11 January 1997), in this volume. Similarly, in a study of five American cities, Portney and Barry find that strong local party structures afford greater minority political incorporation than citywide issue organizations. Kent Portney and Jeffrey Barry, 'Social Capital and the City,' Edwards, Foley and Diani (eds), *Beyond Tocqueville* (Hanover: University Press of New England, 2001).

84 Bétéille, in this volume, p. 210.

Because citizenship in India is so severely compromised by inequality, liberal society is diminished. Citizenship is little more than a legal title for many Indians, so the 'basic ethic of civil society can hardly be said to exist in any meaningful way' observes Dipankar Gupta. 'It is impossible to be civil in an uncivil society'.[85]

Those who share Gupta's critique of modern civil society differ, however, on remedies. Theorists critical of the emphasis on individual rights in western liberalism which they think alien and/or elitist in the Indian context, look for some form of collective democracy or recognition of group rights. Partha Chatterjee and Rajni Kothari look outside modern institutions to movements and organizations arising from the grassroots. Kothari argues for a return to India's cultural roots in the villages to identify indigenous institutions capable of representing the diversity of India's collective life.[86] Chatterjee looks instead for 'new forms of democratic institutions and practices in the mediating field of political society that lie between civil society and the nation-state.'[87] From a more statist perspective, Neera Chandhoke argues that in a society with such inherited group-based inequalities as India, the state must raise marginalized groups to a position of collective equality before rights of individuals within these groups can hold any meaning.[88]

Gupta and Gurpreet Mahajan, on the other hand, focus on state protection of individual citizenship. They are critical of any tendency to romanticize the hierarchy and power struggles in Indian villages or the authenticity of politicized masses. Nor, answering Béteille, do they think intermediary bodies can protect individuals from abuse of power or majoritarian exclusionary practices. Mahajan observes that 'the state alone' can create conditions that are necessary to protect the institutions of civil society.'[89] It must address the inequalities that compromise liberty and the capacity of citizens to participate in democratic governance.

---

[85] Gupta, in this volume. Béteille's piece in this volume is a revision of his original statement written in answer to criticisms that he neglected citizenship and the state.

[86] Rajni Kothari, *State Against Democracy: In Search of Humane Governance* (Delhi; Ajanta Publishers, 1988)

[87] Chatterjee, 'Beyond the Nation?', in this volume, p. 144.

[88] Chandhoke, 'Languages of Civil Society.'

[89] Gurpreet Mahajan, in this volume.

Agreeing that the problem lies with the nature of governance, Krishan Kumar has questioned whether the concept of civil society is even needed:

> If we are concerned about the abuses of state power, with recognizing and promoting pluralism and diversity, with defending rights and enabling individuals to act politically, what is wrong with the language and terms of such concepts as constitutionalism, citizenship and democracy.[90]

His concern is not parsimony but mistaken strategy. He argues that attempts to rebuild civil society from below are misguided attempts to avoid politics.

Unlike the two previous conceptions of civil society—as associations and as moral schools—the Indian debates place the state at the centre of attention. Its cultural appropriateness, its overweening demands for uniformity and compliance, its weak capacity to address the social and individual inequalities that diminish citizenship, and its openness to capture by illiberal forces are all at issue. These concerns draw from the tradition of analysis identified with Hegel and updated by such contemporary political scientists as Samuel Huntington, Juan Linz, and Alfred Stepan. Without an effectual and legitimate state, the political scientists argue, civil society is not able to create the sense of national community or commitment to public interest needed for democratic governance.[91] The civil society debates restore to these analyses a critical idea from classical liberal theory, the need for the state to accept limits.

The other major theme in the Indian debates is the issue of inequality. Mark Edwards has challenged the credibility of any concept of civil society that does not come to terms with differentials in power within a society. The reciprocity and dialogue embodied in the notion of civility, he argues, can only happen when the participants approach each other from positions of relative equality. Voice, security, and rights are the pre-conditions for participation in the conversation among citizens envisaged by proponents of civil society.[92]

90 Kumar, p. 391.

91 Samuel Huntington, *Political Order in Changing Societies* (New Haven: Yale University Press, 1968) and Linz and Stepan, ibid.

92 Michael Edwards, ibid.

CIVIL SOCIETY AS AN ORGANIC FLOWERING FROM HISTORICAL ROOTS

Finally, there are theorists and political leaders who work from the assumption that civil society is defined by its historical sociology. They identify the bases of western civil society in specific features of European history, suggesting that differing histories elsewhere make the development of civil society unlikely or impossible. This assumption has fed both western-based predictions of a 'clash of civilizations' between western civil societies and Islamic cultures, and Asian elites' rejection of liberal civil society as culturally alien.[93]

The metaphor of the social contract which underlies western conceptions of civil society may be traced to the development of capitalism and bourgeois society in eighteenth-century Europe. New economic elites demanded the right to self-regulation of commerce, while calling upon the state to follow rules of procedure guaranteeing freedom from arbitrary state action. In Western Europe, these new merchants and townsmen allied with the king against the aristocracy, in exchange for civil liberties in the towns.

Structures established earlier in western civilization predisposed Europe to this societal self-organization.[94] Among these were the separation of church and state established under early Christianity, competition among the small states after the fall of the Roman empire, and the dispersion of power in medieval Europe among many countervailing forces in feudal society. Segmentation of power prevented the construction of an overarching imperial framework and fostered cultural and political variability among the various units.

When these western theorists look outside Europe, they tend to look at culture, not history.[95] They read the texts of Islam and perceive that the vision of a singular religious truth denies space for mundane politics, failing to note the many different ways Islamic communities have adapted to political circumstances. Yet Hefner's account of Indonesian Islam shows that communities founded through trade differed greatly from those founded by conquest, providing a basis for

[93] Samuel Huntington, *The Clash of Civilizations and the Remaking of the World Order* (New York: Simon and Schuster, 1996) and Garry Rodan, in this volume.

[94] John Hall, 'The Nature of Civil Society,' *Society* (May/June 1998), pp. 32–41.

[95] Hall, ibid.

pluralism and civil autonomy that was disrupted by colonialism.[96] Similarly, Yahya Sadowski argues that classical orientalists studying the Middle East ignore the impact of colonialism in deindustrializing the Ottoman and Qajar empires. The view that the obstacles to development are internal and unchanging is an essentialism that follows from their dismissal of western colonialism and imperialism.[97] The Latin American variant of this argument attributes its unstable authoritarian politics to a combination of 'late' development and Iberian tradition, ignoring how concentration of wealth in colonial trading cities prevented development of competing power centres and social pluralism.[98]

Looking at India, these theorists have adopted the Brahmanic version of caste in India: pollution taboos, hierarchical ordering, and withdrawal from the state.[99] They are unaware of the evidence from historical anthropology about patterns of mobility, contestation, and blurring of identities among caste groups. New Indian history, on the other hand, demonstrates that caste was rigidified under colonialism as the British sought to categorize, systematize, and privatize society for their rule.[100]

The same theorists of the western tradition often forget that the habits of moderation, negotiation, and tolerance which now constitute civility were absent during much of European history. Tolerance arose not from conviction but stalemate in the religious wars of the seventeenth century. Indeed, Robert Hefner concludes that Europe compares poorly with imperial China, which had a much better ability to cope with religious difference.[101] Political stability was achieved in England only after a century of civil war, treason trials, and regicide. And the dispersion of power among states led to international rivalries that brought the explosive development of

[96] Robert Hefner, 'A Muslim Civil Society?' in Hefner (ed.), pp. 285–321.

[97] Yahya Sadowski, 'The New Orientalism and the Democracy Debate,' *Middle East Report* (July–August 1993), pp. 14–20.

[98] Philip Oxhorn, 'From Controlled Inclusion to Coerced Marginalization: The Struggle for Civil Society in Latin America,' John Hall (ed.), *Civil Society* (Polity Press, 1995), p. 256.

[99] Hall, p. 37.

[100] Susan Bayly, *Caste, Society and Politics in India from the Eighteenth Century to the Modern Age* (New York: Cambridge University Press, 2001).

[101] Robert Hefner, 'On the History and Cross-Cultural Possibility of a Democratic Ideal,' in Hefner (ed.), p. 13.

colonialism, ethnonationalism, and the wars of the twentieth century. Civil society was not preordained nor culturally embedded nor continuously present in Europe. It was the result of political settlements made and broken at various points in history.

Structural Bases for Civil Society in the Third World

An optimistic assessment of the possibilities for civil society in the third world is made by sociologists studying the structural changes of modernization. They suggest that the process of modernization leads to differentiation among the various sectors of society, providing a basis for pluralism. Higher levels of education lead to greater expectations about government and greater capacity to participate in national politics. Growth of the market undermines concentrated state power. The assertion of private ownership rights stimulates demands for political rights and freedoms. Middle class and professional groups brought into existence by development lead the process of democratizing politics. The results are a shift in the balance of power between the state and society, a change in the nature of associational forms, and a redesigning of the political system along democratic lines.[102] The predicted outcome is a civil society.

Without this structural transformation, civil society is fragile and probably transient. Stimulated by outside examples, civil society may flourish for a while due to a gap in governmental controls, but it cannot last. This is the pessimistic analysis of observers of Zambia which, for a while, appeared to offer the promise of liberal democracy in Africa. Civil society groups there grew as the authoritarian Kaunda regime declined, and eventually formed a coalition that brought a change in government. All these groups were still rooted in or dependent on the state, however, with no socio-economic basis to sustain their autonomy nor coherence to sustain their alliance. Gordon White argues that without these structural supports, civil society cannot survive.[103]

Observers of actual politics in East and Southeast Asia caution, however, that these increasingly modern societies demonstrate that structural change provides no certain path to democracy as predicted. Capitalist development there is creating a differentiated middle class,

---

[102] Gordon White, 'Civil Society (I),' pp. 375–90.
[103] Gordon White, 'Civil Society (II),' p. 68.

a business class with a diverse range of strategies, and an increasingly assertive wage labour sector. The response to these pressures varies across the region, however, depending on the regimes' capabilities and strategies. In Singapore, the regime has co-opted business and middle classes through elaborate mechanisms of selective consultation legitimated by appeals to social harmony and Asian values. Garry Rodan envisages that authoritarian regimes in much of Asia may be able to reach political accommodations with some groups without fundamental changes in authoritarian rule.[104]

Cultural Bases for Civil Society in the Third World

Any effort to assess the relevance of the concept of civil society outside the west must acknowledge the enthusiasm for it reported at the outset. While some of these voices have adopted explicitly western models, many have situated their claims in the context of their own cultural traditions. As Rodan reports, the South Korean human rights movement argues that democracy has deep roots in Asian cultures, including in the works of Confucius. In Burma, Nobel Peace Laureate Aung San Suu Kyi critiques western materialism in arguing for forms of democracy that draw from local knowledge and traditions. In other cases, the global human rights movement has provided the language, defending itself from criticisms of its western origin by linking the liberal concept of human rights to economic and social rights, environmentalism, and critiques of globalization. Robert Hefner calls this a process of contextualization and hybridization, not imitation of western models.[105]

In most societies one can find precursors of civil society in their history and culture. Arab societies have a long tradition of autonomy for all kinds of community groups, including men of religion, guilds, ethnic groups, and charitable institutions. Notables managed intercommunal conflicts and mediated between government and people, reducing the pressures of the absolutist state.[106] Pre-Maoist China had a complex layering of intermediate associations that included organizations of intellectuals, traditional trade organizations, irrigation

104 Rodan, in this volume.

105 Hefner, in this volume.

106 Saad Eddin Ibrahim, 'The Troubled Triangle: Populism, Islam and Civil Society in the Arab World,' *International Political Science Review*, 19(4), 1998, p. 376.

societies, and secret societies, as well as organizations based on clan or lineage. Many of these were horizontal associations cutting across communal ties.[107] Confucian values established strong norms of civility for relationships between groups.

Within the traditions of India are many components of civil society: attitudes of tolerance between social groups, conceptions of a self-regulating society under a limited state, and a kind of individualism in the Hindu doctrine of responsibility for one's own religious destiny through personal choices made on this earth. Islamic concepts of equality and respect for the autonomy of groups provide other bases on which to build idioms for a new civil society discourse.

Gandhi used these cultural materials to rework the concept of civil society to build a political community in India. His ashram, his prayer meetings, his confessional autobiography, his fasts and other exemplary performances served to enact the values he sought to propagate.[108] Gandhi's reformulation of civil society illustrates the process of cultural globalization evident elsewhere. It is never merely a transfer, but a reworking shaped as much by local context as the culture of origin. As civil society is articulated outside the west, the balances struck between public and private goods, individual and collective rights, equality and freedom differ and change in the process of institutionalizing general principles of democratic civility.[109]

Cultural resources provide only half of the equation, however, for all these societies have lived under some form of authoritarian state. In the third world, as in European history, the possibility of civil society depends more on existing political settlements between state and society than on cultural precursors. Hefner observes, 'It is not the ancient beat of associational drums that determines democracy's rhythms, nor some inimitable archaeology of philosophical ideas, but a thoroughly contemporary circle of organizations and values.'[110]

INVESTIGATING CIVIL SOCIETY AND DEMOCRACY

The conceptual literature on civil society is richly suggestive of possible relationships with democracy, but these must be assessed empirically

---

[107] Gordon White et. al. *In Search of Civil Society* (Oxford: Clarendon Press, 1996), p. 16. (In this volume).

[108] Rudolph and Rudolph, in this volume.

[109] Hefner, p. 40.

[110] Ibid., p. 41.

to discern their fruitfulness as explanations of social reality. The social science literature on civil society is not as developed as the political theory, but significant studies are now appearing. Robert Putnam's massive study of Italy, *Making Democracy Work*, concluded from a variety of statistical and historical studies that civil society makes democratic government more effective.[111] The debates generated by this work have led to considerable new empirically based scholarship on civil society. Two sets of circumstances may be distinguished, transitions (or lack of) to democratic government and deepening of democracy.

Democratic transition in Latin America substantiates the theoretical premise that civil society leads to democracy. According to Kamrava and Mora, its bureaucratic authoritarian regimes proved unwilling and, with the adoption of fiscal restraints to combat inflation, unable to serve popular needs. With the state pulling out of the economy, people became less materially involved with the state. The social spaces vacated by the regimes were filled by grassroots organizations doing community organizing, running soup kitchens, and providing a range of other social services. What distinguished the civil society sector at this time in history, as opposed to earlier periods of corporatism, is that the new organizations arose independently from the state. Therefore, unlike earlier, they did not retreat into alliances with the oligarchy when confronted with pressures from below. After its adoption of liberation theology, the Catholic church provided important ideological and organizational support to these organizations as part of its social reform and human rights agenda. Concurrent changes in the left in favour of democracy following the end of the Cold War provided support for a commitment to democratic civil society. Eventually disaffection within the regimes lowered their resistance to liberalization and democracy.[112]

In China, transition to any form of democracy is still in question. The market economy and loosening state controls are bringing forward an escalating array of civil society groups, both groups pressing for liberal government and others with more nefarious agendas. The state is responding through a combination of repression and incorporation.[113] After the Tiananmen Square protest in 1989, government

[111] Robert Putnam, *Making Democracy Work: Civic Traditions in Modern Italy* (Princeton: Princeton University Press, 1993).

[112] Kamrava and Mora, in this volume.

[113] White, in this volume.

imposed a centralized system of codified regulations to control the activities of new organizations. Now it is seeking to shift the emphasis from control to a corporatist conception of complementarity, with explicit references to the Japanese model of government/business relations. There are, however, numbers of organizations in the interstices or on the margins of the system—informal, unrecognized, suppressed, illegal, or criminal—that are expanding beyond the state's capacity to incorporate them.

Gordon White judges that movement toward an autonomous civil society sector will be difficult because of the diversity among associations, many of which are reluctant to forego government patronage. He argues that the viability of effecting a stable and peaceful transition to less authoritarian government depends not only on the emergence of reformist leadership in the Communist Party of China, but also on the ability of the associational sectors to agree on new political arrangements. These arrangements can draw on China's cultural resources for democracy, its social capital of horizontal associations, and its moral emphasis on civility. But as Robert Weller argues, these resources will not suffice to create a civil society without both state and society making commitments to limited government and democratic inclusion.[114]

The Chinese analysis brings together the two sets of issues that are problematic in other democratic transitions as well. One is the nature of civil society. Its organizations must draw together on a common agenda and articulate culturally valid commitments to democracy. Lack of cohesion and willingness to be selectively co-opted by the state are problems arresting democratic transition in Indonesia and Africa as well. From Indonesia Hefner reports that strong disagreements among Muslim groups about the role of religion in politics enabled government to divide the Islamist movement for many years, and now prevents the Islamic groups from working out a consensus on an enduring basis for democratic government.[115] In Africa, Jean Bayart reports that the deep cultural, religious, and regional differences and intellectuals' willingness to compromise with the state have prevented development of any common cultural frame of

---

[114] Robert Weller, 'Horizontal Ties and Civil Institutions in Chinese Societies,' in Robert Hefner (ed.) *Democratic Civility* (New Brunswick: Transaction Publishers, 1998), p. 243.

[115] Hefner, 'Indonesia,' in Hefner (ed.), ibid., p. 315.

reference among civil society groups. Instead, societies 'chip away at the state from below' by local revolts, declining productivity, migrations, informal exchange, and religious revivals outside state control.[116] And in the Middle East, observers report that without an inclusive mobilization across civil society nor leadership articulating commitments to democracy, rising social groups are turning to radical Islamic organizations that deny pluralism and the separation between state and society intrinsic to liberal democracy.[117]

Secondly, without changes in the state, civil society cannot itself bring about democracy. There must be some form of state withdrawal to provide civil society organizations with protected space to grow and freedom to negotiate their differences. As in China, Hefner concludes that years of authoritarian rule in Indonesia restricted the space allowed needed for civil society groups to negotiate their differences. And there must be sufficient access to the resources and authority of the state to draw protesting groups into working within the system. In the Middle East, young male urban migrants and educated unemployed are finding no access to participation or services provided by the closed, corporatist state.[118]

Social Capital and Civil Society in India

In India, research has focused on the quality of democracy among its states. The states share a longstanding constitutionally democratic system with protected space for civil society and strong intellectual commitments to liberal democracy, but differ markedly in effectiveness and responsiveness to citizens' needs. To investigate these differences, civil society research has focused on the theory of social capital brought forward by Putnam.[119]

Hans Blomkvist's surveys in five states of India enable him to test Putnam's thesis. His data support the associational conception over the normative one, in that concrete social relationships correlate better with responsive government than prevalent attitudes of generalized trust in people. Blomkvist suggests that among Indian villagers,

[116] Bayart, p. 119.

[117] Kamrava and Mora, ibid.

[118] Ibrahim, ibid.

[119] Hans Blomkvist and Ashok Swain, 'Investigating Democracy and Social Capital in India,' *Economic and Political Weekly* (25 February 2001), 36(8), p. 640. See papers in this issue for other investigations of social capital in India.

tangible connections with people outside the household are important for making democracy work.[120] And, contrary to previous scholarship admiring of leftist governments in India, he finds that social capital explains government responsiveness better than the ideology or class basis of government. Thus capitalist Gujarat and leftist Kerala, both with high social capital, have more responsive government than leftist West Bengal with its low social capital.

Anirudh Krishna's study of Rajasthani villages adds another dimension to this analysis. He finds that social capital is significant but insufficient as an explanation of democratic responsiveness. Villages with high social capital but lacking energetic young leaders to represent their interests to outside authorities were not able to develop access to development resources. Those villages with a combination of dense social networks, capable new agents, and literacy performed well over a broad series of development measures.[121]

Ashutosh Varshney's study of communal conflict in six Indian cities provides further insight.[122] His study responds to political observers in India who, worried about the increasing expression of communal animosity by civil society organizations, have questioned the value of civil society for democracy. Varshney distinguishes between bonding (intra-ethnic, segmentary) civil society and bridging (inter-ethnic) civil society. Cities with extensive existing business, professional, and social ties between Hindus and Muslims, he finds, are more able to preserve social peace than those whose civil society is segmented along religious lines. He also distinguishes between formal associations and informal, everyday interactions, and finds associational engagement among members of different social groups a 'sturdier bulwark of social peace' than informal networks across the same groups. They provide an 'institutionalized peace system' that works in public arenas and synergistically with the police in defusing tensions, squelching rumours, and preventing escalation of violence.

[120] Hans Blomkvist, 'Social Capital, Civil Society and Degrees of Democracy in India,' 2001, in this volume.

[121] Anirudh Krishna, 'Moving from the Stock of Social Capital to the Flow of Benefits: The Role of Agency,' *World Development*, 29(6), p. 938. For a more general analysis of the need to understand how solidarity bonds at the social level can become effective in accessing the state, see Peter Evans, 'Government Action, Social Capital and Development: Reviewing the Evidence on Synergy,' *World Development* (1996), 24(6), p. 1124.

[122] Varshney, in this volume.

Can one identify the historical roots of responsive governance and intercommunal civil society, as Putnam did in Italy? Peter Mayer has constructed an index of civic community (electoral turnout, inter-party collaboration, newspaper readership) and governmental performance among the Indian states.[123] Following Putnam's argument that dense associational life builds civic community, he investigates whether those states with historically high membership in cooperatives now have higher levels of civic community and institutional performance. Contrary to the associational analysis, he finds that early literacy is more important, suggesting that educational traditions are more significant than social capital traditions (read: associational memberships) in building civic involvement.

STRENGTHENING DEMOCRATIC CIVIL SOCIETY IN INDIA

Guidance for democratizing and strengthening civil society depends on the analyses of the sources and nature of civil society. Theorists who see civil society as an organic flowering from an historic base suggest there is little scope for conscious construction. If there is not a pre-existing Tocquevillian spirit of association among the population, legal protections for civil society would be empty procedural gestures. Theorists viewing civil society as a special kind of political culture provide a broad but diffuse template for action. Cultures are multidimensional, holistic, and non-rational, replete with possibilities for distortion and backlash. Thirdly, the purely associational conception risks naively ignoring the political context that crucially shapes the outcomes of organization.

Those who have theorized civil society as a form of state society interaction provide a basis for more politically aware strategies. Mark Robinson argues that if voluntary development agencies in Indian civil society were to perceive their role as participants in an ideological contestation over the nature of the state in India, they might be more effective in upholding the values of secularism, accountability, and concern for marginalized peoples that they espouse. He worries that while militant nationalists and proponents of global capital are moving effectively across civil and political society to serve undemocratic

123 Peter Mayer, 'Human Development and Civic Community in India: Making Democracy Perform,' *Economic and Political Weekly* (24 February 2001), p. 691.

purposes, voluntary agencies refrain from alliances with secular pro-poor advocacy organizations for fear of attracting conflict and appearing political. In so doing they are less able to protect the communities they wish to serve and also fail to make a needed contribution to debates on governance.

For a government building democracy, the civil society materials suggest the importance of self-limitation and trust in citizen action. Civil society organizations need room for experimentation, contestation, and negotiation. While one might prefer that civil groups be internally democratic, experience suggests that intervention to determine internal procedures or requirements for extensive reporting risk diminishing the autonomy of civil society and thus its value to democratic functioning. Further, government should review its modes of providing services so that it does not effectively lock citizens into groups they might wish to exit. Nancy Rosenblum would have government protect pluralism by ensuring that access to basic services such as education or health care does not depend on associational memberships. Thus India's various requirements of identifying with a caste group to access reserved privileges or with a religious group for legal protections may be destructive of civil society.

Most important for government is to do what only it, with it's centuries-old experience, can. This is to attend to the society-wide factors that affect people's capacity for citizenship and democratic participation: the distribution of social and economic power, the public law systems that provide a framework for advocacy and defence of rights, and the provision of health and education for all citizens. These are tasks that governments know how to do. As Peter Mayer remarks, 'Unlike social capital, for the creation of which we lack proven technologies, we have centuries of experience in forming educated populations.'[124]

What then is the promise of civil society? Would a strengthened civil society bring or sustain democracy? Would it deepen democracy? Or increase popular well-being? The evidence we have considered weighs against such optimism. Associational groupings may be self-interested and unavailable to the poor. Nor are they necessarily internally democratic or respectful of individual autonomy and choice. Finally, given the financial pressures on states in the south to reduce their economic commitments, can we expect civil society

124 Mayer, p. 691.

organizations to succeed in securing greater state investment in the well-being of its citizens.[125]

It would appear that a more modest expectation is in order. From the Lockean perspective, civil society groups concerned with civil and political liberties may monitor the fairness and legality of government procedures. From the perspective of Montesquieu, followed by Walzer and Rosenblum, they may increase opportunities for citizens to solve problems locally, explore and change identities, and adapt to contingencies. Most importantly, civil society provides space for critical public conversations about the goals and values of governance—if the pre-conditions for conversation are present. Such expectations seem eminently worthy of support.

---

125 See Geoffrey Hawthorne's sober assessment of the decline of state capacities, 'The Promise of "Civil Society" in the South', Kaviraj and Khilnani.

I

Conceptualizing Civil Society

2

MODES OF CIVIL SOCIETY*

Charles Taylor

In the last decade or so, people have begun to talk a lot again of civil society. They are invoking, of course, not the age-old term, used for centuries as synonymous with 'political society,' but rather the contrastive notion which figures in the philosophy of Hegel. Civil society in this sense exists over against the state, in partial independence from it. It includes those dimensions of social life which cannot be confounded with, or swallowed up in the state.

It is perhaps not hard to understand why this term should return today. Indeed, it emerges from several sources. In societies suffering under Leninist tyranny, it articulated the hopes of those fighting to open spaces of freedom. Originally, when the chances of doing away with these power structures altogether seemed remote, the notion 'civil society' expressed a programme of building independent forms of social life from below, free from state tutelage. This was the thinking current in the Solidarity movement in Poland, for instance, in the early 1980s. But there is also a widespread conviction that this

* This paper was presented to the Center Forum of the Center For Psychosocial Studies (Chicago) on 11–12 November 1989, and is No. 31 of Working Papers and Proceedings of the Center For Psychosocial Studies in Greg Urban and Benjamin Lee (eds), under the title 'Invoking Civil Society.'

independence of society is not only a necessary recourse under tyranny, that it should be an important feature of a democratic Poland as well. And so the invocation of the term has not ceased with the turnover of power; on the contrary, it has only just begun.

Independently, the idea has also sprung up in the west. From one point of view, this might seem surprising, I mean from an 'eastern' perspective. For viewed from inside those Leninist societies, 'civil society' was alive and flourishing in the west. In fact, in using the term, Eastern Europeans wanted to invoke something of the history and practice of the western democracies as a model. The notion was first, that in the west there already is a civil society, and second, that this contemporary reality is the heir to a centuries-long development which found expression in the distinction between civil society and state.

There is a lot of truth in both these claims, but to get at their truth we have to modulate the meaning of 'civil society'. This turns out to be a more complex and many-faceted idea than one might have thought at first. The nuances are worth exploring, because they colour the models of the political process that we want to steer our lives by in coming decades.

To take the first claim: civil society already exists in the west. Yes, there is in western societies a web of autonomous associations, independent of the state, and these have an effect on public policy. But there has also been a tendency for these to become integrated into the state, the tendency towards what has been called (often in a slightly sneering tone, because of the origins of this term in Fascist Italy) 'corporatism'. States like Sweden, Holland, West Germany, but also many others, have gone some way to integrating trade unions, employers' associations, and the like into government planning. To speak of integration 'into the state' may be tendentious here; some people see it as a loss of government independence to special interests. But in fact what occurs is an interweaving of society and government to the point where the distinction no longer expresses an important difference in the basis of power or the dynamics of policy-making. Both government and associations draw on and are responsive to the same public. For instance, issues of national incomes policy which are debated between management and labour unions in tripartite negotiations with government as the third party can also be debated in Parliament, where the same social forces are represented in the form of, e.g., Social Democratic and Conservative parties. In fact, these two loci of negotiation/debate are generally complementary; the issue about corporatism could be phrased as the question: how much of the crucial negotiation takes place outside of Parliament?

Of course, there are lots of associations in western societies which are not involved in corporatist-type negotiations. Some of these are capable of having an impact on policy by lobbying or public campaigns, while others are marginal and easy to ignore. But the drift towards corporatism in modern industrial democracies consists in the first category, the associations with potential clout being more and more integrated into the process of decision-making. It makes sense for a democratic government to consult before deciding, not only to determine the most popular policy, but also to soften the edges of confrontation with the losers, who will at least have the sense that they have been listened to and will be listened to again.

I

So the first claim I mentioned above, that civil society already exists in the west, is more problematical than it appeared. Exploring it has brought greater clarity on the scope of this concept. But the second claim is also not simply true, and it would be worth exploring this one at even greater length.

The second claim was one about the western tradition. The (relative) freedom we enjoy is seen as having sources deep in the history of the west, and in particular in the conceptions of society which go back to medieval Christendom. These sources can be articulated with something like the conception of civil society. In the context of contemporary Eastern Europe, the obvious pole of comparison is Russia. At successive stages, Russia obviously took a different political path from western polities. The development of an independent noble class, of free cities, and hence of a regime of 'Estates' was cut short at crucial moments by the state-building of Ivan the Terrible, and later by Peter the Great. Subsequent initiatives aimed at joining the west were repressed by Nicholas I and, of course, Lenin. A mainstay of western development, that is, a church really independent of political authority, never existed in the Orthodox tradition.

So runs the story; and it obviously has a great deal of truth to it. And particular relevance to the situation of Eastern Europe; at least to Hungary, Poland, Czechoslovakia, and East Germany. These societies developed in close cultural contact and symbiosis with Western

Europe. They share analogous institutional developments and some of the same ideals. For instance, republican ideals of self-rule were present in Poland and enshrined even in the name of the pre-partition state, the Rzeczpospolita Polska. The poignant fate of these societies in the post-war era was to have been forced to accept a political system which was alien, in fact of Russian origin, which ran against the grain of those societies, and was the cause of endless conflict. The aspiration to greater freedom in these societies is in effect synonymous with the aspiration 'to rejoin Europe. That is why it finds natural expression in a view of the European political tradition, and in the notion of 'civil society'.

A. The medieval notion of society is one of those which has turned out to be important in the development of the west, What is important about it is in a sense a negative fact: that society is not defined in terms of its political organization. The underlying issue is this: what gives a society its identity? What are the features without which it would cease to be a society, or would become a wholly different one? In many civilizations and eras, these questions are answered in terms of political structure. For both the Greeks and the Romans, the identity of society was defined by its *politeia*, its political constitution. Under the empire, unity came from a common subjection to authority, although the fiction that this authority came from an act of the people was maintained. Now to the extent that a society is defined by its political organization, to that degree it is in principle permeable by political power. It lacks a principle of resistance to the invasive force of sovereign political authority. Just being politically defined is hardly a sufficient condition of this kind of take-over by despotic power, as the Greek *polis* attests. It is rather that the basis for a certain kind of limitation on this power is lacking, should the conditions ever ripen for its advance.

Now unlike the ancient conceptions, the notion that developed in the early Middle Ages was of a society in which political authority was one organ among others. Royal authority for instance was *singulis major*, but *universis minor*. This idea, that society is not identical with its political organization, can be seen as a crucial differentiation, one of the origins of the later notion of civil society, and one of the roots of western liberalism.

B. This differentiation was carried further by one of the most important features of Latin Christendom. This was the development of an idea of the church as an independent society. In principle, the inhabitants of Christendom were Christian. But these same people were organized in two societies—one temporal, one spiritual—of which neither could be simply subordinated to the other. This was, of course, a formula for perpetual struggle, and in the course of this, extravagant claims were made for one side or the other, including an arrogation *plenitudo potestatis* to Papal authority on the part of Innocent III. But the underlying common understanding remained within the Gelasian definition of 'Two Swords.' There were two sources of authority, both granted for different purposes by God. Each was subordinate to the other for some purposes and supreme for others. Western Christendom was, in its essence, bi-focal.

Alongside these two pervasive features, there were particular facets of medieval political arrangements which with hindsight appear important.

C. One is the development of a legal notion of subjective rights. This was linked to the peculiar nature of feudal relations of authority. The relation of vassalage was seen in a quasi-contractual light. The superior had obligations as well as the inferior. To repudiate these obligations on his part was a felony, as much as for the vassal. So inferiors were seen as the beneficiaries of obligations, privileges which were enjoyed by them as a kind of property. This is the origin of the western notion of subjective rights. It starts off as a notion of purely positive law, before being transposed by the 'natural rights' doctrines of the seventeenth and eighteenth centuries. But it meant that medieval sovereigns faced a society which was partly defined as a skein of rights and duties, which imposed on them the necessity of winning consent for important changes. This, along with (D) the existence of relatively independent, self-governing cities, brought about (E) the standard political structures of medieval polities, in which a monarch ruled with the intermittent and uncertain support of a body of Estates, which had to be called together from time to time to raise the resources he needed to govern and wage war. This dyarchy constituted another, purely secular dualism, linking the political structure to society at large.

We can recognize our roots in all of this, but it did not ensure a trouble-free progress to modern liberal democracy. Between us and that time lies the great early modern attempt over most of Europe to set up 'absolute' monarchies. Kings won the power to raise taxes without calling the Estates, built standing armies on these resources, which in turn made their power harder to challenge. Around 1680, this looked like the wave of the future; it must have seemed to many that only this kind of state could be militarily effective. Moreover, influential theories justified this new model of political society. On one hand, the concepts of Roman law, favouring monarchical power, become dominant. On the other, Bodin and Hobbes develop a notion of sovereignty which quite undermines or supersedes the medieval understanding of society (A). The notion comes to be accredited that a society in order to exist at all must be held together by sovereign power, that is by a power which is not limited by any other. In other words, the identification of society with .its political organization returns, and in a form which is unambiguously favourable to despotism. Important vestiges of A emerge in social contract doctrines where society is accorded existence prior to government, as it is with Grotius and Pufendorf. This is the feature of the contract theory which Hobbes wanted to suppress. But even with Grotius and Pufendorf, the 'contract of subjection' is seen as setting up absolute power, against which society has henceforth no legal recourse.

Meanwhile, throughout this period, a satellitization of the church is taking place in a number of Protestant countries, and the very division of Christendom undermines the idea which was at the heart of B, viz., that everyone belongs to a single alternative society.

As I said above 'absolute' monarchies were really rather limited exercises in despotism, seen in the light of twentieth-century dictatorships. They did away with D and E, but remained limited by C, the entrenched traditions of rights. Of course, nothing assured that C in turn would not be eroded if absolutism pursued its further course. That important stream of reform thinking in the eighteenth century that looked to 'Enlightened Despotism' to reorder society on rational lines was hostile to traditional rights, wanted them swept aside in the name of reason. But absolutism couldn't run its course. What undermined it was the military, and behind that the economic success of the at first relatively minor powers who operated on another, more consensual model, especially England and the Low Countries. In that sense, the end of the eighteenth century may have parallels with the end of the twentieth.

Around this alternative model, there crystallized a number of antiabsolutist doctrines. The most celebrated and influential was that of Locke. He in a sense transposed and renewed both A and B and brought them back into political theory in a new form. A returns in Locke in the unprecedentedly strong form that defines government as a trust.[1] Society exists before government; it issues from a first contract which takes individuals out of the state of nature. This newly-formed body then sets up government. This may be defined as supreme, but it is in fact in a fiduciary relation to society. Should it violate its trust, society recovers its freedom of action.

But Locke also re-introduces a transform of B. Prior to all political society humans form a kind of community. They are constituted as such by being under natural law, which is enjoined on them by God.[2] We are made a community, in other words, by our enjoyment of natural rights. This community is in fact defined as a transform of C, now written into the order of things rather than simply inscribed in positive law. Any particular political society has to respect this higher law, since those who set it up were bound by it, and they could not pass on powers they did not have.

Locke is, of course, still using the term 'civil society' in its traditional sense, where it is synonymous with 'political society'. But he is preparing the ground for the emergence of the new, contrastive sense a century later. This contrast arises out of the anti-absolutist doctrines of the eighteenth century, but in two rather different, even to some extent, antithetical ways. One develops out of Locke's embryonic notion of mankind as a pre-political community. Locke's state of nature is not the scene of devastation portrayed by Hobbes. It lacks security, and that is why humans are driven to set up government. But otherwise it is the possible scene of great progress in what was later called 'civilization', of economic development, the division of labour, the development of money, and the accumulation of property. This idea could be and was developed in the eighteenth century into a picture of human social life in which much that is valuable is seen as coming about in a pre- or non-political realm, at best under the protection of political authority, but by no means under its direction.

There was another source of the contrast, which we can perhaps most handily identify with Montesquieu. His portrait of 'monarchy' in the *Esprit des Lois* offers an alternative anti-absolutist doctrine to

[1] See *The Second Treatise of Civil Government*, paras 221–2, in Peter Laslett, (ed.), *Locke's Two Treatises of Government*, 2nd ed. (Cambridge: Cambridge University Press 1967), p. 430.

[2] See *Second Treatise*, para 172, where Locke speaks of 'the common bond whereby humane kind is united into one fellowship and societies,' in Laslett, op. cit., p. 401.

Locke's. Unlike Locke, he assumes a strong monarchical government which is irremovable. The important issue turns on whether this government is unchecked, and veering towards despotism, or whether it is limited by law. But limitation by law is ineffective unless there exist independent bodies which have a standing in this law, and are there to defend it. The rule of law and the 'corps intermediaries' stand and fall together. They mutually support each other. Without law, bodies like Parliaments and Estates like the nobility have no standing; without such bodies and Estates, the law has no effective defenders. The free monarchy (a pleonasm for Montesquieu, since the unfree one is a despotism) is in equilibrium between a powerful central authority and an interlocking mass of agencies and associations with which it has to compose.

Montesquieu's theory draws on different elements of the tradition from Locke's. It is based on elements C, D, and E of the medieval constitution. Indeed, the debate in France, which ran for centuries, over the rise of absolutism was seen as one which pitted a doctrine of continuity with the ancient constitution, inherited originally from the Frankish conquerors, against models drawn from Roman law. Montesquieu saw himself as reformulating the 'German' case. Speaking of the English constitution which he admired, Montesquieu says that it was derived from the ancient Germans. 'Ce beau système a été trouvé dans les bois.'[3] What he doesn't need to draw on at all is A and B. Society is not defined independently of its political constitution. On the contrary, the free society is identified with a certain such constitution.

For all the importance of the medieval constitution to him, in this respect Montesquieu thinks more like an ancient. The *polis* too was defined politically. The very terms we use show this to be a tautology. This vision of things allowed no place *for* a distinction between civil society and the state—a nuance that would have been incomprehensible to a Greek or Roman. Montesquieu, along with many anti-absolutists of his era, was an admirer of ancient freedom. But he did not make this his model alternative to absolute rule. His genius was rather to have articulated a third standard, in some ways antithetical to the *polis*, which was nevertheless one of freedom and dignity for the participant. Monarchy was antithetical to the republic because the

3 *De l' Esprit des Lois*, livre XI, ch. 6, in *Oeuvres Complètes*, Paris: Seuil 1964, p. 590.

latter supposed 'vertu', a dedication to the public good, as well as austere mores and equality; while monarchy requires a lively sense of one's own rights and privileges, and thrives on the difference of status and display of wealth and power, which are bound up with 'honneur'. Patriotic virtue was the motive force which kept the society free in the ancient republic, because it led people to defend the laws to the death against internal and external threats. The lively sense of one's own rights and status was what protected freedom in the modern monarchy, because it was what made the privileged resist royal encroachment and feel shame in obeying any order which derogated from their code.

So while retaining a thoroughly political definition of society, like the ancients, Montesquieu laid the ground for the civil society/state distinction which was very alien to the ancients. He did this with a view of society as an equilibrium between central power and a skein of entrenched rights.

Both these anti-absolutist doctrines are reflected in the distinction which was eventually drawn around the turn of the century, and found its most celebrated statement in Hegel's *Philosophy of Right*. But in fact, they sit uneasily together in this new concept of civil society. There is a tension between them, and between the different models of a free society which can be articulated with this new concept.

II

Thus two streams come together into 'civil society'. Let's call them the L-stream and the M-stream respectively, after the figures I have (perhaps somewhat arbitrarily) chosen to represent them. What I would like to do here is map this convergence and highlight some of the tensions.

The central feature of what I am calling the L-stream is the elaboration of a richer view of society as an extra-political reality. One facet of this elaboration has dominated the discussion of the nature of 'civil society' until quite recently. That is the development of a picture of society as an 'economy', that is, as a whole of interrelated acts of production, exchange, and consumption which has its own internal dynamic, its own autonomous laws. This crystallizes in the eighteenth century with the work of the Physiocrats, and more definitively, with Adam Smith. Just how great an intellectual revolution is involved here can be measured in the transformation of the meaning of this term. 'Economics' is etymologically the art of household management; it designated a particular field of prudent administration. The 'nomos'. was that imposed by the manager, the head of household or *oikos*. It already involved one revolution in thinking to begin to consider whole kingdoms as like households, needing to have their production and consumption 'managed' in this way. This gives us the jump to 'political economy'. But the important revolution is to a view of this domain as in a sense organizing itself, following its own laws of equilibrium and change. The 'nomos' in the world now comes to resemble its use in a term like 'astronomy', referring us to an 'autonomous' domain of causal laws. The modern 'economy' is born, as a domain with its own inherent organization.

This gives a new twist and a new force to the idea of society as enjoying an extra-political identity. The 'economy' now defines a dimension of social life in which we function as a society potentially quite outside the ambit of politics. Of course, there are differences among the practitioners of the new science as to how autonomous it ought to be. Even Adam Smith was in favour of much more state regulation than his popular reputation today allows. But this intellectual revolution allows us to raise the issue of economic autonomy; without this notion of the economic as governed by its own laws, the issue couldn't even be framed. Now everyone thinks in these terms, interventionist and free-enterpriser alike. They differ only in their assessment of the likely outcome of unregulated flow, and hence of the need or lack of it for remedial action of a more or less radical kind. Even Marx, indeed especially Marx, has a theory of the unimpeded flow. It is a disaster scenario, and is laid out in *Capital*.

This provided an important part of the content of the new concept of civil society, at least of its L-facet. It figures in Hegel's formulation, where the self-regulating, entrepreneurial economy is given a central place on this level of society. Marx took over Hegel's concept and reduced it almost exclusively to this, and it is partly due to Marx's influence that 'civil society' was for so long defined in purely economic terms. But this represents an impoverishment of Hegel's concept. This also owed something to the M-stream, so that his civil society incorporated bodies engaged in conscious self-management—the Corporations—which were also integrated in their own way into the state.

But I want to return to this later, when we look at the tension between the two streams. Right now, it is important to see that even in what I am calling the L-stream, the economy is not the only component. What is also of great importance in the eighteenth century is the development of an autonomous public with its own 'opinion'. This involves a quite new use of the notion of the 'public'. This term designates what is of common concern, and not just objectively or from an outsider's perspective, but what is commonly recognized as of common concern. So public is what matters to the whole society, or belongs to this whole society, or pertains to the instruments, or institutions or loci by which the society comes together as a body and acts. So plainly the political structure of a society is public, its executive organs, the loci of its legislative power, and whatever spaces of assembly these require, from the agora in which the *ekklesia* meets to the court where a king exercises his rule. These are loci of what one might call public space.

The new notion of opinion in the eighteenth century defines a quite different model of public space. Through the circulation of newspapers, reviews, and books among the educated classes, and scattered, small-scale face-to-face exchanges in salons, coffee houses, and (in some cases) political assemblies, there emerges a sense of the nation, or its literate segment, an opinion which deserves to be called 'public'. Public opinion, as originally conceived, is not just the sum of our private individual opinions, even where we spontaneously agree. It is something which has been elaborated in a debate and discussion, and is recognized by us all as something we hold in common. This element of common recognition is what makes it public in the strong sense.

This is also what gives it its force, a new force in history. Its novel aspect is the one relevant to our concerns: public opinion is elaborated entirely outside the channels and public spaces of the political structure. More radically, it is developed outside the channels and public spaces of any authority whatever, because it is also independent of that second focus of European societies, the church. Governments were, of course, used to facing the independent power of religious opinion, articulated by churches. What was new was this opinion which presented itself as that of society, but which was elaborated through no official, established, hierarchical organs of definition.[4]

[4] This whole development has been interestingly discussed by Jürgen Habermas in his *Strukturwandel der Öffentlichkeit*, Berlin: Luchterhand 1962.

Like the economy, public opinion was here to stay. And although some thinkers envisaged a kind of absolute rule which would align itself on enlightened opinion, in fact in the long run, free opinion and absolute power do not consort too well together. But it cannot be just forgotten, and so contemporary despotisms are forced not only to suppress public opinion, but also to counterfeit it. Official newspapers write editorials and report meetings and resolutions, all of which purportedly come spontaneously from the individual authors and initiators. The orchestrated character of all this has to be hidden from view. Such is the prestige of public opinion.

The self-regulating economy, and public opinion, these are two ways in which society can come to some unity or co-ordination outside of political structures. These give body to the Lockean idea, which in turn has medieval roots, that society has its own identity outside of the political dimension. It seems to follow from this that political authority ought to respect the autonomy of society in the spheres where it is manifest. This involves a new kind of limitation of this authority. It was always understood as limited in Christendom by the church, to some degree or other; and also by rights ascribed to individuals or corporations. But the political was the only domain previously in which secular social purpose could be articulated and carried out. To the extent that these new spheres of non-political social identity become recognized, this is no longer the case.

Indeed, the new space of public opinion, mediated by printed materials, can be the source of a more radical challenge, questioning the primacy of political structures on their own ground. Previously, it was axiomatic that societies found their political identities and defined their political direction through and in the traditionally established political structures, and only there—whether these were royal courts or parliaments or some combination of the two. Unofficial pressure might be exercised through agitation and pamphleteering, but this did not challenge the principle that the authoritative locus for defining political ends lay in the established bodies. With the development of the new space of public opinion, more far-reaching claims begin to be made. It has been argued,[5] for instance, that in early eighteenth-century America, a new form of discourse emerges in newspapers and pamphlets. It is a discourse which

[5] I have drawn here on the interesting discussion in Michael Warner, *The Letters of the Republic*, Cambridge, MA: Harvard University Press, 1990.

implicitly arrogates to this print-sustained space the power and duty to define the goals of the people and to call the established bodies to book for their deviations from these. The discourse is cast in the traditional rhetoric of republicanism, but under this familiar cover a radically new formula is being advanced. In republican societies, the people did indeed criticize and control their officers, but assembled in the *ekklesia* or general meeting. This was itself a governing body, the foundational one. Now the powers of the assembled people are being arrogated to a new print-mediated public space, unembodied in any traditional structure, or indeed, face-to-face meeting of any kind. The political identity of society shifts to an unprecedented locus. Whether or not this analysis holds of the eighteenth-century British American colonies, something like this shift has plainly become central to modern democratic self-understanding.

This congeries of ideas about the economy and public space constituted one of the strands in the new notion of 'civil society' which was distinguished from the state. It comprised a public, but not politically structured domain. The first feature was essential: civil society was not the private sphere. Where Aristotle distinguishes *polis* from *oikos*, and only the first is a public domain, Hegel distinguishes three terms *Sittlichkeit*: family, civil society, and the state. Civil society is not identical with the third term, the *polis*, but it is not with the first term either. That is why I argued earlier that any definition of civil society in sense one, which identifies it simply with the existence of autonomous associations free from state tutelage, fails to do justice to the historical concept. This defines a pattern of public social life, and not just a congeries of private enclaves.

This notion of civil society, the L-variant, can inspire radical political hopes: sometimes of an anti-political kind. Even Locke saw the political structure as an emanation of a society which in one sense was already political, because people had put their power to enforce the Law of Nature in common, but had as yet no political structure. With the enriching of the concept, we can formulate the idea that society has its own pre-political life and unity which the political structure must serve. Society has the right and power to make and unmake political authority, according to whether it serves or fails to serve.

This is the radical doctrine of Thomas Paine. In a somewhat less radical variant, something like this was acted on by the Americans in their war of independence. It was less radical, because the decision to rebel was taken by political authorities in the thirteen colonies. The early modern idea, that a rebellion against a supreme authority in violation of its trust could be carried out by duly constituted subordinate authority (e.g., the central notion of the *Vindiciae contra Tyrannos*), would also have served to justify the rebellion. Americans saw themselves as fighting for established right against usurpation. But in fact, the language they adopted, that of 'We, the People', had a more radical impact. It seemed to draw the revolutionary conclusion from the L-variant: the people have an identity, they have purposes, even (one might say) a will, outside of any political structure. In the name of this identity, following this will, they have the right to make and unmake these structures. The duality of focus in the western concept of society, which goes back in different forms to the Middle Ages, finally takes on its most revolutionary formulation.

This has become a commonplace of modern thought. Between 1776 and now, the notion of a people's pre-political identity has taken a new and much more powerful form, that of the nation. We now speak of this right to make and unmake structures as the right of self-determination. No one today dares deny this in principle, however suppressed it may be in practice.

But radical hopes could also take an anti-political form. One could dream of the non-political spheres of society becoming more and more autonomous, more and more self-sufficient. Taken to the extreme, this offers a vision of a society without politics, where the government of men gives way to the administration of things, as Saint Simon articulated it, followed by Engels. In less extreme fashion, one could hope for a society in which the development of industry and commerce would serve to tie people together in peace on a growing scale, and thus drastically reduce the role of government, lessening its policing function and doing away with war altogether.

The eighteenth-century developments I described earlier, which gave us the notions of economy and public opinion, also developed a notion of 'civilization'. A 'civilized' society was partly so in virtue of its political constitution—and indeed, the term in some respects replaces the earlier French expression 'état policé'. But 'civilization' included a lot more, to do with pacification, enlightenment, the development of production, arts and sciences, and polished mores. Within the self-definition of modern Europe as civilized, in contrast to other societies and to its own past, the virtues of peaceful production bulked large, and the older warrior virtues were seen in an unfavourable light. European society gained in polish as it turned its back on these and on the honour ethic which accompanied them. But it was also the honour ethic which gave the political life intrinsic value. For the new social ethic of peaceful productivity, as we see for instance with the Utilitarians, political structures had purely instrumental significance. The less we needed them the better.

So two rather different kinds of political hopes arise from this notion of society as having a pre- or non-political identity. The one moves towards the norm of self-determination; the other towards the goal of marginalizing the political. So we can now see why the L-stream was not the only one which fed the new concept of civil society. It was not just that these hopes each in its own way undermine the very distinction civil society/state. This they did, of course. Radical self-determination swallows up the state in society, in a supposed common will; while the goal of marginalization is to approach anarchy as closely as possible.

But it is also, much more importantly, that both these hopes pose a threat for freedom, and the distinction was introduced in the first place in the context of counter-absolutist thought. One recurring threat to freedom has come from the politics of what would later be called the general will. This *idée force*, as elaborated by Rousseau, fuses the idea of a people's will independent of all political structure with the ethic of ancient republicanism, and draws its power from both. Rousseau invokes the pre-political in the very non-ancient idea of a social contract, of society as constituted by will, as well as in his understanding of nature as inner voice. He invokes the ancient ethic of virtue in the ideal of a transparent face-to-face political society. This latter, of course, drops out of the picture as unrealizable in the modern world. What remains is the notion of a popular will as the ultimate justification for all political structures and authority.

The most thoroughgoing destruction of civil society has been carried out in the name of some of the variants and successors of this idea in the twentieth century, notably the nation and the proletariat. A strange and horrifying reversal has taken place, whereby an idea whose roots lie in a pre-political conception of society now can justify the total subjection of life to an enterprise of political transformation. And in less spectacular form, the power of the state has often been enhanced by its self-definition as the instrument of the national will.

But in a more subtle way, the politics of marginalizing politics has also been seen as posing a threat to freedom. This is particularly so when the sphere of society in the name of which the political is being marginalized is that of the self-regulating economy. For in this domain the disposition of things in society as a whole is seen as arising not out of any collective will or common decision, but by an 'invisible hand.' To leave our collective fate to blind economic forces can be portrayed as a kind of alienation. On top of this, all those whose allegiance is to an ideal of the political life as a good in itself will see the marginalization of politics as a kind of abandonment of what is most valuable in life, a flight from the public into the narrower and less significant sphere of private satisfactions, seeking the 'petits et vulgaires plaisirs' of which Tocqueville speaks.[6]

Marx, who developed a theory of alienation, himself subscribed to his own version of a world without politics. Tocqueville articulated the most influential view in which the dangers implicit in both the kinds of hopes the L-theory generates have been explored and related. The modern democracy of the general will can degenerate, he argues, into a kind of 'despotisme doux'[7] in which citizens fall prey to a tutelary power which dwarfs them; and this is both cause and effect of a turn away from the public to the private which although tempting represents a diminution of their human stature.

Those who are thus dissatisfied with the L-variant of the notion of civil society are induced to turn to Montesquieu. Tocqueville can be seen as the greatest disciple of Montesquieu in the nineteenth century. But already Hegel in his dissatisfaction with the L-variant had drawn on Montesquieu. Hegel, like Marx after him, couldn't believe in the benign effects of an autonomous, unregulated economic sphere. And he produced his own variant of the civic humanist doctrine that the life of the citizen had value in itself. At the same time, his theory of modern life, in distinction from the ancients, turned on the differentiated development of this non-political public sphere, which related us in our separate, non-political identities. The result was the Hegelian concept of civil society. This was a separate sphere, but not self-sufficient. Not only did its constituent economic processes need regulation, which was undertaken partly within civil society, but this society could escape destruction only by being incorporated in the higher unity of the state, i.e., the society as politically organized.

---

6 See *De la Démocratie en Amérique*, Paris: Flammarion 1981, Vol. II, IVe partie, ch. VI, p. 385.

7 *De la Démocratie en Amérique*, Vol. II, IVe partie, ch. VI, p. 384.

Hegel combines both the L- and the M-streams in his concept of civil society. If the L-concept, to repeat, turns on the idea of a non political dimension to society, Montesquieu's contribution is the picture of a society which is defined by its political organization, but where this is constitutionally diverse, distributing power among many independent sources. It is important here too that there be independent associations for non-political purposes. But their significance is not that they form a non-political social sphere, but rather that they form the basis for the fragmentation and diversity of power within the political system. What is relevant is not their life outside, but the way they are integrated into the political system, and the weight they have in it. Montesquieu's 'corps intermédiaires' are in fact 'amphibious' bodies. They have a life outside the political structure, and this is indeed their primary purpose, and the basis of their strength. But it is crucial to the health of the polity that they also play a role within it.

Thus the different elements of Hegel's political society take up their role in the state, make up the different Estates and form the basis for a differentiated constitution, whose formula was partly inspired by Montesquieu. In this way, we avoid both the undifferentiated homogeneity of the general-will state, which Hegel thought must lead inevitably to tyranny and terror, and also the unregulated and ultimately self-destructive play of blind economic forces, which seemed to menace England.

With Tocqueville the Montesquieuian heritage is even clearer. The only bulwark against mild despotism is associations. Voluntary associations for all purposes are valuable. But their significance is that they give us the taste and habit of self-rule. And so associations for political purposes are essential. But if they are to be really loci of self-rule, they have to be non-gigantic and numerous, and exist at many levels of the polity. This itself should be decentralized, so that self-government can be practised also at the local and not just national level. If it dies out on the former, it is in danger on the latter. 'Dans les pays démocratiques, la science de l'association est la science mère.'[8]

III

So our notion of civil society is complex. It is an amalgam of two rather different influences, which I have called the L-stream and the

8 De la Démocratie en Amérique, Vol. II, IIe partie, ch. V, p. 141.

M-stream. It clearly goes beyond the minimal definition 1 earlier. But it hovers between the other two because of its dual origin. For the purposes of deconstructing a Leninist dictatorship, anyone of these definitions will do. But when we come to ask how the concept of civil society relates to the freedom of western liberal democracies, we find a more complex story.

We can see now why the question I discussed at the outset, whether we in fact have a functioning independent civil society in the west, was not so easy to answer. Among the other reasons is the fact that there are rather different definitions of what this independence involves, which have equally strong warrant in our two-streamed tradition. No easier to answer is the question of what role a concept of civil society has to play in the future defence of freedom.

It is tempting to think that it is almost guaranteed a role, just because of its place in the complex intellectual and institutional background of western liberty. The distinction between civil society and the state is indeed important to the western tradition, not just because of all the roots of the idea in earlier epochs of western history, but more especially because it has been central to the different forms of counter-absolutist thinking. Indeed, it owes its existence and relevance to the development in the west of reforming absolutism, of what has been called 'the well-ordered police state'[9] in the seventeenth and eighteenth centuries. It made no more sense in the context of the *polis*, or the medieval polity, than it did in a host of traditional non-western polities. It arose, one might say, as a necessary instrument of defence in face of the specific *threats* to freedom implicit in the western tradition. But precisely to the extent that the modern state is still drawn to a vocation of mobilizing and re-organizing its subjects' lives, the distinction would seem to be guaranteed a continuing relevance.

Thus one can argue that the distinction is essential to our conception of what it is to preserve freedom. But it has also been shouldered aside or sidetracked by supposedly simpler and more arresting definitions of a free society, which turn on the idea of a general will, or a politics-free sphere. These emerge from the same sources as the idea of civil society, but have each taken on a radically different cast.

[9] See Marc Raeff, *The Well-Ordered Police State*, New Haven: Yale University Press, 1983. Of course, the term is used not in its twentieth-century sense. 'Police' translates the eighteenth-century German 'Polizei', which covered state action ordering the lives of its subjects rather than that directed to suppressing violence.

On one hand, there is the 'Jacobin' notion of democracy, that people are free only when they constitute together a common will, which ought in principle to be unlimited, since it is the expression of their freedom. To erect reserved areas where this will cannot enter is to establish zones of potential privilege, in which relations of domination and alienation can arise. The power of the general will to establish the conditions of freedom 'est la condition qui donnant chaque citoyen à la patrie, le garantit de toute dépendance personnelle.'[10] This is the model which, through its Marxist transformation,[11] underlies Leninism. But in another variant it has also animated extreme forms of nationalism.

On the other side stands a mode of liberalism which is attracted to the model of a self-regulating social life. Our goal ought to be to disintricate the state as much as possible from society, to allow maximum space for individual freedom on one hand, and the benign, self-adjusting forces at play between them on the other. Among the latter, the market has paradigmatic status. I have drawn these two images in extreme form. Obviously, they can work their attractive force also in much more moderate and multifaceted political conditions. But part of their power comes from their simplicity. For that very reason, while they are at daggers drawn, each tends to identify the other as the only alternative. The more complex moral world to which neither properly applies is not acknowledged. Former adepts of Marx often convert into fervent followers of Hayek. To make the notion of civil society central to our political discourse today, we have to be able to reject these seductively limpid formulae.

There is, in fact, a wide range of other possibilities, of potential 'third ways' including an alternative version of liberalism of Tocquevillian provenance. Where the 'Jacobin' view draws on the republican tradition of political freedom, but uses it to subdue civil society, and where 'negative' liberalism depreciates political freedom altogether, Tocqueville reformulates the ideals of republican freedom in a context of fragmented, decentralized power whose formula derives from the M-stream. Montesquieu's 'corps intermédiaires,' originally for the most part bastions of privilege, have become self-governing associations. Civil society is not so much a sphere outside political

10 *Du Contrat Social*, Book I, ch. VII.
11 We can see this, for example, in *Zur Judenfrage*.

power; rather it penetrates deeply into this power, fragments and decentralizes it. Its components are truly 'amphibious.'

I suppose I haven't managed to hide very effectively my preference for this third model over the first two. I hope the first now stands discredited, but I fear the second may gain from its demise. If this were to happen, the civil society notion would be sidetracked and drained of much of its force. Its weight as a counter-thrust to bureaucratic power would be neutralized. And an important constituent of our political tradition, the ideal of political freedom, would atrophy.

But that doesn't mean that the idea of civil society which we want to recur to is a simple, unified one. We can't just opt for the M-against the L-stream. Both of them are deeply woven into our political traditions and way of life. The force of the L-idea is too great and too obtrusive to be altogether denied. Rather the choice would seem to lie between a view of civil society almost exclusively concerned with the L-stream, and one which tries to balance both. In the first category fall those critics of 'corporatist' politics on the right who aim to roll back the power of the state. In the second are found the contemporary followers of Tocqueville, some of whom along with a bewilderingly diverse variety of utopians end up on the ecological left, but who are also distributed through the centre of many western societies.

As the preoccupation with civil society continues in both east and west, as the discussions in the two areas interpenetrate more and more, as is surely bound to happen, we must hope that this second option will emerge as the dominant one. Only in this way will we be able to incorporate into our political structures the multifaceted western tradition of freedom.

3

THE IDEA OF CIVIL SOCIETY
*A Path to Social Reconstruction**

Michael Walzer

My aim in this essay is to defend a complex, imprecise, and, at crucial points, uncertain account of society and politics. I have no hope of theoretical simplicity, not at this historical moment when so many stable oppositions of political and intellectual life have collapsed; but I also have no desire for simplicity, since a world that theory could fully grasp and neatly explain would not, I suspect, be a pleasant place. In the nature of things, then, my argument won't be elegant, and though I believe that arguments should march, the sentences following one another like soldiers on parade, the route of my march will be twisting and roundabout. I shall begin with the idea of civil society, recently revived by Central and East European intellectuals, and go on to talk about the state, the economy, and the nation, and then about civil society and the state again. These are the crucial social formations that we inhabit, but we don't at this moment live comfortably in any of them. Nor is it possible to imagine, in accordance with one or another of the great simplifying theories, a way to choose among them—as if we were destined to find, one day, the best social

* This essay was given as the Gunnar Myrdal lecture at the University of Stockholm, Sweden, October 1990.

formation. I mean to argue against choosing, but I shall also claim that it is from within civil society that this argument is best understood.

The words 'civil society' name the space of uncoerced human association and also the set of relational networks—formed for the sake of family, faith, interest, and ideology—that fill this space. Central and East European dissidence flourished within a highly restricted version of civil society, and the first task of the new democracies created by the dissidents, so we are told, is to rebuild the networks: unions, churches, political parties and movements, cooperatives, neighbourhoods, schools of thought, societies for promoting or preventing this and that. In the west, by contrast, we have lived in civil society for many years without knowing it. Or, better, since the Scottish Enlightenment, or since Hegel, the words have been known to the knowers of such things but they have rarely served to focus anyone else's attention. Now writers in Hungary, Czechoslovakia, and Poland invite us to think about how this social formation is secured and invigorated.

We have reasons of our own for accepting the invitation. Increasingly, associational life in the 'advanced' capitalist and social democratic countries seems at risk. Publicists and preachers warn us of a steady attenuation of everyday cooperation and civic friendship. And this time it's possible that they are not, as they usually are, foolishly alarmist. Our cities really are noisier and nastier than they once were. Familial solidarity, mutual assistance, political likemindedness—all these are less certain and less substantial than they once were. Other people, strangers on the street, seem less trustworthy than they once did. The Hobbesian account of society is more persuasive than it once was.

Perhaps this worrisome picture follows—in part, no more, but what else can a political theorist say?—from the fact that we have not thought enough about solidarity and trust or planned for their future. We have been thinking too much about social formations different from, in competition with, civil society. And so we have neglected the networks through which civility is produced and reproduced. Imagine that the following questions were posed one or two centuries ago to political theorists and moral philosophers: what is the preferred setting, the most supportive environment, for the good life? What sorts of institutions should we work for? Nineteenth- and twentieth-century social thought provides four different, by now familiar, answers to these questions. Think of them as four rival ideologies, each with its own claim to completeness and correctness. Each is importantly wrong. Each neglects the necessary pluralism of any civil society. Each is predicated on an assumption I mean to attack: that such questions must receive a singular answer.

DEFINITIONS FROM THE LEFT

I shall begin, since this is for me the best-known ground, with two leftist answers. The first of the two holds that the preferred setting for the good life is the political community, the democratic state, within which we can be citizens: freely engaged, fully committed, decision-making members. And a citizen, on this view, is much the best thing to be. To live well is to be politically active, working with our fellow citizens, collectively determining our common destiny— not for the sake of this or that determination but for the work itself, in which our highest capacities as rational and moral agents find expression. We know ourselves best as persons who propose, debate, and decide.

This argument goes back to the Greeks, but we are most likely to recognize its neo-classical versions. It is Rousseau's argument or the standard leftist interpretation of Rousseau's argument. His understanding of citizenship as moral agency is one of the key sources of democratic idealism. We can see it at work in a liberal such as John Stuart Mill, in whose writings it produced an unexpected defence of Syndicalism (what is today called 'workers' control') and, more generally, of social democracy. It appeared among nineteenth- and twentieth-century democratic radicals, often with a hard populist edge. It played a part in the reiterated demand for social inclusion by women, workers, blacks, and new immigrants, all of whom based their claims on their capacity as agents. And this same neo-classical idea of citizenship resurfaced in the 1960s in New Left theories of participation, where it was, however, like latter-day revivals of many ideas, highly theoretical and without much local resonance.

Today perhaps in response in the political disasters of the late sixties, 'communitarians' in the United States struggle to give Rousseauian idealism a historical reference, looking back to the early American republic and calling for a renewal of civic virtue. They prescribe citizenship as an antidote to the fragmentation of contemporary society—for these theorists, like Rousseau, are disinclined to value the fragments. In their hands, republicanism is still a simplifying creed. If politics is our highest calling, then we are called away from every other activity (or, every other activity is redefined in political terms); our energies are directed toward policy formation and decision-making in the democratic state.

I don't doubt that the active and engaged citizen is an attractive figure—even if some of the activists that we actually meet carrying placards and shouting slogans aren't all that attractive. The most penetrating criticism of this first answer to the question about the good life is not that the life isn't good but that it isn't the 'real life' of very many people in the modern world. This is so in two senses. First, though the power of the democratic state has grown enormously, partly (and rightly) in response to the demands of engaged citizens, it can't be said that the state is fully in the hands of its citizens. And the larger it gets, the more it takes over those smaller associations still subject to hands-on control. The rule of the demos is in significant ways illusory; the participation of ordinary men and women in the activities of the state (unless they are state employees) is largely vicarious; even party militants are more likely to argue and complain than actually to decide.

Second, despite the singlemindedness of republican ideology, politics rarely engages the full attention of the citizens who are supposed to be its chief protagonists. They have too many other things to worry about. Above all, they have to earn a living. They are more deeply engaged in the economy than in the political community. Republican theorists (like Hannah Arendt) recognize this engagement only as a threat to civic virtue. Economic activity belongs to the realm of necessity, they argue, politics to the realm of freedom. Ideally, citizens should not have to work; they should be served by machines, if not by slaves, so that they can flock to the assemblies and argue with their fellows about affairs of state. In practice, however, work, though it begins in necessity, takes on a value of its own—expressed in commitment to a career, pride in a job well done, a sense of camaraderie in the workplace. All of these are competitive with the values of citizenship.

The second leftist position on the preferred setting for the good life involves a turning away from republican politics and a focus instead on economic activity. We can think of this as the socialist answer to the questions I began with; it can be found in Marx and also, though the arguments are somewhat different, among the utopians he hoped to supersede. For Marx, the preferred setting is the cooperative economy, where we can all be producers—artists (Marx was a romantic), inventors, and artisans. (Assembly-line workers don't quite seem to fit.) This again is much the best thing to be. The picture Marx paints is of creative men and women making useful and beautiful objects, not for the sake of this or that object but for the sake of creativity itself, the highest expression of our 'species-being' as *homo faber*, man-the-maker.

The state, in this view, ought to be managed in such a way as to set productivity free. It doesn't matter who the managers are so long as they are committed to this goal and rational in its pursuit. Their work is technically important but not substantively interesting. Once productivity is free, politics simply ceases to engage anyone's attention. Before that time, in the Marxist here and now, political conflict is taken to be the superstructural enactment of economic conflict, and democracy is valued mainly because it enables socialist movements and parties to organize for victory. The value is instrumental and historically specific. A democratic state is the preferred setting not for the good life but for the class struggle; the purpose of the struggle is to win, and victory brings an end to democratic instrumentality. There is no intrinsic value in democracy, no reason to think that politics has, for creatures like us, a permanent attractiveness. When we are all engaged in productive activity, social division and the conflicts it engenders will disappear, and the state, in the once-famous phrase, will 'wither away.'

In fact, if this vision were ever realized, it is politics that would wither away. Some kind of administrative agency would still be necessary for economic coordination, and it is only a Marxist conceit to refuse to call this agency a state. 'Society regulates the general production,' Marx wrote in *The German Ideology*, 'and thus makes it possible for me to do one thing today and another tomorrow... just as I have a mind.' Because this regulation is non-political, the individual producers are freed from the burdens of citizenship. They attend instead to the things they make and to the cooperative relationships they establish. Exactly how one can work with other people and still do whatever one pleases is unclear to me and probably to most other readers of Marx. The texts suggest an extraordinary faith in the virtuosity of the regulators. No one, I think, quite shares this faith today, but something like it helps to explain the tendency of some leftists to see even the liberal and democratic state as an obstacle that has to be, in the worst of recent jargons, 'smashed.'

The seriousness of Marxist anti-politics is nicely illustrated by Marx's own dislike of syndicalism. What the syndicalists proposed was a neat amalgam of the first and second answers to the question about the good life: for them, the preferred setting was the worker-controlled factory, where men and women were simultaneously citizens and producers, making decisions and making things. Marx seems to have regarded the combination as impossible; factories could not be both democratic and productive. This is the point of Engels's little essay on authority, which I take to express Marx's view also. More generally, self-government on the job called into question the legitimacy of 'social regulation' or state planning, which alone, Marx thought, could enable individual workers to devote themselves, without distraction, to their work.

But this vision of the cooperative economy is set against an unbelievable background—a non-political state, regulation without conflict, 'the administration of things.' In every actual experience of socialist politics, the state has moved rapidly into the foreground, and most socialists, in the west at least, have been driven to make their own amalgam of the first and second answers. They call themselves *democratic* socialists, focusing on the state as well as (in fact, much more than) on the economy and doubling the preferred settings for the good life. Because I believe that two are better than one, I take this to be progress. But before I try to suggest what further progress might look like, I need to describe two more ideological answers to the question about the good life, one of them capitalist, the other nationalist. For there is no reason to think that only leftists love singularity.

A Capitalist Definition

The third answer holds that the preferred setting for the good life is the marketplace, where individual men and women, consumers rather than producers, choose among a maximum number of options. The autonomous individual confronting his, and now her, possibilities—this is much the best thing to be. To live well is not to make political decisions or beautiful objects; it is to make personal choices. Not any particular choices, for no choice is substantively the best: it is the activity of choosing that makes for autonomy. And the market within which choices are made, like the socialist economy, largely dispenses with politics; it requires at most a minimal state—not 'social regulation,' only the police.

Production, too, is free even if it isn't, as in the Marxist vision, freely creative. More important than the producers, however, are the entrepreneurs—heroes of autonomy, consumers of opportunity—who compete to supply whatever all the other consumers want or might be persuaded to want. Entrepreneurial activity tracks consumer preference. Though not without its own excitements, it is mostly instrumental: the aim of all entrepreneurs (and all producers) is to increase their market power, maximize their options. Competing with one another, they maximize everyone else's options too, filling the marketplace with desirable objects. The market is preferred (over the political community and the cooperative economy) because of its fullness. Freedom, in the capitalist view, is a function of plenitude. We can only choose when we many choices.

It is also true, unhappily, that we can only make effective (rather than merely speculative or wistful) choices when we have resources to dispose of. But people come to the marketplace with radically unequal resources—some with virtually nothing at all. Not everyone can compete successfully in commodity production, and therefore not everyone has access to commodities. Autonomy turns out to be a high-risk value, which many men and women can only realize with help from their friends. The market, however, is not a good setting for mutual assistance, for I cannot help someone else without reducing (for the short term, at least) my own options. And I have no reason, as an autonomous individual, to accept any reductions of any sort for someone else's sake. My argument here is not that autonomy collapses into egotism, only that autonomy in the market-place provides no support for social solidarity. Despite the successes of capitalist production, the good life of consumer choice is not universally available. Large numbers of people drop out of the market economy or live precariously on its margins.

Partly for this reason, capitalism, like socialism, is highly dependent on state action—not only to prevent theft and enforce contracts but also to regulate the economy and guarantee the minimal welfare of its participants. But these participants, insofar as they are market activists, are not active in the state: capitalism in its ideal form, like socialism again, does not make for citizenship. Or, its protagonists conceive of citizenship in economic terms, so that citizens are trans-formed into autonomous consumers, looking for the party or programme that most persuasively promises to strengthen their market positions. They need the state but have no moral relation to it, and they control its officials only as consumers control the producers of commodities, by buying or not buying what they make.

Because the market has no political boundaries, capitalist entrepreneurs also evade official control. They need the state but have no loyalty to it; the profit motive brings them into conflict with democratic regulation. So arms merchants sell the latest military technology to foreign powers, and manufacturers move their factories overseas to escape safety codes or minimum-wage laws. Multinational corporations stand outside (and to some extent against) every political community. They are known only by their brand names, which, unlike family names and country names, evoke preferences but not affections or solidarities.

A NATIONALIST RESPONSE

The fourth answer to the question about the good life can be read as a response to market amorality and disloyalty, though it has, historically, other sources as well. According to the fourth answer, the preferred setting is the nation, within which we are loyal members, bound to one another by ties of blood and history. And a member, secure in membership, literally part of an organic whole— this is much the best thing to be. To live well is to participate with other men and women in remembering, cultivating, and passing on a national heritage. This is so, on the nationalist view, without reference to the specific content of the heritage, so long as it is one's own, a matter of birth, not choice. Every nationalist will, of course, find value in his or her own heritage, but the highest value is not in the finding but in the willing: the firm identification of the individual with a people and a history.

Nationalism has often been a leftist ideology, historically linked to democracy and even to socialism. But it is most characteristically an ideology of the right, for its understanding of membership is ascriptive; it requires no political choices and no activity beyond ritual affirmation. When nations find themselves ruled by foreigners, however, ritual affirmation isn't enough. Then nationalism requires a more heroic loyalty: self-sacrifice in the struggle for national liberation. The capacity of the nation to elicit such sacrifices from its members is proof of the importance of this fourth answer. Individual members seek the good life by seeking autonomy not for themselves but for their people. Ideally, this attitude ought to survive the liberation struggle and provide a foundation for social solidarity and mutual assistance. Perhaps, to some extent, it does: certainly the welfare state has had its greatest successes in ethnically homogeneous countries. It is also true, however, that once liberation has been secured, nationalist men and women are commonly content with a vicarious rather than a practical participation in the community. There is nothing wrong with vicarious participation, on the nationalist view, since the good life is more a matter of identity than activity—faith, not works, so to speak, though both of these are understood in secular terms.

In the modern world, nations commonly seek statehood, for their autonomy will always be at risk if they lack sovereign power. But they don't seek states of any particular kind. No more do they seek economic arrangements of any particular kind. Unlike religious believers who are their close kin and (often) bitter rivals, nationalists are not bound by a body of authoritative law or a set of sacred texts. Beyond liberation, they have no program, only a vague commitment to continue a history, to sustain a 'way of life.' Their own lives, I suppose, are emotionally intense, but in relation to society and economy this is a dangerously free-floating intensity. In time of trouble, it can readily be turned against other nations, particularly against the internal others: minorities, aliens, strangers. Democratic citizenship, worker solidarity, free enterprise, and consumer autonomy—all these are less exclusive than nationalism but not always resistant to its power. The ease with which citizens, workers, and consumers become fervent nationalists is a sign of the inadequacy of the first three answers to the question about the good life. The nature of nationalist fervour signals the inadequacy of the fourth.

CAN WE FIND A SYNTHESIS?

All these answers are wrongheaded because of their singularity. They miss the complexity of human society, the inevitable conflicts of commitment and loyalty. Hence I am uneasy with the idea that there might be a fifth and finally correct answer to the question about the good life. Still, there is a fifth answer, the newest one (it draws upon less central themes of nineteenth- and twentieth-century social thought), which holds that the good life can only be lived in civil society, the realm of fragmentation and struggle but also of concrete and authentic solidarities, where we fulfill E. M. Forster's injunction, 'only connect,' and become sociable or communal men and women. And this is, of course, much the best thing to be. The picture here is of people freely associating and communicating with one another, forming and reforming groups of all sorts, not for the sake of any particular formation—family, tribe, nation, religion, commune, brotherhood or sisterhood, interest group, or ideological movement—but for the sake of sociability itself. For we are by nature social, before we are political or economic beings.

I would rather say that the civil society argument is a corrective to the four ideological accounts of the good life—part denial, part incorporation—rather than a fifth to stand alongside them. It challenges their singularity but it has no singularity of its own. The phrase 'social being' describes men and women who are citizens, producers. consumers, members of the nation, and much else besides—and none of these by nature or because it is the best thing to be. The associational life of civil society is the actual ground where all versions of the good are worked out and tested...and proved to be partial, incomplete, ultimately unsatisfying. It can't be the case that living on this ground is good in itself; there isn't any other place to live. What is true is that the quality of our political and economic activity and of our national culture is intimately connected to the strength and vitality of our associations.

Ideally, civil society is a setting of settings: all are included, none is preferred. The argument is a liberal version of the four answers, accepting them all, insisting that each leave room for the others, therefore not finally accepting any of them. Liberalism appears here as an anti-ideology, and this is an attractive position in the contemporary world: I shall stress this attractiveness as I try to explain how civil society might actually incorporate and deny the four answers. Later on, however, I shall have to argue that this position too, so genial and benign, has its problems.

Let's begin with the political community and the cooperative economy, taken together. These two leftist versions of the good life systematically undervalued all associations except the demos and the working class. Their protagonists could imagine conflicts between political communities and between classes but not within either; they aimed at the abolition or transcendence of particularism and all its divisions. Theorists of civil society, by contrast, have a more realistic view of communities and economies. They are more accommodating to conflict—that is, to political opposition and economic competition.

Associational freedom serves for them to legitimate a set of market relations, though not necessarily the capitalist set. The market, when it is entangled in the network of associations, when the forms of ownership are pluralized, is without doubt the economic formation most consistent with the civil society argument. This same argument also serves to legitimate a kind of state that is liberal and pluralist more than republican (not so radically dependent upon the virtue of its citizens). Indeed, a state of this sort, as we shall see, is necessary if associations are to flourish.

Once incorporated into civil society, neither citizenship nor production can ever again be all-absorbing. They will have their votaries, but these people will not be models for the rest of us—or, they will be partial models only, for some people at some time of their lives, not for other people, not at other times. This pluralist perspective follows in part, perhaps, from the lost romance of work, from our experience with the new productive technologies and the growth of the service economy. Service is more easily reconciled with a vision of human beings as social animals than with *homo faber*. What can a hospital attendant or a school teacher or a marriage counsellor or a social worker or a television repair-person or a government official be said to *make*? The contemporary economy does not offer many people a chance for creativity in the Marxist sense. Nor does Marx (or any socialist thinker of the central tradition) have much to say about those men and women whose economic activity consists entirely in helping other people. The helpmate, like the housewife, was never assimilated to the class of workers.

In similar fashion, politics in the contemporary democratic state does not offer many people a chance for Rousseauian self-determination. Citizenship, taken by itself, is today mostly a passive role: citizens are spectators who vote. Between elections they are served, well or badly, by the civil service. They are not at all like those heroes of republican mythology, the citizens of ancient Athens meeting in assembly and (foolishly, as it turned out) deciding to invade Sicily. But in the associational networks of civil society—in unions, parties, movements, interest groups, and so on—these same people make many smaller decisions and shape to some degree the more distant determinations of state and economy. And in a more densely organized, more egalitarian civil society, they might do both these things to greater effect.

These socially engaged men and women—part-time union officers, movement activists, party regulars, consumer advocates, welfare volunteers, church members, family heads—stand outside the republic of citizens as it is commonly conceived. They are only intermittently virtuous; they are too caught up in particularity. They look, most of them, for many partial fulfillments, no longer for the one clinching fulfillment. On the ground of actuality (unless the state usurps the ground), citizenship shades off into a great diversity of (sometimes divisive) decision-making roles; and, similarly, production shades off into a multitude of (sometimes competitive) socially useful activities. It is, then, a mistake to set politics and work in opposition to one another. There is no ideal fulfillment and no essential human capacity. We require many settings so that we can live different kinds of good lives.

All this is not to say, however, that we need to accept the capitalist version of competition and division. Theorists who regard the market as the preferred setting for the good life aim to make it the actual setting for as many aspects of life as possible. Their singlemindedness takes the form of market imperialism; confronting the democratic state, they are advocates of privatization and laissez-faire. Their ideal is a society in which all goods and services are provided by entrepreneurs to consumers. That some entrepreneurs would fail and many consumers find themselves helpless in the marketplace—this is the price of individual autonomy. It is, obviously, a price we already pay: in all capitalist societies, the market makes for inequality. The more successful its imperialism, the greater the inequality. But were the market to be set firmly within civil society, politically constrained, open to communal as well as private initiatives, limits might be fixed on its unequal outcomes. The exact nature of the limits would depend on the strength and density of the associational networks (including, now, the political community).

The problem with inequality is not merely that some individuals are more capable, others less capable, of making their consumer preferences effective. It's not that some individuals live in fancier apartments than others, or drive better-made cars, or take vacations in more exotic places. These are conceivably the just rewards of market success. The problem is that inequality commonly translates into domination and radical deprivation. But the verb 'translate' here describes a socially mediated process, which is fostered or inhibited by the structure of its mediations. Dominated and deprived individuals are likely to be disorganized as well as impoverished, whereas poor people with strong families, churches, unions, political parties, and ethnic alliances are not likely to be dominated or deprived for long. Nor need these people stand alone even in the marketplace. The capitalist answer assumes I that the good life of entrepreneurial initiative and consumer choice is a life led most importantly by individuals. But civil society encompasses or can encompass a variety of market agents: family businesses, publicly owned or municipal companies, worker communes, consumer cooperatives, non-profit organizations of many different sorts. All these function in the market even though they have their origins outside. And just as the experience of democracy is expanded and enhanced by groups that are in but not of the state, so consumer choice is expanded and enhanced by groups that are in but not of the market.

It is only necessary to add that among the groups in but not of the state are market organizations, and among the groups in but not of the market are state organizations. All social forms are relativized by the civil society argument—and on the actual ground too. This also means that all social forms are contestable; moreover, contests can't be won by invoking one or another account of the preferred setting—as if it were enough to say that market organizations, insofar as they are efficient, don't have to be democratic or that state firms, insofar as they are democratically controlled, don't have to operate within the constraints of the market. The exact character of our associational life is something that has to be argued about, and it is in the course of these arguments that we also decide about the forms of democracy, the nature of work, the extent and effects of market inequalities, and much else.

The quality of nationalism is also determined within civil society, where national groups coexist and overlap with families and religious communities (two social formations largely neglected in modernist answers to the question about the good life) and where nationalism is expressed in schools and movements, organizations for mutual aid, cultural and historical societies. It is because groups like these are entangled with other groups, similar in kind but different in aim, that civil society holds out the hope of a domesticated nationalism. In states dominated by a single nation, the multiplicity of the groups pluralizes nationalist politics and culture; in states with more than one nation, the density of the networks prevents radical polarization.

Civil society as we know it has its origin in the struggle for religious freedom. Though often violent, the struggle held open the possibility of peace. 'The establishment of this one thing,' John Locke wrote about toleration 'would take away all ground of complaints and tumults upon account of conscience.' One can easily imagine groundless complaints and tumults, but Locke believed (and he was largely right) that tolerance would dull the edge of religious conflict. People would be less ready to take risks once the stakes were lowered. Civil society simply is that place where the stakes are lower, where, in principle at least, coercion is used only to keep the peace and all associations are equal under the law. In the market, this formal equality often has no substance, but in the world of faith and identity, it is real enough. Though nations don't compete for members in the same way as religions (sometimes) do, the argument for granting them the associational freedom of civil society is similar. When they are free to celebrate their histories, remember their dead, and shape (in part) the education of their children, they are more likely to be harmless than when they are unfree. Locke may have put the claim too strongly when he wrote, 'There is only one thing which gathers people into seditious commotions, and that is oppression,' but he was close enough to the truth to warrant the experiment of radical tolerance.

But if oppression is the cause of seditious commotion, what is the cause of oppression? I don't doubt that there is a materialist story to tell here, but I want to stress the central role played by ideological singlemindedness: the intolerant universalism of (most) religions, the exclusivity of (most) nations. The actual experience of civil society, when it can be had, seems to work against these two. Indeed, it works so well, some observers think, that neither religious faith nor national identity is likely to survive for long in the network of free associations. But we really don't know to what extent faith and identity depend upon coercion or whether they can reproduce themselves under conditions of freedom. I suspect that they both respond to such deep human needs that they will outlast their current organizational forms. It seems, in any case, worthwhile to wait and see.

STILL A NEED FOR STATE POWER

But there is no escape from power and coercion, no possibility of choosing, like the old anarchists, civil society alone. A few years ago, in a book called *Anti-Politics*, the Hungarian dissident George Konrad described a way of living alongside the totalitarian state but, so to speak, with one's back turned toward it. He urged his fellow dissidents to reject the very idea of seizing or sharing power and to devote their energies to religious, cultural, economic, and professional associations. Civil society appears in his book as an alternative to the state, which he assumes to be unchangeable and irredeemably hostile. His argument seemed right to me when I first read his book. Looking back, after the collapse of the Communist regimes in Hungary and elsewhere, I can easily see how much it was a product of its time— and how short that time was! No state can survive for long if it is wholly alienated from civil society. It cannot outlast its own coercive machinery; it is lost, literally, without its firepower. The production and reproduction of loyalty, civility, political competence, and trust in authority are never the work of the state alone, and the effort to go it alone—one meaning of totalitarianism—is doomed to failure.

The failure, however, has carried with it terrible costs, and so one can understand the appeal of contemporary anti-politics. Even as Central and East European dissidents take power, they remain, and should remain, cautious and, apprehensive about its uses. The totalitarian project has left behind an abiding sense of bureaucratic brutality. Here was the ultimate form of political singlemindedness and though the 'democratic' (and, for that matter, the 'communist') ideology that they appropriated was false, the intrusions even of a more genuine democracy are rendered suspect by the memory. Post-totalitarian politicians and writers have, in addition, learned the older anti-politics of free enterprise—so that the laissez-faire market is defended in the east today as one of the necessary institutions of civil society, or, more strongly, as the dominant social formation. This second view takes on plausibility from the extraordinary havoc wrought by totalitarian economic 'planning.' But it rests, exactly like political singlemindedness, on a failure to recognize the pluralism of associational life. The first view leads, often, to a more interesting and more genuinely liberal mistake: it suggests that pluralism is self-sufficient and self-sustaining.

This is, indeed, the experience of the dissidents: the state could not destroy their unions, churches, free universities, illegal markets, *samizdat* publications. Nonetheless, I want to warn against the anti-political tendencies that commonly accompany the celebration of civil society. The network of associations incorporates, but it cannot dispense with, the agencies of state power; neither can socialist cooperation or capitalist competition dispense with the state. That's why so many dissidents are ministers now. It is indeed true that the new social movements in the east and the west—concerned with ecology, feminism, the rights of immigrants and national minorities, workplace and product safety, and so on—do not aim, as the democratic and labour movements once aimed, at taking power. This represents an important change, in sensibility as much as in ideology, reflecting a new valuation of parts over wholes and a new willingness to settle for something less than total victory. But there can be no victory at all that doesn't involve some control over, or use of, the state apparatus. The collapse of totalitarianism is empowering for the members of civil society precisely because it renders the state accessible.

Here, then, is the paradox of the civil society argument. Citizenship is one of many roles that members play, but the state itself is unlike all the other associations. It both frames civil society and occupies space within it. It fixes the boundary conditions and the basic rules of all associational activity (including political activity). It compels association members to think about a common good, beyond their own conceptions of the good life. Even the failed totalitarianism of, say, the Polish communist state had this much impact upon the Solidarity union: it determined that Solidarity was a Polish union, focused on economic arrangements and labour policy within the borders of Poland. A democratic state, which is continuous with the other associations, has at the same time a greater say about their quality and vitality. It serves, or it doesn't serve, the needs of the associational networks as these are worked out by men and women who are simultaneously members and citizens. I shall give only a few obvious examples, drawn from American experience.

Families with working parents need state help in the form of publicly funded day care and effective public schools. National minorities need help in organizing and sustaining their own educational programs. Worker-owned companies and consumer cooperatives need state loans or loan guarantees; so do (even more often) capitalist entrepreneurs and firms. Philanthropy and mutual aid, churches and private universities, depend upon tax exemptions. Labour unions need legal recognition and guarantees against 'unfair labour practices.' Professional associations need state support for their licensing procedures. And across the entire range of association, individual men and women need to be protected against the power of officials, employers, experts, party bosses, factory foremen, directors, priests, parents, patrons; and small and weak groups need to be protected against large and powerful ones. For civil society, left to itself, generates radically unequal power relationships, which only state power can challenge.

Civil society also challenges state power, most importantly when associations have resources or supporters abroad: world religions, pan-national movements, the new environmental groups, multinational corporations. We are likely to feel differently about these challenges, especially after we recognize the real but relative importance of the state. Multinational corporations, for example, need to be constrained, much like states with imperial ambitions; and the best constraint probably lies in collective security, that is, in alliances with other states that give economic regulation some international effect. The same mechanism may turn out to be useful to the new environmental groups. In the first case, the state pressures the corporation; in the second it responds to environmentalist pressure. The two cases suggest, again, that civil society requires political agency. And the state is an indispensable agent—even if the associational networks also, always, resist the organizing impulses of state bureaucrats.

Only a democratic state can create a democratic civil society; only a democratic civil society, can sustain a democratic state. The civility that makes democratic politics possible can only be learned in the associational networks; the roughly equal and widely dispersed capabilities that sustain the networks have to be fostered by the democratic state. Confronted with an overbearing state, citizens, who are also members, will struggle to make room for autonomous associations and market relationships (and also for local governments and decentralized bureaucracies). But the state can never be what it appears to be in liberal theory, a mere framework for civil society. It is also the instrument of the struggle, used to give a particular shape to the common life. Hence citizenship has a certain practical pre-eminence among all our actual and possible memberships. That's not to say that we must be citizens all the time, finding in politics, as Rousseau urged, the greater part of our happiness. Most of us will be happier elsewhere, involved only sometimes in affairs of state. But we must have a state open to our sometime involvement.

Nor need we be involved all the time in our associations. A democratic civil society is one controlled by its members, not through a single process of self-determination but through a large number of different and uncoordinated processes. These needn't all be demo-cratic, for we are likely to be members of many associations, and we will want some of them to be managed in our interests, but also in our absence. Civil society is sufficiently democratic when in some, at least, of its parts we are able to recognize ourselves as authoritative and responsible participants. States are tested by their capacity to sustain this kind of participation—which is very different from the heroic intensity of Rousseauian citizenship. And civil society is tested by its capacity to produce citizens whose interests, at least sometimes, reach farther than themselves and their comrades, who look after the political community that fosters and protects the associational net-works

In Favour of Inclusiveness

I mean to defend a perspective that might be called, awkwardly, 'critical associationalism.' I want to join, but I am somewhat uneasy with, the civil society argument. It can't be said that nothing is lost when we give up the singlemindedness of democratic citizenship or socialist cooperation or individual autonomy or national identity. There was a kind of heroism in those projects—a concentration of energy, a clear sense of direction, an unblinking recognition of friends and enemies. To make one of these one's own was a serious commit-ment. The defence of civil society doesn't seem quite comparable. Associational engagement is conceivably as important a project as any of the others, but its greatest virtue lies in its inclusiveness, and inclusiveness does not make for heroism. 'Join the associations of your choice' is not a slogan to rally political militants. And yet that is what civil society requires: men and women actively engaged—in state, economy, and nation, and also in churches, neighbourhoods, and families, and in many other settings too. To reach this goal is not as easy as it sounds; many people, perhaps most people, live very loosely within the networks; a growing number of people seem to be radically disengaged—passive clients of the state, market dropouts, resentful and posturing nationalists. And the civil society project doesn't confront an energizing hostility, as all the others do; its protagonists are more likely to meet sullen indifference, fear, despair, apathy, and withdrawal.

In Central and Eastern Europe, civil society is still a battle cry, for it requires a dismantling of the totalitarian state and it brings with it the exhilarating experience of associational independence. Among ourselves what is required is nothing so grand; nor does it lend itself to a singular description (but this is what lies ahead in the east too). The civil society project can only be described in terms of all the other projects, against their singularity. Hence my account in these pages, which suggests the need (1) to decentralize the state so that there are more opportunities for citizens to take responsibility for (some of) its activities; (2) to socialize the economy so that there is a greater diversity of market agents, communal as well as private; and (3) to pluralize and domesticate nationalism, on the religious model, so that there are different ways to realize and sustain historical identities.

None of this can be accomplished without using political power to redistribute resources and to underwrite and subsidize the most desirable associational activities. But political power alone cannot accomplish any of it. The kinds of 'action' discussed by theorists of the state need to be supplemented (not, however, replaced) by something radically different: more like union organizing than political mobilization, more like teaching in a school than arguing in the assembly, more like volunteering in a hospital than joining a political party, more like working in an ethnic alliance or a feminist support group than canvassing in an election, more like shaping a co-op budget than deciding on national fiscal policy. But can any of these local and small-scale activities ever carry with them the honour of citizenship? Sometimes, certainly, they are narrowly conceived, partial and particularist; they need political correction. The greater problem, however, is that they seem so ordinary. Living in civil society, one might think, is like speaking in prose.

But just as speaking in prose implies an understanding of syntax, so these forms of action (when they are pluralized) imply an understanding of civility. And that is not an understanding about which we can be entirely confident these days. There is something to be said for the neo-conservative argument that in the modern world we need to recapture the density of associational life and relearn the activities and understandings that go with it. And if this is the case, then a more strenuous argument is called for from the left: we have to reconstruct that same density under new conditions of freedom and equality. It would appear to be an elementary requirement of social democracy that there exist a *society* of lively, engaged, and effective men and women—where the honour of 'action' belongs to the many and not to the few.

Against a background of growing disorganization—violence, homelessness, divorce, abandonment, alienation, and addiction—a society of this sort looks more like a necessary achievement than a comfortable reality. In truth, however, it was never a comfortable reality, except for the few. Most men and women have been trapped in one or another, subordinate relationship, where the 'civility' they learned was deferential rather than independent and active. That is why democratic citizenship, socialist production, free enterprise, and nationalism were all of them liberating projects. But none of them has yet produced a general, coherent, or sustainable liberation. And their more single-minded adherents, who have exaggerated the effectiveness of the state or the market or the nation and neglected the networks, have probably contributed to the disorder of contemporary life. The projects have to be relativized and brought together, and the place to do that is in civil society, the setting of settings, where each can find the partial fulfillment that is all it deserves.

Civil society itself is sustained by groups much smaller than the demos or the working class or the mass of consumers or the nation. All these are necessarily fragmented and localized as they are incorporated. They become part of the world of family, friends, comrades, and colleagues, where people are connected to one another and made responsible for one another. Connected and responsible: without that, 'free and equal' is less attractive than we once thought it would be. I have no magic formula for making connections or strengthening the sense of responsibility. These aren't aims that can be underwritten with historical guarantees or achieved through a single unified struggle. Civil society is a project of projects; it requires many organizing strategies and new forms of state action. It requires a new sensitivity for what is local, specific, contingent—and, above all, a new recognition (to paraphrase a famous sentence) that the good life is in the details.

4

RETHINKING THE PUBLIC SPHERE
A Contribution to the Critique of
*Actually Existing Democracy**

Nancy Fraser

INTRODUCTION

Today in the United States we hear a great deal of ballyhoo about 'the triumph of liberal democracy' and even 'the end of history.' Yet there is still quite a lot to object to in our own actually existing democracy, and the project of a critical theory of the limits of democracy in late-capitalist societies remains as relevant as ever. In fact, this project seems to me to have acquired a new urgency at a time when 'liberal democracy' is being touted as the *ne plus ultra* of social systems for countries that are emerging from Soviet-style state socialism, Latin American military dictatorships, and southern African regimes of racial domination.

Those of us who remain committed to theorizing the limits of democracy in late-capitalist societies will find in the work of Jürgen Habermas an indispensable resource. I mean the concept of 'the public sphere,' originally elaborated in his 1962 book, *The Structural*

---

* Craig Calhoun (ed.), *Habermas and the Public Sphere*, Cambridge, MIT Press, 1992.

Transformation of the Public Sphere, and subsequently resituated but never abandoned in his later work.[1]

The political and theoretical importance of this idea is easy to explain. Habermas's concept of the public sphere provides a way of circumventing some confusions that have plagued progressive social movements and the political theories associated with them. Take, for example, the longstanding failure in the dominant wing of the socialist and Marxist tradition to appreciate full force of the distinction between the apparatuses of the state, on the one hand, and public arenas of citizen discourse and association, on the other. All too often it was assumed in this tradition that to subject the economy to the control of the socialist state was to subject it to the control of the socialist citizenry. Of course, that was not so. But the conflation of the state apparatus with the public sphere of discourse and association provided ballast to processes whereby the socialist vision became institutionalized in an authoritarian-statist form instead of in a participatory-democratic form. The result has been to jeopardize the very idea of socialist democracy.

The idea of 'the public sphere' in Habermas's sense is a conceptual resource that can help overcome such problems. It designates a theatre in modern societies in which political participation is enacted through the medium of talk. It is the space in which citizens deliberate about their common affairs, and hence an institutionalized arena of discursive interaction. This arena is conceptually distinct from the state; it is a site for the production and circulation of discourses that can in principle be critical of the state. The public sphere in Habermas's sense is also conceptually distinct from the official economy; it is not an arena of market relations but rather one of discursive relations, a theatre for debating and deliberating rather than for buying and

---

[1] Jürgen Habermas, *The Structural Transformation of the Public Sphere: An Inquiry into a Category of Bourgeois Society*, trans. Thomas Burger with Frederick Lawrence (Cambridge: MIT Press, 1989). For Hambermas's later use of the category of the public sphere, see Jürgen Habermas, *The Theory of Communicative Action*, Vol. 2, *Lifeworld and System: A Critique of Functionalist Reason*, trans. Thomas McCarthy (Boston: Beacon Press, 1987). For a critical secondary discussion of Habermas's later use of the concept, see Nancy Fraser, 'What's Critical About Critical Theory? The Case of Habermas and Gender,' in Fraser, *Unruly Practices: Power Discourse, and Gender in Contemporary Social Theory* (University of Minnesota Press, 1989).

selling. Thus this concept of the public sphere permits us to keep in view the distinctions among state apparatuses, economic markets, and democratic associations, distinctions that are essential to democratic theory.

Oddly, Habermas stops short of developing a new, post-bourgeois model of the public sphere. Moreover, he never explicitly problematizes some dubious assumptions that underlie the bourgeois model. As a result, we are left at the end of *Structural Transformation* without a conception of the public sphere that is sufficiently distinct from the bourgeois conception to serve the needs of critical theory today.

I shall identify four assumptions underlying the bourgeois conception of the public sphere, as Habermas describes it, that this newer historiography renders suspect. Next in the following sections I shall examine each of these assumptions in turn. Finally, in a brief conclusion I shall draw together some strands from these critical discussions that point toward an alternative, post-bourgeois conception of the public sphere.

I shall argue that the revisionist historiography neither undermines nor vindicates *the* concept of the public sphere *simpliciter*, but that it calls into question four assumptions that are central to the *bourgeois, masculinist* conception of the public sphere, at least as Habermas describes it. These are as follows:

(i) The assumption that it is possible for interlocutors in a public sphere to bracket status differentials and to deliberate *as if* they were social equals; the assumption, therefore, that societal equality is not a necessary condition for political democracy.

(ii) The assumption that the proliferation of a multiplicity of competing publics is necessarily a step away from, rather than toward, greater democracy, and that a single, comprehensive public sphere is always preferable to a nexus of multiple publics.

(iii) The assumption that discourse in public spheres should be restricted to deliberation about the common good, and that the appearance of private interests and private issues is always undesirable.

(iv) The assumption that a functioning democratic public sphere requires a sharp separation between civil society and the state.

Let me consider each of these in turn.

OPEN ACCESS, PARTICIPATORY PARITY, AND SOCIAL EQUALITY

Habermas's account of the bourgeois conception of the public sphere stresses its claim to be open and accessible to all. Indeed, this idea of open access is one of the central meanings of the norm of publicity. Of course, we know both from revisionist history and from Habermas's account that the bourgeois public's claim to full accessibility was not in fact realized. Women of all classes and ethnicities were excluded from official political participation on the basis of gender status, while plebeian men were formally excluded by property qualifications. Moreover, in many cases women and men of racialized ethnicities of all classes were excluded on racial grounds.

What are we to make of this historical fact of the non-realization in practice of the bourgeois public sphere's ideal of open access? One approach is to conclude that the ideal itself remains unaffected, since it is possible in principle to overcome these exclusions. And in fact, it was only a matter of time before formal exclusions based on gender, property, and race were eliminated.

This is convincing enough as far as it goes, but it does not go far enough. The question of open access cannot be reduced without remainder to the presence or absence of formal exclusions. It requires us to look also at the process of discursive interaction within formally inclusive public arenas. Here we should recall that the bourgeois conception of the public sphere requires bracketing inequalities of status. This public sphere was to be an arena in which interlocutors would set aside such characteristics as differences in birth and fortune and speak to one another as if they were social and economic peers. The operative phrase here is 'as if.' In fact, the social inequalities among the interlocutors were not eliminated but only bracketed.

But were they really effectively bracketed? The revisionist historiography suggests they were not. Rather, discursive interaction within the bourgeois public sphere was governed by protocols of style and decorum that were themselves correlates and markers of status inequality. These functioned informally to marginalize women and members of the plebeian classes and to prevent them from participating as peers.

Here I think we encounter a very serious difficulty with the bourgeois conception of the public sphere. Insofar as the bracketing of social inequalities in deliberation means proceedings as if they don't exist when they do, this does not foster participatory parity. On the contrary, such bracketing usually works to the advantage of dominant groups in society and to the disadvantage of subordinates. In most cases it would be more appropriate to *unbracket* inequalities in the sense of explicitly thematizing them—a point that accords with the spirit of Habermas's later communicative ethics.

The misplaced faith in the efficacy of bracketing suggests another flaw in the bourgeois conception. This conception assumes that a public sphere is or can be a space of zero degree culture, so utterly bereft of any specific ethos as to accommodate with perfect neutrality and equal ease interventions expressive of any and every cultural ethos. But this assumption is counterfactual, and not for reasons that are merely accidental. In stratified societies, unequally empowered social groups tend to develop unequally valued cultural styles. The result is the development of powerful informal pressures that marginalize the contributions of members of subordinated groups both in everyday contexts and in official public spheres.[2] Moreover, these pressures are amplified, rather than mitigated, by the peculiar political economy of the bourgeois public sphere. In this public sphere the media that constitute the material support for the circulation of views are privately owned and operated for profit. Consequently, subordinated social groups usually lack equal access to the material means of equal participation.[3] Thus political economy enforces structurally what culture accomplishes informally.

If we take these considerations seriously, then we should be led to entertain serious doubts about a conception of the public sphere that purports to bracket, rather than to eliminate, structural social inequalities. We should question whether it is possible even in principle

[2] In *Distinction* Pierre Bourdieu has theorized these processes in an illuminating way in terms of the concept of 'class habitus.'

[3] As Habermas notes, this tendency is exacerbated with the concentration of media ownership in late-capitalist societies. For the steep increase in concentration in the United States in the late twentieth century, see Ben H. Bagdikian, *The Media Monopoly* (Boston: Beacon Press, 1983) and 'Lords of the Global Village,' *The Nation* (12 June 1989). This situation contrasts in some respects with countries with television owned and operated by the state. But even there it is doubtful that subordinated groups have equal access. Moreover, political and economic pressures have recently encouraged privatization of media in several of these countries. In part, this reflects the problems of state networks having to compete for 'market share' with private channels airing US-produced mass entertainment.

for interlocutors to deliberate *as if* they were social peers in specially designated discursive arenas when these discursive arenas are situated in a larger societal context that is pervaded by structural relations of dominance and subordination.

What is at stake here is the autonomy of specifically political institutions vis-à-vis the surrounding societal context. Now one salient feature that distinguishes liberalism from some other political-theoretical orientations is that liberalism assumes the autonomy of the political in a very strong form. Liberal political theory assumes that it is possible to organize a democratic form of political life on the basis of socio-economic and socio-sexual structures that generate systemic inequalities. For liberals, then, the problem of democracy becomes the problems of how to insulate political processes from what are considered to be non-political or pre-political processes, those characteristic, for example, of the economy, the family, and informal everyday life. The problem for liberals is thus how to strengthen the barriers separating political institutions that are supposed to instantiate relations of equality from economic, cultural, and socio-sexual institutions that are premised on systemic relations of inequality.[4] Yet the weight of circumstance suggests that to have a

---

[4] This is the spirit behind, for example, proposals for reforms of election-campaign financing aimed at preventing the intrusion of economic dominance into the public sphere. Needless to say, within a context of massive societal inequality, it is far better to have such reforms than not to have them. However, in light of the sorts of informal effects of dominance and inequality discussed above, one ought not to expect too much from them. The most thoughtful recent defence of the liberal view comes from someone who in other respects is not a liberal. See Michael Walzer, *Spheres of Justice: A Defense of Pluralism and Equality* (New York: Basic Books, 1983). Another very interesting approach has been suggested by Joshua Cohen. In response to an earlier draft of this essay, he argued that policies designed to facilitate the formation of social movements, secondary associations, and political parties would better foster participatory parity than would policies designed to achieve social equality, since the latter would require redistributive efforts that carry 'deadweight losses.' I certainly support the sort of policies that Cohen recommends, as well as his more general aim of an 'associative democracy.' The sections of this paper on multiple publics and strong publics make a case for related arrangements. However, I am not persuaded by the claim that these policies can achieve participatory parity under conditions of social inequality. That claim seems to me to be another variant of the liberal view of the autonomy of the political, which Cohen otherwise claims to reject. See Joshua Cohen, 'Comments on Nancy Fraser's "Rethinking the Public Sphere"

public sphere in which interlocutors can deliberate as peers, it is not sufficient merely to bracket social inequality. Instead, a necessary condition for participatory parity is that systemic social inequalities be eliminated. This does not mean that everyone must have exactly the same income, but it does require the sort of rough equality that is inconsistent with systemically generated relations of dominance and subordination. *Pace* liberalism, then, political democracy requires substantive social equality.[5]

I have been arguing that the bourgeois conception of the public sphere is inadequate insofar as it supposes that social equality is not a necessary condition for participatory parity in public spheres. What follows from this for the critique of actually existing democracy? One task for critical theory is to render visible the ways in which societal inequality infects formally inclusive existing public spheres and taints discursive interaction within them.

Equality, Diversity, and Multiple Publics

So far I have been discussing what we might call 'intra-public relations,' that is, the character and quality of discursive interactions within a given public sphere. Now I want to consider what we might call 'inter-public relations,' that is, the character of interactions among different publics.

Let me begin by recalling that Habermas's account stresses the singularity of the bourgeois conception of the public sphere, its claim to be *the* public arena, in the singular. In addition, his narrative tends in this respect to be faithful to that conception, since it casts the emergence of additional publics as a late development signalling fragmentation and decline. This narrative, then, like the bourgeois conception itself, is informed by an underlying evaluative assumption, namely, that the institutional confinement of public life to a single, overarching public sphere is a positive and desirable state of affairs, whereas the proliferation of a multiplicity of publics represents a departure from, rather than an advance toward, democracy. It is this

---

(unpublished manuscript presented at the meetings of the American Philosophical Association, Central Division, New Orleans, April 1990).

[5] My argument draws on Karl Marx's still unsurpassed critique of liberalism in section 1 of 'On the Jewish Question.' Hence the allusion to Marx in the title of this essay.

normative assumption that I now want to scrutinize. In this section I shall assess the relative merits of a single, comprehensive public versus multiple publics in two kinds of modern societies: stratified societies and egalitarian multicultural societies.[6]

First, let me consider the case of stratified societies, by which I mean societies whose basic institutional framework generates unequal social groups in structural relations of dominance and subordination. I have already argued that in such societies, full parity of participation in public debate and deliberation is not within the reach of possibility. The question to be addressed here then is: what form of public life comes closest to approaching that ideal? What institutional arrangements will best help narrow the gap in participatory parity between dominant and subordinate groups?

I contend that in stratified societies, arrangements that accommodate contestation among a plurality of competing publics better promote the ideal of participatory parity than does a single, comprehensive, overarching public. This follows from the argument of the previous section. There I argued that it is not possible to insulate special discursive arenas from the effects of societal inequality and that where societal inequality persists, deliberative processes in public spheres will tend to operate to the advantage of dominant groups and to the disadvantage of subordinates. Now I want to add that these effects will be exacerbated where there is only a single, comprehensive public sphere. In that case, members of subordinated groups would have no arenas for deliberation among themselves about their needs, objectives, and strategies. They would have no venues in which to undertake communicative processes that were not, as it were, under the supervision of dominant groups. In this situation they would be less likely than otherwise to 'keep their wants inchoate.' This would render them less able than otherwise to articulate and defend their interests in the comprehensive public sphere. They would be less able than otherwise to expose modes of deliberation that mask domination by, in Mansbridge's words, 'absorbing the less powerful into a false 'we' that reflects the more powerful.'

This argument gains additional support from revisionist historiography of the public sphere, up to and including that of very recent

6 My argument in this section is deeply 'indebted to Joshua Cohen's perceptive comments on an earlier draft of this paper in 'Comments on Nancy Fraser's "Rethinking the Public Sphere".'

developments. This historiography records that members of subordinated social groups—women, workers, peoples of colour, and gays and lesbians—have repeatedly found it advantageous to constitute alternative publics. I propose to call these *subaltern counterpublics* in order to signal that they are parallel discursive arenas where members of subordinated social groups invent and circulate counterdiscourses to formulate oppositional interpretations of their identities, interests, and needs.[7]

Let me not be misunderstood. I do not mean to suggest that subaltern counterpublics are always necessarily virtuous. Some of them, alas, are explicitly anti-democratic and anti-egalitarian, and even those with democratic and egalitarian intentions are not always above practising their own modes of informal exclusion and marginalization. Still, insofar as these counterpublics emerge in response to exclusions within dominant publics, they help expand discursive space. In principle, assumptions that were previously exempt from contestation will now have to be publicly argued out. In general, the proliferation of subaltern counterpublics means a widening of discursive contestation, and that is a good thing in stratified societies.

I am emphasizing the contestatory function of subaltern counterpublics in stratified societies in part to complicate the issue of separatism. In my view, the concept of a counterpublic militates in the long run against separatism because it assumes a *publicist* orientation. Insofar as these arenas are *publics*, they are by definition not enclaves, which is not to deny that they are often involuntarily enclaved. After all, to interact discursively as a member of public, subaltern or otherwise, is to aspire to disseminate one's discourse to ever widening arenas. Habermas captures well this aspect of the meaning of publicity when he notes that, however limited a public may be in its empirical manifestation at any given time, its members understand themselves as part of a potentially wider public, that indeterminate, empirically counterfactual body we call 'the public at

[7] I have coined this expression by combining two terms that other theorists have recently effectively used for purposes consonant with my own. I take the term 'subaltern' from Gayatri Spivak, 'Can the Subaltern Speak?' in *Marxism and the Interpretation of Culture* in Cary Nelson and Larry Grossberg (eds), (Chicago: University of Illinois Press, 1988), pp. 271–313. I take the term 'counterpublic' from Rita Felski, *Beyond Feminist Aesthetics* (Cambridge: Harvard University Press, 1989).

large.' The point is that in stratified societies, subaltern counterpublics have a dual character. On the one hand, they function as spaces of withdrawal and regroupment; on the other hand, they also function as bases and training grounds for agitational activities directed toward wider publics. It is precisely in the dialectic between these two functions that their emancipatory potential resides. This dialectic enables subaltern counterpublics partially to offset, although not wholly to eradicate, the unjust participatory privileges enjoyed by members of dominant social groups in stratified societies.

So far I have been arguing that, although in stratified societies the ideal of participatory parity is not fully realizable, it is more closely approximated by arrangements that permit contestation among a plurality of competing publics than by a single, comprehensive public sphere. Of course, contestation among competing publics supposes interpublic discursive interaction. How, then, should we understand such interaction? Geoff Eley suggests that we think of the public sphere (in stratified societies) as 'the structured setting where cultural and ideological contest or negotiation among a variety of publics takes place.'[8] This formulation does justice to the multiplicity of public arenas in stratified societies by expressly acknowledging the presence and activity of 'a variety of publics.' At the same time, it also does justice to the fact that these various publics are situated in a single 'structured setting' that advantages some and disadvantages others. Finally, Eley's formulation does justice to the fact that in stratified societies the discursive relations among differentially empowered publics are as likely to take the form of contestation as that of deliberation.

Let me now consider the relative merits of multiple publics versus a single public for egalitarian, multicultural societies. By 'egalitarian societies' I mean non-stratified societies, societies whose basic framework does not generate unequal social groups in structural relations of dominance and subordination. Egalitarian societies, therefore, are societies without classes and without gender or racial divisions of labour. However, they need not be culturally homogeneous. On the

---

[8] Geoff Eley, 'Nations, Publics, and Political Cultures.' Eley goes on to explain that this is tantamount to 'extend[ing] Habermas's idea of the public sphere toward the wider public domain where authority is not only constituted as rational and legitimate, but where its terms are contested, modified, and occasionally overthrown by subaltern groups.'

contrary, provided such societies permit free expression and association, they are likely to be inhabited by social groups with diverse values, identities, and cultural styles, and hence to be multicultural. My question is under conditions of cultural diversity in the absence of structural inequality, would a single, comprehensive public sphere be preferable to multiple publics?

To answer this question, we need to take a closer look at the relationship between public discourse and social identities. *Pace* the bourgeois conception, public spheres are not only arenas for the formation of discursive opinion; in addition, they are arenas for the formation and enactment of social identities.[9] This means that participation is not simply a matter of being able to state propositional contents that are neutral with respect to form of expression. Rather, as I argued in the previous section, participation means being able to speak in one's own voice, and thereby simultaneously to construct and express one's cultural identity through idiom and style.[10] Moreover, as I also suggested, public spheres themselves are not spaces of zero-degree culture, equally hospitable to any possible form of cultural expression. Rather, they consist in culturally specific institutions, including, for example, various journals and various social geographies of urban space. These institutions may be under-

[9] It seems to me that public discursive arenas are among the most important and underrecognized sites in which social identities are constructed, deconstructed, and reconstructed. My view stands in contrast to various psychoanalytic accounts of identity formation, which neglect the formative importance of post-Oedipal discursive interaction outside the nuclear family and which therefore cannot explain identity shifts over time. It strikes me as unfortunate that so much of contemporary feminist theory has taken its understanding of social identity from psychoanalytic models, while neglecting to study identity construction of relation to public spheres. The revisionist historiography of the public sphere discussed earlier can help redress the imbalance by identifying public spheres as loci of identity reconstruction. For an account of the discursive character of social identity and a critique of Lacanian psychoanalytic approaches to identity, see Nancy Fraser, 'The Uses and Abuses of French Discourse Theories for Feminist Politics,' *Boundary 2*, 17(2), (Summer 1990): 82–101.

[10] For another statement of this position, see Nancy Fraser, 'Toward a Discourse Ethic of Solidarity,' *Praxis International* 5, No. 4 (January 1986): 425–9. See also Iris Young, 'Impartiality and the Civic Public: Some Implications of Feminist Critiques of Moral and Political Theory' in *Feminism as Critique*, Seyla Benhabib and Drucilla Cornell (ed.), (Minneapolis: University of Minnesota Press, 1987), pp. 56–76.

stood as culturally specific rhetorical lenses that filter and alter the utterances they frame; they can accommodate some expressive modes and not others.[11]

It follows that public life in egalitarian, multicultural societies cannot consist exclusively in a single, comprehensive public sphere. That would be tantamount to filtering diverse rhetorical and stylistic norms through a single, overarching lens. Moreover, since there can be no such lens that is genuinely culturally neutral, it would effectively privilege the expressive norms of one cultural group over others and thereby make discursive assimilation a condition for participation in public debate. The result would be the demise of multiculturalism (and the likely demise of social equality). In general, then, we can conclude that the idea of an egalitarian, multicultural society only makes sense if we suppose a plurality of public arenas in which groups with diverse values and rhetorics participate. By definition, such a society must contain a multiplicity of publics.

However, this need not preclude the possibility of an additional, more comprehensive arena in which members of different, more limited publics talk across lines of cultural diversity. On the contrary, our hypothetical egalitarian, multicultural society would surely have to entertain debates over policies and issues affecting everyone. The question is: would participants in such debates share enough in the way of values, expressive norms, and therefore protocols of persuasion to lend their talk the quality of deliberations aimed at reaching agreement through giving reasons?

In my view, this is better treated as an empirical question than as a conceptual question. I see no reason to rule out in principle the possibility of a society in which social equality and cultural diversity coexist with participatory democracy. I certainly hope there can be such a society. That hope gains some plausibility if we consider that, however difficult it may be, communication across lines of cultural difference is not in principle impossible, although it will certainly become impossible if one imagines that it requires bracketing of differences. Granted, such communication requires multicultural literacy, but that, I believe, can be acquired through practice. In fact, the possibilities expand once we acknowledge the complexity of cultural

[11] For an analysis of the rhetorical specificity of one historical public sphere, see Michael Warner, *The Letters of the Republic: Publication and the Public Sphere in Eighteenth Century America* (Cambridge: Harvard University Press, 1990).

identities. *Pace* reductive, essentialist conceptions, cultural identities are woven of many different strands, and some of these strands may be common to people whose identities otherwise diverge, even when it is the divergences that are most salient.[12] Likewise, under conditions of social equality, the porousness, outer-directedness, and open-endedness of publics could promote intercultural communication. After all, the concept of a public presupposes a plurality of perspectives among those who participate within it, thereby allowing for internal differences and antagonisms and discouraging reified blocs.[13] In addition, the unbounded character and publicist orientation of publics allows people to participate in more than one public, and it allows memberships of different publics partially to overlap. This in turn makes intercultural communication conceivable in principle. All told, then, there do not seem to be any conceptual (as opposed to empirical) barriers to the possibility of a socially egalitarian, multicultural society that is also a participatory democracy. But this will necessarily be a society with many different publics, including at least one public in which participants can deliberate as peers across lines of difference about policy that concerns them all.

In general, I have been arguing that the ideal of participatory parity is better achieved by a multiplicity of publics than by a single

[12] One could say that at the deepest level, everyone is *mestizo*. The best metaphor here may be Wittgenstein's idea of family resemblances, or networks of crisscrossing, overlapping differences and similarities, no single thread of which runs continuously throughout the whole. For an account that stresses the complexity of cultural identities and the salience of discourse in their construction, see Nancy Fraser, 'The Uses and Abuses of French Discourse Theories for Feminist Politics.' For accounts that draw on concepts of *métissage*, see Gloria Anzaldua, *Borderlands: La Frontera* (1987) and Françoise Lionnet, *Autobiographical Voices: Race, Gender, Self-Portraiture* (Ithaca: Cornell University Press, 1989).

[13] In these respects, the concept of a public differs from that of a community. 'Community' suggests a bounded and fairly homogeneous group, and it often connotes consensus. 'Public,' in contrast, emphasizes discursive interaction that is in principle unbounded and open-ended, and this in turn implies a plurality of perspectives. Thus, the idea of a public can accommodate internal differences, antagonisms, and debates better than that of a community. For an account of the connection between publicity and plurality, see Hannah Arendt, *The Human Condition* (Chicago: University of Chicago Press, 1958). For a critique of the concept of community, see Iris Young, 'The Ideal of Community and the Politics of Difference,' in *Feminism and Postmodernism*, Linda J. Nicholson (ed.), (New York: Routledge, Chapman and Hall, 1989), pp. 300–23.

public. This is true both for stratified societies and for egalitarian, multicultural societies, albeit for different reasons. In neither case is my argument intended as a simple post-modern celebration of multiplicity. Rather, in a case of stratified societies, I am defending subaltern counterpublic formed under conditions of dominance and subordination. In the other case, by contrast, I am defending the possibility of combining social equality, cultural diversity, and participatory democracy.

What are the implications of this discussion for a critical theory of the public sphere in actually existing democracy? Briefly, we need a critical political sociology of a form of public life in which multiple but unequal publics participate. This means theorizing about the contestatory interaction of different publics and identifying the mechanisms that render some of them subordinate to others.

PUBLIC SPHERES, COMMON CONCERNS, AND PRIVATE INTERESTS

I have argued that in stratified societies, like it or not, subaltern counterpublics stand in a contestatory relationship to dominant publics. One important object of such inter-public contestation is the appropriate boundaries of the public sphere. Here the central questions are: what counts as a public matter? What, in contrast, is private? This brings me to a third set of problematic assumptions underlying the bourgeois conception of the public sphere, namely, assumptions concerning of appropriate scope of publicity in relation to privacy.

Let me remind you that it is central to Habermas's account that the bourgeois public sphere was to be a discursive arena in which 'private persons' deliberated about 'public matters.' There are several different senses of 'private' and 'public' in play here. 'Public,' for example, can mean (1) state-related, (2) accessible to everyone, (3) of concern to everyone, and (4) pertaining to a common good or shared interest. Each of these corresponds to a contrasting sense of 'private'. In addition, there are two other senses of 'private' hovering just below the surface here, (5) pertaining to private property in a market economy, and (6) pertaining to intimate domestic or personal life, including sexual life.

I have already talked at length about the sense of 'public' as open or accessible to all. Now I want to examine some of the other senses, beginning with (3), of concern to everyone.[14] This is ambiguous between what objectively affects or has an impact on everyone as seen from an outsider's perspective, and what is recognized as a matter of common concern by participants. The idea of a public sphere as an arena of collective self-determination does not sit well with approaches that would appeal to an outsider's perspective to delimit its proper boundaries. Thus it is the second, participant's perspective that is relevant here. Only participants themselves can decide what is and what is not of common concern to them. However, there is no guarantee that all of them will agree. For example, until quite recently, feminists were in the minority in thinking that domestic violence against women was a matter of common concern and thus a legitimate topic of public discourse. The great majority of people considered this issue to be a private matter between what was assumed to be a fairly small number of heterosexual couples (and perhaps the social and legal professionals who were supposed to deal with them). Then feminists formed a subaltern counterpublic from which we disseminated a view of domestic violence as a widespread systemic feature of male-dominated societies. Eventually, after sustained discursive contestation, we succeeded in *making* it a common concern.

The point is that there are no naturally given, priori boundaries here. What will count as a matter of common concern will be decided precisely through discursive contestation. It follows that no topics should be ruled off limits in advance of such contestation. On the contrary, democratic publicity requires positive guarantees of opportunities for minorities to convince others that what in the past was not public in the sense of being a matter of common concern should now become so.[15]

What, then, of the sense of 'publicity' as pertaining to a common good or shared interest? This is the sense that is in play when Habermas characterizes the bourgeois public sphere as an arena in which the topic of discussion is restricted to the 'common good' and in which discussion of 'private interests' is ruled out. This is a view of the public sphere that we would today call civic-republican, as

14 In this essay I do not directly discuss sense (1), state-related. However, in the next section of this essay I consider some issues that touch on that sense.

15 This is the equivalent in democratic theory of a point that Paul Feyerabend has argued in the philosophy of science. See Feyerabend, *Against Method* (New York: Verso, 1988).

opposed to liberal-individualist. Briefly, the civic-republican model stresses a view of politics as people reasoning together to promote a common good that transcends the mere sum of individual preferences. The idea is that through deliberation the members of the public can come to discover or create such a common good. In the process of their deliberations, participants are transformed from a collection of self-seeking, private individuals into a public-spirited collectivity, capable of acting together in the common interest. On this view, private interests have no proper place in the political public sphere. At best, they are the pre-political starting point of deliberation, to be transformed and transcended in the course of debate.[16]

This civic-republican view of the public sphere is in one respect an improvement over the liberal-individualist alternative. Unlike the latter, it does not assume that people's preferences, interests, and identities are given exogenously in advance of public discourse and deliberation. It appreciates, rather, that preferences, interests, and identities are as much outcomes as antecedents of public deliberation; indeed, they are discursively constituted in and through it. However, the civic-republican view contains a very serious confusion, one that blunts its critical edge. This view conflates the ideas of deliberation and the common good by assuming that deliberation must be deliberation *about* the common good. Consequently, it limits deliberation to talk framed from the standpoint of a single, all-encompassing 'we,' thereby ruling claims of self-interest and group interest out of order. Yet, as Jane Mansbridge has argued, this works against one of the principal aims of deliberation, namely, to help participants clarify their interests, even when those interests turn out to conflict. 'Ruling self-interest [and group interest] out of order makes it harder for any participant to sort out what is going on. In particular, the less powerful may not find ways to discover that the prevailing sense of 'we' does not adequately include them.'[17]

16 In contrast, the liberal-individualist model stresses the view of politics as the aggregation of self-interested, individual preferences. Deliberation in the strict sense drops out altogether. Instead, political discourse consists in registering individual preferences and in bargaining, looking for formulas that satisfy as many private interests as possible. It is assumed that there is no such thing as the common good over and above the sum of all the various individual goods, and so private interests are the legitimate stuff of political discourse.

17 Jane Mansbridge, 'Feminism and Democracy,' p. 131.

In general, there is no way to know in advance whether the outcome of a deliberative process will be the discovery of a common good in which conflicts of interest evaporate as merely apparent or the discovery that conflicts of interest are real and the common good is chimerical. But if the existence of a common good cannot be presumed in advance, then there is no warrant for putting any strictures on what sorts of topics, interests, and views are admissible in deliberation.[18]

This argument holds even in the best-case scenario of societies whose basic institutional frameworks do not generate systemic inequalities; even in such relatively egalitarian societies, we cannot assume in advance that there will be no real conflicts of interest. How much more pertinent, then, the argument is to stratified societies, which are traversed with pervasive relations of inequality. After all, when social arrangements operate to the systemic profit of some groups of people and to the systemic detriment of others, there are prima facie reasons for thinking that the postulation of a common good shared by exploiters and exploited may well be a mystification. Moreover, any consensus that purports to represent the common good in this social context should be regarded with suspicion, since this consensus will have been reached through deliberative process tainted by the effects of dominance and subordination.

In general, critical theory needs to take a harder, more critical look at the terms 'private' and 'public.' These terms, after all, are not simply straightforward designations of societal spheres; they are cultural classifications and rhetorical labels. In political discourse they are powerful terms frequently deployed to delegitimate some interests, views, and topics and to valorize others.

This brings me to two other senses of 'private,' which often function ideologically to delimit the boundaries of the public sphere in ways that disadvantage subordinate social groups. These are sense (5), pertaining to private property in a market economy, and sense

---

[18] This point, incidentally, is in the spirit of a strand of Habermas's recent normative thought, which stresses the procedural, as opposed to the substantive, definition of a democratic public sphere; here the public sphere is defined as an arena for a certain types of topics and problems. There are no restrictions, therefore, on what may become a topic of deliberation. See Seyla Benhabib's account of this radical proceduralist strand of Habermas's thought and her defence of it as the strand that renders his view of the public sphere superior to alternative views: Benhabib, 'Models of Public Space: Hannah Arendt, the Liberal Tradition, and Jürgen Habermas,' in *Habermas and the Public Sphere*, Craig Calhoun (ed.).

(6), pertaining to intimate domestic or personal life, including sexual life. Each of these senses is at the centre of a rhetoric of privacy that has historically been used to restrict the universe of legitimate public contestation.

The rhetoric of domestic privacy would exclude some issues and interests from public debate by personalizing and/or familializing them; it casts these as private, domestic or personal, familial matters in contradistinction to public, political matters. The rhetoric of economic privacy, in contrast, would exclude some issues and interests from public debate by economizing them; the issues in question here are cast as impersonal market imperatives or as 'private' ownership prerogatives or as technical problems for managers and planners, all in contradistinction to public, political matters. In both cases, the result is to enclave certain matters in specialized discursive arenas and thereby to shield them from broadly based debate and contestation. This usually works to the advantage of dominant groups and individuals and to the disadvantage of their subordinates.[19] If wife battering, for example, is labelled a 'personal' or 'domestic' matter and if public discourse about it is channelled into specialized institutions associated with, say, family law, social work, and the sociology and psychology of 'deviance,' then this serves to reproduce gender dominance and subordination. Similarly, if questions of workplace democracy are labelled 'economic' or 'managerial' problems and if discourse about these questions is shunted into specialized institutions associated with, say, 'industrial relations' sociology, labour law, and 'management science' then this serves to perpetuate class (and usually also gender and race) dominance and subordination.

This shows once again that the lifting of formal restrictions on public-sphere participation does not suffice to ensure inclusion in

[19] Usually, but not always. As Joshua Cohen has argued, exceptions are the uses of privacy in *Roe v. Wade*, the US Supreme Court decision legalizing abortion, and in Justice Blackmun's dissent in *Bowers*, the decision upholding state anti-sodomy laws. These examples show that the privacy rhetoric is multivalent rather than univocally and necessarily harmful. On the other hand, there is no question but that the weightier tradition of privacy argument has buttressed inequality by restricting debate. Moreover, many feminists have argued that even the 'good' privacy uses have some serious negative consequences in the current context and that gender domination is better challenged in this context in other terms. For a defence of privacy talk, see Joshua Cohen, 'Comments on Nancy Fraser's "Rethinking the Public Sphere".'

practice. On the contrary, even after women and workers have been formally licensed to participate, their participation may be hedged by conceptions of economic privacy and domestic privacy that delimit the scope of debate. These notions, therefore, are vehicles through which gender and class disadvantages may continue to operate subtextually and informally, even after explicit, formal restrictions have been rescinded.

STRONG PUBLICS, WEAK PUBLICS: ON CIVIL SOCIETY AND THE STATE

Let me turn now to my fourth and last assumption underlying the bourgeois conception of the public sphere, namely, the assumption that a functioning democratic public sphere requires a sharp separation of civil society and the state. This assumption is susceptible to two different interpretations, according to how one understands the expression 'civil society.' If one takes that expression to mean a privately ordered, capitalist economy, then to insist on its separation from the state is to defend classical liberalism. The claim would be that a system of limited government and laissez-faire capitalism is a necessary pre-condition for a well-functioning public sphere.

We can dispose of this (relatively uninteresting) claim fairly quickly by drawing on some arguments of the previous sections. I have already shown that participatory parity is essential to a democratic public sphere and that rough socio-economic equality is a precondition of participatory parity. Now I need only add that laissez-faire capitalism does not foster socio-economic equality and that some form of politically regulated economic reorganization and redistribution is needed to achieve that end. Likewise, I have also shown that efforts to 'privatize' economic issues and to cast them as off-limits with respect to state activity impede, rather than promote, the sort of full and free discussion built into the idea of a public sphere. It follows from these considerations that a sharp separation of (economic) civil society and the state is not a necessary condition for a well-functioning public sphere. On the contrary and *pace* the bourgeois conception, it is precisely some sort of interimbrication of these institutions that is needed.[20]

20 There are many possibilities here, including such mixed forms as market socialism.

However, there is also a second, more interesting interpretation of the bourgeois assumption that a sharp separation of civil society and the state is necessary to a working public sphere, one that warrants more extended examination. In this interpretation, 'civil society' means the nexus of nongovernmental or 'secondary' associations that are neither economic nor administrative. We can best appreciate the force of the claim that civil society in this sense should be separate from the state if we recall Habermas's definition of the liberal public sphere as a 'body of private persons assembled to form a public.' The emphasis here on 'private persons' signals (among other things) that the members of the bourgeois public are not state officials and that their participation in the public sphere is not undertaken in any official capacity. Accordingly, their discourse does not eventuate in binding, sovereign decisions authorizing the use of state power; on the contrary, it eventuates in 'public opinion,' critical commentary on authorized decision making that transpires elsewhere. The public sphere, in short, is not the state; it is rather the informally mobilized body of non-governmental discursive opinion that can serve as a counterweight to the state. Indeed, in the bourgeois conception, it is precisely this extra-governmental character of the public sphere that confers an aura of independence, autonomy, and legitimacy on the 'public opinion' generated in it.

Thus the bourgeois conception of the public sphere supposes the desirability of a sharp separation of (associational) civil society and the state. As a result, it promotes what I shall call *weak publics*, publics whose deliberative practice consists exclusively in opinion formation and does not also encompass decision making. Moreover, the bourgeois conception seems to imply that an expansion of such publics' discursive authority to encompass decision-making as well as opinion making would threaten the autonomy of public opinion, for then the public would effectively become the state, and the possibility of a critical discursive check on the state would be lost.

That, at least, is suggested by Habermas's initial formulation of the bourgeois conception. In fact, the issue becomes more complicated as soon as we consider the emergence of parliamentary sovereignty. With that landmark development in the history of the public sphere, we encounter a major structural transformation, since a sovereign parliament functions as a public sphere *within* the state. Moreover, sovereign parliaments are what I shall call *strong publics*, publics whose discourse encompasses both opinion formation and decision-making. As a locus of public deliberation culminating in legally binding decisions (or laws), parliament was to be the site for the discursive authorization of the use of state power. With the achievement of parliamentary sovereignty, therefore, the line separating (associational) civil society and the state is blurred.

Clearly, the emergence of parliamentary sovereignty and the consequent blurring of the separation between (associational) civil society and the state represents a democratic advance over earlier political arrangements. This is because, as the terms 'strong public' and 'weak public' suggest, the force of public opinion is strengthened when a body representing it is empowered to translate such 'opinion' into authoritative decisions. At the same time, there remain important questions about the relation between parliamentary strong publics and the weak publics to which they are supposed to be accountable. In general, these developments raise some interesting and important questions about the relative merits of weak and strong publics and about the respective roles that institutions of both kinds might play in a democratic and egalitarian society.

One set of questions concerns the possible proliferation of strong publics in the form of self-managing institutions. In self-managed workplaces, child-care centres, or residential communities, for example, internal institutional public spheres could be arenas both of opinion formation and decision making. This would be tantamount to constituting sites of direct or quasi-direct democracy, wherein all those engaged in a collective understanding would participate in deliberations to determine its design and operation.[21] However, this would still leave open the relationship between such internal public spheres cum decision-making bodies and those external publics to which they might also be deemed accountable. The question of that relationship becomes important when we consider that people affected by an undertaking in which they do not directly participate as agents may nonetheless have a stake in its *modus operandi*; they therefore also have a legitimate claim to a say in its institutional design and operation.

---

[21] I use the expression 'quasi-direct democracy' to signal the possibility of hybrid forms of self-management involving the democratic designation of representatives, managers, or planners held to strict standards of accountability through, for example, recall.

Here we are again broaching the issue of accountability. What institutional arrangements best ensure the accountability of democratic decision-making bodies (strong publics) to *their* (external, weak, or, given the possibility of hybrid cases, weaker publics?[22] Where in society are direct democracy arrangements called for, and where are representative forms more appropriate? How are the former best articulated with the latter? More generally, what democratic arrangements best institutionalize co-ordination among different institutions, including co-ordination among their various complicated publics? Should we think of central parliament as a strong superpublic with authoritative discursive sovereignty over basic societal ground rules and co-ordination arrangements? If so, does that require the assumption of a single weak(er) external superpublic (in addition), not instead of, various other smaller publics)? In any event, given the inescapable global interdependence manifest in the international division of labour within a single shared planetary biosphere, does it make sense to understand the nation-state as the appropriate unit of sovereignty?

I do not know the answers to most of these questions, and I am unable to explore them further in this essay. However, the possibility of posing them, even in the absence of full, persuasive answers, enables us to draw one salient conclusion: any conception of the public sphere that requires a sharp separation between (associational) civil society and the state will be unable to imagine the forms of self-management, inter-public co-ordination, and political accountability that are essential to a democratic and egalitarian society. The bourgeois conception of the public sphere, therefore, is not adequate for contemporary critical theory. What is needed, rather, is a post-bourgeois conception that can permit us to envision a greater role for (at least some) public spheres than mere autonomous opinion formation removed from authoritative decision-making. A post-bourgeois conception would enable us to think about strong *and* weak publics, as well as about various hybrid forms. In addition, it would allow us to theorize the range of possible relations among such publics, which would expand our capacity to envision democratic possibilities beyond the limits of actually existing democracy.

22 By 'hybrid possibilities' I mean arrangements involving very strict accountability of representative decision-making bodies to their external publics through veto and recall rights. Such hybrid forms might be desirable in some circumstances, though certainly not all.

CONCLUSION: RETHINKING THE PUBLIC SPHERE

Let me conclude by recapitulating what I believe I have accomplished in this essay. I have shown that the bourgeois conception of the public sphere as described by Habermas is not adequate for the critique of the limits of actually existing democracy in late-capitalist societies. At one level, my argument undermines the bourgeois conception as a normative ideal. I have shown first that an adequate conception of the public sphere requires not merely the bracketing, but rather the elimination, of social inequality. Second, I have shown that a multiplicity of publics is preferable to a single public sphere both in stratified societies and egalitarian societies. Third, I have shown that a tenable conception of the public sphere must countenance not the exclusion, but the inclusion, of interests and issues that bourgeois, masculinist ideology labels 'private' and treats as inadmissible. Finally, I have shown that a defensible conception must allow both for strong publics and for weak publics and that it should help theorize the relations among them. In sum, I have argued against four constitutive assumptions of the bourgeois conception of the public sphere; at the same time, I have identified some corresponding elements of a new, post-bourgeois conception.

At another level, my argument enjoins four corresponding tasks on the critical theory of actually existing democracy. First, this theory should render visible the ways in which social inequality taints deliberation within publics in late-capitalist societies. Second, it should show how inequality affects relations among publics in late-capitalist societies, how publics are differentially empowered or segmented, and how some are involuntarily enclaved and subordinated to others. Next, a critical theory should expose ways in which the labelling of some issues and interests as 'private' limits the range of problems, and of approaches to problems, that can be widely contested in contemporary societies. Finally, the theory should show how the overly weak character of some public spheres in late-capitalist societies denudes 'public opinion' of practical force.

In all these ways the theory should expose the limits of the specific form of democracy we enjoy in late-capitalist societies. Perhaps it can thereby help inspire us to try to push back those limits, while also cautioning people in other parts of the world against heeding the call to install them.

5

CIVIL SOCIETIES
*Liberalism and the Moral Uses of Pluralism**

Nancy L. Rosenblum

INTRODUCTION

There is no single, systematic theory of the relation between liberal
government and civil society—'that sphere of autonomous institutions, protected by the rule of law, within which individuals and
communities possessing divergent values and beliefs may coexist in
peace' (Gray, 1993a, p. 157).[1] Political theorists are typically less concerned with the direction of causality than with the general proposition that liberal government and civil society are reciprocally
supportive. Since secondary associations may be neither liberal nor
liberalizing, one way of sharpening this proposition is to say that their
mutually beneficial relations—stability, normative reinforcement, and
shared participation in forming the moral dispositions of liberal citizens—depends upon congruence between public norms and institutions and the internal life and organization of associations.[2] In political

---

* *Social Research*, 61(3) (Fall 1994).

1 For a survey of approaches, see Putnam, 1993.

2 'Only a democratic state can create a democratic civil society; only a
democratic civil society can sustain a democratic state' (Walzer, 1991, p. 302). In
this volume.

theory, the degree of congruence recommended (or, alternatively, of incongruity embraced, as I will argue) is variable and depends on the liberal purposes civil society is thought to serve.

Variation in the degree to which associations ought to incorporate liberal norms and practices is a critical feature of liberal thought and the subject of this essay. But it is important to note at the outset that liberal theorists agree on at least the broad parameters of congruence. Liberal government does not require the internal life of every association to conform to public norms and practices by prohibiting discrimination, enforcing due process, encouraging liberal private life (outlawing polygamous marriage as 'patriarchal'), favouring democratic authority (congregational churches over hierarchic ones or worker control over other forms of management). Liberalism does not command strict congruence everywhere and 'all the way down.' But neither do associations have unlimited autonomy to govern their own affairs; even churches are subject to an array of public laws. Liberal government may accommodate (though rarely) particular groups and sub-communities by granting exemptions from specific general obligations, but separatist self-rule and 'internal exile' fall outside this parameter. There is also broad agreement about the other parameter, where civil society makes incursions on government. Liberal government must be representative, but that is consistent with wide variations in the extent to which public institutions are expected to mirror or incorporate ever-changing social pluralism. And if all sorts of semi-public/semi-private organizations engage in activities such as education and welfare that qualify as 'state action,' the devolution of public responsibility to secondary associations always supplements the activities of what liberals agree must be a strong state and is subject to political revision.

Within these very general parameters, the associations considered crucial to the support of liberalism and the kind and degree of congruence or incongruity wanted depend on the purposes civil society is said to serve. One purpose dominates liberal thought today, particularly theories of American liberalism: civil society's role in the cultivation of moral dispositions judged essential to a flourishing liberal democracy.[3] In this essay, I propose a typology of contemporary liberal accounts of the moral purposes of civil society, each of which has a characteristic position on the question of congruence. I

[3] For key essays on the subject, see Rosenblum, 1989.

argue that messy, unsystematic 'elective civil society' with its exploitation of incongruity has the advantage over 'democratic' and 'mediating' types.

THE MORAL PURPOSES AND PSYCHOLOGICAL DYNAMICS OF CIVIL SOCIETY

The orthodox liberal focus on the political conditions that permit social and cultural diversity and on the political functions of associations as buffers against government power and participants in interest group politics has been replaced by preoccupation with the constitutive effects of associational life. The familiar social science question of congruence is recast by political theorists in exclusively moral terms. The unifying idea is that pluralism is normative as well as empirical, and that the associations of civil society can foster personal moral development, social connectedness, and civic values that support liberalism. Official 'seedbeds of civic virtue' cannot do the work of character-formation and community-building alone, the argument goes, and the reproduction of citizens on which the stability and flourishing of liberalism depends goes on in the networks of civil society. Once the preserve of conservatives, the claim that 'in the modern world we need to recapture the density of associational life and relearn the activities and understandings that go with it' is received sympathetically rather than disparaged as reactionary by liberals or as 'bourgeois' or 'bad privacy' by the left (Walzer, 1991, p. 304).

THREE CIVIL SOCIETIES

What does liberal theory have to say? A three-part typology of 'democratic,' 'mediating,' and 'elective' civil society is useful (though the usual cautions about mixed types and merely illustrative cases apply). In *democratic civil society*, secondary associations are schools of virtue. The principal business of civil society is shaping citizens with a sense of political efficacy, a capacity for public deliberation, and an inclination to deliberate on behalf of the common good.[4] To this end, they should be internally liberal-democratic 'minipublics' oriented toward public arenas of discussion and policy-making. In some accounts, civil society excludes institutions that are not internally

[4] For an extended discussion, see Rosenblum (1944). For a brief early version of this typology, see Rosenblum (1993b).

democratic and that represent partial interests by definition—corporations, for example, whose political participation and speech rights should be regulated. Alternatively, non-conforming associations could be reformed, in this example through worker control, shareholder democracy, or public interest representation on corporate boards (Michelman, 1988; Sunstein, 1988). 'The encouragement of an ongoing and popular civic consciousness can be treated as an explicit goal of institutional design, affecting both public and private institutions.' Accordingly, one account of democratic civil society recommends that government recognize and financially support groups that represent important social perspectives and contribute to the quality of decision-making by focusing public discussion on the common good (and sanction groups that do not demonstrate allegiance to liberal-democratic public norms). Strong state action shapes the organized representation of fragmented or excluded interests and encourages the organized to be more other-regarding (Cohen and Rogers, 1992, pp. 421, 425).

Plainly, the crucial political question raised by theories of democratic civil society is how much congruence between liberal-democratic norms and the organization and activities of groups should be enforced by law? Where is the line set dividing the internal affairs of a church or trade union from its regulable activities? If this question is not dependably addressed or the answer is elusive, it is not surprising; *liberal* democracy is at issue and anxiety about liberty is understandably aroused, since the logic of congruence underlying this view of civil society is clear. If families are schools of justice, gender inequality must be erased through shared parenting and a fair division of paid and unpaid domestic labour (Okin, 1989). Religious groups should be constrained from participating in politics unless they frame their arguments in universal, secular terms (Audi, 1989, p. 265). The Jaycees or Rotary Clubs cannot successfully invoke First Amendment rights of association to control their memberships by excluding women as full associates; association can be legally compelled because like many other voluntary associations they are 'private boot camps for citizenship' (Sullivan, 1988, p. 1720). Social and cultural identity groups should be represented in every governmental and quasi-public arena where social goods are distributed so that their 'voices' (but not vulgar interests) are heard (Young, 1990).

Liberal democracy is less a mirror of pluralist society than a tutor and creator of democratic civil society. Indeed, in some accounts, secondary groups and associations appear as virtual artifacts of government, owing their constitutive purposes to public policy.

In *mediating civil society*, the idea is just the opposite: to orient people toward the social networks believed to inculcate civility, sociability, and responsibility, which hold any society and particularly pluralist liberal democracy together. Churches, neighbourhood groups, and cultural and ethnic associations assume responsibility for articulating and addressing an expansive array of needs and interests, caring for the elderly and educating children, say. Civil society mediates between those functions reserved to government and those pursued by individuals alone or in private life. The label 'decentralization' does not apply here, because associations are social, not governmental; the label 'privatization' is inapt, too, because we are supposed to recognize the public face of civil society.

Mediating civil society instils habits of responsibility and cooperation above all, and these are compatible with the cultivation of a variety of particularist values and personal qualities in social formations ranging from cultural subcommunities to workplaces. Moreover, secondary associations are not expected to cultivate political virtues, and social collaboration need not translate into political representation. In Gray's version, it is not necessary to have a vigorous democracy at all for civil society to flourish; authoritarianism will do. So congruence need not be strict. On the other hand, mediating civil society does not positively invite incongruity or embrace pluralism for its own sake. The point is not 'protectionism' out of regard for the autonomy of cultural communities, solicitude for the authentic life of associations, or acceptance of a group's own interpretation of what is necessary for its survival or self-respect as a requirement of justice. Independence is not granted economic institutions for the sake of efficiency or choice. Rather, because tacit socialization in liberal dispositions is not enough, certain secondary associations are encouraged to take on the necessary task of moral education. Thus, 'functionally traditionalist' groups instil a sense of belonging and concern for the well-being of others; market arrangements cultivate civility (Galston, 1992).

The distributive question remains, of course, whether government should recognize, tax, legally sanction, subsidize, and support these social networks? Should liberal government actively foster the associations of civil society, and how? Gray argues that given a legal framework that includes machinery for private litigation, and official restraint so that government does not crowd out social roles and responsibilities or foment 'a political war of redistribution,' civil society will flourish. He is appalled by grabbiness and 'state-subsidized ghettos' and would leave not only economic institutions but all associations to themselves (Gray, 1993c, p. 17; Gray, 1993d, p. 266). He sees no acceptable middle ground between very limited government and corporatist Behemoth. Other advocates of mediating civil society are not so repulsed by the jockeying of pluralist politics or so fearful of either aggressive state 'capture' or passive clientelism that they want associations to turn from politics and government to opt out. They prescribe government funding for both religious and secular public education, charitable organizations, or retirement schemes so long as accommodation and support is distributed among social groups in a way that cannot be construed as a special privilege (McConnell, 1992).

Even if we assume, as theorists of mediating civil society apparently do, that groups and associations arise spontaneously, it is doubtful whether their commitment to liberalism is also spontaneous. But solicitude for associational life is not matched by solicitude for liberal values and institutions. Gray considers the conditions that encourage associations but not the conditions that lead associations to support liberal government arid its public norms, especially when these impose some cost on a group's local culture. Proposals for public funding and support provide reasons why associations might have a commitment to liberal government sufficiently strong to weigh in against their loyalty to their own at home and abroad, though this rationale is seldom explicit. In short, social networks should not only be internally cooperative, nurturing their own, they should cooperate with one another. 'Social-capital,' such as trust, norms, and networks, must redound to liberal political society as a whole, not associations as self-segregated enclaves, The very reason some liberals want mediating civil society should make them sensitive to the need for strong political integration and public support.

The problem with 'democratic civil society' is that it gives undue priority to political participation, depreciating other uses of civil society—private relations and personal satisfactions, economic ambitions, cultural identity, ideology, and individual expressivism. The danger is the colonization of social life by political culture. The problem with 'mediating civil society' is that enthusiasm for associational life eclipses the political and legal institutions necessary to sustain it. The danger is the balkanization of public life and insufficient attachment to the public institutions of liberal democracy.

Both approaches ignore the lessons of Hegel's moment: arrant self-interest, fearful anomie, and gripping group affiliation coexist in civil society and require different correctives. In their separate ways, democratic and mediating pluralism chasten egotism, provide attachments, widen outlooks, and enlarge sentiments, which is why both may be useful at times, and neither is a substitute for the other. But they do not exhaust the possibilities for the moral uses of civil society; indeed, they give little hint of the complex dynamics that inform the third approach.

On my view, which I call *elective civil society*, incongruity is the condition for generating liberal dispositions, and the key to liberal civil society is the moral uses of pluralism by men and women personally and individually. Liberal government must create a climate for the ongoing formation of new associations and for shifting involvements among them. Freedom of association will often lead to democratic participation and to mediating structures that foster concrete moral beliefs and provide caring communities. But the beneficial experience of pluralism does not stop with these.

What is the argument for incongruity and movement among associations and spheres? From the perspective of the moral uses of pluralism, compelling support for elective civil society comes from an unexpected place: the vicissitudes of individual moral development. If there are good political and psychological reasons for thinking that no single constitutive context is determinative of moral disposition, that one experience of association can compensate for the deprivations and depredations of another, that except for cruel and violent settings, almost any association has potential for being either constructive or destructive of liberal dispositions depending on whether the obstacle in an individual case is narrow self-interest, gripping affiliation, or anomie, then we should be cautious about concluding that incongruities between associational and public life are beyond the pale on the grounds of moral effects alone. It follows that if some associations inhibit liberal virtues, not all illiberal settings do; that even those may not be debilitating for all members and may even perform vital moralizing and socializing functions for some; that vices may not be unamenable to containment and correction. No single type of association is the sole support for liberalism, because the social and psychological sources of anti-liberalism are diverse. No single dynamic is at work, and no dynamic is at work all the time for every individual; whether the experiences of pluralism are complementary or compensatory is variable and generally unpredictable.

The uses of authority for moral development is just one aspect of the personal uses of pluralism, but it gives a taste of what is at issue. J. S. Mill drew a simple distinction between the moral needs of children and adults, arguing that paternalism enables children to attain the maturity of their faculties. But we know that experiences of authority serve self-development in more complicated ways. The moral effects of different types of authority vary from person to person, which is why we select a particular teacher or school for a child or seek out a physician-patient relation that is paternalistic or collaborative, to say nothing of the implicit choice we make about dependence when we choose a particular man or woman as partner, husband, or wife.

Deep needs (and good reasons) for various authority relations obviously continue into adulthood, which psychologists now say has its own developmental tasks. Writings on mentor relations describe how authority can facilitate the transition to full responsibility, and we know that some people work productively within a defined hierarchy and others under conditions of cooperation or even isolation.[5] At different points in their lives, and depending on personal as well as social circumstances, people feel more secure, confident, and self-respecting in one sort of authority relation than another. It bears mentioning that it is not always weakness, infirmity, or moral cravenness to choose to be subject to authority even in situations where autonomy is expected of us or considered ideal.[6] This thought should be familiar from John Rawls' account of 'the morality of authority' and 'the morality of association' 'We sometimes doubt the soundness of our moral attitudes when we reflect on their psychological origins,' Rawls observes, 'thinking that these sentiments have arisen in situations marked say by submission to authority, we may wonder whether they should not be rejected altogether.' But moral sentiments will cease to be regarded as neurotic compulsions 'if we understand the essential features of the psychology of moral development' (Rawls, 1971, pp. 514–15).

[5] The authors of *Habits of the Heart* demonstrate that membership in conservative churches is a response to the felt need for outer control as protection against a felt chaos of internal and external demands. Less apparent is the fact that the same person may profit from all of these at some time (Bellah, Madsen, Sullivan, Swidler, and Tipton, 1985, pp. 236, 414).

[6] See Rosenblum (1987, p. 124).

The question for liberalism is whether and how experiences of civil society come together in the lives of individuals. Individual vicissitudes make moral education variable and unpredictable. But the emergence of liberal dispositions is not a matter of serendipity, and, by itself, the existence of a pluralist array of associations may not contribute to shaping liberal dispositions since the *experience of pluralism* is necessary. The crucial considerations are the extent to which individuals' lives are bound up with a single group or association, whether membership inhibits or encourages others, what experiences of associational life are accessible, and the facility of shifting involvements. Since it is not clear whether a dynamic of compensation or reinforcement is at work, prediction, much less a general theory of civil society, may be impossible. But it is at least plausible to say that the experience of pluralism cultivates the habit of differentiating among spheres and adjusting moral conduct to them. Even if we are subject to (or inflict) prejudice, arbitrariness, or deference in one domain, we may also be able to exhibit tolerance, say, in public arenas and fairness in hiring.

But a background of strong liberal public culture and public policy is necessary to support the personal experience of pluralism. What sorts of things serve this purpose? Elective civil society assumes that our standing as citizens is unaffected by changes in affiliation or by lack of affiliation; thus, the objection to proposals for group rights and representation is not that they are unjust (affirmative action may be justifiable), but that distributing public rights and benefits on the basis of ascriptive group membership tends to freeze associations and make it difficult for individuals to change or multiply affiliations. Social policy can encourage the moral uses of pluralism by disconnecting health care benefits and pensions from specific employment, for example, or insisting that even self-contained religious communities pay minimum wages and contribute to social security taxes, so that their members are not economically constrained from leaving (Rosenblum, 1993a).

The idea of a connection between moral disposition and pluralism is nothing new—there is Mill's argument for the conditions of self-development and Adam Smith on the connection between markets and virtues. The present task is to think more expansively, and with greater attention to moral psychology, about the formation of liberal dispositions under conditions of modern pluralist civil society.

6

BOWLING IN THE BRONX
*The Uncivil Interstices between Civil and Political Society**

Laurence Whitehead

INTRODUCTION

What do we understand by the term 'civil society'? How does it arise? How is it related to pluralism, democracy, and democratization? If it has a tendency towards disintegration or self-destruction, does that threaten the consolidation of democratic regimes, or dies it merely exacerbate anxieties about the quality of our 'really existing' democracies (polyarchies)? If it develops a capacity for self-preservation, does that necessarily reinforce the deepening of political democracy, or could it come at the expense of the universalism and non-discrimination required for democratic authenticity?

This contribution offers a very general—and provisional—overview of these issues. Its point of departure is the discrepancy between our inclusive view of citizenship and our tacitly more restrictive view of the requirements of civil society.

Modern liberal constitutionalism extends the scope of citizenship (formal political rights) to virtually all adults within the relevant

* Robert Fine and Shirin Rai (eds), *Civil Society*, London, Frank Cass, 1997.

jurisdiction. In a world of territorial states the exceptions to this rule are at a grave disadvantage. Typically, therefore, such exceptions (for example, the incarcerated, the certifiably insane or incompetent, refugees, and asylum seekers) are narrowly defined and carefully delimited. If it were otherwise and categories of exception were loosely defined or easily extendible, then broad segments of the political community might feel their citizenship rights to be potentially under threat and might therefore become mobilized to defend an extended franchise. Historically, after all, the present almost universal and inclusionary conception of citizenship rights was only brought about through pressure and agitation by and on behalf of those who were initially excluded or marginalized from the territorial political community. The result is that nowadays the overwhelming majority of contemporary representative polities are strongly biased towards universality. In other words, they contain a strong presumption against the withdrawal of citizenship rights. This is true both of long-established democracies (polyarchies), and also of the many fragile and newly established constitutionally and potentially democratic regimes (neo-democracies).

However, although modern citizenship may assume the guise of universality, the same cannot be said for membership of 'civil society'. That, at least, is the claim upon which this analysis is based. The distinction between an inclusionary conception of citizenship (and therefore of 'political society'), and a more selective or restrictive view of what constitutes civil society will of course depend upon how the second category is defined. The discussion therefore begins with a brief review of the competing possibilities, all of which imply something narrower than universal citizenship. All of which, in other words, admit a third category of 'uncivil citizens', or persons enjoying political rights, but not submitting themselves to the constraints imposed by 'civil society'. Since there appear to be no single consensual definition of our second category there are alternative views of what from these constraints may take, but in some from or other they must surely include a requirement of 'civility'. The study therefore proposes a working definition which incorporates this requirement. It then proceeds to consider the implications of incivility, both for our understanding of 'civil society' and for our theorizing about the relationship between civil society and democratization.

The underlying assumption is that whether or not this particular working definition is adopted, on my reasonable account there will necessarily remain a substantial gap between universalistic conceptions of modern political society, and more restrictive or extracting notions of civil society. The interstices between these two social forms will favour the production of multiple variants of 'incivility' (a residual category derived from the notion of civil society, which may therefore need to be disaggregated and deconstructed). The discussion concludes that the quality and stability of both contemporary neo-democracies—and indeed of long-standing 'polyarchies'—is likely to be materially affected by the solidity and structure of civil society, and that these characteristics in turn will be heavily conditioned by the nature and strength of the challenges arising from the 'uncivil interstices'.

The weaknesses of civil society, and the dangers posed by various forms of 'incivility' are particularly evident in many neo-democracies. In both the post-authoritarian and the post-communist experiences efforts at democratization are frequently overshadowed by the emergence or proliferation of anti-social forms of individualism and group organization that substitute for, or even seek to subvert, the forms of civil associationalism celebrated by theorists of 'civil society'. An internationally recognizable shorthand for this flourishing of incivility can be found in the term 'mafia'. Were this a straightforward matter of criminality it would be of limited significance to students of politics, however difficult it might be for the police to handle. But it becomes of central concern when the requirements of democratization include the extension of political and citizenship rights to large sectors of the population who not only may have no prior experience of democratic politics, but also have few resources to escape mafia-type networks of political co-optation and control. It is also of central concern where uncivil forms of association are left over from the disintegration of the *ancien régime*, or arise in the course of political struggle between groups who are 'disloyal' to the prevailing (if fragile) constitutional order. The incentives to organize intolerant and uncivil forms of associationalism are particularly strong where claims to privilege and property are politically contestable; where servants of the old regime still seek impunity for past misdeeds, and fear revenge; and where the present justice system seems incapable of upholding a broad and impartial rule of law. These are all, of course, characteristic conditions to be found in many neo-democracies.

However, the discussion is not directed solely, or even mainly, to the travails of the many societies currently attempting to consolidate their fragile new democracies. The long-established polyarchies of the

OECD area also manifest sharp disjunctions between the scope of their civil and political societies. Italy, as the original home of the mafia, has recently manifested the destabilizing macro-political potential of the uncivil interstices in a particularly dramatic form.[1] But such incivility takes many forms and appears in most polyarchies. For example, in France once of the most sensitive issues has become the spread of street violence through the *banlieux* of almost all the large urban centres, particularly where youth unemployment and Islamic traditions coincide. The French police now keep monthly records of the incidents they deal with in the 1017 *quartiers* which have been classified as '*sensitifs*'. July 1995 was a record month with 955 such incidents—the norm is around 500.[2] Nor is Britain exempt,[3] nor even the United States, particularly in some derelict inner city wastelands. Indeed, the title of this chapter has been chosen to highlight the weaknesses of civil associationalism in parts of America not foreseen by Tocqueville.[4] The Bronx has been singled out in the hope of avoiding the exoticism that would arise from situating discussions of civil society in the context of such stereotypical 'Third World' locations as El Alto (La Paz), the Baixada Fluminese (Rio), or Guguletu (Cape Town). The assumption is that once we have gone bowling in the Bronx we are most of the way to understanding the relationship between civil society and democracy in Bolivia, Brazil, and South Africa as well.

1 For a useful and up-to-date compilation of the intricacies, including institutional and regional disaggregation and a discussion of the Andreotti trials, see Luciano Violante (ed.), *Mafie e antimafia: Rapporto '96* (Rome: Laterza, 1966).

2 *Le monde*, 30 December 1995, p. 6.

3 Britain, like many long-established 'polyarchies', extends political rights (rights to vote and organize) to substantial communities that reject its constitutional authority and that consider it legitimate to practice 'uncivil' forms of political opposition. Sínn Féin, Heri Batasuna, and the Corsican nationalists all illustrate this pattern of incivility.

4 The title is also a reference to Robert Putnam's 'Bowling Alone: Democracy in America at the End of the Twentieth Century', in D. Rueschemeyer and Marilyn Rueschemeyer (eds), *Participation and Democracy: East and West* (Armonk, NY: M. E. Sharpe, 1995). Putnam concludes that in the USA

> participation has fallen (often sharply) in many types of civic associations, from religious groups to labour unions, from women's clubs to fraternal clubs, and from neighbourhood gatherings to bowling leagues. Virtually all segments of society have been afflicted by this lessening in social connectedness... (which) seems a likely contributor to many of the social and political ills now afflicting America, and perhaps to those besetting other advanced democracies, as well.

THE LACK OF CONGRUENCE BETWEEN 'CIVIL' AND 'POLITICAL' SOCIETY

All the rival meanings just discussed, and certainly the working definition I have finally selected, point to forms of voluntary (or at least uncoerced) associative organizations that we are most unlikely to find distributed evenly across the geographical and social terrain covered by the modern territorial state (the 'polity'). Uneven development is more or less self-evident in the realm of commerce and the division of labour. It is also a virtually inescapable characteristic both of Hegel's corporations and of Tocqueville's newspaper co-ordinated local associations. The same is true if we regard church-sponsored collectivities as a crucial component of civil society; these are more densely concentrated in some areas, and in some social strata, than in others. Similarly, working class labour unions and forms of community organizations tend to be geographically concentrated. Equally, if we follow Parsons in stressing the centrality of educational institutions (especially universities), again we will encounter uneven social coverage. Schmitter's definition carries the same implication, in that the four conditions he specifies are more reliable fulfilled in some social settings than in others (especially 'civility', but also dual autonomy, etc.). Although some of these patterns of distribution may be offsetting (strong working class associations where higher educational coverage is weak, etc.) others are cumulative. In fact all these definitions seem to imply that civil society will be 'denser' in Hampstead than in Brixton, in Santa Monica that in East Los Angeles. For however we specify the precise components of civil society, some sections of the citizenry will be over-supplied with 'dense associative life', while others will be under-provided. (This is probably true even of Habermas's 'life-world of communicative interaction' though it is hard to be certain.)[5]

Neither the market nor the state can be relied upon to even out this uneven social distribution of voluntary associationalism. Not the

[5] In his account of what he calls the 'structural transformation of the public sphere', Habermas views civil society as the arena in which pluralistic public opinion makes itself felt as an independent source of power. But of course some voices express themselves more loudly than others in the arena of public opinion, and not all the opinions expressed in an unconstrained public arena will be equally 'civil': Jürgen Habermas, *Strukturwandel der Öffentlichkeit* (Frankfurt: Suhrkamp, 1993).

market because it obeys consumer sovereignty, which is skewed towards high income earners. Not the state, because the sovereign assembly is also typically skewed towards the most articulate and best-organized groups in the polity (indeed parliamentarism has not infrequently been both praised and criticized as the best form of government for securing the ascendancy of civil society over the republican will). More fundamentally, theorists of associationalism who wish to preserve its voluntary and participatory features therefore resist centrally imposed standardization, and see state regulation as a threat to liberty.[6] But in that case what countervailing mechanism can they point to, to even out the inequalities of civil society? The hopeful assertion that since voluntary associations are beneficial, those who lack them can be taught or encouraged to create them, seems to me a flimsy counterweight.

As we know from countless studies of policing and the administration of justice, even those legal rights which are formally uniform throughout the modern polity are in practice somewhat selectively distributed. Poverty, race, underprivileged family background, and so forth provide virtually universal negative markers even in the most consolidated and 'social democratic' of nation-states. Robert Putnam has recently drawn attention to the evidence of strong regional and local variations in the quality of civic life in different parts of Italy, and Francis Fukuyama has sketched a framework for making similar comparisons internationally.[7] In most neo-democracies the main attributes of civil society tend to be highly concentrated in specific sites; are often reserved to a minority of the population; and are not infrequently derived from privileges conferred by a pre-democratic structure of power. And insofar as the 'rule of law' constitutes an essential component of civil society, publicly provided and impartial justice is typically an aspiration rather than a realized achievement across broad swathes of the social landscape in most 'really existing' democracies. (As Cohen and Arato reluctantly admit, although 'fundamental rights must be seen as the *organizing principle*

[6] For a vigorous recent presentation of this case see Paul Hirst, *Associative Democracy: New Forms of Economic and Social Governance* (Massachusetts: University of Massachusetts Press, 1994).

[7] Robert Putnam, *Making Democracy Work: Civic Traditions in Modern Italy* (Princeton, 1994) and Francis Fukuyama, *Trust: New Foundations of Global Prosperity* (L. Hamish Hamilton, 1995).

of a modern civil society a civil society in formation...[as in Eastern Europe recently] may for a time have to do without a settled structure of rights'.)[8]

Not only is civil society unevenly distributed across social space at any particular moment of time, it also develops unevenly, and according to a logic that is distinct from that of state formation, over time. Obviously each diverse definition of civil society outlined above embodies a distinctive implicit theory of historical causation, and indeed it is more than likely that somewhat different processes were involved in the generation of north Italian civic traditions from those that produced Tocueville's small town America, or the emerging civil society of post-communist Poland. All that need concern us here is the conclusion that, whichever historical route may have been followed, the resulting patterns of associative life and social communication will be highly structured, with insiders, traditionally favoured sectors, and marginal or excluded sectors. Depending on where one is located in relation to this structure of privilege and opportunity, and how flexible and open it prove to be, one may either view the resulting civil society as the most authentic expression and durable guarantee of a political democracy or the most flagrant negation of its universalistic promise.[9]

In contrast to the incremental, organic, uneven, and perhaps reversible rhythms of development that characterize the growth of civil society, modern political regimes are frequently constituted at short notice, as coherent interdependent structures, and with pretensions to uniform coverage across their respective territorial jurisdictions. The 'new states' created in Europe after 1918, or in Africa and Asia after 1945, provide many recent illustrations of this thesis, but it applies also to many neo-democracies created in the wake of the Soviet collapse of 1989/91. In nearly all such cases the claims of uniform coverage and of formal political equality for all citizens within the new jurisdiction, were initially to some extent no more than aspirations,

[8] Jean L. Cohen and Andrew Arato, *Civil Society and Political Theory* (Cambridge, MA: MIT Press, 1992), pp. 440–2.

[9] On a recent visit to South Africa I was struck by the richness and stability of the civic society that had sheltered the whites—and even perhaps the coloureds of Cape province—under *apartheid*, while actively and energetically suppressing the possibilities of peaceful association for the none-white majority. Protestant Ulster probably displays a somewhat comparable polarity in civic provision, in this case legitimated by a universal suffrage that guaranteed Catholic subordination.

or legal fictions, for much of the subject population. Nevertheless these new political guidelines of territorial sovereignty and civic equality were in principle created at a specific moment (for example, through the writing of a constitution), after which they acquired instant universality. In the cases that concern us here, it was a full panoply of democratic political rights that were ostensibly conferred upon a newly created citizenry. Yet the sudden creation of new inclusionary political societies may well not coincide with any pre-existing maps of dense associative life. The obvious question therefore follows: how are the associative and communicative *practices* of 'civil society' related to the aspirational or juridical *fictions* of 'political society' in new democracies? If there is more than one historical route to the establishment of a civil society, it would seem to follow that there could be more than one way in which civil society is related to the construction of a democratic political regime.

Evidently, there could be a slow growth of civil society which eventually creates the conditions for the eventual implantation of political democracy. (This is the Whig interpretation of British history; it also applies to one dominant view of the democratization of Spain.) But there could also be a reverse sequence, through which a formal political regime would first be implanted, and only sub-sequently would civil society—perhaps nurtured by a protective liberal state—gradually mature. (This would seem a standard western model for theorizing the democratization of many post-communist state; it could also apply to such 'protectorate' experiences as the democratization of Puerto Rico and Hawaii.) Other combinations are also theoretically possible—a civil society which attains a high level of development, without ever culminating in a democratic regime (Hong Kong, for example); a civil society which develops on the basis that its freedoms and rights can only be secure if non-members are excluded from political participation (be they Tamils, Palestinians, Turkish Cypriots, Muslims, or 'Bantus'). Where new political frontiers are incongruent with older maps of associative life, it is just as likely that peripheral or cross-border civil societies will be damaged as that core civil societies will be reinforced. Viewed in this broadly com-parative manner, there seems no strong reason—either theoretical or empirical—for presuming the existence of only one strongly deter-minate relationship between civil society and political democracy. If the two are so readily separable, and in principle, incongruent, we need to examine more closely the interstices between them.

'UNCIVIL SOCIETY' AND POLITICAL DEMOCRACY

In those social locations where civil society is weak or absent, the reverse of Schmitter's four conditions apply—namely (1) encroachments on dual autonomy; (2) which subvert the capacity for deliberation; and may encourage (3) usurpation; and (4) incivility. This abstract formulation embraces a great variety of more specific possibilities, since threats to civil society can come from many—and often multiple—sources, and can be driven by political, socio-economic, or even by technological processes.[10] Consider this quick listing of some of the most celebrated historical examples—the Nazi party's subversion of civil society in Weimar Germany; followed by the Socialist Unity Party (SED) in post-1945 East Germany; the mafia in republican Sicily; Catholic clerical conformism—in, say, rural Ireland; Islamic fundamentalism in the *bidonvilles* of the Maghreb; state-imposed conformity in Singapore; and some would add media-manipulated docility in Eisenhower's America, amoral familism in the Philippines, or caste-based exclusionisms in some parts of South Asia. This list should not be read as lumping all these diverse phenomena into an undifferentiated amalgam of 'threats to western liberty', nor should one lightly endorse all the specific historical and social judgements of responsibility that it implies. In a grounded analysis of any specific case we should expect to find multiple causation and some degree of structured determination, rather than just the will of a single illiberal agency. In the instances listed above, about half were examples of encroachments from above (the state) and half from below (illiberal society). In general one should expect some interaction between these two sources of constraint.

There is also a range of unintentional, non-political, or 'structural' threats to civil society which are tediously familiar, but still require some listing—unemployment (which is hardly conducive to civility, or collective deliberation); criminality (which erodes dual autonomy, encourages usurpation); monopolistic systems of local social control (which regardless of political intent block off deliberation, foster intolerance, obscure the legitimacy of alternative viewpoints); the atomizing effects of market supremacy, and so forth. Again, the purpose of this list is not to amalgamate all these structures into an

---

10 If Putnam's friends no longer go bowling, this is at least in part because so many rival entertainments are now supplied to them electronically and at home.

undifferentiated threat, nor to imply that they are either separately or conjointly determinate. On the contrary, the purpose is to demonstrate their heterogeneity and fragmentation. For this implies that civil society will always be under pressure from multiple sources, and that in any modern polity it is always likely to coexist with substantial and persisting sources of incivility. It is never likely to achieve uniformity of coverage throughout any full-scale nation-state; and therefore it will always require an organized capacity for self-defence and self-reproduction if it is to secure and preserve its political hegemony.

In a modern democracy these pockets or strata of incivility also possess political rights and are entitled to their share of representation in the making of public policy. Depending, therefore, on their size and their capacity for political articulation, they will help steer the course of democratic government. They may indeed shape the rules and affect the resources allocations that underpin the civil part of society. For example, if we regard 'autonomous deliberation' as one of the most essential ingredients of a robust civil society, political democracy may well empower political forces which have no interest in fostering such practices, but may instead view them as either wasteful or even threatening. Similarly, there can be no guarantee that electoral majorities will always favour the preservation of the 'civility' so dear to well-educated minorities. On the contrary one sector's 'autonomy and civility' can easily be reinterpreted by another sector of society as elitist privilege, needing to be levelled.

The recent reinstatement in office, via competitive elections, of no more than lightly 'reformed' communist parties in various East European neo-democracies, serves to highlight this persistent tension between the rival claims for our allegiance of civil society and political democracy. Eminent liberal theorists, such as Gray and Gellner, have all invoked visions of civil society as counterposed to communism, that can be read as delegitimizing such electoral outcomes.[11]

---

[11] In his last book Ernest Gellner trenchantly sets out the two rival theoretical claims to validation, and asserts his clear choice:

> Theorists of democracy who operate in the abstracts, without reference to concrete social conditions, end up with a vindication of democracy as a general ideal, but are then obliged to concede that in many societies the ideal is not realizable.... Is it not better to state the conditions that make the ideal feasible, or even mandatory, and start from that? Civil society is a more realistic notion,

Similarly, in an analysis centred on capitalist democracy, although Schmitter tends to present civil society as normally and in the long run positive for democratic consolidation, he also acknowledges the separateness of the two processes, and the potential for friction between them. 'Civil society, however, is not an unmitigated blessing for democracy. It can affect the consolidation and subsequent functioning of democracy in a number of negative ways.' Among these he includes:

(2) It may build into the policy process a systematically biased distribution of influence... .

(3) It tends to impose an elaborate and obscure process of compromise upon political life, the outcome of which can be policies which no-one wanted in the first place and with which no-one can subsequently identify... .

(5) Most dangerously it 'may prove to be not one but several civil societies—all occupying the same territory and polity, but organizing interests and passions into communities that are ethnically, linguistically or culturally distinct—even exclusive'.[12]

The two foregoing paragraphs have presented strikingly counterposed normative images of the relationship between civil society and democracy. In the first, 'civil society' is the bearer of liberty, and is threatened by the mechanical application of majoritarian politics in a society with a still prevailing uncivil inheritance. In the second, the consolidation of political democracy is taken as the desirable goal, and 'civil society' can therefore be scrutinized and evaluated according to the quality of its potential contribution, which could be negative. On the first view, the stronger the civil society the

---

which specifies and includes its own conditions.... Because it highlights those institutional pre-conditions and the necessary historical context 'Civil Society' is probably a better more illuminating slogan than democracy. Ernest Gellner, *Conditions of Liberty: Civil Society and Its Rivals* (London: Allen Lane, 1994), pp. 188–9.

But Gellner's imprecise specifications relate only loosely to the ideals of democratic theory.

12 Mimeo, 'On Civil Society and the Consolidation of Democracy: Ten Propositions' (Stanford Department of Political Science, July, 1995), p. 14. Note that these negative potentialities tend to run counter to the positive attributes emphasized by Schmitter's initial definition. Here non-usurpation becomes policy bias; deliberation becomes opacity; and civility becomes tribalism. It is difficult to sustain an idealized image of civil society, while also reflecting its multiple and ambiguous manifestations and its lopsided impact on the working of the larger polity.

better, even if it is inherently 'denser' in some social locations than in others. On the second view, only those forms of civil society that contribute to the consolidation of a high quality of political democracy are clearly desirable. Other forms may be too inegalitarian, too pushy and disorienting, or even too 'uncivil', to be desirable. Indeed sound democratization could require far-reaching reform, and perhaps even the weakening, of inherited systems of dense associative life.[13]

The first account makes the implicit assumption of an overbearing state. Civil society therefore needs strengthening against that source of threat to its 'dual autonomy'. In the second account, by contrast, the state is implicitly assumed to lack strong authority. It is therefore the capture of civil society by particularistic interests that presents the main threat to dual autonomy.

Since these two possibilities are both theoretically and empirically plausible, we may conclude that the moral significance we can assign to civil society is indeterminate (perhaps even 'essentially contested'), at this abstract level. A reasoned evaluation will depend in part on where the observer is located in the social structure, and on how a particular civil society functions and relates to the broader political system. Perhaps it would be better for US democracy if we all went out to bowling clubs together more often. But while on the Upper East Side of Manhattan a natural focus of community deliberation would be excessive tax burdens and wasteful social spending, in the Bronx a different form of civility might be more likely to emerge. The impediments to effective collective action would almost certainly prove quite different in the two cases as well.

[13] Carlos M. Vilas provides some striking illustrations of this viewpoint, in an overview of the neo-democracies of Central America; 'Prospects for Democratization in a Post-Revolutionary Setting: Central America', *Journal of Latin American Studies*, Vol. 28, Part 2 (1996), pp. 461–503. He portrays local oligarchies founded on tight inherited structures of social exclusivity that have learnt to parade the rhetoric of market democracy as a public discourse masking their continued supremacy, while their more intimate social practices perpetuate deeply undemocratic values. Compare E. Gyimah-Boadi on the weaknesses of civil society in Africa: 'preliberal or antiliberal values...tend also to pervade the modern and secular civil associations...tendencies of some key civil associations...to refuse to establish "rational" bureaucracies; to "anoint" rather than elect (including those involved in prodemocracy work) their executives; and to endow their leader with "life" chairmanships', 'Civil Society in Africa', *Journal of Democracy*, 7(2), (1996), p. 129.

One way to cope with this diversity is to say that any collective deliberations that are not subversive, and that do not fall outside the law, are as legitimate as any others. Of course, in order to achieve positive results within a liberal constitutional framework, it will be necessary to win over many diverse interests. Some forms of deliberation will therefore be more successful (because more persuasive, or more skilfully targeted) than others. But ineffective and unpersuasive forms of deliberation are also permitted, provided they do not infringe a small number of clearly defined legal prohibitions. In principle this is indeed the way democratic regimes should define the scope of tolerated deliberations. But can the same criterion serve to delimit the scope of debate within 'civil society'? Following the definition adopted in this discussion it would seem not.

On most definitions (including the one used here) it would be more plausible to say that some forms of discussion which are not illegal in a democracy are nevertheless 'uncivil', and threatening to such crucial norms as non-usurpation and interpersonal toleration. Thus various forms of religious fundamentalism may have to be tolerated within a democracy, but cannot be regarded as pat of a modern liberal 'civil society'. A rich family can plot to buy up a newspaper, and then use it to discredit their enemies, and with care the whole operation may be carried out within the law, but this would involve no manifestation of dual automony, or of civility. Public officials can collude to withold information that the electorate 'ought' to know (in order to make well-founded political choices), and again this may be done within the limits of the law, but it could still be 'uncivil'. In fact, the very question of how rigorously the law will be enforced in various settings may also be subject to uncivil manipulation which remains within the bounds of constitutionally permitted action.

In short, in the realm of collective discourse, as much as in the realm of social structure, there is a gap between the narrow coverage that properly pertains to our various conceptions of 'civil society' and the broader coverage required of the democratic polity. On the other side of that gap we can identify 'uncivil' deliberations, and 'uncivil' social strata. The precise boundary between the civil and the uncivil may be hard to define even in principle, and all the more so in practice. Alliances of convenience can be expected from, time to time, spanning that boundary (as when the least civil of media barons are courted by the most respected of liberal institutions on some issue of common interest, or when fundamentalists seek the protection of civil libertarians). But a boundary there must be, if 'civil society' is to carry any of the moral or sociological connotations assigned to it by its theorists. If so, then the activities which lie on the other side of that boundary—in what I have called the 'uncivil interstices between civil and political society'—may be of great significance for the quality and stability of the democracy as a whole. This section has attempted to illustrate the extent of such effects even in well-established western democracies. By extension one could argue that in neo-democracies such uncivil interstices occupy a much large social space, often more than that occupied by the emerging civil society itself.[14] In order to analyse the scope for 'democratic consolidation' in such societies we therefore need to attend to the political manifestations of 'uncivil society' in emerging democracies. We also need to consider how the scale and power of this 'uncivil' society may affect the content and characteristics displayed by whatever form of civil society can accompany it. The final section of this contribution outlines some preliminary ideas on this issue.

CIVIL SOCIETY AND THE 'OTHER'

If civil society is characterized by its capacity for deliberation, and for collective action (within the limits set by non-usurpation and civility) then we must expect it both to deliberate and to act on perceived threats to its existence, or to its capacity for future development. Such threats might be attributed primarily to 'traditional society' and its habitual constraints, or to the 'modern state' with its rationalizing and atomizing propensities. But, particularly in neo-democracies, they might also be located in the 'uncivil' (but neither private-traditional nor public-bureaucratic) interstices of the new political community.

Each of these alternative diagnoses invokes an alternative model (or theory) and implies a particular strategy of self-perpetuation. In

[14] Giorgio Alberti of the University of Bologna has based his conception of *movimentismo* in Peru and Argentina on an analogous argument (see his '"Movimentismo" and Democracy: An Analytical Framework and the Peruvian Case Study' (Mimeo, CESDE, Bologna, October, 1995). Guillermo O'Donnell coined the term 'brown areas' to refer to the large sectors of Latin American society where uncivil conditions prevail; 'On the State, Democratization and Some Conceptual Problems: A Latin American View with Glances at Some Postcommunist Countries', *World Development*, 21(8), (1993), pp. 1355–69.

any particular instance these three rival conceptions may be found in contention within the councils of a given 'civil society'. When traditional family and particularist loyalties are defined as the central problem to be overcome, 'state strengthening' strategies may seem acceptable, particularly those that strengthen the 'public sphere' by guaranteeing impersonal civic rights and reinforcing the rule of law. But when (as in post-communist neo-democracies, and also in Latin American neo-liberal discourse) the overbearing state is regarded as a greater menace, then deregulation, privatization, and state shrinking will be preferred. In principle these may also involve enhancement of some kind of 'public space' where autonomous agents can interact without manipulation, and so here too it could be said that impartial legality and rights are implied, but it makes a great difference that such rights are asserted *against* the state, rather than under its protection, and that the justice system is liable to be subjected to the same austerity and market testing as the rest of the state bureaucracy.[15] For in these conditions the resulting 'rule of law' will be above all responsive to the requirements of commerce, rather than to those of state directed rationality.[16] In the language of Habermas, this would lead to cultural impoverishment and the 'colonization of the life-world' from which modern civil society is supposed to emerge.

As the norm of 'dual autonomy' makes clear, civil societies are always to some extent under pressure from both sides, from traditional particularism and from the intrusive state. The preservation and enlargement of an autonomous realm requires a steady flow of resources and recruits, directed with vigilance and continuity of purpose. Civil society consists of multiple self-perpetuating centres of association,

[15] Compare the Czech debate over 'civil society' in which President Havel tries to promote the concept as a corrective to excessive emphasis on purely market relationships, while Prime Minister Havel equates democracy with individual freedom, including freedom from social engineering in the name of civil society; Vaclav Havel, Vaclav Klaus and Petr Pithart, 'Rival Visions', *Journal of Democracy*, 7(1), (1996), pp. 18, 20.

[16] Recall the liberal pluralism of Durkheim for whom it was the state which 'creates and organizes and makes a reality' of the individual's natural rights, indeed its 'essential function' was to 'liberate individual personalities', by offsetting the pressure on them of local domestic, ecclesiastical, occupational and other secondary groups (while the latter were also needed to offset the potential tyranny of the state); Steven Lukes, *Emile Durkheim* (London: Allen Lane, 1973), p. 271.

competing as well as cooperating in order to promote their rival interests and to project their alternative conceptions of autonomy, civility, and self-preservation. Some such centres will shrink from particularism but hope to benefit from enlightened state activism; others will firmly resist state direction, but see little ham in allying with aspects of social traditionalism. Within each civil society alternative perspectives and priorities will compete for ascendancy with fluctuating success as the external environment is perceived to change.

But what if , as in many neo-democracies, the major threat to civil society comes—or at least is perceived to come—neither from statism nor traditional particularism, but from a majoritarian incivility of the modern kind? This refers to such phenomena as the impersonal irresponsibility of modern commercialized mass media; the impulsiveness of an uprooted and disoriented electorate; the short-termism of speculative financial markets; and the insecurity generated by well-organized crime, typically lodged in such strategic sectors as arms trafficking, money laundering, and the narcotics trade? Norms of dual autonomy, rational deliberation, civility, and Cohen and Arato's 'universal fundamental rights' may all come under siege from potentially majoritarian incivilities of this kind, which cannot for the most part be attributed directly to either of the two long-standing sources of threat against which civil society has typically been organized. As stressed in this discussion, this third alternative challenge to civil society can now be found everywhere—even in the most secure and developed of liberal democracies. Some theorists emphasize the importance of global integration, and the erosion of the authority of the nation state, as the dominant new tendencies at work. That might help to account for *some* of the elements of majoritarian incivility listed above, but by no means all, in my opinion. Particularly in neo-democracies it is often the manner in which the authoritarian regime foundered, and the uncivil inheritances it left in its wake, that prove more critical than the erosion of the nation state as such.

In neo-democracies emerging civil societies are, by definition, incipient and untested. The norms of dual autonomy, independent deliberation, and civility were little cultivated under authoritarian rule (except perhaps among some very privileged minorities under what Linz termed 'limited pluralism'), and so they had to be promoted and upheld in the face of official repression. That often provided an intense learning experience for activist minorities, and often their social influence exploded when the authoritarian regime left power.

But at best they were a select group, not all of them deeply socialized in the norms of civility, and the choices they faced during the helter-skelter of democratization dispersed them into widely scattered activities. (The virtual disintegration of the Solidarity bloc in Poland after 1989 seems a paradigmatic case.) Competing with them for influence in post-transition public life were many active groups schooled in less civil norms—pragmatists from the authoritarian power structure; revanchistes, chauvinists, and fundamentalists from other sectors of the opposition; the new rich, often engaged in 'primitive accumulation'; carpetbagging foreign advisers with no durable commitment to the local society; and so on. The list could be extended further, but the point is already clear. In such setting whatever 'civil society' may have been precariously established will be fragile and under siege from all sides. It will have to contend with a democratic polity mostly populated by actors whose commitment to civility is questionable or absent.

Long before this 'civil society' can be stabilized and entrenched, the polity will have produce a succession of foundational decisions that will heavily constrain subsequent patterns of political interaction. No doubt certain forms of constitutional engineering may improve the prospects of a viable civil society (for example, though a well-crafted bill of rights, or perhaps through parliamentarism or federalism). Similarly some strategies of economic modernization are likely to be more supportive than others (for example, law-based schemes of open regionalism, deregulation, some forms of privatization). But there is no single or guaranteed prescription applicable to all cases, nor should the health of civil society be the only point for consideration when choosing between these alternatives. In practice, other considerations will usually prove decisive. There is equally no single unique way in which the leaders of an incipient civil society must necessarily respond to the internal contradictions and external constraints that they face, but the range of alternatives compatible with survival and eventual growth are sure to be limited and inhibiting. In some cases strong civil societies may nevertheless be erected over the longer term, but not under conditions of their own choosing. In Gellner's language, the conditions for a realistic civil society may not permit the realization of the civil society *ideal*.

Constitutional government based on universal suffrage would normally imply that those who wish to realize an ideal of public conduct should promote their cause through a political party or at least via the electoral process. But the norms of 'dual autonomy' and 'non-usurpation' that we have attributed to civil society imply that the term should not be extended to embrace political organizations that compete for public office. Moreover, in many neo-democracies some of the most effective vote-winning organizations lack a tradition of commitment to the norm of 'civility', and/or permit very little 'deliberation' over their internal affairs. There is therefore, in general, no particular reason to expect an 'elective affinity' between a vigorous civil society and electorally successful political parties. Certainly in various cases we may find that the emergence of a more broadly based civil society is followed by the establishment of democratic political parties which proceed to legislate in accordance with a civil society ideal. But two other models are equally plausible, namely (i) an antagonism between the architects of civil society and successful party leaders; or (ii) a compartmentalization of the two spheres.[17] The relationship between civil society and party politics clearly requires careful analysis, which has not been possible in this paper.[18] But we can at least warn against the error of reductionism here.

So what if the 'other' against which the thinking heads of civil society can organize themselves is neither the coherently intrusive state, nor the inertia of unthinking tradition, but rather the insecurity, rootlessness, arbitrariness, and perhaps even the social cannibalism, that have come to be associated with many post-transition liberalized societies? What kind of civil society, based on what organizing principles, can survive and develop in the face of this modern anomic 'other'? A Hobbesian 'city' perhaps united only by its fear of the surrounding war of all against all? Hegelian guilds? Or a Marxian bourgeoisie? A Tocquevillean network of local associations (and bowling clubs)? Or even Habermas's 'life-world of communicative

[17] These three alternatives have been elaborated by Carlos A. Forment, 'Civil Society and the Invention of Democracy in Nineteenth Century Cuba' (mimeo, Princeton, September, 1995).

[18] My approach has been to exclude all political parties from 'civil society' on the grounds that they compete for national office. An alternative would be to include those political parties (and only those) who represent the interests of substantial sectors of civil society. This would involve making some invidious distinctions between political parties. Does the Italian Communist Party express the interests of a major element in civil society, or dies it displace and suborn those interests? Is this stable over time, or variable? How do we prove one interpretation rather than the other?

interaction'? Each of these tends to privilege a particular sociological category—specialists in security, master craftsmen, capitalists, local journalists, intelligentsia, and so forth—and none of them seem self-evidently applicable to neo-democracies as a whole. Each may suggest a fragment of the potential whole, but none gives clear guidance as to the principles upon which it might be integrated. In practice different forms of civil society are likely to prove relatively viable in different neo-democracies. But in general it may be concluded that the most effective principles of integration are more likely to come from without, rather than from within. That is to say, those forms of civil society which can cope best with the pressures of uncivil majoritarianism have the best prospects. Whether they can also live up to the idealistic hopes vested in them by so many recent theorists is another matter.

7

BEYOND THE NATION?
OR WITHIN?*

Partha Chatterjee

It is only by separating the two interrelated issues of civil society-modernity and political society-democracy that we will begin to see the dimensions of power and political strategy without an awareness of which the proposals to 'move beyond the nation' are quite likely to strengthen inequalities and defeat the struggle for democracy the world over.

I

'We need to think ourselves beyond the nation', declared Arjun Appadurai in the first sentence of his 1993 essay 'Patriotism and Its Futures'.[1] If we are to take seriously Appadurai's proposal to rethink the linguistic imaginary of the territorial state, one of the ways might be to take a fresh look at some of the conceptual components that

* *Economic and Political Weekly*, 4–11 January 1997.

1 Arjun Appadurai, 'Patriotism and Its Futures' *Public Culture*, 5(3), 1993, pp. 411–29, now included in Appadurai, *Modernity at Large Cultural Dimensions of Globalisation*, University of Minnesota Press, Minneapolis, 1996, pp. 158–77. All page references to Appadurai in my text are from this book.

claim to tie together local structures of community with territorial nation-states. Let me bring these up here: family, civil society, political society, and the state. These are classical concepts of political theory, but used, we know, in a wide variety of senses and often with much inconsistency. I must clarify here the sense in which I find it useful to employ these concepts in talking about contemporary political formations.

Hegel's synthesis in the *Philosophy of Right* of these elements of what he called 'ethical life' spoke of family, civil society, and the state, but had no place for a distinct sphere of political society. However, in understanding the structure and dynamics of mass political formations in twentieth-century nation-states, if seems to me useful to think of a domain of mediating institutions between civil society and the state. The sharpness of the nineteenth-century distinction between state and civil society, developed along the tradition of European anti-absolutist thinking, has the analytical disadvantage today of either regarding the domain of the civil as a depoliticized domain in contrast with the political domain of the state, or of blurring the distinction altogether by claiming that all civil institutions are political. Neither emphasis is of help in understanding the complexities of political phenomena in large parts of the contemporary world.

I find it useful to retain the term 'civil society' to those characteristic institutions of modern associational life originating in western societies that are based on equality, autonomy, freedom of entry and exit, contract, deliberative procedures of decision-making, recognized rights and duties of members, and such other principles. Obviously, this is not to deny that the history of modernity in non-western countries contains numerous examples of the emergence of what could well be called civil-social institutions which nevertheless do not always conform to these principles. Rather, it is precisely to identify these marks of difference, to understand their significance, to appreciate how by the continued invocation of a 'pure' model of origin—the institutions of modernity as they were meant to be—a normative discourse can still continue to energize and shape the evolving forms of social institutions in the non-western world, that I would prefer to retain the more classical sense of the term 'civil society' rather than adopt any of its recent revised versions.[2] Indeed,

---

[2] An account of some of these versions is given in Jean L. Cohen and Andrew Arato, *Civil Society and Political Theory*, MIT Press, Cambridge, Massachusetts, 1994.

for theoretical purposes, I even find it useful to hold on to the sense of civil society used in Hegel and Marx as bourgeois society (*burgerliche gesellschaft*).

An important consideration in thinking about the relation between civil society and the state in the modern history of formerly colonial countries such as, for example, India is the fact that whereas the legal-bureaucratic apparatus of the state has been able, by the late colonial and certainly in the post-colonial period, to reach as the target of many of its activities virtually all of the population that inhabits its territory, the domain of civil social institutions as conceived above is still restricted to a fairly small section of 'citizens'. This hiatus is extremely significant because it is the mark of non-western modernity as an always incomplete project of 'modernization' and of the role of an enlightened elite engaged in a pedagogical mission in relation to the rest of society.

But then, how are we to conceptualize the rest of society that lies outside the domain of modern civil society? The most common approach has been to use a traditional/modern dichotomy. One difficulty with this is the trap, not at all easy to avoid, of dehistoricizing and essentializing 'tradition'. The related difficulty is one of denying the possibility that this other domain, relegated to the zone of the traditional, could find ways of coping with the modern that might not conform to the (western bourgeois, secularized Christian) principles of modern civil society. I think a notion of political society lying between civil society and the state could help us see some of these historical possibilities.

By political society, I mean a domain of institutions and activities where several mediations are carried out. In the classical theory, the family is the elementary unit of social organization: by the nineteenth century, this is widely assumed to mean the nuclear family of modern bourgeois patriarchy. (Hegel, we know, strongly resisted the idea that the family was based on contract, but by the late nineteenth-century the contractually formed family becomes the normative model of most social theorizing in the west as well as of reformed laws of marriage, property, inheritance, and personal taxation. Indeed, the family becomes a product of contractual arrangements between individuals who are the primary units of society.) In countries such as India, it would be completely unrealistic to assume this definition of the family as obtaining universally. In fact, what is significant is that in formulating its policies and laws that must reach the greater part of the population, even the state does not make this assumption.

The conceptual move that seems to have been made very widely, even if somewhat imperceptibly, is from the idea of society as constituted by the elementary units of homogeneous families to that of a *population*, differentiated but classifiable, describable, and enumerable. Michel Foucault has been more perceptive than other social philosophers of recent times in noticing the crucial importance of the new concept of population for the emergence of modern governmental technologies. Perhaps we should also note the contribution here of colonial anthropology and colonial administrative theories.

Population, then, constitutes the material of society. Unlike the family in classical theory, the concept of population is descriptive and empirical, not normative. Indeed, population is assumed to contain large elements of 'naturalness' and 'primordiality'; the internal principles of the constitution of particular population groups is not expected to be rationally explicable since they are not the products of rational contractual association but are, as it were, pre-rational. What the concept of population does, however, is make available for governmental functions (economic policy, bureaucratic administration, law and political mobilization) a set of rationally manipulable instruments for reaching large sections of the inhabitants of a country as the targets of 'policy'.

Civil social institutions, on the other hand, if they are to conform to the normative model presented by western modernity, must necessarily exclude from its scope the vast mass of the population. Unlike many radical theorists, I do not think that this 'defect' of the classical concept needs to be rectified by revising the definition of civil society in order to include within it social institutions based on other principles. Rather, I think retaining the older idea of civil society actually helps us capture some of the conflicting desires of modernity that animate contemporary political and cultural debates in countries such as India.

Civil society in such countries is best used to describe those institutions of modern associational life set up by nationalist elites in the era of colonial modernity, though often as part of their anti-colonial struggle. These institutions embody the desire of this elite to replicate in its own society the forms as well as the substance of western modernity. It is a desire for a new ethical life in society, one that is in conformity with the virtues of the enlightenment and of bourgeois freedom and whose known cultural forms are those of secularized western Christianity. These are apparent in most of the arguments used by early nationalist elites in colonial countries for setting up new institutions of secular public life. It is well recognized in those arguments that the new domain of civil society will long remain an exclusive domain of the elite, that the actual 'public' will not match up to the standards required by civil society and that the function of civil social institutions in relation to the public at large will be one of pedagogy rather than of free association.

Countries with relatively long histories of colonial modernization and nationalist movements often have quite an extensive and impressive network of civil social institutions of this kind. In India, most of them survive to this day, not as quaint remnants of colonial modernity but often as serious protagonists of a project of cultural modernization still to be completed. However, in more recent times, they seem to be under a state of siege.

To understand this, we will need to historicize more carefully the concepts of civil society, political society, and the state in colonial and post-colonial conditions.

II

The explicit form of the post-colonial state in India is that of a modern liberal democracy. It is often said, not unjustifiably, that the reason why liberal democratic institutions have performed more creditably in India than in many other parts of the formerly colonial world is the strength of its civil social institutions that are relatively independent of the political domain of the state. But one needs to be more careful about the precise relationships involved here.

Before the rise of mass nationalist movements in the early twentieth century, nationalist politics in India was largely confined to the same circle of elites that was then busy setting up the new institutions of 'national' civil society. These elites were thoroughly wedded to the normative principles of modern associational public life and criticized the colonial state precisely for not living up to the standards of a liberal constitutional state. In talking about this part of the history of nationalist modernity, we do not need to bring in the notion of a political society mediating between civil society and the state.

However, entwined with this process of the formation of modern civil social institutions, something else was also happening. I have explained elsewhere how the various cultural forms of western modernity were put through a nationalist sieve and only selectively adopted, and then combined with the reconstituted elements of what was claimed to be indigenous tradition.[3] Dichotomies such as spiritual/material, inner/outer, alien/indigenous, etc. were applied to justify and legitimize these choices from the standpoint of a nationalist cultural politics. What I wish to point out here in particular is that even as the associational principles of secular bourgeois civil institutions were adopted in the new civil society of the nationalist elite, the possibility of a different mediation between the population and the state was already being imagined, *one that would not ground itself on a modernized civil society.*

The impetus here was directly political. It had to do with the fact that the governmental technologies of the colonial state were already seeking to bring within its reach large sections of the population as the targets of its policies. Nationalist politics had to find an adequate strategic response if it was not to remain immobilized within the confines of the 'properly constituted' civil society of the urban elites. The cultural politics of nationalism supplied this answer by which it could mediate politically between the population and the nation-state of the future. In the Indian case, the most dramatic and effective form of this mediation was represented by what I have elsewhere described as the Gandhian moment of manoeuvre.[4]

This mediation between the population and the state takes place on the site of a new political society. It is built around the framework of modern political associations such as political parties. But, as researches on nationalist political mobilizations in the Gandhian era have shown repeatedly, elite and popular anti-colonial politics, even as they came together within a formally organized arena such as that of the Indian National Congress, diverged at specific moments and spilled over the limits laid down by the organization.[5] This arena of national politics, in other words, became a site of strategic manoeuvres,

[3] *The Nation and Its Fragments: Colonial and Postcolonial Histories*, Princeton University Press, Princeton, 1994.

[4] *Nationalist Thought and the Colonial World*, Zed Books, London, 1986.

[5] One set of studies of Indian nationalist politics that explicitly addresses this 'split in the domain of politics' is contained in the volumes of *Subaltern Studies* and in several monographs written by historians contributing to that series.

resistance, and appropriation by different groups and classes, many of those contests remaining unresolved even in the present phase of the post-colonial state. The point is that the practices that activate the forms and methods of mobilization and participation in political society are not always consistent with the principles of association in civil society.

What then are the principles that govern political society? The question has been addressed in many ways in the literature on mass mobilizations, electoral politics, ethnic politics, etc. In the light of the conceptual distinctions I have made above between population, civil society, political society, and the state, we will need to focus more clearly on the mediations between population on the one hand and political society and the state on the other. The major instrumental form here in the post-colonial period is that of the developmental state which seeks to relate to different sections of the population through the governmental function of *welfare*. Correspondingly, if we have to give a name to the major form of mobilization by which political society (parties, movements, non-party political formations) tries to channelize and order popular demands on the developmental state, we should call it *democracy*. The institutional forms of this emergent political society are still unclear. Just as there is a continuing attempt to order these institutions in the prescribed forms of liberal civil society, there is probably an even stronger tendency to strive for what are perceived to be democratic rights and entitlements by violating those institutional norms. I have suggested elsewhere that the uncertain institutionalization of this domain of political society can be traced to the absence of a sufficiently differentiated and flexible notion of community in the theoretical conception of the modern state.[6] In any case, there is much churning in political society in the countries of the post-colonial world, not all of which are worthy of approval, which nevertheless can be seen as an attempt to find new democratic forms of the modern state that were not thought out by the post-enlightenment social consensus of the secularized Christian world.

III

In order to look more closely at what I see as the new movement of political society and the desire for democracy it represents, and also

[6] *The Nation and Its Fragments*, ch. 11.

to bring the discussion back to the supposed crisis of the nation-state and the possibility of post-national formations, let me put forward three theses that might be pursued further. These are three theses that arise from the historical study of modernity in non-western societies.

(1) The most significant site of transformations in the colonial period is that of civil society; the most significant transformations occurring in the post-colonial period are in political society.

(2) The question that frames the debate over social transformation in the colonial period is that of modernity. In political society of the post-colonial period, the framing question is that of democracy.

(3) In the context of the latest phase of the globalization of capital, we may well be witnessing an emerging opposition between modernity and democracy, i.e., between civil society and political society.

The implications of these theses will, I believe, diverge in important ways from the proposals for creating post-national forms of government. If one looks closely at the descriptions of the crisis-ridden nation-state in different parts of the contemporary world, one will find two sets of interrelated arguments. One is about the failure of effective governability. This has to do, in terms of the functions listed above, with the failure of the state to provide for the 'welfare' of populations. The second set of arguments relates to the decay or lack of appropriate civil social institutions that could provide a secure foundation for a proper relationship between autonomous individual lives in society and the collective political domain of the state. This is where complaints are made about the authoritarian or tyrannical role of the nation-state. The two sets of arguments are often collapsed into a single prognosis, as in Appadurai, about the failure of nation-states to arbitrate between globality and modernity. I will argue that there are actually two kinds of mediation that are being expected here—one, between globality and modernity, and the other, between globality and democracy. The two—at least apparently—cannot be performed by the same set of institutions. This, as I see it, is the current crisis of the nation-state.

We can trace this crisis, in terms of the conceptual elements I have set out above, for at least two different sites—one, the old nation-states and liberal democracies of the west (including Australia and New Zealand), and the other, the countries, mostly ex-colonial, of Asia and Africa and those of the former socialist bloc in Eastern Europe and Central Asia. In the first case, the historical yardstick is provided by a description (abstract and often idealized) of a sort of normative equilibrium where civil society and state were well demarcated and properly balanced. This is the liberal description of the 'constitution' that supposedly provides both an abstract universal theory and a historically embedded, nation-specific, instance of the actual and more or less permanent substantive content of political life. This relatively stable normative equilibrium is now often seen as having been disturbed by the new immigration of the last three decades. As residents, the new immigrants have free access to the institutions of civil society, but are often insufficiently educated in or unappreciative of its practices. As populations, they are beneficiaries of governmental welfare activities but do not always have a commitment to or solidarity with the political community of the host nation. As citizens, their political loyalties are seen as being suspect and many do not even want citizenship if they can enjoy the economic and social advantages of residence. Here, transnational solidarities among immigrant groups, in fact, become evidence for the charge that they are inappropriate subjects of the nation's civil and political life. This has created a crisis both for the universalist assumptions of civil society and for the particular cultural content of nationhood. One response to this has been to recognize the change in historical situation and redefine the substantive content of civic and political life through an active effort at 'multiculturalism'. But there has also been the attempt to curb immigration, deny citizenship to many immigrants and even restrict the access of residents to (the presumably universalist) civil social and welfare institutions.

In the case of the formerly colonial countries of Asia and Africa, the dominant approach is to apply the same yardstick of the abstract model of the modern nation-state and place the different actually existing states on a scale of 'development' or 'modernization'. The overwhelming theme is one of lack, sometimes with an additional story that describes the recent decay of a moderately satisfactory albeit inadequate set of institutions. But the lack, as I said before, is of two kinds—one in the domain of governmentality, the other in that of an effective civil society. For a considerable part of the 1960s and 1970s, modernization demanded primarily, often exclusively, a rapid expansion of the government functions of the developmental state legitimized by its claims to represent and strengthen the nation as a whole. By the 1980s, the complaints were getting strong that the absence of an autonomous domain of civil social institutions had made the nation-state tyrannical. And where the nation-state was failing to perform even its governmental functions, as it many countries in Africa, the situation was one of anarchy and mass social disaster. Proper modernization will have to ensure a more balanced development of both state and civil social institutions.

A considerable part of transnational activities today take place in the domain of non-state institutions under the sign of the modernization of civil social formation. These are the activities of a transnational public sphere whose moral claims derive from the assumed existence of a domain of universal civil society. Many United Nations agencies, non-governmental organizations, peace-keeping missions, human rights groups, women's organizations, free speech activists, operate in this moral terrain. As such, they act as an *external* check on sovereign powers of the nation-state and occupy the critical moral position of a global civil society assessing the incomplete modernity of particular national political formations. This is the standpoint that produces the most aggressive charges of the nation-state failing to successfully mediate between globality and modernity.

The charges derive their ideological power from a universalist conception of the right of autonomous and self-determining individuals balanced against the powers of the state and, by extension, of the rights of autonomous groups against the dominance of large political formations. Often the arguments are used with blatant cynicism as in US political interventions in different parts of the world. But many transnational activities and movements pursuing demands for social and cultural rights for individuals or groups seek to open up and institutionalize precisely such a sphere of global intervention framed by a universalist notion of rights and grounded in a global civil society.

Even though there is much celebratory rhetoric and high moral passion associated with these visions of global modernity, the political-strategic implications of a move from 'transnational tendencies' or post-national formations are largely elided. Comparing our present world-historic moment with that of, let us say, 'the expansion of Europe' two or three centuries ago, it would not be farfetched at all to notice similarities in the moral–cultural drive to spread 'modernity' throughout the world.

The contrary tendencies I am pointing out—those that look within rather than beyond the nation-state—are also strong features of the contemporary world. In particular, they are tendencies that operate in the very heart of western nation-states and liberal democracies, just as they are the driving force of politics in many non-western countries. They are located on a different site, not the moral-cultural ground of modernity and the external institutional domain of a global civil society, but rather the ground of democracy and the internal domain of national political society. What these tendencies in many countries around the world show up are the glaring inadequacies of the old forms of democratic representation, not only in the less modernized countries of the non-western world but in western democracies themselves. There is much contestation over new claims and entitlements, those that were not part of the earlier liberal consensus on state-civil society relations. In many cases, the new claims directly contradict and violate universal 'modern' conventions of civil society. The historical task that has been set by these movements is to work out new forms of democratic institutions and practices on the mediating field of political society that lies between civil society and the nation-state.

The framework of global modernity will, it seems to me, inevitably structure the world according to a pattern that is profoundly colonial; the framework of democracy, on the other hand, will pronounce modernity itself as inappropriate and deeply flawed. An important observation that Arujn Appadurai often makes concerns the way in which transnational tendencies have made deep inroads into contemporary western societies and rendered currently existing nation-state forms inadequate. In particular, talking about the cities of the western world, Holston and Appadurai have recently noticed the abandonment of the notion of shared public space as an attribute of citizenship and the retreat into segregated private spaces. They have also correctly perceived this as an issue that is directly connected with the question of the democratic negotiation of citizenship under conditions of globalization.[7] My argument in this presentation is that it is only by separating the two interrelated issues of civil society–modernity and political society–democracy that we will begin to see the dimensions of power and political strategy that underlie this question. Without this awareness, the proposals to 'move beyond the nation' are quite likely to strengthen inequalities and defeat the struggle for democracy the world over.

---

[7] James Holston and Arjun Appadurai, 'Cities and Citizenship', *Public Culture*, 8(2), Winter 1996, pp. 187–204.

8

CIVIL SOCIETY
*Cultural Possibility of a Modern Ideal**

Robert Hefner

Few questions more clearly preoccupy our age than how to facilitate civil, free, and democratic interaction among the citizens of plural societies. In recent years, the importance of this challenge has become globally apparent. In the late 1980s and early 1990s, we were witness to a transformation of international politics more fundamental than any since the end of the Second World War. The collapse of European communism, the break-up of the Soviet Union, widespread programmes of economic restructuring, and efforts to advance human rights and the rule of law throughout the world—these and other developments at first seemed to herald a new and brightly democratic era in global politics.

CONDITIONS OF A MODERN POSSIBILITY

Perhaps no phrase has figured more prominently in this literature on the social prerequisites for pluralism and democracy than has 'civil society.' Though writers differ on its details, most agree in describing civil society as an arena of friendships, clubs, churches, business

* *Society*, 35(3), 1998.

associations unions, and other voluntary associations that mediate the vast expanse of social life between the household and the state. This associational sphere is seen as the place where citizens learn habits of free assembly, dialogue, and social initiative. If managed properly, it is suggested, civil society can also help to bring about that delicate balance of private interests and public concern vital for a vibrant democracy.

Rarely has so heavy an analytic cargo been strapped on the back of so slender a conceptual beast. The disparate uses to which the idea of civil society has been put make a cool assessment of its utility difficult, to say the least. However, while showing that the concept has a certain slipperiness, recent research indicates that the idea of civil society can be given sociological precision, and that it is an important ingredient in any effort to understand the conditions of modern democracy's possibility. To realize its promise, however, the concept must be given firmer sociological and cross-cultural moorings. Too much of the theoretical writing on civil society has been more concerned with summarizing technical debates among professional philosophers than it has in demonstrating that those ideas inform real political practice. Similarly, much of the debate on civil society has been conducted within a philosophical framework of uniquely European provenance, without bothering to ask how much of the framework is transferable to non-western societies—or even whether such a framework does justice to the varieties of western politics. A sociological approach to civil society may do well to be less stratospheric in its philosophical pretensions, but more socially realistic in its insights.

Recent research on civil organization and democracy offers us five lessons of generalizable importance. At a time when the question of democracy's cross-cultural possibility is being widely debated, the lessons highlight both the peculiarities of the western experience and the prospects for the diffusion of democratic ideals beyond the western world.

CIVILITY AND SELF-ORGANIZATION

Since its initial stirrings in ancient Greece and Rome, western political theory has developed as if the communities to which it applied were culturally homogeneous entities with securely agreed borders. Though both ancient Greece and Rome developed from simple republics into multicultural empires, their political theories remained premised on a vision of close-knit communities sharing language, culture, and religion. Surprisingly, this homogenizing bias persisted in the liberal theory that emerged in the West in the eighteenth and nineteenth centuries. As Michael Walzar has noted, liberal writers were 'ready enough to acknowledge a plurality of interests,' but they were 'strikingly unready for a plurality of cultures. One people made one state.'

In reflecting on the prospects for civility and democracy, then, it is useful to remind ourselves that pluralism is by no means a uniquely modern problem. Though Durkheimian stereotypes of traditional societies imply otherwise, societies in which people from varied religious, ethnic, linguistic, and racial backgrounds live within a single political order have existed at least since ancient times. More recently, such states as Mughal India, the Ottoman empire, West African Asante, and Majapahit Java all incorporated a diverse array of peoples and cultures, and were involved with a social and economic macrocosm extending far beyond their borders. Though often established through conquest and domination, most of these plural societies went on to develop more pacific arrangements for accommodating the varied groupings comprising their whole. Though precise arrangements differed, most organized interaction across social divides through categorizations and hierarchies that segregated populations into large social blocks defined in terms of religion, ethnicity, tribe, gender, caste, and other ascriptive markers. These categories then became the basis of assigning people differential rights of participation in the political order. To borrow an image from John Hall, pre-modern political integration was usually organized around a civility of 'social cages.' Recently the anthropologist F. G. Bailey has reminded us (in his *The Civility of Indifference*, Cornell 1996) that interaction across social divides was also facilitated through a 'civility of indifference'; social groupings were as much ignored as they were caged. In either case, however, pre-modern polities were usually based on a strategic balance of separation and inequality.

With its Christian church, Roman legal heritage, and politics of kingdom and manor, pre-modern Europe was considerably less pluralistic than many of these imperial counterparts in Asia, West Africa, and the Middle East. This relative homogeneity was not merely the consequence of natural circumstances, moreover, but reflected a history of sometimes violent suppression of religious, ethnic, and cultural differences. With its anti-heresy campaigns, mass killings of witches, and chronic inaccommodation of Muslims and Jews, pre-modern Europe can claim no special genius in resolving the problem of pluralism. If this generalization is true for the pre-modern era, however, the same cannot quite be said for all recent European experiments in civility. In the early modern era a few regions in Western Europe attempted to develop new and quite distinctive forms of political cohesion. In the aftermath of the European Enlightenment, in particular, efforts were made to promote ideals of a civic nature, grounded on the triplicate values of freedom, equality, and tolerance.

Unfortunately, however, history shows rather clearly that these early experiments in democratic civility failed to extend rights of participation to whole categories of people, including, most famously, women, the propertyless, and racial and ethnic minorities. Other interests competed with civic ideals to structure politics in sometimes contradictory ways. Despite this shortcoming, however, the fact remains that the effort to conjoin rights of democratic participation with tolerance and equality represented a historically unprecedented formula for political integration, and is the basis of the values we know as democratic civility.

Indeed, though its principles may be violated or ignored, democratic civility is not an ideological illusion nor mere instrument of hegemonic control. On the contrary, it is an idea that has mattered in modern history, and mattered greatly. Post-modern and Foucauldian political theorists do a great disservice to democratic struggles when they assert that modern politics involves little more than the ever-greater intrusion of the state and hegemonic 'discourses' into our public and private lives. The modern west has witnessed repeated and valiant struggles to extend rights of political participation to heretofore excluded social groupings. More remarkable yet, in this century civil democratic ideals have spread throughout the world with a speed and intensity that mark them as among the most important 'globalizations' of our time. Whereas a century ago civil ideals were foreign to most of the world's political cultures, today ideas bearing at least a family resemblance to those of democratic civility have their supporters in almost every corner of the globe. Here, then, is a development as world-transforming as the modern emergence of capitalism and nationalism, yet of which we have an astoundingly incomplete grasp.

In attempting to explain the contagious spread of democratic ideals, some scholars have placed special emphasis on their western genealogy. Some have even suggested that civil and democratic ideals can only be realized in western cultural settings. This assessment of democracy's cross-cultural possibility, however, is probably unduly pessimistic as regards the non-western world, and a bit too generous as regards the west. The identification of civil ideals as 'Western', first of all, risks overlooking the fact that democratic and egalitarian values are even today not the only ones animating Western culture, and not long ago were far from secure. Equally serious, such a culturalist approach to politics overlooks a basic lesson from the sociology of knowledge, namely that though ideas originate in the minds of individuals, their institutionalization in public life depends on a broader 'political economy of meaning,' whereby some ideas are publicly amplified, while others are suppressed. Thus, to understand the conditions of democracy's possibility requires that we attend to the interaction of culture and social structures that first facilitated just such an institutionalization of democratic ideals. Having done this, we can then ask whether a similar dynamic of structure and culture might not be occurring in portions of the non-western world today.

In several recent essays, John Hall has done much to address these last questions. He shows that, in Western Europe, the development of a culture of democratic civility depended upon the prior emergence of a variety of civil-societal structures. Building on the work of Max Weber and Ernest Gellner, Hall's *Power and Liberties: The Causes and Consequences of the Rise of the West* (California 1985) makes the point that from early on, circumstances predisposed Western Europe toward a pattern of 'societal self-organization' whereby large portions of the European populace regulated their affairs free of state meddling. This self-organization was in the first instance facilitated by the absence of any pan-European imperial structure in the aftermath of the Roman empire. The resulting 'pluricentric' political map, as Hall has described it, was in part the product of the ecological fragmentation of the European continent, which made effective control of Europe's scattered regions difficult. But it was also related to the military and administrative vigour of the local state systems which survived in the aftermath of Rome. Contrary to the pattern of imperial China, once established, Europe's regional states proved skilled at resisting those who dreamed of a restored imperium.

Western Europe enjoyed other advantages in matters of societal self-organization. Hall notes that, unlike the states of classical Islam, Western Christianity institutionalized a separation of ideological and political power, and this separation diffused power out even further from the state. The church was deeply involved in public and political matters. Christian norms facilitated trust and collaboration across Western Europe's expanse, and church representatives provided vital legal services for merchants and lords. However, while Byzantium witnessed numerous Caesaropapist pacts, the western church concluded that its interests could be better served through a strategic collaboration with many local states rather than full institutional union with one. The church's efforts to defend its own interests thus worked to limit the power of secular states.

Another precedent for Western Europe's civil organization was the fact that, by the late medieval period, when kings sought a greater centralization of power, they faced a well-entrenched array of countervailing forces. The church and feudal lords enjoyed extensive rights to property and influence, and both groups were reluctant to relinquish these privileges. In addition, in a few parts of late medieval Europe, the growth of commerce and towns created wealthy urban centres of unusual independence and initiative. Faced with assertive burghers and a restless peasantry, kings in East and Central Europe forged an unholy alliance with the feudal aristocracy, preserving the bondage of the manor and destroying the dynamism of towns. In northwestern Europe, however, rivalries among centralizing rulers led a few kings to conclude that they could best enhance their power by distancing themselves from the landed aristocracy, and allowing merchants and towns a measure of liberty. Inasmuch as they prospered, the towns offered the state new revenues and a significant advantage over their political rivals. The resulting formula—enhanced royal power through urban liberties and economic initiative—also worked to strengthen the legal-mindedness of Western European society.

Sceptics might argue that this historical sociology displays a misleading selectivity in its arrangement of facts. Some might wonder, for example, just how this model would account for Europe's persecution of the Jews, bloodshed between Protestants and Catholics, nineteenth-century class conflict, and the twentieth century's wars of nation and race. Hall has responded to these criticism by arguing that civil society in Europe was never all-or-nothing, but chronically incremental. He notes, for example, that civil society gained 'self-consciousness' in the bitter battle against 'politico-religious unification drives' in the aftermath of the Reformation. Faced with fierce class struggles and nationalist wars, civil society in Europe effectively collapsed in the late nineteenth and early twentieth century. The collapse in part occurred, Hall argues, because ruling elites were unwilling to heed the winds of change and allow the entry of popular classes onto the national stage. The collapse was thus more a colossal elite blunder than it was a failure of the European system as a whole, which otherwise enjoyed extensive civil freedoms.

One might suggest a somewhat less rosy reading of this same historical evidence, however, one that has the advantage of bringing us closer to an understanding of what is required for democratization around the world today. History shows us that the qualities of civic self-organization did indeed have deep historic roots in some parts of Western Europe. However, even as late as the twentieth century, this social capital was not sufficient to stabilize European politics into an enduring pattern of freedom, tolerance, and social participation. Civil organization there was, but a fully democratic civility there was not.

The multipolar state organization that facilitated urban commerce and the Protestant Reformation, one must remember, also allowed Europe's religious wars to rage unresolved for decades. On this point, Europe's record compares rather poorly with imperial China, which showed a much better ability to domesticate religious difference. Later, Europe's structural fracturation facilitated the explosively competitive growth of colonialism and ethnonationalism, culminating in a war in which one of the world's most affluent societies annihilated an entire segment of the European population. European self-organization and multipolaxity ensured an important measure of liberty for some people, it seems, but it also created a fertile ground for imperial and national rivalries, with decidedly uncivil consequences at home and abroad. Viewed from this perspective, Western Europe achieved an only segmentary civility, not a uniformly democratic one.

Modern European history thus provides a first and largely cautionary lesson on democracy and civility. The dispersion of powers and the balancing of forces associated with self-organization do indeed provide important supports for civility and participation. Left to themselves, however, these structural conditions often create no more than segmentary freedoms, enjoyed by only a portion of the populace. The broader achievement of citizen equality requires at least two other things: the scaling up of civil values into a certain kind of state, and a broadly based civic culture. Though deeply dependent on it, these two influences are not reducible to societal self-organization, but have a political and sociological integrity quite their own.

CIVIL SOCIETY AGAINST THE STATE?

From a historical perspective, the recent popularity of the idea of civil society in politics and academia is a matter of no small irony. Having received much attention during the European Enligtenment, the phrase had long since ceased to fire the imagination of real-world political figures, and by the first years of this century the phrase had been relegated to the dusty shelves of western academia. Or so it seemed until the revolutions of 1989–91 swept communist parties from power throughout Eastern Europe. In the aftermath of the communist collapse, there appeared a generation of Eastern Europeans confident of little more than that they desired prosperity, disliked communism, and believed that both goals might be well served by promoting this curious entity called civil society.

The idea of civil society had first appeared on the Eastern European scene a few years prior to the 1989 revolutions. Its earliest promoters included poets, writers, clergy, academics, and labour leaders involved in the struggle against, to borrow a phrase from the political theorist John Keane, the 'command states' that dominated this region. Among this diverse group only a few academics were interested in the bookish genealogy of the idea. What ordinary people found appealing was the phrase's promise of something of which they felt long deprived. Civil society evoked images of freedom to speak and associate without fear. It conjured up images of a public life in which the words and actions of ordinary citizens would be duly acknowledged by the state. It spoke, in short, to a painful absence in Eastern Europeans' lives.

There was a bittersweet irony to Eastern Europeans' embrace of the civil society ideal. Many of the concept's promoters had first encountered the phrase in state-mandated classes on Marxism. Marx did have much to say about civil society. He characterized it as a sphere of private, bourgeois satisfaction. In eighteenth-century German writing, *burgerliche Gessellschaft* had ambiguous connotations, blending the meanings of citizen and bourgeois, political participant and self-interested economic actor. In his comments on civil society, Marx shifted the conceptual weight of the phrase away from its connotations of participatory citizenship toward those of economism and self-interest. In Marx's eyes, the privacy of civil society was above all that of narrow self-interest; its freedom was a freedom for a few premised on the exclusion of the many.

It was a symptom of the depth of their disaffection that so many Eastern Europeans resisted official cannons and heard civil society as a positive ideal. The ideal struck deftly at the pretensions of the Eastern European regimes. These were states, after all, that affirmed the right of the vanguard party and thus the state to command society. Theirs was an authority of denials: denial of a legal and political difference between state and civil society; of rights of free association and speech; of economic initiative other than that under party control; and of public values other than those franchised by the state. By the time of communism's collapse, of course, many regime spokespersons had ceased to believe in the vanguard role of the party and the mobilizational state. But the principle of the party-state remained, and, not inconveniently, could be deployed whenever societal forces threatened state hegemony.

In the face of such state pretensions, it is not surprising that some Eastern European activists articulated their desire for civil society in anti-statist and even anti-political terms. At times they spoke as if what were required for civil decency was not just the dismantlement of the totalitarian state, but an abolition of politics itself. The appeal of such a naively privatist ideal is of course not unique to Eastern Europe. As de Tocqueville first remarked, it has been an intermittent feature of populist imaginings in, among other places, the United States.

But events in post-communist Europe indicated just why this antipolitical impulse is, in the end, so antithetical to the decency and freedom enjoined by civil ideals. Throughout Eastern Europe, the unity once enjoyed by the dissident community gave way in the post-communist era to a cacophony of voices. Disputes over state programmes pitted secularists against the religious, libertarians against welfare social democrats, fiery anti-communists against careful constitutionalists, and everywhere it seemed, deal-making insiders against democratic reformers. In countries like the former Yugoslavia, leaders turned ethnonationalist slogans against their rivals, destroying the social decency for which citizens had long yearned. Post-communist civility was proving more elusive than many had imagined.

In this there is an important second lesson on civil society and the state. However great the temptation to flee the public for the pleasures of the private, civil freedoms are deeply dependent upon a civil state. In this sense, and contrary to some sloganeering characterizations, there is no zero-sum opposition between civil society and the state. On the contrary, civil society requires a state that is both strong and self-limiting. It must be self limiting in the sense that it does not monopolize society's powers, drawing all vital personnel, services, and enterprise back into itself. But a civil state must also be strong, in the sense that it is capable of safeguarding the freedoms of association and initiative on which a vigorous public life depends. It is a banal but important truth that, contrary to certain libertarian imaginings, these freedoms are not 'free' in the sense that they are the spontaneous outcome of independent human association. The recent history of Afghanistan and Rwanda shows all too painfully that a weak or crippled state can be an invitation to factionalist butchery rather than a source of liberty. Civil society needs a civil state, because public life can be threatened by societal forces as much it can the state.

Indeed, democratic civility is only imaginable within the horizons of an effectively functioning modern state. Pre-modern states may be capable of explosive bursts of power, but they lack the infrastructure for a uniform and, therefore, equitable administration across their expanse. From our modern vantage point, this should not seem surprising. After all, even in modern democracies, the state's ability to guarantee civil rights for all citizens is often but partial. As in America's violence-plagued cities, some citizens may find themselves deprived of life and liberty, often at the hands of their neighbours in 'civil' society.

In the final days of Eastern European communism, it is not surprising that dissidents overlooked arguments like these on the fragile interdependency of civil society and constitutional states. It was all too easy to imagine that freedom was a flight from the political into the delights of the private. Indeed, early on in the post-communist transition, the concept of civil society lost much of its allure, as the once united dissident coalition dissolved, citizen engagement declined, and problems of practical government became woefully apparent. A wave of ethnic and religious hatred swept across parts of the region, often manipulated by rival wings of the political elite. The worst such cases provided a doleful reminder of our second principle of modern civility: that civil society requires the legal vigilance and regulatory safeguards of an engaged citizenry and a civilized state.

GLOBALIZATION VIA LOCALIZATION

While events in Eastern Europe unfolded with their own logic, the prominence of civil society slogans in the region's pro-democracy movements attracted the attention of activists in other parts of the world. Indeed, with the idea of democracy itself, the diffusion of the phrases 'civil society' became a dramatic example of the much celebrated process of cultural globalization. However, the uses to which the concept was put illustrate that cultural globalization is never merely a matter of untransformative diffusion, but a process in which the item transferred is shaped as much by local context and usage as it is by its place of origin.

In the late 1980s and early 1990s, the idea of civil society caught on in many non-western countries despite enormous problems of cultural translation. In the case of China, the American anthropologist Robert Weller has observed that Confucianism in China left little ideological room for a distinction between state and society, 'except in the way that fathers can be distinguished from sons.' As late as the nineteenth century, there was still no plausible way to translate civil society into Chinese. Indeed, even today, the term is translated through a variety of, as Weller puts it, 'awkward neologisms.'

But all is not culturally relative; nor is the popularity of the phrase a simple effect of western cultural hegemony, as China's leadership might suggest. Illustrating once again that globalization proceeds by way of hybridized contextualization, Weller and other China scholars have shown that some of the concepts of civil society made the passage quite well from the west because elements of them were already 'there' in Chinese social practice, thought in an as yet unamplified form. Despite the lack of official ideological precedents, China has long had an array of horizontal ties beyond the family, including those of kinship, friendship, and dialect group. Though these social precedents had never been elaborated into an explicit ideology of civic associationalism (official or populist), their values and relationships existed at the interstices of public life. In Weller's excellent phrase, they were 'an undeveloped possibility.' Not coincidentally, Chinese and Taiwanese involved in new democratic movements invoked these same precedents to provide cultural resonance for their appeals. Theirs was an effort to recover, amplify, and redirect meanings submerged in the myriad practices of everyday life.

China thus provides a general lesson on the cross-cultural prospects for civil ideals. At first glance, the example seems to confirm the pessimism of some cultural particularists about the impossibility of meaningful translation across distant cultures. In translating the values of civil society, 'awkward neologisms' remain approximations at best, and miniature acts of cultural imperialism at worst. However, under closer inspection, things do not look nearly so bad. Viewed from the ground of everyday practice rather than the dizzying heights of official canons, the normative diversity of even traditional societies is far greater than classical sociological models imply. In all societies there are values and practices that hover closer to the social ground and carry unamplified possibilities, some of which may have egalitarian or democratic dimensions. These low-lying precedents may not appear in high-flying slogans or official political statements. Nonetheless, they may in some sense be available for engagement and reflection by those who aspire to alternatives ways. As with China's pro-democracy movement, under conditions of growing global communications, local actors may seize on exogenous idioms to legitimate principles of equality and participation already 'present' in social practice, if in an undeveloped, subordinate, or politically bracketed manner.

In commenting on such attempts at democratization, some might be tempted to speak of the triumph of western values or the irreversible progress of 'westernization.' Native conservatives might see things similarly, and condemn yet another instance of spiritual pollution. But what is really at play in such processes is a far more complex interaction between the local and the (relatively) global. For local actors, the 'global' concept of democracy or civil society is meaningful because it evokes, extends, and legitimates some local potentiality.

It was through just such a dialogue of the local and the transnational that such concepts as civil society, participatory democracy, and human rights spread in the early 1990s from Eastern Europe to Latin

America, East Asia, Africa, and the Middle East. Needless to say the concepts were not used in a manner consistent with the bookish genealogies preferred by some western academics. Often they served as a kind of aspirational shorthand for ideas of equity, participation, and public fairness. However, despite this variation, there were family resemblances across these varied usages. Indeed, the past few years have provided an important third lesson on civility and democracy: that, contrary to the claims of some occidentalist naysayers, the aspiration for civil decency is anything but uniquely western. Notwithstanding its varied genealogies, this simple hope has become a powerful force in politics around the world.

DEMOCRACY WITHOUT CLOSURE

It was in the United States and Western Europe, however, that the idea of civil society underwent its most florid evolution in the aftermath of the Cold War. In what ranks as one of the more important developments in western political discourse since the Second World War, people rallied to the idea of civil society from both the political left and right. Here again, of course, supporters of the idea often understood it in different ways. The differences in emphasis, however, did not easily map out along the conventional divides of left and right. In numerous instances left-liberals and conservatives gave common voice to calls for local participation, public virtues, and civil decency.

To illustrate the complexity of this refiguration, it is useful to look for a few moments at some of the earliest enthusiasts of civil democratic ideas on the post-Marxist left. Some in this camp were attracted to the idea of civil society by what they regarded as an analogy between Eastern Europeans' struggles against statist tyranny and their own efforts to promote women's rights, sexual freedom, racial equality, and environmental protections. However, for most on the democratic left, the situation in Eastern Europe was not so much a source of inspiration, as a wake-up call for a more critical reflection on Marxism. Most western socialists had, of course, long since argued that the real-and-existing socialism of Eastern Europe should be distinguished from other socialist possibilities. Inasmuch as capitalism also varies in its impact according to the legal and political environment in which it is embedded, this qualification seemed reasonable.

However, as communist regimes in Eastern Europe teetered toward collapse, and as the full extent of their deformation of democratic ideals became apparent to even the most stalwart apologists of Leninism, writers on the democratic left began to ask more boldly whether the abuses of state-socialism were not themselves already implicit in Marx's ideas on state and civil society. These critics took issue with Marx's obsession with seizure of state power as the key to emancipation, noting that the resulting unification of political, economic, and cultural power in one structure was a formula for tyrannical abuse. They also rejected Marx's essentialization of class as the always-dominant line of exclusion and inequality in society, emphasizing instead that religion, ethnicity, gender, and race can also serve as fault-lines for inequality. Finally, and most relevant for our present discussion, many repudiated Marx's equation of civil society with exclusion and domination, insisting that civil society could be a line of defence not only for elites but for all citizens. Through these and other critiques, a self-consciously post-Marxist left emerged. Uncomfortable with even a residual identification with Marxism, some among these critics dropped the post-Marxist label in favour of a phrase they felt conveyed the positive content of their principles: radical democracy.

'Radical democracy' expresses well the ambitions and ambiguities of this influential stream in the contemporary revival of civil democratic ideas. Rejecting Marx's critique of civil society, radical democrats insist that the western left must adopt a new position on liberal democracy. In her *Dimensions of Radical Democracy: Pluralism, Citizenship, Community* (London: Verso, 1992), for example, the French political theorist Chantal Mouffe takes many of her colleagues on the left to task for denouncing liberal ideals and for romanticizing revolution. 'If the Left is to learn from the tragic experiences of totalitarianism it has to adopt a different attitude toward liberal democracy, and recognize its strengths as well as reveal its shortcomings. ...[T]he objective of the Left should be the extension and deepening of the democratic revolution initiated two hundred years ago.'

As illustrated by her reference to Enlightenment-era revolutions, Mouffe and her colleagues distance themselves from the relativist fashions popular among some social theorists. Some among the latter, she observes, see the heterogeneity of culture as so exhaustive as to render judgments as to the merits of one set of political values over another impossible. The ethical grounds for condemning even as odious a figure as Adolf Hitler thus become unclear. 'Such an extreme form of pluralism,' Mouffe writes, 'according to which all interests, all opinions, all differences are seen as legitimate, could never provide the framework for a political regime. For the recognition of plurality not to lead to a complete indifferentiation and indifference, criteria must exist to decide between what is admissible and what is not.' Erik Olin Wright has made a related point, arguing that the 'post-modernist rejection of "grand narratives"' and 'emancipatory values' encourages a cynical corrosion of democratic and egalitarian ideals.

It is important to note that Mouffe's general point is applicable to a broader range of issues in the civil society revival than those of interest to radical democrats alone. At the heart of the civil democratic vision lies the idea that, even as we legitimate pluralism, not everything can be relativized. Though, as John Hall has argued, civil society enjoins a mild relativism on some values, it must retain an unambiguous commitment to others, including the values of freedom, equality, and tolerance of difference. But a problem remains. Societies change, and the balance among democracy's core values may as well. Over the past century, western democracies have struck and restruck significantly different balances among the triad of equality, freedom and tolerance of difference. Such adjustments are neither automatic nor untroubled. People respond to new circumstances differently, and may reach quite different conclusions as to which balance of democratic values is best for our age. The fabric of civil society can be torn by such disputes, and democracy itself put in jeopardy.

The difficulties involved in achieving a stable balance among civil values is ironically apparent in the arguments of radical democrats themselves. What makes radical democracy 'radical' is that its supporters seek to extend the liberty and equality associated with citizenship beyond their usual domains of liberal application. Freedom and equality are to be promoted in schools, businesses, and homes, not just in electoral politics. In keeping with this activist understanding of citizenship, radical democracy places great emphasis on the creative role of 'new social movements' in democratic life. These include the women's movement, gay and lesbian rights, environmentalism, multiculturalism, and movements for other groupings seen as heretofore excluded from mainstream politics. Though their critics sometimes argue that radical democrats invoke new social movements as functional equivalents of Marxism's proletariat, there is an important difference. Radical democrats reject Rousseauian utopianism, and see the demands of new social movements not as irrecuperable contradictions in the political system, but as shortcomings to be corrected through a deepening commitment to equality and justice.

Conservative—and left—liberals often react to radical democratic projects with unease. Among other things, they fear that the highlighting of group identities through which radical democrats promote greater inclusion may, despite itself, corrode the values of individual dignity and group equality. In fact the example illustrates a larger tension, one endemic to all discussions of civil democracy. The values of liberty, equality, and tolerance in plurality are highly general, to say the least. As first principles, they come with few instructions as to where they should apply, or how they might be balanced in the varied policies and programmes a citizenry must devise. This would not be a problem, of course, if the principles always worked in synergistic harmony, the promotion of one necessarily enhancing the others. However, the past century of turmoil in eastern democracies shows clearly that these first principles come with no such compatibility guarantee. Private property may reinforce liberty and autonomy under some circumstances, but be corrosive of freedom and equality under others. Affirmative actions to promote the collective well-being of one disenfranchised group may under certain circumstances be detrimental to individual freedoms and equality, even for the members of such marginalized groups. Similarly, demands for gender and sexual equality may excite legitimate concern among religious minorities who insist that the promotion of sexual liberty within their temples and mosques violate their right to self-determination.

These are not just blemishes on the radical version of liberal democracy, but tensions endemic to the civil democratic tradition as a whole. In radicalizing democracy, radical democrats only make this general tension more apparent. Thus, for example, when promoting the extension of pluralism to the widest range of social relations, some radical democrats seem unaware of how the radicalization of pluralism can relativize freedom and equality. Not all people protected by pluralism clauses will agree that liberty and equality should also be maximized. Similarly, radicalization of popular political participation is no guarantee that the resulting political order will be civil or free, as the treatment of minorities in modern democracies has repeatedly illustrated. Freedom, equality, and plurality come with no guarantee of triplicate compatibility.

That civil democracy does not inalterably specify a balance among its principles is a source of chronic tension in modern democracies. But it is this very quality that underscores the importance of our fourth lesson on democratic civility. For it is precisely at this point, at what seems to be the most vexing of impasses in modern politics, that the virtues of democratic civility become most apparent. Civil theory may not offer a final definition of the good, or a definitive resolution of the proper balance among its first principles. Yet it is this inability to absolutize that makes all the more imperative the establishment of a sphere of uncoerced association, speech, and exchange in which different ideas of the good can be debated and tried. As Michael Walzer has put it, civil society can serve as this 'setting of settings' in which people are free to experiment, associate, and debate. From there, the results of such experiments may be communicated to other citizens, and, in at least some cases, to the policies of the state.

None of this provides a definitive resolution of civil-democracy's axiological conundrum. But it is this very impossibility that gives special urgency to our efforts to uphold the freedoms through which citizens debate and adjust the balance among their values.

HETEROGENEOUS EMBEDDINGS

That democracy requires some kind of culture and organization to be realized in society is an idea that strikes most sociologists and anthropologists as so patently obvious as to be trivial. For scholars in these disciplines, it is a commonplace of analysis that all societies require some minimal ground rules to smooth social interaction. In recent years anthropologists and sociologists have come to recognize that culture is far more unbounded and heterogenous than once thought, and subject to more force and contestation. While these insights have complicated our understanding of culture, they have done little to diminish this analytic confidence that, like fish in water, every politics, including civil democracy, requires a culture.

Though sociologists and anthropologists share this conviction, the fact remains that characterizing the culture and organization conducive to democracy and civility has proved difficult. In part this reflects the fact that, given the division of academic labour, the recent academic revival of interest in civil society and democracy began in the field of political philosophy. There is nothing wrong with this, but, as noted above, it has meant that much writing on civil society as been less concerned with sociological realism than it has with debating the relative grounds for one imagined liberalism as opposed to another.

Recently, however, some political theorists have taken their colleagues to task for this putatively irrealist bias. One sustained example of just such a critique has emerged in the debate between communitarians and liberals. Communitarians' arguments are varied, but in general they fault mainstream liberals for identifying the grounds for civil politics in such culturally anorexic terms as to imperil democracy's health. Thus communitarians claim that liberal theory's emphasis on autonomy and individual rights to the exclusion of other social goods leads conventional liberals to tolerate developments in law, the market, and morals corrosive of the very virtues on which a decent and participatory society depends. Though this critique is by no means peculiar to them, communitarians oppose what they see as this trend toward sociological and ethical laissez-faire. For them, the idea of civil society is a clarion call for heightened citizen education and participation. Communitarians also take issue with the idea that all variants of liberal democracy are equally individualistic, suggesting instead that philosophical liberalism often misrepresents the variety of normative traditions at work in real-and-existing western democracies.

Arguments of this sort often strike philosophical teetotalers in sociology and anthropology as of little importance for what they do. However, by forcing researchers to go off the beaten philosophical path and examine the actual practice of politics, the liberal-communitarian debate has inadvertently produced a small mountain of evidence showing that modern democracies actually depend upon associations and values more varied than those of a Hobbesian nature. This complicates rather interestingly our task of understanding just what cultures and organizations are compatible with civil democracy.

The Netherlands example illustrates this point rather nicely. Philosophical commentators on the idea of civil society are often surprised to learn that until recently the Netherlands—an origin-point for many western ideas on republican freedom and economic liberalism—had a political system organized around state-supported social 'pillars.' The pillars were vertical social structures based on the Netherlands' four major religious groupings: Roman Catholics, orthodox Protestants, liberal Protestants, and secular humanists. Recently, efforts have been made to get the state to recognize a fifth pillar for the Netherlands' small Muslim community. The pillars are social and not ecclesiastical organizations, each of which is headed by a non-clerical administrative board. Originating in the last century's struggles among Dutch religious communities, today the pillars administer funds provided by the state for religious education and social services.

As its origins the pillar structure was socially emancipatory and democratic—at least inasmuch as it provided the Roman Catholic and orthodox Protestant minorities with protections from the majoritarian tyranny of liberal Protestants. In actual operation, however, the structure was managed by pillar leaders in a way that was, as the Dutch sociologist Anton Zijderveld puts it, 'rather authoritarian and elitist,' even though it allowed a 'remarkable social and political pacification.' Moreover, the impact of the pillars was not confined to churches and schooling. Zijderveld observes that 'even the labour market' was informally organized around the pillars. All in all, it seems, Dutch civility was grounded on structures that were vertical, collectivistic, and, less singularly preoccupied with individual autonomy than many philosophical liberals recognize.

The combination of the de-churching of Dutch society, which began in the 1960s, and baby boom anti-authoritarianism has recently made the pillars less popular and brought about, as Zijderveld puts it, a 'concomitant rise of a typically modern individualization.' From our comparative perspective, however, what is so fascinating about the Dutch example is that it shows once again that civil ideals are never simultaneously absolutized in all social spheres. If the latter were possible, western civil societies would show none of the variation that they do in their relative balance of liberty, equality, and group versus individual rights. Indeed, the unimaginable might be conceivable: Americans and Britons would agree on gun-control policies.

All this brings us to a fifth and final conclusion: that the institutional nest that supports democratic civility has varied considerably across time and space, and involved different value balances. Philosophical idealists might see this as a fatal flaw in real-and-existing democracy, wondering how politics can flourish if freedom, equality, and tolerance are not maximized in all social spheres. The failure of American society for much of its history to resolve the status of its African-American citizens shows that this can be a serious and even tragic problem. But this does not deny the basic point that, like modernity itself, civil democracy is not one structure or normative system, but many. We call some societies 'civil' because, though precise arrangements vary, they show a family resemblance in their commitment to freedom, equality, and tolerance.

The Dutch example can be used to make two final observations, the first on the kinds of social organization conducive to democratic civility. An often-heard argument in recent years is that horizontal or lateral social ties are the key to a healthy civil polity; vertical linkages, by contrast, are undemocratic. However, the Dutch example shows us that not all verticalism is antithetical to civil decency. As in the Netherlands, some vertical structures may not only coexist with civil organizations, but, by preserving the peace or building bridges over troubled waters, actually help to strengthen civility and democracy. The key to determining just when and where verticalism is good is the values toward which it is oriented, and the procedures through which it operates. Robert Putnam and others quite rightly remind us that patron-clientage is corrosive of civility and trust. But not all vertical structures are of a clientalist sort. Some can strengthen civility and democracy if they operate in a transparent and procedurally responsive fashion.

A similar qualification should be made to our understanding of horizontal organizations. Though long identified as the essence of civil organization, some small-scale organizations—like America's extremist militias—may become breeding grounds for the virus of hatred and intolerance. More is required of horizontal associations than structural laterality if they are to reinforce democracy. Their organization must nurture not only participation, but a participation that reinforces a commitment to equality, freedom, and tolerance.

There is a final paragraph to these five lessons on civil society. It is that the values of civil society are, by their very nature, ever-unfinished. This is so not merely because the ideals of civil democracy come with no guarantee of triplicate compatibility. That is part of it. But the indeterminacy also reflects the fact that societies change, so that the balance of forces underlying one civil compromise shifts and people perceive old arrangements in a new light. Thus, the pillar system is no longer popular among Dutch youth because it is seen as authoritarian rather than protective of their religious rights (in which they have lost interest). Or, similarly, gender roles seen by some people as central to western civility are today being questioned by others who would elevate individual autonomy above family cohesion.

DEMOCRATIC CIVILITY'S FUTURE

The controversies that accompany such re-equilibrations can tear a society apart. However, with the right dose of democratic civility, the instability can also be a source of strength, demonstrating a society's ability to accommodate new interests, new personnel, and new ideas of the good.

Taken together, these five lessons on democratic civility imply that it is less the beat of ancient associational drums that determines democracy's rhythms than it is a thoroughly contemporary circle of organizations and values. If this is true, it means that civility and participation can be enhanced through strategic interventions at any number of points in the democratic circle—by building civil associations, supporting countervailing institutions, diffusing wealth and decentralizing economic initiative, strengthening the judiciary, defending a free press, and, always, fostering a leadership and citizenry committed to these very goals. Even in the smoothest-running political systems, democracy is not all-or-nothing, but enduringly incremental.

Equally important, the lessons of modern history suggest that the aspiration for democratic civility depends less on a culture unique to the west than it does on social and cultural conditions widespread in our age. In its most general form, the urge to which democratic civility responds is the desire for participation and self-determination. This desire is neither unique to our age nor universal. However, in our time social change has become so pervasive that some people in virtually all nations have come to look to civil ideals as an ethical compass amidst the roaring flux. No single 'determinant in the last instance' can explain this appeal. On the contrary, all evidence indicates that this thirst for dignity and participation arises through varied circumstances: as settled villages give way to mobile urbanizations; as kinship collectivities become optative ties of family; as mothers become 'working' mothers; as economies of command become competitive; as public voices become multiple.

Plural in its organizations and meanings, there is no single modernity; nor is there one final formula for civility-in-democracy. However, the restructuration of life worlds that characterizes our age has become so massive that it guarantees that, more than any prior epoch, large numbers of people find themselves drawn to ideals of a civil and democratic sort. In actual usage, of course, the precise expression of such ideals varies. So too does the balance societies strike between public and private goods, and individual and collective rights. But this only shows that it is contextual and hybridizing processes, not imitation or diffusion, that are the real key to democracy's contemporary 'globalization.'

The evidence of these studies leads me to a final, normative observation, one with which I am not sure all my fellow contributors would agree. It is that we supporters of civility and democracy must show greater confidence in the relevance of these ideals for our age. That confidence has nothing to do with the alleged occidental origins of democratic ideals, a mythic charter that, I have suggested, only clouds the issue by telling non-westerners that their own experience is not what is most directly relevant to democracy's possibility. Rather than discursive genealogies, our democratic confidence should be based on the conviction that the appeal of freedom, equality, and tolerance-in-plurality is not narrowly circumscribed, as argued by some prophets of the new civilizational relativism. Civil ideals are appealing because they respond to circumstances and needs widespread in our world.

This is not to say that the outcomes of today's struggles are guaranteed. Ours will remain an age of democratic trial, and, for better or for worse, history's verdict will vary. But of this we should feel sure: that aspirations for dignity and civility are not civilizationally circumscribed, but will remain a powerful force in world politics and culture for many years to come.

9

CIVIL SOCIETY AND ITS AVTARS
What Happened to Freedom and Democracy?*

Gurpreet Mahajan

In contemporary social and political theory civil society is almost always associated with democracy. Yet, there continue to exist vast differences of opinion about what civil society is and the precise manner in which it is linked to democracy. For some theorists, civil society represents autonomous associations that exist independently of the state, associations which curtail the power of the state while simultaneously allowing individuals and groups in society to manage their affairs directly. By this reckoning, civil society is another name for voluntary associations of all types, from football associations and theatre groups to trade unions, churches, and caste panchayats. Irrespective of the goals that these associations pursue and without consideration to the way they impact upon the freedom and rights of all citizens, all forms of collectivities are seen as agencies of civil society and weighted positively. What is perhaps equally problematic is that in this framework proliferation of associations and non-government agencies become the hallmark of democracy. Instead of ensuring that the state provides equal rights to all citizens, its retreat from the public arena is presented as being a condition necessary for strengthening and reinventing democracy.

* *Economic and Political Weekly*, 15 May 1999.

In contrast to this fairly popular conception of civil society there exists another viewpoint: one where the condition of civility is the presence of rule of law. A variety of institutions—from hospitals to schools—that exist outside the state and possess a rational legal structure of organization constitute the realm of civil society. Here the presence of an open system of stratification along with a stance of neutrality become the primary attributes of civil society. Just why should an open system of stratification be the distinguishing feature of civil society and not the state? And why should civil society be placed outside the state? These are questions that remain imponderables within this framework. After all, democracy challenges existing hierarchies based on status, land, and birth, and seeks to institute a more open system based on equal rights of citizenship. Consequently, within a democracy all social and political institutions are expected to abide by this norm of openness. Assuming that civil society heralds the presence of an open and secular system, there is little reason to separate civil society from the state. Why should civil society be placed outside the domain of the state which enunciates the law? Faced with dilemmas of this kind, one needs in fact to ask whether civil society is, or must be seen as, an identifiable zone that lies outside the state? Is it an arena that is equidistant from religious and political institutions? Is it a synonym for voluntary and non-state associations? Is self-management the chief attribute of institutions of civil society? Is civil society the arena of struggle and participation? Above all, why is civil society considered to be an integral and indispensable aspect of democracy? These are questions that need to be addressed if we are to make sense of the concept of civil society and to understand its privileged status within democratic theory.

INDIVIDUAL RIGHTS AS THE CONDITION OF CIVILITY: LOCKE AND HEGEL ON CIVIL SOCIETY

The term 'civil society' became a part of the general political discourse in sixteenth and seventeenth-century Europe. At this time theorists of democracy invoked this concept to define a democratic form of government rooted in the rights of citizens. In the thirteenth century when the established Roman Catholic church exercised considerable hegemony over social and political life, the concept '*societas civilis*' was coined to depict a zone which was free from papal influence, and was governed by laws that were not of divine origin. As such, civil society symbolized the autonomy of the temporal realm in relation to the ecclesiastical. Within civil society people had the right to choose their king and be governed by laws that pursued the minimum shared interests of the people [Colas 1997: 9–21]. At this stage, civil society heralded the process of secularization which paved the way for the construction of a democratic polity. It questioned the centrality that was previously accorded to religious institutions and religious explanations, and allowed for the emergence of an alternative pattern of society and government. Later theorists built upon this conception and by the seventeenth century civil society came to designate a distinct form of political society—one in which the rights of individuals received primacy over all else. This conception of civil society emerged most forcefully in the writings of John Locke, and it formed the basis of much of the subsequent thinking on civil society and democracy.

Writing in the late seventeenth century, Locke differentiated civil society both from the state of nature as well as from political society. At a general level Locke maintained that civil society comes into existence when men, possessing the natural right to life, liberty and estate, come together, sign a contract, and constitute a common public authority. The public authority, or the supreme sovereign established through a voluntary contract, has the right to promulgate and administer laws that are required to exercise and enjoy rights that are given to men by nature. Locke contrasts this civil society with the state of nature: in the latter, men have equal natural rights but there is no legal authority that can uphold these rights and punish its offenders. Since the natural state of human existence lacks rules and institutions that secure the freedom of rights-bearing individuals, it represents an uncivil condition.

The existence of a publicly recognized political sovereign, an established system of law and a mechanism for punishing the offenders of that law, constitutes the minimum condition for the existence of civility in society, but by itself it is insufficient for the emergence of a civil society. For Locke, the presence of law and governance in accordance with law transform a collective body into a political society. However, the existence of civil society requires more than the rule of law. Civil society emerges only when the citizen's right to life, liberty, and property is guaranteed by law [Locke 1924: 44–62]. To put the same thing in another way, legal recognition and protection of the natural rights of individuals transform a political society into a civil society.[1] A civil society exists for the sake of securing the rights of men, and within it the actions of the sovereign are supposed to create conditions by which individuals can enjoy their rights and liberty fully. Consequently, a political society in which the basic rights of citizens are not recognized or given priority by the sovereign does not constitute a civil society.

Understood thus, civil society is a specific kind of political society: one where the rights of individuals receive primacy over all else. And it is this principle of 'primacy to rights' that distinguishes civil society from other forms of political society, collective bodies, community institutions and associations. Further, as a collectivity predicated on the principle of individual rights, civil society does not stand outside the state. In other words, it is not a domain external to the state, standing against it trying to curtail its powers. Instead, the presence of civil society announces the emergence of the modern democratic state. As civil society signifies a collective body that cherishes individual rights and legally protects the freedom of its members, it symbolizes a condition that is necessary for the existence of a democratic state.

Standing at the head of the liberal democratic tradition, Locke did not advocate universal adult franchise or equal citizenship rights. However, his theory provided a principle—namely, the primacy of rights—that was subsequently used to challenge existing patterns of social and political discrimination while simultaneously curtailing the arbitrary use of power by the political sovereign. The emergence of a political society that gives precedence to the natural and inalienable rights of citizens thus heralded the emergence of a secular democratic state—one where the concern for individual liberty could be combined with social equality.

Locke had conceived civil society as a democratic state in which the rights of individuals receive priority. Writing in the nineteenth century, G. W. F. Hegel reaffirmed this idea albeit by interrogating the liberal Lockean understanding of freedom, law, and state. Like his predecessor, Hegel maintained that civil society represents a system of relations that support and enhance freedom of all. However, he

---

[1] Reflecting on the transition from political society to civil society. Rousseau argues that this move produces a remarkable change in man. 'It puts justice as a rule of conduct in the place of instinct, and gives his actions the moral quality they previously lacked' [Rousseau 1968: 64].

disagreed with Locke's negative conception of law and freedom. According to Hegel, Locke counterpoises individual subjective will to universal law. The latter is presented as being external to the self; that is, as an object that constrains the subjective particular will. Hence, in Locke's writings universality enters only as a 'negative category' [Hegel 1953: 33] that limits the self-will; and law appears to be in conflict with subjective will and freedom. Hegel challenges this view by questioning the apparent contradiction between particular will and law. Acknowledging the primacy of the subjective particular, Hegel maintains that the universal (embodied in law) must emerge from self-will. Indeed for Hegel the universal law represents 'reflective' or 'self-conscious' will.

Beginning with this understanding, Hegel defines civil society as a form of ethical life in which the subjective and the objective coexist in harmony. This harmony is possible because civil society embodies a system of relations built upon the mutual recognition of the rights of the self and the other. Within civil society the self acknowledges the other, forges a link with it and recognizes the rights of each subjectivity—the self and the other. This recognition of rights allows for the construction of a system through which the idea of freedom is actualized in the world. Civil society becomes the objective embodiment of the idea of freedom in the world as it represents institutions and structures that acknowledge the mutual rights of the self and the other.

Seen thus, civil society, for Hegel, is a collective body, or for that matter, any collective body, whose members are conceived as 'self-subsistent persons' [Hegel 1953: 148]. The fact that the members of civil society are, and have the status of, distinct self-subsistent individuals, distinguishes this collectivity from the family. Although there are occasions when Hegel refers to civil society as the 'universal family' [Hegel 1953: 148], he maintains that it (civil society) 'tears the individual from his family ties, estranges the members of the family from one another...' [Hegel 1953: 148]. Underlining the idea that civil society is neither an expanded family nor an extension of the latter, Hegel argues that civil society does not arise out of natural ties of kinship and community. Instead it develops in the 'course of their actual attainment of selfish ends' [Hegel 1953: 123].

Since civil society emerges in the pursuit of individual interests, subjective particularity is retained within it and the universal law emerges as a mode of sustaining that particularity. It is the ability to retain and accommodate the subjective particularity that differentiates civil society, as a form of collective life, from ancient political systems and patterns of organization.

...[F]or example, the allotment of individuals to classes was left to the ruling class, as in Plato's Republic, or to the accident of birth as in the Indian caste system. Thus, subjective particularity was not incorporated into the organization of society as a whole; it was not reconciled in the whole, and...it shows itself there as something hostile, as a corruption of the social order. Either it overthrows society, as happened in the Greek states and in the Romance Republic; or else, should society preserve itself in being as a force or a religious authority, for instance, it appears as inner corruption and complete degeneration, as was the case to some extent in Sparta and is now altogether the case in India [Hegel 1953: 133].

By comparison, in the modern world where civil society exists, 'subjective particularity is upheld by the objective order in conformity with it and is at the same time allowed its rights...' [Hegel 1953: 133]. Rights, in the latter context, are granted to individuals and to corporate bodies that arise out of the voluntary associations of individuals.

Further, as was mentioned earlier, in civil society interaction between individuals is shaped by the mutual recognition of the rights of the self and the other. As such, a system of rights links individuals with each other and one group with another. 'My individual rights, whose embodiment has hitherto been immediate and abstract, now similarly becomes embodied in the existent will and knowledge of everyone, in the sense that it becomes recognized' [Hegel 1953: 136]. One might also add that in civil society the rights of the self are postulated without detriment to the rights of the other and encoded in law. Indeed, the law provides 'knowledge of what is right, or more exactly, of our legal rights (*Rechtens*)' [Hegel 1953: 136], and it is through law that the abstract right 'steps into a determinate mode of being. It is then something on its own account, and in contrast with particular willing and opining of the right, it is self-subsistent and has to vindicate itself as something universal' [Hegel 1953: 140].

For Hegel, the universal (in this instance, the law), can only be vindicated when it is accepted and endorsed in particular cases. Consequently, for him, the administration of justice constitutes an important moment of civil society. The court of justice exists to ensure that, irrespective of private interests, the abstract right embodied in law forms the basis of individual and collective action in society. Given the significance of this task in the life of civil society, Hegel argues that the members of civil society 'have the right in *judico stare* and correspondingly, a duty of acknowledging the jurisdiction of the court and accepting its decision as final when his own interests are in dispute' [Hegel 1953: 141]. In other words, in civil society individuals have an obligation to abide by the decisions of the court because by administering law the courts restore rights to their due position in society. And, it is through the administration of justice that the unity between the subjective particular and the universal is achieved in society.

Within the Hegelian framework, rights come with certain obligations for the self and the collectivity. In the case of civil society, for instance, individual members have rights of their own and at the same time they have an obligation to respect equal rights of other members. This obligation compels them to acknowledge the jurisdiction of the courts and accept the decisions of the latter. Hegel elaborates the theme of rights and accompanying duties by taking the case of a corporation—an institution that symbolizes, in Hegel's view, the spirit of civil society. Even though members of the corporation are separate, self-subsistent persons, with the right to life and property, the welfare of fellow associates is the responsibility of each member. In fact, for Hegel, the wealthy have an obligation to assist the poorer members. 'Within the Corporation the help which poverty receives loses its accidental character and the humiliation wrongfully associated with it. The wealthy perform their *duties* to their fellow associates and thus riches cease to inspire either pride or envy...' [Hegel 1953: 154]. On the other side, the collective body as a whole is expected to provide for the livelihood and welfare of all its members: it must 'protect its members against particular contingencies.' [Hegel 1953: 15] and 'provide education requisite to fit others to become members' [Hegel 1953: 15].

Civil society has the right and duty of superintending and influencing education, inasmuch as education bears upon the child's capacity to become a member of society.... Similarly, society has the right and duty of acting as trustee of those whose extravagances destroy the security of their own subsistence or their families [Hegel 1953: 148].

In general terms it is the responsibility of civil society to ensure that all its members enjoy the 'broader freedom and especially the intellectual benefits of civil society' [Hegel 1953: 150]. If it fails to fulfil this duty and sections of the population fall below the minimum subsistence level, then it is the task of public authority and wealthier classes to provide assistance to the former by providing them the opportunity to work. Given these attributes, civil society is a special kind of collective body and institutions within it, such as, the corporation, are special kinds of associative bodies. For one, it is governed neither by kinship ties nor by the blind forces of the market. Instead it represents collective bodies, associations and institutions, that are premised on a system of individual rights. Second, the collective entities of civil society exist to secure the freedom and welfare of its members. Even as they allow for the pursuit of individual needs and desires, they seek to ensure that individual goals are pursued in a manner compatible with the rights of all its members. The civil society exists to protect individual life and liberty and it places an obligation upon its members to share that goal and to act to realize it in society. As such, what binds the members of civil society together are not ties of kinship but the common concern for the welfare and freedom of all.

From the seventeenth to the nineteenth century most political theorists regarded the right to property as an essential individual right. Locke and Hegel were no exceptions. Like several of their contemporaries they maintained that it was the concern of civil society to protect property. For both of them freedom meant protection of life, liberty, and property. Besides defending an individual's right to property they also upheld the instrument of contract. According to Hegel, contract, unlike simple ownership of property, was a form of relationship based on the mutual recognition of the freedom of the self and the other. In property ownership or possession there exists only the abstract will; that is, the freedom of a single person related only to himself. On the other hand, in the device of the contract we have a situation where two persons exist in their capacity as owners. Consequently, they need to act in conformity with a common will and without detriment to the rights of either [Hegel 1953: 38–9]. Since contract requires mutual recognition of the rights of the different parties, it had a special place in civil society. The defence of contract in the workplace or market and the accompanying defence of the right to property, in the writings of Locke and Hegel, served the interest of the bourgeoisie. In fact their work seemed to suggest that the instruments that were central to the capitalist mode of production were expressions of freedom and compatible with the concerns of civil society. At times, the primacy accorded to the right to property in civil society reinforced the view that the latter was an expression of the bourgeois order: that is, a system in which rights-based political institutions were coupled with industrial organization of capital.

There is of course little doubt that the concept of civil society, as it emerged in the writings of Hegel, was compatible with, if not supportive of, the bourgeois system; but what is equally important is that civil society was not a synonym for free market, unregulated competition or the pursuit of mere profit. Hegel, in particular, was emphatic on this count. He maintained that civil society emerges for the sake of satisfying individual needs. However, when people realize that their needs can only be fulfilled by 'means of the others' [Hegel 1953: 123], a system of interdependence develops. Within it, 'the livelihood, happiness and legal status of one man is interwoven with the livelihood, happiness and rights of all' [Hegel 1953: 123]. Initially, single needs are satisfied through work performed by craftsmen, but as division of labour evolves, manufacturing, or mass-production to satisfy particular needs also grows in society. This, in turn, results in the business of exchange, wherein separate utilities are exchanged primarily through money as it 'actualises the abstract value of all commodities...' [Hegel 1953: 132]. Hegel recognized the role of producers and the business class but he also realized that control by public authority was necessary to ensure a fair balance between the interests of the producers and the consumers. In particular, public authority was needed to defend people's rights as purchasers and for 'management of goods inspection' [Hegel 1953: 147]. Above all else, 'control from above' [Hegel 1953: 147] was needed to ensure that business is not reduced to 'mere self seeking' [Hegel 1953: 147, 153], and that all individuals have the possibility of sharing in the general wealth of society. Consequently, the corporation was regarded as a distinct entity and rights were granted to it, but at the same time, it was expected to function 'under the surveillance of the public authority' [Hegel 1953: 152].

For Hegel, police or the public authority was an integral part of civil society and there was no question of civil society functioning without the presence and regulation of that public authority [see Pelczynski 1976: 10]. What was designated by the advocates of free market as state interference was seen by Hegel as the principle of universality operating in civil society. Without the presence of public authority, Hegel feared that civil society would cease to be a collective body. It would not be able to secure the rights and welfare of its members. What also needs to be remembered in this regard is that the civil society, for Hegel, embodied the spirit of fraternity. While it allows for the production of wealth and property, it exists to secure the freedom and welfare of all its members; and its is these considerations that place severe constraints upon profit-making and free market. The concern of freedom and welfare also create space for the principle of redistribution to operate in society, thereby ensuring that the ideals of justice and equality permeate the life of civil society.

The writings of Hegel have a special place in the debates on civil society not simply because contemporary discussions take their lead from him, but because he, more than others, elucidates the idea of civil society and reflects upon its relationship with democracy. His analysis gives a systematic and coherent form to the theme that had, in one way or another, been associated with civil society in previous usages: namely, that the idea of 'freedom for all' animates civil society. Tracing the genealogy of the concept of civil society. Dominique Colas points out that all through the sixteenth and seventeenth century the concepts of civil society and fanaticism appear together and always in opposition to one another [Colas 1997: 9]. Challenging the latter, civil society stands for the expansion of individual freedom. At first, the expression of freedom results in the displacement of the theological world-view and attempts to secularize social and political phenomena. Subsequently, Locke links the realization of freedom with protection of natural, inalienable rights of man. Hegel carries this idea forward and collectively these theorists assert that civil society denotes a structure of relationships in which the rights of individuals receive primacy and are recognized and upheld by law.

In elaborating this view of civil society Hegel clarified that civil society involved the existence of institutional arrangements that were built neither upon the principle of hierarchy nor upon a closed system of stratification. Furthermore, he showed that there was a symbiotic relationship between the state and civil society. The state apparatus, in particular, law and public authority, was a part of civil society, and vice-versa, the spirit of freedom that civil society represents permeates the state. As such, the two moments determine each other. Civil society points to the existence of a particular kind of state and the law promulgated by the state regulates and secures the conditions which give civil society its distinct form.

Hegel had articulated this position most clearly but he was not the only one to stipulate a nexus between the state and civil society. Before him, Locke had used the term 'civil society' to denote a state that endorsed the rights of individuals; and as Knox points out, several theorists of the eighteenth century used the concept of civil society in contexts 'where we would normally speak of the state' [Knox 1953: x). That is, for them it was an aspect of the state. Hegel distinguished between the state and civil society; however, he saw them as two moments of ethical life that were imbued by the same spirit. In both of them one could glimpse, albeit in different ways, the universality of the idea of freedom.

The close connection between state and civil society postulated in these writings was backed by the assumption that the state symbolized a rational order, 'the actuality of concrete freedom' [Hegel 1953: 161]. Within it the 'personal individuality and the particular interests not only achieve their complete development and gain explicit recognition of their right...but...they also pass over of their own accord into the interest of the universal' [Hegel 1953: 160]. Like many analysts of the eighteenth century, Hegel did not view the state simply as a symbol of legitimate authority expressing the sovereignty of the ruler, or as an instrument of coercive power. For him the state signified a structure which upholds and protects the freedom and rights of the individuals. While its law embodies the conditions of objective freedom, its institutions secure subjective freedom that allows individuals to pursue their particular ends. Consequently, for him as well as many of his immediate contemporaries, the state and civil society were closely related. In fact, one was a part of the other; and, more importantly, both were embodiments of the idea of freedom.

DISILLUSIONMENT WITH THE STATE REPRESENTATIONS OF CIVIL SOCIETY IN THE TWENTIETH CENTURY

From the seventeenth to the nineteenth century, a limited democratic state, and even a constitutional monarchy, was perceived to be a vehicle of democratization and secularization. Based on the consent of the people, however restricted that might be, the democratic state was seen as a symbol of public freedom, challenging closed systems of stratification and traditional forms of organizations rooted in the principle of hierarchy and exclusive privileges. Political philosophers from Locke to Hegel endorsed this conception of the state. However, the second half of the twentieth century witnessed a loss of faith in the institution of the state, and this led to a reconsideration of the earlier conception of civil society. Rethinking on the concept of state and civil society occurred in three quite diverse contexts: (i) as a corollary of the Marxian understanding of the relationship between economic interest and political institutions; (ii) in an attempt to revitalize participation of citizens in western democracies; and (iii) in totalitarian regimes of socialist societies.

Till the nineteenth century, civil society represented a network of relations—structures and institutions—based on the principle of individual rights. Since the language of rights could be appropriated by subordinated groups to challenge their exclusion from the political arena, it was an important means of empowering individuals. It stimulated the growth of institutions that functioned on the principle of social equality and, at the same time, it protected the individual against abuse of power by another person, a corporation, or the state. As a body rooted in the principle of equal rights, civil society represented a collectivity that was committed to the ideal of equal liberty. While it allowed for the pursuit of private interests, its also guarded the common concern for the freedom and welfare of all members. However, this conception of civil society was seriously challenged within Marxism. Within this framework, civil society came to be portrayed primarily as the domain of particular interests and not collective freedom.

In 'The Critique of Hegel's Philosophy of Right', Marx emphasized the nexus between economic interests and political institutions. Focusing on the right to property sanctioned by civil society, he maintained that the latter lacked the ability to express universal interests common to society as a whole [Marx 1977: 81]. Like the capitalist state, it remained the voice of the ruling class. Gramsci developed this idea further, albeit by associating the state with instruments of direct coercion and civil society with the creation of hegemony [Gramsci 1975: 12–13]. While the apparatus of state relies on coercive power to legally enforce discipline on groups, civil society organizes 'spontaneous consent given by the great masses of the population to the general direction imposed on social life by the dominant fundamental group' [Gramsci 1975: 12]. For Gramsci, the preponderance of civil society over the state allowed western societies to generate consent without relying heavily on direct coercion and domination. By comparison, direct intervention by the state and frequent reliance on the coercive power of the state remained the characteristic features of the east.

The distinction between the east and the west that was postulated here, and endorsed by the other Marxists [Anderson 1976–7] was subsequently questioned by French sociologists, particularly Pierre Birnbaum. The latter differentiated between western states and argued that in highly institutionalized and differentiated states, such as, France, a 'strong' state was accompanied by a relatively 'weak' civil society. Here the state dominated over all aspects of social and community life and presented itself as a 'machine for dominating civil society' [Birnbaum 1988: 72]. It controlled, regulated, and oversaw the activities of the civil society. This enabled a quicker realization of the ideal of universal citizenship, and, at the same time, created space for collective action directed against the state. In sharp contrast to this, in countries like Britain or America, a less differentiated and 'weak' state was attended by a relatively 'strong' civil society. In these polities, the institutions of civil society, for example, the trade unions, manage their own affairs by reaching collective agreement with their employers [Birnbaum 1988: 78]; as a result the state is not called upon to rule in disputes. Indeed the state acts as a 'locus for the representation of a range of different interests' [Birnbaum 1988: 186]; it allows pressure groups and associations of all kinds to make themselves heard. Consequently, societal corporatism spreads without clashing with the state. However, pluralism gets limited to some extent as some interests are legitimized at the expense of others [Birnbaum 1988: 187] and the state is able to exercise considerable influence over the members of those socio-economic groups which are favoured.

Birnbaum postulates an inverse relationship between the state and civil society. A highly institutionalized and differentiated state has a weak civil society; it gives relatively less space for the self-management of societal groups and institutions, while a less differentiated and institutionalized state allows greater expression to the associations and interests groups in society. However, what is perhaps significant is that in a weak state but strong civil society, collective action is less likely to be directed against the state. The state becomes the direct target of movements in polities with a relatively weak civil society. Since the presence of a strong civil society acted as a deterrent against political mobilizations that oppose the state, Birnbaum argued that the institutions of civil society could not be depended upon to democratize society. Indeed, civil society was just a dependent variable that had to be taken into account while explaining different patterns of political mobilization and collective action.

In sharp contrast to this perspective, advocates of 'associative' democracy [Hirst 1994] invest hope in the agencies of civil society. According to these theorists the centralized and highly bureaucratized modern state does not allow citizens to participate and govern themselves. By locating decision-making in the hands of a few civil servants and experts, it has taken away from the citizens that which must rightfully belong to them in a democracy. To reverse this trend champions of associative democracy seek to limit the state by giving powers of decision-making to 'communities of place and interest' [Hirst 1994: 20]. Strong, voluntary communities provide, in their view, the means of 'delivering a decentralized welfare state and regenerating regional economies' [Hirst 1994: 26; also see Steward 1996].

Besides, smaller communities allow citizens to debate discuss, and deliberate upon issues that affect their lives and immediate environment directly. They also enable members of the group to build trust and exchange information that is necessary for proper decision-making [Barber 1984]. The point that needs to be underlined is that the 'new communities' that these theorists seek to build and strengthen have little in common with the traditional communities based on ascriptive identities. Indeed, supporters of associative democracy do not attempt to recreate communities around traditional identities and patterns of loyalty. As such, this model is predicated on the success of the democratic project of social equality. To put it in another way, these analysts begin with the belief that democratization has dislodged previous social hierarchies and systems of inclusion and exclusion. Consequently, the small communities that they attempt to activate are, in a sense, 'new' communities for they are the product of an open rather than a closed system. Furthermore, these new forms of community life acknowledge their members as equal rights-bearing individuals. Thus, the principle of equality permeates institutions at all levels and allows for the creation of a decentralized democratic polity.

The voices of associative democracy are dissatisfied with the centralized, imposing and alienating structures of the modern bureaucratic state. Hence they seek to energize local bodies and associations in the hope of transferring a greater degree of decision-making power to the citizens in western democracies. Activating a variety of different institutional structures and forums—from neighbourhood councils to parent–teacher associations and church organizations—is thus seen as a way of enlivening citizenship and limiting the Leviathan. As small, local communities become the main units of democratic governance, it is assumed that the state would withdraw and become a necessary but secondary public power [Barnett 1996].

A third conception of state and civil society emerges in socialist societies faced with totalitarian regimes—the most striking example being Poland. Here the state does not appear as the embodiment of freedom, rather it represents a force restricting and actively curbing civil and political liberties of individual citizens. Under these circumstances, the state is pitted against civil society—an entity that expresses, struggles for, and protects individuals rights and freedom [Spullbeck 1996; Hall 1995]. In the struggle for political democracy a variety of diverse associations and bodies, from labour unions to the Catholic church, are placed together under the category of civil society as each of them contributes to the forces that are resisting and fighting against the totalitarian state.

For the critics of the totalitarian state, civil society stands outside the state and exists in sharp contradiction to it. Indeed the task of civil society is to transform the state completely by making it responsive to the rights of the individual. Hence, what identifies the institutions of civil society is their shared perception that the state is the repository of coercive force which is frequently directed against the citizens. The fact that the state is a potential and actual transgressor of individual liberty and that its might must be collectively challenged gives coherence to the otherwise diverse units of civil society. Although a non-hierarchical and open system of stratification is not always a characteristic feature of these institutions and collectivities, yet, each of them endeavours to fight against totalitarianism as it exists in these societies. Consequently, civil society is seen as an instrument of democratization, a symbol of 'perestroika', that can energize the struggles for individual liberty and assist in the gradual transition to a more open and democratic polity.

As is evident from the discussion above, in each of these three representations the conception of the state is significantly revised. As a result the accompanying idea of civil society is also altered. Although civil society remains a correlate of democracy, it is now represented as a domain that exists outside the state, if not, against the state. Till the nineteenth century most theorists viewed civil society as a particular form of political community: one is which rights of individuals receive primacy and institutions are based on the explicit recognition and acknowledgement of these rights. As such, civil society embodied a norm that defines the democratic state. Indeed, in this incarnation, civil society was closely associated with the process of democratization because the principle in which it was anchored—namely, the primacy of individual rights—offered a means of challenging prevailing forms of inter-group inequalities as well as a way of displacing structures of inequality that exist within traditional communities.

In the twentieth century, the centrality accorded to rights previously is displaced with the notion of direct participation and self-management. The shift to an associative model of democracy makes civil society the domain of church, family, and voluntary associations [Barber 1996: 147]. It reduces civil society to a 'space that we occupy when we go about our daily business when we are not engaged in politics (voting, jury service, paying taxes) or in commerce (working, producing, shopping, consuming)' [Barber 1996: 149]. It is perhaps necessary to underline that this conception of civil society has emerged in a context where traditional structures of loyalty and community identity have, to a considerable extent, broken down; and the principle of formal equality, rooted in the notion of equal rights of citizens and an individualistic ethic, has been widely accepted and incorporated in the practices of the state. The church, for instance, appears as an institution of civil society only when it does not exercise a hegemonic influence over the social domain. Once it is transformed into a voluntary congregation, it appears as an association that can be a vehicle of civil liberties. Thus, in democracies of the west, the shift from a rights-based conception of democracy to an associative one is preceded, or accompanied, by the democratization of state and society. And it is only with the realization of the democratic project that associations like the church are able to operate and manage their affairs in conformity with the principles of non-discrimination and equal rights. As a result, even when civil society is placed outside the realm of the formal structures of political power, it continues to be permeated by the ethic of freedom and equal rights that the democratic state is expected to manifest and uphold. It is only in totalitarian regimes that the civil society and state appear as adversaries, poised against each other.

CIVIL SOCIETY AS AN INSTRUMENT OF HUMANE GOVERNANCE

As was noticed earlier, social and political theory in the second half of the twentieth century has been characterized by a loss of faith in the institution of the state. This sentiment is evident not only in western democracies but also in third world democracies, like India. Here too, disenchantment with the state forms the backdrop to the revival of interest in civil society [Gupta 1997]; indeed it is a recurrent and common theme in the writings on civil society. The disillusionment with the state is expressed by Marxists and non-Marxists alike. For theorists of the Marxist persuasion, the post-colonial bourgeois state in India cannot accommodate the interests of the weaker sections of society. The democratic struggles of the people are accordingly placed in civil society. The latter becomes the 'leitmotif of movements struggling to free themselves from unresponsive and often tyrannical post-colonial elites' [Chandoke 1998: 30]. Manoranjan Mohanty refers to this domain, where the democratic demands have a salience, as 'creative society'. The latter expresses the demands for a decentralized, responsive, and participatory state [Mohanty 1998: 74]. For other analysts, most notably, Rajni Kothari, the path of development that the state in India has adopted is deeply flawed: the focus on 'market efficiency', 'profitability', 'development' and 'national security' [Kothari 1988a: 2] has made the Indian state unresponsive, if not hostile, to the basic rights of the common man. Indeed, with a large repertoire of coercive apparatuses the state frequently violates and suppresses the essential liberties of the people. Against such an undemocratic and elitist state, civil society is placed as the arena where the marginalized protest and struggle for their essential human and democratic rights.

In each of these perspectives civil society is the domain of popular participation, albeit outside of the formal institutional structures of the state. Marxists believe that it offers avenues for resisting and challenging the hegemony of the ruling class, while social scientists like Rajni Kothari see it as a way of empowering the common man. In case of the latter, civil society appears as the 'take-off point for humane governance' [Kothari 1988a: 3]; it includes, within its ambit, a variety of contemporary social movements—such as, human rights movements, ecology movements, women's movements and the peace movement—which seek to restore the principles of good life in the conduct of human affairs. At the same time, the civil society also incorporates a 'network of voluntary, *self-governing* institutions in *all* walks of life' [Kothari 1988a: 202; emphasis added]. Collectively, these organizations provide the 'grass roots model of *mass politics*... in which *people are more important* than the state' [Kothari 1988b: 212; emphasis added]. Kothari clearly associates civil society with people-centric institutions; consequently, he incorporates within it all those forums in which people participate directly and manage their own affairs. Since the accent is almost exclusively on people's participation, panchayats, even caste panchayats, voluntary associations, and NGOs of all hues and colours are regarded as agencies of civil society that strengthen democracy. What brings these diverse institutions together is the fact that they stand outside the state, offering an alternative to state-sponsored and state-managed to organizations; in fact they open 'alternative political spaces outside the usual arenas of party and government' [Kothari 1988a: 45].

Kothari wishes to empower the institutions of civil society as they offer an alternative to the bureaucratic and unresponsive state machinery. Like several western scholars of the twentieth century, his writings on civil society express a loss of faith in the state. To quote him, the 'state has lost its role as an agent of transformation, or even as a protector and mediator in the affairs of civil society. In fact, one finds that the whole relation between the state and civil society is increasingly visited by a growing coercion of the state apparatus' [Kothari 1988b: 209]. It is under these circumstances that he pins his hopes on smaller village level bodies, panchayats, and non-governmental agencies, and assumes that these institutions of direct participation would 'transform the nature and scope of the state' [Kothari 1988b: 142] so that the latter can act in accordance with popular sentiments.

Like many social theorists in the west, Rajni Kothari maintains that a highly bureaucratized state restricts and does not augment avenues of popular participation. Instead of guaranteeing freedom, its authoritarian structure curbs individual liberty. Against this state, civil society is presented as the arena of self-management and active participation. It is perhaps necessary to remember that Kothari pins his hope on civil society because the Indian state has failed: it has belied people's expectations and has been an ineffective agent of social and economic transformation. As such, the move towards civil society is primarily a negative one: prompted mainly by a loss of faith in the state. Further, while searching for an alternative to the state, Kothari postulates a dichotomy between people and state elite; the former are represented as marginalized and subjugated masses. The postulated dichotomy captures the neglect of the village as a unit of economic and political life, but, at the same time, it ignores the conflict of interests that exist in caste and community divided villages. Consequently, the critique of state and centre-managed development ends up postulating a romantic picture of homogenized village communities that are immune to the struggles of power that infest the machinery of the state.

In Kothari's writings, civil society emerges as an alternative to the state. Conceived in this form, it is equated with non-state, non-government organizations and associations through which people participate directly and manage their own affairs. Since institutions that are independent of the state and government exist in a variety of different political systems, civil society does not appear in this framework as a correlate of democracy. Indeed, this perspective suggests that civil society was strong in pre-modern India as it was governed through traditional community institutions that allowed people to manage their own affairs with little interference from the political regime. The fact that Kothari does not distinguish between different kinds of institutions that exist in the social arena fosters the impression that all collectivities, from football clubs and caste panchayats to student unions, Ramlila *mandalis*, and temple organizations, are agencies of democratization. That some of these bodies operate on the principle of hierarchy and exclusion is a consideration that is almost always left out of the discussion on civil society.

To some extent this confusion exists in most conceptions of participatory democracy. However, in the Indian context the clubbing together of diverse organizations and community structures under the rubric of civil society poses a special problems. In western democracies community identities and institutional structures have either disappeared or been compelled to function in accordance with the minimum framework of democratic equality prescribed by the state. Consequently, social institutions and even religious bodies, like the church, have been transformed into voluntary associations. However, in India, where the task of ensuring inter-group and intra-group equality still remains unfulfilled, empowering all types of social and religious institutions tends to hinder the realization of democratic equality. What matters in a democracy is the nature of social and community institutions; the principles on which they function rather than their numbers of degree of autonomy is the crucial consideration. The theorists of civil society, from Locke to Hegel, realized this. Hence, they associated civil society with the displacement of traditional identity-based institutions with those that operated on principles of social non-discrimination. By neglecting this dimension, Rajni Kothari indirectly legitimizes groups and institutions that do not operate on the democratic principle of equality.

Within a democracy, active and direct participation of citizens in decision-making is a valued good, but it must also be realized that the majority is not the best guarantor of equal rights. Participation allows for the expression of popular will but it also ensures that the decision of the majority prevails. In societies where community membership determines, or at least shapes choices, the framework of rights needs to be given priority. If democracy is to function as a system that delinks distribution of political privileges from social ascriptive identities, civil society must rest upon the explicit recognition of equal rights of citizens.

Rajni Kothari does not deny the significance of equal rights and civil liberties in a democracy. In fact he would like to strengthen the framework of citizens' rights. However, in endorsing a participation-based conception of associative democracy that is currently espoused by several liberals in the west, he neglects the implications of this view in the Indian context. To repeat the argument, participation is intended to energize communities; however, with the breakdown of religious hegemony and older forms of communities based on ascriptive identities, western theorists of democracy assume that new forms of community have emerged in these societies: communities that are not based on the principle of hierarchy and exclusion. Non-state associations, neighbourhood councils, and institutions of local self-government are sought to be strengthened in this context. The shift from rights to participation poses relatively fewer problems in western societies because of the changes that have already been introduced in the social and public arena. However, in countries like India where ascriptive community identities and institutions are politically recognized and religion plays an important role in the life of the communities, it yields more disturbing results. Here, the emphasis on direct participation in non-state associations, rather than the presence of collectivities that function on the principle of equal rights of citizens, justifies a communitarian ethic that leaves the structures of intra-group inequalities intact.

INTERMEDIARY INSTITUTIONS AND CIVIL SOCIETY

While most social scientists in India associate civil society with voluntary and non-government bodies in the social arena that allow individuals to participate directly and manage their own affairs, André Béteille differentiates between the diverse forms of intermediary institutions in order to situate civil society in the modern discourse on individual liberty and social equality. According to him, every society has a number of mediating institutions that link individuals to each other and negotiate between citizens and the state. 'A society with only individuals (citizens) at one end and the nation (or state) at the other would not only be difficult to live in but also difficult to conceive' [Béteille 1996: 14]. Hence, the presence of mediating institutions is a universal feature of all human societies. However, the nature of these organizatons and institutions undergoes a fundamental change with the coming of democracy: instead of being closed structures based on the principle of hierarchy and exclusive privileges, they become 'open and secular institutions.

They are open in the sense that membership in them is independent of such considerations as race, caste, creed and gender; selection to positions of respect and responsibility...are based, at least in principle, on open national competition. They are secular in the sense that their internal arrangements are not governed by religious rules or religious authorities [Béteille 1996: 17].

The emergence of open and secular institutions is conducive to the growth of civil society.

For Béteille then, the existence or proliferation of mediating institutions per se is not enough. Civil society is dependent upon the strength of those mediating institutions that are open to all categories of citizens and whose functioning is controlled neither by the state nor by religious authorities. Apart from being institutions that are not rooted in relations of kinship, caste, or religion, these are arrangements that are, to use a Habermasian phrase, equidistant from state and religion. Their autonomy lies in the fact that they are neither controlled by state nor directed by religious rules. They have a distinct identity of their own which is recognized publicly, and they function in accordance with institutionally prescribed rules and laws that are also known to all its members. In contemporary India, Béteille sees banks, universities, hospitals, municipal corporations, schools, newspapers, professional associations as examples of these new institutions that are conducive to the well-being of civil society.

The merit of Béteille analysis is that it distinguishes unambiguously between institutions of civil society and other types of mediating institutions in society. Unlike many of his contemporaries in India, he associates civil society with the modern concern for individual liberty within the framework of a secular society [Béteille 1995: 562–4]. Accordingly, the institutions of civil society are valued as free associations of citizens in pursuit of particular ends. To put it in another way, they are not envisaged as units of direct participation or self-management, rather they surface as expressions of individual autonomy. Hence, their presence constitutes an essential moment in the process of democratization. In linking civil society with individual freedom and social non-discrimination, Béteille tries to return to the ideas that informed the thinking on civil society in the eighteenth and nineteenth century. However, he is unable to escape the scepticism that characterizes twentieth-century views on state. Taking a cue from Weber, he sees state as the repository of coercive force, or, at best, an embodiment of sectional interests. Consequently, he separates and distances civil society from state. Indeed, Béteille sees both state and religious institutions as enemies of civil society. He begins his analysis by stipulating that civil society refers to institutions that are neither controlled by the state nor governed by religious norms. This bracketing of state with religious institutions is indeed quite problematic and it poses serious problems in the Indian context. It delegitimizes the state and law, and lends credibility to the view that the state must not interfere in the functioning of associations and community bodies—a conclusion that is favoured strongly by the communitarian perspectives in India. In fact, the latter have appropriated the idea of non-interference by the state to defend the autonomy of communities, including religious communities, even when they do not endorse the minimum conditions of equal citizenship [Mahajan 1998: 177–8]. Even though Béteille is interested in protecting the autonomy of open and secular institutions in society, his argument lends support to the communitarian perspective that has scant respect for the latter.

Besides, it must be noted that the policy of political non-interference was particularly relevant at a time when state and church worked closely together to establish the hegemony of one religious group within the nation state. However, once that alliance was fractured and the state was compelled to endorse the principle of religious tolerance and formal equality, the state played an important role in secularizing the polity. In France, for instance, the state became an ally of the non-conformists and religious non-believers in their struggle against the established hegemony of the Catholic church [Acomb 1967]. It also played a crucial role in the secularization of the educational institutions. In other words, unlike religious institutions that have no interest in augmenting the bonds of citizenship, the democratic state can be, and historically it has been, a catalyst in creating and securing conditions that are necessary for strengthening civil society. What is needed then is to find ways of compelling the state to perform this task because open and secular institutions cannot be expected to function effectively in a context where the state is hostile to it. To a considerable extent, Hegel recognized this and for this reason he postulated a symbiotic relationship between state and civil society.

André Béteille tends to ignore Hegel in this regard. Following de Tocqueville he views the presence of plural public associations in civil life to be the hallmark of a healthy democracy. In his analysis of democracy in America, de Tocqueville maintained that free associations flourish in democratic nations where the principle of equality exists. 'The principle of equality, which makes men independent of each other, gives them a habit and a taste for following in their private actions no other guide than their own will' [de Tocqueville 1945: 304]. Consequently, in these societies they have a natural inclination for free institutions. On the other hand, '[I]n aristocratic societies men do not need to combine in order to act, because they are strongly held together. Every wealthy and powerful citizen constitutes the head of a permanent and compulsory association, composed of all those who depend upon him or whom he makes subservient to the executions of his designs' [de Tocqueville 1945: 115]. Béteille does not reflect upon these conditions that allow for the growth of plural associations. Looking through Weberian lenses he assumes that adherence to institutional norms coupled with the existence of a rational–legal structure is all that is needed for institutions of civil society to function effectively. Examining the functioning of civil society institutions in India, he argues that the absence of the latter has prevented these institutions from acquiring a 'personality of their own, separate from the personalities of their creators' [Béteille 1996: 20]. These institutions have been ineffective as they have failed to set their own agenda and act in accordance with institutional rules and procedures.

CONCLUSION

While it is true that in an organization governed by a rational–legal structure, the institution receives priority over the individual, however, the compulsion to enforce this structure, to abide by institutional norms and to retain the open and secular character of institutions can come only from the universality of law. And, universal laws cannot, as Keane points out, emerge spontaneously from civil society; their formulation and application entails the involvement of the state [Keane 1988]. Besides, the state alone can create conditions that are necessary to protect the institutions of civil society from internal disruptions [Blaney and Pasha 1993]. As such, it is difficult to detach civil society from the state or to conceive it without the latter. Indeed the institutions of civil society are, and must be viewed as, parts of the democratic constitutional state. When this dimension is lost and civil society is presented as rule-governed intermediary institutions, the concern for social equality and non-discrimination falls by the wayside. As Dipankar Gupta points out, there can be rules that 'promote rational efficiency but are indifferent to considerations of citizenship' [Gupta 1997: 306]. To make institutions responsible to the claims of equal citizenship, it is necessary to follow Hegel's lead and see civil society as a moment in the ethical life of the democratic state.

To conclude, smaller participatory bodies may provide avenues for greater interaction between the decision-makers and the people and free associations of citizens may allow for the pursuit of diverse particular interest. But to secure individual liberty along with social equality, neither increased participation nor diversity of intermediary bodies is enough. Both remain inadequate in protecting the individual against abuse of power; indeed each of them can be appropriated to sanction majority practices and unequal structures of power. To safeguard against this possibility, it is necessary to go back in history and retrieve a rights-based conception of civility.

10

CIVIL SOCIETY AND ITS INSTITUTIONS*

André Béteille

CONCEPTS AND TERMS

The idea of civil society—or at least the term 'civil society'—has acquired a certain currency in discussions of society and politics in India. It was not widely used in the Indian context until very recent times, and those who use the term now do not always make its meaning clear, often leaving the reader in some perplexity. The general impression conveyed in these writings is that civil society is something desirable, that it should be given room for expansion and protected from forces hostile to it.

In the tradition of western writing on the subject going back to the eighteenth century, civil society is a historical and not a universal category of human existence. It is not something that exists everywhere or has existed at all times. European writers of the eighteenth and nineteenth centuries, such as Adam Ferguson and G. W. F. Hegel, made some effort to identify and describe the conditions under which civil society came into existence in the west, even though they might not all use the term in exactly the same way. There has hardly been any discussion of when and under what conditions civil society came

* André Béteille, *Antinomies of Society: Essays on Ideologies and Institutions* (Delhi: Oxford University Press, 2000).

into existence in India, and, in the absence of such a discussion, the term is inevitably used somewhat promiscuously.

It may be said, of course, that in discussing the relationship between society and politics in India, we do not need to bind ourselves to the conventions of terminology established in the west. Those conventions have changed in the last two hundred years, and contemporary discussion of the subject in the west may be too narrowly focused on the particularities of western society for its conclusions to be usefully applied in the Indian situation. At the same time, social theorists in India draw freely from the general repository of terms and concepts, with or without acknowledgement, and it is best, while using a term from that repository, to keep in mind the meanings that have usually been associated with it. Moreover, Indian scholars need to explain, at least to themselves, the meanings they attach to the terms they employ so that their discussions with each other may be fruitful. If there is to be a distinctively Indian meaning of the term 'civil society', that too needs to be specified.

One reason for the ambiguity of usage is that the writings of Indian authors echo, consciously or unconsciously, the views of various western authorities who, as I have already indicated, have not all approached the subject from the same angle. A second and related reason lies in the differences of disciplinary perspective among those who speak and write about the subject. 'Civil Society', if it is to mean anything at all, must mean some form or aspect of human society, and it should therefore be of interest to sociologists, but so far Indian sociologists have written little on the subject. Political theorists, who are concerned more centrally with the state, have given greater attention to it while examining the relationship, whether of harmony or antagonism, between state and civil society. My own approach to the subject reflects my interest not so much in the state as such as in the institutions of society. It is in short the approach of a sociologist, and while it is not the only possible approach, it has its uses.

In retrospect, it is easy to understand why the initial impulse of looking at civil society came from the political scientists, for in India it arose largely from a disenchantment with the state. This may be seen most clearly in the work of Rajni Kothari (1988a, 1988b), arguably India's most influential political scientist. Those who were young at the time of independence had expected a very great deal from the transfer of power in 1947. Many of them became bitterly disappointed when they saw that no miracle accompanied the change from a colonial to a national state. They watched with dismay as the apparatus of government became corrupt and inefficient, and in some respects even more oppressive than it was under the British.

Some have come to believe that what the government has failed to do should be left in the care of the market. But such a belief is not universally held among social theorists in India, many of whom now regard both state and market with an even measure of suspicion. For them, the real wealth of the nation consists of neither the state nor the market, but the people. In this perspective, bringing civil society into operation simply means creating a more active and a more participatory role for the common people, and especially for the poorest and the lowliest among them. One can easily detect the influence of Gandhian thought in this perspective, although Gandhi himself did not use the concept of civil society explicitly.

Since I have a somewhat different conception of civil society, I would like to indicate very briefly an alternative source of the recent interest in the subject. Here too, the impulse came from a disenchantment with the state, in this case the state that was to create and sustain the world of real socialism in Eastern Europe. By the eighties it had become apparent even to left leaning intellectuals in the west that the socialist state had taken a heavy toll of both individuals and institutions. This could no longer be attributed to the 'cult of personality' or the evil propensities of particular individuals; its causes had to be sought in some fundamental failure of society in those countries.

Liberal democracy has survived and prospered in the west because it has respected the autonomy and the plurality of institutions. The socialist state under Stalin not only swallowed up the commanding heights of the economy, but brought virtually all public institutions, such as universities, scientific laboratories, hospitals, publishing houses, and newspapers, under its command and control. This caused untold hardship to individuals, and it impoverished and degraded society as a whole. For those who reflected on this experience—as also the experience of Germany under Hitler—civil society was not simply a matte of bringing the people back in, but also of safeguarding the autonomy and plurality of institutions.

I would like to make a quick note here of two common points brought up by the discussion so far. Firstly, most current discussions of civil society rest on a positive evaluation of it. Secondly, underlying that positive evaluation is the tacit assumption of a kind of elective affinity between civil society and democracy. I doubt that there would be many promoters of civil society in India—or anywhere else—if they felt that the interests of democracy might be injured by it. Civil society shows the societal face, as it were, of democracy; its political face, including not only the government but the various organs closely associated with it, has shown so many ugly scars in India recently that it is understandable that many should pin their hopes for democracy on civil society.

The positive evaluation of democracy and of civil society does not extend fully to the state itself. There is undoubtedly an element of ambiguity in the relationship between state and civil society. Although none would wish to promote civil society at the expense of democracy, there are, as we have indicated, at least some in India who might wish to promote it at the expense of the state, not just the present, somewhat unsatisfactory one in the country, but the state as such. Viewed in historical and comparative terms, the state will appear to have acted negatively as well as positively on civil society. Its contribution had been negative, not to say destructive, in the Soviet Union under Stalin and in Germany under Hitler, but in the Scandinavian countries, in the Netherlands, and in the United Kingdom, its role in the twentieth century has been on the whole beneficial. I do not believe that the state has had only a negative effect on civil society in India in the last fifty years. It has been ineffective rather than destructive.

FRAMEWORK OF ANALYSIS

The framework within which the idea of civil society must be examined provided by the three-fold relationship between (a) state; (b) citizenship; and (c) mediating institutions. Each is important in its own right, but it is only in their mutual association that the three together provide the setting for the operation of civil society. The importance of state and citizenship is obvious, and does not call for any further clarification at this point. The dependence of both state and citizenship on mediating institutions is no less important, although this may not be apparent at first sight.

State

Civil society, as I understand it, cannot be sustained without the rule of law, and the ultimate guarantor of the rule of law is the constitutional state. This simply means that there must be an impersonal order that secures for all members of society the equal protection of the laws and equality before the law. In such an order nobody is outside the law, and nobody is above it. The highest public official is, at least in principle, subject to the same law as the lowliest member of society. Where the rule of law is in practice violated habitually by the very public officials who are its designated overseers, the costs have to be borne not only by the constitutional order but by civil society as well.

If the state is to play its part as the guarantor of the rule of law, it must have its own structure of authority. It is in the nature of the modern constitutional state to have its own division of functions and powers. The idea of the separation of powers is a familiar one in modern constitutional theory, and its justification lies in the diversity of functions that the state is required to perform. No state can perform those functions unless it is vested with the appropriate powers, but those powers are in the present case powers of the office rather than the person.

Some separation of powers is essential if the distinction between the office and the person, and the rule of law that requires that distinction, is to be maintained. It is impossible to determine in advance the full range of functions that the state may be called upon to perform. The modern state has everywhere shown a certain expansionist tendency. It expands the range of its functions, and in that way justifies the expansion of its powers. On the other hand, the very idea of civil society presupposes a certain separation of functions between the state and itself. A constitutional state is simply one which sets limits to its own functions and powers.

In the twentieth century, the totalitarian state has squeezed civil society out by appropriating functions—and the corresponding powers—in an increasing range of domains: production, distribution, education, science, culture and so on. The idea of civil society rests on an appreciation of the differentiation of society, not on the denial to the state of the powers and functions appropriate to it. Of course, powers and functions are never exactly balanced among the different domains except in the mind of the philosopher. In the real world, the state may appropriate powers in a certain domain—let us say higher education—and yet perform the required functions very inadequately. Conversely, demands may be made that the state expand its range of functions and simultaneously reduce its powers. In India, those who attack the state for concentrating more and more powers also expect it to provide education and employment to all those who wish to have it.

The constitutional state can work only through an apparatus which is a system of graded authority. This is gall and wormwood to all those who believe that since, in a democracy, the state is of the people, it should be at one with them—particularly the common, ordinary people—and not set itself apart from them. The gradation of authority and the abuse of power are, of course, two different things, but in newly created democracies, they are easily confused, and the functionaries of the state become the natural targets of the hostility towards 'elitism'.

Citizenship

Not only the constitutional state, but citizenship as well is a novelty in India's long historical existence. The two ideas found their most complete expression in the same charter, namely, the constitution of India, although they had both been in the air for some decades before the adoption of the Constitution in 1950.

We will not appreciate the significance of citizenship as a social historical, and jural category if we fail to recognize its novelty. Traditional Indian society was a society of castes and communities, and not a society of citizens. The significance of citizenship for the present discussion lies simply in this, that without citizenship, civil society is impossible.

The subordination of the individual to the group was a feature of most, if not all, pre-modern societies. The individual as an autonomous legal and moral agent, entitled to respect and responsibility in his own right, is not the starting point of social evolution, but the end-product of a long historical process. That process faces many obstacles in India where the loyalties due to caste and community are not only very strong but often reinforced by the democratic process itself. The rights of citizenship can be respected only in a society in which the autonomy of the individual is valued.

It is obviously impossible to assign an exact date to the birth of the modern concept of citizenship, but the French Revolution of 1789 was an important landmark. As is well known, the Revolution looked back to the world of Roman antiquity for many of its images and metaphors. But the fact is that it reinvented the concept of citizenship by presenting it in a universalistic idiom. The modern concept of citizenship expresses the principle of universality in a manner completely alien to that of classical antiquity. It denies slavery, and it overrides all distinctions of race, caste, creed, sex and place of birth. Universal citizenship is a modern idea, unknown to the ancient and medieval world, certainly in India.

I have elsewhere explained the distinction between equality and universality (Béteille 1994). The idea of 'equal citizenship' is at bottom an expression of the principle of universality. It cannot and indeed does not seek to cancel out all distinctions of wealth, esteem, or power. But it does seek to ensure at least three things: (a) that each member of society be treated 'as an end in himself, and never as a means only'; (b) that certain basic rights and capacities be available to all members of society; and (c) that positions of respect and responsibility be open to every member of society irrespective of birth or social antecedent.

The idea of citizenship was introduced into India, but only as a germ, by the British in the nineteenth century. The main channels for its transmission were the law courts, the institutions of higher education, and the press. It is remarkable how quickly it secured a toehold in an unpromising and incongenial environment. Among the principal social obstacles to it were the caste system and the joint family system, especially under the rule of Mitakshara. It cannot be too strongly emphasized that citizenship is not just a universalizing but also an individualizing concept. Throughout the nineteenth century, such appeal as it had was confined almost entirely to the urban intelligentsia. The extent of its diffusion beyond that circle until the middle of the twentieth century is not very easy to assess.

The British introduced the Indian intelligentsia to the idea of citizenship, but denied them its substance. This contradiction was felt acutely by the leaders of the nationalist movement and quickened in them the urge for self-rule which alone would enable them to cease being second-class citizens and become full citizens in their own country. No one has expressed the contradiction more eloquently than Nirad C. Chaudhuri who dedicated his *Autobiography* to the memory of the British empire which, he wrote, 'conferred subjecthood on us but withheld citizenship; to which yet every one of us threw out the challenge: *"civis britannicus sum"*' (Chaudhuri 1951: v). With the end of empire and the adoption of a new constitution, Indians changed from being subjects into becoming citizens in the formal sense. But historical experience everywhere has shown that the form of citizenship is not the same as its substance.

The political and legal passage from subjecthood to citizenship does not lead automatically to the conversion of a society based on caste to one based on citizenship. For it is not only the hierarchical ranking of castes that stands in the way but also the subordination of the individual to the group. The leaders of the nationalist movement rightly believed that they could not build a new society unless they got rid of the two impediments of colonialism and casteism. The second impediment has proved to be more obdurate than the first.

Speaking in the constituent assembly on the eve of India's independence, Pandit Govind Ballabh Pant drew attention to the threat to citizenship from the assertion of group identities. When he said, 'There is the unwholesome and to some extent a degrading habit of thinking always in terms of communities and never in terms of citizens', his remarks were greeted with cheers (Constituent Assembly Debates 1989: 332). At that time it was easy to blame the British for suppressing the claims of citizenship and playing upon group interests in the name of minority rights. But we have been on our own for more than fifty years, and citizenship still remains precariously balanced in the face of caste and community.

Mediating Institutions

A society with only individuals (or citizens) at one end and the nation (or state) at the other would be difficult not only to live in but also to think about. Every society has its own internal arrangements: its groups, classes, and communities; its associations, organizations, and institutions; and its networks of interpersonal relations, linking the different parts to each other and to the whole. Here I would like to stress only the variety and complexity of these internal arrangements. Some of them are ephemeral and bind only a few persons to each other; others are very extended in scale, have great continuity over time, and are highly visible. Indeed, when the sociologist speaks of society, it is these various arrangements, rather than the individual or the nation, that he has most often in mind.

Reacting strongly against the demand for quotas based on caste and community, the much respected Gandhian, Kaka Kalelkar had argued as chairman of the first all-India Backward Classes Commission that only the individual and the nation should count in public affairs. He had stated that 'nothing should be allowed to organize itself between these two ends to the detriment of the freedom of the individual and the solidarity of the nation' (Kalelkar 1956: iv). Put in this form, the statement stands as a serious misrepresentation of human society. No society, least of all Indian society, is merely an atomistic aggregate of individuals. Today, what makes the inhabitant of this country an Indian in the formal sense is the fact that he is a citizen of India; but that would amount to little in the absence of the innumerable bonds by which he is tied to particular persons and particular places. A citizen of India may live abroad, adopt the citizenship of another country, and renounce his Indian citizenship; but he might still think and feel that he is an Indian so long as those particular bonds are cherished and sustained.

It is not my argument that mediating social arrangements are a unique feature of what I describe as civil society; they are a universal feature of all human societies everywhere. I have also indicated that they are of many different kinds. Among these, I would like to devote special attention to what I call institutions. An institution is a social arrangement with a distinct identity, a distinct internal structure and culture, and a life-span extending well beyond the lives of its individual members. Mediating institutions are of many different kinds, and only some, and not all, contribute to the health and well-being of civil society.

In the traditional order of Indian society, there were many different kinds of structures and institutions by which the individual was linked with other individuals and with the wider society. This is so well known that it hardly requires reiteration. Nevertheless, I would like to stress the importance of groups with more or less closed and fixed boundaries, pre-eminent among which were village, caste, and joint family. What should be noted in particular is that the attachment of the individual to the group was based in each case on the principle of hierarchical subordination.

In pre-modern societies, whether in India or Europe, the individual was firmly embedded in a social matrix: he was not a detached or free-floating monad. The process of modernization, with which the emergence of citizenship and the constitutional state are associated, detaches the individual by loosening, at least to some extent, the bonds of his attachment to that matrix. Here I cannot do better than to quote Tocqueville: 'Aristocracy had made a chain of all the members of the community from the peasant to the king; democracy breaks that chain and severs every link of it' (Tocqueville 1956: II, 99). The ideal of hierarchical integration was a commonplace of medieval European thought, and it has been memorably depicted by Jan Huizinga in his classic study, *The Waning of the Middle Ages* (Huizinga 1924).

Among all the societies known to history, it was in the Indian that the work of hierarchical integration found its most complete realization. Now when people look back fondly on the integrated communities of the past, they tend to forget the hierarchy; and when they attack the iniquities of the past, they tend to overlook the integration. The problem we face today is that of constructing and sustaining an integrated society on the basis of equality instead of hierarchy; it was a problem over which Tocqueville agonized in France more than a hundred and fifty years ago. The view that equality and unity are inseparable is a modern myth rather than a conclusion of social science.

Hierarchical integration was maintained in India through the social institutions of kinship, caste, and religion. Caste has been represented by generations of sociologists and social anthropologists as the pre-eminent institution of India, and it reached into every aspect of Indian social life. But caste did not stand alone, being related on one side to kinship and on the other to religion. Caste may be viewed as a metaphorical extension of kinship, for all the members of a subcaste are related, at least in their own belief if not demonstrably, by ties of blood and marriage. And, for two thousand years, the rules of caste were the rules of religion, at least among the Hindus. Caste, kinship, religion combined to give a distinct character to all social relations, associations, and networks in India.

The mediating institutions that I consider to be congenial, if not indispensable, to the growth of civil society are very different from those based on kinship, caste, and religion. They are open and secular institutions. They are open in the sense that membership in them is independent of such considerations as race, caste, creed, and gender: selection to positions of respect and responsibility in a university, a research laboratory or a public hospital, to pick only a few examples, is based, at least in principle, on open competition. They are secular in the sense that their internal arrangements are not regulated by religious rules or religious authorities.

New institutions of the kind I am now describing began to emerge gradually under the influence of colonial rule from the middle of the nineteenth century onward, first in the presidency towns of Calcutta, Bombay, and Madras; from there they spread their influence elsewhere. They included schools, universities, hospitals, banks, municipal corporations, professional associations, newspapers, publishing houses, and others of many different kinds. To be sure, their growth was facilitated by the introduction of a new legal order and new economic opportunities. But their appeal lay no less in the fact that they offered a new ideal of social life and a new model of social association.

The new institutions began to extend their influence, and when the country became independent in 1947, the drive was not for a return to the old social order, but for development and modernization. The building of new, open and secular institutions was an integral part of that drive. It was supported by a new system of education that provided avenues of economic advancement to aspiring individuals mainly from the upper castes. One cannot emphasize too strongly the part played in it by the emerging middle class imbued with a new outlook on life. The history of civil society is inseparable from the history of the middle class, not only in India, but everywhere. To repeat, the term used by Hegel for what we are here describing as civil society was 'bürgerliche Gesellschaft', literally 'bourgeois society'.

It is evident that the new social arrangements—institutions, associations, networks of interpersonal relations—did not displace all the old ones based on kinship, caste, and religion even among the most advanced sections of the urban middle class, not to speak of other sections of Indian society. It is in some sense remarkable how quickly the new social arrangements with which I am now concerned made room for themselves in a society whose basic design and social morphology were so greatly at variance with them. Perhaps there was something congenial in the heteromorphic and open-ended character of Hindu civilization that allowed the accretion of new social and cultural components without fully assimilating them. The state also played an important part in encouraging their adoption in the early years of independence in keeping with its commitment to the modernization of Indian society. I have earlier indicated that the state may play either a positive or a negative part in the development of civil society. No two states could be more different in their orientations to civil society than the Republic of India under Nehru and the Peoples' Republic of China under Mao.

The well-being of civil society depends upon the emergence of open and secular institutions, and on their differentiation from each other. Not only should the domains of finance, education, research, communications and so on be differentiated from each other, but within each domain there should be institutions of more than one kind, and preferably several of each kind. Thus, the institutions of administration and of politics should be differentiated from each other, and there should be a plurality of political parties and associations. To revert to a well-worn example, a one-party system, even where it claims to represent the interests of the people as a whole, is not a party system at all.

In civil society, the plurality of institutions goes hand-in-hand with the autonomy of institutions. To be sure, this autonomy is both relative and dynamic. The state has in the present century acted as the most serious threat to the autonomy of the kind of institutions about which I have spoken. This does not mean that no accommodation is possible between the state and the other institutions of society. Mutual accommodation is indeed essential for the health and well-being of both state and civil society.

The long-term evolutionary trend, as I have argued, is towards the differentiation of society. But the long-term trend does not provide guarantees against reverses and setbacks in the short term. There have been examples of institutions moving towards differentiation and autonomy, and then being brought back in line and even swallowed up by the state. In the twentieth century, where the state has most often damaged or destroyed the autonomy of mediating institutions, it has done so almost invariably in the name of the people.

In seeking to be consistent in maintaining the distinction between the state and mediating institutions, I may have given rise to a misunderstanding which I would like to dispel before proceeding further. It will be a serious error not to recognize the fact that the state is itself an institution, homologous at least in certain respects with many of the institutions with which I have just dealt. For many political theorists, the state is not only an institution, it is the pre-eminent institution. The sociologist, by contrast, hesitates to assign pre-eminence to any one of the major institutions of society, although that does not mean that we must assign equal importance, either historically or functionally, to each and every institution.

CIVIL SOCIETY AND RELIGION

In our times, it is not just the state, but also religion that has acted as a threat to civil society. Where church and state have acted in conjunction, as in Iran, they have severely damaged both the autonomy of institutions and the freedom of individuals. Nothing can be more inimical to civil society than the combination of religion and politics. At the same time, the relation between religion and civil society, somewhat like the one between state and civil society, is a relation of ambivalence rather than of inherent contradiction.

In writing about mediating institutions, I kept the state aside because, obviously, the state cannot mediate between itself and the citizen. I also kept religion aside because I dealt by choice with 'open and *secular*' institutions. Indeed, secular principles define not only the mediating institutions about which I wrote, but also the constitutional state and citizenship as I understand them. The constitutional state is governed not by religious authority or religious regulations, but by man-made laws: the prospects of civil society are at best uncertain in a state whose legitimacy rests on religion. Moreover, citizenship in the sense given to it here is defined independently of religion: a citizen may be of any religion or have no religion at all.

The state as such is not an enemy of civil society; it is only when the state seeks to dominate every sphere of life and to control every institution and every individual that it becomes a threat to civil society. Religion as such is not an enemy of civil society; it is only when it seeks to encompass every aspect of society and to regulate every individual and every institution that religion stifles the growth of civil society. Historically, both church and state have been extremely powerful institutions. Civil society has grown not by destroying them, but by creating and inhabiting spaces outside their direct control.

Those who wrote about civil society in the eighteenth and nineteenth centuries did not generally regard religion as an enemy of civil society. Many of them were religious believers who favoured religious tolerance. This was largely the case with the Scottish moral philosophers of the eighteenth century. Alexis de Tocqueville believed that religion contributed positively to the growth of democratic institutions in America, but he also pointed out that it was most effective where there was a separation of church and state (Tocqueville 1956: I, 308–14).

In the western countries where civil society as we know it had its origins, an important step in its emergence was the separation of church and state. The church gradually relaxed its hold not only over the state but over many of the other institutions of society. The university provides a good example of what I have in mind, although many other examples may be found. From the Middle Ages, when they were founded, till well into the nineteenth century, the universities of Oxford and Cambridge were governed in accordance with religious rules. The members of a college, both senior and junior, had to be Christians, and church service was an important part of its life. This is now no longer the case, although some traces of religious symbolism may still be found, particularly in the older colleges. Many other institutions that have come up in the western countries in the last hundred years have been secular since birth.

Secularization has been viewed by some religious believers as the beginning of the end of religion. But it may also be viewed as part of a long-term process of differentiation which allows religion to retain its pre-eminence within its own domain, but not over every domain. The Indian constitution is a secular constitution only in the sense that it denies religion pre-eminence in every domain, and not in the sense that it denies to religion what is due to it in its own domain. It gives every religion an equal place, and at the same time insulates certain domains from regulation and control by religion.

If civil society is to be based on the acceptance of a plurality of institutions, it would be contrary to its spirit to wage a war against religious institutions. The refusal to tolerate religion can hardly be an answer to religious intolerance. The brutal assault on the church in the Soviet Union and elsewhere in Stalin's time was a denial and not an assertion of the spirit of civil society. And when the tide turned in the eighties, in Poland, the German Democratic Republic and elsewhere, the church played a significant part in the revival of civil society.

Religious tolerance and the respect for religion are fundamental components of the culture of civility to which, as we have seen, some authors have given a prominent place in their conception of civil society. In a country like India, where historical and demographic considerations require the co-existence of communities professing and practising distinct faiths and rites, secular institutions are difficult to sustain, but they are no less indispensable for that reason. Their survival depends upon a culture of civility, and the state alone cannot create or sustain that culture. The culture of civility is a culture of tolerance: militant atheism is no less alien to it than the glorification of holy war.

Secular institutions and the culture of civility often lack the energy and vitality that come from unshakeable religious faith. Where those institutions are weak and infirm and have to work in an incongenial environment, they become easy targets of attack, not only from outside but also from within. In such an environment, they have to make many compromises, if only to survive, and they are then attacked 'from the religious point of view' for making those very compromises and for being venal and corrupt. Proponents of secular ideas and institutions can never offer the promise of an incorrupt and unblemished future society with the same conviction with which religious believers can. The political appeal of such a promise may of course have little to do with the actual conduct of those who make it, and there is little evidence to show that religious institutions as they are, in India or elsewhere, are less corrupt, less venal, and less feeble than other institutions.

The real challenge to civil society comes from those religions that advance totalizing claims. These totalizing claims are, of course, not pressed with equal insistence by all religions, or by any religion at all times. On the whole, the religions of the book, the monotheistic religions, have pressed those claims more strongly than the others, but rarely, if ever, with full consistency. But where it comes to advancing totalizing claims, we cannot take any religion, monotheistic or polytheistic, for granted; even the most seemingly accommodating among them might feel that the time has come to take the world in its grasp and give it a firm moral foundation. Religious ideologues learn quickly from each other, not only the lessons of compassion and humility, but also those of bigotry and intolerance. Even so, religious institutions themselves have shown a great capacity to outlive the ebb and flow of the intolerance of religious ideologues.

CIVIL SOCIETY AND COMMUNITIES OF BIRTH

I have spoken of open and secular institutions and, more briefly, of religious institutions, and have stressed their great variety and multiplicity. But those institutions taken together do not exhaust all the space that lies between individual and society. There are also communities that occupy an important place in the wider society and act upon its individual members in a variety of ways.

India has been described as 'the land of the most inviolable organization by birth' (Weber 1958: 3). It is also a land in which the individual has been subordinated to the community to an unusual degree. Communities of birth exist in all societies, but they do not have everywhere the same salience that they have had in India and some other societies. Among communities of birth, I include those based on clan, tribe, caste, sect, and also religion. They are all bound together by ties of real or putative kinship. They are very different from secular institutions such as the university, the bank, and the political party, and also different from religious institutions such as the temple, the church, and the monastery.

I would like to make a brief observation on religious communities, including sects. No doubt religion is a matter of faith, even personal faith. But it is not only a matter of personal faith since it cannot be sustained for long without institutions governed by distinctive rules and practices. Finally, religion is also a matter of membership in a community. A religious community is not necessarily or in principle a community of birth. In fact, the religious sect begins typically on the basis of personal and voluntary acts of subscription. But in course of time, the sect too becomes for all practical purposes a community of birth. Particularly in times of political turmoil, the individual's loyalty to his religion is more often a matter of loyalty to his community of birth than to any particular doctrine or practice.

What is true of the religious community in this respect is even more true of clan, caste, and tribe. Although the three are not the same, it is of interest to note that they have been persistently confused with each other in the ethnographic literature on India. Membership in all three is acquired at birth, and one cannot choose at will to be a member of a particular tribe, caste, or clan as one can, at least in principle, opt for a religion other than that of one's forebears.

The elementary family is the building block of all the three types of community just referred to. It is a social unit of universal significance, present in one form or another in all human societies. In India, as in many other parts of the world, it does not stand alone, but is embedded in a wider matrix of kinship and marriage. The clan, the caste, and the tribe may all be viewed as kinship systems writ large or as metaphorical extension of the family.

Civil society, whether in India or the west, has to accommodate the family. No one has, to my knowledge, recommended the abolition of the family as a condition for the advance of civil society, although the family has been attacked on other grounds. But to what extent can the extensions of kinship, real or metaphorical, be accommodated by civil society as here understood? More generally, what should be the place of communities of birth in a society committed to open and secular institutions?

Where the claims of kinship have a strong social appeal, they are carried over, overtly or covertly, into public domains in which they are not wholly appropriate. They manifest themselves in various ways in the domain of politics. The son, the daughter, and, surprisingly, even the widow are widely acknowledged to have a natural claim to the highest political office in many Asian countries that have resolutely renounced the monarchical principle. This happens even when the claimant has shown little aptitude or inclination for politics in his previous career. It cannot be explained solely by the personal ambitions of the claimant or the coterie which promotes his or her claims; millions of persons, including many who are totally non-partisan, feel that the son, the daughter, or the widow has a rightful claim which should not be denied.

In a society where the sentiment of kinship is so strong and its ties are so extensively reckoned, it is difficult to fully insulate any part of the public domain from its claims. It is difficult to say to what extent the working of public institutions such as banks, hospitals, universities is vitiated by benefits being granted or withheld, not in accordance with the rules of those institutions but in conformity with the claims of kinship. But the proper working of those institutions according to their own norms does not require the denial of the claims of kinship, no matter how extensive, in those domains that are appropriate to them. Again, as with religion, so also with kinship: the development of open and secular institutions calls for the differentiation of society, not for the war of one part of society against another. Further, the well-being of civil society in India does not require its kinship system to become an exact replica of the European or the American kinship system.

Caste is of course much more than a kin group in the literal sense of the term. The caste system has in many ways dominated the structure of Indian society for centuries. It has been changing over the last hundred and fifty years, but has by no means disappeared.

It has been widely noted that while the ritual aspects of caste have declined greatly in significance, its political aspects have gathered strength (Fuller 1996). Not only are the distinctions of caste still widely manifest, the sentiment of caste has acquired a new lease of life on account of its continuing involvement in electoral politics, and through it, in public life in general. This is a more serious challenge to the growth of civil society in India than the state's hunger for power.

I have already indicated that caste and citizenship are antithetical principles. The normative basis of caste and of the open and secular institutions on whose success the vitality of civil society depends are also at odds with each other. Does this mean that civil society cannot take root in Indian soil unless caste is first uprooted from it? It certainly means that unless the state as well as the other open and secular institutions of society are substantially insulated from caste, the prospects of civil society will remain uncertain.

In part, the claims of caste insinuate themselves into public institutions such as universities, hospitals, banks in the same way in which the claims of kinship do. The scale on which this happens is difficult to estimate even approximately, and it obviously varies a very great deal from one institution to another, and possibly also from one part of the country to another. It has analogues in other parts of the world, including countries such as the USA, the Netherlands, and Belgium. It is often viewed as a form of corruption, and is both criticized and accommodated.

But the penetration of caste and community into what are designed to be open and secular institutions may not take place only through the back door; they may also enter through the front door, and that too on a fairly extensive scale. The colonial regime had introduced quotas based on caste and community in public service well before independence. Those quotas had on the whole been viewed with disfavour by the leaders of the nationalist movement. When Kaka Kalelkar had declared that nothing should be allowed to stand between the individual and the nation, what he had in mind were not the open and secular institutions discussed earlier, but castes and other communities of birth. He tried to prevent the intrusion of caste into the public domain, but failed. Whether the trend introduced into public life by V. P. Singh's government in 1990 will fade away or gather strength, only time can tell.

DEMOCRACY AND CIVIL SOCIETY

I began by pointing out that the idea of civil society has in our times become inseparable from that of democracy. It became evident from the beginning of the nineteenth century onward that democracy is not just a form of government, but a whole way of life. This insight was first fully articulated in the work of Alexis de Tocqueville who showed how democracy alters the texture of society, its institutions, its customs and manners, and the very character of interpersonal relations. From this point of view it may be said in a very broad way that civil society represents the societal as against the political aspect of democracy.

Again, as I pointed out at the beginning, in India, the recent interest in civil society has arisen less from a natural curiosity about changes in the inner life of society than from a concern over the problems and prospects of Indian democracy. It has arisen because many persons have begun to feel that democracy is facing a crisis, and that this crisis has been created, or at least intensified by the state. It is in civil society that these persons invest their hope for rescuing democracy from an oppressive state and its uncaring elite. They believe that civil society already exists, only that it is lying dormant among the common people and needs to be awakened so that democracy may be restored to its rightful place. Others believe that creating civil society in India is and has been an uphill task because it involves the care and nurture of new institutions in an inhospitable social and cultural environment.

Much of the confusion over what we should mean by civil society arises from the failure to maintain a clear distinction between two different conceptions of democracy, the constitutionalist and the populist. We started at independence with a constitutionalist conception of democracy, but have since moved some distance in the direction of a populist one. As I have already noted, the Emergency and its aftermath provided a kind of watershed. More and more persons began to represent not only the state as the enemy of democracy but public institutions in general as enemies of the common people. In this environment, those who seek to make the case for civil society from the constitutionalist point of view must learn to sail against the wind.

When India became independent after a long period of colonial rule, there was understandable optimism about the prospects of all-round economic and political development through constitutional means. But India's archaic and ponderous social hierarchy proved far more resistant to modernization than had been anticipated, and modernization itself brought new and unforeseen social problems in its wake. Economic growth was slow, and the fruits of that growth continued to be unequally distributed between individuals and among communities. The politics of parties and elections, far from dissolving the boundaries between castes and communities, deepened the awareness of those boundaries. As more and more laws came to be enacted, their inability to overcome the obduracy of custom became more and more apparent.

By treating the constitution lightly, the Emergency strengthened the appeal of populism. The politics of caste and community, till then viewed as a barely tolerable evil, became legitimized in the name of social justice. Such open and secular institutions as had begun to take their faltering steps in an incongenial environment came under severe attack for being unrepresentative, elitist and against the real interests of the people. Politicians began to undermine the very institutions from which they derived their sustenance, and many intellectuals who were modernized to their fingertips began to attack modernity itself.

Constitutional democracy depends upon respect for rules and procedures and for the gradations of legitimate authority in the state and in other public institutions. Populism represents all established authorities as fortresses against the exploited and the oppressed, and all rules and procedures as instruments of vested interests. It has little regard for the functional requirements of the kind of open and secular institutions about which I have written. It seeks instead to promote democracy through the direct empowerment of the people, and especially of disadvantaged, disesteemed, and marginalized communities. Populism is at once emancipationist and antinomian in its orientation; it has little regard for civility and for the rights of the citizen as an individual.

11

CIVIL SOCIETY OR THE STATE
*What Happened to Citizenship?**

Dipankar Gupta

CIVIL SOCIETY AGAINST THE STATE

How can one account for the surge of literature on civil society these days? In India Rajni Kothari was one of the first to revive this concept. Around the same time the term was also doing the rounds in western academic circles, gathering strength with each turn. Today there is a plethora of literature on this subject, and, perhaps because of it, a general confusion about what 'civil society' is supposed to mean.

It is tempting to dismiss all this as yet another fad. To do so would be a pity for it would block out the many sociological issues that the literature on the subject brings out. These sociological factors also help us understand why the term is enjoying such popularity today.

It is true, as many observers have noted, that the disenchantment with the state is a major reason for the contemporary interest in civil society (Keane 1988; Seligman 1992: 12, Blaney and Pasha 1993: 3–24, Chandhoke 1995: 31; Hann 1996: 4). In developed western democracies this disenchantment is largely because of the surfeit of consumerism leading people to wonder what happened to certain

* Ramachandra Guha and Jonathan Parry, *Institutions and Inequalities*, Delhi: Oxford University Press, 1999.

natural simplicities (e.g. Seligman 1992). Along with such consumerist excesses the state has acquired panoptic powers of surveillance akin to Foucault's dystopia.

Such powers at the top, aided in no small measure by technological supports, undermine the viability of democratic participation through modern institutions. The state thus begins to resemble an incubus which cannot quite be shaken off. In the totalitarian regimes of Eastern Europe and the Soviet Union, this image was even stronger (see Spulbeck 1996). All of this put together explains why the concept of civil society emerged in these societies in such hostile opposition to the state.

In countries like India, the state is not a good word either. The reasons in this case are almost the reverse of the ones in the European situation. Over the past five decades the Indian state has been unable to deliver in spite of repeated promises. In fact, some would go on to argue, things have become much worse. Technological advance has been monopolized by an elite section in India. It is this stratum that controls the state and influences its functioning.

The majority of Indians, on the other hand, only witnessed the negative consequences of technology, and in that sense have been its victims. Instead of heeding to the needs of the majority the Indian state is busy aggrandizing itself and its functionaries. It does so in the name of democracy, but in reality has scant respect for it. Instead of promoting unity the state is basically divisive in its orientation as it constantly seeks to marginalize communities and estrange them from each other (see 1988a, 1988b, 1991; Nandy 1984, 1989).

This disenchantment with the state has, however, taken different manifestations. In some cases it has resulted in a recall of sentiments and structures of the past (Seligman 1994; Kothari 1988b, 1991). In other cases, quite conversely, there is a demand for the strengthening of intermediate institutions that would realize the promise of constitutional democracies (Béteille 1996). Ernest Gellner, in his recent contribution on civil society, also lauds the institutions of constitutional democracies of the advanced western world, but leaves behind the impression that such arrangements cannot really be exported to other shores (Gellner 1994).

The truth however is that it is not studies of this kind that have given the concept of civil society its second wind in academic circles the world over. The reason for the resurgence of this term is that it is generally viewed in terms of a return to a traditional moral ordering of community relations. The emphasis is now on moving away from a universalistic discourse, which is laden with technological domination, to one of moral sentiments based on shared mutuality and trust (Seligman 1992: 12).

Rajni Kothari expresses this view rather forthrightly when he says that civil society must draw

> upon available and still surviving traditions of togetherness, mutuality and resolution of differences and conflict—in short, traditions of a democratic collective that are our own and which we need to build in a changed historical context. This is the basic political task facing Indians—the creation of a civil society that is rooted in diversity yet cohering and holding together. (Kothari 1991: 29).

If the concept of civil society today is largely charged by a return to tradition then that by itself is no minor irony. When the term 'civil society' was first referred to by Locke, Rousseau, and, then most elegantly, by Hegel, it was to inaugurate a break from a hierarchical and medieval past and a movement into a more public spirited era. In a civil society the individual is a member of a family, part of a corporation, but, most importantly, a free citizen in a constitutional republic (see Anderson 1996: 102).

When the odd study on civil society in India today does pay attention to the need for constitutional democracy (Béteille 1996), emphasis is placed on the role of modern rational-legal intermediate institutions, These institutions could be the corporate structure of the economy, the judiciary, the municipality, the various institutions of local self-governance, the university, and so on (ibid.). For Béteille, the hope for modern Indian society lies in the elaboration and proper functioning of these rational-legal intermediate institutions.

The state, it seems, cannot be quite trusted upon to uphold the autonomy of such institutions, though it established them in the first place. Béteille finds that over the years these institutions have been internally perjured by the state's political interference (Béteille 1991). They must therefore, be freed from these political imperatives if they are to stand up on their own and be true to their basic institutional logics. It is only by reviving these institutions that the promise of liberal democracy can be attained. In which case then these intermediate institutions need not be viewed as tributaries of the state structure but, on the contrary, can now be independently valorized. We are therefore, in the heart of a paradox. Rational-legal intermediate institutions are independently good for constitutional democracy even if the state, which originally set them up, is not always quite so. These institutions are rather like endangered species that need to be protected from statist depredations. This has important consequences, especially for the notion of citizenship in a developing country. But more of that in a while.

CIVIL SOCIETY AND COMMUNITY TIES

The dominant trend in current renditions on civil society clearly privileges community ties based on custom over modern constitutional arrangements. In all such cases, custom, and even tradition, are primordial wells of fraternity and mutual trust. As the modern constitutional state is now suspect, it is almost natural that institutions prior to it should be viewed kindly in a friendly light. Contract theorists and later Hegel, followed by Liberal thinkers, all saw tradition as essentially irrational for it constrained human freedom. Now, however, as depicted by many modern-day civil-society protagonists, it is in traditional mores and customs that moral authenticity resides. Clearly this revulsion to the modern state, which goes all the way to the other side, is reminiscent of the romantic reaction to the state, science and technology that Heidegger, and to some extent Husserl, popularized in early-twentieth-century Europe.

One can see elements of this even in Jurgen Habermas's *Theory of Communicative Action* (1984) though he does not invoke the concept of civil society in any fundamental way. Nevertheless Habermas argues that societies are characterized by system-integrating and symbolic-integrating functions. Symbolically integrating aspects are those such as family and interpersonal relations which are based on consensus. System-integrating ones are those that relate to political power and the economy. Traditionally, according to Habermas these two modes of integration functioned in tandem, but modern societies have uncoupled them. The 'life world', which is the zone of consensus and easy inter-subjectivity, is now overwhelmed by the system-integrating forces of money and power.

The contemporary conjoining of tradition with the concept of civil society sees the world in a similar way. It is against the background of disillusionment with the state that the tendency to romanticize 'society' must be positioned. As a consequence those aspects of society least touched by the state seem more 'civil', precious and authentic.

India provides a hospitable locale for such a point of view. Not only has the post-colonial state in India been a great disappointment, but tradition is beckoning from every nook and cranny of this society. The rationalist Jawaharlal Nehru was short of patience on any kind of traditional swill, but what has the Indian state achieved in the past five decades of independence? Rather than take a jaundiced, unsympathetic attitude towards tradition one should look at it instead as a source of social bonding. Protagonists of civil society in India now argue that if we have lost our bearings as a nation it is because we were so dismissive of our cultural roots.

This point of view can be misread as belonging to the same species of thought which in Europe has spawned 'new social movements'. There is a major difference between the two and that should be cleared up right away. In new social movements attention is on how to revive intermediate institutions of modernity without necessarily exalting tradition. Yet the new social movements are not concerned with the need to capture state power (for example in Touraine 1992). These movements in Europe seek to pressure intermediate institutions to respond to popular will, and in that sense restrain the arbitrary and undemocratic use of state power. There is no focused attempt anywhere to divorce these intermediate institutions from the state. Instead these institutions are now being reminded that in their original condition they were supposed to be the vehicles of popular initiatives.

The concept of civil society generated by new social movements does not necessarily deny or even undermine the validity of modern state apparatuses. The new social movements in the west challenge unpopular state action by invigorating intermediate institutions of the state. These may be the local council, municipalities, action groups at the borough or neighbourhood level, or unions and special-interest activist forums. All of these are recognized aspects and appurtenances of modern democratic states. Trade unions, or interest groups, or local self-government councils were not set up to oppose the state, but perceived as so many agencies through which the state receives its inputs from 'agentic individuals' (Seligman 1992: 5).

What is new about the new social movements is that while they oppose overbearing and unresponsive governments in power, they have no desire to question the legitimacy of the modern state, or to directly take over state power. They remain firmly rooted within these intermediate institutions and work to keep them active so that they do not fall into disuse from either complacency or neglect.

THE CALL FOR HUMANE GOVERNANCE

What is the majority slant on civil society in India? Civil society is generally understood by Indian academics as a realm which is inimical to modernity and its creations. As the constitutional state is also a modern phenomenon it too is extremely suspect. Civil society thus lies in traditions and customs that are either before the state or outside the state. As the Indian state has failed on many fronts, the temptation to revile it and its many institutions as unmitigatedly evil is rather difficult to resist. Some of the best known exponents of civil society as embodying customary and traditional ties are Rajni Kothari, Ashis Nandy, and D. L. Sheth. Their writings on this subject have generated wide-ranging debate. As we shall soon see the question of civil society in India draws in matters relating to affirmative action (or positive discrimination), relationship with minorities, and the authenticity of the Indian nation-state itself.

It is not easy to compress the large repertoire of civil society experts in India for their arguments have evolved over time and are often reactions to concrete political events. There is yet another difficulty. Very often, with the exception of André Béteille (1996) and Partha Chatterji (1997), references and allusions to civil society are made somewhat independently of the tradition and provenance of the term in western scholarship.

The concept of civil society in India draws its charge as a cultural critique of the Indian state. In critiques of this sort India's history and its peculiar cultural genius serve as points of departure. Anything that does not quite square with this is immediately suspect. Rajni Kothari, the leading figure in this regard, argues that the crisis of governance in contemporary India has come about because the state is insensitive to the myriad diversities of the subcontinent. Instead of being alert to these differences the state tries to stifle them in the name of political unity (Kothari 1988a: 2223). But it is not unity that it really wishes to bring about. The state's real project is homogenization—cultural, political and social.

These homogenization efforts by the state negate the culture and talent of the people and foist instead a techno-managerial structure on them. The state's increasing reliance on the urban industrial class has led to the bifurcation of two Indias—one urban and the other rural (ibid.: 2227). It is obvious that Kothari's sympathies lie with the latter. It is also in rural India that civil society functions best. It is in the villages, away from the prying and destroying eyes of the techno-managerial urban elite, that the negative genius and dispositions of the Indian people can be found in their near pristine condition.

The prospects, therefore, for humane governance are remote in the modern Indian nation-state (and by extension all modern states) as it prioritizes the compulsions of the profit-seeking market (Kothari 1988b: 2, 39). Humane governance, on the other hand, should give primacy to endogenous impulses and aspirations as these emerge spontaneously from the people. Instead the Indian nation-state brutally marginalizes all those who do not fall in line. It is in these marginalized zones that the true impulses of civil society lie. To quote Kothari:

Civil society's ordering of politics and governance is, in my view, the take-off point for humane governance. Such a re-entry is what contemporary social movements strive for. Human rights movements, ecology movements, women's movements, the peace movement are all about restoring the first principles of the 'good' and the 'good life' in the conduct of human affairs. Such sources of regeneration... *lie more in the South than in the North, more in women than in men, more in the marginalized than in the powerful, more in ethnic identities and submerged civilizations than in dominant cultures.* (ibid.: 3, emphasis mine)

For Kothari then the state is quite unambiguously an alien construct. This prompts him to repose confidence in non-governmental organizations as they are closer to the marginal and subjugated people and hence better turned to the stirrings of civil society (ibid.: 71, 109–10). D. L. Sheth too delves into the merits of non-governmental organizations for they are free from the power-seeking homogenizing logic of the state (1984: 259–62). Ashis Nandy complements this point of view by arguing that the western-oriented people in India first look to the state and adjust their culture moorings (1984: 2078–80). In a later essay entitled 'The Political Culture of the Indian Nation State', Nandy develops this idea further. According to him the 'culture of politics has in recent years depended more and more on a mix of Indian high culture and the metropolitan culture of the nation-state. The traditional dialectic of the Brahminic and the non-Brahminic, the classical and the folk, the textually prescribed and the customary practice has been bypassed' (1989: 9). As a result, instead of diversity we now find a 'scaled down homogeneity...(and a) constant search for grand technological and organizational feats as evidence of the cultural superiority of the new elites' (ibid.).

RETURN TO TRADITION

The need to invigorate civil society with tradition gives tradition a gloss that modernization theorists, Marxists, and liberals (such as Béteille) would strenuously object to. Even the espousal of minority rights by harkening to traditional values, *pace* Kothari and Nandy, constitutes quite a novelty. To argue that tradition housed values of tolerance, fraternity, and broad-minded good will is bound to take the uninitiated by complete surprise. While such a view was aired previously from conservative and even reactionary quarters, it is now being endorsed even by zealous advocates of the 'subaltern peoples'.

In a country generally acknowledged to be the most hierarchical, rigid, and oppressive among known human civilizations the claim is now being made that Indian tradition exerted, on balance, a healthy respect for peoples' initiatives and aspirations. The ignominy of caste, ritual widow burning, child marriage, and the subjugation of women are calmly overlooked. Even the sacerdotal texts known for foisting Brahminic and male-centred prescriptions and ideologies are now seen as founts of wisdom and compassion. Ancient Hindu texts such as the *Manusmriti* and the *Yagnavalkyasmriti*, which actively campaigned for a Brahminic and masculine social order, are being reinterpreted as being popular in origin and accommodative of diverse points of view (see Kishwar 1994: 2148).

There is, however, another kind of tradition and custom which appears much more congenial, at least at first glance. Many peasant communities, such as the Jats and Gujars of north India, have tried to come out with their own versions of civil code. For example, the Jats gathered in 1993 in Sisana, Haryana to formulate a code that would be binding on all Jats (see Gupta 1997: 145). This gathering of Jat clan heads decided to ban dowry, liquor vends and liquor consumption, as well as extravagant marriage ceremonies. Details on how different rituals should be conducted were elaborately spelt out. Some of this would certainly appear very laudable to many, especially the strictures against dowry and ostentatiousness.

This, however, is not all. As we read on we find that the document also endorses that women should be educated, but it severely opposes any hint this education should make them financially or socially independent. Women's education is recommended not because they can then become better mothers and help their children with school work. Further, the Sisana document does not favour the free mixing of sexes or co-educational schools. It also maintains that after marriage a girl loses all rights to her natal home and to her father's property. If, for some reason, a marriage goes wrong and it cannot be patched up, the offending party should be boycotted (for the full Sisana document see Gupta 1997: 200–3).

Looking back now it becomes quite clear that the injunctions against dowry and against extravaganzas were as inflexible and intolerant as those against women's independence and inheritance. The community spokesmen not only ordained that certain ceremonies must be held, but also explicitly laid down the modalities of their performance. Failure to comply would make the offending party liable to social boycott. Therefore, though there might be elements in tradition which look good from afar, they are not really manifestations of either goodwill or tolerance. More than anything else, tradition and custom once again come through as unbending for they can only demand complete obedience.

In communitarian renditions of civil society, however, it is only modern institutions that were wrong. Not just that, in the Indian case, even the Indian nation-state is seen as a conceptual and empirical monster. That different linguistic, religious, and regional communities, with their divergent notions of the social good, are boxed into a single nation-state, demonstrates to these critics the state's oppressive callousness towards marginal and non-conformist aspirations. As primordial (or ascriptive) identities define the horizon of meaning, the state must necessarily be dismantled if authenticity, humaneness, and popular initiatives are to rule again. Stated in such terms, civil society resembles 'the state of nature' that Locke so distrusted (Locke 1967). Civil society is also all about the 'heart', about 'enthusiasm' and 'natural simplicity' that Hegel so unambiguously distanced himself from (see Hegel 1945: 95, 125). Moreover, when civil society is seen as tradition, the internal contradictions between communities and within communities are completely overlooked. Communities are seen as self-regulating and non-contradictory. The horizon of tradition is packed with only well-meaning individuals sworn to fraternity and principles of tolerance (see Taylor 1979: 157–9; MacIntyre 1981: 205).

Though Partha Chatterji's understanding of civil society is different from that of the cultural critics, there is much in common between them. Chatterji considers civil society to be part of modernity and modernity alone. For this reason he sees civil society even in institutions set up during the period of colonial rule in India (1997).

In Chatterji's opinion, civil society has been cornered by the better-off sections and members of the elite. This is why he has a negative view of modernity and all those who work and employ modern institutions. In this he is one with Kothari, Nandy, and the cultural critics of the Indian state. There is of course the difference between Chatterji's notion of civil society and those of the cultural critics. But this could be seen largely as a terminological matter as their larger positions seem to coincide.

For Chatterji civil society is modern institutions, for which reason, he argues, one must break out of it by relying on political initiatives which are outside of these institutions. The end result is very much the same. Like Nandy, Kothari, and Sheth, Chatterji too is very critical of modernity. If Kothari and Sheth look to grass-roots movements as an alternative to the stifling technocratic managerial state, Chatterji pins his hopes on an autonomous political realm to accomplish much the same. It is not very clear whether in establishing the autonomy of the political, Chatterji too would like to plumb the depths of tradition. In spite of terminological differences and a certain ambiguity on some points, there is an obvious similarity between Chatterji's view and those of Kothari, Nandy, and Sheth. Both points of view distrust the modern state and its projects, and both believe that the answer lies outside the purview of modern institutions. The die is cast in terms of the elites versus the authentic masses.

It is also quite apparent then that Rajni Kothari or Ashis Nandy would like to preserve some of the gains of the Enlightenment with respect to freedom and dignity, but without the modern state. Therefore, while they find virtues in tradition they would not make common cause with straightforward revivalists. This nostalgia for tradition on the one hand and the desire to be free on the other is a first class contradiction they seem to be oblivious of. As Marx explained in *Grundrisse*, it is impossible now to return to ancient Greece as we can no longer be naïve enough to give up our freedoms (Marx 1973: 111).

That the majority of Indian scholarship on civil society insists on being naïve from a safe distance is what makes it reminiscent of European romantic revivalists of the nineteenth and early twentieth centuries. This also explains why proponents of civil society in India have no sympathy for the functioning of modern organizations and institutions as they are all seen as agencies of oppression. Therefore affirmative action is advocated in its most uncritical form without a thought how the well-being of intermediate institutions can be protected (see Béteille 1991 for a critique). As institutional efficiency is considered to be just a mask which the techno-managerial sector dons in order to ruthlessly homogenize the subject and marginalized population, there seems to be no need to worry unduly about it.

De Tocqueville on Intermediate Institutions

At this point it is necessary to consider André Béteille's contribution to the subject of civil society. I believe Béteille is largely reacting against the manner in which the cultural critics have romanticized the concept of civil society and linked it quite unabashedly with tradition. So far Béteille's is a rather lonely voice in the Indian debate on civil society, but his vast academic reputation, and the erudition he brings to bear on the subject call for close attention. To set Béteille against the rest therefore seems like a good manoeuvre to get significant conceptual issues out in the open. Béteille's route to civil society is very different from the one considered so far. He recalls the classics, but finds his point of inspiration, not in Hegel or Rousseau, but in Alexis de Tocqueville's study of American democracy (de Tocqueville 1954). For this reason a slight digression into de Tocqueville is perhaps called for.

Though de Tocqueville's experience of America was on the whole a positive one, he feared the excessive power that the American state had the potential of acquiring. To that end he argued that democratic associations be kept fit and in readiness so that the state could be curbed if and when the occasion arose. Absolute power should not be vested in any single authority, which is why checks and balances are required. As democratic states tend to give the legislature too much power, democratic associations and voluntary organizations are necessary to exercise countervailing pressure. In this case it is not clear if these intermediate associations or institutions are agencies of the state structure, or are outside the state. It would appear that for de Tocqueville the intermediate institutions possessed a rationale quite independent of the modern democratic state.

For de Tocqueville intermediate institutions were coeval with the modern state, but not necessarily its outgrowths. Instead they emerged because of the customs and manners of the people. It is in this sense that de Tocqueville found America quite unique. As its immigrant population was largely influenced by the puritanical outlook of the Pilgrim Fathers, there was a natural abhorrence towards centralization of power and other forms of aggrandizement. De Tocqueville was convinced that this popular mind-set could be trusted to act as a deterrent against the American state becoming too powerful. Any time an issue comes up, local councils and voluntary organizations spontaneously emerge to debate and discuss the matter.

It is also possible to make the case that, for de Tocqueville, democratic associations functioned as agencies of the state to help realize its various goals. But these two positions are quite distinct. In one case democratic associations curb the excesses that a democratic state is prone to commit, and in the other case these associations link individuals to the state as active members of the citizenry. Of course, one never exists empirically without the other. The question really is of emphasis and direction. Nevertheless, as will be argued later, this conceptual distinction has important practical consequences as well.

Further, de Tocqueville's study presents another complicating factor. De Tocqueville quite clearly made the case that democracy required, at least in the exemplary American situation, a specific cultural make-up in terms of customs and manners. This cultural factor was therefore prior to the establishment of the democratic state. Indeed, without it any attempt towards the establishment of a democratic regime would be severely limited. This was why de Tocqueville often despaired at the efforts of the French Revolution to set up an enduring democracy. In other words, the customs and manners of the American people could also be considered as a primordial given whose natural genius led towards the establishment of a democratic society.

The use of de Tocqueville in Edward C. Banfield's work, *The Moral Basis of a Backward Society* (1958) also encourages this position. Recalling, de Tocqueville, Banfield argues that only a rich associational life can be the mainstay of modern societies. A rich associational life emerges when individuals interact with one another through institutions such as local councils. Interaction through primordial institutions does not bring about the kind of associational life that Banfield is talking about. It is for this reason that he does not see much hope for the so-called 'backward societies'. These backward societies may have tradition, but not an associational life that brings about enlightened self-governance as in the modern state.

To paraphrase Banfield, a rich associational life comes about only through modern intermediate institutions. It is through the multifarious ties that these institutions sponsor that public trust is generated. This is what allows modern society and the state to function the way they do. Therefore, in the ultimate analysis, the founts, or agencies, of a rich associational life *lie outside* the modern state, though they are coeval with it. If anything, it is this rich associational life which gives rise to the modern state. More recent works, such as those of Putnam, practically lift the essence of Banfield's arguments and recast it in the context of 'social capital' (Putnam 1993).

On the other hand for Locke, Rousseau, and Hegel (and even perhaps Adam Smith and Ferguson), intermediate institutions of democracy were not just coeval with the modern democratic state, indeed their express intent was to link the individual to the state as free citizens. It is the modern constitutional democratic state that created free citizens. In earlier regimes there were people but not citizens. Locke's point that democracy grew out of the disenchantment with the 'state of nature' should not mean that democratic impulses were already present as a cultural given in pre-democratic societies. Citizenship, democracy and intermediate institutions therefore come together in one fell swoop.

Intermediate institutions not only make it possible for the modern state to realize itself, they also help individuals to realize their essential freedoms. Hegel stated this position most forthrightly as he saw intermediate institutions as substantiations of the ethical imperatives of the modern state (Hegel 1945: 157; see also Rousseau 1968: 62–5).

Thus while Hegel and Locke would both agree that the nostalgia for the past, as in the romantics, is highly misplaced; while they might both agree that such intermediate institutions cannot be found in the state of nature; nevertheless Locke maintained a 'hire and fire' view of the state, while for Hegel the state was the ultimate repository of the ethical imperatives of freedom. What, however, unites Locke with Hegel against de Tocqueville is that for both the intermediate institutions were born of the same drive and impulses that brought about the modern state. For de Tocqueville, however, the customs and manners of Americans were democratic to begin with and the American state emerged as a consequence.

Unlike de Tocqueville, in classical conceptualizations of civil society the intermediate institutions do not stand apart from the state. This is as much true of Hegel as it is for Rousseau and Locke. Indeed, in all such cases the valorization of institutional autonomy, whether of the judiciary or of the market-place, draws sustenance from the axiomatic assumption that the state alone can guarantee essential freedoms to the individual. Without prefiguring this, institutional autonomy would lack a full-fledged rationale. This is why autonomy does not mean that institutions should pull in different directions. Instead their specific drives possess resonance and body because institutions emerge from the collective of which they are a part. It is only in a modern constitutional state that institutional autonomy is at once a symptom and result of social cohesion. As such freedoms were inadequately realized in the 'state of nature', there is no longing or nostalgia for the revival of tradition in any mainstream classical exponent of civil society.

To be fair, de Tocqueville's promotion of intermediate institutions was also forward looking. But if his head were not so firmly set against turning back, one is not very sure where his heart would have led him. De Tocqueville's position on Algeria clearly furthered the forward-looking view (see Richter 1963). However, when it came to the passing away of the *ancien regime* in France he regretted that certain profound human values had been lost forever. This is what separates him from Locke, Rousseau, Adam Smith and Hegel. Hegel was perhaps the most unequivocal of them all when he wrote that civil society is not about 'natural' 'simplicity' (1945: 125), nor is it based on the 'superficial' philosophy which teaches that the opposite of knowledge, the heart and the enthusiasm, are the true principles of ethical action' (ibid.: 95).

INTERMEDIATE INSTITUTIONS AND THE STATE

We are better equipped to appreciate André Béteille's contribution to the debate on civil society in India. In a manner reminiscent of de Tocqueville Béteille argues that the well-being of modern institutions can be guaranteed only if civil societies are understood as comprising truly autonomous bodies (Béteille 1996, 1991). In doing so Béteille is emphasizing the need to be wary of giving in to traditional solidarities and associations as they are inimical to the functioning of modern institutions. Some of these modern institutions, according to Béteille, are universities, judiciaries, medical hospital, and corporations (ibid.). But Béteille is not only drawing attention to the fact that traditional solidarities undermine the well-being of modern institutions, he is also blaming the Indian state for eroding the autonomy of the institutions that it had once set up. It is significant to note in this connection Béteille's overt reliance on de Tocqueville, his rather unenthusiastic references to Locke, and his studied and deliberate distancing from Hegel.

First, and quite naturally, de Tocqueville. In a de Tocquevillean manner Béteille is for upholding the institutional autonomy of intermediate institutions for that would be the most effective guarantee against a demagogic state. The Indian state, Béteille believes, has given in to mass political pressures and to sectarian and communitarian forces. Such a state would necessarily undermine the well-being of intermediate institutions, which is where civil society lies. In order to protect civil society it is important to keep these institutions autonomous and independent of state control.

One reason why Locke is not immediately attractive to Béteille is probably because Locke, like Adam Smith, favoured a kind of minimalist state (see also Nozick 1974). Given India's late entry into the modern world, and its extreme poverty, the state in India is expected to intervene as a mobilizing instrument to alter the existing state of affairs and realize developmental goals.

Unhappy though Béteille is with the performance of the Indian state he is not yet willing to give up on it as a vital mobilizing agency. Where Béteille is disappointed is not only with the state's inability to perform but also with the manner in which it has infected intermediate institutions with its compromising political proclivities. The issue uppermost on his mind is how to protect these intermediate institutions from the pressures of mass politics.

This also explains why Béteille is suspicious of Hegel and Gramsci. In the latter case it is perhaps justifiable, as Gramsci saw civil society as an instrument for exercising the will of the state. In this connection it needs also to be said that Marx's notion of civil society is very different from that of Hegel. For Marx civil society is rather simplistically understood as anything that is outside of the state (Marx and Engels 1969a: 38, 77). This even includes the simple family and the tribe. Civil society does not emerge in Marx with the dawn of constitutional democracy and with the idea of freedom. It has been there all the time, through history.

Hegel, however is completely different. The civil society is for him not worth the candle if it does not manifest the ethic of freedom of which the state is the highest repository and the 'actuality of the ethical idea' (Hegel 1945: 155). Hegel's version of civil society talks of no greater good than actualizing the ethics of individual freedom.

It should be made clear though that this freedom is not of the kind that the hero enjoys, but a freedom that human beings can attain in association such that they can fully realize themselves (Hegel 1945: 108; see also Rousseau 1968: 62, and Durkheim 1957: 71). The majesty that Hegel sees in the state is not because of its coercive abilities but rather because it is the highest realization of freedom. According to T. M. Knox, Hegel's most erudite exegete: 'It cannot be too often emphasized that Hegel's philosophy culminates not with the state but with art, religion and philosophy, which lie beyond the state and above it' (Knox, translator's notes, in Hegel 1945: 305).

That Hegel has been loudly appropriated by the likes of Lenin or Gramsci does not mean that Hegel himself would have in any way condoned the erosion of individual freedom. In fact it is in Hegel that one finds the most systematic rationale for the autonomy of intermediate institutions that Béteille and most true liberals cherish. According to Hegel, these institutions form part of the civil society compact as they manifest the ethical imperatives of freedom which radiate outward from the state. It is the civil society that gives freedom to the citizen. A citizen is not just a free-market agent, nor just a rational-legal human being. The freedom that the state gives to its citizens is the freedom to develop socially valuable assets irrespective of the accidents of birth. Walzer is quite right when he says that 'civil society is a setting of settings: all are included none is preferred' (1992: 98).

INSTITUTIONAL AUTONOMY OR CITIZENSHIP

What Béteille's appeal for maintaining the well-being of institutions lacks is a rounded rationale that grounds these intermediate institutions in a larger perspective. It is not enough to say that if the constitutional state wants to attain its stated legal ends it must protect the well-being of institutions. The point really is how to understand institutional well-being. After all, it is possible to set high standards of institutional efficiency and well-being without taking the citizen into account. The efficiency and well-being of institutions need not benefit society as a whole. These intermediary institutions could just as well look after themselves and set up perfectly idiosyncratic norms. In fact a range of such alternative possibilities can be found in Nozick's critique of 'do good' liberalism (1974: 207–8, 247).

The fact that the Indian state has constantly whittled down institutional autonomy for sectional political advantages has led Béteille to valorize institutional autonomy as a good in its own right. This is tantamount to rejecting the state as an aspect of civil society. That would have been all right except that citizenship gets short shrift for no fault of its own. This is the unintended consequence of Béteille's position. Citizenship is the unfortunate casualty as institutional autonomy no longer needs the state for its actualization.

The interesting feature is that both Béteille and the cultural critics distrust the modern state for one reason or another. This justifies to a great extent, even explains away, the Indian state's inaction as far as being responsible to the public is concerned. In effect it lets the state off the hook for it is no longer pressured to perform for the welfare of its citizens, or to realize citizenship. Proceeding strictly on Béteille's lines one cannot adequately justify public funding for education, health, and internal security. The state is only petitioned to stay out of the functioning of intermediate institutions after it has put in place a 'system of rational, impersonal law' (Béteille 1996). For Béteille what counts the most is that these intermediate institutions be characterized by impersonal rules of efficiency. It does not really matter whether or not they pay attention to public welfare. In fact, on closer examination it appears that these are not so much intermediate institutions as they are simply modern organizations.

A clear implication of this stand is that all well-run organizations are good provided they are technologically forward looking, and allow the best within the respective organizations to emerge. These institutions are intermediate because they are neither enmeshed by the compromises of politics that the state is encumbered with, nor are they compelled to give in to archaic demands and obligations of traditional associations, which is characteristic of Indians in 'their state of nature'. They are intermediate not because they link the state with the citizens—with the public, but rather because they fall conceptually, in between.

Though Béteille ostensibly relies on de Tocqueville, his real hero is Max Weber. It is a system of rational-legal authority that Béteille would like to see implemented through intermediary institutions. While a constitutional democratic state must have at its core a rational-legal framework, it is not as if it works in the same way if the direction were to be reversed. A rational-legal system does not necessarily need a constitutional democratic state. It may be realized through the market, and through facilities like the Golf Club. The most important feature of a rational-legal structure is that it should abide by rules that are not traditional, familial, or particularistic. A market economy fulfils these criteria, so does a system where merit plays the most important role. To appreciate that rational-legal institutions are not necessarily democratic in character one has only to read Nozick (1974).

From Béteille's treatment of intermediate institutions it appears that as long as these institutions work efficiently they are worthy of protection and need to be encouraged. Efficiency can be understood in a variety of ways and several of them have little to do with citizenship, which, as T. H. Marshall (1977) once said, 'has a tendency towards equality'. If one were to go by Béteille's position, these modern institutions could well function along lines inimical to the interests of citizens in general. They could quite feasibly have a tendency towards inequality. In India we see many examples of this, particularly in the establishment of expensive private schools and hospitals. These institutions, which should cater for the welfare of the citizens, instead service only an affluent minority. Béteille's autonomous intermediary institutions would then begin to resemble Chatterji's version of civil society. In Chatterji, as we noted earlier, civil society has to do with modernization and not with citizenship.

As the institutions of civil society are intermediate (in the Tocquevillean sense), it is not inconsistent that Béteille's notion of citizenship should be primarily a legal one. In Béteille one does not get a clear sense that these intermediate institutions are manned by those who are first citizens and then experts. What appears more important is that the installations be autonomous and manned by qualified functionaries. The fact that the institutions of civil society must first and foremost give substance to citizenship is relegated to the background. In which case it is hard to find a logical connection between institutional well-being and national or collective well-being. It is only in Hegel's understanding of civil society, as we said earlier, that we find a clear rationale for the reconciliation of the universal and the particular in an ethical community.

CIVIL SOCIETY AND THE ETHIC OF FREEDOM

In the Hegelian understanding of civil society, intermediate institutions possess autonomy intrinsically because they are aspects of a democratic state and not because these institutions are opposed to it, or have an independent provenance of their own. According to Hegel, the autonomy of the institutions of civil society emerged because the ethics of freedom permeated through them. It is this ethic that made for individual growth but within a collective of which the constitutional democratic state was the highest expression.

This ethic of freedom, for Hegel, can be experienced in the family, in the corporation, and of course, in its highest form in the state (Hegel 1945). The family, corporation, and state do not mark the stages in the development of civil society, as it is often interpreted. They are instead 'moments' of the ethic of freedom which beat synchronously in all of them (see also Marx and Engels 1969a: 34 for a clarification of 'moments'). At one point Hegel even says that the family and the corporation are 'the two fixed points round which the unorganized atoms of civil society revolve' (p. 154). The family is no longer simply an institution of sexual gratification and patriarchal oppression, but one where altruistic ties of blood and marriage are in consonance with the rights of citizens (p. 148). The corporation is not just market-oriented and self-seeking in its disposition (pp. 151. 153), but contracts and relates according to policies which do not undermine the well-being of citizens. The corporation is thus constantly under the 'surveillance of the public authority...' (p. 152). Nor is the state autocratic, bureaucratic, or demagogic. The state in which civil society manifests itself is a constitutional democratic institution (pp. 160 ff). If one were to draw freely from Rawls and Dworkin, one might go on to say that such a state guarantees its citizens the freedom and opportunity to acquire socially valuable assets as members of a fraternity (see Rawls 1971: 102, 128; and Dworkin 1977: 141–50).

The state, corporation, and the family are essential prerequisites for the ethic of freedom to organize and reproduce itself. For example, a developed civil society even converts the church into an association like any other association, and 'brings it into the domain of the state' (Hegel 1945: 171). The church, no matter what its denomination, is not an·alternative source of temporal power, but an institution catering to the spiritual needs of individuals. The disunion between the state and the church is in Hegel's view 'the best piece of good fortune which could have befallen either...' (p. 1/4).

Hegel's position on the family and the church helps us once again to mark our distance from the communitarians. A sophisticated version of communitarianism may not demand a wholesale return to tradition. Instead it might contend that one must be sensitive to tradition and custom in order to recover what is best in them. It would then appear that it is possible to lift bits and pieces of tradition and append them to modern institutions. The problem then would be how to bind the diverse logics of tradition and modernity and cement them together in the same society. Even sophisticated communitarians have really no answer to this question. Indeed, I believe, communitarians of all hues are not sensitive to such issues and therefore fail to problematize them.

At this point Hegel can help us again. It is not as if Hegel said that with civil society everything arises anew. Hegel did not argue that in civil society institutions like the church and the family should be extirpated simply because they originated in tradition. This is what Marx had recommended in the *Communist Manifesto*. On the other hand, for Hegel, institutions like the family and the church continue to coexist with civil society, but their *raison d'être* is completely transformed by the ethic of freedom. It is not the best of tradition that is continuing in the present, but that the present has transformed the past and forced it to work along modern lines.

In all such 'moments' the citizen is clearly the principal protagonist. In each of these instances civil society demonstrably protects the citizen's freedom to acquire and develop socially valuable assets, regardless of traditional loyalties related to birth and creed. Even the most private domain of the family is intrinsically converted by considerations that are essentially 'public' in nature. This is yet another instance of the distance between Hegel and Marx on the notion of civil society. For Marx, the development of history involved the dissolution of the family. Marx saw the family primarily as the site of patriarchal oppression and no more (see Marx and Engels 1969b: 123). For Hegel though, the family transforms itself once it becomes a 'moment' of the ethic of freedom. Patriarchy slips away, but the family remains. Likewise, the church in civil society can no longer lay claim to temporal power or even command spiritual allegiance. Its survival depends on accepting the right to choice of worship, and tending to the spiritual needs of those who willingly associate with it.

This also clarifies our reservations against Partha Chatterji. According to Chatterji even institutions set up by colonial governments should be considered as agencies of civil society. What needs to be pointed out is that these agencies and institutions can be instruments of modernization, but they do not involve citizens. In this sense Partha Chatterji too overlooks the close link between civil society and citizenship (Chatterji 1997: 30–4, esp. 33). Civil societies may be linked to the project of modernization, but at a remove. Their primary task is to constitute a community of citizens bound by the ethics of freedom and not by particulars of hierarchy and tradition, or by the rational-legal calculus of the market-place.

As Béteille is quick to dismiss Hegel, he overlooks the importance that citizenship gives to the ethic of freedom. It is not security, nor mutual consent—but freedom—which is realized through the collective. It is this, and rational-legal institutions, that make citizens. Otherwise one could have citizens without a democratic state. This clarification is not found in de Tocqueville, nor in Max Weber, but only in the writings of Hegel.

For Kothari and the cultural critics the matter is quite straightforward. As humaneness and authenticity are found primarily in tradition and custom, the cultural critics have little sympathy for the well-being of modern institutions. For them efficiency is just a word coined by self-seeking technocrats with their heads in the western world. This is why the conception of the public is absent in their works, which are otherwise redolent with references to the masses and to the marginalized and subjugated sections of the population. The need to maintain standards of modern institutions is a laughable ambition sneeringly dismissed. As there is nothing civil about these institutions there is little point in upholding their efficiency. The cultural critics would instead promote a policy that would favour the deprived and the marginals to capture these institutions and make good while they can. If the better off could have used it for themselves, why not the less fortunate?

This, essentially cynical, view of modern institutions can be upheld only if one logically looks beyond the modern state and its apparatuses as agencies of humane governance. This the cultural critics do for they believe that the modern democratic, constitutional state is a technocratic behemoth out to crush the true sources of civil society. Logically then, the cultural critics are consistent. Politically, however, their position is unrealizable, and not simply because it is regressively communitarian. The horizon of communities does not include democratic values and choice, though it provides security, often of the patron–client variety. The citizen really is nowhere in the picture.

CIVIL SOCIETY AS AN EMPIRICAL OR ANALYTICAL CATEGORY

The divide between the Hegelian view of civil society and those inspired by either communitarian principles or by de Tocqueville has other ramifications too. For Hegel, civil society functioned more as an analytical category which is realized in empirical institutions, whereas for the others civil society is limited to certain definite aspects of empirical reality. Hegel's civil society is a manifestation of the ethic of freedom. This ethic is also capable of realization in the corporation, family, or state. It was crucial for Hegel to demonstrate that something as private as a family was an instance of the ethic of freedom as was civil society and the state. So for Hegel the ethic of freedom was not limited to a finite number of institutions. The ethic of freedom was rather a principle, a rationale, an ethic, that permeated society and all its institutions.

This is why Hegel's civil society is neither specific primordial communities nor a defined set of rational–legal institutions. This does not mean that it was a piece of conceptual jugglery entirely up in the air. On the contrary, as Hegel often laboriously pointed out, a concept was worthwhile only if it was empirically realizable. The concept of civil society too must be empirically realizable, but that is not the same as saying that it rests only in certain empirical locales. Unlike both Kothari and Béteille, the Hegelian position would not in advance limit civil society to certain kinds of communities and primordial ties, nor to a specified set of rational-legal organizations. Instead, it would find instances, or 'moments', of civil society wherever the ethic of freedom (which valorizes the citizen) is manifest. Naturally, such an ethic is incompatible with primordial communities as they cannot incorporate freedom of choice in any meaningful way. But such an ethic is not intrinsically hostile to rational-legal institutions. It needs to be recalled, however, that not all rational–legal institutions are sensitive to citizenship and to the ethic of freedom.

LETTING THE STATE OFF THE HOOK

Civil society as an ethic of freedom manifests itself in the modern democratic constitutional state by creating citizens and by upholding institutional autonomy. This fact has not always been fully appreciated in India. The gross inadequacies of the Indian state tempt one to reach out to primordial unities or to intermediate institutions. What this does in effect is to take some of the heat off the state and let it off the hook. This is rather surprising considering the fact of India's economic backwardness, and also considering that most people in India still depend directly and indirectly on the state, inefficient though it is, at a variety of levels. This is true for the rich as well as for the poor. Therefore, in practical terms the state is still a critical mobilizing agency. In such a situation one would have expected intellectual energy to be directed towards pressuring the state rather than to letting it off the hook, either by valorizing traditional associations and communities, or by seeking to protect the autonomy of intermediate institutions as an end (or a good) in itself.

One principal reason for this outcome is the great differences that exist between classes, communities, and regions in this country. This makes the idea of citizenship very hard to realize in practice. The intersubjectivity that John Rawls felt was so essential to ingrain the basic tenets of citizenship (Rawls 1971: 102) is constrained by the immense variations in lifestyles and expectations. There is no viable common base on which differences can develop and flourish. In this connection it is worthwhile to recall that Durkheim's organic solidarity was possible only when society had a prior basis in mechanical solidarity (Durkheim 1933). Citizenship confers an equality of status. Citizenship can be more than just a legal provision only when a minimum set of resemblances exist between people (see ibid.: 298, 405).

This set of resemblances are constituted of practices that allow everybody to develop socially valuable attributes. This is a matter of *right*. Further, a state in a civil society would consistently strive to increase the pool of socially valuable assets among its citizenry through appropriate *policies*, such as those of affirmative action or reservations. The stress all the while is on increasing social wealth in terms of an enhanced quality of life among individuals as citizens, in which case no policy is good in itself. It is good only so far as it can add to the pool of socially valuable assets.

If the notion of civil society in India is not intrinsically linked with citizenship, the way it is in many western democracies, this is largely because a minimum set of resemblances between the people of this country appears almost impossible to obtain. For instance D. L. Sheth finds that 'the "civil space" for the enforcement and protection of rights of individual citizens is by and large restricted to the politically and economically organized sectors of the society...' (Sheth 1991: 34). In Sheth's opinion it is only these economically well-organized sections that have benefited from modernization. But Sheth stops a little too early. What needs to be emphasized is that if the benefits of civil society are restricted to just these sections in spite of constitutional democracy it just shows that the project of civil society is far from being complete. As freedom in this case is being realized only by a minority, and not by the people as a whole, the basic ethic of civil society can hardly be said to exist in any meaningful way. It is impossible to be civil in an uncivil society.

This is why it is so important to launch a concerted full-blown critique against the modern Indian state for allowing citizenship to languish as little more than a legal title. But instead of pressuring the state to deliver to its citizens, the tension of the moment tempts one to promote an alienated and reactive mood. This mires one in either protecting institutional well-being or, what is infinitely more danger-ous, in valorizing tradition.

When civil society is seen as intrinsically related to citizenship, it is easier to appreciate where modernization has gone wrong, or the distance it has yet to traverse in countries like India. This is a sounder way of examining the weaknesses of post-colonial societies than by opposing modernization against tradition, or by simply exalting the modern. When democracy no longer encourages the well-being of citizens along the lines of civil society it is largely because the ethics of freedom are being subverted by technological rationality, or by market principles, or by the majority principle, or by the pure and dogmatic assertions of communal or group equality (as in caste-based politics). None of these is compatible with the ethic of civil society, nor with the cultivation of citizenship.

It is true that most post-colonial democracies are far from near perfect in realizing citizenship. Cultural critics such as Kothari, Nandy, and even Chatterji, respond to this by recommending a return to traditional and customary ties. In doing so communities are revived uncritically with all their anti-individualistic and often hierarchic assumptions. As the state has already been condemned as a ruthless modernizer there is no pressure on it to deliver. The search for deliverance is on elsewhere, in other 'natural' realms.

Beginning from an entirely different position Béteille too lets the state off the hook by placing primary emphasis on institutional well-being. The state is only requested to stay clear of such institutions and let them function autonomously without hindrance. Quite unwittingly perhaps, Béteille's de Tocquevillean grounding of civil society leads him to uphold the drives of experts and not the aspirations of citizens.

The only real alternative is to force the state to respond to its citizens and not let it off the hook. Pierre Bourdieu once made a similar point while warning the new-social-movement activists that a cultural rewriting of meaning would be an effete exercise without challenging the state and forcing it to deliver (Bourdieu 1985: 723–44). After all, as Hegel clarified, the state is not 'a mere mechanical scaffolding' (1945: 170), but a vital source for realizing the ethics of freedom. Walzer put this across rather nicely when he writes that the state is not a mere framework for civil society. It is also the instrument of the struggle, and it gives 'a particular shape to the common life. Hence citizenship has a certain practical pre-eminence—among all our actual and possible memberships' (1992: 105). Therefore, if the project civil society is to be saved, and along with it the freedom accorded to citizenship, it can only be done through the constitutional democratic state and not by intermediate institutions outside it, or through traditional forums 'before' it.

THE CONSTRUCTION OF FRATERNITY AGAINST FRATERNITY AS A GIVEN

The communitarian cultural critics, however, quite consciously steer clear of any substantive commitment to the notion of citizenship. For them the fraternity that is embedded in traditional and customary ties within a community forms the basis of a moral and authentic social order. Fraternity is thus a given and not something that has to be worked upon and arrived at. They ignore the many instances of tyranny and intolerance in the pre-modern period. Richard Burghart has vividly illustrated the persistent antagonisms between rival sects and communities in pre-modern India. For instance, in the Nashik Kumbh Mela festival of 1813, hostilities between Hindu Saivites and Vaishnavites led to the death of many *sadhus* belonging to rival sects (Burghart 1996: 127). Indeed, one can safely go on to say that such sectarian conflagrations were quite common in earlier pre-modern times, particularly during festivals (see also Subrahmanyam 1996). The cultural critics, with their strong communitarian bias, overlook such details and see only a seamless fraternity in tradition.

A true liberal follower of constitutional democracy believes, however, that fraternity is not a primordial given, but something to be attained by deliberate policies (for example, Rawls's 'difference principle'; see Rawls 1971: 105–6). The fraternity thus constituted by constitutional democracies is not of blood brothers but of citizens. It is one that is *based on individual rights and not on birth rights*. Even Marx was very dismissive of the idea that the proletariat could of its own accord create a socialist revolution. In his view all such attempts would degenerate to petty-bourgeois revolts and no more. Working-class solidarity does not grow spontaneously but requires a close and deliberate study of history and society.

It is necessary to ask why fraternity is never taken as a given by liberal philosophers. Traditional societies were governed by fixed, hierarchic principles which were generally in consonance with a closed natural economy. A person's status was known in advance and there was little one could do but obey the rules of the estate, or the community, that one was born into. The question of choosing one's profession, estate, or cultural lifestyle was largely non-existent. The cultural and economic statuses that people were born into locked them in fixed structural locations from which there was little scope for escape.

When peace reigned in such societies it was a peace between these entrenched differences which were largely insurmountable. The most benign condition in such a situation was one of peace between diverse groups. The possibility of such a peace was however dependent on the extent to which people adhered to their station in society and led their lives incognito. Diversity of social ambitions between groups were settled by wars. Once the war was over, and the distinction between the victor and vanquished clearly established, communities and classes fell in place and observed the rules of living in multiple solitudes.

A modern society is completely different. Now choice is the essence of life as citizens are imbued with the ethic of freedom. This makes both horizontal and vertical mobility most commonplace. Public spheres are created where people of hitherto diverse cultural backgrounds are thrown in together under conditions of anonymity. Quite naturally rules of interaction have to be renegotiated. This time these rules cannot take the fixed hierarchic estate model as its standard, but must begin with individuals. Fraternity must be constructed afresh and on principles entirely different from those based in tradition. The past is not at all a reliable guide in such a situation.

In fact all the pre-existing fraternities are extremely suspect and need to be dissolved if true citizenship is to emerge.

Even if one were to overlook the various inegalitarian elements in tradition it still does not make its revival a viable proposition. The secularization of society, the creation of public spaces, the development of the structures of the nation-state make such projections appear largely wistful, if not plainly utopian, in character. If we do not want to succumb to the naïveté that Marx mentioned in *Grundrisse* it is best to heed the specifics of an epoch and realize the inevitability of the constitutional democratic state. It is also important to note that after one has tasted citizenship, however fleetingly, it is impossible to return to the past.

Civil Society as an Alternative Ideal

A final word on the contemporary relevance of the term 'civil society'. The importance that civil society is receiving from academics the world over is largely, as we said, because of the general disillusionment with the state. There is, however, a further reason for the revival of this term from its earlier classroom obscurity. The disillusionment with the state is not simply a kind of frustration with the apparatuses and structures of governance, but also with ideals that have sustained democracies for over several decades. The failure of capitalism and socialism as pure ideals must also be factored in to properly appreciate the return of civil society.

For about seven decades democracy was ideologically charged not so much with notions of pure liberalism as with the differences between capitalism and socialism. Both sides claimed democracy to be their own. But neither socialism (as in the Soviet Union or Eastern Europe), nor capitalism (as in America) was able to establish fraternity on an enduring and self-generating basis. In this sense both capitalism and socialism have lost much of their shine, though it is only overtly acknowledged that socialism has lost out.

Civil society has moved in to fill the space thus been vacated. Civil society, no matter in which rendition, promises an ideal that can provide a way for the future. This is why it is necessary to seriously acknowledge and examine the many contributions on this subject in recent years, and not sneer at them as instances of academic hype. In our view the aperture that civil society opens allows us to see more clearly the problems of our times. It also helps us to seek out ways for overcoming them.

12

THE 'CIVIL' AND THE 'POLITICAL'
IN CIVIL SOCIETY*

Neera Chandhoke

The main objective of this essay is to interrogate some of the dominant conceptualizations that have come to cluster around the concept of civil society in recent theory. Due to a variety of historical factors, these conceptualizations have romanticized the concept to a large extent. In the process, any meaningful or politically relevant discussion of civil society has often been obfuscated. The essay problematizes the notion of civil society as the 'third sphere' in recent theory, and illustrates the argument with recent examples from India, with the intention of restoring some of the important insights that should logically attend any serious understanding of the concept.

INTRODUCTION

We have, since the 1980s, witnessed alongside the resurgence of civil society, a somewhat uncritical celebration of the concept to such an extent that it has become a *consensual* concept. But when concepts become consensual they become problematic. Indeed, if a variety of dissimilar groups such as international funding agencies, non-governmental organizations (NGOs), and institutions of the state

* *Democratization*, 8(2), Summer 2001.

on the one hand, and left-leaning liberals, trade unions, and social movements on the other, subscribe equally to the validity of the concept, it is time to worry. It is time to worry for if groups who should otherwise be disagreeing on the concept come to agree on it, the concept must have been *flattened* out to such an alarming extent that it loses its credibility. In other words, the concept of civil society may have, through consensus, become slack.

Cohen and Arato in a, by now well-known, definition, refer to a 'third realm' differentiated from the economy and the state as civil society.[1] Civil society as the space for associational life is, on the face of it, neither contaminated by the logic of politics nor that of economics. For both logics have been found wanting, mired as they are in the politics of conflict, on the one hand, and the politics of competition, on the other. Civil society in the hands of these two authors becomes a normative model of a societal realm different from the state and the economy and having the following components: (1) plurality: families, informal groups, and voluntary associations whose plurality and autonomy allow for a variety of forms of life; (2) publicity: institutions of culture and communication; (3) privacy: a domain of individual self-development and moral choice; and (4) legality: structures of general laws and basic rights needed to demarcate plurality, privacy and publicity from at least the state and, what may appear more tendentious, from the economy too.[2]

Let us now in the course of an exploration of civil society overturn this assumption by raising the following questions. Can we assume that civil society possesses a distinct logic of its own, which is in sharp contrast to that of the state or the market? Can we correspondingly assume that it is quite as autonomous of other spheres as much as we would like it to be? These questions are significant because the answers may hold important implications for our comprehension of what civil society is and for the way we think of civil society as a *political project*. In effect, what is being suggested here is that our *normative expectations* about the sphere of civil society should not derange our analysis of *actually existing civil societies*. We should in other words learn to probematize the sphere exactly as Hegel, Marx, and Gramsci had done, even if the results of our investigation may not prove to be

---

[1] Jean Cohen and Andrew Arato, *Political Theory and Civil Society* (Cambridge: MIT Press, 1992), p. 18.

[2] Ibid., p. 346.

entirely satisfactory for our political or indeed academic concerns. But, on the other hand, we cannot allow our political passions and normative concerns to obfuscate our understanding of this sphere, for that may lead us into tediously repetitive dead ends.

Admittedly, the idea of civil society as an autonomous third sphere, with its attending imagery of solidarity, empathy, and self-organization is immensely attractive. For only if we accept this as our basic premise, can we proceed to assume that atomized and imper-sonal societies can be emancipated from the alienation that besets them. It is only then that we can hope that warm, perhaps intimate, relationships among people can be restored. Indeed, the concept of civil society seems peculiarly apt when it comes to realizing the project associated with Habermas: of rescuing and regenerating the life world. What makes it attractive, writes Adam Seligman, is 'its assumed synthesis of private and public "good" and of individual and social desiderata. The idea of civil society thus embodies for many an ethical ideal of the social order, one that, if not overcomes, at least harmonizes the conflicting demands of individual interest and social good.'[3] As we shall see, the shadow of Adam Smith and his *Theory of Moral Sentiments* (1759) looms large over these con-ceptualizations.

But howsoever attractive and seductive the idea of civil society as a third sphere of human interaction may be, howsoever radically novel in its conceptualization and design it may appear, howsoever much it may seem to provide an answer to our pressing and intrac-table problems, the idea itself is deeply problematic. For it brings up not only the problem of boundary maintenance between spheres, it also throws up the additional problem of how overlapping bound-aries can possibly contain separate and discrete logics. In the subse-quent section, I argue that this kind of separation between spheres of individual and collective life is both misplaced and confusing. In effect, it can blur our grasp of civil society to a large extent.

THE CONSTITUTIVENESS OF CIVIL SOCIETY

The question that we need to ask at this stage of the argument is simply the following: can we think of *any* sphere of human activity

---

3 Adam Seligman, *The Idea of Civil Society*, New York: Free Press, 1992.

as either autonomous or as marked by a different logic? The assumptions behind the 'third sphere' argument presumably is that whereas people once they are out of the household enter into transactions with other members in civil society, these interactions will not be marked by either conflict, mediation, or compromise that is the stuff of politics. Nor will they be characterized by competition over scarce resources, which is the stuff of economics. This kind of bounding off of civil society leads to some confusion, for we will have to presuppose that each and every sphere of human action is marked by a different sectoral and organizational logic. And it is precisely this that is reiterated by Cohen and Arato when they write that 'economic activities in the substantive sense are (at least in part) included in civil society, but economy as a formal process is outside of it'.[4]

They go on to suggest that while the borders between the economy and civil society are not sealed off, the economy can be differentiated from civil society. This really means that at some point, and at some site, civil society may be engaged in economic transactions, but this is not a *general* feature of civil society; it may be, however, an *occasional* one. What is important is that the ethos of the market does not constitute civil society. Further confusion piles up when they suggest that we should separate the political, that is, non-state society from civil society. Not only is civil society not political, the domain of politics does not affect it. Besides, we now have another site of human association added to the three spheres: the public sphere that is the non-state sphere of politics. In this four-fold classification of collective life, civil society as the realm of warm, sociable, and personalized associational life is markedly different from the economy, the public sphere, and the state, though on occasion members of civil society may execute activities that spill over into the other domains.

Other conceptualizations of civil society fill in the 'third sector' with voluntary groups and refer to it as the 'voluntary sector' or the 'non-profit sector'. Here professional non-governmental organizations, foundations and philanthropies shoulder welfare and community re-building activities, provide education, health, and community development in a mode that is different from the state. But, once again, this sphere is supposed to function in isolation from, or even

[4] Ibid., p. 75.

counter to, the logic of the market and the state.[5] Indeed, multilateral funding agencies have tried to build up this sphere as an alternative to the state by funding non-governmental agencies and bypassing the 'third world' state in the process. Some groups do not seek to bypass the market, since the rolling back of the state from both civil society and the market forms an integral part of this agenda. Other *avatars* of civil society vigorously promote the activities of non-governmental organizations as providers of services and upholders of democracy, as an alternative to the market. In any case, civil society is definitely de-linked from the state and in some cases from the market.

In sum, whatever we fill civil society with—associations, voluntary agencies, or social movements—it continues to be thought of as the third sphere, neither related to the state and market nor constituted by them. In other words, it emerges in such formulations as something uncontaminated by those impulses that characterize other domains of human interaction. Here people can sort out their problems at the level of the neighbourhood, community, and the workplace with some prospect of reconciliation, for civil society is presumably neither conflictual nor marked with power relations as the other spheres are.

Now by the logic of this argument, collective life, that is the part of life where individuals come into contact with each other outside the household, can be separated into distinct arenas of activity. Each sphere possesses its own logic and its own momentum and no sphere either influences the other or constitutes the other. Collective life can thus be conceptualized as the h.h. (household) + c.s. (civil society) + e (the economy) + p (politics that includes the public sphere as well as the state). The perspective on collective life is—to put it mildly—additive.

Certainly, we can accept such separation as a heuristic device. We can in effect think of various spheres of human interaction in terms of the *different* ways in which human beings make their own history. So we can, speaking purely theoretically, refer to different sets and kinds of interaction in the household, the economy, in civil society, and in politics. What, however, should be resisted is the implication that these sectors of human activity do not constitute each other, or

---

[5] For a representative collection of essays on this theme, see Andrew Clayton (ed.), *NGOs, Civil Society and the State. Building Democracy in Transitional Societies* (Oxford: Intrac, 1996).

that they are marked by an exclusive and discrete logic that differs from site to site of such interaction. Therefore, whereas we can with some legitimacy conceptualize civil society as a site where people associate in ways that are distinct from the way they associate in the economy or in the political sphere, we can hardly assume that civil society is either emancipated or abstracted from the ethos that permeates these two spheres. There are at least eight reasons for this.

(1) State as Enabler of Civil Society

At an obvious level, civil society needs at the least a politico-legal framework that institutionalizes the normative pre-requisites of rights, freedom and the rule of law. Think of constitutions, judiciaries, and even the police, which are required for any meaningful implementation of civil liberties. But this framework, note, is provided by none other than the state. Therefore, ironically, the very state that civil society supposedly positions itself against, *enables* the latter in the sense that it provides the legal and the political settings for the sphere to exist and maintain itself. The shades of the great philosopher Hegel who suggested that the state is a *pre-condition* for the existence of civil society prove especially strong here.[6] The autonomy of civil society from the state emerges as an optical illusion.

If we accept this point, we cannot help but concede that this power of setting the frame of civil society gives the state immense capacity to define which kinds of civil society organizations are permissible under law. Thus, whereas in India the state can accept organizations of industrialists such as the Federation of Indian Chambers of Commerce or the Confederation of Indian Industries with a great deal of felicity, while it can accept even striking university teacher unions struggling for higher salaries, it has a definite problem in respect of groups that challenge the legitimacy of the system. For unless we subscribe to the liberal fallacy that the state is a disembodied institution abstracted from society, we have to accept—as discussed below—that the state codifies the power relations in society. It is simply a condensate of power, though its identity as a codifier of power gives

---

[6] This is ironic because for Hegel the state is what it is—the embodiment of universality—because civil society is what it is, namely the domain of particularity containing the seeds of universality. But ultimately it is the state that becomes the condition for civil society. See Neera Chandhoke, *State and Civil Society. Explorations in Political Theory* (Delhi: Sage, 1995), ch. 4.

it a particular status as well as a fair amount of autonomy from the power equations in society. Therefore, it will not axiomatically tolerate any challenge to the structuration of power in society.

It is not surprising that the Indian state has proved notoriously coercive when it comes to, for example, organizations of the landless peasants seeking redistributive justice. It has, for instance, stigmatized Naxalite groups representing the far left, who are fighting for the rights of the landless peasants, as criminal. It has indeed banished them to the utter darkness that constitutes the periphery of civil society. Here, in this unlit and dismal space, groups possessing no rights whatsoever are hounded by the law and the police, killed in police encounters and denied the protection that should in principle be extended to any citizen of the state. True Naxalites use violence to accomplish their objectives. But no one stops to consider *why* they need to use violence. Is it because they have experienced violence as a constitutive element of both state and civil society? Is it because the state simply does not heed the voices of the most under-privileged and disempowered sections of Indian society—the so-called 'low caste' landless peasantry oppressed by the so-called upper castes, on the one hand, and the propertied classes, on the other? [often the two overlap]. But it is a different matter when representatives of the commodified peasantry seek higher procurement prices or cancelling of loans. When it comes to withdrawing the generous subsidies granted to this section of the peasantry, we witness utter furore in Parliament and the press, simply because in today's India it is this group that exercises political influence, even direct political power, at the state level. Towards them, the Indian state is scandalously soft.

This offensive discrimination makes sense only when we comprehend that the domain of civil society is delineated by the state itself. And states simply happen to have their own notions of what is politically permissible, what is culturally permissible and what is socially permissible. And whereas these notions will *enable* some sections of civil society, they will necessarily *disable* others. State action, therefore, possesses momentous consequences for civil society inasmuch as it has the power to lay down the boundaries of what is politically permissible. It simply has the luxury of shaping the structure of civil society organizations to a formidable extent. And civil society may indeed be alarmingly constrained when it comes to ideas of what is politically permissible. What currency can we then give to the idea of a 'third' and presumably autonomous sphere in this context.

(2) Limits on Civil Society Autonomy

Of course, actors in civil society have the right under law to challenge state-given notions of what is politically permissible, *provided* that they do so in ways that cohere with the legal limits of political action. They can use the permitted means of opposition, such as moving courts, public action, and marches. This is a given under any condition of liberal democracy that is an indispensable pre-requisite of civil society. What, however, civil society actors cannot do is to challenge the state in ways that it does not allow—militancy, for instance, howsoever justified this militancy may be in the face of the brute exercise of state power and that of the privileged groups in civil society itself. Obviously, both discourses and political action in civil society have to function within certain parameters. For the penalties for transgressing these boundaries are far too high. Groups who transgress these boundaries are always likely to be excluded to the space beyond the horizons of civil society. And this space happens to be dark, damp, and rather mouldy, much like the medieval dungeons in Europe to which the Catholic church expelled 'heretics'. Here we find neither rights nor justice, just the naked exercise of brutal police and military power.

Therefore, we can suggest with some justification that the much-vaunted autonomy of civil society is constrained from the word go. Within the frontiers of what is politically permissible, of course, actors in civil society can exercise constant vigilance against arbitrary exercise of power, check and monitor violations of human rights, demand accountability, demand that the state delivers what it promises, and battle unjust policies. They can do all this as long as, recollect, they respect the frontiers laid down by the state—frontiers that may exclude rather than include, disempower rather than empower.

(3) Civil Society Needs the State's Support

However, we also need to accept that the relationship between the state and civil society need not be only one of opposition. For actors in civil society *need* the state for various purposes. Or that the relationship between the two can with perfect reason be collaborative and cooperative. This is understandable, for a women's group can hardly demand fresh rights for, say, gender justice, without the corresponding demand for state protection and the setting up of appropriate institutions. Or civil society organizations can scarcely carry out developmental work without the state providing them with resources, personnel and management. Alternatively, civil society groups fighting, say, violations of civil liberties, will *need* the state to punish offenders, need human rights commissions, sympathetic judges, and a sensitive police for their objectives. Various groups engaged in providing literacy to the people would of necessity look to the state for both funding as well as institutionalizing their efforts in the form of the right to primary and adult education. A number of other such examples could be cited, but the point is clear enough.

In effect, the argument here is that civil society actors will draw upon the state both to reform state institutions—to redress violation of human rights for instance—and to reform civil society itself, for example, through enacting laws restricting sexual harassment in the workplace. This means—and this is a point that is not generally grasped by many advocates of civil society—that the state *frames the limits of civil society, as well as frames social initiatives in civil society.* Even Walzer, with his somewhat romantic view of civil society as 'the setting of settings' and the realm of 'concrete and authentic solidarities' where 'all are excluded and none is preferred', accepts realistically that 'civil society requires political agency'. The state, he agrees, is an indispensable agent, 'Even if', he hastens to add, 'the associational networks also, always, resist the organizing impulses of state bureaucrats'.

(4) Civil Society and Nationalism

However, that associational networks always resist the organizing impulses of state bureaucrats is not clear. For one of the uncomfortable realities of political life is that states not only lay down agendas, but that they employ a variety of means to garner and garnish acceptance, and hence legitimacy, for these agendas. Gramsci, recollect, lent the term 'hegemony' to this in his by now famous formulation. This formulation proves more than apt when we witness the manner in which the current government in India has raised nationalism to a high pitch of hysteria, through the exploitation of first the nuclear explosion at Pokhran 1998 and then the war with Pakistan in Kargil in 1999.

In mid-May 1998, under the Bharatiya Janata Party (BJP)-led government, a nuclear device was exploded in Pokhran. Immediately the country was swept by a powerful storm of 'national pride' at having gatecrashed the exclusive nuclear club. Even as themes relating to the nation, national conceit, and jingoistic exuberance reached absurd proportions,[7] all this contributed towards the consolidation of a belligerent culture, initially propelled by the *Sangh Parivar*[8] since the late 1980s. Members of the *parivar*, for instance, wanted to scatter the dust from the site of the explosions all over the country, till someone pointed out to them that the dust was radioactive and bound to harm. In all this euphoria and games of one-upmanship that overtook civil society, reservations expressed by the anti-nuclear movement that the production of weapons of mass destruction was morally, politically, and strategically suicidal, were brushed away contemptuously, and dismissed as anti-patriotic. There is, in today's nuclearized India, no room for debate. We witness only the imposition of a particularly mindless nationalistic fervour that has been in major measure propelled both by the state and complaint groups in civil society.[9]

Similarly, the discovery in mid-1999 that Pakistan's armed forces had invaded Kargil in India's northern border, was to reinforce the spirit of assertive nationalism. As the country was invaded by the Kargil fever, with hundreds of young men queuing up to go and fight the invader in the north, even as anger against Pakistan erupted in

[7] Prime Minister Vajpayee suggested that we add scientists to the slogan crafted in the mid-1960s of *jai jawan, jai kisan*, which is a slogan that hails the peasant and the soldier. Now it would be *jai jawan, jai kisan*, and *jai vigyan*, the latter being the hindi term for science. It is interesting that the slogan of hailing the soldier had been formulated after the successful war with Pakistan in 1965. That of hailing the peasant was added after the accomplishment of the 'green revolution', which made India self-sufficient in food grains in the same decade.

[8] The *Sangh Parivar* refers to the complex of right wing organizations that subscribe to and propagate the idea of *Hindutva* or majority nationalism, and who believe that the rightful inheritor of the nation is the majority community. These organizations—the Rashtriya Swayam Sevak Sangh or the RSS (of which more later), the BJP as the political wing, the Vishwa Hindu Parishad, and the Bajrang Dal—have been involved in a systematic campaign against religious minorities, on the one hand, and the building up of majority sentiments, on the other.

[9] See the special issue of the journal *Seminar*, No. 468 (August 1998), for a collection of perspectives on Pokhran II.

several unpalatable ways, the rage against our neighbour was displaced to target the Muslim minority in the country.[10] The Kargil incident furthered the already communalized atmosphere in the country to an alarming extent. All this was supremely gainful for the government. For even as discourses in civil society came to be dominated by Kargil, a fertile ground for the BJP to come back to power in the September 1999 election was assiduously prepared. A report on an opinion poll carried in the national weekly *Outlook* was to state before the elections of September 1999 that '[P.M.] Vajpayee, fuelled by Kargil, will be the singular engine of the BJP's return...just seven months ago...Vajpayee was widely pitted as a nice man but a poor P.M. .... Today the nation's collective memory doesn't seem to stretch beyond Kargil; at best, to the bomb'.[11]

The problem is that both the events at Pokhran and Kargil have institutionalized and legitimized a particularly mindless cultural nationalism[12] in India's civil society. Even as this genre of nationalism seeks to cast a strong shadow of suspicion on the minorities within the country, it dismisses those who question the shape of this nationalism as anti-national. Overtaking civil society in India, this nationalism—both exclusive and insular to a frightful degree—strongly bears the imprimatur of the state. Narrow in scope, chauvinistic in content, stereotypical in form, and constructed around the homogenizing impulse, cultural nationalism attempts to accomplish two feats. It seeks to construct majorities and minorities out of a plural, heterogeneous, and loosely articulated society, and it seeks to institutionalize fissures between the two constructed groups on the basis of stereotypes and stigmata. Events at Pokhran and Kargil were to consolidate this. In the process, the BJP-led government has managed to legitimize a deep-seated intolerance in India's civil society, as

10 One of the right wing groups who has enjoyed power in Maharashtra—the Shiv Sena—demanded that the noted and respected film actor Dilip Kumar *prove* his loyalty to the country by returning the sign of honour bestowed upon him by the government of Pakistan, the Nishan-e-Pakistan. It is difficult to escape the conclusion that the fact that he is a Muslim was enough to cast suspicion on his credentials as a 'patriotic Indian'.

11 Ishan Joshi. 'A Wee Swing to the Right', *Outlook* (16 August 1999), pp. 28–9.

12 This was particularly evident in the complete identification of the BJP with the armed forces, who it was widely perceived had made sacrifices for the sanctity of the borders.

evinced in the fact that criminal and murderous attacks on other minorities such as the Christians have grown.[13] And the tragedy is that with some notable exceptions, the majority of the inhabitants in our civil society seem resigned to the prospect of a majoritarian India, even as the possibility of a meaningful debate on such vital issues is foreclosed. Or at least the pendulum has perceptibly swung in favour of cultural nationalism and against democratic ideologies.

Civil societies we will have to accept, albeit with some amount of discomfort, can be organized in ways that are not healthy for civil society itself. Popular support for state sponsored action in civil society breeds somewhat unfortunate consequences for all those groups who oppose the state or dominant trends within the sphere. But theorizations of civil society as an autonomous sphere simply neglect to see how the sphere can be colonized by the legitimizing strategies of the state.

(5) Politics and Power in Associational Life

Moreover, the idea that associational life is always the source of democratic activism, that can be counterposed to the arbitrary state, is one that is riddled with ambiguity. Should we assume that civil society is not permeated with politics and with power, all of which curtails democratic activity in definite ways? Think of patriarchy that consolidates itself in the sphere of civil society and in the household, or the practices of caste, ethnicity, and race that mould interpersonal relationships, or class equations that are always weighted against democratic groups. Or should we assume that politics and power in associational life is not as stultifying as when it is wielded by the state?

---

[13] A series of attacks on Christian institutions in December 1998, was followed by the burning alive of a missionary, Graham Stewart Staines, and his two teenaged sons in Manoharpur in the state of Orissa on the midnight of 22 January 1999, all in the name of *Hindutva*. Whereas the leadership was quick to condemn the brutal killings, they explained them away in terms of resentment against forced conversions. This is laughable when we recollect that despite a long presence in India, Christianity has managed to convert a little over two per cent of the people. It is not mere coincidence that attacks on Christians began to acquire a frequency around the time the BJP settled into power in the central government. In Gujarat, 28 churches were destroyed in one month and this was accompanied by attacks on the community in other parts of the country. See the cover story by Ishan Joshi, 'Mob Rule', *Outlook* (8 February 1999), pp. 12–18.

But as any astute observer will tell us, society itself is riddled with power equations of all kinds—those of patriarchy, class, caste, and religion. Surely in a post-Foucauldian age we should be able to accept this. For society, as Michel Foucault argued when directing our attention away from visible and formalized codes of power, is saturated with power, that is ubiquitous and immanent, and that has neither a beginning nor an end.

The individual is not to be conceived as a sort of elementary nucleus, a primitive atom, a multiple and inert material on which power comes to fasten or against which it happens to strike.... In fact, it is already one of the prime effects of power that certain bodies, certain gestures, certain discourses, certain desires, come to be identified and constituted as individuals.[14]

This individual is not the opposite of power; he is one of its prime effects. The individual whose equality, justice, and freedom civil society is supposed to uphold, is already in himself the effect of a subjugation that is much more profound than himself. If this argument makes sense, then civil society as the associational aspect of society cannot be conceptualized as free from or abstracted from power relationships.

(6) State, Power and Society

There is more a profound issue at stake here. I suggest we will not be able to understand the complexities of civil society unless we understand what the state is. And the state, as Marx was to tell us a long time ago, is not suspended in mid-air from society, so that other spheres of society can function independently of it. It is neither disembodied nor disembedded from the power structures of society, for the *state both condenses as well as codifies the power of the social formation*. If this is so, we need to note that *the power codified at the level of the state is gathered up and condensed from society*. State power, in other words, rests on a constellation of power in society.

Certainly, the state cannot be reduced to power structures in society, for it plays a key role in producing, codifying, and constructing power. The specificity of the state lies in the fact that it codifies

14 Michel Foucault, 'Body/Power', in Colin Gordon (ed.), *Foucault on Power/ Knowledge: Selected Interviews and Other Writings 1972–1977*, trans. Colin Gordon, Leo Marshall, John Mepham and Kate Soper (Brighton: Harvester, 1980), p. 98.

a dominant set of power relations in society, gives to them fixity, and therefore, gives society stability. For instance, in a society marked by proprietors of property, the state will endeavour to secure property rights against those groups who challenge these rights, in the form of, say, laws, or the judicial process that privileges the right to property. The state thus possesses the power to select, categorize, crystallize, and arrange social power in formal codes and institutions. This gives to the state its status specificity and its own distinctive brand of power. In contrast to society where power balances are precarious and unstable, since they are prone to challenges from subordinated groups, the state grants a certain coherence, howsoever minimal, to the power relations of society. As both a concentrate and a codifier of power, the state materializes as a discrete form of power. In effect, since the state through a set of specifically political practices confers fixity to otherwise unstable social blocs in society, society is constituted through the state and exists within the parameters laid down by the state.[15]

However, we also need to remember that this power is not conjured up out of thin air, and that it is always drawn from society, from the nodal points of power relations that define a social order. Any perspective that disregards this is bound to suffer from myopia, for it detaches social and economic from political power. If this is so, then the state as the codified power of the social formation is not detached from civil society where power is expressed and contested, it is the apex organization of power. And if this is so, then civil society cannot be abstracted from the state and defined as a separate sphere. For the two are organically connected through structures of power. The relationship is reciprocal, with the state reflecting the dominant power equation in civil society, and these power equations getting a fresh lease of life through a state that is in complicity with the structuration of power.

(7) The Darker Side of Social Capital

Therefore, all those theories that tell us that associational life is the answer to state power because associations are democratic per se are misplaced because they give us an erroneous picture of civil society. Consider Robert Putnam's celebrated analysis of social

[15] This has been discussed in some detail in Chandhoke, *State and Civil Society*, ch. 2.

capital.[16] Putnam conceives of civil society, in the sense of dense networks of associations, as generating what he calls social capital. Defining social capital as any feature of social relations that contributes to the ability of society to work together and accomplish certain goals, Putnam suggests a correlation between the density of social associations that manage to bridge social cleavage, the creation of civic culture, and strong democracy. High levels of civic engagement, argues Putnam, contribute to the sustaining and fostering of democracy.

This is not a new idea. Civic republican thinkers suggested long ago that the vibrancy of any democracy rests on the cultivation of moral virtue, moral commitments, and the fostering of public spiritedness among citizens. But this is not the thrust of Putnam's argument, for he relies solely on the density of associational life as an indicator of high levels of citizen participation in democratic life. Associationalism produces, according to him, habits of cooperation, trust, social networks, and norms: in sum social capital, which is an indispensable pre-requisite for democracy.

Now, the concept of social capital as originally outlined by James Coleman,[17] had suggested that it is a feature not of individuals but of social relations. Coleman had in effect argued that social capital is context-dependent. Professional transactions among bankers, for instance, will be marked by the norms of reciprocity and trust. The existence of these norms constitutes a resource, since it facilitates financial transactions in society. This resource we term social capital. However, and this is a point we need to register, the banker need not carry trust with him to other social contexts, to land transactions with a crafty property dealer, for example. Outside a specific context, norms and values may not translate themselves into social capital simply because they inhere in particular sets of social relationships. People need not necessarily internalize these values, it is enough that in a given setting they behave according to these values, or behave as they are expected to behave. But, warns Coleman, it is important to note that this capital is unevenly distributed in a society, and not everyone has equal access to it.

16 Robert, D. Putnam, *Making Democracy Work: Civil Traditions in Modern Italy* (Princeton, NJ: University of Princeton Press, 1993); Robert D. Putnam, 'Bowling Alone: America's Declining Social Capital', *Journal of Democracy*, 6(1), 1995, pp. 65–78.

17 James Coleman, 'Social Capital in the Creation of Human Capital', *American Journal of Sociology* (1998), pp. 95–1120.

More importantly, cautioned Coleman, not all forms of social capital are equally valuable as resources to facilitate individual or collective action. The concept, as we can see, becomes a morally neutral category in the hands of Coleman. It can facilitate transactions among a group of fascist organizations as much as it can be employed by a group of human rights activists to the same effect. Further, access to various forms of capital is shaped substantially by inequalities of social location such as race, gender, class, or geography. Neither can we aggregate social capital to produce some measure of the resources available in and to a society. Putnam, on the other hand, attaches normative weight to the concept of social capital by abstracting it from social contexts and attributing it to individuals. He not only reduces the concept to associational life per se; he concentrates on only that form of life that permits civic engagement. Or he limits his focus to that kind of social capital that produces the civic spirit. He thus moves away from Coleman's formulation that emphasizes socially embedded and context-specific resources.

His theory of social capital in general assumes that the more we *connect* with other people, the more we trust them and vice-versa. Generalized social trust in each other, trust in public officials, and tolerance which trust requires as a precondition are integral components of social capital, which has in turn a beneficial effect on citizen participation. Social capital, in other words, is the source of healthy democratic activity that breeds participation.

However, several questions arise at precisely this moment to cast doubts on Putnam's thesis. For one, how do people build trust and reciprocity in associational life in independence from wider contexts? After all, the state can launch projects of political repression, or propel shifting patterns of cultural hegemony, all of which lead to fissures in civil society. Certainly economic disasters can be propelled by the economy. All this can radically alter the balance between groups in civil society even as social conflict over resources can bedevil relations of reciprocity and trust.

Consider for a moment how the politics of 'Mandalization' in India, which by reserving jobs in the public sector for the 'Other Backward Castes' (the OBCs) in addition to the reservations for the scheduled castes, split Indian society irremediably. As the central government headed by Prime Minister V. P. Singh in 1990 implemented the recommendations of the Mandal Commission for job reservations, civil society in India witnessed the onset of immense rage and *angst*. Young people, most of them students, occupied strategic sites in New Delhi's busy traffic intersection, even as they mounted a diatribe against what they called the sheer incompetence and inefficiency of the OBCs. Several young people died as they set themselves on fire in protest. The country was overcome with the politics of wild, disrespectful, and acrimonious protest. Competition for scarce resources had rendered civic life completely uncivil. Rather than trust and reciprocity, we saw nothing but anger and distrust, rendering dreams of social capital into nightmares.

Two years later the Hindu right wing in the country—the complex of organizations known as the *Sangh Parivar*—accomplished their objective of bringing down the Babri Mosque in Ayodhya. The act itself was preceded by large-scale mobilization over a period of at least five years through the utilization of several means: political theatricals, provocative oratory, and spectacles such as chariot processions—the *rath yatra*. The present (at the time of writing) home minister L. K. Advani journeyed through the country in one such car-turned-chariot making impassioned speeches for recovering history by demolishing the mosque, which it was claimed had been built on a temple of God Ram, by the Mughal emperor Babur. As Advani commenced the chariot procession young men offered him a cup of blood signifying readiness to achieve martyrdom. The stage was slowly but surely set for the communalization of India's already fragile civil society, a communalization that has unleashed completely when the mosque was brought down in December 1992. Communal riots said to be the worst since the partition of India in 1947 engulfed the country. We could see no trust here, only the hermeneutics of suspicion and the politics of hate in India's civil society. No civility, but the gradual cleavage of society along religious and caste lines. And all this was brought about through social associations.

Mandalization and Mandirization in India in the 1990s have drastically furthered the fault-lines in the country and created cleavages in associational life. Both these events had somewhat disastrous consequences for civil society even as people who had learnt to live together, despite different caste and religious persuasions, were torn apart by the politics of hatred. We can hardly accept Putnam's assumption that social associations function to further civic engagement, just as we cannot agree with the theorists of civil society and civil society as a third sphere is comfortably bounded off from politics and the state.

Moreover, if we confine our attention only to social associations that are beneficial to civic management, we not only engage in moral irresponsibility, we also achieve a distorted understanding of civil society. For if civil society consists of associational life per se, then we have to accept that associations of every stripe and hue exist in this space. Patriarchal forces exist alongside feminist groups. Religious fascists exist along with movements against communalism. Class oppression exists alongside groups organized to fight for redistributive justice. And pro-state associations that further and strengthen the dominant project of society exist alongside those groups that challenge the legitimacy of the state. Some social groups further civic engagement, other inhibit it, some expand the domain of civil society by bringing in formerly disadvantaged groups, and yet others debar these groups from civic life. For the enemies of democratic life exist in civil society itself, even as groups well organized to make demands and perhaps in a position to have these demands satisfied, strive to impose their mandate upon the sphere.

Let us look briefly at the organization—the Rashtriya Swayam Sevak Sangh (RSS), whose membership, overlapping as it does with the membership of the top leaders of the BJP, currently exercises power in India. The RSS does not tire of telling us that it is not a political but a cultural organization, whose professed aim is to create a Hindu identity that is proudly aware of its cultural heritage. However, the pursuance of this very task makes the RSS the 'fountainhead of aggressive Hindu communalism'.[18] Based upon a firm rejection of the idea that the religious minorities have equal rights as citizens, the RSS and its affiliates subscribe to the views of the founder of modern day *Hindutva*—V. D. Savarkar. In 1923, Savarkar had defined a Hindu as one who regards India as both his Fatherland as well as his Holyland—*pitribhumi* and *punyabhumi*. But this cannot be the case for the Christians and the Muslims, he argues, for their Holy Land is in far away Arabia and Palestine. Therefore, India can never be Fatherland as well as Holy Land for

[18] Tapan Basu, Pradip Dutta, Sumit Sarkar, Tanika Sarkar, and Sambuddha Sen, *Khaki Shorts and Saffron Flags: A Critique of the Hindu Right* (Delhi: Orient Longman, 1993), p. 2. Also see B. D. Graham, *Hindu Nationalism and Indian Politics, The Origins and Development of the Bharatiya Jana Sangh* (Cambridge: Cambridge University Press, 1990); Walter K. Andersen and Shridhar D. Damle, *The Brotherhood in Saffron, The Rashtriya Swayamsevak Sangh and Hindu Revivalism* (Boulder, CO: Westview, 1980).

minorities.[19] By this verbal sleight of hand, the minorities are pushed out of the boundaries of the nation. And the nation we have to accept is one of the constitutive ideologies of civil society. Consequently, civil society has either no place or a subordinate place for minorities.

A highly disciplined, closed, and hierarchical organization, the RSS has silently but surely trained its cadres to work for the establishment of a Hindu state, through attempts to forge a regenerated and strong or machismo Hindu culture throughout the country. Using disciplinary modes such as the morning drill,[20] and participating in what is euphemistically called nation-building activities, the RSS seeks foremost to subordinate the individual to the collective. 'Physical training in the RSS is only the means to the end of a psychological drill leading to a total surrender of individuality to what the RSS likes to call the "ideal".'[21] In claustrophobic small towns marked by a trade cum professional milieu, the authors of the monograph *Khaki Shorts and Saffron Flags* point out, 'any alternative culture seems, quite simply, non-existent: the young men move from communal minded families to schools and colleges full of RSS teachers, and RSS *shakhas* provide, practically, the only other source of recreation, leisure–time socialization, and intellectual training'.[22] Aimed at effecting a fusion between religion and nationalism, the ideology, and the practices of the RSS run completely counter to the values of civil society, values that seek to promote freedom, plurality, dialogue, tolerance, secularism, and democracy.

Internally the body is marked by a complete lack of democracy, the command structure is totally centralized, the ethos is militaristic to an alarming degree and unthinking obedience surrounds its activities. Indeed, when it was set up in the 1920s, Hedgewar, the first president or the *sarsanghchalak*, built the internal structure of the RSS along the lines of revolutionary terrorist groups. Externally, the

---

[19] V. D. Savarkar, *Hindutva! Who is a Hindu?* (Bombay: Veer Savarkar Prakashan, 1969, first published 1923).

[20] This highly ritualized physical training called the *shakha* is performed at identical times by RSS cadres throughout the country. Alongside the enactment of myths glorifying Hindu matyrs who have laid down their life for the country, stories and slogans, the *shakha* trains young men in the art of wielding the lathi or the staff, the sword, the javelin, and the dagger. The ultimate aim is to make the Hindu militantly powerful and aggressive.

[21] Basu et al., *Khaki Shorts*, p. 34.

[22] Ibid., p. 36.

organization concentrating as it does on targeting religious minorities has contributed largely to the communalization of civil society in India. And we cannot regard the RSS as a group which is not of civil society, for this sphere, as theorists like Walzer never tire of telling us, excludes no one and includes everyone. If this is so, we are compelled to conclude that civil society organizations need not be democratic at all, need not subscribe to the values of the sphere at all, and need not heed the calls to counter the state at all. For it is precisely organizations such as the RSS that have prepared civil society for the politics of majoritarianism.

Further, if we were to characterize healthy associational life only on the basis of the thickness of bonds within associations, as Putnam suggests, we realize uncomfortably that the most communal of organizations such as the RSS or indeed minority fundamentalist organizations are characterized by thick bonds of social solidarity. Research on the RSS has told us in great detail how the organization functions in a familial-like structure, concerned with the most intimate details of its member's existence, and intent on cultivating the ethics of care among the members. And certainly the Ku Klux Klan or the Mafia, as any reader of Mario Puzo's remarkable novel *The Godfather* can tell us, is characterized by strong bonds of caring for and nurturing each other.

In effect, if we take as our referent point the idea that social organizations are the reason for civil society to exist, then we have to accept that the sphere contains every kind of group. We can hardly expel, say, the various chambers of commerce from civil society. They are as much a part of civil society as groups of the working classes fighting for a better living. We can scarcely expel groups of agro-industrialists who benefit from the Narmada dam from civil society and admit the Narmada Bachao Andolan (the NBA).[23] But this will mean that civil society, far from being the realm of solidarity and warm personalized interaction, is itself a fragmented, divided, and a hierarchically structured realm. Here we will find organizations of the dominant classes existing alongside organizations of the dominated who are battling for survival; we find patriarchal structures existing

[23] The NBA has launched a massive social movement since the late 1980s in western India against the complex of dams being built on the river Narmada, which has displaced almost a 100,000 people and that promises to displace many more thousands of tribals residing in the area.

alongside women's groups struggling for a place in the sun; we find caste- and race-based groups along with democratic movements fighting for dignity.

(8) Civil Society as Defender of State Power

Civil society emerges in this perspective not as the *site of sociability* per se, though this may well be an unintended consequence of associational life. It emerges as a *site for struggle* between the forces that uphold power equations and those that battle these equations in an attempt to further the democratic project. It is important to realize that dominant groups in civil society, far from constituting a sphere that is oppositional to the state, actually defend and extend state power in the domain of civil society.

COMING TO TERMS WITH THE 'CIVIL' IN CIVIL SOCIETY

If the argument made so far proves to be at all persuasive, then it follows that civil society must be understood in the following way.

First, civil society as associational life cannot be identified with democracy per se. On the other hand, it is a *pre-condition* for democracy inasmuch as it constitutes both a site for democracy and a cluster of values and institutions that are intrinsic to democracy. Let me put this another way. Democracy requires as a pre-condition a space where various groups can express their ideas about how society and politics should be organized, where they can articulate both the content as well as the boundaries of what is desirable in a good society. Correspondingly, individuals and groups should possess the right to conceptualize in conditions of relative freedom their notions of the desired and the good society.

The absence of this site would mean the absence of democracy, for it would mean that people do not possess either access to a space, or to the freedom that is necessary for democratic interaction. Imagine a society that calls itself democratic and yet denies to its own people the opportunities to associate in freedom in order to carry out discussions or contestations on what should constitute the good life. That is why in authoritarian states the struggle for civil society primarily demands the consolidation of a space where people in association with others can debate and contest their own versions of the political. It is this dimension of the struggle that is indicated by the phrase civil society 'against the state'.

The achievement is by no measure a mean one. People demand that regimes recognize the competence of the political public to chart out a discourse on the content and the limits of what is politically permissible. Civil society in this instance stakes a claim to autonomy from the state, that people have the right to associate with each other, that this right should be recognized by the state, and that the state should institutionalize this natural right in the form of the legal freedom to associate. Correspondingly, civil societies have demanded the institutionalization of this right in the shape of the rule of law, rights, justiciability. All this may be necessary but not enough for democracy.

For one reason, formal democracy as critical theorists have pointed out in great detail can prove an illusion. Freedom and rights can mean the freedom of the propertied classes to carry out their projects of exploitation. Freedom can enable fascist groups to communalize society. The rule of law can be employed by amoral leaderships to debar substantial chunks of the people from the rights of citizenship. And the market, as any critical theorist knows, is supremely insensitive to those who cannot buy or who cannot sell. All this can render civil society supremely uncivil and rotten.

Secondly, this does not mean that we dispense with the argument, it merely means that formal democracy, which the concept is based upon, is supremely insensitive to power equations in civil society. Some groups possess overlapping political, material, and social power; others possess nothing—not even access to the means of subsistence. Civil society, therefore, cannot look only to the state, it needs must look inwards, at the power centres within its domain, which may be in complicity with the state, and battle them.

Therefore, what civil society does afford us is the provision of both a site as well as the values, which can help us to battle with the inequities of the sphere itself. Therefore, if the project of *Hindutva* hegemonized civil society to some extent, civil society also provides a space for anti-communal groups to struggle against this particular formulation, howsoever unequal the battle may seem to be at the present moment.

Thirdly, note that we witness a rather profound transformation in the notion of politics in such and related processes. Politics is not about what the state or the dominant classes do or do not do. In other words, politics is not about the capacity of power to do what it wills with people. Politics is about how ordinary men and women think about, conceptualize, debate, and contest how people belonging to different persuasions, classes, and interests live together in society in conditions of justice and civility.

Let me expand upon this. Politics in one obvious and rather simplistic sense is about competition over state power. Or it is about the decision-making process in the state, about the content of these decisions and about the ways the holders of state power decide the fate of entire societies. This notion would restrict the notion of power to the formal and the visible domain of the state. But at a deeper level politics is about the experiences of everyday life. That is, politics is about how people translate their experiences into the expressive, politics is about how the dominant groups seek to retain their power. And politics is about the struggle of the dominated people to live in dignity. Therefore, civil society and its attendant norms of publicity, accountability, rights, and rule of law becomes a staging ground for a struggle between democratic and anti-democratic forces. We ignore this aspect of civil society at the risk of distorting our understanding of the sphere.

But this makes civil society valuable only as a site and as a cluster of values intrinsic to democratic life. For civil societies are what their inhabitants make of them, always keeping in mind that their thoughts and their social practices will be permeated by the logic of both the state and the market. Civil society is constituted by the politics of power as much as it is constituted by the politics of protest. And it is this aspect of civil society that transforms it, in Hegelian terms, into the 'theatre of history'.

CONCLUSION

This essay has argued that the idea that civil society constitutes an independent sphere of existence may distort our understanding of the sphere. For though we tend to divide spheres of human interaction into segments, and though we accept that human beings act in different ways in different segments, we need to register that these spheres are mutually constitutive of each other. For this reason it is argued that civil society is only ambiguously the source of democratic activism, for we are likely to discover in this sphere structures of power that tie up with the state. Therefore, civil society emerges as a deeply fractured and hierarchically structured domain of social associations.

However, there is some value to the idea of civil society, because it provides the preconditions of formal democracy. And, though formal democracy is not sufficient for our purposes, it is an essential component of social and political structures. For it provides the space for democratic elements both to challenge power equations in the sphere as well as to transform the sphere itself.

But for this we have to accept that it is not enough that there *be* a civil society, or even a civil society that is independent of the state. Civil society is not an institution, it is rather a process whereby the inhabitants of the sphere constantly monitor both the state and the monopoly of power in civil society. Democratic movements have to constantly widen the spaces from where undemocratic practices can be criticized, and for this purpose they have to exercise both vigilance and criticality. They have to be Janus-faced, looking to the state and the market as well as inwards. In the process civil society constantly reinvents itself, constantly discovers new projects, discerns new enemies, and makes new friends. It is not something that once constructed can be left to fend for itself because it is a process. And this is important, for civil society is an essential pre-condition for democracy.

II

Empirical Investigations

13

MARKET REFORMS AND THE EMERGENT CONSTELLATION OF CIVIL SOCIETY IN CHINA*

Gordon White, Jude Howell, and Shang Xiaoyuan

WAS THERE A 'CIVIL SOCIETY' IN PRE-REVOLUTIONARY CHINA?

There has been considerable debate among historians about whether a 'civil society' of any description existed in pre-revolutionary China, concentrating mainly on the phase of rapid social, economic, and political change during the last phase of the Qing dynasty and the Republican period—from the overthrow of Qing rule in 1911 to the revolutionary success of the CCP in 1949. This has been prompted partly by a desire to look for historical precursors of the social organizations which have emerged during the post-Mao reform era, but also for historical precedents for the kind of political mobilization mounted by urban social forces during the Democracy Movement of 1989. Our intentions here are similar and in this section we shall draw on the Chinese and foreign historical literature on this same period,

---

* Gordon White et al. (eds), *In Search of Civil Society: Market Reform and Social Change* in *Contemporary China*, Oxford, Clarendon Press, 1997.

first, to investigate the extent to which intermediate organizations of the type we have identified with civil society can be identified in the late Qing and Republican periods and, second to analyse their character, their roles in society, and their relationships with the state.

The picture is one of diversity and dynamic change. Over the period as a whole one can detect an increasingly complex layering of intermediate associations. The reach of the Qing state was broad but shallow, allowing social space for the operation of a diverse realm of intermediate organizations with a variety of relationships with the state, ranging from outright opposition to playing a bridging role between state and society. These traditional organizations were based on trade, kinship, ethnicity, region or homeplace, religion or cultural/intellectual pursuits. They included organizations of intellectuals (*xueshe* and *shuyuan*), traditional trade organizations (*hangbang*, *hanghui*, *huiguan*, *huisuo*), irrigation societies (*shuihui*), secret or 'black' societies (such as the Qingbang and Hongbang), and complex kinship organizations based on clan or lineage (*zongzu*).

The weakening of the imperial state, commercialization, and the rise of new urban centres in the late Qing period led both to a diversification of associational life as traditional associations adapted and new types of 'modern' association emerged to play an increasingly important role in both politics and social life. Beginning towards the end of the nineteenth century and mushrooming in the first decade of the twentieth century, for example, certain organizations of intellectuals became more active and influential, publishing newspapers, organizing petitions, lobbying officials, and the like. As organizations they embodied both traditional and modern elements, using traditional titles such as *xuehui*, *xueguan*, and *xueshe* and often being based on personal connections or home-regions. In the first decade of this century, new chambers of commerce (*shanghui*) appeared with the stimulus and support of the late Qing government and took on an increasing role in the provision of public services and social governance generally.[1] After the end of the dynasty they

---

[1] From 1902 the number of chambers of commerce at country town level and above grew to 871 according to official statistics. Under this level, there were smaller chambers of commerce in market towns (*jizhen*). One Chinese historian (Zhu Ying 1991: 55) estimates that the total number of chambers of commerce at all levels was probably not less than 2000 by 1912, with approximately 200,000 merchants as members. For an excellent western discussion of the role of merchant associations in the late Qing, see Rowe (1993).

were followed by a plethora of new organizations such as trade unions (*gonghui*), peasants' associations (*nonghui*), bankers' associations (*yinhang gonghui*), and women's organizations[2] which were structured along modern lines following their western counterparts.[3] These new organizations both overlaid and interpenetrated with their traditional counterparts. Old social organizations, such as the intellectuals' academies, trade guilds, secret societies, and kinship organizations, not only persisted but in many cases increased their social influence. The resulting sphere of intermediate associational life was very heterogeneous in terms of its social constituencies, its social roles, and its relationships with the state.[4]

This emerging constellation of social organizations covered wide areas of social life, such as political and public affairs, sports and leisure, various religions, charities, and so on.[5] Most important social groups were involved in social organizations, such as intellectuals, business people, professionals, workers, peasants, women, and even children; among these, chambers of commerce occupied a particularly important position in terms of numbers and influence. Moreover, social organizations operated not only in large cities such as Shanghai and Beijing, but also is many smaller towns, especially in the relatively developed areas in south China.

Given the diversity, and the fact that during the first half of the twentieth century the Chinese political system experienced successive convulsions and transformations, it is impossible to come up with a simple characterization of relations between these social organizations and the state. However, we can discern a broad political dynamic of associational life which divides into two periods according to changes in the relationship between state and society. The first stage was from the beginning of the century to 1927, before the Nationalist regime established its power, and the second stage was the period of

[2] To take newspapers as one indication of their social impact, no less than 110 different kinds of women's newspapers and magazines were published in Beijing between 1905 and 1949. The earliest one was the *Beijing Women's Newspaper* (*Beijing Nubao*) published in 1905.

[3] e.g. the chambers of commerce followed the model of foreign chambers of commerce in the leased territories in China.

[4] There is a vigorous debate among western historians about the relationship between these associations and the late Qing state. For some of the main protagonists in the debate, see Wakeman (1993), Rowe (1993), and Huang (1993).

[5] Ministry of Society (1944).

Nationalist rule on the mainland from 1927 to 1949. During the first stage, the balance of power was shifting away from the state towards society. Social organizations developed as representatives of a rapidly changing and increasingly assertive society, gradually became more independent and in many cases ended up in direct opposition to the state. As one example of gradually growing autonomy, take the case of the chamber of commerce in Tianjin in the late Qing period: this began as an official commercial bureau (*shangwuju*), then became a semi-official commercial public house (*shangwu gongsou*) and finally became an independent merchant organization, the General Federation of Chambers of Commerce (*shangwuzonghui*). The latter joined with merchant organizations in other large cities to establish the Chinese Federation of Chambers of Commerce (*Zhonghua Shanghui Lianhehui*).[6] The rise of chambers of commerce in other cities, such as Shanghai, followed a similar pattern (Zhu 1989: 62). These chambers of commerce played very active roles in certain social movements against foreign business incursion in the late Qing and were a main force in the movement to push the Qing government to establish a parliament and issue a constitution, and the movement for local self-governance. Later, social associations played a powerful role in certain key anti-government movements during the next two decades, notably the May Fourth Movement which was initiated by students' organizations, was later joined by worker and business organizations in Beijing and Shanghai, and soon spread across the country.[7] During the May Thirtieth Movement of 1925, students' federations, business associations, and trade unions jointly organized a large-scale strike in Shanghai and the movement soon spread to other cities.[8]

In all these movements, not only were new types of social organization expressing a powerful and independent political voice, but they were also coming into intermittently radical confrontation with successive governments, sometimes resulting in large-scale massacres. This was an era when the political dynamic of civil society was operating powerfully and the elements of an emerging 'public sphere' were growing stronger (intellectual salons, native-place clubs,

[6] Tianjin Municipal Archives (1992), 2.

[7] Republic of China Centre for the Activities of Popular Organizations (1961), 53.

[8] David Strand (1989: 185–7) describes the participation of 500 groups and associations in the May Thirieth Movement in Beijing in 1925 which were organized according to 'circles' (*jie*) of the city's population.

temples, and teahouses). It was also a period when the differences between social groups were often overshadowed by a joint opposition to governments (and the imperialist governments behind them). This tradition of opposition was to continue over the next decades, partly through popular mobilization in the Nationalist areas against the Japanese and, most powerfully, through the growing communist revolutionary movement which linked together social forces in both cities and countryside. However, at least in the areas controlled by the Nationalist government, there was a counter-trend in relations between state and society. In this second stage, from 1927 onwards, the Nationalist regime changed its political strategy from one which had sought to develop strong social organizations to support its bid for national power to a new one which sought to consolidate its rule by shifting the balance of power towards the state through a combination of repression and incorporation.

Thus social organizations were vetted according to certain official political standards and many of them were suppressed.[9] On the one side, radical organizations were disbanded either peacefully or coercively, sometimes with bloodshed. On the other side, the Nationalist government used laws, regulations, and other methods to incorporate social organisations into the new political system.[10] These efforts at incorporation and subordination intensified during the anti-Japanese war (1937–45). According to the 'Organisational Law of People's Organizations in a Special Period' (1941), political controls were strengthened: by requiring social organizations to be supervised by relevant government departments as well as to register with departments of the Ministry of Society at different levels; by making

[9] e.g. trade unions in Guangdong province were divided into two categories, 'red' and righteous', and in 1927 110 'red' trade unions were disbanded in Guangzhou city, leaving only 'righteous' trade unions to function. In Shanghai, not only were radical trade unions disbanded 1927, but also the independent Shanghai General Chamber of Commerce was reorganized by the Nationalist government in 1931 after four years of conflict with the Shanghai capitalists. (Xu and Qian, 1991: 390–401).

[10] Examples were the Trade Union Law of 1930, the Law of Peasants' Association of 1931, the Law on Chambers of Commerce of 1930, the Organizational Outline of Autonomous Students' Associations of 1931, and laws regulating other social (such as professional, cultural, educational, and charity) organizations. Immediately after the issue of the new Trade Union Law, both the members of trade unions and their members radically declined (Xu 1930: 47).

membership of professional organizations, such as the Lawyers' and Journalists' Associations, obligatory; and by stipulating government involvement in regulating organizational procedures and appointing staff. Table 13.1, based on official statistics from the penultimate year of the anti-Japanese war and covering only the area under Nationalist control, gives a rough idea of the number and kinds of national-level social organizations which had registered with the Ministry of Society (Ministry of Society 1944: 3). Controls were to remain in operation during the period of civil war between the Nationalists and Communists up to 1949.

TABLE 13.1
People's Organizations in the Rear Areas, 1944

	No. of organizations	Members
Total	26,126	5,575,076
Among them:		
Peasant organizations	7139	2,814,970
Fishermen's organizations	102	34,357
Trade unions	3359	885,310
Commercial and industrial organizations	9892	379,624
Professional organizations*	2138	157,437
Social organizations**	3496	1,303,378

Note: Rear areas are areas behind the Nationalist-controlled battlefront.
* including organizations such as associations of doctors, lawyers, nurses, and accountants.
** including cultural, religious, philanthropic, women's, sports, and health organizations, and so on.

Given the complexity of Chinese society's associational sphere and the changes in state–society relations, it is not surprising that the political roles of specific social organizations varied greatly according to sector and over time. While at no point during this period could it be said that they were granted or were able to secure the institutionally guaranteed rights and freedoms characteristic of a liberal democratic political order, certain associational sectors did enjoy varying degrees of autonomy and influence. During periods of political change and turmoil, social organizations operated to increase the voice and visibility of specific social groups, play a gadfly role in watershed political movements, and provide support for competing political parties. Alternatively, social organizations could also act as agents of social governance, particularly business associations at local levels. For example, in some more developed areas, such as Shanghai, Guangzhou, Suzhou, or the North-East, local chambers of commerce had their own courts, budgets, and armed forces.[11] They bore part of the responsibility for looking after local public affairs as an alternative or complement to the government, in areas such as public security, road construction, fire brigades, and poverty alleviation. These and other associations could also act as officially recognized representatives of their constituencies in relations with the state or other social organizations, particularly during the short period of stable Nationalist rule (for example, in negotiations between business and labour). In these situations, the boundaries between the private (*si*) and the public (*gong*) spheres became muddied.

The picture that emerges from this broad-brush survey is of a constellation of associational life which is highly complex, dynamic, diverse, and contradictory. This is exactly what one would expect in the case of a large, regionally diverse society undergoing rapid but uneven socio-economic change and convulsive political transformations. This is an ambiguous and multifaceted associational heritage for the communist era after 1949, with no single pattern of association or of state–society relations to be easily distilled from it. If one were looking for incipient corporatism in an intermediate associational sphere in which government and social organizations intermingled, one could find it in the late Qing or the Nationalist heyday, particularly in relations between local governments and business associations;[12] if one were looking for progressive associations aiming at overthrowing or transforming regimes in power, one could find them, particularly among organizations of intellectuals, workers, and peasants. The attempt to force this heritage into a single mould is probably fruitless and a more nuanced analysis needs a great deal more historical work. At a very general, however, one can highlight the multiplicity of 'sectors' of associational life—traditional, modern, and mixed;

[11] See Strand (1993, 32–3) for details of the armed merchant corps in Guangzhou.

[12] The theme of autonomy and dependence is a central focus of debate about civil society among western historians of China: e.g. see the debate between Huang (1993), Wakeman (1993), and Rowe (1993), concerning the autonomy or not of business associations in the late Qing period.

radical to liberal, conservative, and reactionary; legal to semi-legal and underground; incorporated to autonomous, oppositional, and subversive. One can also discern two patterns of state–society relations: during periods of political decay, to use Samuel Huntington's term (1968), oppositional social movements involving coalitions of organized social groups have arisen to challenge the state and demand reform or revolution; during periods of state reform or consolidation, notably the Nationalist heyday of 1927–37, there have been attempts by the state to create and/or incorporate social organizations within a broad framework of societal regulation and control. At local levels, this resulted in certain associations playing an important role in social governance. Their degree of autonomy shifted according to time and circumstance and, as Rowe (1993: 148) concludes, 'The balance between autonomy and state control was thus never clearly defined, but was in practice the result of a process of continual negotiation.' These general patterns have echoes in the experience of the People's Republic.

CHINESE SOCIAL ORGANIZATION ON THE EVE OF THE REFORMS: THE MAOIST HERITAGE

In the post-Liberation period, the CCP either disbanded or repressed pre-existing forms of social association and established a new institutional system which, intermittent upsurges of organized discontent notwithstanding, prevented the operation of social organizations which could meet our criteria of 'civil society'.

Chinese society on the eve of the reforms had certain distinctive characteristics deriving from its dual character as a modernizing agrarian society organized along state socialist lines. Over 80 per cent of the population lived in the countryside in 1978 while 71 per cent of the labour force worked in agriculture or related activities. Overlaying and reinforcing the sectoral divide between urban and rural economies was a bimodal ownership system of state and collective enterprises: the urban economy was dominated by state and large-collective (quasi-state) enterprises while the rural labour force mainly worked in producer collectives organized on a residential basis. The result was a segmented society which was divided into two homogenous sectors, each with different sets of occupations, levels of income, and conditions of work. This segmentation was enforced by means of pervasive controls over population movement and occupational mobility. In the urban sector, employees tended to stay in the same enterprise for life; indeed, they often married their workmates and their children often inherited their jobs. In the rural sector, peasants were restricted to their home villages through a highly effective system of household registration (*hukou*), which made it very difficult to seek employment in the cities or in other provinces except on a temporary basis. In consequence, Chinese society on the eve of the economic reforms was highly immobile.

While this society contained strong elements of inequality in terms of income, power, and status,[13] Chinese social structure was relatively egalitarian as a consequence of official policies to compress the social structure by preventing the rise of certain groups which would have widened social differentials (such as private business people, urban marginals, or a landless rural proletariat) and to homogenize each existing social group by imposing uniform conditions of work on them and restricting income differentials (for example, through egalitarian policies on wages in industry and workpoints in agriculture). There was also a comprehensive attempt to establish a 'floor' for the population as a whole by providing security of employment, basic welfare services, and some kind of guaranteed income, albeit often at very low levels.

Underlying all this was a distinctive institutional principle, characteristic of state socialist societies elsewhere, the phenomenon of *verticality* whereby all members of society were incorporated into hierarchically organized institutional systems. At the macro level, this was based on centralized bureaucratic 'systems' (*xitong*) emanating from the centre like spokes from the hub of a wheel; at the micro level it was based on the work 'unit' (*danwei*) in the cities and the agricultural collective (*jiti*) in the countryside which encompassed the lives of individuals in comprehensive ways. This principle of vertical incorporation created a system of social 'encapsulation', which restricted the capacity of individuals, institutions, and groups in one system or sector to form 'horizontal' links with their counterparts elsewhere.[14] While certain formal institutional mechanisms were designed to cut across and integrate this columnar edifice, notably the

[13] For analysis of social differentiation in the late Maoist era, see G. White (1978), and Whyte and Parish (1984).

[14] For the idea and operation of social encapsulation, see G. White (1987), Shue (1989), and Vogel (1989: ch. 12).

Communist Party, for ordinary individuals and institutions the main form of lateral transcendence was through informal connections based on personal ties (*guanxi*) between members of different institutional sectors.[15] Overall, the system of institutional control and ideological mobilization was so pervasive that it was hard to see any clear distinction between state and society; the former pervaded the latter like a nervous system pervading a body. To the extent that we can identify points of separation between the two spheres—such as the difference between an ordinary peasant and a commune cadre—these were often blurred and transcended by informal ties and personal networks.

In sum, Chinese society at the end of the Maoist era was relatively homogeneous and egalitarian, highly segmented, vertically encapsulated, and immobile. The state system pervaded and dominated society and there were no clear lines of demarcation between state and society. To the extent that markets create a more differentiated and fluid sphere of 'horizontal' relationships between social actors engaged in autonomous transactions and endowed with power over economic resources, it could be expected that the economic reforms would pose a fundamental challenge to the previous patterns of social organization and state–society relations.

THE SOCIAL IMPACT OF ECONOMIC REFORM: THE SOCIETAL IMPETUS FOR CIVIL SOCIETY

To a considerable extent, these expectations have been borne out by the experience of the reform era. The spread of market relations through the fostering of a private sector and a commercially oriented collective sector, an increase in the autonomy of public enterprises, the introduction of foreign investment, the decollectivization of agriculture and price liberalization have altered the fabric of society, rendering it more complex, fluid, and differentiated.[16] The domestic reforms and the policy of openness to the outside world have created new sources of wealth and alternative avenues of personal opportunity. No longer is it necessary to be a party member or Communist Youth League cadre to advance one's career within the state sector,

---

15 For an analysis of *guanxi*, see Gold (1985).

16 For a general analysis by a Chinese sociologist of changes in the structure and dynamics of Chinese society during the reform era, see Li Qiang (1993).

gain access to higher education, or enjoy access to such privileges as cars or spacious housing. Increasingly these and other social goods can be purchased on the market by those who have taken advantage of the new opportunities on offer. For those with business acumen, skills, and drive the market offers the possibility of making money on a scale and within a time-frame not dreamed possible before. The result has been a growing redistribution of power and resources in society: away from party/state officials towards public-sector managers, private/collective entrepreneurs, self-employed business people, and those with foreign connections or marketable professional and technical skills.

The process of commodification—in Chinese terms, 'marketization' (shichanghua)—of goods, labour, capital, and (to a limited degree) land has led to increasing levels of social differentiation, social and geographical mobility, and social and regional inequality. New groups and strata have emerged with their own distinct interests and sources of wealth: for instance, 'new rich peasant' households in the rural areas, private and 'collective' entrepreneurs in both cities and countryside, and more independent members of 'liberal professions' such as medicine, accounting, and the law. Although the vast proportion of the population have benefited materially from the reforms, some have benefited more than others and there is a widespread consciousness of growing inequalities between regions and social strata. Whilst China now has many millionaires, it also has over 60 million people below the poverty line. While this officially recognized poverty is predominantly rural and limited to poorer regions in the interior, there are also new categories of 'poor' emerging, most notably in the mid-1990s an unprecedented spread of urban poverty estimated as affecting 12 million people.

Chinese society has become more fluid and dynamic in both geographical and occupational terms. People are much more on the move than before and there is much greater interchange between social groups. Urban workers have left their jobs in the public sector to start small business; officials and professionals have left their secure but increasingly unrewarding jobs on the government payroll to seek their fortunes in the private or collective sectors (the phenomenon of 'plunging into the sea', xia hai). The previous controls over population flows enforced through the system of household registration were also breaking down in the 1990s. In consequence, peasants from rural hinterlands have left for local towns and cities creating a growing 'floating population' existing within the interstices of urban life; people from poor regions have moved within and between provinces in search of a better life; and young peasants have been recruited from across the country to work in the Special Economic Zones and other open areas along the coast. The numbers of 'floating population' have vastly increased and the large cities now have large temporary or transient populations. For example, certain areas of Beijing are now called Xinjiang village or Zhejiang village because they are areas where migrants from these provinces are concentrated.[17] In those parts of Guangdong province where large numbers of migrant workers have flooded in from the interior, a new kind of 'class system' has emerged with the migrants forming a 'proletariat' and the local population a 'petty bourgeoisie' (Smart 1993).

These social changes have multiplied potential sources of social conflict and brought feelings of insecurity and discontent among more vulnerable or disadvantaged sections of the population. The *nouveaux riches* have flaunted their wealth through conspicuous consumption of designer clothes, luxury vehicles, and trips abroad. The cellular phone and pager have come to symbolize a new generation of Chinese yuppies while enterprising farmers in the suburban countryside have turned their money into three-storyed houses equipped with air-conditioners, video recorders, and freezers. The cost of weddings has soared in the reform era, with an urban wedding already costing 5000–6000 *yuan* by the mid-1980s. (Davis 1993: 65). The growth of advertising and increasing availability of an ever-wider range of consumer goods have contributed to a change in values and expectations. Materialism, self-enrichment, competitiveness, and individualism have gradually displaced the Maoist principles of egalitarianism, collectivism, altruism, and cooperation. The opportunities to pursue personal interests in the economic sphere and the increasing exposure to western culture and living standards have combined to strengthen the sense and legitimacy of having individual wants. These new influences provide new sources of identity which cut across the rigid categories of the Maoist era and allow new forms of common experience and association.

These changing aspirations have had contradictory effects. On the one hand, there has been a desperate race for riches; on the other hand, as the slower runners have fallen behind, the race has fuelled

[17] *New China News Agency*, Beijing, 14 July 1993.

a deep dissatisfaction and envy, referred to as the 'red eye disease' (*hong yan bing*), reinforcing a traditional suspicion that pursuit of individual interests fosters immorality. These trends have generated social unrest and instability, accompanied by a widely perceived decline in standards of public order and morality. In consequence, by the mid-1990s the Chinese state was facing a more volatile and assertive population and increasingly widespread social unrest in both cities and countryside which was threatening to reach critical proportions.[18]

While Chinese society was becoming more ungovernable, moreover, the institutional capacity of the party/state was declining in tandem. Official corruption was increasingly pervasive, contributing to a generalized decline in the moral authority of state institutions and their legitimating ideology. The party leadership has been unable to create a new version of the official ideology which could adapt to and incorporate changes in social structure and attitudes. The reforms also weakened the key institutions which controlled and encapsulated the population in the pre-reform era: the party apparatus itself, the official 'mass organizations' under its control, and the basic work environment of the vast majority of the population—the 'unit' in the cities and the 'collective' in the countryside. The expansion of the private and 'small-collective' sectors and greater social mobility have meant that a growing number of people are able to fend for themselves outside the state system. This encourages a spirit of separateness and independence and generates a sense of group as well as individual identity. Members of the 'floating population' are also increasingly beyond the reach of official systems of social control. Rural migrants are able to bypass the *hukou* system by staying in makeshift dwellings, the houses of urban relatives, or in rented shared rooms. Numbers have reached such proportions that local neighbourhood offices and residents' committees in the cities are unable to keep pace.

Overall, these changes have created a social soil which is potentially fertile for the growth of new forms of social association. Attitudes towards self, society, and state have changed radically; social groups

---

[18] During 1993 and 1994, warnings about mounting social unrest were increasing on all sides. For one account from an official youth journal, e.g. see Liu Dafu, 'The key to unshakeableness for 100 years is unshakeableness for 10 years,' *Zhongguo Qingian* (*Chinese Youth*), 1 (1993), excerpts of which are translated in BBC, *Summary of World Broadcast: Far East* (hereafter *SWB: FE*), 1668.

and interests have diversified, in the process becoming more autonomous and potentially more assertive in relation to the party/state. Social space for the organization and articulation of social interests has been opened up by a dual process whereby social groups and individuals gain greater independent power over resources on the one hand and the control capacity of state institutions declines on the other. Here one can identify a powerful societal impetus to the emergence of social organizations characteristic of civil society: new types of intermediate association which represent the interests and aspirations of evolving social forces and are a means whereby the latter seek greater autonomy from, and influence over, the party/state. Indeed, as we shall see later, large numbers of new intermediate social organizations have sprouted like bamboos after the rain since the beginning of the reforms. To this extent, the 'market hypothesis' of the emergence of civil society would seem to be viable.

THE STATE IMPETUS TOWARDS CHANGES IN SOCIAL ORGANIZATION

Our research has revealed, however, that analysis of the rise of new social organizations based on a causal sequence of markets→social change→civil society is too simplistic and one-dimensional. While we have argued that there has been a decline in the legitimacy and capacity of the official political institutions and ideology, the reaction of both political leaders and state officials to the reforms has been far from passive. At all levels, they have actively sought to come to terms with social changes, co-opt and co-operate with new social forces, ameliorate, or rein in growing tensions between state and society, channel growing pressures for access and participation, and avert the political danger posed by a decline in governability and control. This has meant a powerful *state impetus* towards reshaping patterns of social association, party reinforcing and partly countervailing the societal impetus.

The political dynamic of civil society during the reform era found expression in an official strategy of political liberalization which decreased the degree of direct politicization of society and provided greater space for intellectual debate, cultural creativity, professional expertise, and economic entrepreneurship. Given our focus on the market dynamic of civil society, however, our particular interest here is in the ways in which state institutions have sought to adapt to the spread of the market economy and the social consequences thereof. There is an official rhetoric which specifies desired changes in the relationship between state and society/economy, based on a series of wide-ranging proposals about the need to 'separate government from enterprise', 'transfer government functions', establish a 'small government, big society', streamline the state apparatus, reduce the number of state personnel and establish a professional 'civil service'. While there has been some patchy progress towards achieving these goals, the actual behaviour of state officials and institutions and the real changes in relations between them and society/economy have been complex and contradictory, diverging in many ways from official intentions. To a considerable extent this reflects important changes in the state apparatus as a whole: a pervasive diffusion and decentralization of power vertically between layers of government and horizontally between departments. Specific governments, agencies, and officials have acquired their own autonomy and intentions and have adapted to central demands for institutional reform on the one side and market pressures and opportunities on the other side in ways which are multifaceted and often creative and 'entrepreneurial'.[19] These changes have involved both formal and informal realignments and intermeshing with emergent social forces. Though we recognize the pervasive importance of the informal/personal dimension of realignments between state officials and social actors, our research has mainly concentrated on formal institutions.[20]

How have state institutions and officials behaved in relation to new types of social association which have emerged along with the spread of market relations? Two aspects of state behaviour are particularly important: repression and incorporation. Certain expressions of organized social opposition and unrest, particularly those resulting from the political dynamic of civil society, have been dealt with repressively, most dramatically in the Beijing Massacre on 4 June 1989. As the conversations of CPP leaders at the time allegedly reveal, they found the political challenge mounted by demands from students and workers for autonomous organizations free from the controls conventionally exerted on 'mass organizations' particularly threatening. For

[19] For discussion of the 'entrepreneurial state', see Blecher (1991) and G. White (1991a).

[20] The work of David Wank (1992; 1995) has been particularly important on the informal, personalistic dimension of state–society realignments.

example, Li Peng is reported as having said: 'If we recognize the "College Students Autonomous Federation" just because the students insist on it, then we will be most likely to recognize a solidarity trade union if the workers insist on their demands, won't we?' Yao Yilin allegedly added that 'Peasants will establish peasants' organizations as well, then China will become another Poland. For this reason, we must never give in.'[21] In this particular, explicitly political form, civil society levelled a rapier at the heart of the institutional logic of Marxism-Leninism. Resort to naked armed force on the scale of 4 June apart, however, repression also takes the everyday forms of selective victimization, constant surveillance, harassment, and the implicit threat of swoops and clampdowns.

But the Chinese party/state has also adapted to new socio-economic realities through a generalized, but disaggregated, process of incorporation. As we shall see, the reform era has seen the emergence of a plethora of new-style 'social organizations' whose origins and relationship to state institutions embody the main elements of a pattern of organized relations between state and social groups which has elsewhere been described as 'corporatism'. The essential elements of corporatism have been defined by Schmitter (1974: 93–4) as follows:[22]

Corporatism can be defined as a system of interest representation in which the constituent units are organized into a limited number of singular, compulsory, non-competitive, hierarchically ordered and functionally differ-entiated categories, recognized or licensed (if not created) by the state and granted a deliberate monopoly within their respective categories in exchange for observing certain controls on their selection of leaders and articulation of demands and supports.

[21] For an account published by the Hong Kong press, see Lin Musen, 'A CCP document reaffirms the Tiananmen massacre', *Cheng Ming*, 1 February 1992, in *SWB: FE*, 1305. Other more reformist, CCP leaders such as Wan Li were allegedly more sympathetic to the idea of autonomous student organizations in 1989: for example, see Lo Ping, 'Wan Li on the June 4 Lesson', *Cheng Ming*, 1 June 1993, pp. 12–13, in *SWP: FE*, 1706.

[22] Another frequently cited definition is that provided by Stepan, based on his work on Latin America (1978: 46): 'Corporatism refers to a particular set of policies and institutional arrangement for structuring interest representation. Where such arrangements predominate, the state often charters or even creates predominate interest groups, attempts to regulate their number, and gives them the appearance of a quasi-representational monopoly along with special prerogatives.'

There are several key elements in this notion of corporatism: (1) it is a specific institutional approach to organizing the relationship between the state and social groups/interests in which the state plays a more or less dominant role in defining and maintaining that relationship; (2) it is a form of 'interest intermediation' in the sense of a specific set of institutional mechanisms designed to channel and represent social interests to the state; (3) the institutions are distinctive in that they are licensed by the state to enjoy a representational monopoly with regard to a specific social group or interest, thereby excluding or marginalizing other organizations making a similar claim; (4) the officially recognized social organizations enjoy a degree of guaranteed autonomy within their demarcated spheres and are also granted special privileges therein, but they must in turn agree to obey certain rules and restrictions governing their activities and structures laid down by the state. It is also commonplace to further distinguish between different forms of corporatism, notably: (a) those in more authoritarian contexts in which the role of the state is overwhelmingly dominant and the relationship with social organizations is heavily top-down—'state corporatism'—and those in more democratic contexts in which social interests have more power and autonomy and there is more give-and-take in their relationships with the state—'societal corporatism' (Schmitter and Lehmbruch 1979); and (b) more 'inclusionary' and 'exclusionary' forms which differ in terms of the range of social interests included in corporatist institutions (Stepan 1978; Pempel and Tsunekawa 1979).[23]

The notion of 'corporatism' has been applied to post-Maoist China, for example, by Unger and Chan (1993), and (1994).[24] The idea is well worth pursuing not merely as a way of describing the institutional

[23] There are several other clarifications of the concept of corporatism which need to be made if the idea is to be at all useful; e.g. as in the case of 'civil society', there is a difference between 'corporatism' as an ideal-type description and as a set of actual institutions which may fall far short of the ideal and, on closer inspection, turn out to be insubstantial or downright rickety. Corporatist institutions differ widely in their reach: some may extend to encompass a large proportion of social interest whereas others may only cover one sector, leaving an unorganized and more 'pluralist' sector outside. Moreover, the specific forms of incorporation may vary in relation to different sets of interests, as Bianchi (1989) has shown in the Egyptian case.

[24] Howell has also discussed the applicability of the notion of corporatism elsewhere (1994a).

dynamics of transition in state socialist societies generally, but also as a potentially new version of a wider East Asian form of state–society co-ordination observed in Japan, South Korea, and Taiwan.[25] However, if one regards 'corporatism' as a comprehensive, national political project consciously and systematically adopted by state authorities, one should be cautious about applying the term too readily to post-Maoist China. Moreover, as we shall see below in our discussion of the 'incorporated sector' of social organizations, to the extent that there is a Chinese form of corporatism, it has been given a distinctive shape by the concrete circumstances of economic reform and the disaggregated nature of the state's response to these. During our detailed analysis, therefore, we prefer to use the less systematic terms 'incorporation' or 'corporatist arrangements' to capture this process.

Repression and incorporation do not exhaust the range of state reactions to its changing socio-economic environment. What has been lacking—and this is important if one is seeking 'civil society' in any fully developed sense—is decisive move on the part of the party/state authorities to recognize the freedom and autonomy of social organizations as an institutionalized principle of the political order. Within this limitation, however, state responses have been multidimensional and have interacted with societal pressures to create a social scene characterized by a wide variety of intermediate organizations which have developed along with and as a consequence of the Dengist reforms. These organizations have different types of relations with a party/state machine which is itself undergoing profound institutional changes. The purpose of the next section is to paint this social scene using a broad brush to provide an overall context for the detailed case-studies which are to follow in later chapters.

THE RISE OF AN INTERMEDIATE SPHERE: THE CIVIL SOCIETY CONSTELLATION

In contemporary China it is difficult to find ideal-type 'civil society' organizations that fully embody the principles of voluntary participation and self-regulation, autonomy, and separation from the state. Though organizations with this kind of potential do exist, they are only able to operate within the interstices or outside the realm

25 e.g. consider some of the contributions to MacIntyre (ed.) (1995).

of state controls and their activities are hampered thereby. Within the official realm, however, the principle of a fully autonomous social organization has not been formally recognized. While the official regulations for the registration of new-style social organizations do go some way towards granting them an institutionalized status by recognizing them as 'legal persons' (*faren*), the registration procedures to which they are subject are highly restrictive. All officially recognized social organizations are thus, to a greater or lesser degree, controlled by and dependent on state institutions. Outside that realm, there are organizations that are excluded from official recognition yet live a limbo life of informal activity; there are organizations that, while disapproved of officially, are none the less tolerated or winked at by the authorities; and there are underground organizations subject to repression. Yet each of these categories of social organization embodies, to varying degrees, the characteristic associational qualities of 'civil society'. This partial and piebald 'civil society' is made up of a complex and rapidly changing social constellation with many layers and many different types of relationship between them and the state.

If we categorize these layers according to the nature of their relationship with the party/state, the range is from what we call 'caging', through (various degrees of) incorporation, to (more or less intermittent) toleration and repression. Let us discuss each category in terms of this gradation.

1. *The caged sector: the mass organizations.* The old-style 'mass organizations' (*qunzhong zuzhi*) of the pre-reform era, namely the All-China Federation of Trade Unions (ACFTU), the All-China Women's Federation (ACWF), and the Young Communist League (YCL), had been subordinated to the Communist Party as the three main 'pillars' of its organized base of social control and support. These organizations had their roots in the pre-Liberation era when the Communist Party operated as an underground organization in opposition to the Nationalist Party. After 1949, as in pre-Liberation days, they were designed to serve primarily as 'transmission belts' between the party and society, communicating party policy downwards and transmitting the opinions of their members upwards, according to the heavily top-down Leninist principle of 'democratic centralism'. Like the party itself, these mass organizations became bureaucratized and their cadres functioned in effect as state officials, appointed and remunerated by the state. As such, they had virtually no organizational

autonomy and any attempt to become more assertive, as in the case of the trade unions in the early and mid-1950s, provoked a political clampdown. During the Cultural Revolution decade, they virtually ceased to exist as organizations even in this highly circumscribed form. Their lack of autonomy leads us to reject any characterization of previous role in terms of 'corporatism', preferring rather the image of incarceration within a rigid Leninist institutional cage.[26]

In the earlier part of the reform era, until 1989, a combination of political liberalization and rapid socio-economic change created both pressures on and opportunities for these organizations to become more assertive in the interests of their social constituencies. In the case of the trade unions and the women's federation, these trends grew stronger in the years immediately before Tiananmen and during this period they responded by seeking greater autonomy and voice in relation to the party. This movement was checked by the conservative backlash after the Beijing Massacre in 1989 and Leninist controls were reimposed on the two organizations. During the years immediately after Tiananmen, both organizations continued to seek to represent the interests of their constituencies, but this time by seeking a closer rather than more distant relationship with the party. However, this relationship was becoming more difficult to sustain in the mid-1990s as the pace of economic reform accelerated and their authority came under increasing challenge from rival organizations—autonomous unions and informal women's groups—which could lay much greater claim to be the 'real' representatives of their members' interests. As of the mid-1990s, these two mass organizations had reached a crucial crossroads: to continue as a subordinate agency of the party or to strike out on their own in search of greater autonomy and credibility.[27]

[26] By contrast, Anita Chan (1993) has argued the applicability of 'state corporatism to the previous relationship between the party and the mass organizations.

[27] In our studies of ACFTU and ACWF in Chapters 3 and 4 of our book *In Search of Civil Society: Market Reform and Social Change in Contemporary China* (Oxford Clarendon Press, 1996), we document this process in detail. As for Young Communist League, it suffered a great loss of political influence and social appeal during the reform era because the Party no longer regarded it as a crucial channel of political recruitment. Moreover, joining the Party was no longer the only way for people to make their way up in society in any case, so the previous role of YCL as a pathway to upward mobility was increasingly obsolete. Official policy

2. *The incorporated sector: the new social organizations.* A new stratum of officially recognized 'social organizations' (*shehui tuanti*) has rapidly emerged at both national and local levels, including business, and trade associations, professional associations, academic societies, friendship circles, sports, recreational, and cultural clubs—a new phenomenon on the Chinese social scene.

In spite of much misleading official vocabulary about their being 'popular organizations' (*minjian tuanti*) and, when describing them to foreigners, 'non-governmental organizations' (NGOs) (*Feizheng Fu zuzhi*), closer inspection reveals a continuum of different mixes between what one might call of the state and the societal element of each organization. All of them have to be officially registered to carry on their activities and all are subject to varying degrees of governmental penetration or control. At one extreme, there is a minority of organizations which are totally controlled by the government (*guanban*) which are essentially extensions of the state machine. One might call them GONGO—'government organized non-governmental organizations'. At the other extreme is a minority of organizations which are not considered important enough to be worth controlling on a continuing basis (usually friendship, recreational, academic, or cultural groups) which operate in ways more resembling NGOs elsewhere. Most social organizations contain a mixture of both components, roughly called semi-governmental/semi-popular (*banguan banmin*) or just 'semi-official'. Overall, as of mid-1994 at least when the last phase of this research was conducted, the state component was predominant within this mix, though there was evidence that the balance was shifting in favour of the societal component.

If judged in terms of our criteria of civil society, these organizations are ambiguous and heterogeneous entities. Rather than constituting an associational sphere which primarily embodies the growing power and assertiveness of social forces emerging from radical market reforms, they are an institutional terrain in which the interests and objectives both of increasingly influential social forces and of still powerful state institutions are interwoven. As such they constitute

---

also encouraged the depoliticization of youth and their involvement in activities—occupational, cultural, and recreational—which they could increasingly obtain on the market and not through the good offices of YCL. It is difficult to believe that YCL has any future whatsoever. For a local case-study of the decline of YCL, see White (1993a).

a socially ambiguous institutional sphere which 'braids' state and society in new and heterogeneous ways.[28] They owe their hybrid existence to a mixture of pressures and motivations. As our detailed analysis will show later, the impetus to form social organizations in the early years of the reform era often came 'from below'—from social groups themselves—and to the extent that their formation was encouraged by the state, it was more often than not the result of decentralized decisions by individual local governments or administrative departments rather than a mere response to official policy signals from the centre. While these decisions sometimes reflected an agency's desire to lessen its administrative burden or expand its operational range, particularly during the 1990s social organizations also provided a convenient home for surplus or ageing personnel at a time when the official staff establishments (*bianzhi*) of government departments were under increasing pressure.

Moreover, although there were early, centrally inspired efforts to use social organizations to manage potentially troublesome groups (such as the rapidly expanding self-employed sector), the main central impetus to rationalize the process on a nation-wide basis came later and mainly reflected a desire to rein in and regulate a process of organizational proliferation which was seen as threatening to get out of control. This did not mean that the new social organizations had been wholly independent or unregulated before; most had been established under the sponsorship of state institutions at different levels of government and had been subject to relatively *ad hoc* sectoral or local regulation. The pressure for national regulation began to build up in the mid-1980s, but was given a strong push by the events of early 1989. In the aftermath of Tiananmen, there was a hasty effort to identify, discipline, cull, restructure, and monitor social organizations through a system of compulsory registration administered by departments of Civil Affairs. The post-Tiananmen impetus was to impose a centralized system of codified, nationally uniform regulations to control the creation and activity of new social organizations.

The major motive behind these regulations was the desire to establish control over a potentially threatening social phenomenon, and in practice the registration process has operated as a powerful mechanism to subordinate and exclude officially unacceptable forms of social organization. However, the imposition of a regulatory

---

[28] He Baogang (1993), calls this organizational sphere 'semi-civil society'.

system has been accompanied by an increasingly explicit official rationale which resembles a more coherent notion of 'corporatism'. This emphasizes the complementarity between social organizations and the state as components of a new system of socio-economic regulation. The noted economist Xue Muqiao articulated this idea systematically in 1988, arguing that in the economic sphere social organizations could 'serve as a bridge between the state and the enterprises' in a new form of 'indirect regulation and management of the economy which avoided both the previous deficiencies of Stalinist directive planning and the future dangers of anarchic markets (Xue 1988). In retrospect, this can be seen as a counter-argument to a view of social organizations current in the mid-1980s which emphasized their democratic potential.[29] A corporatist construction of social organizations is thus a conservative notion, emphasizing social stability, regulation, and harmony, which has gained currency during the 1990s. In the industrial sphere, it has become part of a general movement to 'transfer the functions of government organs', whereby social organizations become in effect an intermediate level of an integrated system of economic governance linked with the state on one side and enterprises on the other. Movement in this direction (notably the transformation of certain central light-industrial ministries into 'general associations') has brought China to resemble the pattern of state–business relations characteristic of other East Asian economies, notably those of Japan and South Korea. Indeed, Japan has been cited as a positive model for emulation by Chinese policy-makers.

Whether we use the term 'corporatism' or not, however, the undeniable strength of a 'state impetus' towards incorporation during the reform era has contributed to the formation of a burgeoning stratum of intermediate social associations which embody the forces and interests of both state and society. While official recognition of 'social organizations' has been a force for co-optation and control, it has also operated as a screening device to exclude organizations seen as unnecessary, unacceptable, or threatening. Thus the 'incorporated'

---

[29] For example, see 'Social organizations are an important force for establishing a socialist democratic system, *Renmin Ribao* (*People's Daily*), 29 April 1988, cited in Shue (1994: 87). Social organizations were also an important part of the plan for a 'big society' to counterpoise a 'small government' devised by Liao Xun for implementation in the new province of Hainan (Brodsgaard 1993).

sector must be set within the wider context of a 'counter-world' of alternative organizations which is already in existence and expanding rapidly. It is to this world that we turn in the next two sections.

3. *The interstitial, 'limbo' world of civil society.* Particularly during the period leading up to Tiananmen and in the early to mid-1990s when the pace of economic reform accelerated, there was a rapid growth of urban associations which have either not achieved formal official recognition or have achieved it only through connections with sympathetic agencies or individuals. One dramatic example was the growth of 'salons' of intellectuals in 1988–9 which provided much of the thought and some of the organizational initiative behind the political mobilization of early 1989. These operated through informal connections and meetings and intermittently through formal public events such as conferences and seminars. In the early 1990s, this type of informal association took a less explicitly political form, and operated through an increasingly dense system of networks of likeminded people (such as journalists, artists, rock musicians, homosexuals, artists, martial arts specialists), often focusing on specific locations such as clubs, karaoke parlours, dancehalls, and bars as well as private homes. For example, one particular areas of expansion was that of women's groups. Some of these have been organized formally and found shelter as 'second-level associations' under the formal auspices of an officially recognized social organization; others have been encouraged and protected by the official Women's Federation. But the early 1990s have also seen the emergence of informal, unrecognized women's groups without official sponsors, small salons which meet to discuss issues specific to women. Other interstitial associations include those in formation which are intending to seek official recognition, those that are having difficulty obtaining registration and those that have failed the registration procedure.

While the above phenomena would be characteristic of cities and larger towns, the rural areas have also seen a proliferation of semi-formal and informal associations throughout the reform era. These include traditional organizations based on lineage and clan, or ethnic group; Buddhist and Daoist religious groups based on existing, reconstructed, and new temples and shrines; informal local 'cliques' and brotherhoods; and local-place associations (*tongxianghui*), some of which have been transplanted to the cities where they provide an organizational basis for rural migrants. Some of these organizations have caused concern to the local authorities: for example, when disputes between single-clan villages have led to armed fights between them;[30] when traditional religious practices have interfered with state policies (such as that of encouraging cremation over burial); or where local 'cliques' and brotherhoods have become involved in gambling and other forms of crime. However, it is very common for local authorities, including party officials, either to wink at the resurgence of these pre-revolutionary forms of association, or actively to support and even participate in them. Local officials may use these ties to strengthen their own authority and build up their locality. For example, party officials in Muslim areas may promote religious revivals to benefit from preferential policies or to encourage potentially lucrative contracts with Islamic countries in the Middle East. Entrepreneurial local officials in coastal provinces with large migrant populations overseas use *tongxianghui* to encourage business contracts and attract capital from overseas Chinese.[31] These pre-revolutionary forms of social association do constitute a growing organizational sphere which embodies the basic characteristics of 'civil society'. However, as in the case of urban social organizations, relationships between them and the local state vary a great deal, ranging from mutual suspicion and uneasy coexistence to active co-operation and mutual support.

This interstitial pattern of association was becoming denser in the mid-1990s and its growth more rapid, fostered by the breakneck pace of economic and socio-cultural transformation during this period. It constitutes a kind of associational 'counter-culture' in waiting. In the cities, the key role in its expansion is being played by members of the intelligentsia and emergent professional strata, groups whose potential social influence is increasing as they become more integrated with the world of business through their growing propensity to 'plunge into the sea' of commerce and industry.[32] The emergence of

---

[30] For example, an official in the Judicial Department of the Zengcheng country government in Guangdong province, interviewed in March 1994, admitted that fights between single-clan villages posed a threat. For a Chinese account of rural kinship organizations, see He Qinglian (1993).

[31] This practice was recently observed by Howell in Fujian province in the late 1980s and by White and Shang during a field-visit to Zengcheng country in Guangdong province in March–April 1994.

[32] For analyses of the relationship between intellectuals and the emergence of this new associational sphere, see Kelly and He (1992) and Bonnin and Chevrier (1991).

this associational sphere not only reflects the increasing diversity and assertiveness of these and other social forces, but also suggests that the social space they occupy is expanding beyond the ability of the party/state to control. Although they are subject to periodic harassment, one can argue that by the mid-1990s the trend was becoming irreversible.

4. *The suppressed sector: underground civil society.* This sphere consists of organizations subject to active repression or punitive surveillance. It is highly diverse, including a wide variety of political and social organizations as well as secret societies and other criminal organizations. The form and degree of official repression vary. In some cases, it involves monitoring, with coercive action kept as an option in reserve. A document reportedly issued by the CCP in mid-1992, for example, drew attention to the rise of 'spontaneous mass organizations which were neither officially reported to nor sanctioned by government organs' which required close surveillance. These included organizations such as the All-China Qigong Association, the National Alliance of Demobilized Servicemen of the Rural Areas, the Association of Urban Unemployed, and the Association of Individual Households. While these kinds of organization do not pose an explicit threat to the regime, they are perceived as potentially dangerous because they have been organized independently and embody groups which could potentially cause trouble (notably demobilized soldiers who have a long history of self-organization and public activism, going back to the Hundred Flowers Movement).[33]

Other organizations are classified as hostile agencies and are rigorously suppressed by the security services. Many of these are the heritage of the repression of 4 June and its aftermath, when governments in Beijing and other cities took steps to identify and suppress organizations involved in the mobilizations of early to mid-1989.[34] However, there was already an accumulation of banned organizations before 1989 and others have appeared since. An internal document issued by the Ministry of Public Security in 1993 and leaked in the Hong Kong press, reported that over the period from June 1986 to September 1992 the public security forces had banned 1370 'illegal organizations of all kinds' and a further sixty-nine had either

[33] Yang Po, 'CCP takes strict precautions against 'rebellion' by non-governmental mass organisations', *Cheng Ming*, 8 June 1992, in *SWB: FE*, 1409.

[34] For a valuable survey of these organizations, see Walder (n.d.).

voluntarily disbanded or surrendered to the police. In spite of these measures, however, the document reported that illegal organizations were still spreading 'like a prairie fire'. It directed particular attention to sixty-two 'hostile forces opposing the socialist system', which included political and social organizations from the 1989 Democracy Movement (such as the National Autonomous Federation of Workers), and assorted 'ultra-leftist reactionary' organizations, relics of the Maoist period, with names such as the Defend MaoZedong Doctrine Alliance and the Jiangxi Red Uprising Column. The list also included regional/ethnic organizations such as the Xinjiang Justice Party and the Independent Party of Inner Mongolia and religious organizations such as the China Christian Association and China Catholic Association.[35]

Religious sentiment spread rapidly in the early to mid-1990s in both urban and rural areas. Public opinion surveys reported an upsurge of interest in religion, particularly among young people. Religious organizations have proliferated in the early to mid-1990s—Christian, Islamic, Buddhist, and Daoist—and the authorities responded with a mixture of repression, toleration, and attempts to incorporate them into the officially recognized religious bodies. Many of these organizations belong to the interstitial sector, but there has been a rapid spread of underground 'spontaneous churches' which the authorities have attempted to crack down on, with limited success.[36] Regional policies towards grass-roots religious organizations have varied significantly, with authorities in Guangdong apparently showing more tolerance than those in other provinces such as Sichuan which have been more repressive.[37]

There has been a comparably rapid spread of secret societies and other criminal fraternities and gangs. A circular reportedly issued by the Ministry of Public Security in 1992 claimed that there were over 1830 underworld organizations of various types, some of them having

[35] 'On cases of underground illegal organisations cracked and banned or surrendering themselves to the police over recent years', reported in *Cheng Ming*, Hong Kong, 1 January 1993, in *SWB: FE*, 1581.

[36] For attempts to control national-level religious organizations, see Lu Yusa, 'Tension in spring—utmost 'solicitude' is shown for national churches', *Tangtai*, Hong Kong, 15 June 1994, in *SWB: FE*, 2028.

[37] For the Sichuan case, see *Zhongguo Xinwenshe* (*China News Agency*), Beijing, 25 March 1993 (in *SWB: FE*, 1964) which reports a change of policy in the direction of religious liberalization after a decade of conflict and repression.

as many as 30,000 members and operating not only across regions but also internationally, particularly through co-operation with Triad organizations in Hong Kong.[38] These organizations are regarded as dangerous not merely because of their characteristic involvement in vice and crime, but also because of their overseas connections and their sporadic political involvements (for example, in smuggling Democracy Movement activists out of China after 4 June).

In general, illegal organizations have spread rapidly in the early to mid-1990s and have clearly outrun the capacity or the inclination of the authorities to control them. Some of them, such as the criminal secret societies, would be illegal under any form of political system, and some, such as remnant 'ultra-leftist' and Democracy Movement organizations, represent a clear political challenge. However, like their interstitial counterparts, many of them represent the associational urges of a rapidly changing society which is increasingly restless and resentful of restrictions. The regime faces a catch-22 situation. On the one hand, suppression is increasingly unfeasible and, even where effective, is often counter-productive; on the other hand, toleration will allow a widening range of organizations to increase their influence and exert stronger pressures for official recognition, thereby undermining the party/state's capacity to maintain its institutional monopoly over society. This catch-22 provides a powerful political dynamic towards not only the formation of civil society in terms of new, more independent social organizations, but also towards pressuring the authorities to change the political framework to provide some form of institutionalized guarantees for their existence and operational autonomy.

SOME CONCLUDING REMARKS ON THE INTERMEDIATE SPHERE

One can argue strongly that there is a strong and growing intermediate sphere of social association in China which embodies, in different ways and to differing degrees, the basic characteristics of a 'civil society'—those of voluntary participation and self-regulation, autonomy, and separation from the state. It is equally true that this

---

[38] 'Circular on Resolutely Banning and Cracking Down on the Organisations and Activities of Secret Societies', reported in *Cheng Ming*, Hong Kong, 1 May 1992, in *SWB: FE*, 1385.

organizational realm is partial and incipient in the sense that many of the organizations described to not embody these characteristics to the full, nor do they operate in a political context which guarantees them the right to do so. This emergent associational universe is very diverse, containing sectors which are both 'traditional' and 'modern', urban and rural, national and grass-roots, political and non-political, progressive and reactionary, liberal and ultra-leftist, open and underground. These associational sectors also vary widely in the types of relationship they have with the party/state, ranging across a wide spectrum from the caged, through the incorporated and interstitial, to the suppressed sectors. There is a kind of 'core–periphery' arrangement with a relatively well-integrated, but increasingly restless core of caged and incorporated associations, and a large and rapidly growing periphery of associations which are relatively fragmented and are kept so by non-recognition, surveillance, and repression. To this extent, there is no simple or single way of characterizing relations between the state and social organizations.

The sociological conception of civil society has its limitations as a description of current Chinese society. It tends to provide partial and static snapshots which blind us to important elements of the reality and cannot capture the dynamics of a rapidly changing social universe. Though we found evidence of new forms of association characteristic of an emergent civil society which the central hypothesis suggested, we found that this was but one part of a broader, more complex, and contradictory process of institutional change. The dichotomous ideal-type model of civil society may be useful in framing general questions about the nature of specific social organizations, but it ill accords with our finding that the defining characteristics of civil society vary along an associational continuum rather than being sharply delineated along yes–no lines. Moreover, social organizations in the burgeoning incorporated sector constitute an institutional terrain in which state and society are intermingled and braided, blurring the distinction between them. That said, however, it is too hasty to dismiss the paradigm of civil society as some misplaced product of allegedly western dichotomous thinking. Although the organizational realities are not dichotomous, the substantive issues raised by the idea of civil society—the importance of organizational autonomy and voluntary membership—are clearly important to Chinese observers. For many Chinese interviewed, the recognized social organizations are lapdogs of the state and cannot be described as popular organizations (*minjian tuanti*), the latter term being reserved for truly independent associations in the interstitial and illegal sectors. As such, the ideal-type notion of civil society which we put forward at the outset as a potentially useful interpretative framework for assessing the social and political substance of intermediate associations is in fact shared by both external researchers and internal participants.

As a structural analysis, however, the civil society paradigm does focus one's attention too exclusively on formal associations and needs to be situated within a wider awareness of the dense networks of informal relationships which pervade both state and society. The relationship between the formal and informal spheres of association is crucial in understanding how relations between state and society have evolved over the past two decades. We have shown how the recognized social organizations have constituted a terrain in which state institutions and social groups have overlapped and interpenetrated in different mixes, from official to semi-official to popular. Along with this has come a far more pervasive and influential form of interpenetration between state officials and social actors through personal connections. In analytical terms, this process further weakens the relevance of the public–private distinction embedded in the paradigm of civil society. In practical terms, it provides the sociological basis for the spread of corruption during the reform era. It is too simple to see this in terms of personal morality. One should also see it as a systemic consequence of the failure to establish new forms of institutionalized interaction between state and society in a period when the need for these was increasing at an exponential rate. One can argue that these personal connections and the corrupt behaviour they may embody represent the costs of not allowing the development of a richer and more independent realm of formal associations. It is not surprising, therefore, that the extent of corruption increased when the scope of associational life was restricted after Tiananmen, notwithstanding increasingly desperate official campaigns to stamp it out. From this perspective, corruption is a by-product of associational repression and this connection bears out some of the arguments made by those who stress the political virtues of a formal, institutionalized civil society as a potential source of pressure for clean and accountable government.

To understand the development of civil society in contemporary China, moreover, we need to go beyond a structural analysis to investigate the dynamics of the process. The shifting constellation of intermediate associational life described above reflects the operation of both. The market dynamic has opened up socio-economic space, endowed social actors with resources and the power to use them, created the basis for new horizontal forms of social interaction and weakened the vertical controls embodied in the old institutional regime. This process is visible both in the cities and in the more dynamic rural areas. The political dynamic has fluctuated over time between periods of relaxation and restriction, respectively encouraging and repressing the impulse towards the formation of intermediate organizations. During the early years of the reforms, the new atmosphere of political relaxation was particularly crucial both in allowing the resurrection of previous social organizations, such as the trade unions, ACWF, and the Federation of Industry and Commerce, but also in encouraging the emergence of new ones. By the mid-1980s, the two dynamics were beginning to reinforce each other as new market-based forces—particularly urban small-scale business, larger-scale private enterprise in the more dynamic coastal cities, and commercial agriculture and small-scale industry in the countryside—helped to underpin a proliferation of new forms of social organization and to maintain a relatively liberal political atmosphere. From 1989 onwards, however, the two dynamics came into conflict as the conservative post-Tiananmen leadership sought to rein in the perceivedly threatening associational impulses of the earlier phases by means of incorporation and repression. As the economic reforms regained their momentum from early 1992, the market dynamic of civil society intensified and came into conflict with a regime which had scant interest in political reform. The result was an increasingly tense situation of associational repression with two types of consequence: first, the state's attempt to control existing social organizations by maintaining controls over mass organizations and subjecting new social organizations to a strict system of registration sapped their institutional vitality and undermined their social credibility; and, second, through its regulatory and repressive apparatus, the state marginalized or drove underground many genuinely popular associations.

The associational repression of the post-Tiananmen era operates in different ways for each layer of associations, depending on the specific nature of its relationship with the party/state. Each layer has its own particular dynamic: the institutional prisoners in the caged sector are facing increasingly strong pressures to choose between autonomy and dependence; the balance of power within the incorporated layer is shifting gradually in favour of the societal component; and the interstitial and illegal layers are nibbling away at at the state's capacity to control and coerce. These movements suggest the image of tectonic plates shifting before an earth tremor. In their different ways, these two dynamics are moving in a direction which presages major changes in the balance of power and the nature of the relationships between state and society in contemporary China. The party/state's coping strategy—a combination of incorporation and repression—has channelled and staunched the rise of organized social forces, but also proving increasingly problematic as the pace of socio-economic change accelerated in the mid-1990s.

TOWARDS CHINESE CORPORATISM?

The political resistance to the market dynamic of civil society went beyond fluctuations between liberal and conservative phases in CCP policy. The political response involved a deeper impetus on the part of institutions throughout the state apparatus towards shaping and controlling the emergence of intermediate organizations. Our research made us realize that our initial focus on the emergence of civil society was one-sided in that it diverted attention away from changes in the structure and behaviour of the state. Indeed, at times we felt that we had set out in search of civil society only to find corporatism. State institutions have responded to the new socio-economic environment resulting from the reforms not only by refusing to let the old mass organizations off the leash, but also by attempting to create and/or co-opt new social organizations. Registered associations were penetrated by the state and social organizations more truly characteristic of civil society were marginalized or repressed. Yet is this 'corporatism' worthy of the name, and, if so, is it taking a distinctively Chinese form?

It is true that we have found processes operating at all levels of the party/state system that embody central elements of the conventional corporatist practice. As the state's partner in an emerging institutional nexus, the officially recognized social organizations do exhibit many features of corporatist model. They are regarded by state agencies as a bridge between themselves and specific social sectors; they enjoy a representational monopoly in their particular sphere; they receive certain privileged benefits from the state, but must in turn fulfil certain responsibilities; they enjoy a more or less limited degree of autonomy which is delineated and policed by state agencies. It is true that this formal system co-exists with and is much less influential than the informal ties between state and society based on personal connections, but then this coexistence is a feature of other corporatist systems in East and South East Asia (MacIntyre 1994: 4). Yet we are still uncomfortable about referring to 'Chinese corporatism'. If there is a Chinese corporatism, it may well be a rickety and piebald phenomenon, for several reasons.

If we accept that corporatism is usually a matter of institutional design by state élites with certain conscious aims, this accords to some extent with Chinese experience in that the sponsorship of a certain stratum of social organizations does reflect a conscious response on a the part of political and administrative élites to the new environment created by market reforms. Many of these organizations, such as professional and academic associations, are one consequence of a strategic political decision to grant greater recognition to, but still retain control over, increasingly influential professional strata. Others reflect a generalized attempt by the party/state to come to terms with growing sectoral differentiation in the economy and the rise of new economic forces such as self-employed, new-collective, and large-scale private business people.

However, this does not mean that there has been a systematic and clear-minded attempt to establish a form of socialist corporatism as part of the reform programme. The process of incorporation has been much more incremental, disjointed, implicit, and haphazard than that. The overall impulse towards incorporation is by no means consistent; it reflects four overlapping but also potentially conflicting rationales which motivate state behaviour: (1) a political rationale reflecting the desire to co-opt rising social forces and control a growth of associations which could pose a threat to the political status quo; (2) a managerial rationale aimed at creating new institutional mechanisms to regulate an increasingly complex and fluid socio-economic system; (3) a developmental rationale seeking to involve emergent socio-economic forces in programmes of state-led economic growth;[39] and (4) a bureaucratic rationale which reflects the institutional

---

[39] Jean Oi (1992) has provided a valuable analysis of the politico-economic motives underlying local state corporatism in China.

responses of specific state agencies to the contradictory pressures of economic reform. While each of these rationales operates at all levels of the political system, they also operate in uncoordinated and dispersed ways which both reflect and intensify fault-lines within that system. Thus there are powerful impulses towards local or community corporatism, from the large city down to the small rural town, which may fuel conflict with higher levels and intensify competition with other localities. Similarly, the pervasive impetus towards departmental corporatism at all levels can serve to impair the coherence of governments, helping to convert them into a conglomeration of competing bureaucratic bailiwicks. Thus the various modes of incorporation operate both to integrate and to disarticulate the operations of the party/state. It is corporatism of a fragmented and fragmenting kind, which reflects the increasingly fragmented, pluralist nature of the Chinese state system as a whole.

Thus it is misleading to talk of the emergence of a Chinese corporatism as a conscious and coherent project. The idea of incorporation is not a central element of the overall ideological framework of the socialist market economy; the process of incorporation is only one element in a more complex restructuring of relationships between state and society/economy and not the most important at that; the incorporation of social organizations at the national level is weak and across the country the commitment to incorporation is uneven across sector and region. Moreover, to the extent that there is a consistent thrust to incorporation, the process is not only highly statist but also very selective and exclusionary. Only a relatively small stratum of associations make the grade and other forms of association are excluded. The registered social organizations are like a thin layer of marzipan on a very large cake.

Nor can we speak of a Chinese corporatism as some stable institutional *fait accompli*. Both state and society are in flux and the relationships between them are constantly changing. Comparative experience suggests (for example, Bianchi 1989) that corporatist systems are hard to establish and prone to instability and disintegration. In the Chinese context, there is a constant tension between official regulations and the changing reality of social organizations and society, the latter acting constantly to render the former obsolete. For example, the requirement that there should be only one association of its kind in each area is often challenged by competing associations and officially designated monopolies are increasingly being undermined by the rise of second-level associations which attach themselves to a first-level host association. Similarly, it is increasingly difficult to maintain departmental corporatism in a situation in which market participants are expanding outside the traditional reach of a department and relations between them are becoming more competitive. These pressures are weakening any effort towards a more systematic corporatist project even as it begins to take shape. It is here that the contradiction between the horizontal market dynamic of civil society and the vertical institutional logic of the previous system is particularly visible.

Moreover, there is evidence that the balance between the (now dominant) state and the (now subordinate) societal components of recognized social organizations is shifting in the mid-1990s. Government agencies at all levels are trying to reduce the burden of supporting social organizations financially, prompting the latter to make an effort to find their own sources of revenue and become more autonomous as a matter of institutional survival. This involves setting up their own business, exploiting any real estate at their disposal, and providing paid services to their members. These new activities in turn push them to be more sensitive to the needs and interests of their own social constituencies and, because less dependent on the state, less beholden to it. The associations we studied clearly varied in their ability to do this and there is likely to be a shake-out as the more fortunate and entrepreneurial organizations gain strength and the more flaccid or ill-situated ones wither on the institutional vine. The fittest which survive are likely to have an institutional capacity and resilience which bodes well for their longer-term future.

As the extent of government control over social organizations gradually recedes, moreover, the power of social interests is increasing, a phenomenon particularly visible in the spheres of private business and the professions. For example, the growing influence of trade associations is visible, particularly in the localities, in both the urban and rural areas. These can provide tangible benefits to their members in terms of access to state agencies, market information and promotion, business contracts, prevention of 'unfair' competition, establishment and monitoring of standards, technical services, and the like. The rising power of the liberal professions is also visible: for example, lawyers are increasingly moving out of government service to establish their own private partnerships and the number of lawyers is expected to double (to 100,000) by the year 2000. Private medicine and education are also expanding rapidly.[40] Semi-official and private newspapers and journals have also proliferated over recent years, outrunning the capacity of the state to control and regulate them, and journalists have become increasingly vocal in agitating for greater freedom and legal protection.[41]

All these trends may be gradually converting the recognized sector of social organizations into associations of a more civil nature. To the extent that corporatist controls are maintained, this would imply a transition from the state corporatism to societal corporatism. However, this changing balance may undermine the very basis of incorporation itself, opening up the possibility of a proliferation of alternative and competing organizations which arise to challenge the current associational monopolies. Given the escalating difficulties in maintaining monopolies over a socio-economic system which is increasingly complex, competitive, and volatile, this latter scenario would hardly be surprisingly.

CIVIL SOCIETY AND POLITICAL CHANGE

We have identified an intensifying process of associational repression which has been gaining force since the clampdowns after Tiananmen. Pressure from social groups to have their voices heard and to form their own associations have mounted throughout society, but they have not yet found adequate channels for expression. Part of the tragedy of Tiananmen was that it marked a lost historical opportunity—comparable to the repression of the Czechoslovakian reforms in 1968—to allow social organizations to operate as agents of gradual social and political democratization within a continued one-party framework. Instead of being harbingers of democracy, however, recognized social organizations were converted into another echelon of state control. The tension between state and society has increased in consequence and associational repression has given rise to increasingly pervasive outbursts of spontaneous activity—demonstrations, riots, protests, sit-ins, beatings, and fights—in both urban and rural

[40] For a report on the expansion of private schools in Beijing, e.g., see the report in *NCNA*, 23 March 1994, in *SWB: FE*, 1984.

[41] For a report on the demand for legal protection by journalists in Guangdong province, see *Lian He Bao*, Hong Kong, 10 December 1993, in *SWB: FE*, 1872.

areas. The image of a boiler building up a dangerous level of steam pressure is an apt one.

What are the implications of these trends for the question we raised at the outset about the relationship between the rise of civil society as a sociological entity and the establishment of a civil society in the sense of a political society which legitimizes the free operations of social associations through the rule of law and guaranteed civil and political rights (in effect some form of liberal democracy)? Have the associational consequences of market reforms created pressures for redefining the relationship between state and society through political reform and can these pressures be the basis for constituting a democratic polity? The sociological civil society we have identified has an ambiguous political potential. It contains the seeds of both political construction and collapse. On the one hand, state and intermediate associations continue to intermesh through the official mass organizations and the incorporated social organizations. On the other hand, the tensions between an authoritarian state and the burgeoning interstitial and illegal sectors of civil society are mounting and the capacity of the state to manage them is dwindling. The former scenario offers the possibility of a gradual political evolution whereby recognized associations gain greater political autonomy and social credibility, and the range of legitimate associations gradually widens. In this scenario, there would be a gradual convergence of the four associational sectors into an institutionalized form of civil society in which rights of social association are guaranteed and protected. The latter scenario points towards the prospect of an increasingly acute and generalized political struggle between state and society leading to some form of takeover or collapse rather than an orderly transition to an alternative, more democratic polity.

The current character of China's incipient civil society poses problems for a smooth political transition because it is so diverse, fragmented, and potentially destabilizing. To this extent, civil society is as much of an obstacle as an impetus to democratization. For example, too many officials in the old mass organizations are unwilling to break the umbilical tie with the party and they thereby lose credibility in eyes of their constituencies; and too many leaders in the registered social organizations are unwilling or unable to seek greater autonomy from their state sponsors and assume greater accountability to their members. So long as these associational sectors remain so deeply enmeshed with and dependent on the state, they will be an obstacle to political reform; the gap between them and the underclass of interstitial and illegal organizations will widen and the possibilities for peaceful and stable political transition will be weakened. In the event of a collapse of the CCP regime, the mass organizations and many associations in the incorporated sector would be likely to collapse with it and their intermediary roles would be occupied by currently submerged or repressed organizations which would rush in to fill the vacuum.

But the latter are themselves divided and ambivalent on the issue of political reform. For example, while some of the underground political organizations may be in favour of liberal democracy, others advocate a return to Maoist politics or, in the case of ethnic separatist organizations, a break-up of the existing political community. Moreover, certain key potential counter-élites—most notably the new private entrepreneurial strata—have shown little interest in the prospect of radical political change because their interests are bound up with the stability of the current process of market reform under the auspices of an authoritarian regime with which they are deeply entangled.[42] As Wang Shaoguang (1991) has pointed out, civil societies in general—and Chinese civil society in particular—are riven by conflicts and inequalities and have a potential for a wide variety of different types of politics, of which democracy is but one. The tendency towards idealizing the political potential of civil society should be resisted.

The ideological climate among political reformers in China has moved in a more sober and conservative direction over recent years. After the radical political fervour of Tiananmen died away, there has been a growing consensus that, if a process of political liberalization and democratization is to take place, it should be gradual, managed process. This does not merely represent the desire of political élites either to cling to their power or go out gracefully (or at least comfortably). To a considerable extent it also represents the fears and conflicts inherent in China's incipient civil society: the new entrepreneurial class worries that radical political change might lead to instability, mass rule, or a recalcitrant labour force; the industrial working class fears that it might lead to a rapid erosion of its relatively privileged position in society, and greater insecurity and exploitation

[42] This point is made cogently by Solinger (1992) and demonstrated by Wank (1995) in his case study of Xiamen.

by capital; and intellectuals and professionals fear that it could lead either to chaos or to rule by an illiterate numerical majority.

Given these antagonisms, comparative experience suggests that a stable and peaceful political transition—involving liberalization or democratization—can most effectively be achieved through a process of political bargaining and accommodation between key élites in state and civil society.[43] The balance of power between the two sectors varies from country to country. In the Soviet case, for example, a democratic transition was sponsored and organized by reformist elements within the existing political elites, in a situation in which civil society in any organized form was virtually non-existent. In South Korea, the state élites of the *ancien régime* retained a commanding position in the transition but were forced to deal with an increasingly assertive business élite in the *chaebol* sector and opposition politicians bolstered by widespread mobilization of public support by social organizations such as labour unions and church groups. In Zambia, by contrast, the previous one-party system was collapsing and it was the élites of civil society—from the unions, church groups, and business—who sponsored and commanded the transition to democracy. (G. White 1995). In terms of the balance between state and civil society, China may perhaps be situated somewhere between the Soviet Union and South Korea: the key élites of the Leninist regime—in the party, the state bureaucracy, and the military—are still the overwhelmingly dominant political force, but the new social groups and organizations resulting from the economic reforms are creating an increasingly influential counter-force: the democratic intellectuals active in 1989 and before; the emergent business sector and its potentially influential organizations such as the various entrepreneurs' associations, the trade associations and the Federation of Industry and Commerce and its affiliates; the growing professional strata who are highly organized in associations and rapidly gaining occupational autonomy; and the trade unions with their strong roots in urban factories and their growing awareness of the need to act on behalf of their constituency or face dissolution.

The viability of this scenario of bargained or crafted transition depends partly on the emergence of a reformist leadership within the

---

[43] For comparative experience on the political dynamics of democratic transitions, see O'Donnell, Schmitter, and Whitehead (1986), Przeworski (1991) and Huntington (1991).

CCP which is willing to read the writing on the wall and come to terms with new socio-political forces through institutional change. It also depends on the ability of influential social forces, both old and new, to come together and agree on the form of new political arrangements. By so doing, the organizations of civil society and their leaders can play a crucial constitutive role not only in impelling and organizing the transition to a democratic polity, but also in defining its distinctive institutional shape and political character. The form of democratic order which emerges—in particular the extent to which democratic procedures overlay substantive democratic processes—depends heavily on the range of social groups included in this initial compact: for example, whether or not workers' organizations are involved, or whether the peasantry is able to find a cohesive associational voice. It also depends heavily on the kind of political society to which the interests and associations of civil society give rise—in particular the new political parties which arise to link civil society with the state and take over the role formerly played by the CCP. The nature of this political society is important is determining not only the political character of the new polity but also its stability.

Even more fundamentally, the organized forces of civil society can also play a crucial constitutive role in establishing a new system of societal organization to replace the institutions of the Marxist-Leninist era. As Émile Durkheim (1893–1964) warned in his discussion of the transition from 'mechanical' to 'organic' solidarity, in a context of rapid socio-economic transformation the previous institutions which hold a society together lose their efficacy and relevance and there is danger of social anomie. In its most acute form, this would mean of a collapse of Chinese society into its basic components—not merely into localities or communities, but still further down to the level of networks and families. As in the case of Durkheim's professional associations (Durkheim 1992), intermediate associations have the potential to provide a new source of social cohesion to fill the institutional vacuum, not only by providing new links between state and society but also by reconstituting Chinese society itself in an era of potentially convulsive change. From this admittedly optimistic perspective, the organized forces of emergent civil society could be the architects of the new post-communist China. However, given their current diversity and potential for conflict, the transition to a new political order is likely to be a rough and rocky one.

14

CIVIL SOCIETY AND OTHER POLITICAL POSSIBILITIES IN SOUTHEAST ASIA*

Garry Rodan

In the last decade we have witnessed the end of the Cold War and the collapse of various authoritarian regimes in Eastern Europe, Latin America, and East Asia. Not surprisingly, this has lead to a great deal of attention in policy and academic circles to the prospects of political liberalization outside the established liberal democracies. A crucial aspect of the debates around this question involves the newly-industrializing countries of East Asia. Much has been made of the way rapid industrialization has brought with it social transformations, such as expanded and more diverse middle classes, that have manifested in pressures for greater political pluralism. Indeed, many theorists contend that the demise of authoritarian rule in East Asian societies such as South Korea and Taiwan not only reflects the close nexus between economic development and 'democratization' but also broadly mirrors the future for Southeast Asian NICs in their wake. The emergence of civil society, involving organizations independent of government and giving expression to a more complex and differentiated society, is seen as a crucial ingredient in this 'democratization.'

* *Journal of Contemporary Asia*, 27(2), (1997).

This projection, and the theoretical sources which underlie it, are open to contest from a variety of perspectives. However, one of the most concerted attempts to refute it has come in the form of a set of culturalist arguments about the existence of an 'Asian alternative' to 'western liberalism'. Put simply, it is contended that core Asian values rooted in traditional culture militate against the establishment of liberal 'democracy in the region. In this view, there is certainly no inevitable flourishing of civil society in Asia as capitalist development advances. While this view is understandably popular among custodians of authoritarian rule in East and Southeast Asia, it enjoys wide appeal inside policy and academic circles in the established liberal democracies too.

In this study, we critically examine the proposition that the cultural distinctiveness of Asia poses an obstacle to civil society. It will be argued that while there certainly is no inevitable flourishing of civil society in Asia as capitalist development proceeds, this is not a function of any cultural predisposition of Asian societies. Rather, historical factors have meant that relationships between the middle and business classes and the state in East and Southeast Asia are unlikely to reflect the dominant patterns of early industrializing countries. More particularly, there are means other than civil society through which the aspirations for political change might be accommodated, of which selective co-option of social forces is the most prevalent. Political pluralism, in other words, may be possible without a vibrant civil society.

At the same time, the capacity of authoritarian regimes to promote and institutionalize alternatives to civil society in East and Southeast Asia is not uniform. The different constellations of social and political forces in the region are manifesting in various combinations and strengths in the pressures for civil society. Contrary to the Asian values line, the region is likely to be increasingly marked by political diversity, including the possible emergence of more extensive civil societies in some cases. There are social forces which are increasingly resistant to, or not amenable to, co-option by the state. The Asian values discourse, at least as it is employed by authoritarian leaders in Asia, is an ideological response to this—an attempt to undermine the legitimacy of such challenges by effectively labelling them 'unAsian' or 'alien.'

Yet if the emergence of civil society is a possible, though not an inevitable by-product of capitalist development in Southeast Asia, it must be underlined that civil society contains politically diverse elements. Contrary to the popular positive connotations attached to civil society, groups that exist outside the state have divergent values and agendas, not all of which are marked by political tolerance or liberal democracy. Indeed, some forces within civil society hold to blatantly elitist and anti-democratic values. They may seek the right to operate independently of the state to shape the exercise of state power and influence public policy, but this does not mean they endorse the rights of all independent organizations to do likewise. Nor does it mean their internal organizational structures of practices reflect democratic or egalitarian principles.

Let us now turn our attention to how this concept might assist in an understanding of contemporary social and political developments in East and Southeast Asia. At one extreme of the related debates we have an expectation of an imminent and liberalizing civil society as capitalist development gathers momentum. At the other extreme we have, in effect, the proposition that civil society— or at least a liberalizing civil society—is culturally alien to Asia and must be avoided lest social discipline and economic development give way to chaos.

PRESSURES FOR POLITICAL PLURALISM AND THE REVIVAL OF 'ASIAN VALUES'

Democratic economic development in much of East and Southeast Asia since the 1960s has set in train social transformations involving new centres of economic and political power, as well as new divisions and conflicts. This has translated into new pressures on authoritarian rule, not just from emerging business and middle classes seeking the greater institutionalization of the rule of law, transparency in government and the curtailment of corruption, but also from organizations representing labour, women, environmentalists, and social justice and human rights activists. Broadly speaking, there has been an upsurge of political opposition, but significantly without the sort of strategic influence of communists, socialists, and radicals that has characterized previous historical phases of opposition (see Hewison and Rodan, 1994). Certainly, liberal democratic ideas feature prominently within the political philosophies and aspirations of many of these social forces, although they are one element of a wider complex. What is crucially important is that these social forces have agitated for the right to influence public policy. That has generally required some sort of reassessment of state–society relations by authoritarian leaders.

The complexion and strength of these pressures have obviously varied throughout East and Southeast Asia, as have the responses by authoritarian regimes facing such challenges. Thus, throughout the region we have witnessed a differential mix, importance and character to political parties, social movements, NGOs, and organizations co-opted into some sort of political relationship with the state. We can expect the contrasting mixes in the forms and substances of political opposition in each society to produce even more divergent political trajectories as capitalist industrialization consolidates and reflects local constellations of social and economic power.

A major distinction is likely to be drawn, however, between societies in which changes in state–society relations permit significantly greater independent political space—where civil societies expand—and those where more extensive and ingenious forms of political co-option are devised. Clearly developments in Taiwan, South Korea and to a lesser extent, Hong Kong, have been much more facilitative of independent political spaces than Singapore, Malaysia, and Indonesia, for example. In the former, interest groups representing labour, business, and professionals, together with an assortment of social movements and NGOs are playing an increasingly active political role, in some respects surpassing political parties. By contrast, in the latter, what concessions have been made to political pluralism have often involved extensions to state structures themselves. This has taken quite elaborate form in Singapore to selectively sanction wider consultation with elements of the business and middle classes. Here the ruling People's Action Party (PAP) is attempting to shore up elitism at the same time as it widens the incorporation of social forces into state structures (Rodan, 1992). But in Indonesia, recent labour strikes, as well as public demonstrations over press bans, serve as a reminder that, outside the city-state, the viability of corporatism is likely to be more fully tested.

Since the 1980s, the fortunes of authoritarian regimes have certainly suffered in the region, starting with the collapse of the Marcos regime in the Philippines and followed by the fall of military and civilian dictatorships in South Korea, Taiwan, and Thailand. Events in 1989, culminating in the Tienanmen Square massacre, also underlined the more than residual opposition to authoritarian rule in China. Then, following twenty-eight years of military dictatorship, the National League for Democracy NLD) had a landslide electoral victory in Burma in 1990. Despite tight controls on campaigning and the house arrest ten months earlier of its leaders, the NDL picked up 392 out of 485 seats while the pro-military National Unity Party won just ten seats. While the military prevented the elected leaders from taking office, this was another powerful rebuff for the idea that Asians have some cultural predisposition towards 'strong government.' Meanwhile, and in defiance of Chinese authorities preparing to regain sovereignty in mid-1997, elections in 1991 and 1995 in Hong Kong also appear to have whetted an appetite for greater political representation.

In these circumstances, it is understandable that authoritarian leaderships remaining in the region might feel a little nervous about the patterns of change around them and anxious to dissuade their own populations from emulating any of these experiences. This is the context in which a discourse about 'Asian values' has surfaced which, in essence, portrays challenges to authoritarian rule emanating from civil society as culturally alien to Asia. Ironically, it is not that long ago that theorists were documenting what they saw as the impediments to modernization presenting by traditional cultures (see Finkle and Gable, 1966), including 'Asian values.' It is even more ironic that for some of these writers the very diversity of Asian in social, political, and cultural terms was part of the problem. Accordingly, Ho (1977, p. 13), for example, argued that:

It is therefore more appropriate to use the term 'Asian Values' to denote not a particular set of attitudes, beliefs and institutions which all Asian people share in common, but rather to refer to the great diversities which characterize Asian *values* as such, and which in the context of this discussion, pose serious difficulties to the task of modernizing Asia for social, economic and political development.

It was precisely this diversity which led John Steadman (1969) as early as 1969 to argue in *The Myth of Asia* that 'The most obvious signs of unity in Asia are, paradoxically, those of Western influence.'

The contemporary focus on 'Asian values,' however, not only attempts to distil essential cultural elements across the region, but puts a decidedly more favourable gloss on them. Thus we are told that such 'Asian' cultural characteristics as group rather than individual orientation, the importance of the family, the propensity to adopt consensual rather than competitive decision-making processes, and emphasis on education and saving have underscored political stability and economic development (Hofheinz and Calder 1982; Lee Kuan Yew cited in Zakaria 1994; Mahathir and Ishihara 1995; Mahbubani, 1995; Goh 1994; Berger and Hsiao, 1990; Koh 1993). While the particular combination of characteristics may vary from one account to another, the common theme to these portrayals is the notion that social and political organization is hierarchical or controlled from above. Furthermore, this is presented as a natural state of affairs, since it is rooted in Asian culture. This 'top-down' model of social and political organization infers at best a limited place for a civil society housing social groups or individuals that place demands on the political and social elite. Indeed, obligations to the state are stressed, thereby obviating the need for societal demands to be conveyed via independent organizations.

Adherents to the 'Asian values' thesis both inside and outside East and Southeast Asia have tended to characterize Confucianism as the cultural underlay to these particular values, raising questions about where the non-ethnic Chinese communities fit in this schema. Significantly, the essentials of 'Asian values' have been defined principally in opposition to what is commonly referred to as 'western liberalism' which is seen, amongst other things, to be characterized by excessive individualism and a propensity for protestation and open political conflict. The consistent reference to 'western liberalism' conveys the clear message that liberalism is an 'alien' set of social and political values for which 'real' Asians have a cultural aversion.

The concerted attack on liberation reflects the fact that political forces in East and Southeast Asia have generally moderated, compared with previous attempts to carve out greater space for civil society. In the past, the spectre of communism or arguments about the primacy of initiating economic development have been drawn on to justify authoritarian rule and curtail political pluralism in much of the region. However, the social forces associated with the current push for political space, particularly from the middle and business classes, largely involve groups and individuals with a strong stake in the consolidation and deepening of capitalism. These challenges to authoritarian rule cannot be so easily dismissed, hence the new critical focus on liberalism and its juxtaposition with 'Asian values.' In this exercise, attempts to carve out civil society space are depicted as a mimic of foreign ideas, incompatible with the cultural basis of Asian polities and societies.

In emphasizing the utility of 'Asian values' to the maintenance of authoritarian rule, it cannot be denied that there are other factors behind this turnaround in the meaning and application of 'Asian values' since the heyday of modernization theory. The intervening decades have witnessed significant changes, including rapid economic development and a favourable repositioning of Asia within the global political economy. Projections of an 'Asian century' abound. It is understandable that many people within these predominantly post-colonial societies should derive pride from this, not least the leaders. Nor should we be surprised that greater institutionalization of economic and political relationship in the region should ensue. Notions of an 'Asian renaissance' and the recent establishment of the Commission for a New Asia (1994) gives vivid expression to this changing mood. But we should be careful to distinguish the shared experience and consciousness of late but spectacular industrialization from shared culture. Attempts to foster regional identity which promote the idea of cultural homogeneity will continue to confront a complex reality and invite observations like that of former Japanese Ministry of Trade and Industry (MITI) official, Naohiro Amaya. According to him, '"Asia" is a geographical word. Asian nations share nothing in common' (cited in Jameson, 1992).

Beyond Elite Culture in Asia

The attempts to articulate 'Asian values' has relied heavily on liberalism as a point of departure and has been deficient in specifying the positive, definitive characteristics of 'Asian culture' that permeate social and political organizations in the region. This is not so surprising, given that the region is comprised of a series of adapted systems fundamentally shaped by liberal democratic and communist ideas. Any attempts to identify the 'consensual Asian' from the government runs into this problem (Mallet, 1994). The difficulty is compounded by the fact that the region's most vocal and influential proponents of 'Asian values' have had to embark on something of a cultural rediscovery themselves to address this issue. It is an acute irony that Singapore's most western-educated elite are at the pivot of the campaign for 'Asian values.' Apart from Lee Kuan Yew, this included Goh Chok Tong, Kishore Mahbubani, Chan Heng Chee, Tommy Koh, George Yeo, and Bilahari Kausikan. Yet in the 1980s, when the PAP government decided to introduce Confucianism into the secondary education syllabus, this was only possible with the help of outside experts. The atmosphere has certainly changed. During the 1960s and 1970s, when the opposition political party, Barisan Sosialis, had significant support amongst those educated in the Chinese language medium, the PAP was particularly vigilant against anything roughly approximating Chinese chauvinism (see Bloodworth, 1986).

To the extent that 'Asian values' have been appropriated in reaction to the perceived threat of liberalism, the absence of real definition to the alternative Asian model is not a fundamental problem. Indeed, from a political and ideological point of view it is paramount that the notion be retained at as abstract and vague a level as possible. Nevertheless, this does produce some interesting ambiguities and contradictions. Take for instance Lee Kuan Yew's position on the liberal democratic notion of the separation of powers. This is one of the fundamental ingredients of liberal democracy, but not one ever claimed as central to 'Asian values.' Indeed, recently the Mayor of Seoul, Dr Cho Soon (cited in Australian, 15 November 1995, p. 15) argued that the traditional absence of this concept in Asian necessarily meant that the development of democracy in the region could not replicate western experience. Yet, as international newspaper proprietors have discovered to their considerable cost, nothing is more likely to provoke the authorities in Singapore than to cast doubts on the independence of the judiciary from the executive. Yet surely there are a host of plausible political arguments for not placing central importance on the separation of powers if you feel no compunction to defend liberalism and are confident about a defensible political alternative.

This uncertainty about what actually constitutes the 'Asian alternative' underlines that the principal dynamic behind the revival of 'Asian values' by authoritarian leaders is to negate the perceived appeal of liberalism within Asia. Not surprisingly, then, these leaders find themselves not just at odds with other Asians who reject the attempt to depict their views as 'alien,' but also with those who take seriously the question of how cultural heritages in Asia shape contemporary possibilities. In a recent lecture in Singapore, Professor Tu Wei-ming of Harvard University, one of those experts who had earlier been consulted by Singapore's authorities on Confucianism, raised very serious doubts even about the validity of Confucianism as the basis of critique of 'the west'.' To be relevant today, Tu argues,

Confucian tradition needs to be creatively transformed by some of the values of the European Enlightenment, including human rights, freedom, liberty and due process of law. If this can be achieved, without sacrificing such spiritual resources as family cohesion and respect for elders, then Tu believed Confucianists would then, and only then, have earned 'the right and responsibility to be critical of excessive individualism, litigiousness and social disintegration' (cited in *Straits Times*, 22 March, p. 22, 1995).

A more direct refutation of the attempt to harness Confucianism and Asian cultural traditions to an attack on liberalism has been undertaken by other Asian political figures themselves. Indeed, former presidential candidate and leading dissident and human rights campaigner in South Korea, Kim Dae Jung, has turned the argument on its head. In an explicit response to Lee Kuan Yew's published views in the American journal *Foreign Affairs*, Kim (1994) argues that democracy has deep roots in Asian cultures and philosophies, including the works of Confucius, Lao-tzu, and Mencius. In China and Korea, a country prefecture system had been in place for 2000 years when western societies were still being ruled by feudal lords. Far from Asia's cultural traditions obstructing liberal democracy, Kim maintains they contain the intellectual ideological bases for a major contribution to a new 'global democracy.'

Kim's high profile, like that of President Ramos of the Philippines, who has also clashed with Lee Kuan Yew over the latter's anti-democratic prescriptions for the region [see *Far Eastern Economic Review*, 10 December 1992, p. 29 and Hong Kong human rights campaigner and Legislative Councillor Christine Loh (1993)], gives these intra-Asian disputations a certain visibility. However, there also exists a range of other oppositions within Asia to the 'Asian values' thesis. Take, for example, the issue of human rights. The position adopted by Asian governments in the Bangkok Declaration in March 1993, prior to the United Nations World Conference on Human Rights, emphasized the importance of historical, cultural, and regional specificities in the interpretation of human rights (see Freeman, 1995). This amounted to a serious qualification to the idea of human rights as universal, and included arguments about the importance of social stability and economic development rather than abstract individual freedoms as the primary basis of gauging human rights. The message was clear: the west should not try to impose its culturally-specific standards on other countries.

Regional NGOs responded immediately to re-assert the universality of human rights across cultures (see Ghai 1995; Muntarbhom, 1993). In July the following year, and despite the efforts of Thai authorities to jettison the gathering (see *Thai Development News*, No. 25, 1994, pp. 68–70), the *Southeast Asian NGOs Forum on Human Rights and Development* in Bangkok issued a further statement which extended the challenge to regional governments on human rights. The statement included condemnation of the repressive State Law and Order Restoration Council (SLORC) in Burma and the occupation of East Timor by Indonesian authorities. Moreover, while these NGOs accepted the importance of linking human rights with social and economic rights, as the Asian governments had earlier insisted, they drew on this principle to call for more equitable distribution of income, environmentally-sustainable development, and the removal of gender discrimination. Clearly, within the region there are individuals and groups who see a case for critically evaluating the liberal concept of human rights, but as a basis for social and economic reform agendas few authoritarian regimes would welcome. Indeed, as Ghai (1995, pp. 64–5) has argued, the sensitivity of authorities in Asia to debate over human rights is grounded on concern about the potential of this to question the structures of power and authority embedded in material disparities, corruption, the influence of international capital, and other objects of popular animosity.

The attempt by authoritarian leaders in Asia, then, to dismiss dissenting views on human rights on the basis that they simply echo mainstream 'western liberal' opinion does not hold up to scrutiny. Liberalism is a significant political force in the region and, as the formation in 1994 of both the Forum of Democratic Leaders in the Asian Pacific (FDL-AP) and the Council of Asian Liberals and Democrats (CALD) illustrates, it has the potential to assume more formal networks across the region. However, other challenges to authoritarian rule exist, inspired by notions of democracy and development that go beyond liberal individualism. Various NGOs involved in social and economic development throughout much of Asia involve efforts to promote participatory democracy (see Clark, 1991; Hewison 1991; Eldridge, 1995). In the endeavour to sustain local communities, economic and political decentralization is a priority for many in Asia. As Callahan (1994) points out, there are grassroots alternatives to the notions of 'Asian democracy' propagated by elites which draw on local knowledge and traditions in Asia.

Illustrating this point, Aung San Suu Kyi (1994)—one of Asia's most popular political figures—insists that democracy takes a variety of forms and should not simply be equated with one dominant form. Indeed, even in the west the forms vary significantly, and we should expect the same in Asia. However, this cannot be used to justify authoritarian rule. Rather, she contends that 'People's participation in social and political transformation is the central issue of our time.' Moreover, Aung's critique of what Lee Kuan Yew and other proponents of 'Asian values' would regard as 'western decadence' is seen in very different terms:

Many of the worst ills of American society, increasingly to be found in other developed countries, can be traced not to the democratic legacy but to the demands of modern materialism. Gross individuals and cut-throat morality arise when political and intellectual freedoms are curbed on the one hand while on the other fierce economic competitiveness is encouraged by making material success the measure of prestige and progress.

Such a critique has obvious relevance for much of Asia where economic individualism generally faces less constraints than in established liberal democracies in which environmental groups and others exert a general influence to protect wider community interests. The philosophical contrast between Aung and Lee is a dramatic but nevertheless poignant reminder of the diversity that the generalizations of 'Asian values' obscure. Such authentic expressions of Asian opinion obviously pose a special problem for the credibility of 'Asian values.'

The point of the above is not to establish the 'real' Asian values but to instead emphasize there are a number of different political voices in Asia. The advocates of the 'Asian values' thesis are correct in claiming connections between the ideas within Asia that reject this thesis and ideas within the west. But this is no less true of the ideas encapsulated in 'Asian values.' The views championed by advocates of 'Asian values' are not an 'Asian alternative' to 'western liberalism' but an 'alternative in Asia' to liberalism. As will be explained below, the same attacks on liberalism can be found in the west itself.

SUPPORT IN THE WEST FOR 'ASIAN VALUES'

Of no less importance in this 'Asian values' rhetoric is the depiction of liberalism as absolutely and equally ascendant throughout 'the west.' Yet behind this convenient monolith, there are considerable differences in the constellation and strength of political forces and ideas from American to Europe, for example, which pose varying domestic challenges to liberalism and incite serious debates over the nature of liberalism itself among its supporters. At their core, these challenges and debates centre around the fundamental and unresolved disputes over the relative rights and responsibilities of individuals and the state: precisely the same set of questions underlying political and ideological contestation in Asia today and embodied in the content of 'Asian values.' It is linking up of ideological forces across 'East' and 'West' in the prosecution of positions taken in these fundamental disputes, not a clash of cultures, which is unfolding. Critical in this is an amalgam of conservative and neo-liberal forces seeking in the west to reverse a range of social and political reforms of the post-war period that resulted from certain social democratic and liberal pressures (Rodan, 1995).

The integration of Asia into domestic ideological and political battles in the established liberal democracies has gathered momentum as the economic fortunes of the former increasingly stand in sharp contrast with those of the latter. Some observers, like American economist Paul Krugman (1995), have argued that this will prove a short-lived growth spurt owing to structural limitations to these Asian economies. Whether this argument holds or not, it has understandable appeal, particularly for those theorists who view political liberty as a functional requirement of sophisticated capitalist development. But a host of policy-makers and academics have come to the conclusion that the competitiveness of the 'Asia model' simply compels some pragmatic adjustments in 'the west', while neo-liberals and conservatives have ready-made solutions which resonate with various 'Asian values'. Gellner (1994) quite explicitly makes the point that a modern, industrialized society cannot only exist without a civil society, but it can indeed flourish.

The discourse of 'Asian values' also provides a tempting rationale for governments and their bureaucrats, anxious to extend economic relations with Asia, moderating public positions on human rights in an attempt to avoid diplomatic friction. Academics with specialist knowledge about Asian cultures can also feel empowered by the opportunity to 'unlock the mysteries of the east' that this debate presents. And there are assorted radicals whose animosity towards imperialism leads them also to sympathize with attacks on 'the west' (see Robison, 1993). So there are a variety of seductions in 'Asian values' outside the region.

This harnessing of the 'Asian values' debate to domestic politics has been quite explicit in Australia where, for the last decade, economic restructuring has been closely tied to the idea of economic relations with Asia. A variety of politicians, journalists, business leaders, academics, judges, and other prominent figures have weighed in with recommendations on how Australian society needs to be reformed in response to, or emulation of, Asian development (see Rodan and Hewison, 1996). Increasingly, the same process is reflected in the United States, Britain, and Europe. Recently, the Chairman of the UK House of Commons Foreign Affairs Committee, the Conservative Party's David Howell, gave one of the most direct and comprehensive such statements in altering Europeans to imminent 'Easternization.' According to Howell (1995), this is 'not just about adopting the business techniques of those now in the ascendant, the Asian dynamos, but about some of the values and attitudes which lie beneath their success both as economies and societies.' Not surprisingly, this leads amongst other things to the endorsement of 'the greater security which flows families and neighbourhoods' ahead of the welfare state (Ibid.).

The point is that much of the force behind the 'Asian values' debate stems precisely from the fact that these values have international, transcultural meaning and appeal. Without a recognition that these values resonate with ideologies and interests outside the region, it would be difficult to understand why such thoroughly 'westernized' proponents of these values as Lee Kuan Yew would not have their credentials to speak on behalf of 'Asia' more seriously scrutinized, if not dismissed. So notions of 'Asian values' are not only being deployed in an attempt to marginalize, if not obstruct, emerging political oppositions within much of Asia. They are also incorporated into established liberal democracies in the ongoing battle for ideological ascendancy between competing liberal, conservative, and social democratic forces. It is this combined political significance of 'Asian values' that makes it so influential and important a debate, and that also exposes as myth the proposition that such values are culturally distinct.

CHANGING STATE–SOCIETY RELATIONS IN SOUTHEAST ASIA

Having made the points that there is no endemic cultural aversion to civil society in Asia and that civil society has enjoyed relative prosperity at previous times in the histories of East and Southeast

Asia, this is not to suggest that it will inevitably flourish as capitalist revolutions consolidate. Nevertheless, complex social transformations associated with capitalist development do necessitate political changes to state–society relations. The increasingly numerous and differentiated middle class, which encompasses a range of professionals, public and private bureaucrats, and the self-employed is a major dimension of this. So too is the development of business classes involving more diverse and sophisticated domestic and global accumulation strategies. The expansion of wage labour is a further aspect of these social transformations beginning to assert themselves in some cases. Such new interests and identities are manifesting in pressures for influence over the policy process, as well as precipitating new tensions involving social groups and classes adversely affected by changing patterns of social and economic power.

An expanded civil society is one possible scenario to accommodate this, though clearly not the one preferred by authoritarian leaders in Southeast Asia, who look askance at recent trends in South Korea, Taiwan, or even Hong Kong. To differing extents, alongside the growth in political parties in these three East Asian societies, independent trade unions, interest groups and/or non-government organizations are exerting a significant influence over the political process. If civil society is to be resisted in Southeast Asia, other forms of social and political organization, which do not involve the same measure of independence from the state, must be effectively institu-
ionalized. But while governments in most of Southeast Asia may share a preference for resisting the expansion and diversification of civil society, the capacities to do this are not uniform. The brief and selective examination of this question below not only makes this point, but underlines that where any significant concessions are being made to greater independent political space, this has essentially involved comparatively privileged elements of society.

At one extreme of the spectrum in Southeast Asia we have Singapore. Here, new mechanisms have been developed to widen the structures of co-option, but on a very selective basis. A variety of institutional arrangements facilitate consultation with professionals, business groups, and ethnic organizations in the public policy process, including the appointment of nominated members of parliament (NMPs), wider use of parliamentary committees, and a government-sponsored think tank. Significantly, though, this consultation is depicted by authorities as a functional process which draws on expertise. It is sharply contrasted with the sanctioning of interest-based politics. Probably the only significant exception to this pattern of the state extending its umbrella to rein in more of society involve the Nature Society of Singapore and the Association of Women for Action and Research. These small non-government organizations (NGOs), both dominated by cautious middle class activists with politically moderate objectives have been able to enter the political process in a limited way.

Meanwhile, avenues for organized, independent political contestation by, and on behalf of, the under-privileged in Singapore remain extremely difficult, not the least through fear of enforcement of the Societies Act which bars engagement in 'politics' by organizations not registered for such a purpose. Attempts by lay religious organizations in the late 1980s to represent the interests and concerns of guest workers was enough to precipitate an extensive internal security crackdown. The government controlled National Trades Union Congress (NTUC) remains the fundamental voice of labour. Consequently, growing concerns over the last decade about widening material inequalities may have translated into greater electoral support for the PAP's formal political opponents, but these parties cannot draw on, or connect with, independent social organizations with complementary reform agendas. This is the fundamental limitation of electoral politics: its severing from any organic connection with civil society.

Beyond the small city state, the constraints on independent political activity are not quite as effective or complete, although co-option of emerging social forces is also a dominant theme. In particular, since the mid-1980s Southeast Asia has witnessed the rapid expansion of business and professional organizations. In Indonesia and Thailand, at least, some of these groups have achieved considerable power. MacIntyre (1991) has demonstrated how industry associations and business groups have been able to use the Indonesian state's corporatist structures to derive benefits for their members. This, he argues, effectively amounts to expanded political representation. Anek (1992) also maintains that, in the Thailand case, business associations have become autonomous of the state, acting as interest groups, even if there are 'close and supportive relations between the government and organized business.'

The point such developments underline is that, whether it takes the form of opening up civil society or extending the state's structures of co-option, any increased political representation that has taken place has been occurring on a selective basis. It has generally excluded the underprivileged. However, the extension of the market economy within Southeast Asia and the unequal social and economic effects of it are likely to increasingly generate pressure for the protection and advancement of disadvantaged social groups. Yet, as a legacy of decades of authoritarian rule, the institutionalized incorporation of organized labour into the structures of the state is well advanced throughout Southeast Asia. The under-privileged—who are not always wage labourers but can also include peasants, merchants, and various categories of self-employed—therefore have to look for other groups to represent their interests. Thus, either in conjunction with—or in place of—trade unions, NGOs engaged in social and economic development and, to a lesser extent, social movements, have emerged as significant political influences in the region.

The roles of developmental NGOs in Southeast Asia vary, from high profile activism in the Philippines and Thailand to a more moderate role in Indonesia and Malaysia, limited in Singapore, and virtually non-existent in Burma and Laos. Moreover, as some analysts have pointed out (see Kothari, 1989; Sasono, 1989; Rahnema, 1989), many so-called NGOs engaged in social and economic development in the region have either been co-opted by government or are self-promoting or self-interested. However, in view of the tight clamp on overtly political activities and the very nature of work undertaken by many of these organizations, they have come to assume an important unofficial political function. The personnel of such organizations are mostly drawn from urban intellectuals and middle class groups. But, as Sasono (1989, p. 19) points out, these people nevertheless act in a class-based manner, working for the poor, and taking risks, knowing the political and economic costs involved. A new NGO ideology has evolved out of their work. Many have learnt that development practice cannot be neutral and that empowerment of the poor, disorganized, and disenfranchised is the key to 'real' development. In addition, poverty has been defined as a political issue, since poverty has a lot to do with powerlessness. Many working in these NGOs have concluded that development projects are more successful 'if they are based on people's own analysis of the problems they face and their solutions' (Clark 1991, p. 102).

In essence, this suggests an approach to participation, representation, and collective action, where political action on a national or even international stage is necessary. This challenges the elitist ideology of meritocracy, so powerful in the Singapore case, which is used to justify selective functional representation in the political process to those with expertise. It also makes it imperative for such NGOs to try and expand political space. In Southeast Asia this has involved the building of coalitions with religious and women's groups, environmentalists, trade unions, and others in attempts to shape public policy.

This last observation leads to the point that, despite the continued difficulties for independent trade unions throughout Southeast Asia, they have not been completely blunted. Rising labour activism in Indonesia attests to this, with trade unions like the PPBI (Centre for Working Class Struggles) and SBSI (Indonesia Prosperous Workers' Union) playing a critical role. Importantly, though, this has been one component of an increasing breadth of oppositional forces, particularly within Indonesia but generally throughout the region. Growing links between the student and labour movements in Indonesia are expressed through the activities of such organizations as the PPBI and the YMB (Foundation for Mutual Progress) for example. Together with developmental NGOs like the SISBIKUM and YAKOMA they complicate the New Order's corporatist designs for labour, albeit under constant threat of repressive reprisals from the state. The student movement in Indonesia, whose potential ranks are bolstered by the expansion of the middle class, is also integrating itself with peasant organizations via a range of NGOs involved in social and economic development. But if the urban middle class in Indonesia is increasingly forming political coalitions with less privileged sectors, and even playing a strategic role in this coalition, these links are nevertheless still ad hoc, often clandestine, and insecure.

In neighbouring Malaysia, while a comparable alliance between the student and labour movements is absent, the urban middle class is, however, a limited force for the broadening of political contestation. Here we see significant middle class involvement and leadership in what attempts have been made to open up the space of civil society. Lawyers and other professionals have attempted to advance concern about civil rights, environmental degradation, women's rights, corruption, and the social consequences of economic development. Prominent independent organizations trying to influence public policy, wherein the middle class plays a strategic role, include Aliran, the Environmental Protection Society of Malaysia, Selangor Graduates Society, Consumer Association of Penang, National Council of Women's Organizations, and the Association of Women Lawyers.

Recent Southeast Asian history contains some striking illustrations of the potential for NGOs to play decisive political roles when circumstances are favourable. In Thailand, for example, NGOs played leading and co-ordinating roles in the events of 1991 and 1992 which eventually led to the demise of a military government. Earlier, in 1986, NGOs played a similar role in overthrowing the Marcos regime. Notwithstanding this, alongside the much more extensive NGOs in South-Korea and Taiwan, where there has been a flowering of social movements, NGO structures are modest. In both these East Asian societies, consumer, environmental, human rights, women's student, and social justice movements have fuelled remarkable social and political dynamics. Between 1990 and 1995, hundreds of NGOs emerged in South Korea and there are now more than twenty environmental organizations alone. Significantly, in both South Korea and Taiwan, these important organizations in the mobilization of popular opinion have eschewed links with political parties, even though the latter have a more important role to play in the competition for power than their counterparts in Southeast Asia. So the sharp separation of party politics from broader social and political life is a feature across East and Southeast Asia.

The point to emphasize here, however, is that while NGOs and social movements may be less influential in Southeast Asia, they nevertheless are in existence and they may yet have a greater impact if the assorted mechanisms of co-option fail in their political accommodation of new and more diversified social forces. Furthermore, as capitalist industrialization advances in Southeast Asia, issues relating to income distribution, pollution, public transport, and other social infrastructure are likely to loom larger. It remains to be seen how effective corporatist structures will be in satisfactorily defusing these issues. At the very least, it would seem that structures to actually ascertain diverse social opinion are necessary to give any semblance of credibility to the idea by authoritarian leaders that public policy is arrived at by consensus rather than contestation. This in itself would involve significant political change.

CONCLUSION

For historical reasons, social, political, and economic developments in Southeast Asia necessarily contrast in certain respects from the processes that accompanied development in the earlier industrializers of the established liberal democracies. But claims that Asian cultural predispositions render competitive political processes unworkable in East and Southeast Asia are a different matter. Such claims must themselves be put in historical context—a context of growing and increasingly complex political pressures on authoritarian structures in East and Southeast Asia. In the past, tight political controls were rationalized by authoritarian leaderships in much of developing Asia as a necessary temporary trade-off to enable economic development to take root. But with the economic transformation of Asia, this argument is much less tenable, especially as it has brought with it greater social complexity and associated pressures for political plural-ism. Changes of some form or degree in state–society relations are thus inevitable.

Yet these pressures comprise diverse social groups and political aspirations, not all of which lead in the direction of liberal democracy or a liberal civil society. Thus, authoritarian regimes in Southeast Asia may be able to reach political accommodations with some groups—either by extending the mechanisms of state co-option or by selec-tively opening up the space of civil society—without fundamental changes to authoritarian rule. Wider political participation could be reconciled with the consolidation of hierarchical and elitist political structures. In this scenario, major sections of society would remain politically marginalized.

Indications are, however, that throughout Southeast Asia the state corporatist direction is likely to face challenges. A variety of non-government organizations are emerging, including organizations that actively promote the interests of social groups adversely affected by the inequalities of the market economy. Their continued exclusion from the political process—even from co-option—undermines claims of an 'Asian' alternative to liberal democracy based on consensual politics. More importantly, it remains to be seen whether this sort of exclusion will prove politically effective over the longer term as the capitalist revolution in Southeast Asia matures. In contrast with the notion of an 'Asian' alternative, it is likely that there will be increased differen-tiation in the nature of state–society relations across the region. Central in this will be the relative margin and character of civil society. Authoritarian rule is by no means a necessary casualty of advanced capitalist development, but growing social complexity and the inescap-able social frictions of market economies will at least compel a com-mensurate increase in its political sophistication if it is to survive.

15

CIVIL SOCIETY AND DEMOCRATIZATION IN COMPARATIVE PERSPECTIVE
Latin America and the Middle East*

Mehran Kamrava and Frank O. Mora

If the latest democratic wave has been on a global march since the early to mid-1980s, it has either completely skipped the Middle East or has yet to make its introduction into the region. Amid the seemingly global democratic euphoria, the Middle East remains an authoritarian stronghold, where various non-democratic political systems cling on to power with unsurpassed tenacity and remarkable power. Worse yet, they seem to encounter little in the way of popular pressure to democratize, with political leaders either riding high on popular legitimacy or, if not endowed with Khomeini-like charisma, governing over societies that appear politically docile and uninterested in pursuing democratic agenda. What accounts for this seeming lack of desire on the part of Middle Easterners to actively seek after democratic political systems, particularly now that democracy is a tangible political reality in so many previously undemocratic places?

This paper examines the question of democratization in two regions of the world that have seen completely different patterns of

* *Third World Quarterly*, 19(5), 1998.

political rule and evolution in the course of the past few decades. Democratic transitions require two developments; one involving the state, the other society. In the case of the state, transition may develop from complete breakdown or paralysis, as it did in Argentina, Bolivia, and Uruguay. It may also develop when the state finds itself with no viable alternative in dealing with pressures from below and abroad, such as Brazil, eastern Europe, and South Korea. Insofar as societal dynamics are concerned, civil society organizations (CSOs) need to emerge either before the transition takes place or before the consolidation of a new system. Both developments were present in Latin America; neither has occurred in the Middle East. To our knowledge state–society relations in Latin America and the Middle East have not been comparatively studied yet. This paper is a response to a clarion call for more cross-regional comparisons that have been conspicuously scarce in the literature.[1] Most cross-regional studies have compared industrial development and democratization in Latin America with East Asia, Southern Europe, and Eastern Europe.[2] This unique

[1] J. A. Bill, 'The study of Middle East politics, 1946–1996: a stocktaking', *Middle East Journal*, 50(4), 1996, pp. 501–2; and P. Smith, 'The changing agenda for social science research on Latin America', in P. Smith (ed.), *Latin America in Comparative Perspective: New Approaches to Methods and Analysis*, Boulder, CO: Westview Press, 1995. A research programme organized by the Centre for Iberian and Latin American Studies (CILAS) at the University of California, San Diego is publishing a series of volumes that 'demonstrate the desirability and the feasibility of analyzing Latin America in comparative perspective, in conjunction with other regions, and in global perspective, in the context of worldwide processes'.

[2] See, for example, G. O'Donnell, P. C. Schmitter and L. Whitehead (eds), *Transition from Authoritarian Rule*, 4 Vols, Baltimore, MD: Johns Hopkins University Press, 1986; E. Baloyra (ed.), *Comparing New Democracies: Transition and Consolidation in Mediterranean Europe and the Southern Cone*, Boulder, CO: Westview Press, 1987; G. Gereffi & D. Wyman (eds), *Manufacturing Miracles: Paths of Industrialization in Latin America and East Asia*, Princeton, NJ: Princeton University Press, 1990; D. Rueschmeyer, E. H. Stephens & J. D. Stephens, *Capitalist Development and Democracy*, Chicago, IL: University of Chicago Press, 1992; S. Mainwaring, G. O'Donnell & J. S. Valenzuela (eds), *Issues in Democratic Consolidation: The New South American Democracies in Comparative Perspective*, South Bend, IN: University of Notre Dame Press, 1992; R. Gunther, P. N. Diamandorous & H. J. Puhle (eds), *The Politics of Democratic Consolidation: Southern Europe in Comparative Perspective*, Baltimore, MD. Johns Hopkins University Press, 1995; A Lijphart & C. Waisman (eds), *Institutional Design in*

comparative study of civil society and democratization in Latin America and the Middle East is an attempt to fill this scholarly void.

Any study of this magnitude must necessarily remain at a certain level of generalization. This paper focuses neither exclusively on Latin America nor on the Middle East, but rather on the comparative development of a number of forces that have made democratization possible in parts of one region while keeping it absent from another. Within itself, each region is rich in the plethora of diverse social, economic, and political dynamics that are found in its different countries. While mindful of these differences and their attendant consequences for such political phenomena as corporatism, civil society, and democratization, our goal here is to highlight regional comparisons that make further detailed study possible.

By placing the two regions in a comparative perspective, we will disprove the idea of Middle Eastern particularism. Rather, the argument maintains that the historical, economic, and political contexts in which state–society relations have occurred made political liberalization and transition to democracy the only viable option in Latin America but not in the Middle East. We focus on the performance and/or functional breakdown of the state in the two regions, and examine how political and economic factors combined to give birth to a dense and democratic civil society in Latin America but have impeded the development of a similar phenomenon in the Middle East. The breakdown of societal functions of the authoritarian state, as in Argentina, or the retreat of the state from its functions because of political and or/economic crises and policies, as in most other South American authoritarian regimes of the early 1980s, provided the population with a breathing space for political expression, organization, and participation. The masses looked for societal alternatives, and an increasingly democratic civil society emerged as a result. In the Middle East, however, the collapse of the state has not been nearly as total, with Middle Eastern leaders retaining enough political, economic, and cultural sources of legitimacy to be able to supplant much of the potential appeal that burgeoning civil society organizations might have. Exclusionary

New Democracies: Eastern Europe and Latin America, Boulder, CO: Westview Press, 1996; and J. Linz & A. Stepan, *Problems of Democratic Transition and Consolidation: Southern Europe, South America, and Post-Communism Europe*, Baltimore, MD: Johns Hopkins University Press, 1996.

politics and economic crises, in other words, expedited the break-down of bureaucratic–authoritarian politics in Latin America, forcing society to seek alternatives and opening the way for democratic pressures from below. Invariably all Middle Eastern states, however, have been able to maintain those corporatist arrangements through which they keep key social groups beholden to them, thus discouraging them from indirectly undermining their own interests.

STATE, CIVIL SOCIETY, AND DEMOCRATIC TRANSITIONS

Recent years have witnessed a proliferation of studies on the role of political, economic, social, and cultural dynamics in bringing about processes of democratic transition. While many of these studies differ on the degree of importance that they attribute to the various forces responsible for the democratization process, most agree that, at some point in the transition, either before the actual demise of the non-democratic state or afterwards, civil society develops and plays a crucial role in influencing the political system.[3] For most democratic theorists, who tend to see democratization processes and outcomes as contingent on the confluence of international and domestic actors and development (democratic contagion, state breakdown, class actors, pacted negotiations, etc.), a democratic civil society develops *after* the actual process of transition from an authoritarian to a democratic state has taken place.[4] There have been others, however, arguing mostly from a sociological and cultural perspective, who maintain that civil society frequently develops before, and is in fact a main cause of, the transition to a democratic system.[5] In either case, both camps agree that civil society is one of—if not *the*—crucial

[3] See, for example, E. Gellner, *Conditions of Liberty: Civil Service and its Critics*, New York: Penguin, 1994; J. Hall (ed.), *Civil Society: Theory History, Comparison*, Cambridge: Polity Press, 1995; I. Budge & D. McKay (eds), *Developing Democracy*, London: Sage, 1994; and K. Tester, *Civil Society*, London: Routledge, 1992, to mention only a few.

[4] G. O'Donnell & P. Schmitter, *Transitions from Authoritarian Rule: Tentative Conclusions about Uncertain Democracies*, Baltimore, MD: Johns Hopkins University Press, 1986, p. 48; B. Geremek, 'Civil society then and now', *Journal of Democracy*, 3(2), 1992, pp. 3–12; L. Diamond, 'Rethinking civil society: toward democratic consolidation', *Journal of Democracy*, 5(3), 1994, pp. 4–17.

[5] See, for example, C. Bryant, 'Civic nation, civil society, civil religion', in Hall (ed.), *Civil Society*, pp. 136–57.

phenomena that takes shape and becomes influential during processes of democratic transition.

Civil society organizations—defined here as self-organizing and self-regulating groups with corporate identities that are autonomous from the state—may exist within any given social or political setting. But for them to become politically relevant, and more importantly, to become agents of democratization, they must have three additional, specific characteristics: (1) they themselves must operate democratically,[6] encompassing and respecting pluralism and diversity, thus in turn bestowing the virtues of democracy on their own members; (2) they must complement their own issue-driven agendas with implicit or explicit demands for political democracy, therefore adding to the pressures the state feels in opening up; and (3) they need either to gather sufficient powers on their own or, better yet, be complemented by other CSOs, in a process of horizontal relations of civil society within itself.[7] Civil society, in other words, cannot by itself spark the overthrow of an authoritarian system and replace it with a democratic one. Neither can interest groups, which often have narrowly defined and specific agendas, simply take the place of political parties and replicate their functions. For democratic pressures on the state to develop, civil society—while still retaining its political autonomy and its identity—must work with and through what Alfred Stepan calls 'political society'. Stepan defines political society as the politicization of CSOs for the specific purposes of constructing a democratic state apparatus.[8] Civil society must view political society as legitimate and be willing to work with and through it. As this paper will demonstrate later, one may find a plethora of CSOs in the Middle East (as well as in Africa), ranging from tribal confederacies to freemasons and syndicates belonging to tradition merchants (bazaaris). However, not meeting the three additional pre-conditions outlined above, none of these groups has so far served as a viable medium for societal democratization or for increasing demands on the state to become more representative and/or accountable.

The democratic contingency of civil society organizations relates to a second proposition, this one dealing with their initial appearance

[6] H. Eckstein, *The Theory of Stable Democracy*, Princeton, NJ: Princeton University Press, 1961.

[7] A. Stepan, *Rethinking Military Politics: Brazil and the Southern Cone*, Princeton, NJ: Princeton University Press, 1988, p. 7.

[8] Ibid., pp. 3–4.

and subsequent rise in numbers. For CSOs to appear and become agents of political liberalization, four sets of conditions must be in place. In broad terms, they include the weakening of the state resulting from its failure to deliver its promises or to fulfil many of its functions; the cultural alienation of the state from society; political effects of economic adjustment and liberalization; and the existence of social actors able and willing to mobilize various constituents for specific goals that may be local or even national in scope. There are some functions that every state performs—the provision and building of infrastructure, for example—and there are functions that it promises to perform—stimulating economic growth and enhancing its citizens' standards of living. Civil society organizations tend to develop in response to an actual or perceived breakdown in the functions of the state in some specific area, be it in the protection of the environment, helping the indigent, sponsoring literacy classes or religious seminars, helping expectant mothers, providing health care to needy communities, and so on. Thus they emerge and organize themselves to satisfy those needs and functions which the state has been unable or unwilling to deliver. CSOs also develop when existing state-affiliated or even largely independent organizations appear tainted in the popular eye (political parties, the church, women's rights groups, etc.) because of their apparent or actual connections with the state. In these circumstances, people begin to look for other alternative venues for political organization, expression, and participation, often joining or organizing themselves into self-help groups. By serving as alternative sources of information and communication, many of these organizations directly challenge the interests and legitimacy of the state and erode its capacity to dominate and control society.[9] Thus the deterioration of the state creates the conditions for the (re)emergence of civil society.[10] This is precisely what happened with the Catholic and Protestant churches in Latin America and with labour unions in Eastern Europe, resulting in either splinter groups within the church hierarchy or in unofficial labour organizations (e.g. Solidarity), or both. However, the situation in the Middle East is completely different, with most Middle Eastern states having

[9] A. Portes & Kincaid, 'The crisis of authoritarianism: state and civil society in Argentina, Chile, and Uruguay', *Research in Political Sociology*, 1, 1985, p. 54.

[10] G. Ekiert, 'Democratization processes in East Central Europe: a theoretical reconsideration', *British Journal of Political Science*, 21, 1991, pp. 26–55.

effectively tied their own corporate identity with that of most or some of the more powerful social groups and organizations (e.g. the religious establishment), therefore curtailing much of society's independence and autonomy.

If autonomy has to do with the amount of power that state and society have in comparison to one another, then the state's ownership of, or control over, the various economic resources found in society is of utmost importance. Most democratic transitions—with a few notable exceptions, such as Argentina, Brazil and Southern Europe—are usually preceded by extensive economic liberalization programmes that once initiated, signal the state's willingness to roll back some of its functions.[11] Economic liberalization entails two facets: on the one hand, it is a product of the large-scale failure of state-led capitalism and of import-substitution industrialization (ISI); on the other hand, it results in the transfer of economic decision-making and power to market forces and social actors, therefore potentially empowering civil society.[12] When economic liberalization takes place under conditions of political stress and instability, as it did in Latin America in the mid-1980s, it is often a sign that the old implicit or explicit bargains between political leaders and their key support groups are not working, and that existing assumptions about the 'rules of the game' can and indeed need to change.[13] Moreover, as some of these authoritarian governments embarked upon belt-tightening structural adjustment reforms, as Pinochet did in Chile in the early 1980s, much of the social costs of fiscal reform were inflicted upon the popular sector. Under these circumstances, civil society is given no alternative but to look inward in order to find cooperative solutions to the decline in the living standard of its constituents.[14] In crisis situations,

11 Several scholars have aptly noted these exceptions, e.g. J. M. Maravall, C. Bresser-Pereira & A. Przeworski, *Economic Reforms in New Democracies*, New York: Cambridge University Press, 1991, pp. 77–131. It is important to note that economic liberalization in Chile began with the imposition of the authoritarian state.

12 A. Przeworski, *Democracy and the Market: Political and Economic Reforms in Eastern Europe and Latin America*, Cambridge: Cambridge University Press, 1991, p. 182.

13 S. Haggard & R. Kaufman, *The Political Economy of Democratic Transitions*, Princeton, NJ: Princeton University Press, 1995, p. 7.

14 P. Oxhorn, *Organizing Civil Society: The Popular Sectors and the Struggle for Democracy*, University Park, PA: Pennsylvania State University Press, 1995, p. 44.

it is also a signal to other economic actors that they can, if they so choose, defect from the old political alliance on which the non-democratic state relies. In other words, 'the inability to avoid or adjust successfully to economic crisis increases the probability that authoritarian regimes will be transformed and reduces the capacity of authoritarian leaders to control the process of political change, including the terms on which they exist'.[15] The potential ramifications for CSOS could be far-reaching, particularly in light of the increasingly freer environment within which they operate and the mounting pressures on the state. The breakdown of paternalistic, ISI strategies prompt the state to scale back its role, thereby reducing its ties to society (e.g. subsidies, etc.). Civil society is no longer tied materially to the state, thus allowing it to organize itself in an autonomous fashion.

Finally, CSOs are made up of social actors, some of whom are located strategically in society in terms of their cultural prestige, their access to communication networks, and means of mass mobilization, and the degree to which they can safeguard their autonomy from the state. Some of the more notable social actors that belong in this category include clergymen, intellectuals, community activists, union organizers, and the like. Having the opportunities and the facilities to organize into independent action from the state is one thing; doing so democratically and for larger democratic goals is quite another. Just because CSOs exist does not mean that their individual or collective efforts will automatically amount to democratic pressures on the state. To facilitate a democratic transition, CSOs must inculcate the norms of tolerance, trust, moderation, and accommodation. Contingency comes into play again, with some actors being democratically inclined at some points and in some contexts while others less so. The comparative role of the clergy within Latin America at different times and between Latin America and the Middle East is most illustrative. Up until the late 1960s and the early 1970s, few clerics in Latin America were terribly concerned with their countries' deplorable political predicaments and the widespread lack of social justice. In fact, in many Latin countries the church formed one of the main corporate groups on which the authoritarian state relied for its legitimacy. However, with changes in the social agendas of the church after

---

[15] Haggard & Kaufman, *The Political Economy of Democratic Transitions*, pp. 7–8.

Vatican II and the 1968 conference of bishops in Medellin, and the subsequent growth of Liberation Theology, many Latin American priests became agents of social awakening and vocal proponents of demands for political representation and social justice.[16] The situation in the Middle East is quite different for although many clergymen there jealously guard their independence from the state and, especially in recent years, have seriously challenged the powers and legitimacy of the political elite, few are interested in giving popular currency to the ideals of democracy and in bringing about truly representative political systems.[17]

In the early to mid-1980s, when many of the transitions to democracy were set in motion, all four conditions needed for the flourishing of civil society organizations could be readily found in most Latin American countries. In turn, they helped facilitate the growth and increasing influence of grass-roots organizations such as Ecclesiastical Base Communities (CEBs), Mothers of Plaza de Mayo in Argentina, the Movement of the Friends of the Neighbourhood in Brazil, and the Association of Democratic Women in Chile. At a time when the Latin American state was confronting acute political and economic crises of its own, society was grappling with a series of indigenous developments that made it assume an overall democratic posture vis-à-vis the weakened state. The state–society negotiations that ensued were almost bound to have democratic outcomes, especially in the light of the retreating state's increasingly narrow options—domestically, internationally, and economically—the concurrent emboldening and empowering of social actors, and the perpetuating momentum of what had steadily become a full-blown, democratic movement. In short, in Latin America a dense civil society developed and became

16 D. Levine, *Religion and Political Conflict in Latin America*, Chapel Hill, NC: University of North Carolina Press, 1986. It is important to note that the development of this social awakening in the church did not develop with the same intensity throughout Latin America, and did not necessarily flourish in direct response to military regimes. The church in Argentina and Bolivia was not as inclined towards social activism as the institution in Colombia and Central America.

17 This point deserves much fuller treatment than the scope of this paper allows. For two differing views on this, see J. Miller, *God Has Ninety-Nine Names: Reporting From a Militant Middle East*, New York: Simon and Schuster, 1996; and J. Esposito & J. Voll, *Islam and Democracy*, Oxford: Oxford University Press, 1996.

more articulate and powerful as the crises facing the state became more profound. Reinforced by a long heritage of familiarity with the concept and practice of democracy in the region, the coming political transition was likely to result in a representative democracy.

The situation in the Middle East has been quite different, however. Although some conditions favourable to the development and spread of democratically inclined civil society organizations have been present in a few Middle Eastern countries, many more have been conspicuously absent. The contrasts with Latin America are particularly striking. Whereas bureaucratic–authoritarian states in Latin America failed completely in the very domain that was meant to be the mainstay of their legitimacy—the economy—the rentier, corporatist states of the Middle East have been able to continue drawing rent revenues, albeit at much smaller rates compared with a decade or so ago, and to make good on the implicit and explicit promises that underlie their popular legitimacy. Most Middle Eastern states have also been able to manipulate enough cultural norms and premises—be they Islam or charisma, nationalist sentiments or patrimonialism—still to retain evocative and emotional ties with the broad strata of society, something which the military-based states of Latin America could only dream of. Moreover, while there has been some economic liberalization in the Middle East, it has been neither enough nor in a direction that would result in a meaningful rolling back of the extensive reaches of the state. In sharp contrast to Latin America, therefore, the overall conditions for the development of a democratic civil society are not currently present in the Middle East and the CSOs that are found there (e.g. those belonging to the religious *ulema*, *bazaari* merchants, professional associations, etc.) tend to be interested in pursuits other than democratic ones.

CIVIL SOCIETY IN LATIN AMERICA

Civil Society in Latin America is not a recent phenomenon. In fact, Latin America was the first region of the Third World to develop a semi-autonomous, semi-democratic civil society, dating as far back as 1870.[18] This may well have to do with the fact that Latin America

---

[18] For an analysis of the early development of civil society in Latin America, see R. C. Çonde, *The First Stages of Modernization in Spanish America*, New York: Harper and Row, 1974; R. Duncan, *Latin American Politics: A Developmental Approach*, New York: Praeger, 1976.

has been in the process of political development much longer than any other region, since it was the first to gain independence during the first quarter of the nineteenth century—in most cases more than a century before many nations in Africa, Southeast Asia, and the Middle East. However, a democratic civil society as defined above, as an agent of democratization, did not begin to develop until the late 1960s.

There is no question that the degree to which civil society has developed in Latin America varies from one country to the next. Certainly, civil society has not only developed but has internalized democratic values more in Argentina, Chile, Costa Rica, and Uruguay than in Guatemala and Paraguay. The differences rest in the historical process of industrialization/modernization, socio-economic development and social differentiation, to name just a few. However, there are some important generalizations that can be made, particularly concerning countries which were under an authoritarian regime until the mid-1980s, about civil society and democratization in Latin America. An important claim made in this paper is that civil society in many Latin American countries not only developed because of state breakdown, weakening, or retreat, but, as the Chilean case demonstrates, in spite of the state. Despite attempts by the state to politically demobilize or deactivate society, at a minimum, enclaves of autonomous political organization and activity expanded under tremendous pressure or neglect from the state.[19] Organized labour was one of the most important sectors that, despite being weakened in Argentina, Chile, and Uruguay, were not eliminated. They proved able to mobilize workers against the regimes, providing an important nucleus for resistance by other groups in society.[20] Once again, this was typically the case in the more industrialized countries of Latin America, specifically the bureaucratic–authoritarian regimes of South America, but it does not preclude similar processes in other Latin American countries.

[19] On the development of civil society under an authoritarian regime, see S. Eckstein (ed.), *Power and Popular Protest: Latin American Social Movements*, Berkeley, CA: University of California Press, 1989; J. Corradi, P. W. Fagen & M. A. Garreton (eds), *Fear at the Edge: State Terror and Resistance in Latin America*, Berkeley, CA: University of California Press, 1992.

[20] P. Drake, *Labour Movements and Dictatorships: The Southern Cone in Comparative Perspective*, Baltimore, MD: Johns Hopkins University Press, 1996.

Civil Society Organizations in Latin America

The growth of civil society in Latin America has been linked to the process of socio-economic development, initially sparked by the expansion of the export sector (1880–1930) and then accelerated by the modernizing processes of industrialization and capitalist development (1930–60). These processes generated profound social changes and gave rise to various actors demanding expression and political inclusion.[21] Once state power was consolidated in the 1880s Latin America embarked on a process of agricultural and/or mineral export expansion, setting into motion subtle but important transformations in society. The growth of the middle sectors (i.e. merchants, shopkeepers, and small businessmen) and of urbanization, which accompanied the expansion of the export economy, were the foundations upon which civil society began to develop around the turn of the century.[22] With the newly emerging urban groups of employees and professionals, or workers in transport and early manufacturing, civil society became stronger and the weight of previously excluded sectors steadily increased.[23]

The acceleration of modernization and industrialization, in its second and more profound stage from 1930 to 1960, gave rise to some new and more differentiated social forces that further altered the social structure and nature of state–society relations. The growth of commerce helped stimulate the emergence of a new class of business people who began to organize into associational and/or professional groups that challenged the powers of the traditional oligarchs, especially large landowners. Starting in the 1930s in some countries and later in others, the growth of ISI, along with urbanization, brought forth further expansion of the middle and working classes, particularly state employees (product of state expansion), private white collar employees, professionals and intellectuals, along with artisans, shopkeepers, and small entrepreneurs. As Rueschemeyer,

---

[21] C. Anderson, *Politics and Economic Change in Latin America*, Princeton, NJ: Van Nostrand, 1967: David Rueschemeyer, et al., *Capitalist Development and Democracy*.

[22] J. Johnson, *Political Change in Latin America: The Emergence of the Middle Sectors*, Stanford, CA: Stanford University Press, 1958.

[23] G. Germani, *The Sociology of Modernization: Studies on Its Historical and Theoretical Aspects in Latin America*, New Brunswick: Transactions Books, 1981.

Stephens and Stephens maintain, 'industrialization raised the potential for pressures for democratization, particularly for greater political inclusion, because it strengthened civil society by increasing the size and the interaction among the middle sectors and the working class'.[24] This process was most pronounced in the early industrializing nations of Mexico and South America: Argentina, Brazil, Chile, and Uruguay. In the agricultural-export economies of Central America, the state and clientelistic parties shaped the political articulation of a less diversified and differentiated civil society.[25]

The process of socio-economic development accelerated and expanded to other countries of Latin America throughout the mid-1990s. However, this second phase in the development of civil society did not spark a sustainable process of democratization because its political effects were mediated by pre-existing political and institutional structures, most of which were still controlled by traditional, anti-democratic elites—particularly the party system—and by the tradition of state intervention in society. Additionally, civil society was paralyzed by its own inability or unwillingness to organize democratically and to articulate a democratic agenda. In the case of Mexico, for instance, middle sector organizations representing groups such as government employees, teachers, private farmers, small merchants, and professionals were organized into the corporatist National Confederation of Popular Organizations (CNOP), which in turn formed the basis for the 'popular sector' of President Lazaro Cardenas' Revolutionary Party of Mexico (PRM).[26] In these regimes, trade unions were the first to be co-opted and incorporated into the corporatist state because of their potential to undermine and threaten the status quo.[27]

In some cases, civil society groups were not immune to the idea of inviting military intervention or seeking alliances with the oligarchy in order to avert pressure from the 'uneducated lower classes' and

[24] Rueschemeyer et al., Capitalist Development and Democracy, p. 166.

[25] V. Bulmer-Thomas, The Political Economy of Central America Since 1920, Cambridge: Cambridge University Press, 1987, pp. 68–100.

[26] R. Spalding, 'The Mexican variant of corporatism', Comparative Political Studies, 14, 1981, pp. 139–61.

[27] V. Alba, Politics and the Labour Movement in Latin America, Stanford, CA: Stanford University Press, 1968, pp. 67–96; K. Erickson, The Brazillian Corporative State and Working Class Politics, Berkeley, CA: University of California Press, 1977.

to obtain (or maintain) certain material and political privileges.[28] In fact, these middle sectors feared 'premature democratization', that is, a democratic process that they could not control in the face of challenges from radical trade unions and organized peasants.[29] Thus, despite growing industrialization during the 1930s and 1940s, civil society developed neither autonomous organizations nor an effective democratic political articulation through societal or party organizations at the national level. Proto-democratic pressures from popular groups remained weak until well into the 1960s.

There has been a paradoxical relationship between authoritarian rule and the development of civil society in Latin America. Ironically, it would be the experience of the repression of military authoritarian regimes, particularly bureaucratic–authoritarian, that would finally produce a fully developed and autonomous civil society, making it an important agent of democratization by contributing to the erosion of authoritarian rule. Where the bureaucratic–authoritarian regimes were successful in generating further industrialization and socio-economic development (as in Argentina, Brazil, and Chile), civil society grew stronger and after the initial phase of repression started to simmer down pressures for liberalization and democratization re-emerged.[30] As authoritarianism waned, CSOS proliferated in the form of self-help or non-governmental organizations that sought to provide an alternative venue of information, communication, and social assistance to individuals and groups suffering from political repression and economic exclusion.[31] A case in point was the development of Chilean grass-roots neighbourhood organizations known as *poblaciones* which became active near the end of Pinochet's rule in the 1980.[32] Subsequently, as in the case of the Movement of the Friends of the Neighbourhood in Nova Iguaçu, Brazil, these organizations, with the

[28] C. Wagley, 'The dilemma of the Latin America middle class', in C. Wagley (ed.), *The Latin American Tradition*, New York: Columbia University Press, 1968, pp. 194–212.

[29] C. Veliz, *The Politics of Conformity in Latin America*, London: Oxford University Press, 1976, p. 72.

[30] Rueschemeyer, *et al.*, *Capitalist Development and Democracy*, p. 217.

[31] L. Landim, 'Nongovernmental organizations in Latin America', in R. Camp (ed.), *Democracy in Latin America: Patterns and Cycles*, Wilmington: Scholarly Resources, 1996, pp. 207–22.

[32] C. Schneider, *Shantytown Protest in Pinochet's Chile*, Philadelphia, PA: Temple University Press, 1995.

assistance of the Catholic church, established strong horizontal relations within civil society that contributed to the pluralism and diversity of forces demanding inclusion, participation and, eventually, democracy from below.[33]

Once in power, bureaucratic–authoritarian regimes sought to radically change both the political system as well as the social and economic structures in existence.[34] In order to accomplish these agendas they tried to exclude economically and to destroy politically any organizational potential that autonomous societal groups might have had. They thus resorted to heavy-handed repression and implemented economic austerity and export policies. In Argentina, Brazil, Chile, and Uruguay these regimes 'proved to be extremely effective at fragmenting, atomizing, and inhibiting, potential oppositional collectivities'. In the initial period of bureaucratic authoritarianism, therefore, civil society 'lost its capacity to generate new political and economic initiatives while the power of the state grew'.[35] As a result, civil society as a whole and its political articulations were significantly weakened in all these cases. Only in Brazil was civil society able to reconstitute its institutions, after a very brief period of repression, while the state continued to acquire additional capacity. In the other cases, particularly in Chile, the state was able to demobilize civil society through a combined strategy of repression, on the one hand, and the restructuring of Chilean capitalism and state–society relations on the other.[36] In Chile, the state retreated or broke its ties to civil society through the use of extensive repression and through what Alfred Stepan characterizes as the 'marketization' of its functions.[37]

[33] S. Mainwaring, 'Grassroots popular movements and the struggle for democracy: Nova Iguaçu', in A. Stepan (ed.), *Democratizing Brazil: Problems of Transition*, New York: Oxford University Press, 1989, pp. 168–204; and J. Burdick, 'Rethinking the study of social movements: the case of urban Christian base communities in urban Brazil', in A. Escobar & S. Alvarez (eds), *The Making of Social Movements in Latin America: Identity, Strategy, and Democracy*, Boulder, CO: Westview Press, 1992, pp. 171–84.

[34] G. O'Donnell, *Modernization and Bureaucratic-Authoritarianism*, Berkeley, CA: Institute of International Studies, University of California, 1973.

[35] A. Stepan, 'State power and the strength of civil society in the Southern Cone of Latin America', in P. Evans, D. Rueschemeyer and T. Skocpol (eds), *Bringing the State Back In*, New York: Cambridge University Press, 1985, p. 317.

[36] K. Remmer, *Military Rule in Latin America*, Boulder, CO: Westview Press, 1991.

[37] Stepan, 'State power and the strength of civil society', p. 323.

The military's policies of deindustrialization and state retrenchment' weakened civil society and its capacity to articulate demands for political change. In the process of restructuring the economy, the state rescinded its previous social functions.[38] For the first time since the 1920s the state turned its back on society, leaving civil society no alternative but to organize self-help groups and cooperate in finding common solutions to common social needs. The absence of institutionalized linkages civil society made it difficult for the authoritarian regime to contain domestic demands for reform. In short, by attempting to disarticulate civil society, these regimes unwittingly contributed to the formation of autonomous and pluralistic societal organizations. By the mid-1980s, these organizations were sufficiently empowered to have become agents of democratization.[39]

Civil Society and Democracy in Latin America

One element that contributed to the growth of civil society organizations with more-or-less oppositional agendas within the context of authoritarian regimes, particularly in Brazil and Chile, was the profound changes within the Catholic church.[40] After the 1968 Bishop's Conference in Medellin, the church in Latin America adopted an agenda for the poor that emphasized social reform, justice, and a stronger stance against human rights violations by the state. Through the formation of Christian base communities, the level of organization of marginalized groups was raised considerably in such places as Central America and Brazil. The participatory practices of these base

[38] For a discussion of state–society relations during the Pinochet dictatorship, see H. Fruhling, 'Repressive policies and legal dissent in authoritarian regimes: Chile 1973–1981', *International Journal of Sociology of Law*, 12, 1984, pp. 351–74; J. Valenzuela & A. Valenzuela (eds), *Military Rule in Chile: Dictatorship and Opposition*, Baltimore, MD: Johns Hopkins University Press, 1986; M. Garreton, *The Chilean Political Process*, Boston, MA: Allen and Unwin, 1989.

[39] M. Garreton, 'Popular mobilization and the military regime in Chile: the complexities of the invisible transition', in S. Eckstein (ed.), *Power and Popular Protest: Latin American Social Movements*, Berkeley, CA: University of California Press, 1989.

[40] D. Mutchler, *The Church as a Political Force in Latin America*, New York: Praeger, 1971; B. Smith, *The Church and Politics in Chile*, Princeton, NJ: Princeton University Press, 1982; S. Mainwaring, *The Catholic Church and Politics in Brazil, 1916–1985*, Stanford, CA: Stanford University Press, 1986.

communities predisposed their members to demand opportunities for participation in the political process. These base communities in Brazil became the foundations upon which other societal groups, like trade unions and neighbourhood associations, learned to organize and from which resources could be transferred horizontally from one sphere of civil society to others.[41] This contributed to the pluralism and diversity of civil society.

Concurrent with changes in the church were highly consequential changes occurring within the left. As Francisco Weffort has noted, the contagiousness of the horizontal relations of civil society within itself and the successful democratization of Latin America would not have been possible without the overwhelming majority of the left undergoing a deep ideological reassessment, the upshot of which was a 'revalorization' of democracy not just as a temporary tactic but as a permanent value.[42] In other words, if it were not for the Latin American left leaving behind its militancy and revolutionary rhetoric, the military and their allies would not have felt 'safe' in allowing political liberalization.[43] This is another crucial area of difference in the emergence and evolution of civil society in the Middle East and Latin America: whereas in Latin America the left adopted democracy for its intrinsic as well as popular values, Middle Eastern opposition groups have yet to do so (see below).

Finally, severe economic difficulties played an important role in the strengthening of civil society and in the transition of democratic rule in virtually every country except Chile.[44] Mounting economic difficulties encouraged opposition within the private sector and contributed to the mobilization of broader social and electoral movements. The powers of society grew in relation to the weakening and delegitimation of the authoritarian regime. In the case of Brazil, for instance, significant industrialization led to a new, much more diverse,

[41] T. Bruneau, *The Church in Brazil: The Politics of Religion*, Austin, TX: University of Texas Press, 1982; R. D. Cava, 'The "People's Church", the Vatican, and Abertura', in Stepan (ed.), *Democratizing Brazil*, pp. 143–67.

[42] F. Weffort, *Qual Democracia?* São Paulo: Companhia Das Letras, 1992, pp. 42–69.

[43] For a discussion of the Latin American left and its changes in rhetoric, strategies, and goals, see J. Castaneda, *Utopia Unarmed: The Latin American Left after the Cold War*, New York: Knopf, 1993.

[44] Haggard and Kaufman, *The Political Economy of Democratic Transition*, pp. 45–74.

complex and interrelated economy, in turn creating new sources of wealth and power outside the state, thus changing the social structure of wealth and power outside the state, thus changing the social structure and values that encouraged democratization. Once the economy entered the recessionary period of the early 1980s, these forces were unleashed and began demanding political space and representation. In other words, by the mid-1970s in Brazil, 'it was precisely those sectors which benefitted most from the years of the economic miracle that were the most vocal in demanding a return to democratic rule'.[45] In the end, as in Argentina and Bolivia, the decisive turning points in the process of authoritarian withdrawal occurred when rampant corruption, economic crisis and civilian political opposition had seriously weakened the commitment of military leaders to the original authoritarian project.

The austerity policies adopted by some regimes to correct fiscal imbalances and high rates of inflation also contributed to the formation of an autonomous and democratic civil society. These authoritarian regimes, already weakened by defections and by their inability to deliver economically, were forced to take unpopular deficit-reduction measures that hurt the most marginalized strata of society. The political consequences of the austerity measures only further weakened and delegitimized these military governments and strengthened the resolve and organizational capacity of civil society as pressure for reform left these regimes, particularly in light of defections from the ruling coalition, with no other viable option than to embark upon a process of democratic transition.[46]

The growth of democratic civil society in Latin America during the Third Wave is linked to a number of historical, socio-economic, and political factors that enabled society to open its own spaces for political organization and expression in spite of efforts by repressive states to deny independent political activity. In many ways, the highly exclusionary military regimes of South America accelerated and helped consolidate a process that had been well underway since the early part of the century. The lack of socio-political alternatives

[45] S. Mainwaring, 'The transition to democracy in Brazil', *Journal of Interamerican Studies and World Affairs*, 28, September 1986, p. 152.

[46] G. Richards, 'Stablization crises and the breakdown of military authoritarianism in Latin America', *Comparative Political Studies*, 18(4), 1986, pp. 449–85.

coupled with state hostility and neglect of social functions offered CSOs no other option than to establish independent and horizontally included CSOs. Though not as dense, civil societies in less institutionalized polities, such as in Central America and Paraguay, where clientalism still impedes the development of a truly democratic civil society, are demonstrating higher levels of political organization and participation that are contributing to the democratization of their states.

CIVIL SOCIETY IN THE MIDDLE EAST

In the Middle East, there have historically been three civil society organizations that have enjoyed considerable autonomy and independence from the state. They are the clergy (*ulema*), tribes and tribal confederacies, and traditional merchants known as the *bazaaris*. Despite their historical longevity, however, the circumstances within which these and other CSOs have interacted with the state in the Middle East have rendered them largely ineffective as forums for the emergence and spread of democratic ideals. The Middle Eastern state has had a pattern of evolution, especially since the Second World War, that has been decidedly different from that of the Latin American state. Whereas the Latin American state had to concoct enemies domestically, the Middle Eastern state had and continues to have real and tangible enemies outside its borders. Whereas the Latin American state took a laissez-faire approach to the domestic forces of culture and society, thus leaving people to fend for themselves, the Middle Eastern state has gone directly after culture, manipulating its every aspect—from Islam to charisma, clientalism, and patronage—to enhance its own source of legitimacy. Finally, whereas the Latin American state was single-minded in its pursuit of ISI, the Middle Eastern state instituted a mixed economy, supported by an ever-expanding bureaucracy, that enabled it to retain considerable economic leverage over social actors and other potentially autonomous groups. The end result has been a depoliticization of CSOs in the Middle East. CSOs remain largely independent of the state, but the state's own active social and political agendas have given the CSOs little reason even to become political, much less agents for democratization.

A comparative analysis of the Middle East reveals two general types of economies in the region: those of the conservative sheikhdoms of the Arabian peninsula, whose incredible oil wealth has prompted one observer to label them as 'oil monarchies',[47] and the less wealthy, more differentiated economies found in the rest of the region. Because of their different capacities and sources of legitimacy in relation to society, these two groups of states have gone about dealing with CSOS in quite different ways. One group, namely the oil monarchies, has used petrodollars to establish an extensive welfare apparatus through which it has sought to placate and buy off, rather successfully, most independent CSOS. In fact, as far back as the 1950s, in order to address the growing disquiet of the population caused by profound changes in economic and social relations, the states of the Arabian peninsula began to utilize economic planning and development as a form of institutionalized social control.[48] For their part, the states with less affluent economies have resorted to a mixture of populism and repression to emasculate independent or oppositional groups. In either case, the historical development and current predicament of CSOs do not bode well for transition to democracy.

State–society Relations in the Middle East

In contrast to Latin America, formal independence came rather late to the Middle East, from the 1920s to the 1940s, and was soon followed by a host of radical and transformative revolutions throughout the 1950s and 1960s. The Nasserist revolution of 1952 in Egypt inspired similar events in Iraq in 1958, in Syria in 1963, in Sudan in 1964, and in Libya in 1969. Meanwhile, highly populist regimes came to power in the Maghreb following the withdrawal of the French from the region, beginning with Tunisia and Morocco in 1956 and Algeria in 1962. Invariably, the incoming inclusionary states launched massive industrialization and modernization campaigns and sought to enhance their control over society by building up a mammoth, modern bureaucracy. State-led capitalism became the order of the day, and, accordingly, most urban classes became directly or indirectly dependent on the state and its patronage. From 1952 to 1970, for example, during Nasser's rule, the Egyptian bureaucracy grew from employing 250,000 individuals to providing jobs for over

---

[47] F. G. Gause, *Oil Monarchies: Domestic and Security Challenges in the Arab Gulf States*, New York: Council on Foreign Relations Press, 1994.

[48] J. Ismael, *Kuwait: Dependency and Class in a Rentier State*, Gainesville, FL: University Press of Florida, 1993, p. 134.

1,200,000. The number of state-owned corporations also jumped from one in 1957 to 46 in 1970.[49] In Sudan the number of state employees similarly grew from 176,408 in 1955-6 to 408,716 in 1976-7.[50] Through successive land reforms, existing feudal classes were destroyed and replaced by urban capitalists who owed much of their economic status and prestige to the state. The bureaucratic middle class that also emerged, most of it employed in the civil service, was also heavily dependent on the state and its pursuit of rentier economic policies.[51]

These economic and political developments only reinforced the historically urban character of politics in the Middle East, and, consequently, tribal and other bedouin groups increasingly lost any political significance they once might have had.[52] Nevertheless, as Cantori points out, the state has legitimized some (urban) groups, permitting them to play social roles, while prohibiting others from doing so.[53] Politically largely innocuous, most of these groups consist of associations of physicians, journalists, lawyers, and engineers, most of whose members are reluctant to engage in overtly oppositional activities against the state for fear of losing the few privileges that the state has granted them. This corporatist arrangement, and with it the implicit understanding that has emerged between the various social groups and the state, has come under pressure in recent years in places such as Jordan and Egypt with the ascendance of Islamist activists to leadership positions within many of the independent and professional associations. But, even in these instances, the state has been adept at either isolating its most vocal opponents (as in Egypt) or reducing the overall significance of their oppositional statements

[49] M. Palmer, A. Leila and E. S. Yassin, *The Egyptian Bureaucracy*, Cairo: The American University of Cairo Press, 1988, p. 4.

[50] A. Richards and J. Waterbury, *A Political Economy of the Middle East*, Boulder, CO: Westview, 1990, p. 205.

[51] D. Sullivan, 'Extra-state actors and privatization in Egypt', in I. Harik and D. Sullivan (eds), *Privatization and Liberalization in the Middle East*, Bloomington, IN: Indiana University Press, 1992, pp. 27-8.

[52] K. H. al-Naqeeb, 'Social origins of the authoritarian state in the Arab East', in E. Davis and N. Gavrielides (eds), *Statecraft in the Middle East: Oil, Historical Memory, and Popular Culture*, Miami: Florida International University Press, 1991, pp. 42-3.

[53] L. Cantori, 'Civil society, liberalism and the corporatist alternative in the Middle East', *Middle East Studies Association Bulletin*, 31(1), 1997, p. 37.

(as in Jordan).[54] In any event, 'these groups do not compete with one another horizontally as in the pluralist model but rather have a vertical relationship to the state'.[55]

Equally consequential for the CSOs has been the emergence of two reinforcing political developments, one domestic and the other international. Domestically, a number of Middle Eastern states have at some point had highly charismatic leaders—Muhammad V in Morocco, Nasser in Egypt, Ben Bella in Algeria, Qaddafi in Libya, Bourguiba in Tunisia, and Khomeini in Iran, to name a few—who at least initially instituted inclusionary regimes that combined repression with charismatic populism. The goal of the state was (and in places like Libya and Iraq continues to be) to mobilize mass participation in pursuit of one emotionally-laden project or another (the destruction of the 'Israeli enemy' has long been a favourite). Severely sacrificed in the process was societal autonomy, and even those urban groups with a history of independence from the state—of which the clergy and the *bazaaris* were the most notable—have often found it necessary to toe the state's line. Reinforcing the domestic omnipotence and repressive nature of the state was the volatile international environment of the post-WW II era, fuelled in the Middle East by the Israeli–Palestinian conflict, which has ultimately benefited the region's authoritarian regimes in their pursuit of hegemony over domestic actors. Under the mantle of the Palestinian cause, Middle Eastern autocrats have long solidified their own power-bases internally, branded domestic opponents as Zionist collaborators, and built up the edifice of the state to unprecedented proportions.

Two official power centres emerged in the process. The first was the military, the central fount of official power and the primary institution that supplied the leaders and top officials of the state. Throughout the 1950s and 1960s almost all Arab republics of the Middle East, with the exception of Lebanon, had 'revolutionary command councils' that ran the state. The second power centre was the official party—often the only party allowed to operate—which was designed to balance the repression of the military with popular mobilization and mass political inclusion. Again, Colonel Nasser

[54] M. Kamrava, 'Frozen political liberalization in Jordan: the consequences for democracy', *Democratization*, 5(1), 1998, pp. 138–57.

[55] L. Cantori, 'Civil society, liberalism and the corporatist alternative in the Middle East', p. 37.

and the Arab Socialist Union set the standard, followed by General Assad and the Ba'th party in Syria (in 1963 and again 1970), General al-Bakr and the Ba'th party in Iraq (1963), Colonel Boumedienne and the National Liberation Front in Algeria (1965), and Colonel Qaddafi and his system of *jumhuriyya* (1969). Urban social classes were either repressed and depoliticized, or forcibly or voluntarily mobilized in support of the state's anti-Israeli projects. By the 1970s, the powerful mixture of inclusionary policies on the one hand and brute repression and intolerance on the other had made the state's domination of society nearly complete. The one state in this category that shunned inclusionary policies—that of the Shah of Iran—succumbed to a popular revolutionary movement as soon as it loosened its repressive policies.

The economic ramifications of authoritarianism were equally significant. State capitalism left little room for the growth of a sizeable, autonomous capitalist class. Instead, the numbers of state employees in the bureaucratic and industrial sectors mushroomed, there being no tolerance of independent unions or syndicates of any kind. Much of the private sector activity, meanwhile, took place through relatively small shops and stores (a phenomenon which still continues today), the few employees of which are often drawn from relatives, neighbours, and other acquaintances. Apart from a brief period in the 1940s and 1950s therefore, a sense of workers' solidarity has not fully developed in the Middle East, especially in countries where a single industry—oil—does not dominate the economy (Jordan, Syria, Lebanon, Egypt, Tunisia, and Morocco).[56] Industrialists similarly found themselves curtailed by the intrusive reaches of the state, even after the initiation of economic liberalization policies (known as the *infitah*, or open door) in the mid-1970s and 1980s. Most states simply refined their economic roles and continued to remain 'the largest business "corporation"' within the country.[57]

The record of most Middle Eastern states on divestiture has been modest: several firms in Turkey, Tunisia, and Egypt, a few in (pre-Gulf War) Iraq, but none in Algeria, Syria, or Jordan.[58] For its part,

---

[56] A notable exception was Bahrain, where there were repeated instances of labour unrest throughout the 1960s.

[57] I. Harik, 'Privatization: the issue, the prospects, and the fears', in Harik and Sullivan, *Privatization and Liberalization in the Middle East*, p. 12.

[58] Ibid., p. 17.

after some 20 years of post-revolutionary institutionalization, the Iranian government has not yet decided on the extent of its involvement in the economy, which has nevertheless been consistently high since 1979.[59] With the exception of Turkey (where a limited and highly restricted democratic system has been in existence since 1983), Middle Eastern governments continue to be the biggest employers and retain many of their interventionist economic features. After twenty years of supposedly liberal market economics in Egypt and Tunisia, for example, the public sector still generates some 65 per cent and 60 per cent, respectively of manufacturing output.[60] The limited economic reforms implemented have primarily been designed with tactical political considerations in mind and have not changed the overall nature of the state's involvement in the economy.[61] Nowhere in the Middle East has there been the wholesale implementation of neo-liberal market reforms of the kind that occurred in Latin America in the 1980s. Nevertheless, although the *infitah* improved the lot of many in the upper and upper middle classes, their essentially dependent relationship with the state remained intact. An overwhelming majority of these wealthy industrialists are import–export merchants who continue to rely on the state for securing contracts and acquiring the necessary permits and licences. Even if the risks were not as severe as they are now, few industrialists have much incentive to act against the state.

The relationship of the state to society is based on a somewhat different premise in the oil monarchies. But the outcome—lack of societal pressure for change—is essentially the same. The corporatist arrangement in the oil monarchies has four central axioms. At the top sits the royal family, which dominates and is often indistinguishable from the state (especially in smaller countries such as Oman, Bahrain, Qatar, and Kuwait). The royal family is, in turn, supported by three key social groups: the clergy, whose close association with the state has resulted in the emergence of a so-called 'Official Islam' (*al-Islam al-rasmi*); chiefs and notables from other tribes; and wealthy

59 H. Amirahmadi, *Revolution and Economic Transition: The Iranian Experience*, Albany, NY: Suny Press, 1990, p. 101.

60 I. Harik, 'Privatization', p. 13.

61 H. Barkey, 'Can the Middle East compete?', in L. Diamond and M. Plattner (eds), *Economic Reform and Democracy*, Baltimore, MD: Johns Hopkins University Press, 1995, p. 167.

merchants and industrialists. None of these three groups is willing to challenge an implicit understanding with the state that has long ensured their economic prosperity, social affluence, political inclusion (or acceptance), and physical security. Those openly opposing the regime invariably come from outside these corporatist groups, with many being Islamist activists who question the credentials of the royal family and its Official Islam. Not surprisingly, the state persecutes them with relentless repression.

Formal independence came to the oil monarchies even later than in the rest of the Middle East (Kuwait in 1961, Bahrain in 1970, Qatar and the United Arab Emirates in 1971). Nevertheless, the royal families that eventually dominated the state had already achieved local control and prominence long before the departing British recognized them as the rulers of the region. Upon the assumption of formal power, the royal families based their control of the state on two powerful principles—one economic, the other historical. Historically, the royal families used the apparatus of the state to presents themselves as the 'natural' outgrowth of tribal forces in society, the true representatives of the *essence* of their nation.[62] By so doing, they nullified any potential claims to rulership that other tribal chieftains or local notables might have had, thus eliminating an important source of possible opposition or, for that matter, societal independence. With varying degrees of success, they also sought to cultivate additional legitimacy on religious grounds, presenting themselves as the embodiment of religious piety and righteousness.[63] Although there have been widespread and frequent reports of corruption and immorality in the Gulf court,[64] all the royal families present highly pious and devout images of themselves to their populations. Fortunate to house Mecca and Medina in his territory, in 1986 Saudi Arabia's King Fahd went so far as to adopt the title of 'Custodian of Islam's Holiest Mosques'.[65]

[62] The use of the term 'natural state' here is inspired by Khaldoun Hasan al-Naqeeb, although he uses it in a specific historical context, lasting roughly from the 16th century to the 19th century. See K. H. al-Naqeeb, *Society and State in the Gulf and Arab Peninsula*, London: Routledge, 1990, pp. 6–24.

[63] Gause, *Oil Monarchies*, pp. 12–13.

[64] P. Wilson & D. Graham, *Saudi Arabia: The Coming Storm*, Armonk, NY: ME Sharpe, 1994, p. 56.

[65] Ibid., p. 61. In addition to 'His Majesty', the King dropped other titles, including 'Light of the Kingdom' and 'Object of One's Self-Sacrifice'.

Complementing these subjective sources of legitimacy are concrete ties forged through economic patronage, with the public purse being controlled and distributed under the direct supervision of the royal family. Formal independence meant transferring the oil industry to the control of the royal family, by which time other traditional sources of wealth—pearl diving and overseas trade—had run their course and exhausted themselves. It was only in the 1950s and 1960s, after would-be royal families had already started dominating the oil sector, that economic growth set in and wealthy merchants and industrialists began appearing in the cities. Economic patronage, in fact, can be traced to pre-independence days, although the evolution of the modern state gave it institutional sanction and legitimacy. Currently, throughout the Arabian peninsula the second most afflu-ent echelon of society after the royal family is made up of a class of wealthy, urban-based merchants, followed by chiefs and other no-tables from non-royal tribes.[66] While the merchants owe their economic livelihood to receiving state contracts and maintaining close relations with the royal family, tribal leaders seek various types of patronage for their tribe and royal recognition and acceptance. As a result, the dependence of the upper and middle classes—both civil services employees and import–export merchants—is much more direct and acute in the oil monarchies than in most other Middle Eastern states.

What of the lower classes? Again, it is in the treatment of those in the lower rungs of the economic ladder that the oil monarchies and the other Middle Eastern states differ radically. In inclusionary authoritarian states, it is those in the lower classes—the rural immi-grants, seasonal workers, others in low-wage jobs in the informal sector—which are most susceptible either to the manipulations of the state or the message of the opposition. This is the group which the state wishes it could ignore but cannot afford to do so because of its inherent volatility. Not having comprehensive policies for co-option or inclusion, the state often ignores this underclass until it discovers an underground group (the *Jama' Islami* in Egypt or the Muslim Brotherhood in Syria) to which many of the underprivileged and the disillusioned belong, at which time it seeks to repress and destroy it. In the Gulf, however, the underclass is almost invariably

66 M. Field, *The Merchant: The Big Business Families of Saudi Arabia and the Gulf States*, Woodstock, NY: Overlook Press, 1985.

foreign (whether of Palestinian, Jordanian, Yemeni, Iranian, Indian, or Pakistani origin), its status kept intact and reinforced by strict citizenship laws and socio-cultural segregation.[67] Any hint of political opposition is grounds for deportation and, for those living in the country for generations, the abyss of homelessness. In the Gulf, in short, the lower classes do not matter politically.

The Current Prognosis

The current political landscape in the Middle East differs from that of Latin America in a number of fundamental ways. To begin with, while most Middle Eastern states are authoritarian—Turkey, Lebanon, and Israel being exceptions—none can really be classified as bureaucratic–authoritarian.[68] Thus, unlike the situation in Latin America, the non-democratic states of the Middle East have yet to fall victim to the successes of their own social and economic development policies, with the notable exception of Iran's Shah. As the preceding pages demonstrate, most have managed to retain a degree of functional viability *vis-à-vis* society that has enabled them to maintain power. In essence, despite significant weaknesses, the authoritarian, corporatist states of the Middle East have not reached a complete political deadlock in the same way that most Latin American states had by the early 1980s. Nor have Middle Eastern states embarked on economic liberalization programmes that have transferred greater autonomy and power to social actors. Moreover, most Middle Eastern leaders have been able to complement the institutional basis of their rule with at least one or more socio-cultural dynamic, thus reducing (but by no means eliminating) the need for society-based alternative venues for organization and participation.

A growing variety of autonomous or at least semi-autonomous groups and organizations has, nevertheless, appeared in a number of Middle Eastern societies, ranging from religious endowment organizations to private social clubs. Some observers of the region have even

[67] R. Owen, *Migrant Workers in the Gulf*, London: Minority Rights Group, 1985.

[68] Nevertheless, the political systems that existed in Iran under the Pahlavi monarchs, in Turkey in the 1970s, and in Algeria in the late 1970s and the 1980s did come close to resembling the bureaucratic–authoritarian regimes found in Latin America.

gone so far as to maintain that Middle Eastern leaders are 'facing persistent crises of government', with old political remedies no longer yielding traditional results.[69] Thus 'the new language of politics in the Middle East talks about participation, cultural authenticity freedom, and even democracy'.[70] The number of political parties in some of the regions's countries is in itself and impressive indicator of a 'blossoming civil society': 46 in Algeria, 43 in Yemen, 23 in Jordan, 19 in Morocco, 13 in Egypt, 11 in Tunisia, and six in Mauritania.[71] More impressive, however, are the plethora of professional associations, businessmen's groups, and cultural clubs found especially in Algeria, Egypt, Iran, Israel, Kuwait, Turkey, Yemen, and in the Israeli-occupied territories. Of particular note are Kuwait's *diwaniyyah*, 'a gathering place in leading citizens' homes where men (and in recent years a few women) gather to socialize and share views on a range of topics from sports to politics'.[72]

There are also political parties, syndicates and, more importantly, professional organizations that engage in 'politics by proxy'—Kuwait's University Graduates Society, Qatar's Jassrah Cultural Club, and the Association of Social Professions in the United Arab Emirates.[73] In Jordan, there is a 'growing vibrancy in the civic realm' as demonstrated through 'greater respect for human rights, far greater freedom of expression, the emergence of political parties, the development of political satire (particularly in the theatre), and the multitude of conferences, lectures, panel discussions, and meetings on a variety of topics'.[74] Nevertheless, most observers agree that what has been occurring in Jordan is at best a state-led process of 'managed liberalization' rather than a full-blown democratization.[75] Among the Palestinian communities of the Occupied Territories there has also developed a variety of political shops (*dakakin siyasiyyah*), voluntary cooperatives

---

69 A. R. Norton, 'Introduction', in Norton (ed.), *Civil Society in the Middle East*, Leiden: E. J. Brill, 1995, p. 3.

70 Ibid., p. 5.

71 Ibid., p. 9.

72 Ibid., p. 16.

73 S. E. Ibrahim, 'Civil society and prospects for democratization in the Arab World, in Norton (ed.), *Civil Society in the Middle East*, p. 42.

74 L. Brand, 'In the beginning was the state...the quest for civil society in Jordan', in Norton (ed.), *Civil Society in the Middle East*, p. 184.

75 M. Kamrava, 'Frozen political liberalization in Jordan: the consequences for democracy', *Democratization*, 5(1), 1998, pp. 138–57.

and mass organizations, and various Islamist groups.[76] In fact, some would argue that these 'social formations' when combined, could support 'an infrastructure of political and civic institutions that would support a Palestinian state, whenever that state arrives'.[77]

That these autonomous organizations exist is a certainty; what is doubtful however, is the degree of their viability and their commitment to democracy. To begin with, given the persistence of authoritarian rule in the Middle East, it is doubtful how truly autonomous and detached from the state these organizations can become. In fact, it is doubtful whether 'civil society' is an apt description for these organizations at all. In Kuwait, civil society is at best still 'a work in progress', being pursued by 'quasi-autonomous associations' which operate in system that has 'controlled participatory institutions'.[78] The Syrian state has been even more successful at stifling a civil society, employing in the process the help of the bourgeoisie. Syrian 'elites have opted, so far successfully, to control the revival of civil society through a merely political decompression calculated to preserve, not transform the state'.[79] In Egypt, political parties have had to contend with decreasing political autonomy, on the one hand, and with the tendency of both the state and increasingly vocal number of social actors (e.g. Islamic activists) to punish dissenters.[80] In Tunisia, the potential for civil society's growth remains mixed at best, enjoying, on the one hand, 'a vast network of associations that are training citizens in civisme and civility', while, on the other hand, state elites continue to resist opening up the political process.[81]

The controversy over the very existence or viability of civil society organizations in the Middle East notwithstanding, it is important to remember one of the defining characteristics of the phenomenon of civil society. As noted earlier, not every politically autonomous

---

[76] M. Muslih, 'Palestinian civil society', in Norton, *Civil Society in the Middle East*, pp. 249–58.

[77] Ibid., p. 268.

[78] N. Hicks and G. al-Najjar, 'The utility of tradition: civil society in Kuwait', in Norton, *Civil Society in the Middle East*, pp. 212–13.

[79] R. Hinnebusch, 'State, civil society, and political change in Syria', in Norton, *Civil Society in the Middle East*, p. 242.

[80] M. K. Al-Sayyid, 'A civil society in Egypt?', in Norton, *Civil Society in the Middle East*, p. 290.

[81] E. Bellin, 'Civil society in Tunisia', in Norton, *Civil Society in the Middle East*, p. 147.

societal group is a democratic or democratically-inclined CSO. Some CSOS operate on the assumption that the democratization of the larger polity is in their interest, and therefore pressure the state, whether directly or indirectly, to open up and democratize. There are other similar groups, however, whose interests are highly specific and do not extend beyond protecting certain rights and privileges *vis-à-vis* the state. On the whole, they are not concerned with a general relaxation of state authoritarianism. The most powerful examples of this phenomenon are found not only among many of the groups mentioned above, but, in specific relation to the Middle East (and Africa), among tribal groups and the *bazaaris*.[82] Both these groups tend to be highly interested in curtailing the specific activities of the state insofar as the extent of their own autonomy is concerned. Their chief concern has been securing a more profitable share of the corporatist arrangement in relation to the state and those other groups whom they perceive to be unfairly advantaged. As a result, neither group has so far served as an agent for the democratization of the larger polity, either on its own or in conjunction with other societal actors.

There are, in sum, three broad clusters of forces that have impeded the emergence and growth of a dense, democratic civil society in the Middle East. To begin with, although Middle Eastern states have suffered substantial and deep economic and political reverses since the global recession of the early 1980s, they have managed to retain enough powers to (i) hold onto the reins of power and not be overwhelmed by societal pressures; (ii) manipulate enough social and cultural values to retain just enough popular legitimacy. This touches on a second set of factors responsible for the stunting of CSOs in the Middle East so far, namely the absence of a need, unlike in Latin America, for alternative, non-official or non-state related venues for popular organization, expression, and participation. Middle Eastern states have not severed all their cultural ties with society in the same way that most military-authoritarian regimes did in Latin America. In Latin America, in fact, culture was never a factor in prompting social actors to look or not to look for political alternatives to the state. In the Middle East, however, either through charisma or patrimonialism, connection with Islam or clientelistic populism, the

82 R. Tapper, 'Anthropologists, historians, and tribes people on tribe and state formation in the Middle East', in A. R. Norton (ed.), *Tribes and State Formation in the Middle East*, Berkeley, CA: University of California Press, 1990, p. 67.

state continues to present itself, with varying degrees of success, as an extension and indeed a guardian of some of society's most important norms. This seeming reluctance actively to foster non-state and non-official alternatives is reinforced by the region's pattern of economic development, the third reason for the widespread absence of democratic CSOS. Rentier economics has enabled the state to maintain a mutually beneficial corporatist arrangement with selected social groups, therefore lessening the possibility of demands for radical political change and, by extension, for democratization. The groups outside the 'contract' demanding change are savagely repressed.[83]

CONCLUSION

The forces that determine whether or not civil society organizations can emerge and act as agents of democratization are varied and diverse, often differing according to the particular characteristics of a region or country. Class composition and the nature of economic development, specific societal characteristics and cultural preferences, and the pursuit of certain state policies as opposed to others all appear to be determining factors in the widespread absence, or the emergence and growth, of a dense and democratic civil society. In comparing the two cases of Latin America and the Middle East, all these factors eventually boil down to the structural features and policy agendas of the state. More specifically, in Latin America, where there already existed a historical tradition of autonomous societal activity, it was the bureaucratic–authoritarian state and, later on, its malaise that encouraged and expedited the emergence of truly democratic CSOS. The oppositional left, meanwhile, began experiencing what may best be described as 'ism-fatigue' and discovered that democracy was indeed the only game worth playing. When the breakdown of bureaucratic-authoritarian regimes became imminent, a democratic (and democratizing) civil society was already sufficiently developed to push the new, emerging polity in the direction of democracy.

The contracts with the Middle East are glaring. The region's regimes never fully assumed bureaucratic-authoritarian characteristics, although the Iranian Shah's came close, and the 'ism-fatigue' plaguing Latin activists has yet to get a firm grip in the Middle East. On the one hand, the politics of clientelistic paternalism are still alive

[83] L. Cantori, 'Civil society, liberalism and the corporatist alternative in the Middle East', p. 38.

and well having recently experienced what amount to no more than mere cosmetic adjustments.[84] In both the economic and political realms, dangerously high levels of functional paralysis are still a long way away. On the other hand, most of the emerging autonomous CSOs have yet to fully embrace democracy. Most, in fact, continue to adhere to dogmatic and uncompromising ideological blueprints—religious or otherwise—that are antithetical to democracy. Given the present constellation of social and political forces in today's Middle East, democratization does not appear as a likely possibility in the foreseeable future.

Most Latin American societies, however, have gone through a different experience, both historically and politically. To a large extent, the widespread establishment of bureaucratic-authoritarian regimes in the region, especially throughout South America, was directly responsible for the emergence of alternative, society-based groups which sought to preform the functions that the state could not or would not fulfill. The growth or resurgence of independent organizational life and associational activity starting in the 1970s—what O'Donnell and Schmitter call 'the resurrection of civil society'[85]—has in turn been a key factor in the escalating pressure for democratization that culminated in the transition from authoritarianism in a number of Latin American countries during the past two decades. The growth of autonomous association in Latin America was partly the result of rapid socio-economic modernization under authoritarian regimes. It gave rise to new, more autonomous types of entrepreneurial associations that pulled civil society out of the traditional corporatist structure of the import-substitution industrialization period (1930–60). What perhaps makes this third phase in the development of civil society unique is that for the first time associational life has organized and mobilized itself independently from the state, pressuring and demanding greater representation and accountability from public officials. At least in relation to Latin America, Samuel Huntington's 'third wave' of democratization may be irreversible if this third phase in the development of civil society continues to value and promote democratization.

84 In the late 1980s and early 1990s, for example, the Jordanian government began embarking on a 'democratic experiment' and the Egyptian government sought to emphasize its openness.

85 G. O'Donnell and P. Schmitter, *Transition from an Authoritarian Rule*, pp. 48–57.

16

CIVIL SOCIETY AND IDEOLOGICAL CONTESTATION IN INDIA

Mark Robinson

INTRODUCTION

India is often credited with having one of the most diverse and complex societies in the world, and a populace imbued with multiple and overlapping identities founded on religion, caste, class, and region. This has given rise to a tremendous variety and density of groups, associations, and movements that embody the collective aspirations and normative claims of their members. While these varied expressions of associational life have received considerable attention from social science scholars, their analysis has only rarely been framed with reference to the discourse and practice of civil society. It can be plausibly argued that the concept of civil society is inappropriate as a heuristic device for interpreting indigenous social practices and associational forms, since it derives from theoretical traditions rooted in the evolution of western capitalist societies that have little relevance to the contemporary Indian context. Others are sceptical of the term because it can reduce complex social realities to an over-simplified and unitary organizational form encapsulated by voluntary associations to the exclusion of those founded on ascriptive loyalties (such as caste, religion, and other ethnic categories), and shared normative values centred on democracy and tolerance of difference.

While these qualifications are valid and need to be accommodated by theory, they need not result in the complete rejection of the concept of civil society as an analytical tool that can be employed to useful effect in deepening understanding of non-western associational forms and social practices. Rather, the analysis presented in this chapter is predicated on the assertion that the concept of civil society can be enriched and extended by applying it creatively to the analysis of contemporary Indian social realities. We make three arguments in support of this claim. The first is that, contrary to received wisdom on its putative associational characteristics, civil society should not be narrowly equated with a narrow cross-section of organizations that espouse democratic values and exhibit a shared commonality of purpose centred on the collective pursuit of the public good. While diversity of the organizational type is invariably acknowledged, and at times applauded as a desirable manifestation of associational freedom, organizations founded on ascriptive bonds are invariably excluded from most western definitions.[1] This approach has two main limitations in a country like India: first, religious organizations and ethnic associations founded on caste, kinship, and region, which are a forceful empirical reality, find no place in conventional civil society discourse; and second, civil society is identified with a sub-set of organizations pursuing normative claims that are considered to have some superior validity. We would argue that conceptual narrowness and normative exclusion cloud analytical depth, which is to the detriment of a deeper understanding of contemporary empirical realities.

Our second contention is that civil society should not be reduced to its empirical manifestations in the associational domain, as groups and organizations, but that it extends to the realm of ideology, which is commonly ignored in the conventional use of the term. We argue that civil society in India constitutes a contested realm characterized by conflicting ideologies, organizations, and movements, but that it also provides a vehicle for autonomous citizen action in the public sphere. It thus has a dual character, in that it simultaneously provides space for autonomous citizen action and emancipatory politics outside the state and political parties, and at the same time allows for contestation between organizations pursuing narrower and potentially conflicting ideological agendas.

[1] For a similar critique see C. Hann and E. Dunn (eds), *Civil Society: Challenging Western Models* (London and New York: Routledge, 1996).

The third strand in our argument is that sharply drawn conceptual distinctions between civil and political society, often alluded to in the theoretical literature, appear flawed in the light of Indian realities and historical experience. We seek to extend and illustrate the validity of this argument by demonstrating how groups and organizations wedded to particularist ideological agendas consciously treat the spheres of civil and political society as complementary and interchangeable. Political practice results in a deliberate blurring of the distinctions between these two domains, and questions the assumed separation of organizational practices in civil society on the one hand, and the role of political parties, legislative activity, and elections on the other. While a distinction between the two realms remains useful for analytical and normative purposes, it can also limit our understanding of how consciously designed ideological projects find strategic and organizational expression in civil and political society.[2]

The implication of the argument developed here is that the scope and potential for autonomous citizen action founded on democratic principles and emancipatory politics is shaped by conflict and negotiation between groups pursuing very different ideological agendas within the terrain of civil society, and in the interstices of political and civil society. The balance of power between these contending forces, which is a continuous state of flux, determined by their social composition, the material, ideological, and organizational resources at their disposal, and the character of the state.

The Limitations of Western Political Theory

The concept of civil society used in this chapter is distinct from the liberal tradition, where it is treated as the space where the democratic potential of independent citizen action is realized in the

---

[2] The approach proposed here is consistent with the framework developed by Cohen and Arato in their detailed account of the civil society argument, but with greater emphasis on the conscious and simultaneous utilization of these two domains for ideological and strategic advantage. It should be noted that while their empirical reference points are comparative, they largely draw on experience from Eastern Europe and Latin America, to the exclusion of nonwestern or Asian examples in developing their analysis. Cohen, J. L. and A. Arato, *Civil Society and Political Theory* (Cambridge, Mass. and London: MIT Press, 1992, pp. 78–81).

face of an unresponsive and autocratic state, in opposition to particularistic pressures exerted by groups pursuing self-interested and anti-democratic agendas outside the civil society domain.[3] It is also at variance with the pluralist definition, which views civil society as the organizational expression of a multitude of voluntary groups and associations, since this is to reduce the concept to its most visible manifestation, devoid of normative intent.[4] Both of these approaches inform a conceptualization that is dominant in contemporary discourse, in which civil society constitutes an intermediary sphere of associations located between the family and the state.[5]

The notion that civil society constitutes a domain characterized by ideological and political contestation borrows in part from the Gramscian intellectual tradition. For Gramsci, civil society was a terrain of struggle between class forces contesting for political hegemony, in which the media, schools, unions, and other social and cultural institutions provided an ideological environment conducive to the maintenance of the capitalist mode of production. Civil society was thus a terrain for ideological contestation in which these institutions could sustain capitalist class dominance by asserting the normative virtues of private ownership of the means of production and the commodification of labour, as against the claims of competing anti-capitalist ideologies.

The limitation of this approach, which was grounded in a Marxist analysis of advanced capitalism, is that all forms of contestation in civil society are reduced to a struggle over the attempt of the capitalist class to assert its ideological hegemony in the political realm. Other sources of ideological contestation, emanating from sources of political and social struggles that did not have capitalism as their reference

3 See N. Chandhoke, *State and Civil Society: Explorations in Political Theory* (New Delhi: Sage, 1995), for an excellent overview of these competing perspectives.

4 This approach underpins a commonly-held perception in India and elsewhere that non-governmental organizations and voluntary associations constituting the non-profit or 'third sector', lie at the heart of a democratic civil society, and that other movements and ideologies fall outside of its purview. For a discussion see Van Rooy, A. ed., *Civil Society and the Aid Industry* (London: Earthscan, 1998), pp. 6–30.

5 White, G., 'Civil Society, Democratization and Development (I)', *Democratization*, 1(3), Autumn, 1994.

point, did not figure in Gramsci's conception.[6] While it provides a compelling model for explaining the persistence of capitalist class domination in conditions of liberal democracy and universal suffrage, it is not easily transferable to the non-western context, where capitalism is neither ascendant, nor where class is not the major social cleavage. Nevertheless, the Gramscian approach offers a useful corrective to pluralist or liberal conceptions that have tended to dominate contemporary theoretical debates, which assume either that civil society is a neutral domain inhabited by benign organizations in the voluntary sector, or that it is the locus for democratic political action by autonomous social movements opposed to an invasive and all-encompassing state.

It is the contention of this paper that, not only have contemporary debates concerning civil society been dominated by a western liberal interpretation, but that other significant strands in political theory have been sidelined or ignored. While there are evident limitations in merely replacing one dominant western conceptualization of civil society with another, the Gramscian model provides us with two important conceptual building blocks that can assist in the construction of an approach that is more readily applicable to non-western social and political conditions. These are, firstly, an explicit recognition that ideological contestation can serve to deepen understanding of civil society and its organizational manifestations, and secondly, that struggle for hegemony over the dominant mode of production is but one of a number of terrains in which ideological contestation might feature.

Most conceptions of civil society in the western political tradition have the development of bourgeois society as their principal reference point, either as a sphere of citizen action independent from and counterposed to the state, or as the terrain of struggle over capitalist class domination. One might plausibly argue that in countries where the capitalist mode of production is not fully ascendant, or where bourgeois values have not permeated extensively throughout society, other forms of contestation are likely to predominate. Indeed, in the context of many non-western developing societies, the public sphere may well constitute a realm of contestation between organized social forces, in which the terrains of contestation are multiple and varied,

---

[6] For a detailed discussion see Cohen and Arato, *Civil Society and Political Theory*, pp. 142–59.

and not confined to struggles over capitalist class dominance or the normative assertion of liberal political values. In such contexts, contestation between social forces organized on the basis of religion and ethnicity is often consigned to a pre-modern or primordial realm, whereas civil society is treated as a domain inhabited by modern associations unified by a common affinity to democratic values and consensual politics.

In a departure from dominant traditions in western political theory, it may be possible to develop a conception of civil society which recognizes that the sources of ideological contestation emanate from underlying material and social conditions that combine and interact in very different ways according to a country's historical evolution and experience of state formation. Non-western societies may thus be characterized by multiple forms of contestation that play themselves out in the public realm through concrete associational formations, especially where the ascendancy of capitalism is uncertain or incomplete. Hence, in this conception of civil society, the principal sites of ideological contestation will not be confined to struggles over capitalist hegemony, but will also centre on conflict over religion, nation, and ethnicity, through which organizations and social movements seek to assert their normative claims in these varied terrains of civil society.[7]

While a Gramscian perspective can help to broaden understanding of civil society by focusing attention on the ideological plane as the locus for contestation, this should not obscure the significance of organizational and material factors in shaping the evolution of civil society in particular historical and spatial contexts.[8] Competing normative claims are advanced through various forms of collective

7 See, for example, Mamdani, M., *Citizen and Subject: Contemporary Africa and the Legacy of Late Colonialism* (Princeton, NJ: Princeton University Press, 1996), for a similar line of argument in the African context.

8 For a thoughtful exposition see Bratton, M., 'Civil Society and Political Transitions in Africa', in J. B. Harbeson, D. Rothchild and N. Chazan (eds), *Civil Society and the State in Africa*, Boulder, Co. and London: Lynne Rienner, 1994: 64–71) who argues that the capacity of social groups to accumulate capital is an essential condition for the existence of civil society. In his analysis of the organizational dimension of civil society, Bratton distinguishes between intermediate associations and the institutional linkages between them, which are conditioned by historical experience (most notably the struggle against colonialism in Africa and Asia) and underling economic conditions.

action in civil society, expressed through struggles for political and ideological ascendancy between organizations and movements with differing resources at their disposal. The emergence of these groups is shaped by historical context and economic factors, as well as by conjunctural circumstances that are unpredictable. For example, capitalist development has historically engendered the formation of organizations in civil society that seek to promote the hegemony of competing class interests, such as business associations and trade unions. In non-capitalist developing societies, the major lines of contestation might result from groups formed to protect competing communal interests organized around religion, caste, or tribe. Weak capitalist development is likely to produce a civil society in which organized class interests feature less strongly, as opposed to organizations formed around other social identity markers, since the material base resulting from this form of development cannot easily foster or sustain class-based organizations. When the state displaces private capital as the main agent propelling development, the locus of struggle is different, manifest in contestation among groups founded on ascriptive loyalties for the patronage conferred by access to state resources. Contestation is therefore not exclusively confined to the ideological realm but is expressed through organizations that act as the bearers of normative values and material interests in civil society.

In contemporary India, there are at least three principal sites of contestation: the contested claim to ideological and political supremacy of the Hindu nationalist movement; struggles over the hegemonic claims of capitalism and the developmental state; and resistance to forms of autonomous action that seek to hold the state accountable and responsive to its citizens. In each case, varied forms of ideological contestation emanate from competing normative claims asserted from within civil society, but these are not restricted to the civil society domain. As our three cases demonstrate, these forms of contestation are not restricted to struggles between organized groups in civil society, nor are they insulated from other structures that shape societal relations. Rather, we argue that there is complex dynamic at work, in which civil society provides one terrain in which struggles are played out, but in combination with and in relation to political society, the state, and the market.

Before moving to our cases, it should be noted that there may well be other sites of contestation which are less visible, or that operate at a more localized level. Two such examples are struggles over the assertion of patriarchal values and violence against women, and struggles over caste dominance and social practices, both of which have ideological and organizational manifestations in the public realm. However, it could be argued that these do not constitute separate sites of ideological contestation, but rather inform and permeate the three arenas identified above. For instance, struggles over patriarchal practices permeate ideological contestation over Hindutva supremacy, and the state itself is a terrain of contestation over statutory and legal provisions governing women's rights. Similarly, caste is intricately bound up with subaltern struggles around land and environmental resources, and movements that challenge both the market and the state in promoting developmental strategies that intrude on the economic rights of the poor and marginalized, do not appeal exclusively to class identities.

HINDU NATIONALISM AND CONTESTATION IN CIVIL SOCIETY

Arguably the most important arena of ideological contestation in the public realm in India today concerns the vigorous assertion of Hindutva ideology, centred on the promotion of pan-Hindu identity and nationhood. The principal locus of conflict is between the forces promoting Hindutva ideology and those defending the values of secular nationalism Much of this conflict is played out in the terrain of civil society, and reflects the attempt of pro-Hindutva forces to legitimize the Hindu nationalist project through a variety of related organizations collectively referred to as the *Sangh Parivar*. However, what is significant for our argument is that while the militant Hindu nationalist movement originated in civil society, it consciously developed a parallel strategy of building party organizations to advance the Hindutva agenda in political society in order to capture state power through elections.

The Hindu nationalist movement had its origins in the formation of reform movements like the Hindu Sabhas and the Arya Samaj by the urban middle classes in northern India in the late nineteenth century. In the early part of the twentieth century, the Hindu nationalist movement remained for the most part elite-led and confined to civil society. A strategy of pursuing parliamentary representation for a Hindu constituency was developed in response to the 1909 constitutional reforms that created separate electorates for different religious communities. However, it was not until the formation of the Hindu Mahasabha in the early 1920s that it began to develop a mass base, but more extreme nationalist currents remained very much in a minority.[9]

In the period leading up to independence other organizations with a more avowedly communal agenda came to the fore, such as the Rashtriya Swayamsevak Sangh (RSS—National Social Service Organization). Founded in 1925 in the state of Maharashtra, the RSS consciously developed a cadre-based organization through the creation of a network of small groups (*shakhas*) that met regularly across the whole country. While ostensibly dedicated to promoting a strict regime of physical exercise and healthy living among Hindu youth, the RSS and its front organizations espoused a brand of militant Hinduism that fostered a climate of communal distrust and anti-Muslim sentiment.[10] Its activities were a major contributory factor to the communal riots that wracked many cities in northern and western India, and which grew in intensity in the 1930s and 1940s.

The response to this mobilization of Hindu nationalist sentiment assumed two main forms. One was the formation of militant organizations among Muslims that sought to both defend their communities against the predations of Hindu communal groups, and promote the idea of a separate nation.[11] However, neither form of religious nationalism was successful in mobilizing people on a large scale through appeals to communal sentiments. Both remained minority currents within the domain of civil society though each developed symbiotic relationships with communal parties operating in the political domain, most notably the Hindu Mahasabha and the

---

[9] Zavos, J., 'Searching for Hindu Nationalism in Modern Indian History: Analysis of Some Early Ideological Developments' (*Economic and Political Weekly*, 7 August 1999). On the origins of Hindu nationalism, see, C. Jaffrelot, *The Hindu Nationalist Movement in Indian Politics* (New York: Columbia University Press, 1996) and Graham, B., *Hindu Nationalism and Indian Politics* (Cambridge: Cambridge University Press, 1990).

[10] van der Veer, P., *Religious Nationalism: Hindus and Muslims in India*, Berkeley and Los Angeles: University of California Press, 1994), pp. 71–3.

[11] Pandey, G., *The Construction of Communalism in North India* (New Delhi: Oxford University Press, 1990).

[12] Chandra, B., *Communalism in Modern India* (New Delhi: Vani, 1984).

Muslim League.[12] Part of the explanation lies in the success of the mainstream nationalist movement, which managed to galvanise mass support for independence centred on appeals to religious tolerance, non-violence, and self-reliance. The two major currents in the nationalist movement simultaneously played themselves in the spheres of civil and political society, through the mass movement catalyzed by Mahatma Gandhi and his followers and under the leadership of Jawaharlal Nehru and the Indian National Congress.[13] Another factor, which has until recently received less scholarly attention, is the role played by local associations in fostering tolerance among Hindus and Muslims through shared cultural traditions and religious practices, and the language and practice of commerce.[14] For these various reasons, militant Hindu nationalism never managed to gain a strong foothold among the Indian masses in the pre-independence era. However, as a result of the activities of communal organizations in civil society and allied parties in the parliamentary domain, there was a marked escalation of inter-religious violence. While they were successful in achieving freedom from colonial rule, mainstream nationalist forces in political and civil society proved incapable of preventing the partition of India and the carnage that accompanied the mass transfer of population either side of the new border.[15]

After independence, the militant Hindu nationalist movement went into temporary abeyance, as it was both discredited by Gandhi's assassination and extremist organizations were banned by the Congress government riding on a wave of popularity in the wake of the struggle against colonialism. While Hindu nationalist organizations played a less visible role in the political sphere in the period after independence, the RSS continued to pursue its strategy of building a mass base through local organizations and cultural activities in the civil society domain once it became legalized again. A new organization was formed in 1964—the Vishwa Hindu Parishad (VHP—

[13] For a more detailed examination see Rudolph and Rudolph (in this volume). The communist movement also played a role in countering efforts to stir up communal enmity through vigorous appeals to working class unity and anti-colonialism.

[14] Ashutosh Varshney develops a forceful argument to demonstrate how intercommunal associations centred on trade and commerce have played a critical role in cementing ties across religious boundaries that help to mitigate conflict and violence in certain north Indian cities. Varshney, A., in this volume.

[15] Chandra, *Communalism in Modern India.*

World Hindu Organization)—which had the explicit aim of bringing Muslims into the Hindu fold through aggressive proselytization and spreading the message of Hindu nationalism through cultural activities and rallies. The VHP vigorously sought to extend its appeal to tribals and *dalits* (former untouchables) to counter the influence of Christians and radical left organizations. While these organizations had very different modes of operation, their activities are complementary in that they consciously sought to strengthen the foundations of militant Hindu nationalism within the sphere of civil society. In the process they built up a formidable organizational base with strong material foundations, bolstered by a steady stream of funding from middle class Hindus, both in India and among the Hindu diaspora.

The formation of the Jan Sangh in 1951 represented the first major effort of militant Hindu nationalists to carve out a presence in political society after independence, in recognition that it was necessary to establish its legitimacy on the national political stage and bolster organizational work in civil society.[16] While it registered a modest degree of parliamentary success in the 1950s and 1960s, it was not until the formation of the Janata-led coalition government after the end of the Emergency in 1977 that Hindu nationalists gained a foothold in central government through the allocation of several key ministerial portfolios. This did not last long, however, as the Congress Party under the leadership of Indira Gandhi swept back into power in the 1980 elections. Elements formerly associated with the Jan Sangh created a new political formation calling itself the Bharatiya Janata Party (BJP—Indian Peoples Party), which had the explicit long-term objective of capturing political power through the ballot box. The party made little headway into mainstream politics until the early 1990s when it increased its vote substantially and was able to join the first of several coalition governments at the centre. The BJP consistently expanded its support base throughout the decade with the result that it succeeded in becoming the largest party in the national parliament in the 1996 elections and later assumed a leading role in the 1998 coalition government. Following fresh elections

[16] According to Hansen, 'The motivation on the part of the RSS for entering the political sphere seems to have been the chance to acquire a public voice and political legitimacy and, ultimately, to extend the influence of the organization through its political affiliate.' Hansen, T. B., *The Saffron Wave: Democracy and Hindu Nationalism in Modern India* (New Delhi: Oxford University Press, 1999), p. 127.

in 1999, the BJP formed another coalition government under the leadership of Atal Bihari Vajpayee, securing the lion's share of key cabinet positions.[17]

Over the past two decades there has been a concerted attempt to cement the ideological pre-eminence of militant Hindu nationalism in the public sphere through a variety of institutions in civil society, including the media, educational and research institutions, statutory organizations, and religious bodies. These values are propagated by a set of organizations that are unified in their adherence to the Hindutva ideology (centred on the creation of a theocratic Hindu nation), ranging from a cadre-based political party (the BJP) to groups that have their roots in voluntary action and associational life, such as the RSS and the Vishwa Hindu Parishad, and newer, more extremist, organizations such as the Bajrang Dal. These organizations and movements are currently engaged in a quest for ideological hegemony by employing a variety of complementary strategies in political and civil society. Their goal is to demolish the ideological edifice of secular nationalism and to put in its place a unifying concept of Hindu nationhood.[18]

The response to this sustained attempt at the militant assertion of Hindu nationhood as a dominant ideological discourse has taken

[17] The RSS played a major role in extending the support base of the BJP, reflected in a steady growth of its membership throughout the 1980s and 1990s, though it has major differences with the government on important areas of policy, notably economic reform and foreign investment. T. B. Hansen and C. Jaffrelot, 'Introduction: The BJP After the 1996 Elections', in T. B. Hansen and C. Jaffrelot (eds), The *BJP and the Compulsions of Politics in India* (New Delhi: Oxford University Press, 1998). Senior figures in the BJP-led government, including Prime Minister Vajpayee and other cabinet ministers, publicly reiterated their continued affiliations to the RSS on several occasions after the election victory of 1999.

[18] For example, see Hansen, *The Saffron Wave*. Not all commentators would accept this formulation, however, and argue that coalition government has a moderating effect on Hindu nationalism and that the BJP in particular is not averse to democracy and parliamentary politics. See the various contributions in T. B. Hansen and C. Jaffrelot (eds), *The BJP and the Compulsions of Politics in India* (New Delhi: Oxford University Press, 1998). After the 1999 election the BJP sought to develop its secular credentials by appealing to Muslims and scheduled castes and tribes, but more cynical observers saw this as a ploy designed to build new constituencies for the party and allay concerns about its communal intent.

several forms. One has been a parallel response on the part of minority religious communities threatened by the aggressive articulation of the Hindutva ideology. This has often taken the form of a retreat into fundamentalist assertion of minority religious identity among Muslims, and distancing from the values of secular nationalism that are no longer thought to offer a refuge from Hindu majoritarianism. Particularistic organizations promoting a fundamentalist interpretation of Muslim identity have been formed within civil society, partly to propagate an alternative set of religious values, but also as a protective response to Hindu communalism. The institutions within which this minority religious reassertion takes place are mosques, educational institutions, and the vernacular press, and serve as sites for self-constitution and ideological contestation.

Far less common is a robust defence of secular nationalism as the counterpoint to both Hindutva ideology and minority fundamentalism within civil society. What was formerly a powerful form of normative assertion in its own right, with strong claims to ideological hegemony, now has few vocal adherents within political society, despite continued claims of the Congress Party to embody such values. The ideological and organizational apparatus of secular nationalism, reflected in the practice and discourses of Nehruvian socialism and Gandhian self-reliance, and groups in civil society espousing these values, has progressively diminished under the twin onslaughts of Hindu nationalism and minority religious reassertion.[19] This role has been left to a group of relatively small but politically active organizations in civil society, and to individuals within the media and educational institutions who are contesting attempts by proponents of the Hindutva ideology to insinuate themselves into the fabric of political and civil society. These groupings can be construed as a small sub-category of the voluntary sector, which are numerically insignificant, but engaged in a vigorous campaign to defend, redefine, and extend the principles of secular nationalism. Increasingly, they see their role as guarding against attempts at imposing an ideological hegemony that is both anti-democratic and increasingly intolerant of minority religious and cultural expression. What the outcome of this

---

[19] Newer parties such as the Samajwadi Party and Bahujan Samaj Party seek to build support among other backward classes and scheduled castes, in the process undercutting the support base of political parties seeking to unite Hindu voters around the normative claims of religious nationalism.

struggle will be remains uncertain, but it seems likely that this form of contestation will continue to play itself out in both the civil and political domains.

LIBERALIZATION AND THE MARKET: CONTESTING ECONOMIC REFORMS

The second major arena of ideological contestation in India today is reflected in struggles over the process of capitalist transformation and economic liberalization. The nature of capitalist transformation in the countryside was a matter of heated debate among Indian social scientists in the 1970s and early 1980s. By the close of the decade it was evident that agricultural production had shifted substantially towards the market and that the prevailing pattern of self-sufficient smallholder cultivation was breaking down in the face of the commodification of land and labour. Rural social movements, which sprung up during the course of this transformation, represent the political and material interests of a new 'middle peasantry' on the one hand and the interests of a subaltern class of agricultural labourers and marginal farmers on the other.[20] The new rural rich, many of whom originate from a low caste status, have come to occupy dominant positions in state politics by virtue of their numerical significance and newly acquired material status. The latter have engaged in sporadic protests, which have often turned violent, against the hegemony exercised by the new landholding castes, especially in the central Hindi-speaking states. These were conducted both in the civil society realm by organizations and movements representing the respective and frequently conflicting interests of surplus-producing farmers and landless labourers, but also in the political sphere through parties that were established to represent their interests in state governments. These struggles dominated the ideological discourse of rural civil society in northern India for much of the period after independence, at least until the rise to prominence of the Hindutva movement in the early 1990s.[21]

At the national level, a mixed economy characterized by high levels of state involvement with a vigorous private sector predominated

20 Omvedt, G., *Land, Caste and Politics in Indian States* (New Delhi: Authors Guild, 1982).

21 Brass, T., *New Farmers' Movements* (Ilford: Frank Cass, 1995).

until the late 1980s. Large industrialists accepted the economic status quo and did not mobilize in any significant way against the restrictions placed on private sector activity, partly because they benefited from bureaucratic discretion, but pursued their narrow sectoral interests though business associations for much of the post-independence period. With the advent of economic liberalization in the early 1990s, and a determined attempt by the Narasimha Rao government to reinvigorate the Indian economy through market-oriented reforms, new constituencies were mobilized in the process. This has given rise to intense contestation over the pace and direction of reforms, much of which takes place in the ideological terrain of civil society, between the forces promoting the new economic policy and a freer role for domestic capital on the one hand, and those opposed to the assertion of capitalist hegemony on the other. Among the former are representatives of big business, policy makers, and technocrats who strongly support the new economic policy and who wish to vigorously pursue an agenda based on liberalization and privatization, in part by promoting the acceptability of this set of ideas through the public realm and organs of civil society, such as the media and business associations.[22]

Unionized public sector workers who stand to lose their jobs through rationalization and privatization, and political movements, including those representing sections of the new agricultural elites, constitute the main source of opposition to economic liberalization and opening up the economy to foreign competition. The major trade unions are invariably aligned to political parties that oppose economic reforms, notably the two communist parties. But even if the parent party is committed to reform, as in the case of the Congress in the early 1990s and the BJP in the latter half of the decade, this not guarantee union support. Indeed, the trade union allied with the BJP, the Bharatiya Mazdoor Sangh, has forcefully mobilized dissent against an expanded role for foreign capital in the context of a liberalized economy by invoking *swadeshi* (national self-reliance) sentiments, while at the same time providing ideological and organizational sustenance for the Hindutva movement within civil society.

There is a broad consensus among the major political parties (especially between the Congress and the BJP) on the desirability of

---

[22] See, for example, the essays in Sachs, S., A. Varshney, and N. Bajpai (eds), *India in the Era of Economic Reforms* (New Delhi: Oxford University Press, 1999).

economic reforms. The main point of difference is the speed and direction of reform and the necessity of measures to protect the poor and vulnerable in the transition process. However, within civil society economic reforms remain a source of deep contention, marked by polarization between business associations on the one hand (though not all support liberalization) and trade unions and farmers' organizations on the other. At present the business lobby retains the upper hand with preferential access to policy-makers but politicians remain wary of the potential backlash that a rapid deepening of reforms could provoke in civil society.[23]

CITIZENS AND THE STATE:
NEW SITES OF CONTESTATION

The state itself is becoming an increasingly heated site of ideological contestation in India, in which the forces promoting democratic values based on freedom and equality are counterposed to those seeking to preserve bureaucratic power and discretion within the state apparatus. The former include what liberal theorists would associate with civil society in its classical sense, as an intermediate realm of associations located between the family and the state, which seek to protect citizens from intrusions by an autocratic and unaccountable state, through autonomous civic action designed to protect and extend democratic rights. In organizational terms, this encompasses human rights groups, women's organizations, citizen's groups, and professional associations.

Many human rights organizations first came to prominence in the Emergency declared by Prime Minister Indira Gandhi in 1975, in response to widespread abuse of civil and political rights by the police. Their activities often focused on legal mechanisms as a means of seeking redress for wrongful imprisonment, using the courts for pursuit of justice and defence of individual rights in the face of a state that abrogated the rights of ordinary citizens who had peacefully taken part in the mass movement against Mrs. Gandhi's dictatorial rule led by J. P. Narayan. The post-Emergency period witnessed the formation of a large number of social action groups and movements concerned with upholding the economic and social rights of

[23] For a detailed account of the political repercussions of the reform process see Jenkins, R., *Democratic Politics and Economic Reform in India* (Cambridge: Cambridge University Press, 2000).

disadvantaged sections of the population, especially women, agricultural labourers, tribals, and dalits. Many of these consciously maintained a critical distance from the formal political arena, preferring to pursue a political strategy in the civil society domain.[24] But enthusiasm for this new form of politics waned as groups and movements in civil society proved incapable of forming durable networks that could use a mass base for strategic political advantage. Their intentional separation from political society meant they could exert little influence over public policy in a way that was beneficial to their members at the grass-roots.

Despite their patchy success, newer forms of rural social movements representing poor and marginalized sections of the population have come to the fore in the 1990s. Some of these had their origins in earlier struggles over land rights, common property resources and agricultural wages.[25] The prime source of contestation is the failure of the state to guarantee entitlements to its poorest citizens and to prevent their economic rights from being infringed by state sponsored development schemes, centred on opposition to large dams that result in the forced displacement of tribal peoples and subsistence producers, and commercial timber exploitation. Prominent examples of such struggles include the Narmada Bachao Andolan (Save Narmada Campaign) and the Chipko campaign led by women in the hill areas of northern India. These organizations have sought to complement mass-based struggles against the failure of the state to protect citizens' entitlements through public interest litigation in law courts and by garnering international public opinion, often to great effect.[26] Mass mobilization within civil society has resulted in some success, but powerful interests that favour dam projects and further exploitation of timber resources have sought to counter this mobilization from displaced and affected peoples, by lobbying government authorities and rewarding politicians.

[24] Unia, P., 'Social Action Group Strategies in the Indian Sub-continent,' *Development in Practice*, 1(2), pp. 84–96.

[25] Many of these have been documented in detail by the Society for Participatory Research in Asia (PRIA) as part of a cross-national study of civil society and governance. For a condensed summary see Tandon, R. and R. Mohanty, *Civil Society and Governance* (New Delhi: Sanskriti, 2002).

[26] On the Narmada campaign see Dwivedi R., 'Resisting Dams and "Development": Contemporary Significance of the Campaign Against Narmada Projects in India', *European Journal of Development Research*, 10(3), pp. 135–83.

The 1990s witnessed the emergence of new forms of civil society activism in urban areas with the state as the principal site of contestation. As with the action groups and the social movements of the 1970s and 1980s, this newer set of civil society organizations remained aloof from party politics but, unlike their more radical predecessors, recognized the importance of strategic engagement with the state. These may be typified as citizens' action groups, which emerged in a number of towns and cities in response to growing problems of corruption, poor standards of service delivery, and bureaucratic inertia. For the most part these groups were voluntary organizations led by middle class professionals who wanted to hold municipal authorities to account for poor standards of service delivery and endemic malfeasance. Some developed innovative tools for measuring government performance in the form of independent analysis of municipal budgets and ascertaining citizens' perceptions of the quality of public services. They also sought to influence municipal officials and local politicians through advocacy efforts and media campaigns as a means of improving accountability and standards of service delivery.[27]

The formation of these groups was partly prompted by conjunctural circumstances that created a more receptive environment for their activities. The adoption of economic reforms by the government in the early 1990s increasingly drew into question the efficiency of state-led development and the effectiveness of public sector organizations. The growing international emphasis on good governance provided ideological succour to their activities. Government was no longer immune from public criticism and independent efforts to provide critical oversight were no longer viewed with inherent suspicion. In this particular realm of contestation, media and policy research institutions constitute important sites of opposition to bureaucratic self-interest, through regular press reports and independent studies of poor governance, malfeasance, and abuse, thereby providing an important source of publicity for the work of citizen action groups. Enlightened government officials provide an entry point for strategic engagement on the part of these groups and weaken bureaucratic resistance to reform efforts. Political parties are beginning to see the virtues of pursuing governance reform agenda that potentially

27 For details see Paul, S., *Holding the State to Account: Citizen Monitoring in Action* (Bangalore: Books for Change, 2002).

commands popular support, but remain wary of opposition from public sector trade unions that represent the collective interests of government officials in civil society.

CONCLUSION

In this chapter we have sought to go beyond conventional understandings of civil society in which it is narrowly equated with a set of intermediate associations located between the family and the state. Our principal argument is that the civil society domain does not constitute an organizational vacuum divorced from political society, and that ideology provides an important site of contestation in civil society around which groups and organizations mobilize in conscious pursuit of normatively defined interests. Contrary to received wisdom, we would suggest that religion and ethnicity provide critical reference points for mobilization and contestation within civil society, and that organizations founded on these ascriptive categories should not be dismissed as primordial and thus outside the realm of modern civil society.

The merit of this approach is that it questions a narrow, ethnocentric conceptualization of civil society grounded in western liberal and Marxist approaches, and centred on asserting collective rights of association or in sustaining capitalist class dominance. These aspects are clearly significant, but may be of secondary importance in situations where ethnic and religious identities constitute the primary basis for competing claims for ideological hegemony in civil society. This is not simply to acknowledge that civil society is inhabited by organizations with conflicting normative claims, but to recognize that these are engaged in multiple struggles for ideological supremacy in various arenas of civil society. While we cannot hope to provide full empirical justice to this argument in the confines of this chapter, the three cases we have highlighted demonstrate how struggles for ideological hegemony are not confined to the civil society domain, but also permeate political society and the state.

Our questioning of the presumed dichotomy between civil and political society is not only of theoretical consequence but also has important practical implications for autonomous citizen action and emancipatory politics. In the contemporary discourse on civil society in India the voluntary sector often receives privileged treatment by virtue of its organizational visibility and claimed adherence to upholding the rights and entitlements of its poorest and most vulnerable citizens. Our analysis suggests that the voluntary, non-profit sector is at best a sub-set of organizations within civil society that is primarily engaged in shaping discourse over development practice. Second, with the exception of social action groups, the activities of voluntary sector are for the most part predicated on a consensual approach, in which they seek to work with benign and politically neutral organizations engaged in development work.

For these reasons we would argue that the voluntary sector as presently constituted has only a modest role to play in the three arenas of contestation sketched out above. The developmental and welfare concerns of the voluntary sector have generally precluded it from taking a more active role in struggles over ideological hegemony, in part because these are seen to be political issues and because the sector is generally more comfortable with a consensus-building approach. But the struggles taking place in these three realms profoundly shape the lives of the poor and marginalized communities that the voluntary sector claims to privilege. For example, it is usually poor and vulnerable communities that bear the brunt of communal violence orchestrated by pro-Hindutva forces, they are usually excluded from the benefits accruing from capitalist transformation and economic liberalization, and unresponsive government officials are usually least accommodating to the demands of such groups.

In view of the profound problems of governance in India today it might be incumbent on the voluntary sector, with its mandate of improving the status of poor and marginalized communities, to become more actively engaged in these various spheres of ideological contestation but without compromising its political independence. There may be opportunities for establishing firmer linkages with groups and organizations at the forefront of struggles in civil society over competing visions of national identity, the distributional consequences of economic reform, and state accountability and legitimacy. For example, this might involve linking grass-roots development organizations with activist groups that are striving to maintain intercommunal harmony. It could also take the form of bridge-building between voluntary organizations and citizen action groups that seek to enhance government performance and accountability. Another approach could entail forging closer links between voluntary organizations and trade unions to strengthen their hand in negotiation with industry and to protect those who are retrenched or marginalized as a result of economic reforms. In the process, the voluntary sector could provide much-needed material and organizational support for autonomous citizen action, which might otherwise remain sidelined by ideologically ascendant forces in civil society and an unresponsive and self-perpetuating state.

17

THE COFFEE HOUSE AND THE ASHRAM
Gandhi, Civil Society and Public Spheres

Susanne Hoeber Rudolph
and Lloyd I. Rudolph

Twenty-four hours before he died in 1948, Gandhi proposed to the Indian National Congress, vehicle of the nationalist movement and ruling party of the new Indian nation, that it disband. It should refashion itself, he said, as a social service organization, a Lok Sevak Sangh, controlled from below by a governance structure dominated by panchayats or village committees. Gandhi proposed that the Lok Sevak Sangh be composed of the social service organizations that had been created as part of the nationalist movement: the All India Spinners Association, which provided village level work; the All India Village Industries Association, dedicated to human scale, decentralized, industrial society; the Hindustani Talimi Sangh, for propagating Hindustani as the national language; the Harijan Sevak Sangh, serving untouchables; the Goseva Sangh or cow protection society.[1]

Gandhi was a talented and tireless creator of civil society. He spawned activist networks all his life, wherever he went. His ashrams were the energizing centres of social movements, sending out hundreds

1 R. K. Prabhu and U. R. Rao, compilers, *The Mind of Mahatma Gandhi* (Ahmedabad, Navajivan Press, 1967), p. 354.

of volunteers who in turn generated micro-associations dedicated to social and economic reform at the village level. In his role as the unelected leader of the nationalist movement, he helped create organizational forms for the Indian National Congress which amplified its anti-colonial project to the most remote Indian villages and towns.[2]

With the proposal to dissolve the Indian National Congress, Gandhi turned on one of his own creations, on the association that mobilized Indians to resist and oppose the British imperial state. Independence threatened to convert the Congress from a movement to a party, from an opponent of the (British) state to the engine of the (Indian) state, and a commanding, pervasive, centralized socialist state at that. Gandhi attempted unsuccessfully to forestall that conversion. Why? Parties are amphibious creatures in the associational arena. Opposition parties resemble civil society in that they stand in tension with the government of the day. At the same time, in the role of 'shadow cabinet' and as officially recognized participants in the parliamentary arena, they exhibit an identification with the state. As governing parties, they appropriate and run the state. As a man of civil society, Gandhi targeted the statist face of party.

Civil society is an idea that marks a space separate from the state, either in exchange or in tension with it. Gandhi's stance problematized the state more fundamentally than most proponents of civil society in Europe or America. The manifesto expressed the view that civil society should not only have a space separate from the state; should not only act as critic of and restraint on the state; but that civil society is a more effective agent of social action than the state, creating more appropriate consequences.

Gandhi's proposals for dissolving the efficient, centralized organization he had helped build for the nationalist struggle and for substituting decentralized arenas of action can be deduced from his view of power and his view of human being as moral actor. State power, he believed, is fragile. It depends on the cooperation of the people. Without that cooperation it is helpless. By contrast, society is powerful, the repository of agency, initiative, and will. As Hannah, Arendt who did not particularly consider herself in Gandhi's corner, tells us 'power corresponds to the human ability not just to act but

2 Lloyd I Rudolph and Susanne Hoeber Rudolph, *The Modernity of Tradition; Political Development in India* (Chicago: University of Chicago Press, 1967), p. 234 ff.

to act in concert.' If humans become oppressed, it is because they connive in their own oppression. 'When we say of somebody that he is "in power" we actually refer to his being empowered by a certain number of people to act in their name. The moment the group, from which the power originated to begin with (*potestas in populo*, without a people or group there is no power) disappears, "his power" also vanishes.'[3]

Power does not descend from above. It rises from below, from within society.[4] Forms of governance, then, must strike roots where power and energy are concentrated—below, in the local, within direct control of persons experiencing governance. Gandhi resisted the modernist conclusion that direct democracy—a not unreasonable translation of *swaraj*—is incompatible with modern society and economy. He would not have agreed with Weber that the 'concentration of the means of management' was inevitable.[5] If self-government and the modern prove incompatible, society and economy must be re-aligned. The large scale, the global, the centralized must be resisted and those organizational and economic forms nurtured that are amenable to local control and to the direct influence of civil society. 'Independence must begin at the bottom,' says Gandhi. 'My idea of village *swaraj* is that it is a complete republic, independent of its neighbours for its own vital wants, and yet interdependent for many others for which dependence is a necessity....'[6]

Gandhi's emphasis on civil society also springs from his identification of moral reasoning with voluntarism. Moral thought and

3 Hannah Arendt, *On Violence* (New York: Harcourt Brace and World, Inc., 1969–70), p. 44.

4 Gene Sharp, *The Politics of Non-violent Action, Part I: Power and Struggle* (Boston: Peter Sargent, 1973), p. 8.

5 Most theorists of the modern, from Weber to Nehru, would assert that the inevitable march of rationalization and bureaucratization necessarily goes with centralization. It goes 'hand in hand with the concentration of the material means of management in the hand of the master. This concentration occurs, for instance, in the well-known and typical fashion, in the development of big capitalist enterprises.... A corresponding process occurs in public organizations.' Weber in H. H. Gerth and C. Wright Mills, editors and translators, *From Max Weber* (New York: Oxford University Press, 1946), p. 221.

6 From *Harijan*, 28 July 1946 and *Harijan*, 26 July 1942, in A. T. Hingorani, *Gandhi for 21st Century; the Village Reconstruction* (Mumbai: Bharatiya Vidya Bhavan, Manibhavan Gandhi Sangrahalaya, 1998), pp. 115–17.

conduct are the product of autonomy, of the responsible individual exercising self-control and self-direction. Coercion, presumably including lawful coercion by states, vitiates moral activity. This brings Gandhi into conflict with those Calvinistically toned religious epistemes that posit that the sinner can only come to the true path via the grace of God, and that belief in self-guidance is hubris. For Gandhi, autonomy is a pre-condition of morality.

This paper considers what light the associational forms that Gandhi created shed on the debate about civil society and the public sphere in political and social theory. As John Keane remarks, reflexive, self-organizing non-governmental organizations that some call civil society can and do live by other names in other linguistic and cultural milieux.'[7] How did his 'Indian' variant square with the practice and concept of civil society and public sphere as they have evolved in European history, thought, and practice? Should we stretch the concept of civil society?

CIVIL SOCIETY AND PUBLIC SPHERE AS BOURGEOIS RATIONALITY

The discourse and practice of civil society has had a lively career in the 1990s, passing through numerous incarnations and representations that ranged from revolutionary to collaborative. Civil society, Charles Taylor tells us, refers to a space that exists 'over against the state, in partial independence from it. It includes those dimensions of social life which cannot be confounded with or swallowed up in the state.'[8] Taylor stresses the obstreperous, challenging aspect of civil society, the aspect that showed its face in the Narmada movement in India, in the WTO protests in the US, the contest over electoral corruption in Korea, and the non-violent protests of the Chipko movement. But there are other ways to read it.

The Oxford English dictionary sounds a more gentle tone, stressing the mutuality and *douceur* as aspects of civic society: 'having a proper social order,' keeping 'a certayn civile iustice and friendly love to one another' (Hooker, 1600), or 'reformed, civill, full of good' (Shakespeare,

[7] John Keane, *Civil Society; Old Images, New Visions* (Stanford: Stanford University Press), 1998, p. 55.

[8] Charles Taylor, 'Modes of Civil Society,' *Public Culture*, III, 1, 1990, pp. 59–118, 95. In this volume.

1591, in Two Gentlemen of Verona).[9] The Oxford Dictionary sounds rather like a text for Robert Putnam's or James Coleman's idea of social capital—the capacity to trust and habits of collaboration.[10] It is a vision which expresses itself in Rotary clubs, soccer clubs, Parent Teacher Associations, Lok Sevak Sanghs, associations of and for the homeless, and other friendly associations.

Edward Shills has a more conservative formulation, less focused on popular and associational participation than on the normative mindset appropriate to civility. He stresses the significance of 'a solicitude for the interest of the whole society, a concern for the common good,' underlining obligations to rather than claims against the state.

Transplanting concepts such as civil society and public sphere, born and used in Anglo-American liberal contexts, requires re-calibrating the concept for use in the context of other histories and social structures. When talking about India, we have the excuse that so much of the liberal tradition was transplanted in the course of nineteenth-century nationalist discourse and practice, as also in the constitution of 1950, that the concept of civil society can claim a comfortable home. But definitions of political categories are often captive to their point of first use in a European historical context.[11] As the concept of civil society travels out of its quintessential eighteenth-century European origin to new temporal locations in the twentieth century, and to new cultural locations outside the west, it expresses itself through different cultural forms and takes on different meanings. Indeed it was one of Gandhi's unique talents to give new shape to institutional forms and meanings associated with liberal and democratic spheres.

The version of civil society encapsulated in Jurgen Habermas' earliest ideas about a public sphere will serve as the theoretical backboard off which to bounce Gandhi's associational inventions.[12]

9 *The Compact Edition of the Oxford English Dictionary* (Oxford: Oxford University Press, 1982).

10 Robert Putnam, *Making Democracy Work; Civic Traditions in Modern Italy* (Princeton: Princeton University Press, 1993); James Coleman, *Foundations of Social Theory* (Cambridge, MA: Harvard University Press, 1990).

11 See for example my defence of treating transnational religious movements as an aspect of transnational civil society, in *Transnational Religion and Fading States* (Boulder; Westview, 1997).

12 *The Structural Transformation of the Public Sphere*, translated by Thomas Burger and Frederick Lawrence (Cambridge: MIT Press, 1989).

This early work established Habermas' position as a defender of the enlightenment project of modernity against the critics of the modern, who include Gandhi. Habermas creates and employs categories and representations that highlight the contrast between the Gandhian and European variant of civil society, underlining the re-contextualization of civil society forms.[13]

Habermas, who examined England, France, and Germany, asserted that the public sphere came into being in Europe in the eighteenth century, creating the ground for democratic participation.[14] It was embodied in coffee houses, political clubs, and literary journals.

> There sprang from the midst of the private sphere a relatively dense network of public communication. The growing number of readers...was complemented by a considerable expansion in the production of books, journals and papers.... . The societies for enlightenment, cultural associations, secret freemasonry lodges and orders of illuminati were associations constituted by the free, that is, private decisions of their founding members, based on voluntary membership and characterized internally by egalitarian practices of sociability, free discussion, decision by majority etc.[15]

In these locations, persons who previously led separate lives in private spaces come together and become a public, transcending their private preoccupations and addressing common purposes. The communicative process directed at common questions creates a unified

[13] The 'original' 1962 Habermas has a more restrictive vision of civil society, focusing on narrowly political associations with a strong rationalist and speech-act oriented dimension. The Habermas who appeared at a panel on his work in 1989 had expanded his horizons to include associations with mainly social ends.

> The institutional core of 'civil society' is constituted by voluntary unions outside the realm of the state and the economy and ranging...from churches, cultural associations, and academies to independent media, sport and leisure clubs, debating societies, groups of concerned citizens, and grass-roots petitioning drives all the way to occupational associations, political parties, labour unions, and 'alternative' institutions.

Craig Calhoun, ed., *Habermas and the Public Sphere* (Cambridge, MA: MIT Press, 1996), p. 253.

[14] For an account and analysis of the emergence of opinion and the rise of parties see Lloyd I. Rudolph, 'The Origin of Party: From the Politics of Status to the Politics of Opinion in Eighteenth Century England and America,' Ph.D. Dissertation, Department of Government, Harvard University, 1956.

[15] Habermas, 'Further Reflections on the Public Sphere,' in Calhoun, ed., *Habermas and the Public Sphere*, p. 422.

public. Communicating with each other, social actors learn to share ideas. One can find the organizational form Habermas posits in late nineteenth-century India in major urban centres—in Poona, Bombay, Calcutta, and Madras. Gokhale, Ranade, Tilak, Aurobindo, Surendra Nath Bannerjee: an array of canonical nationalist names is associated with the formation of literary clubs and journals, scholarly societies, service associations, and reform and uplift groups appealing to the educated middle classes.

Habermas, whose volume traced a downward historical trajectory, indicates that such virtuous associational life arises only in limited space and time. He articulates a pessimism as common in the 1960s among conservative American sociologists as among critical Frankfurt Schoolers. Both expected to be overwhelmed by the deluge of mass culture, commodity fetishism, and vulgar interests. Habermas' strong rationalist bias causes him to draw a sharp line between different sorts of opinion and deliberation, received and habitual on the one hand, considered and reflective on the other. Opinion which has always been there differs from this particular moment 'public opinion.'

Whereas mere opinions (things taken for granted as part of a culture, normative convictions, collective prejudices and judgments) seem to persist unchanged in their quasi-natural structure as a kind of sediment of history, public opinion, in terms of its very idea, can be formed only in a public that engages in rational discourse exists.[16]

There is much in Habermas' discourse that implies that public interest can only be arrived at through acts of reasoning that conform to formal notions of rationality and rules of deductive logic. He imagines public intellectuals in engagement with each other. As Eley suggests: 'The faculty of publicness begins with reading, thought, and discussion, with reasonable exchange among equals, and it is this ideal which really focuses Habermas' interest.'[17] Habermas' faith in the power of communicative action makes him a denizen of that German tradition, especially summarized by Hegel, which imagined that the philosopher could, by speech acts and reason, break out of the objectification wrought by social forces such as capitalism and mass culture. That reason, thought, and discussion produce the

[16] Steven Seidman, *Jurgen Habermas on Society and Politics: A Reader* (Boston, MA: Beacon Press, 1989), p. 232.

[17] Geoff Eley, 'Nations, Publics and Political Cultures; Placing Habermas in the Nineteenth Century,' in Calhoun, *Habermas and the Public Sphere*, p. 293.

general interest is a line of argument that rejects consensus based on bargaining. Bargaining implies a deplorable yielding to interest, which does not qualify as a legitimate component of virtuous opinion.

Naturalizing the historical stages characteristic of theories of modernity, Habermas assigns attributes of the public sphere to a specific historical moment:

they developed only in a specific phase of bourgeois society, and only by virtue of a specific constellation of interests could they be incorporated in the order of the bourgeois constitutional state.[18]

Smallish associations marked by 'convivial social intercourse and by a relatively high standard of education' engage in rational consideration of public issues only for a brief, transitional eighteenth-century moment. Then begins the decline. The public sphere is superseded when the bourgeoisie loses its short-lived monopoly of opinion and begins to be pressed by a widening democratization of the public. The forces that obliterate communicative action are mass culture, consumerism, capitalism, the proliferation of private interest. Coffee houses and political clubs are overrun by the competitive and presumably non-rational processes of 'pressure of the streets' and cruder forms of interest confrontation.

Habermas's framing of this move toward democratization is governed by his privileging of the 'rational' over the democratic. The rationality of a proper 'public sphere' will be crowded out by the irrationalities of democratic mobilization. Real deliberation on the common good will be overrun by the narrow interests of organized pressure groups. Public spheres and their rational focus on a common interest are enhazarded by democratization and mass politics.[19]

There is now a propensity among theorists to recognize that the severely rationalist, exclusively bourgeois definition of the public

18 *Jurgen Habermas... a Reader*, p. 232.

19 Habermas speaks of a 'weakening of the public sphere', of the public sphere becoming 'a field for competition among interests in the cruder form of forcible confrontations'; 'Laws that have obviously originated under the "pressure of the streets" can scarcely continue to be understood in terms of a consensus achieved by private persons in public discussion.' Deploring the 'refeudalization' of the public sphere he notes that 'today [publicness] has... been enlisted in the aid of the secret policies of interest groups.' *Jurgen Habermas... a Reader*, p. 236. Much of this is reminiscent of the impatience with political bargaining that lies behind Max Weber's distaste for democratic politics.

sphere which Habermas launched, unduly narrows the idea of the public. It excludes associations from below and associations based on non-print forms of communication. It rejects, as too relativist, the idea of a plurality of associations bearing various visions of the general interest.

Habermas was relatively indifferent to the emergence of a plebeian public sphere. 'The liberal desideratum of reasoned exchange,' Eley suggests, 'also became available for non-bourgeois, subaltern groups, whether the radical intelligentsia of Jacobinism and its successors or wide sections of social classes like the peasantry or the working class.' 'In particular, Habermas' oppositions of "educated/uneducated" and "literate/illiterate" simply don't work because...the liberal public sphere was faced at the very moment of its appearance by...a radical [public] that was combative and highly literate.'[20]

This objection may not go far enough, yielding as it does to the literacy-centrism of elite conceptions of the public sphere. The print media, the bookshop, the coffee houses do not suffice to contain where publics may be found. In the era of mass media, communicative action takes different forms and creates different publics. 'The virtue of publicness could materialize other than by the intellectual transactions of a polite and literate bourgeois milieu.'[21] Ben Lee suggests an alternative conceptualization: 'In many contemporary societies the political public is coextensive with the mass media audience which may be mostly illiterate.'[22] In societies of the south, levels of literacy and forms of social organization need not deter but may reshape the forms that civil society takes.

Habermas' version of civil society envisions a unified process by which the public's deliberations, communicative actions, produce a common conception of a general interest.[23] He does not imagine a variety of differently constituted associations, rallying behind

20 Eley, 'Nations', pp. 304–5.

21 Eley, 'Nations', p. 302.

22 Ben Lee, 'Textuality, Mediation, and Public Discourse,' in Craig Calhoun, ed., *Habermas and the Public Sphere* (Cambridge, MA: MIT Press, 1996, p. 417.

23 He had some doubts about such a single public interest surviving the downward trajectory of society with the assertion of non-public interests: 'The unresolved plurality of competing interests...makes it doubtful whether there can ever emerge a general interest of the kind to which a public opinion could refer as a criterion.' Jurgen Habermas, 'Further Reflections on the Public Sphere,' in Calhoun, *Habermas*, p. 441.

different visions of the public interest. Presumably a multiplicity of publics is really a sign of the assertion of private interest. Habermas names this a process of re-feudalization, invoking the negative valuation which Enlightenment thought imprinted on the feudal.[24] It is a process that leaves behind the models of the public sphere that appeared in eighteenth-century Germany, France, and England. Ahead lie associations from below, not grounded in the literati, non-qualifiers for the public sphere.

Contradictory to this theory of decline, and more sensitive to historical and cultural context, is Ben Lee's conclusion: 'Instead of the degradation of a preexisting bourgeois public sphere... what we see is the coeval emergence of different publics, public spheres, and public spaces, each with their own form of communicative organization.'[25] John Keane goes further:

The ideal of a unified public sphere and its corresponding vision of a territorially bounded republic of citizens striving to live up to their definition of the public good are obsolete. In their place... public life is today subject to 'refeudalization', not in the sense in which Habermas' *Strukturwandel der Offentlichkeit* used the term, but in the different sense of modularization, of the development of a complex mosaic of differently sized, overlapping and interconnected public spheres... .[26]

To summarize, the civil society associations instanced in *Structural Transformations* have a number of attributes which will anchor our discussion of Gandhi's variants of civil society and public sphere. They are voluntary, not coerced; they are located in public spaces— the 'coffee house'—that are explicitly separated from the (private) sphere of house and home; they are marked by an opposition between private and public that impugns the private as the realm of personal interests, disruptive to the public interest; they are skewed toward the intelligentsia, not plebeians, presuming literate if not literary skills; they are grounded in rationalist forms of deliberation which implicitly exclude the force of residual inherited identities— ethnicity and religion—which are seen to live in the arena of private interest.

---

24 Seidman, *Jurgen Habermas*, p. 236.

25 Lee, 'Textuality', p. 416.

26 John Keane, *Civil Society; Old Images, New Visions* (Stanford: Stanford University Press, 1998), p. 169.

INDIAN VARIANTS OF PUBLIC SPHERE
AND CIVIL SOCIETY

How does the theory of public sphere travel in the Indian and in the Gandhian environment? In India the concept of civil society, Partha Chatterjee tells us, 'is best used to describe those institutions of modern associational life set up by nationalist elites in the era of colonial modernity, ...often as part of the colonial struggle.'[27] And indeed, the nineteenth-century specimens of voluntary associations, the Deccan Educational Society, the Brahmo Samaj, the Indian Association, the Prarthana Samaj, and the Poona Sarvajanik Sabha fit rather well with the eighteenth-century rationalist, voluntary, bourgeois, public sphere imagery that Habermas offers. But the nationalist movement, after its transformation into a mass movement in the Gandhian period, spawned many social action initiatives that are not easily contained within the sober, rationalist, descriptors of the public sphere. Liberals like Ranade and Gokhale were one thing, religiously and plebeian toned reformers such as J. G. Phule, Shri Narayana Guru, and Gandhi himself another. Social movements

[27] 'Beyond the Nation? Or Within?' *Economic and Political Weekly*, 4–11 January 1997, pp. 30–4, 32. In this volume. Chatterjee's article recognizes the distinction between the traditional definition of civil society and public sphere and the Gandhian variant of this definition which we are about to elaborate. But he would prefer, apparently in the interest of heuristic sharpness, to 'retain the term civil society [for] those characteristic institutions of modern associational life originating in western societies that are based on equality, autonomy, freedom of entry and exit, contract, deliberative procedures of decision-making, recognized rights and duties of members...' even though non-western countries provide 'numerous examples of the emergence of what could well be called civil-social institutions which nevertheless do not always conform to these principles.' It is a position that denies (on historical grounds? On normative grounds?) the fluidity and adaptability of institutions. This is a different theoretical road than the one adopted in an earlier work in which we argued that 'caste associations' represent a hybrid form of civil society which transgresses the dichotomy between ascribed and voluntary groups. *The Modernity of Tradition: Political Development in India* (Chicago: University of Chicago Press, reprint, 1996). The 'post-midnight' generation of Indian intellectuals, still closer to the colonial experience, tends to read the hybrid nature of many civil society institutions in India as a negative, indicting the colonial contribution to hybridity as inimical. By contrast, the IT generation is producing many observers for whom hybridity appears natural.

were in fact deeply infiltrated by the symbolism, relationships, and practices of a society that was rural, religious, collectively organized, and predominantly illiterate. Bayly, in an argument that provides a historical space for civil society in eighteenth-century India, suggests that such activity was carried on in the arena of religious discourses, the dominant site for ethical reflection and normative practice.[28] Indian associational life in the nationalist era reflected the society into which it was introduced, where realms of life, private/public, religious/secular, chosen/inherited had not been sharply differentiated. Civil society looked different.

One problem in asking the civil society/public sphere question in India is that one is moved, by the eighteenth-century European genealogies of civil society, to look to urban contexts. The rural as an arena does not appear on the horizon, or only marginally. A coffee house in a wheat field? Marx spoke for a general theoretical perspective among modernists when he supposed that peasants did not enter 'into manifold relations with one another.' They were homologous units; like so many potatoes in a sack, they made nothing more cohesive than a sackful of potatoes.[29] They had no 'social capital!'

But India did have strong and pervasive mechanisms of public life, in villages and regional networks, the 'panchayats' that brought together all villagers or village elders to settle conflicts and common affairs, as well as regional caste assemblies which conducted judicial proceedings and proposed economic or political strategies. It became conventional to snigger at the extravagant claims of nationalist historians who claimed isomorphism between the panchayats or sabhas and Greek or Roman republican forums. But these social forms appear to have created an arena for public deliberation where speech acts and persuasion were meant to produce consensus, and do so even today.

Gatherings of respected men...[are] commonly used to settle disputes in Karimpur...those affected by the dispute call together a group of men to act as mediators in the conflict and arrange a settlement. These men should be

---

[28] C. A. Bayly, 'The Indian Ecumene; an Indigenous Public Sphere,' in *Empire and Information; Intelligence Gathering and Social Communication in India, 1780–1870* (Cambridge: Cambridge University Press, 1999), pp. 180–211.

[29] Karl Marx, 'The Eighteenth Brumaire of Louis Napoleon,' *Selected Works* (New York, n.d.), II, p. 415.

aware of the complicated social relationships in which the case is embedded and should aim at a compromise acceptable to all.[30]

These forums were and are communities of unequals, and dominant agrarian families carry disproportionate weight. Members of the village were bound to each other by asymmetrical ties of mutual dependency. In this sense, they violate one of Habermas' more important pre-conditions, that the participants in the public sphere must be free of ties of dependency. Does the fact that the dependency, if asymmetrical, is mutual, soften the objection? As in the polis and the bourgeois public sphere, reaching a 'general interest' in the village commune is predicated on the exclusion or undercounting of inferiors. But the assembly deliberates and attempts to reach a consensus in order to re-establish social harmony, which was until 'yesterday' the village's idea of the general interest.

How about urban contexts? Had they the kind of communicative action, predicated on print media, that enabled the eighteenth-century coffee house, journal, and literary societies on the continent? We know that well into the 1830s and 1840s, lithography had not yet penetrated India. Was this absence significant? Christopher Bayly has explored the nature of publics in eighteenth- and nineteenth-century urban India in the absence of print media. He speaks of the creation of an 'ecumene', a community of written discourse consisting of 'Hindustani-writing literati, Indo-Islamic notables and officers of state' who 'represented the views of bazaar people and artisans when urban communities came under pressure.[31] Such exchanges and debates often revolved around religiously set agendas but 'they were much more than religious polemic...the issue related to religion but

---

[30] Susan Wadley, *Struggling With Destiny in Karimpur; 1925–1984* (Berkeley: University of California, 1994), p. 190. Ralph Retzlaff's monograph in the 1960s was based on the observation of such bodies. *Village Government in India* (Bombay: 1962), pp. 24–5. A more recent account of village panchayats is Bishnu Mohapatra, 'Social Connectedness, Civility and Democracy: A View from an Orissan Village,' unpublished Ms., 'Democracy and Social Capital in Segmented Societies: The Third International Conference,' Vasasalen, Uppsala University, Sweden, 17–19 June 1999. M. N. Srinivas in 'The Social System of a Mysore Village' and Kathleen Gough in 'The Social Structure of a Tanjore Village,' documented the dominance of higher castes in the consensus. In McKim Marriott (ed.), *Village India* (Chicago, 1955). Wadley reports the decay of the ties of dependency that characterized the older village practice.

[31] Bayly, 'Ecumene', p. 182.

in its public manifestations.'[32] 180 Bayly relates the late rise of print media in India to a surplus rather than a shortage of communication forms, speedily propelled across the subcontinent from the northwest to Banaras by news-writers, mail-runners and public recitations.

Indians had created a highly effective information order in which strategically placed written communications reinforced a powerful culture of oral communication ... . Oral exposition, presence and memory were no doubt critical...written media were nevertheless an essential part of North Indian...debate.[33]

Bayly invites us to recognize that there is continuity as well as break between the literate and the non-literate, between notables and officials on the one hand, and the bazaar people and artisans on the other, whose opinions they represent as a matter of importance. It is a connection which carries over into the print media, when in the nineteenth-century some of the 'vernacular press' comes to represent the views of the non-literate. Shahid Amin's detailed account of popular understandings of Gandhi in the twentieth century is based on lengthy vernacular press reports which suggest the connection between sectors characterized by different literacy capacities.[34]

THE ASHRAM AS PUBLIC SPHERE?

Gandhi was attempting to reach beyond the literary elites to a nonliterate mass public. Is deliberation in the public sphere conditioned on literacy? What happens to systems of communication, essential to the formation of civil society, when the potential citizens can neither read or write and before oral/visual mass communication provide another means of communication? When Gandhi was creating a public sphere—in 1900 in South Africa, in the 1920s in India—most villagers and townspeople had neither radio nor television.

Gandhi did not assume a public sphere was conditional on literacy. He was aware that public deliberations and cultural performance reach high levels of complexity under conditions of low literacy.

32 Bayly, 'Ecumene', p. 180.
33 Bayly, 'Ecumene', p. 200.
34 Shahid Amin, *Event, Metaphor, Memory: Chauri Chaura, 1922–92* (Delhi, Oxford University Press, 1996).

Drama (travelling theatre),[35] domestic oral compositions (grandmother's tales),[36] and public oratory (the juridical-cum-civic deliberations of caste and village panchayats) regularly enmesh ordinary non-literate people in cultural production and communication.[37] But to create a 'public' focused on matters of public concern under conditions of non-literacy requires forms of organization different from the coffee house and the literary journal, forms in which exemplification and performance play a visible role.

Gandhi's earliest experiments in creation of a public sphere tried out organizational forms that could be used to attract new constituencies into politics—a very different function than the coffee house's deliberative exchanges among the politicized. His first sites were situated in South Africa, where political participation was restricted to the European bourgeoisie and denied to Africans and Indians. He meant to create a new kind of public space. If the coffee house is the quintessential formation of Anglo-American civil society, the ashram is the special institution of Gandhi's civil society.

Wherever Gandhi's mass politics project travelled, in South Africa or in India, his first step was to create a centre, an ashram—although he did not call it that until he came to India. Here the vanguard participants of his movement could live together, the dedicated and trained resistance professionals who were the key for his major politicization projects, the Delhi Satyagraha, the South African political marches, the salt march. Ashrams are retreats to which those repair who wish to join a community of dedication, usually to a normative or spiritual life, in Gandhi's case also to wider political interests and to social service—projects Gandhi regarded as paired.[38]

---

[35] See Susan Seizer, [Dissertation on travelling village drama troupe] (PhD dissertation in the Department of Anthropology, University of Chicago, Spring 1997).

[36] A. K. Ramanujan (Introduction to book on Folktales).

[37] For a remarkable archive of judicial village rhetoric see the documentary, 'Courts and Councils,' made by the University of Wisconsin and available from their Center of South Asian Studies.

[38] India saw a proliferation of ashrams in the 19th and 20th centuries, institutions which mixed classical models with more recent institutional forms and spiritual needs. The forms also travelled across denominational lines, to Christians and New Agers. For an introduction to the forms and review of historical instances see Richard Taylor, 'Modern Indian Ashrams,' *Religion and Society*, XXXIII, 3 September 1986.

The Gandhian ashrams combined features of European nineteenth-century utopic colonies; the remembered ashram of Kalidasa's fifteenth-century ascetic forest *rishis*; twentieth-century activist NGOs, and the advance bivouac of a guerilla army. The ashrams evolved to perform several tasks: training in discipline of cadres for the large-scale and life-threatening political theatre that was *satyagraha* ('truth-force', non-violent resistance); exemplary enactment of the polity and society to which the movement aspired; commitment to and practice of public service; a site where political leaders met to deliberate on the next step in the movement.

The Gandhian ashram expanded the concept of a public sphere from emphasis on the discursive exchanges of educated men to exemplary performances whose enactment would trigger mass discussions. Satyagrahas were not just large-scale assertions of non-violent resistance. They were vehicles for launching dramatic actions that would politicize millions of people, including uneducated rural and urban folk, alerting them to issues, engaging them in public debate. The ashrams were set up in the context of educating and encouraging a public to assert human rights where they were restricted, by the racist regime of General Smuts in South Africa or the colonial regime in British India. To conduct that education, the ashram set an example—not a quiet, private example, such as that of Kalidasa's peaceful and shady forest retreats—but one whose simplicity, hardship, and political self-sacrifice were meant to be publicly visible.

Gandhi founded two ashrams in South Africa. Phoenix Settlement was established in 1904 under the immediate influence of Ruskin's *Unto This Last*.[39] Tolstoy Farm was established in 1910, named in response to Tolstoy's recognizing Gandhi a spiritual heir.[40] The settlements advertised not only the transnational links of Gandhi's social imagination, but the specific type of socio-political critics he meant to ally with: anti-modernist civil society thinkers. The more ambitious normative goals—to transform the world by transforming the micro-context of everyday life—were linked to more quotidien political ones. Gandhi needed to house and economically sustain the press that produced *Indian Opinion*, the periodic broadsheet of his South Afri-

[39] Mohandas K. Gandhi, *An Autobiography; The Story of My Experiments With Truth* (Boston: Beacon Press, 1993), p. 298.

[40] B. Srinivasan Murthy (ed.), *Mahatma Gandhi and Leo Tolstoy Letters* (Long Beach, CA: Long Beach Publications, 1987), p. 37.

can movement. Also Tolstoy Farm established when it became clear that the freedom struggle in South Africa would be an effort of years, not days, gave a secure retreat to the dedicated satyagrahis and their families who were continually in and out of jail. 'On the one hand there were the Boer generals determined to yield not even an inch of ground, and on the other there were a handful of satyagrahis pledged to fight unto death or victory.' Locating them on the self-sustaining Tolstoy Farm, solved the practical problems of food and shelter even while providing a Benedictine sort of discipline.[41]

When Gandhi brought his freedom project to India, he founded Satyagraha Ashram in 1915 at Ahmedabad.[42] 'I wanted to acquaint India with the method I had tried in South Africa' and the name, 'truth-force,' explained 'our goal and our method of service.'[43] Plague drove the satyagrahis out of Kocharab village in 1917, and they subsequently settled at nearby Sabarmati.[44] When Gandhi turned in 1933 to the condition of the untouchables, Sabarmati was dissolved and renamed Harijan Ashram—using Gandhi's name for untouchables.[45] After three years at Wardha, from 1933-6, where the industrialist Jamnalal Bajaj made available a site, Gandhi's movable community established a new ashram, Sevagram, near Wardha. Segaon was an untouchables' village whose circumstances symbolized the anti-untouchability campaign.[46]

THE ASHRAM AS TRAINING ACADEMY FOR NON-VIOLENT CADRES

The ashrams attracted persons with a vocation for self-sacrifice, often persons with strong political or social values who had participated in Gandhi's early experiments with non-violent resistance to oppressive laws. Many were persons for whom the prospect of communal living seemed attractive. The ashram served as a training academy for

[41] M. K. Gandhi, *Satyagraha in South Africa* (Ahmedabad: Navajivan Press, reprint 1972), p. 213; Martin Green (ed.), *Gandhi in India; in His Own Words* (Hanover: University Press of New England, 1987), p. 176.

[42] *Experiments*, 395–6.

[43] *Experiments*, 396; C. B. Dalal, *Gandhi: 1915–1948; A Detailed Chronology* (New Delhi: Bharatiya Vidya Bhavan, 1971), p. 15.

[44] *Experiments*, 429.

[45] *Chronology*, pp. 102, 104.

[46] Green, *Gandhi in India*, p. 164; *Chronology*, p. 116.

professional resisters and a workshop for fashioning strategies of resistance. Indwellers observed a discipline; they performed common and separate labour on the farm or in the workshops at assigned times to maintain the community; they were schooled to participate in risky political actions. They expected marches, meetings, and public law-breaking acts which would send them to jail. Indeed, jail-going was one of their main vocations. Gandhi occasionally compared them to soldiers; they thought of him as a commander. But the metaphor had limits. The commander's position was much diluted by the fact that all mass actions were preceded by long internal discussion about the expected risks and hardships. Group expectations and pressure to participate were modified by more or less credible assertions that not joining was acceptable. The ashram was a voluntary, not a coercive organization; discipline was helped by the fact that its denizens had self-selected themselves into the ashram and its ethos of self- sacrifice and collective solidarity for a common goal.

The habituation and discipline were not for nothing. Political actions were often dangerous, and the capacity to accept violence had to be cultivated. In 1913, eleven women from Tolstoy Farm and sixteen men and women from Phoenix began the protests against the 'Black Acts' designed to control the movements of the Indian population, against the discriminatory three pound tax, and especially against a judgement of the Cape Supreme Court which retrospectively invalidated Hindu, Muslim, and Parsee marriage, saving only Christian. The decision's consequence was also to invalidate inheritance.[47]

The sixteen person Phoenix party, illegally entering Transvaal, was arrested and given three months at hard labour. The Tolstoy women, all relatively ordinary persons from the large South African Tamil community, played lead roles in a political performance that inducted a whole new non-literate constituency into the fight against racism and for social and political rights. They proceeded to Newcastle in Natal, where they used their linguistic advantage to talk 5000 Tamil and Telugu speaking coal-miners into going on strike. The uncommon appearance of women as political mobilizers—six had babies in their arms, one was pregnant—and outrage at 'the insult offered to our womanhood' caused their call to 'spread like wildfire.'[48] When

---

[47] Satyagraha in South Africa, p. 251 ff.
[48] Ibid., pp. 252, 257.

the women were jailed for three months, their example firmed up the determination of the miners to court arrest. One of the women died and one barely escaped death due to inhuman jail conditions.

The main fruit of the discipline was that despite Gandhi's obvious guiding leadership role, which suggested the ashram was a hierarchical and charismatic form of organization, it could not easily be beheaded. When the authorities arrested Gandhi, as they usually did at the beginning of a mass satyagraha, his co-ordinating role was immediately filled by other adepts; the complex logistical skills associated with guiding thousands in a political march, and above all the routines that kept the peace essential to Gandhi's engagement of opponents, were widely shared by the ashramites.[49]

THE ASHRAM AS EXEMPLAR OF THE IMAGINED SOCIETY

Insofar as the ashram represents public space, it does so in peculiar fashion, its self-sufficiency and domestic rituals dedicated to a partial withdrawal from society, an Indic New Harmony. Yet the withdrawal from society is in preparation for a more complete issuing forth, an exemplary performance, in which the inmates of the ashram publicly enact a standard for society. Ashram society aimed to be exemplary:

Tolstoy Farm was never placed in the limelight, yet an institution which deserved it attracted public sympathy to itself. The Indians saw that the Tolstoy Farmers were doing what they themselves were not prepared to do and what they looked upon in the light of hardship. This public confidence was a great asset to the movement when it was organized afresh on a large scale in 1913.[50]

At Tolstoy Farm, Gandhi invented multicultural India. It became an arena for representing difference as Gandhi hoped it would be experienced in a free Indian society. At Tolstoy Farm, a diversity of private difference yielded to commonality in public space.

The settlers hailed from Gujarat, Tamilnad, Andhra-desh and North India, and there were Hindus, Musalmans, Parsis and Christians among them. About forty of them were young men, two or three old men, five women and twenty to thirty children of whom four or five were girls.[51]

49 For the serial performance of the coordinating roles, see Ibid., pp. 274–86.

50 Gandhi, Ibid. (Ahmedabad: Navajivan Press, reprint 1972), p. 236.

51 M. K. Gandhi, Ibid., p. 215. For a continuation of this ethnic, religious, and social ecumenism, see Martin Green (ed.), *Gandhi in India; in His Own Words* (Hanover: University Press of New England, 1987), p. 177–8.

The Tolstoy accounts are full of the quotidian details of negotiating the integration of private difference into a public space. The practical considerations were, for example, how to arrange feeding? By allowing every family to work their own kitchen, as religious, caste, and culture based differences might dictate? Such practice would increase expenses. If by a common kitchen, which would be more unifying and more economical, how to mediate between meat-eaters and vegetarians? The conundrum appears to have been settled by Gandhi's usual 'gentle persuasion,' not unsurprisingly on the side of vegetarianism. Dish-washing arrangements were partly designed to override residual reservations about purity and pollution: no one was exempted from the cleaning of common dishes.

There was to be one single kitchen, and all were to dine in a single row. Everyone was to see to the cleaning of his own dish and other things. The common pots were to be cleaned by different parties in turn.[52]

More serious in its consequences was the addition of an untouchable family. The gesture has an artificial feel when read in the light of contemporary sensibilities when ex-untouchables reject upper caste sponsorship. Then, such gestures were valuable, but also socially costly for the sponsor. When Gandhi solicited funding among the Gujaratis of Ahmedabad, where the first ashram in India was established, he was taking a risk:

'I made it clear to them that I should take the first opportunity of admitting an untouchable candidate to the ashram if he was otherwise worthy. "Where is the untouchable who will satisfy your condition?" said a *vaishnava* friend self-complacently.'[53]

When Gandhi found such a 'humble and honest untouchable family,' the funding came to an abrupt end. The *vaishnava* friend who had asked the question stopped his contributions, and there was talk of social boycott. Within the ashram, 'my wife and other women did not seem quite to relish the admission into the ashram of the untouchable friends.' The public performance of diversity was costly, and it was indeed public: 'We proclaimed to the world that the Ashram would not countenance untouchability.'[54]

52 Gandhi, Ibid., p. 216.
53 *Experiments*, p. 395.
54 Ibid., p. 399.

The ashram as vehicle of the public sphere also became a species of road show, moving its performances around India and recreating its forms of life at each of the major reform and resistance sites—in Champaran in 1917, in Kheda in 1918, on the salt march in 1930. Part of the road show was the visible practice of simplicity: performing menial work, wearing plain clothes, living in unfurnished environments, doing work for yourself. It was a multi-valenced practice, signifying the asceticism of the religious-seeker, an abjuring of private self-indulgence in favour of the public interest, identification with the least, and a strike at the hierarchical and exclusivist features of Indian culture.

These forms of simplicity were the visible weapon against social injustice. To demonstrate within a pollution-conscious society that all work was worthy, activists performed for themselves the tasks deemed demeaning in caste and class rankings. As volunteers among the poor, the ashram-dwellers saw enactment of simplicity both as a moral obligation and as a strategy for transforming society.

The exemplary performances of simplicity at Champaran, in Bihar, during Gandhi's work on behalf of the indigo labour force are well known. The volunteers whom Gandhi had recruited for this campaign were prosperous upper caste advocates, who helped bring court cases to challenge labour-hostile laws and help take witnesses from the labourers. They assumed serving the movement was compatible with upper caste lifestyles. Writes Gandhi:

The curious ways of living of my companions in the early days were a constant theme of raillery at their expense. Each of the vakils had a servant and a cook, and therefore a separate kitchen, and they often had their dinner as late as midnight. Though they paid their own expenses, the irregularity worried me, but as we had become close friends...they received my ridicule in good part. Ultimately it was agreed that the servants should be dispensed with, that all the kitchens should be amalgamated, and that regular hours should be observed...it was also felt necessary to insist on simple meals.[55]

55 Ibid., p. 417. It is not my objective in this paper to analyse Gandhi's rhetoric, but it is worth pointing out that Gandhi's accounts report no agents: 'It was agreed,' 'it was decided upon.' The various decisions to create a common vegetarian kitchen, at Tolstoy Farm, at Champaran, appear to happen without the active intervention of any advocate or persuador, but rather appear as the fortuitous and appropriate result of a spontaneous consensual expression of ashram souls.

Dr Rajendra Prasad, who became India's first president, was one of the advocates. He wryly recalls trying to figure out how to lower a clay pot by rope into the village well, to the immense amusement of the locals.[56]

These practices demanded a sharing of common social premises: simplicity and abstaining from keeping servants, saving money, dignifying labour, enacting respect for tasks performed by the humble. These practices involved dismantling the separation of public and private spheres. The lawyers who were quite content to give their legal services did not realize, when they signed up with Gandhi, that they had contracted to yield up intimate, status-sustaining personal practices. They had not counted on cleaning their own chamberpots. This public sphere made greater demands than the coffee house, excavating the political meaning of private life-ways, buttresses of the deepest inequalities and oppressions of Indian society.

The ashram's example was also diffused through more conventional messengers of the public sphere: newspapers, the daily press when it reported on the major resistance movements, or through Gandhi's own journal. Its name, *Public Opinion*, signals its place among the key agencies of civil society. Gandhi recognized that an unseen political performatory has no effect. Hence the ashram's withdrawal from the world was conducted very publicly: 'We could not perhaps have educated the local Indian community, nor kept Indians all over the world in touch with the course of events in South Africa in any other way, with the same ease and success as through *Indian Opinion*, which therefore was certainly a most useful and potent weapon in our struggle.'[57] *Indian Opinion*, as the quote reminds us, functioned as a vehicle not merely of national but of transnational civil society, building a constituency in the homeland—especially the Gujarati homeland—for the Indian diaspora in South Africa. His later journals for the Indian campaigns, *Navajivan* and *Young India*, reached a joint circulation of 40,000.[58]

[56] Rajendra Prasad, 'Gandhi in Bihar,' in Homer Jack (ed.), *The Gandhi Reader* (Bloomington, Ind.: University of Indiana Press), pp. 149–59.

[57] Gandhi, *Satyagraha in South Africa*, p. 134. For the massive repercussions in India of the violence committed against the South Africa strikers in 1913, including Viceroy Lord Harding's surprising condemnation of the South African authorities, and G. K. Gokhale's amplification to India of the news he received from South Africa, see *Satyagraha in South Africa*, p. 286.

[58] *Experiments*, p. 474.

The enactment in the ashram of multi-ethnicity, encompassing several Indian regional-linguistic subcultures; of ecumenism, grounded not in a privatization of religion but in a deliberate ethic of mutual respect for publicly practised religiosity; and of cross-caste neighborliness, made the ashram as theatre the model and exemplar of an imagined society.

THE COFFEE HOUSE AND THE ASHRAM: CONTRASTS, CONGRUENCES

The coffee house was the public sphere of literate, educated, middle class political persons. The printed word was their means of communication and action. The reasoned argument was the medium. The ashram by contrast sought to draw uneducated: urban and rural, working and farming people into a public sphere in the context of mass politics. The problem of creating a public sphere, a self-automating civil society, among non-literates propelled Gandhi and his ashram associates to enact, exemplify, amplify political goals in theatrically visible forms, and to create participatory contexts-marches, sit-ins, boycotts—which required political understanding and commitment to goals more than the word.

Among the features that distinguish the ashram from the eighteenth-century political club is the religious grammar in which the ashram is embedded as against the enlightenment rationalism of the club. Yet we ought not draw too sharp a distinction: the Gandhian ashram is about civic virtue, service to a general interest, and the creation of a just society. Gandhi would align with Habermas' understanding of a decline in the public sphere due to the proliferation and institutionalization of private 'interest'. The ashram's idea of service which builds on models of religious obligation as well as self-abnegating asceticism sits somewhat awkwardly with rationalism. Yet it points in a similar direction as the civic virtue face of the public sphere.

By contrast to the coffee house, Gandhi's ashram deliberately challenged the differentiation between private and public that characterizes the modernist public sphere. The ashram is and is not public, a place focused on the political vocation even while engaging all the rounds of life. It is a setting at once familial, even patriarchal; monastic, disciplined by an ecumenical definition of religious commitment; dedicated to social and political change in a polity where illegal political action is the only action possible for a free person. Many of these attributes do not fit with the differentiated, specialized identity conveyed by the coffee house and the political club, unravelled from familial space, from workplace, affected by the marginalization or privatization of religion, and dominated by the discursive activity of educated rationalists. The differentiation between public sphere and private space that appears so central to the European conceptions of civil society since Hegel is indifferently observed.

The revolutionary quality of Gandhi's strategy lay precisely in his transgression of the lines between public and private. That transgression has to be read against the complex meanings of public/private harboured by Indian society—meanings to which conventional European usage is a poor guide. The meaning of privacy is modified by the structure of the family and the pattern of housing and rural settlement. In multi-generational ('joint') families with strong collective norms, surveillance of the most trivial or intimate acts was/is common.[59] How should we conceptualize such transgression? By saying that the family, a private collectivity, invades the privacy of its members? By recognizing a gradation of privacies? By recognizing that the family too—contrary to its assigned position in the western canon—has to be understood as part of the political?[60] The borders of what constitutes privacy become problematic when the family reaches beyond the nuclear unit and constitutes a small community. Again, in villages and hamlets, most quotidien activity is accomplished on verandas or in courtyards, within sight of the neighbours, under surveillance. Privacy is more an urban than a rural phenomenon, and a luxury of the walled-in middle class rather than the open-air poor.

Many nominally private practices—the pulling of the headcloth over the face designating a woman's modesty; the tying of the *dhoti*

[59] See Susanne Hoeber Rudolph and Lloyd I. Rudolph, *Reversing the Gaze; The Amar Singh Diary, a Native Subject's Narrative of Imperial India* (New Delhi: Oxford University Press, 2000), Introduction.

[60] Althusius is one of the few dissenters from the tradition that follows Aristotle, in which the family is *oikos* and pre-political, the polis is public and political. See Johannes Althusius, *Politica*, edited and translated by Frederick. S. Carney (Indianapolis: Liberty Fund, 1995). His pluralist view of the polity as constituted by a graduated set of socio-political units encompasses the family as a basic unit. 'By politics alone arises the wisdom for governing and administering the family', p. 32.

designating caste status; the choice of or mix of *deshi* and *angrezi* dress forms; the participation in a public meal; the marriage of two incompatibly ranked social actors-display in public and for the sake of public certification personal acts that begin in and belong to the private sphere. A narrow view of politics would relegate these to the private. A view of the political that recognizes stability or change in social status/gender status as political acts can not exclude them.[61]

The most fundamental social transformations that Indian reformers have sought to accomplish in the last hundred years have been as much embedded in private as in public spheres: change in gender disparities, in caste exclusions. Major Indian nineteenth-century public figures engaged in the search for just and meaningful social practices amid the conflicting cultural claims that the colonial situation generated. They often affected the public sphere most profoundly by performing some act of private deviation—marrying a widow; crossing the ocean; ignoring the family's conventional demands. As the feminists say, the personal is political. When these individual transgressions proliferated, and reformers sought social legislation to modify oppressive private practices—The Age of Consent Act; the Widow Remarriage Act—the claim of privacy, that intimate spheres are beyond the reach of public scrutiny, or at least beyond the scrutiny of the colonial state, was invoked.[62] What Gandhi did was to assert the opposite, that all private matters—or most—were on the table.

Many of Gandhi's political co-workers in the nationalist cause would gladly have collaborated in the public realm, shielding the more difficult and precious private arena of sectarian, class and caste practices behind the claim of private space. Dismantling the public/private boundary enabled his unabashed invasion of the private practices that drew the boundaries constituting caste and religious difference.

Voluntarism, free entry and exit, are features in which associations operating in a public sphere overlap with the ashram. Ashrams, writes Richard Taylor, 'may be the only traditional kind of Indian

---

61 Not that anyone has any questions these days about the sometimes political nature of the headscarf.

62 M. G. Ranade (1842–1901), who favoured social reform as an appropriate issue for the Indian National Congress, was forced to back off when it became apparent social reform, as against political freedom, would deeply divide the Congress.

association (perhaps along with some bhakti groups) that are outside the...conditions of ascriptive membership—at least in theory, if not always in practice.'[63] Volunteers 'applied' to the ashrams, alerted by the fame of Gandhi's projects. Some arrived in the spirit of novices entering a religious order, some in the spirit of Peace Corps volunteers. Neither ethnicity nor caste nor religion nor nationality qualified or disqualified. Those for whom it was too much or too little, left. Entry by merit, exit by choice.

Voluntarism raises the question of what role leadership plays, whether it is enabling or coercive. The theoretical literature on civil society is relatively silent on this question, but most of it works with the normative assumption of horizontal organization in which peers deliberate.[64] Even scholarship that focuses on free riders in voluntary associations and expects oligarchic tendencies, emphasizes an egalitarian context.[65] How about ashrams? Father Jesudason, who provides a compendium of classical Indian ashram imaginaries, noted 'The continual presence of a Rishi or a man of God reverenced by all for his life of holiness and purity,'[66]—an image which suggests the availability but not dominance of a spiritual guide. On the other hand, popular portrayals of transnational ashrams often project an image of spiritual and material despotism.

Gandhi supplied the role of an ethical and/or spiritual guide. He adapted his style to the cultural and psychological predispositions of his counter-players: peer with some, guru with others.[67] But because

63 Richard W. Taylor, 'Modern Indian Ashrams,' *Religion and Society*, XXXIII, 3 September 1986, p. 20.

64 For a typical and influential version of the assumption of horizontal structure see Margaret E. Keck and Kathryn Sikkink, *Activists Beyond Borders; Advocacy Networks in International Politics* (Ithaca: Cornell University Press, 1998). For a discussion of varieties of networks, horizontal and vertical, see Susanne Hoeber Rudolph and James Piscatori (eds), *Transnational Religion and Fading States* (Boulder: Westview, 1997), pp. 252–5. Robert Putnam attends to the role of elites in local governments in his account of social capital in *Making Democracy Work* (Princeton: Princeton University Press, 1992), pp. 26–37.

65 See Mancur Olson, *The Rise and Decline of Nations; Economic Growth, Stagflation and Social Rigidities* (New Haven: Yale University Press, 1982).

66 Savarirayan Jesudason, *Ashrams, Ancient and Modern: their Aims and Ideals* (Vellore: Sri Ramachandra Press, 1937), p. 6 ff.

67 Susanne Hoeber Rudolph, 'Gandhi's Lieutenants—Varieties of Followership,' in Paul Powers, *The Meaning of Gandhi* (Hawaii: Hawaii University Press, 1971), pp. 41–58.

of the long periods he spent in jail or on the road as a nationalist campaigner, the ashram developed wide experience in self-rule. The *Works* are full of letters written by Gandhi from the road to the inhabitants of the ashrams giving advice, counselling patience in close quarters and among rivals, but expecting the denizens to manage their own affairs.

The ashram's projects were/are based on a more holistic vision than that of the coffee house of how to improve the human condition. In the world of the coffee house, the political is separable from other spheres, from personal vocation, religion, ethnic and other 'primal' solidarities. The ashram embodies the belief, more native to the religious than the political adept, that social change comes about through the ethical and moral transformation of selves rather than through public and political institutions. Gandhi formed his first ashram in the grip of a 'spell' cast by Ruskin's espousal of such a holistic vision.[68] After reading *Unto This Last*, the four political economy essays that constituted Ruskin's slashing attack on market capitalism and modern society,[69] he made himself a promise that reaches well beyond political agendas: 'I determined to change my life in accordance with the ideals of the book.'[70] The ashram was established in part to enable its indwellers to practise a community of virtue: dedicated to the collective good; to the belief that all work is equally worthy; to the conviction that the life of tillers and craftsmen is worth living.[71]

The state is too frail, even impotent, to be the arena of a public good. The locus of true power being the civil society on which the state is ultimately dependent, civil society becomes the proper arena for change. Deliberations in the public sphere are predicated on the assumption of a state that will execute the general interest that evolves. But for the Gandhian ashram, it is the transformation of inner selves, of the will and intent of human actors, that is the path

68 'One of the great prophetic books of the nineteenth century,' which 'pierces through the smoke-screen of classical economics, and reveals true human realities.' Kenneth Clark, *Ruskin Today* (Harmondsworth: Penguin, 1982), p. 265.

69 See Clive Wilmer's review of six books on Ruskin that herald the 'return' of this alternately celebrated and shunned figure, 'Go to Nature,' *Times Literary Supplement*, 7 April 2000, pp. 3–4. For locating the timing of Gandhi's activities see *Chronology*.

70 *Experiments*. p. 298.

71 Ibid., p. 299.

to social change. Thus the worldviews and behaviour that constitute the practice of injustice, such as beliefs in untouchability or extortionate dowry practices are not affected by the weak hand of legislation, but by persuasion and the enactment of justice, routinized in committed associations. Change is more than a political act—for which the coffee house and the political club are sufficient, influencing legislation, public policy, and public sanctions. Change for Gandhi is a societal act engaging subjectivities as well as social structures. Such a political process requires bearers other than the limited and rationalist forms of the eighteenth-century coffee house, pub, and literary society.

18

SOCIAL CAPITAL, CIVIL SOCIETY, AND DEGREES OF DEMOCRACY IN INDIA

Hans Blomkvist

The fall of the Berlin Wall in 1989 meant a political sea change not only in Europe. In many countries democracy has become the only defensible political system; political and scholarly discussions instead centre on what *kind* of democracy is to be preferred, and *how* to achieve a democracy closer to our ideals. In these latter debates the notions of civil society have taken a dominant position (Offe 2000). Claims and counterclaims about the essential or superfluous role of civil society are common but much less frequent are systematic data to support either position.

Closely related to civil society is the concept of social capital. The idea that a group of people sharing networks and norms has a common resource is far from new, but it came into mainstream discussion with Robert Putnam's study of Italy, *Making Democracy Work*. Putnam's study and the notion of social capital have inspired and provoked a landslide of both theoretical and empirical work—including the *Agora Project*. The Agora Project, begun in 1995, is a collaboration between scholars in five academic departments[1] investigating the impact of

[1] *Viz.* the Department of Political Studies, University of the Witwatersrand, Johannesburg, South Africa; Centre for Political Studies at Jawaharlal Nehru

social capital on democratic performance and protest mobilization in India and South Africa, combining quantitative and qualitative research methods. This project did personal interviews with 3200 respondents in 31 localities in five of the then 24 Indian states, *viz.* Gujarat, Kerala, Orissa, Uttar Pradesh, and West Bengal.[2]

To people living in India and others acquainted with the subcontinent it is no news that the 'quality' of its democratic regime varies across this vast country (cf. Varshney 2000). In this paper I will show that these differences in 'democratic quality' at the state level can be explained by variations in social capital endowments.

My argument can be summarized in terms of three interrelated hypotheses:

(i) Formal voluntary associations—civil society—have a positive impact on democratic responsiveness;

(ii) Informal networks have a positive impact on democratic responsiveness;

(iii) Norms of trust have a positive impact on democratic responsiveness.

I also hypothesize that political participation is one important mechanism that influences how social capital resources get transformed into increased democratic responsiveness.

This argument counters two dominant understandings about disparities among Indian states, that they are best explained by either economic development or the political party in power. These are the two most common counter-arguments to the theory of social capital. I briefly discuss the significant (and contested) concepts of democracy, social capital, and civil society. Then I present a model and mechanisms for how social capital may influence democratic performance.

University, New Delhi; the Department of Political Science, Utkal University, Bhubaneswar; the departments of Government and Peace and Conflict Research at Uppsala University in Sweden. We wish to thank the Swedish agency Sida/SAREC for generous financial support of the research. I wish to thank Jean Drèze, Carolyn Elliott, Karolina Hulterström, Sten Widmalm, and Steven Wilkinson for constructive comments on an earlier draft.

2 The interviews were done in early 1998, except in Gujarat where they were done in early 1999. We have also interviewed 1000 respondents in South Africa in early 1998.

After that I confront the model with results from our interview surveys. Finally, I discuss my findings in relation to the two counter-arguments mentioned above.

DEMOCRACY

According to what most academic observers now accept as democracy, 'the continuing responsiveness of the government to the preferences of its citizens, considered as political equals' (Dahl 1971: 1)[3] India is, with minor exceptions, a democracy. But there is a further theoretical problem that is much less discussed by philosophers and political scientists (but cf. Foweraker and Krznaric 2000). Can we say that one particular political system is 'more democratic' than another? Juan Linz and Alfred Stepan note (1996: 6) that '(w)ithin the category of consolidated democracies there is a continuum from low to high quality democracies.' How should we measure this 'democratic quality' or 'democratic deepening' (Heller 2000)?

In principle, any of the three components[4] referred to in the quote from Dahl could be used to evaluate democratic quality: responsiveness, citizens' influence, or political equality. I use the criterion of government responsiveness, which refers to whether the government is responsive to citizen demands. Two measures will be used, an objective—based on statistics of government performance—and a subjective based on citizen perceptions. For the former, we asked our respondents what they saw as 'the most urgent needs in this area' and then compared their preferences with official data from the five states on performance of those policies. For the latter, we asked our respondents 'how interested' they thought the state government 'is in the needs of people like yourself.'

Since this indicator of democracy has been disputed, it is worth emphasizing that it *only* makes sense when we are analysing political systems that are democratic according to the conventional criteria of free elections and political liberties.[5] Policy performance

---

[3] According to this conception, a political system is democratic if it has political and civil rights and free and fair elections; cf. O'Donnell 1993; Beetham 1994; Dahl 1971; Hadenius 1992; Bollen 1993; Tarrow 1996; Berins Collier 1999.

[4] These have been used in a 'democratic audit' in Sweden, cf. Rothstein 1995.

[5] Sidney Tarrow and others criticized this usage by Putnam in his study of Italy (1993), pointing out that 'policy performance is as likely to be positive in

or responsiveness can only serve us in evaluating 'low to high quality democracies'; it cannot distinguish democratic from non-democratic states.

SOCIAL CAPITAL

Social capital refers to trust, networks, and shared norms between two or more individuals (cf. Coleman 1988, 1990; Putnam 1993, 2000). Social capital theory proposes that social connectedness has a strong impact on those societal outcomes which depend on coordination of action, e.g. democratic and economic performance.[6] It facilitates co-ordinated action between individuals and makes collective action problems less difficult. Social capital theory is one important strand in efforts to build an empirically based social theory.[7]

This way of conceptualizing social capital means that associational density or memberships in associations are not synonymous with social capital. Associations are *one form* of social capital; informal networks and shared norms are the other two most important forms of social capital. For the sub-set of formal associations in the sphere between state and the household, I shall use the term 'civil society'.

It is important to draw a line between research on social capital and research on political culture. Political culture has focused on individuals' *values* as the core factor in explaining democracy (cf. Almond & Verba 1963 or Ingelhart 1997). Research on social capital is more promising because it provides less self-evident results. Thus a showing that 'participant political culture' leads to more participation and a better working democracy is not terribly surprising. An empirical finding that social capital is good for democracy is more interesting since we can also hypothesize that social capital could be *harmful* for democracy. Social capital 'enables participants to act

---

non-democratic as in democratic states' (1996: 395). Tarrow's argument constitutes a 'category mistake'. Putnam studied a democratic country according to conventional—including Tarrow's own—criteria.

[6] See Knack & Keefer (1997) who show a strong correlation between data on interpersonal trust and growth of GNP per capita.

[7] 'The really big puzzle in the social sciences' Elinor Ostrom (1998: 9) says, 'is the development of a consistent theory to explain why cooperation levels vary so much.' Controlled experiments have shown that even a single opportunity for the participants to communicate increases cooperation dramatically, and indirectly 'cooperators expect significantly more cooperation than do defectors'.

together more effectively to pursue shared objectives', but 'whether or not their shared goals are praiseworthy is, of course, entirely another matter' as Robert Putnam (1995b: 664f) puts it. It is *an empirical question* whether social capital in fact leads to the beneficial outcomes often assumed. This politically indeterminate nature of social capital, which some critics have seen as a weakness of social capital theory, is actually a theoretical strength.

Does the Theory Travel Well to the South?

Some critics have argued that the theory of social capital—formulated in the west and yielding interesting results in western countries like Italy (Putnam 1993)—is of little relevance in the south. On the contrary I would argue that most Third World societies are *made of* interpersonal trust and networks, the core elements of social capital. The formal institutions of democracy and the market are often found wanting or working in distinctly different ways compared with 'the west'. But here is a theory that strongly emphasizes the *informal* and everyday social interaction as an important explanation for democratic and economic outcomes. Whether these social institutions have different results in countries like India is a matter for study. But it is certainly plausible that knowing and trusting other people is relevant to the nature of democracy in India.

The Model

The model that I will test hypothesizes that variations in individuals' own resources (human capital) and social resources (connectivity to others) affect democratic performance. We hypothesize that they do so through two different 'routes': directly[8] and via effects on political participation.[9] How could social connections have an impact? Putnam suggests three ways: (Putnam 2000: 288). First, social capital allows citizens to resolve collective action problems more easily, in other words, the common social dilemmas where most people reason 'I will do my part if the others do their part.' Social capital also lowers the transaction costs; e.g. the time and effort it takes to find out if

[8] More precisely, via recruitment, monitoring, and government anticipation, social mechanisms, which will be discussed more below.

[9] Therefore Harriss' (2001) critique of social capital theory, including Blomkvist and Swain (2001), of being a(nti) political is unwarranted.

someone ought to be trusted. Thirdly, social connectedness impacts on citizens' awareness of others and the larger world.[10]

In order to identify the contribution made by social capital, we shall seek to eliminate the contribution of socio-economic status, which we know from earlier research (cf. Verba, Nie, Kim 1978), also increases the individual's capacity in the political realm. Thus education and living standard are used as controls in the regression models reported below.

In a schematic form the most important mechanisms are outlined in Figure 18.1.

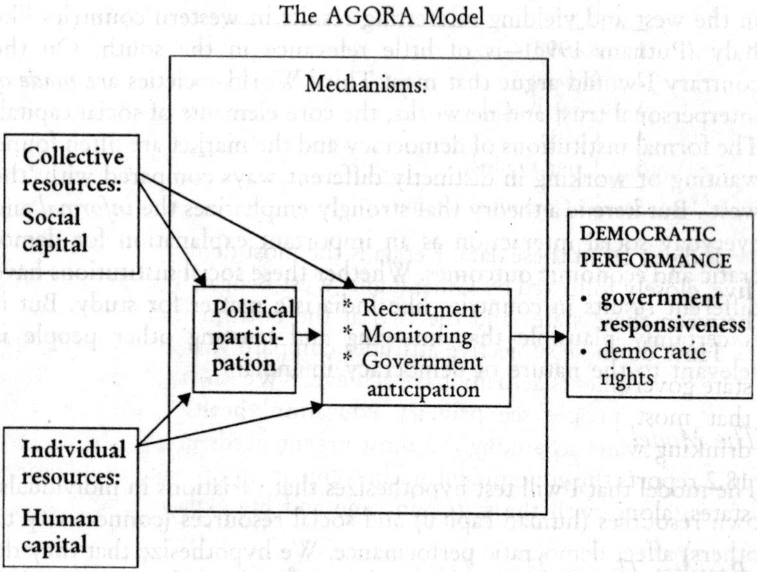

The AGORA Model

Note: Variables written in bold letters are represented by empirical data in the following analysis Human capital—the respondents' education and living standard—is not reported separately but controlled for in the regression analyses later.

FIGURE 18.1: How Social Capital Affects Democratic Performance

The problem with one-point-in-time research is to determine which 'direction' causality goes; what is cause and what is effect? Since

[10] This is corroborated by our data. The size of a person's support network, controlling for education and economic standard, has a significant and positive effect on how often s/he listens to radio news.

time and money do not allow for the ideal method using panel data, we have to rely on past work, theoretical arguments, and common sense. This said, we should not ignore the contribution of 'snap-shot', large-scale research, such as the Agora data set provides. It enables us to outline the general patterns of what 'hangs together'—correlates— and what does not the proportion of people in each state that thinks the state government is 'very interested' and 'quite interested'.

TABLE 18.1
Government Responsiveness (subjective)
Per cent who thinks the state government is interested

Rank		Order
1	Kerala	52
2	Gujarat	47
3	West Bengal	47
4	Orissa	28
5	Uttar Pradesh	23

Source: Computed by author.

Judging from these data, Kerala is the most democratic state of the five, closely followed by Gujarat and West Bengal. The large variance between these states and the two at the bottom is worth noting.

How do these subjective attitudes compare with data on what the state governments actually have achieved? We know from our survey that most people see primary education, health, electricity, and drinking water as among the most urgent needs in their area, Table 18.2 reports the government's achievements in these areas for the five states, along with the state's income and life expectancy.

Results: Theory Meets Data

The Data Set

Five Indian states with a combined population (in 1991) of 309 million people were chosen to give us a sample of the rich economic and political varieties found on the subcontinent.[11] Within the five states

11 Uttar Pradesh and Orissa represent comparatively poor and underdeveloped states where we also assumed social capital would be low. Gujarat on the Indian west coast, the fourth richest state in India, was interesting since its successful cooperative movement might indicate high social capital. West Bengal and Kerala are in the Indian 'middle-range' in terms of development and have been the strong-holds of the Communist Party (Marxist) in India.

TABLE 18.2
Government Responsiveness (objective): Index of policy performance

	Income	Life ex-pectancy	Lite-racy	Vacci-nation	Medical facilities	Water (rural)	Electricity (rural)	Σ
Kerala	119	129	222	156	960	151	420	2153
Gujarat	161	108	151	142	260	143	560	1525
West Bengal	134	111	142	137	130	179	180	1013
Orissa	101	100	121	126	110	128	180	866
Uttar Pradesh	100	101	100	100	100	100	100	701

Notes: The figures are reported as an index where the lowest figure among these five states for each indicator is counted as 100. The other figures are consequently related to this; i.e. the income of 161 for Gujarat means that the average per capita income is 161 per cent of the lowest, that of Uttar Pradesh.

The last column is the summary figure of all the seven indicators; making such a summation builds on the plausible assumption that of each seven 'policy outcomes' is 'weighted' similar by the citizens.

The data refer to the following tables and information in Table A3 in the Statistical Appendix in Drèze & Sen 1995:

Income: Per-capita net state domestic product at current prices, 1991–2

Life expectancy at birth, females, 1990–2

Literacy rate, age 7+, females

Vaccination: Proportion of children aged 12–23 months who have received any vaccination 1992–3

Medical facilities: Proportion of villages with medical facilities 1981

Water: Proportion of households in rural areas having access to safe drinking water, 1991

Electricity: Proportion of rural households with electricity connection, 1991.

Source: Computed by author.

we chose 31 localities[12] to represent important cleavages for each state. Then we chose a voting booth within each locality; from the voting list we drew a random sample of 100 respondents. The respondents were interviewed in their house by Indian students from the respective state, female respondents mainly by female students.[13]

[12] For lack of a better word I use 'locality' here. The word 'district' has a definite administrative and political meaning in India, and our areas are smaller than the district. 31 localities were required to generate statistically meaningful results using ecological analysis.

[13] The questionnaire was translated into five Indian languages: Hindi, Bengali, Oriya, Malayalam, and Gujarati.

Government Responsiveness

Does social capital have the hypothesized impact on democratic performance? I will move 'backwards' in the model presented above: starting with presentation of data on the dependent variable—government responsiveness—then moving on to the intermediate variable—political participation. Finally I will present and discuss data on the independent social capital variables: associational memberships, informal networks, and interpersonal trust. I will start by presenting data by state and then present all respondents together.

Table 18.1 presents the 'subjective' measurement of democratic responsiveness for the five states. We asked our respondents 'How interested do you think the state government is in the needs of people like you?' The respondents were asked to rate this on a 5-point scale from 'Very interested' to 'Not at all interested'. Table 18.1 shows the proportion of people in each state that thinks the state government is 'interested' or 'quite interested'. Judging from these data Kerala is the most democratic state of the five, closely followed by Gujarat and West Bengal. The variance between these states and the two at the bottom is noteworthy.

Table 18.2 gives us information about the extent to which the five state governments have been able to live up to the expectations and wants of their citizens, which I take as a measure of the 'quality' or level of democracy in these five states. It is striking how similar Tables 18.1 and 18.2 are in terms of the states' rank order, even relative distance.

The figures in Table 18.2 do not simply reflect economic wealth. Calculations (not reported here) of how much the different state governments are able to deliver excluding income from the index, and calculating a 'responsiveness index' based on 'development per earned *rupee* in the state' change the rank order of the five states only slightly: Orissa and West Bengal shift positions, otherwise the pattern remains intact. It is thus important to note that Kerala's development is *not* a product of a rich economy, for its per capita income is quite modest; Kerala ranks 10 among the 24 Indian states. The low figure for West Bengal is more surprising since it is a state often described in the literature as a development 'success story'.

From these results we can draw an important conclusion: Achievements and failures measured in objective government statistics match how Indian citizens subjectively evaluate state performance. The attitude taken by our respondents has a strong resonance in what these governments are doing. This result supports the perception of the Indian electorate as being fairly knowledgeable and sophisticated after five decades of democracy and rejects the suspicion that they are an easy prey of elitist propaganda.

Political Participation

We continue 'backwards' in the model and move to the intermediate variable, political participation. We asked our respondents whether during the last five years they had done any of ten specified activities. The proportions in each state who said they had participated some time in seven of these activities are summarized in Table 18.3.

While many of the differences among states might be expected, the results divulge some surprises. The most startling is the low participation rates in West Bengal. Also noteworthy is the comparatively high participation in the 'backward' state of Orissa, and the very high level of violent participation in Uttar Pradesh. Almost eight times as many people in Uttar Pradesh compared to West Bengal say they have taken part in a protest where they have used 'force or violent methods'. Considering what we know of Uttar Pradesh and its politics, this figure probably says more about political estrangement than efficacy.

Social Capital in India

Tables 18.4 and 18.5 report the levels of social capital in the five states. The three major elements of social capital are discussed in turn: formal associations, informal networks, and generalized trust.

Levels of Social Capital

Table 18.4 reports the percentage of our respondents in each state who said they had been a member of a formal association, which we have labelled civil society.

The picture resembles the one from earlier tables: Large variations between the states, with Kerala at the top and Uttar Pradesh in the bottom. The surprisingly low level of participation in West Bengal is confirmed here as well. Somewhat surprisingly, the state of Orissa has a high level of participation in formal associations.[14]

[14] Data on associational memberships in the 1960s in Morriss 1998 interestingly shows a very similar pattern: the rank order of these five states was identical.

TABLE 18.3
Political Participation (per cent)

Activity	Campaign participation	Protest march	Contacted elected representative	Contacted media	Contacted other people	Taken part in sit-in or disruption	Used force or violent methods
Kerala	39	45	55	38	67	35	8
Gujarat	30	6	39	22	36	6	6
Orissa	24	23	34	13	55	9	4
Uttar Pradesh	12	10	3	18	40	44	23
West Bengal	10	13	17	8	35	2	3
Average	23	21	29	20	48	21	9

TABLE 18.4
Participation in Associations (per cent)

Kerala	51
Orissa	46
Gujarat	32
West Bengal	21
Uttar Pradesh	5
Average	31

Note: We asked the question 'Have you actively participated in an association during the last five years?'
Source: Computed by author.

TABLE 18.5
Networks in States
Per cent spending time every day or every week with people

	Support network	Discussion network	Don't know well	Who have a different way of life	Of a different caste	Of a different religion
Kerala	68	72	34	60	89	87
Gujarat	59	43	34	29	54	54
West Bengal	46	40	19	35	61	47
Orissa	62	54	14	22	63	45
Uttar Pradesh	53	54	60	60	0	0
Average	59	54	32	42	57	50

Note: The first column reports the average number of 'supports' (cf. fn. 15) an individual in the respective state has. The index is the proportion of actual support ties in each in relation to the possible number, calculated by dividing the mean size of respondents network in each state by 6, the total number of possible 'supports'.
Source: Computed by author.

Another expression of social capital, or social connectedness, is informal networks. These are likely to be more important than formal associations in a country like India. We asked our respondents questions about three different types of networks—support networks, bridging networks, and discussion networks. A 'support network' is the people you know that can help you with practical things in your everyday life.[15] 'Bridging networks' are connections that cut across the person's ordinary social life or important cleavages in local society like caste and religion.[16] Finally, a 'discussion network' is the people outside of the household that an individual discusses public issues with.[17] The size of such networks varies considerably from one person to another. The idea is that such mundane networks can be activated for other purposes as well, such as spreading information or taking collective action.

The issue of social or interpersonal trust is central in the social capital literature. Some authors view trust as the epitome of social capital (cf. Stolle 2000), and no one questions its usefulness as an all-purpose 'lubricant' to overcome collective action dilemmas. Therefore we asked respondents a set of questions to elicit their trust in people who are Indians, Hindus, Muslims, relatives, and 'my caste' respectively. Table 18.6 reports the percentage in each state who say they trust most other Indians.

TABLE 18.6
Generalized Trust in States
per cent in each state who say they 'trust all or most Indians'

Uttar Pradesh	75
Orissa	51
Gujarat	38
Kerala	32
West Bengal	32
Average	46

Source: Computed by author.

The most striking result is the high proportion in Uttar Pradesh and the low proportion in Kerala who say they trust other Indians.

15 We asked the respondents whether outside their household they had 'someone who could help them with the following free of cost: construction work; arrange a wedding or a funeral; talk about personal matters; get medical advice; get economic advice; get legal advice'. For each person the support network can thus vary from 0 to 6.

16 We asked the respondents how often they spent time (on a five point scale from 'every day' to 'almost never') with 'people you don't know very well; people who have a different way of life; people of a different caste; and of a different religion'.

17 It is operationalized as how often the respondent talks about public issues outside the household; from 'almost every day' to 'never or almost never'.

Does Social Capital have an Impact?

With the help of ordinary least square (OLS) regression analysis, I will investigate where social capital in any of these forms—associations, networks, or trust—has an effect on democratic responsiveness. The following three Tables reveal the following results:

Participation in formal associations does have a statistically significant effect on government responsiveness; *directly* (on both my measurements of responsiveness) as well as *indirectly* via political participation.[18]

The picture is more varied when it comes to informal networks. Discussion networks have an effect on government responsiveness measured both in a 'subjective' as well as an 'objective' way; it also has an effect on political participation. Bridging networks have an effect on the last of these two, but not on the subjective measure of responsiveness. Support networks, finally, have a positive effect on responsiveness measured 'subjectively' and indirectly via political participation, but *not* on responsiveness measured 'objectively'.

The effect of generalized trust[19] on government performance contradicts one of my hypotheses and an important assumption in social capital theory: norms of trust have a *negative* effect (statistically significant) both on the objective measure of government responsiveness, as well as on the respondents' attitude towards whether they think the state government is interested in their needs. Indirectly, via political participation, trust has a positive impact on government responsiveness.

Causal Direction and Mechanisms

These data only show statistical correlations, and are not in themselves proof of causal relationships. In the first two regression models, with subjective and objective government performance as dependent variables, it is likely that the social capital factors cause the government to make a better performance and not vice-versa. When it comes to the third regression model, with political participation as the dependent variable, the causal direction is more difficult to tell. The hypothesis being tested is that participation in associations, discussing

---

[18] Cf. Verba, Nie and Kim 1978, and Chhibber 1999. Analyses not reported here show that political participation has a positive and statistically significant effect on both the measurements of government performance.

[19] The question posed was 'How much do you trust other Indians?'

public issues, mingling with people that are different, or having a 'support network' will increase a person's political participation. But of course, especially in some of the cases cause and effect may be reversed.

TABLE 18.7

Effect of Social Capital Factors on Government Performance
Subjective (OLS regression)

Variable	Coefficient	Standard error
Participation in associations	0.278***	0.059
Trust in Indians	−0.003	0.019
Support network	0.039**	0.015
Bridging network	0.007	0.007
Discussion network	0.084***	0.021
Education	0.008	0.017
Economic standard	0.066	0.037
Constant	2.069***	0.149

Note: Unstandardized b-coefficients are reported, N = 2178, R square = 0.04, * = significant at .05 level, ** = significant at .01 level, *** = significant at .001 level
Source: Computed by author.

TABLE 18.8

Effect of Social Capital Factors on Government Performance
Objective (OLS regression)

Variable	Coefficient	Standard error
Participation in association	176***	21.3
Trust in Indians	−33***	6.5
Support network	6	5.2
Bridging network	42***	2.4
Discussion network	41***	7.5
Education	83***	6.0
Economic standard	77***	13.3
Constant	−166**	53.5

Note: Unstandardized b-coefficients are reported (note the high numbers due to the scale in Table 17.2), N = 2379, R square = 0.29
* = significant at .05 level, ** = significant at .01 level, *** = significant at .001 level
Source: Computed by author.

TABLE 18.9
Effect of Social Capital Factors on Political Participation
(OLS regression)

Variable	Coefficient	Standard error
Participation in association	2.183***	0.094
Trust	0.068*	0.029
Support network	0.184***	0.023
Bridging network	0.045***	0.011
Discussion network	0.373***	0.021
Education	0.087**	0.027
Economic standard	0.098	0.059
Constant	–1.131***	0.237

Note: Unstandardized b-coefficients are reported, N = 2305, R square = 0.35
* = significant at .05 level, ** = significant at .01 level, *** = significant at .001 level
Source: Computed by author.

If we are able to suggest a 'mechanism' linking cause to effect, we stand on much firmer ground (Hedström and Swedberg 1998). I conjecture three mechanisms or processes link social capital and political participation to government responsiveness: recruitment, monitoring, and anticipation. The first is the most manifest. The prevalent values and behavioural patterns in the population at large are likely to influence the persons that get recruited into politics or public administration. Monitoring refers to the more abstract idea that citizens in various ways keep an eye on what the state is doing. If the state is doing something perceived to be wrong, people may react, an ability likely to be affected by the density of social capital. The last process is the most subtle—the state's anticipation. An actor's expectation of what other actors *may* do is as important as it is difficult to study.[20] In a study of two district panchayats, Jonna Lundwall (2002) has demonstrated these mechanisms in operation.

[20] The last two mechanisms refer to the same as Heller (2000: 503f) who writes about the capacity of civil society to create 'spaces and organizations through which subordinate groups can mobilize,' and to curtail 'the repressive capacity of the state'.

Discussion

Succinctly formulated, the following hypotheses have been confirmed statistically:

(i) formal associations have a positive impact on political participation and democratic responsiveness

(ii) informal networks have a positive impact on political participation and in most cases a positive impact on democratic responsiveness

(iii) political participation has a positive impact on democratic responsiveness

(iv) generalized trust has a positive impact on political participation

But, contrary to our expectations and social capital theory, the analysis has also revealed:

(v) generalized trust does not have a positive impact on democratic responsiveness

How do these results speak to the theory about social capital? The results presented show that tangible *connections* with people outside the household are important to 'make democracy work'; when people meet informally and in associations[21] it has an effect on the state's responsiveness and the 'quality' of democracy. But the results reject a central idea in social capital theory—that interpersonal trust affects government responsiveness. The results resemble findings of research done by Yamagishi and Yamagishi (1994) comparing the US and Japan. They found that *trust*—'an expectation of goodwill and benign intent'—is more important in the US and *assurance*—an expectation 'based on the knowledge of the incentive structure surrounding the relationship' (1994: 132) is more important in Japan. Similarly, assurance seems to be more important than trust in India.

Critics of social capital analysis have argued that differences in democratic performance are better explained by economics. Some emphasize the aggregate economic level as the causal factor, while others say that class is the crucial issue; that is, the socio-economic status of the citizens who participate in politics determines whether democracy is conducted 'Kerala style' or 'Uttar Pradesh style' Calculations based on data in Table 18.2 showed that the differences in government responsiveness *remain* when we control for the variations in income level among the five states. Similarly, since I have

---

21 The results are similar to Varshney's (2002), although he explains Hindu–Muslim harmony.

controlled statistically for the respondents' level of education and economic standard in the analyses above, the effect of the social capital variables is what 'remains' when the SES resources are 'taken away' (statistically).

A second critique of the social capital argument[22] makes the simple and plausible claim that politics matters more for democracy than social connections. Atul Kohli (1987, 1990) has argued that the differences between Indian states in terms of policy performance are best explained by the kind of party in power, which he calls the party's 'regime characteristics'.[23] His (1987) extensive and in-depth study of West Bengal, Uttar Pradesh, and Karnataka concludes that leadership, ideology, organization, and class basis of the regime in power 'are the major variables explaining variations in redistributive outcomes' (1987: 223f).

Which is more important for a 'deepening' of democracy—the character of the party regime in power or local resources such as associations and networks? With our data we are in a rare position to speak to this issue. By design we included the two large states that have had a party 'with a difference' in the government for a number of years: Kerala and West Bengal. These two states have for long periods of time been ruled by the Communist Party of India (Marxist); in West Bengal uninterruptedly since 1977 and in Kerala for several periods since early 1957. Both states have been acclaimed in India for vigorous efforts at decentralization and anti-poverty programs.

Categorizing the five states in terms of social capital and nature of the regime yields the four-fold Table 18.10.

[22] Another common argument in explaining the strong differences among the Indian states is to look at path dependence, or historical legacies—not least, the different experiences of caste movements and relations between upper and lower castes (cf. Varshney 2000). I will not discuss that argument further here for lack of space, but more importantly because it can more easily be reconciled with a theory of social capital.

[23] These books do not make any explicit argument against Putnam or social capital (they were written before social capital became a common topic among political scientists). And Kohli is not interested in explaining 'democratic quality' per se; his aim is to explain successful redistributing, or poverty alleviation (1987: 1) in three Indian states. But since Kohli's operationalization of redistribution—'successful implementation of (public) reformist policies' (1987: 230)—is almost identical to how we have defined 'democratic responsiveness' a comparison with his study and theoretical argument is possible.

TABLE 18.10
Social Capital and Political Regime

	Left party in power	No left party in power
High social capital	Kerala	Gujarat
Low social capital	West Bengal	Orissa
		Uttar Pradesh

Since we have controlled for economic factors and since the five states share the same political and constitutional surrounding of the Indian Union one can imagine this as a natural experiment. According to the 'political regime' argument, we expect the two states run by reformist CPM governments to be the most democratically responsive of the five states. Social capital theory, on the other hand, predicts that we find the best democratic performance in Kerala and Gujarat. Therefore, the 'crucial cases' for testing the two different theories are West Bengal and Gujarat.

The data on democratic responsiveness,[24] show that the Gujarat government is markedly more responsive than the CPM-ruled state of West Bengal. The lessons for democratic responsiveness and development are straightforward: most promising is a combination of high social capital and a reformist party in power. If both are not possible, social capital is more promising. With neither, the situation is quite grim. This research also shows the importance of local, informal resources (here labelled social capital) in a politically mobilized environment such as Kerala.[25]

The research refutes any categorical claim that characteristics of the party in power is the vital factor in explaining democratic or government responsiveness. Yet I do not want to replace this claim with another dogma, that social capital is the sole answer. What I do claim is that the data and analysis presented here show that social capital does have an impact on democratic responsiveness in these five states in India.

[24] Calculating an index (not reported here) from the data in Tables 18.1 and 17.2 plus data on 'development per earned rupee' shows that Kerala gets a maximum of 100, Gujarat 70, West Bengal 58, Orissa 45, and Uttar Pradesh 37.

[25] It is therefore also a refutation of Harriss' (2001: 125) surmise that 'The Kerala story constitutes a powerful statement against the currently fashionable ideas about "social capital" and "civil society".'

19

ETHNIC CONFLICT AND
CIVIL SOCIETY
*India and Beyond**

Ashutosh Varshney

Much scholarly work has been done on the topics of civil society and ethnic conflict, but no systematic attempt has yet been made

* This paper was presented at the annual meeting of the American Political Science Association, Boston, 1998, and various versions were also presented in seminars and symposiums at the following universities and other institutions: Chicago, Columbia, Harvard, Illinois (Urbana-Campaign), Michigan (Ann Arbor), MIT, Notre Dame, Oxford, Texas (Austin), Toronto, Uppsala, Yale, the World Bank, and the Ford Foundation (Delhi). Work on the large project of which this article is part was supported by the SSRC–MacArthur Programme in International Security, the US Institute of Peace, the Samuel P. Huntington Fund of Harvard University, and the Ford Foundation. For comments, criticisms, and suggestions, I would like to thank Hans Blomkvist, Kanchan Chandra, Partha Chatterjee, Pradeep Chhibber, Elise Giuliano, Donald Horowitz, Gary King, Atul Kohli, David Laitin, Scott Mainwaring, Anthony Marx, James Morrow, Bhikhu Parekh, Elizabeth Perry, Robert Putnam, Sanjay Reddy, Susanne Rudolph, Jack Snyder, James Scott, Manoj Srivastava, Alfred Stepan, Steven van Evera, the late Myron Weiner, Yogendra Yadav, Crawford Young, and three anonymous reviewers of this journal.

to connect the two.[1] The conclusions of my recent, India-based projects,[2] supplemented by non-Indian materials, suggest that the links between civil society and ethnic conflict are crying out for serious attention. Does civic engagement between different ethnic communities also serve to contain ethnic conflict? Does *inter-ethnic* engagement differ from *intra-ethnic* engagement from the perspective of ethnic conflict? What role do civic organizations play in times of ethnic tensions and why? These questions are not simply of academic relevance, and they have yet to be systematically researched. Given that violence marks many multi-ethnic societies, our research may well have great practical meaning if we can sort out some key relationships.

This paper argues that there is an integral link between the structure of civic life in a multi-ethnic society, on the one hand, and the presence or absence of ethnic violence, on the other. To illustrate these links, two interconnected arguments are made. First, inter-ethnic and intra-ethnic networks of civic engagement play very different roles in ethnic conflict. Because they build bridges and manage tensions, inter-ethnic networks are agents of peace, but if communities are organized only along intra-ethnic lines and the interconnections with other communities are very weak or even non-existent, then ethnic violence is quite likely. The specific conditions under which this argument may not hold will be theoretically specified toward the end. Their empirical relevance can be ascertained only with further research.

Second, civic networks, both intra-ethnic and inter-ethnic, can also be broken down into two other types: organized and quotidian. This distinction is based on whether civic interaction is formal or not. I call the first *associational forms of engagement* and the second *everyday forms of engagement*. Business associations, professional organizations, reading clubs, film clubs, sports clubs, NGOs, trade unions, and cadre-based political parties are examples of the former. Everyday forms of engagement consist of simple, routine interactions of life,

[1] This is not to say that community life *within* ethnic groups has not been studied as part of civil society. A striking recent example, though not the only one, is Michael Walzer, *What It Means to Be American?* (New York: Marsilio, 1992). The view that ethnic (or religious) community life can be called civic is, of course, contested by many. The debate is summarized in Section I.

[2] Ashutosh Varshney, *Ethnic Conflict and Civic Life: Hindus and Muslims in India* (New Haven: Yale University Press, 2002).

such as whether families from different communities visit each other, eat together regularly, jointly participate in festivals, and allow their children to play together in the neighbourhood. Both forms of engagement, if robust, promote peace: contrariwise, their absence or weakness opens up space for ethnic violence. Of the two, however, the associational forms turn out to be sturdier than everyday engagement, especially when confronted with attempts by politicians to polarize people along ethnic lines. Vigorous associational life, if inter-ethnic, acts as a serious constraint on politicians, even when ethnic polarization is in their political interest. The more the associational networks cut across ethnic boundaries, the harder it is for politicians to polarize communities.

The paper also briefly considers how inter-ethnic civic organizations developed in India. Much of India's associational civic structure was put in place in the 1920s, a transformative moment during the freedom movement against the British, when a new form of politics emerged under the leadership of Mahatma Gandhi. After 1920, the movement had two aims: political independence from the British and social transformation of India. Gandhi argued that independence would be empty unless India's social evils were addressed, drawing attention to Hindu–Muslim unity, the abolition of untouchability, self-reliance, women's uplift, tribal uplift, labour welfare, prohibition, and so on. The associational structure of India before Gandhi had been minimal, but the Gandhian shift in the national movement laid the foundations of India's associational civic order. In the process, between the 1920s and 1940s, a host of new organizations came into being.

Historical reasoning, therefore, requires that we draw a distinction between proximate and underlying causation. The role of intercommunal civic networks has been crucial for peace at a proximate level. Taking the long view, however, the causal factor was a transformative shift in national politics. Once put in place by the national movement, the civic structures took on a life and logic of their own, constraining the behaviour of politicians in the short to medium run.

The paper is organized as follows. The first section clarifies three key terms whose meanings are not self-evident: ethnicity, ethnic conflict, and civil society. The second section deals with the puzzle that led me to discover the relevance of civil society for ethnic conflict. The third section summarizes how the puzzle was resolved and presents the arguments that can link ethnic conflict and civil society.

The fourth section presents empirical evidence in support of the arguments made. The fifth section considers causation and endogeneity. The final section summarizes the implications of the project for studies of civil society but also suggests a possible set of conditions under which the basic argument about inter-ethnic and intra-ethnic engagement is unlikely to apply.

CLARIFYING CONCEPTS AND TERMS

The terms 'ethnic conflict' and 'civil society' means different things to different people. To pre-empt misunderstanding, one needs to specify the meaning one is using.

There are two distinct ways in which the term 'ethnic' is interpreted. In the narrower construal of the term, 'ethnic' groups mean 'racial' or 'linguistic' groups. This is the sense in which the term is widely understood in popular discourse, both in India and elsewhere. For example, for politics and conflict based on religious groupings, Indian scholars, bureaucrats, and politicians since the time of the British have used the term 'communal,' not 'ethnic,' reserving the latter term primarily for linguistically or racially distinct groups.

There is, however, a second, broader definition. As Horowitz argues, all conflicts based on *ascriptive* group identities—race, language, religion, tribe, or caste—can be called ethnic.[3] In this umbrella usage, ethnic conflicts range from (1) the Protestant–Catholic conflict in Northern Ireland and the Hindu–Muslim conflict in India to (2) black–white conflict in the United State and South Africa, (3) the Tamil–Sinhala conflict in Sri Lanka, and (4) Shia–Sunni troubles in Pakistan. In the narrower construction of term, (1) is religious, (2) is racial, (3) is linguistic-cum-religious, and (4) is sectarian. In the past the term 'ethnic' would often be reserved for the second and, at best, third conflicts but would not be extended to the first and fourth.

---

3 For an analysis of why, on the basis of a myth of common ancestry, ethnicity can take so many forms (language, race, religion, dress, diction), see Donald Horowitz, *Ethnic Groups in Conflict* (Berkeley University of California Press, 1985), pp. 41–54. One might add that this definition, though by now widely accepted, is not without problems. If all ascriptive divisions can be the basis of ethnicity, can the landed gentry or women's groups be called ethnic? So long as we equate ascriptive identities with ethnic identities, there is no good answer to such questions.

Proponents of the broader usage reject such distinctions, arguing that the form ethnic conflict takes—religious, linguistic, racial, tribal—does not seem to alter its intensity, duration, or relative intractability. Their emphasis in on the ascriptive and cultural core of the conflict, and they distinguish it primarily from the largely nonascriptive and economic core of class conflict. Ethnic conflict may indeed have an economic basis, but that is not its core feature. Irrespective of internal class differentiation, race, language, sect, or religion tends to define the politics of an ethnic groups. Contrariwise, class conflict tends on the whole to be economic, but if the class into which one is born is also the class in which one is trapped until death—and this is true for large number of people—then class conflict takes on ascriptive overtones. Following Horowitz, it is now well understood that the later characteristics apply not to ethnic systems in general but to *ranked* ethnic systems, such as America during the period of slavery, South Africa during apartheid, and India's caste system. Ranked ethnic systems merge ethnicity and class; unranked ethnic systems do not.

The large meaning, one might add, is also increasingly becoming the standard meaning in the social sciences, even if that is not yet true of politics and activism. I will use the term 'ethnic' in this broader sense. In other words, I may distinguish between communal (that is, religious) and linguistic categories, but I will not differentiate between those that are communal and ethnic. Ethnicity is simply the set to which religion, race, language, and sect belong as sub-sets in this definition.

Does 'ethnic conflict,' our second term, have a uniquely acceptable meaning? On the whole, the existing literature has failed to distinguish between ethnic *violence* and ethnic *conflict*. Such conflation is unhelpful. In any ethnically plural society that allows free expression of political demands, some ethnic conflict is more or less inevitable, but it may not necessarily lead to violence.[4] When there are different

---

[4] Indeed, such conflict may be inherent in all pluralistic political systems, authoritarian or democratic. Compared with authoritarian systems, a democratic polity is simply more likely to witness an open expression of such conflicts. Authoritarian polities may lock disaffected ethnic groups into long periods of political silence, giving the appearance of a well-governed society, but a coercive containment of such conflicts also runs the risk of an eventual and accumulated outburst when an authoritarian system begins to liberalize or lose its legitimacy.

ethnic groups that are free to organize, there are likely to be conflicts over resources, identity, patronage, and policies.

The real issue is whether ethnic conflict is violent or waged via the polity's institutionalized channels. If ethnic protest takes an institutionalized form—in parliaments, in assemblies, in bureaucratic corridors, and as non-violent mobilization on the streets—it is conflict but not violence. Such institutionalized conflict must be distinguished from a situation in which protest takes violent forms, rioting breaks out on the streets, and in its most extreme form civil war ensues or pogroms are initiated against some ethnic groups with the complicity of state authorities. Given how different these outcomes are, explanations for institutionalized conflict may not be the same as those for ethnic riots, on the one hand, and for pogroms and civil wars, on the other. Ethnic peace should, for all practical purposes, be conceptualized as an institutionalized channelling and resolution of ethnic demands and conflicts: *as an absence of violence, not as an absence of conflict.* The world would arguably be a happier place if we could eliminate ethnic and national conflicts from our midst, but such a post-ethnic, post-national era does not seem to be in the offing in the near term. Indeed, many post-modern conflicts, even in richer societies, are taking ethnic forms on grounds of authenticity of living styles and distinctiveness of expression.[5]

Though highly popular and much revived in recent years, the concept of civil society also needs to be subjected to critical scrutiny. According to conventional notions in the social sciences, 'civil society' refers to that space which (1) exists between the family, on the one hand, and the state, on the other, (2) makes interconnections between individuals or families possible, and (3) is independent of the state. Many though not all of the existing definitions also suggest two more requirements: that the civic space be organized in associations that attend to the cultural, social, economic, and political needs of the citizens; and that the associations be modern and voluntaristic, not ascriptive. According to the first requirement, trade unions would be part of civil society, but informal neighbourhood associations would not. Following the second requirement, philately clubs and parent-teacher associations would be civic, but a black church or an association of Jews active on behalf of Israel would not.

[5] Ronald Inglehart, *Modernization and Postmodernization* (Princeton: Princeton University Press, 1997).

Should we agree with the latter two proposals? Can non-associational space also be called civic or part of civil society? Must associations, to constitute part of civil society, be of a 'modern' kind—voluntaristic and cross-cutting, rather than ascriptive and based on ethnic affiliation?

The modernist origins of civil society are originally attributed to Hegel's nineteenth-century theoretical formulations.[6] In recent years, however, it has often been suggested that the revival of a modernist notion of civil society derives from debates in Eastern Europe and the English translation of Habermas's *Structural Transformation of the Public Sphere.*[7] Because the concept of civil society has been so important to the field of political philosophy, it is mostly political philosophers who have explored it in recent times.[8] In comparison, the analytic work on civil society in the more empirical fields of the social sciences has not been as voluminous,[9] though the need for it should be quite clear. Only by systematic empirical investigation of the associational and non-associational forms of civic life can we determine whether the functions and forms attributed to civil society in the normative literature exist as more than simply theoretical propositions.

As an illustration of the modernist biases of the conventional definitions of civil society, consider the theoretical arguments of Ernest Gellner, whose writings on civil society have been plentiful

[6] For the early history of the idea, see Adam Seligman, *The Idea of Civil Society* (Princeton: Princeton University Press, 1992).

[7] Jurgen Habermas, *The Structural Transformation of the Public Sphere: An Inquiry into the Category of Bourgeois Society*, trans. Thomas Burger and Frederic Lawrence (Cambridge: MIT Press, 1989). For a debate built around the publication of the English translation, see Craig Calhoun, ed., *Habermas and the Public Sphere* (Cambridge: MIT Press, 1992).

[8] See also Charles Taylor, 'Modes of Civil Society,' *Public Culture* 4 (Fall 1990); in this volume. Michael Walzer, 'The Idea of Civil Society,' *Dissent* 38 (Spring 1991); and Jean Cohen and Andrew Arato, *Civil Society and Political Theory* (Cambridge: MIT Press, 1992).

[9] The debate generated by Putnam's work is finally leading to empirically based scholarship. See, inter alia, Sheri Berman, 'Civil Society and the Collapse of the Weimar Republic,' *World Politics* 49 (April 1997); the special issue on social capital of *American Behavioral Scientist* 39 (April 1997); and Deepa Narayan and Michael Woolcock, 'Social Capital: Implications for Development Theory, Research and Policy,' *World Bank Research Observer* 15 (August 2000).

as well as influential. 'Modularity,' argues Gellner, 'makes civil society,' whereas 'segmentalism' defines a traditional society,.[10] By modularity, he means the ability to transcend traditional or ascriptive occupations and associations. Given a multipurpose, secular, and modern education and given also the objective availability of plentiful as well as changing professional opportunities in post-traditional times, modern man can move from one occupation to another, one place to another, one association to another. In contrast, traditional man's occupation and place were determined by birth. A carpenter in traditional society, whether he liked it or not, would be a carpenter, and all his kinsmen would be carpenters. He would also not generally be involved in associations; and if he were, the association would most likely be an ascriptive guild of carpenters. An agrarian society, argues Gellner, might be able to avoid the tyranny of the state. That is because the power of the state could not reach all segments of a traditional society, given the decentralized nature of production structure, the low level of communication technology, and the relatively self-sufficient character of each segment. But that does not mean that such a society would be 'civil,' for instead of the 'tyranny of state,' it would experience the 'tyranny of cousins.' Civil society concludes Gellner, is not only modern but also based on strictly voluntary associations between the state and family, not on ethnic or religious considerations.[11]

Such claims can be empirically challenged. First, a remarkably large number of studies show that ethnic and religious associations combine ascription and choice. Not all Christians have to be members of a church in a given town, nor all blacks members of a black church. Moreover, it has also been widely documented that ethnic associations can perform many 'modern' functions, such as participating in democratic politics, setting up funds to encourage members of the ethnic group to enter newer professions, and facilitating

10 Ernest Gellner, 'The Importance of Being Modular,' in John Hall, ed., *Civil Society: Theory, History, Comparison* (Cambridge: Blackwell, 1995). This article is a good summary of a large number of Gellner's writings on civil society, written in both the reflective and the activist mode. Many of these writings, including some polemical essays, have been put together in Gellner, *Conditions of Liberty: Civil Society and Its Rivals* (New York: Penguin Press, 1994).

11 For a similar argument, see Edward Shils, *The Virtue of Civility* (Indianapolis, IN: Liberty Fund, 1997).

migration of ethnic kinsmen into modern occupations and modern education.[12]

A similar objection can be raised with respect to the requirement that associations be formal. In much of the developing world, especially in the countryside and small towns, formal associations do not exist. That does not mean, however, that civic interconnections or activities are absent. If what is crucial to the notion of civil society is that families and individuals connect with other families and individuals—beyond their homes—and talk about matters of public relevance without the interference of the state, then it seems far too rigid to insist that this must take place only in 'modern' associations. Empirically speaking, whether such engagement takes place in associations or in the traditional sites of social get-togethers depends on the degree of urbanization and economic development, as well as on the nature of the political system. Cities tend to have formal associations; village make do with informal sites and meetings. Further, political systems may specify which groups may have access to formal civic space and establish organizations and which ones may not. Nineteenth-century Europe provided the propertied classes with access to a whole range of political and institutional instruments of interest articulation; trade unions for workers were slower to arrive.

Some of the spirit of these remarks is conveyed in the commentary generated by Habermas's distinction between the 'lifeworld' and 'systems' in *The Structural Transformation of the Public Sphere*. In its original formulation, the distinction indicated a radical rupture between the significance of everyday interaction and that of interaction made possible by institutions and organizations. The latter, according to Habermas, was associated with a modern public sphere. Everyday interaction made life, but organized interaction made history.[13] The new history of popular struggles launched by those not formally admitted to the public sphere in much of nineteenth-century Europe and America—women peasants, workers, minorities—suggests the limited utility of the original Habermas

[12] For pioneering work on the modernist uses of ethnicity, see Lloyd Rudolph and Susanne Rudolph, *The Modernity of Tradition* (Chicago: University of Chicago Press, 1967); and Myron Weiner, *Sons of the Soil* (Princeton: Princeton University Press, 1978).

[13] See the brief but thoughtful discussion in Harry Boyte, 'The Pragmatic Ends of Popular Politics,' in Calhoun (fn. 7).

distinction.[14] Indeed, in his more recent positions, Habermas has all but dropped his earlier, radical distinction.[15] Street-corner activity can now be viewed as a serious civic form if more organized and institutional civic sites are not available—whether generally or to some particular groups.

The point, of course, is not that formal associations do not matter. One of the arguments of this paper is that they do. But at least in the social and cultural settings that are different from those of Europe and North America, if not more generally, the purposes of activity rather than the forms of organization should be the critical test of civic life. Tradition is not necessarily equal to a tyranny of cousins, and capitalist modernity does not always make civic interaction possible. At best, such dualities are ideal types or based on normatively preferred visions. Empirically speaking, tradition often permits challenging the cousins when existing norms of reciprocity and ethics are violated.[16] Similarly, even capitalist modernity may be highly unsocial and atomizing if people in America stay home and watch soap operas on TV, instead of joining PTAs and other civic organizations.[17] Both informal group activities and ascriptive associations should be considered part of civil society so long as they connect individuals, build trust, encourage reciprocity, and facilitate the exchange of views on matters of public concern—economic, political, cultural, and social. That they may have very different consequences for conflict or peace is an entirely different matter. The latter is an argument about what type of civil society is better for governance and peace, not whether civil society per se is endowed with benign possibilities.

14 Starting with E. P. Thompson, *The Making of the English Working Class* (Harmondworth; Penguin Press, 1968), many such historical works by now exist. For a quick review of how they relate to Habermas, see Mary Ryan, 'Gender and Public Access: Women's Politics in Nineteenth Century America,' and Geoff Eley, 'Nations, Publics, and Political Cultures: Placing Habermas in the Nineteenth Century,' both in Calhoun (fn. 7).

15 Jurgen Habermas, 'Further Reflections on the Public Sphere,' in Calhoun (fn. 7).

16 James Scott, *Moral Economy of the Peasant* (New Haven: Yale University Press, 1978).

17 For an argument along these lines, see Robert Putnam, 'The Strange Disappearance of Civic America,' *American Prospect* 8 (Winter 1996); and idem, 'Bowling Alone,' *Journal of Democracy* 6 (January 1995).

WHY CIVIL SOCIETY? A PUZZLING FEATURE OF ETHNIC CONFLICT

Civil society is a new variable for the study of ethnic conflict. How it emerged as a causal factor in research on Hindu–Muslim relations, therefore, requires a brief explanation of what my project on ethnic conflict sets out to do and why.

Sooner or later, scholars of ethnic conflict are struck by a puzzling empirical regularity—that despite ethnic diversity, some places (regions, nations, towns, villages) manage to remain peaceful, whereas other experience enduring patterns of violence. Similarly, some societies with an impressive record of ethnic peace suddenly explode in ways that surprise the observer and very often the scholar as well. Variations across time and space on the whole constitute an unresolved puzzle in the field of ethnicity and nationalism.

How does one account for such variations? The project selected six cities—three from the list of eight riot-prone cities and three peaceful ones—and arranged them in three pairs. Thus, each pair had a city where communal violence is endemic and a city where it is rare or entirely absent. To ensure against comparing apples and oranges, roughly similar Hindu–Muslim percentages in the city populations constituted the minimum control in each pair. The first pair—Aligarh and Calicut—was based on population percentages only. The second pair—Hyderabad and Lucknow—added two controls to population percentages, one of previous Muslim rule and a second of reasonable cultural similarities. The third pair—Ahmedabad and Surat—was the most tightly controlled. The first two pairs came from the north and south. The third came from the same state of Gujarat, sharing history, language, and culture but not endemic communal violence. All of these cities, at this time, have a population of above half a million, and the biggest, Hyderabad, is a metropolis of over four million people.

RESOLVING THE PUZZLE: THE ROLE OF CIVIL SOCIETY

The pre-existing local networks of civic engagement between the two communities stand out as the single most important proximate explanation for the difference between peace and violence. Where such networks of engagement exist, tensions and conflicts are regulated and managed; where they are missing, communal identities lead to endemic and ghastly violence. As already stated, these networks can in turn be broken down into two parts: associational forms of engagement and everyday forms of engagement. Both forms of engagement, if intercommunal, promote peace, but the capacity of the associational forms to withstand national-level 'exogenous shocks'—such as India's partition in 1947 or the demolition of the Babri mosque in December 1992 in the presence of more than three hundred thousand Hindu militants—is substantially higher.

What are the mechanisms that link civic networks and ethnic conflict? And why is associational engagement a sturdier bulwark of peace than everyday engagement?

One can identify two mechanisms that connect civil society and ethnic conflict. First, by promoting communication between members of different religious communities, civic networks often make neighbourhood-level peace possible. Routine engagement allows people to come together and form organizations in times of tension. Such organizations, though only temporary, turned out to be highly significant. Called peace committees and consisting of members of both communities, they policed neighbourhoods, killed rumours, provided information to the local administration, and facilitated communication between communities in time of tension. Such neighbourhood organizations were difficult to form in cities where everyday interaction did not cross religious lines, or where Hindus and Muslims lived in highly segregated neighbourhoods. Sustained prior interaction or cordiality facilitated the emergence of appropriate, crisis-managing organizations.

The second mechanism also allows us to sort out why associational forms of engagement are sturdier than everyday forms in dealing with ethnic tensions. If vibrant organizations serving the economic, cultural, and social needs of the two communities exist, the support for communal peace tends not only to be strong but also to be more solidly expressed. Everyday forms of engagement may make associational forms possible, but associations can often serve interests that are not the object of quotidian interactions. Intercommunal business organizations survive because they connect the business interests of many Hindus with those of Muslims, not because of neighbourhood warmth between Hindu and Muslim families. Though valuable in itself, the latter does not necessarily constitute the bedrock for strong civic organizations.

That this is so is, one level, a profound paradox. After all, we know that at the village level in India, face-to-face, everyday engagement is the norm, and formal associations are virtually non-existent.[18] Yet rural India, which was home to about 80 per cent of India's population in the early 1950s and still contains two-thirds of the country, has not been the primary site of communal violence. By contrast, even though associational life flourishes in cities, urban India, containing about one-third of India's population today and only 20 per cent in the early 1950s, accounts for the overwhelming majority of deaths in communal violence between 1950 and 1995.

Organized civic networks, when intercommunal, not only do a better job of withstanding the exogenous communal shocks—like partitions, civil wars, and desecration of holy places; they also constrain local politicians in their strategic behaviour. Politicians who seek to polarize Hindus and Muslims for the sake of electoral advantage can tear at the fabric of everyday engagement through the organized might of criminals and gangs. All violent cities in the project showed evidence of a nexus of politicians and criminals.[19] Organized gangs readily disturbed neighbourhood peace, often causing migration from communally heterogeneous to communally homogenous neighbourhood, as people moved away in search of physical safety. Without the involvement of organized gangs, large-scale rioting and tens and hundreds of killings are most unlikely, and without the protection afforded by politicians, such criminals cannot escape the clutches of law. Brass has rightly called this arrangement an institutionalized riot system.[20]

In peaceful cities, however, an institutionalized peace system exists. Countervailing forces are created when organizations such as trade unions, associations of businessmen, traders, teachers, doctors, and lawyers, and at least some cadre-based political parties[21] (different from the ones that have an interest in communal polarization) are communally integrated. Organizations that would lose from

[18] M. N. Srinivas, *Remembered Village* (Berkeley: University of California Press, 1979).

[19] These connections can be proven social scientifically, not legally. The latter requires establishing individual culpability, not obvious links between politicians and gangs as groups.

[20] Paul Brass, *Theft of an Idol* (Princeton: Princeton University Press, 1997).

[21] In a democratic system, political parties would be part of civil society, for not all of them may be linked to the state. In one-party systems, however, parties, even when cadre-based, tend to become appendages of the state, losing their civil society functions. India is a multiparty democracy.

a communal split fight for their turf, alerting not only their members but also the public at large to the dangers of communal violence. Local administrations are far more effective in such circumstances. Civic administrations, for all practical purposes, become the ears and arms of the administration. A synergy emerges between the local wings of the state and local civic organizations, making it easier to police the emerging situation and preventing it from degenerating into riots and killings. Unlike violent cities, where rumours and skirmishes, often strategically planted and spread, quickly escalate into riots, the relationships of synergy in peaceful cities nip rumours, small clashes, and tensions in the bud. In the end, polarizing politicians either do not succeed or eventually give up trying to provoke and engineer communal violence. Figure 18.1 represents the arguments diagrammatically.

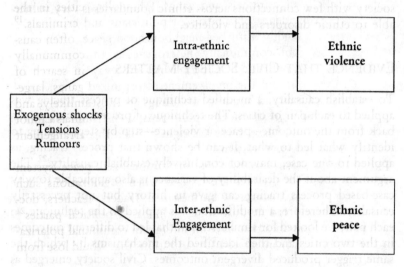

FIGURE 18.1: Civic Life and Ethnic Conflict

This argument, it should be clarified, is probabilistic, not lawlike. It indicates the odds but should not be taken to mean that there can be no exceptions to the generalization. Indeed, pending further empirical investigation, lawlike generalizations about ethnic violence may not be possible at all. Upsetting the probabilities, for example, a state bent on inciting ethnic pogroms and deploying its military may indeed succeed in creating a veritable ethnic hell. My argument, therefore, would be more applicable to *riots* than to *pogroms* or *civil wars*. A theory of civil wars or pogroms would have to be analytically distinguished from one that deals with the more common form of ethnic violence: riots.

Indeed, perhaps the best way to understand the relationship between civic life and political shocks is via an analogy from meteorology. If the civic edifice is inter-ethnic and associational, there is a good chance it can absorb ethnic earthquakes that register quite high on the Richter scale (a partition, a desecration of a holy place); if it is inter-ethnic and quotidian, earthquakes of smaller intensity can bring the edifice down (defeat of an ethnic political party in elections, police brutality in a particular city); but if engagement is only intra-ethnic, not inter-ethnic, small tremors (unconfirmed rumours, victories and defeats in sports) can unleash torrents of violence. A multi-ethnic society with few connections across ethnic boundaries is very vulnerable to ethnic disorders and violence.

EVIDENCE THAT CIVIL SOCIETY MATTERS

To establish causality, a modified technique of process tracing was applied to each pair of cities. The technique of process tracing works back from the outcome—peace or violence—step by step, looking to identify what led to what. It can be shown that process tracing, as applied to one case, may not conclusively establish causality.[22] The argument about the desirability of variance is also applicable to why case-based process tracing can give us history but not necessarily causality. Therefore, a modification was applied to the technique. In each pair, we looked for similar stimuli that led to different outcomes in the two cities and then identified the mechanisms by which the same trigger produced divergent outcomes. Civil society emerged as a causal factor from such comparisons. If we had studied only violent cities, where interconnections between Hindus and Muslims were minimal or absent in the first place, we would not have discovered what intercommunal civic links can do. A controlled comparison based on variance can thus turn process tracing into a method for establishing causality.

---

[22] For a debate on why process tracing will not easily establish causality, see *APSA-CP* (Winter 1997).

SIMILAR PROVOCATIONS, DIFFERENT RESPONSES

The process outlined above was applied to all three pairs in the project. Civic links between the two communities, combined with the use of such links by local administrations, kept tensions from escalating into riots. To explain how this sequence was established, let me concentrate only on the first pair of cities. Presenting all cities together in a stylized fashion will not give a good sense of the process involved.

The first pair consists of Aligarh and Calicut. The former is a riot-prone city in the North Indian state of Uttar Pradesh (UP), and the latter a peaceful city in the South Indian state of Kerala. Calicut has not had a single riot in this century; Aligarh figures in the list of the eight most riot-prone cities. Both cities are roughly 36–8 per cent Muslim, with the remaining population overwhelmingly Hindu.[23] Between 1989 and 1992, when the Hindu nationalist agitation to destroy the Babri mosque in Ayodhya (hereafter referred to as the Ayodhya agitation) led to unprecedented violence in much of India, both cities experienced rumours, tensions, and small clashes. But the final outcomes were very different. In Calicut the local administration was able to maintain law and order. Unfounded rumours circulated in the city that pigs had been thrown into mosques. Similarly, there were rumours that Muslims had attacked the famous Guruvayur temple, a site greatly venerated by Hindus in the state. Such rumours often led to riots in several cities in India and frequently did so in Aligarh. In Calicut the peace committees and the press helped the administration quash the rumours. The storm of the Ayodhya agitation, the biggest since India's partition and one that left hundreds dead in several cities, skirted Calicut and left it unharmed.

By contrast, blinded by a Hindu nationalist fervour during the Ayodhya agitation, the city of Aligarh plunged into horrendous violence. Unlike Calicut's newspapers, which neutralized rumours after investigating them, Aligarh's local newspapers printed inflammatory falsehoods. Two of the largest-circulation Hindi newspapers wrote in lurid detail of Muslim nurses, doctors, and staff of the Aligarh Muslim University (AMU) hospital killing Hindu patients in cold blood.[24] Some Hindus were indeed killed outside the university

---

[23] Calicut also has a small Christian population.
[24] *Aaj*, 10 December 1990; *Amar Ujala*, 11 December 1990.

campus,[25] but nobody was murdered in the AMU hospital.[26] The rumours were believed, however. And gangs of Hindu criminals went on a killing spree. Some of them stopped a train just outside the city, dragged Muslims out, and brutally murdered them. The press under-reported their acts of killing. Although these newspapers were later reprimanded for unprofessional behaviour by the Press Council, the damage had already been done. Gruesome violence rocked the city for several days, leading to nearly seventy deaths and many more injuries.

As in the past, Aligarh's local mechanisms of peace were remarkably inadequate to the task of dealing with an exogenous shock—in this case, the Ayodhya agitation. The criminals who engaged in killing could not be brought to justice. Not only were they protected by politicians, but they also had remarkable journalistic connections—Muslim criminals with the Urdu press and Hindu thugs with the Hindi press. Effective peace committees could not be formed at the city level in Aligarh, for it was difficult even to get the Hindu nationalists and Muslim politicians together. Rumours were often started and then exploited by political organizations. Instead of investigating rumours, the press simply printed them with abandon.

Contrast the situation with Calicut. Two points were common to all accounts given by administrators of Calicut between 1989 and 1992 (as well as those posted there since the mid-1980s) about how the peace was kept. First, politicians of all parties helped establish peace in the city, instead of polarizing communities, as in Aligarh. Second, city-level peace committees were critical to management of tensions.[27]

---

25 'For an Aligarh of Peace,' interview with District Magistrate A. K. Mishra, *Frontline*, December 1990, pp. 22–3.

26 Author interviews with AMU vice-chancellor M. Naseem Farooqui, Delhi, 15 July 1994; several AMU professors, August 1994; and local journalists, August 1994. For a thoughtful review of all such reports appearing in local Hindi newspapers, see Namita Singh, 'Sampradayitka ka khabar ban jana nahin, kahbron ka sampradayik ban jaana khatarnak hai,' *Vartaman Sahitya*, September 1991.

27 Author interviews in Trivandrum with Amitabh Kant, district collector, Calicut, 1991–4, 20 July 1995; Shankar Reddy, police commissioner, Calicut, 1991–4, 22 July 1995; Siby Matthews, police commissioner, Calicut, 1988–91, 21 July 1995; K. Jayakumar, collector, Calicut, 21 July 1995; Rajeevan, police commissioner, Calicut, 1986–8, 21 July 1995. Politicians of the Muslim League and BJP confirmed their participation in peace committees. The political leaders

They provided information to the administration, became a forum at which all were welcome to speak out and express their anger, gave a sense of participation to local actors, and provided links all the way down to the neighbourhood level, where, in addition, citizens formed smaller peace committees.

By contrast, those peace committees that do emerge from below in Aligarh have often tended to be intra-religious, not inter-religious. They are organized at the neighbourhood level to protect co-religionists from a possible attack by other communities and do not facilitate communication with those other communities. Rather, they simply increase the perception of risk and harden the attitudes of those who participate in them. The members of these committees take turns policing their community. The process forms a very different kind of consciousness from what there would be if the committees were inter-religious, since by definition intra-religious committees are based not on inter-religious trust but rather on a lack of such trust. Moving within one's own community, hearing rumours that no one can verify or disprove, staying up in the middle of the night for weeks together, collecting firearms and other small weapons to ensure that retaliation is swift in the event of attack—these activities of intra-religious committees fuel and reflect a communal consciousness, not a consciousness that builds bridges.

The Variety of Civic Networks

Why did the two cities respond so differently? Why did politicians of all kinds cooperate in Calicut but not in Aligarh? Most of all, why did even those politicians of Calicut who stood to benefit from Hindu–Muslim polarization, like the Hindu nationalists of the BJP, avoid working to inflame communal passions and instead cooperate in peace-making efforts? The BJP leader of Calicut admits that Hindu–Muslim polarization would be in his party's political interest because it would lead larger numbers of Hindus to vote for the BJP instead of non-communal parties, as most do currently. But he is also convinced that it would not be wise for his party to systematically initiate the polarizing process, because it might then be blamed for undermining the local peace. If, however, the radical Islamic groups

interviewed were Dr Muneer, Muslim League member of Legislative Assembly since 1991, 23 July 1995; K. Sreedharan Pillai, president BJP, Calicut district BJP committee, Calicut, 25 July 1995.

were to launch a violent campaign, it would doubtless benefit the party and the BJP would be happy to respond in kind.[28]

To understand why the BJP is unwilling to engage in polarizing activities in Calicut, one needs to survey the texture of civic life there. Hindu–Muslim civic integration runs so deep in Calicut (and many would argue, in the state as a whole) that polarization is a highly risky strategy. If a party can be clearly linked to activities destroying the decades-long Hindu–Muslim peace, there is a good chance it will be punished by the electorate. The reverse is true in Aligarh, where the utter weakness of cross-cutting links opens up space for communal politicians to play havoc.

Consider first the quotidian forms of citizen engagement in the two cities. According to survey results, nearly 83 per cent of Hindus and Muslims in Calicut often eat together in social settings; only 54 per cent in Aligarh do.[29] About 90 per cent of Hindu and Muslim families in Calicut report that their children play together; in Aligarh a mere 42 per cent report that to be the case. Close to 84 per cent of Hindus and Muslims in the Calicut survey visit each other regularly; in Aligarh only 60 per cent do, and not often at that. The Hindus and Muslims of Calicut simply socialize more often and enjoy it much of the time, whereas Hindu–Muslim interactions in Aligarh are comparatively thin. Aligarh's statistics on all of these interactions would be much lower if we had concentrated only on the violent neighbourhoods. We see from the few peaceful but integrated neighbourhoods that politics has not destroyed civic interaction in all parts of the town, as some of the neighbourhoods have managed to keep their distance from the hegemonic political trends elsewhere in the town. It should be noted, however, that an overwhelming proportion of respondents over the age of sixty reported that their neighbourhoods in Aligarh had been much more integrated in the 1930s and 1940s.[30] But in the 1930s as politicians started using thugs to spread violence, migration began to communally homogenous localities. Neighbourhood-level intimacy was simply unable to withstand the depredations of the emerging politician–criminal nexus.

[28] Author interview, Sreedharan Pillai, president, BJP district committee, Calicut, 25 July 1995.

[29] Unless otherwise reported, the statistics here and below are from the survey conducted in Calicut and Aligarh.

[30] Forty per cent of the sample was older than sixty, which allowed us to gather recollections of the 1930s and 1940s.

What about the associational forms of engagement? Much like Tocqueville's America, Calicut is a place of 'joiners.' Associations of all kinds—business, labour, professional, social, theatre, film, sports, art, reading—abound. From the ubiquitous traders' associations, to the Lions and Rotary Clubs found in almost all towns in India, to the otherwise rare reading clubs, the head-loaders (porters) association, the rickshaw-pullers association, and even something like an art-lovers association—citizens of Calicut excel in joining clubs and associations. Religiously based organizations also exist, as they do in Aligarh; what is distinctive is the extent of inter-religious interaction in non-denominational organizations.[31]

Consider the economic life of Calicut, which is based primarily on merchandise trade. The city, with a population of about seven hundred thousand in 1995, was dominated by merchants and traders.[32] About one hundred thousand people depended partially or wholly on trade, and, although exact numbers are not available, estimates indicate that the city had between ten and twelve thousand

[31] It may be asked why people in Calicut join inter-religious associations in such large numbers. Since violence and peace constitute the explanandum (the dependent variable) in this analysis, and civic networks, constitute the explanans (the independent variable), I only ask whether causality is correctly ascribed to civic networks or, alternatively, whether it constitutes a case of endogeneity. The question of why people join inter-religious associations in Calicut but not in Aligarh is analytically different. To answer it requires a research design different from the one that investigates why violence or peace obtains in the two places, for the explanandum is violence in one case and associational membership in the other. That said, it is quite plausible to hypothesize that Calicut citizens have greater faith in the 'rational–legal' functioning of the state, and therefore, instead of seeking to change the behaviour of the state by capturing state power, they are confident they can exercise enough pressure on it through associations. It may also be that Calicut citizens identify less with caste and religion today than do the citizens of Aligarh, though historically there is no doubt that caste played an enormously important role in generating struggles for social justice there. For a recent account of the caste basis of such struggles, see Dileep Menon, *Caste, Community and the Nation: Malabar, 1900–1948* (Cambridge University Press, 1995). Finally, integrated civic networks conceivably achieve much more than prevention of communal riots. They may, for example, be related to the better provision of social services in Calicut (and Kerala), but such outcomes are not the main object of analysis in this paper. Only communal violence is.

[32] Calicut has no industry except tiles. It is small in size, with nine factories and about twenty-five hundred workers in all.

traders.[33] It was the rare trader who did not join a trade association. These associations—ranging from organizations of traders who deal in food/grains to those who deal in bullion—were, in turn, members of the Federation of Traders Associations (Vyapari Vyavasayi Ekopana Samithi).

In 1995 as many as eleven out of twenty-six trade associations registered with the federation had Hindu, Muslims, (and Christian) office holders: if the president of the association was from one community, the general secretary was from one of the others.[34] These associations refuse to align with any particular political parties in electoral contests: 'We don't want to enter politics because our unity will be broken. We have debates in our association, so conflicts, if any, get resolved.' Moreover, the depth of engagement was such that many transactions were concluded without any formal contracts. 'Our relationships with Muslim businessmen are entirely based on trust. Payments as large as 10 to 15 lakhs (US$ 30,000–US$ 35,000) are sometimes due. We send bills, but there are no promissory notes valid in the courts of law. Payments come in thirty days. We work through brokers. There is no breach of trust.'[35]

Aligarh also has a traders' association (Vyapar Mandal). In the late 1980s it had about six thousand members. In the 1970s it had even acquired a fair number of Muslim members, who emerged on the business map after the Gulf migration. The association, however, began to engage in infighting over whether it should support and work for a political party, the argument being that supporting a party favourable to traders would benefit all of them. In the 1980s the association finally split into two bodies: a 'secular' organization and a 'non-secular' one, with the non-secular faction joining the BJP and the Muslims turning to the 'secular' faction.[36]

---

[33] These numbers and the information below are based on extensive interviews with the president and general secretary of the Kerala Federation of Trade Associations (Kerala Vyapari Vyavasayi Ekopana Samithi hereafter Samithi). The Samithi is a powerful all-state body, based in all towns of Kerala. The Samithi keeps records and statistics and has a professionally run office. It is rare to find a traders' association run so professionally in North India.

[34] Data supplied by the Samithi, Calicut branch, July 1995.

[35] Author's interview with V. Ramakrishna Erady, wholesale rice dealer, Calicut, 25 July 1995.

[36] Author's interview with Mohammed Sufiyan, former president, Vyapar Mandal, Aligarh, August 1995.

Unlike trade-based Calicut, Aligarh also has a significant industrial sector and is among the largest producers of locks in India. The lock manufacturing is mostly small scale. Moreover, different units specialize in different parts of the manufacturing process. Yet Aligarh has not developed an economic symbiosis between Hindus and Muslims.

It is impossible to estimate the number of people working in Aligarh's lock industry, as no surveys have been conducted.[37] We know from ethnographic work, however, that the workers come from both Muslim and Hindu communities, as do the firm owners. We also know that there is virtually no intercommunal dependence. The informal credit market, normally dominated by Hindu lenders (*mahajan*), was the only Hindu-run economic activity on which some Muslim manufacturer used traditionally to depend. Over the last few decades rotating credit societies have emerged.[38] But these are intra-Muslim societies that build trust within communities, not across them.[39]

If the businessmen are not integrated, what about the workers? Since they numerically constitute a large proportion of the city than the businessmen, inter-religious links formed in trade unions could, in principle, more than make up for an absence of such links among the businessmen. But trade unions hardly exist in Aligarh. Decrepit offices of the local branches of national trade unions, with no staff and little data, greet researchers who study labour activities. By contrast, trade unions thrive in Calicut. The largest unions are linked to two major national trade-union federations: CITU, which is associated with the Communist Party (Marxist), and INTUC, whose political patron is the Congress Party.[40] Both of these unions are

---

[37] It pays to underreport how much labour an industrial unit employs, for under Indian law the small, informal sector does not have to pay pension and other benefits to its workers. Official statistics are thus entirely useless. Foucault's concept of 'popular illegality,' as one keen observer puts it, has caught the fascination of Aligarh's lock manufacturers. Elizabeth A. Mann, *Boundaries and Identities: Muslims, Work and Status in Aligarh* (Delhi and Newbury Park: Sage Publications, 1992), p. 83.

[38] Ibid., pp. 101–2.

[39] Ibid., pp. 84–5.

[40] Exact numbers of unionized members and their religious distribution are almost impossible to come by. Estimates based on the interviews are the best one can do. The description below is based on interviews with labour leaders in Calicut, especially a long and detailed interview with M. Sadiri Koya, state secretary, INTUC, 4 August 1993.

intercommunal. Calicut does have a political party of the Muslims, the Muslim League, which regularly wins general elections. It also sponsors a trade union, the STU. The STU, however, is neither as large as the local units of CITU or INTUC nor as vibrant. It is the weakest and smallest of the three. Muslim workers by and large vote in assembly elections for the Muslim League, but they tend typically to join INTUC or CITU for protection of their labour rights. The Marxist and atheistic character of CITU does not stop them from joining CITU's unions, if they think that CITU will do a better job of fighting for their rights and wages. In the process, they come in contact with Hindu workers, intercommunal links are formed, and a Hindu–Muslim division of the workforce does not take place.

A most unlikely site for unionization—the 'head loaders' or porters—is worth mentioning, for it shows the associational abilities and success of Calicut workers. Distributed over hundreds and thousands of shops and small business units, porters in Indian bazaars are rarely unionized. But they are in Calicut (and in Kerala). In 1995 there were nearly ten thousand head loaders in Calicut—about 60 per cent Hindu and 40 per cent Muslim. Most were part of INTUC and CITU trade unions. There are head loaders in the bazaar in Aligarh, but there they have no associations.

A final and highly distinctive aspect of associational life in Calicut concerns its social and educational activities. The city has had an array of film clubs, popular theatre, and science societies. There is nothing unusual about film clubs—they are popular throughout south India. But societies interested in bringing theatre and science to the masses are rather uncommon. Even more uncommon have been reading clubs. The literacy rate in Kerala today is the highest in India. 'Reading rooms,' a unique Kerala institution, accompanied Kerala's remarkable rise in literacy and formed deep social networks between the 1930s and the 1950s. Young people from most communities would get together several times every week to read newspapers and cultural and political books. The fascinating story of the birth of reading clubs has recently been told by Menon:

Between 1901 [and] 1931, the rise in the numbers of literate was phenomenal. The growing numbers of schools and the rise in literacy found expressions in the numbers of reading rooms that were established both in the country-side and in the town.... One of the novelties in the organization of reading rooms was the [communitarian] drinking of tea, as one person read the newspapers and the others listened.... Tea and coffee lubricated discussions on the veracity of the news and of political questions, and a new culture emerged around the reading rooms. It was premised upon sobriety and knowledge rather than drunken companionship transcending consciousness which characterized the toddy shops. The importance of tea and coffee lay in the fact that they were recently introduced beverages and did not fit into any taboos regarding what could be shared between castes. Tea shops and reading rooms all over Malabar provided [a] common place for people to meet and to drink together regardless of caste [and community]... . The reading rooms emerged as central to both formal attempts at organization by the left wing of the Congress as well as local initiatives.[41]

The cumulative outcome of the reading-room movement is worth noting. In our Calicut sample, as many as 95 per cent of Hindus and Muslims reported reading newspapers—a statistic that is likely to be even higher than in most cities of the richer countries of the world. Calicut today, with a population of over seven hundred thousand has twenty newspapers and magazines![42] By contrast, while most Hindus in the Aligarh sample read newspapers, less than 30 per cent of Muslims did so. Information often travels in the Muslim community by word of mouth. As links with the Hindu community are non-existent, it takes only a few people to spread nasty rumours and make them stick.

To sum up, the civic lives of the two cities are worlds apart. So many Muslims and Hindus are interlocked in associational and neighbourhood relationships in Calicut that peace committees during periods of tension are simply *an extension of the pre-existing local networks of engagement.*[43] A considerable reservoir of social trust is

41 Menon (fn. 39), pp. 145–9.
42 And the state of Kerala has 'a library or a reading room within walking distance of every citizen.' K. A. Isaac, 'Library Movement and Bibliographic Control in Kerala: An Overview' (Paper presented at the International Congress of Kerala Studies, Trivandrum, India, August 1994).
43 It may be suggested that this finding is close to being a tautology: a city is not riot-prone because it is well integrated. This claim, however, would not be plausible for two reasons. First, a conventional explanation, which has long defined the common sense of the field, suggests that for peace, multi-ethnic societies require consociational arrangements. Consociationalism is an argument about segregation at the mass level and bargaining at the elite level, not integration at either level. My argument is very different. Second, religious fundamentalists have often fought violently to 'purify' their communities of influences from other religions in society. Islamic fundamentalists have often sought to undermine Sufi

formed out of the associational and everyday interactions between Muslims and Hindus. Routine familiarity facilitates communication between the two communities; rumours are squelched through better communication; and all of this helps the local administration keep peace. In Aligarh, however, the average Hindu and Muslim do not meet in those civic settings—economic, social, educational—where mutual trust can be forged. Lacking the support of such networks, even competent police and civil administrators look on helplessly as riots unfold.

The other pairs in the project experienced similar processes. The different outcomes, however, resided neither in the absence of religious identities nor in the presence of tensions, provocative rumours, and small clashes. Decisive, rather, was the presence of the intercommunal networks of engagement. Intracommunal networks, by contrast, did not contain, or stop, violence.

ENDOGENEITY AND THE UNDERLYING CAUSATION

Before we accept the argument about civic engagement, two more questions must be explored. First, how can one be sure that the causation did not flow in the other direction? Did communal violence destroy the Hindu–Muslim civic networks in riot-prone towns, or did the presence of such networks prevent violence from occurring? Might we not have a case of endogeneity here? Second, process tracing can at best establish short-run causality. Is the underlying causation different from proximate causation? Are there historical forces that explain the vitality or absence of civic networks? What emerges if we turn the independent variable of the short-run analysis—civic networks—into a variable to be explained historically?

The city of Surat, the third historically peaceful city in the project, helps us address the problem of endogeneity and establishes the short-run primacy of civic networks. In Surat (Gujarat) a nasty riot occurred after the destruction of the Ayodhya mosque, the first such riot in nearly seventy years. An overwhelming proportion of

---

Islam, which has traditionally combined the practice of Islam with the incorporation of neighbouring influences. Communally integrated lives and belief systems have often been seen as a source of tension and conflict rather than peace. For the North American version of the debate, see H. D. Forbes, *Ethnic Conflict* (New Haven: Yale University Press, 1997).

violence, however, was confined to the slums; all 192 deaths took place in the shantytowns. The old city, by contrast, witnessed some arson and looting but no deaths. Subjected to the same stimuli, the pre-existing social networks accounted for the variance within the city.

Surat has experienced an industrial boom in the last twenty years, becoming the small-industry capital of India. Among cities of more than a million people, Surat has registered one of the highest population growth rates since 1980. Migrants from within and from outside the state have poured into the city and settled in the shantytowns. Working in small industrial units and unprotected by the labour laws of the Factory Act, most of these migrants work exceptionally long hours, returning to the slums and shanty-towns only to sleep and eat. There are few institutionalized settings for building civic ties.

When the mosque came down in Ayodhya in December 1992, the slums were the site of awful brutality and violence. In the old city, however, peace committees were quickly formed. The business associations of Surat, whose members live primarily in the old city, are especially integrated. These Hindus and Muslims, who had lived side by side for years and had participated in the old city's business and social life, were able to come together to lower tensions. They set up neighbourhood watch committees and deployed their own resources and organizations in checking rumours and communicating with the administration. As a result, the local administration was more effective in the old city than in the industrial shantytowns, where civic networks were entirely missing and criminals were free to commit acts of savagery and violence.

What about the long-run causation? Have the Hindu–Muslim civic networks always been robust in peaceful towns, directing their Hindu–Muslim politics and making it possible for them to withstand exogenous shocks? Historical research conducted in the cities demonstrates that civic networks—quotidian and associational—determined the outcome in the *short to medium* run, but in the *long* run intercommunal networks were politically constructed. The 1920s were a transformative moment in the nation's politics because it was then that mass politics emerged in India under the leadership of Mahatma Gandhi. Politics before Gandhi had been highly elitist, with the Congress Party a lawyers' club that made its constitutional arguments for more rights with the British in the Queen's English.

Gandhi seized control of the movement in 1920 and quietly revolutionized it by arguing that the British were unlikely to give independence to India until the Indian masses were involved in the national movement. Gandhi talked of two intertwined battles of independence (*swaraj*), one against an external adversary, the colonial power, and another against an internal enemy, India's social evils. He was interested not only in political independence from the British but also in the social transformation of India, arguing that the former could not be meaningful without the latter. He first concentrated on three social objectives: Hindu–Muslim unity, abolition of untouchability, *swadeshi* (buy Indian, wear Indian, think Indian). To these were later added other projects of social transformation: women's welfare, tribal welfare, labour welfare, prohibition, and so on. In the process millions of his followers created a large number of organizations between the 1920s and the 1940s. Before Gandhi the civic structure of India had been quotidian. After the Gandhian moment in the national movement it became associational.

The biggest organization, of course, was the Congress Party, which led the movement politically and developed cadres all over India during the 1920s.[44] The argument about social reconstruction also created a second set of organizations, the voluntary agencies. The Congress Party was primarily political, and organizations that dealt with education, women's issues, the welfare of the tribals and 'untouchables,' self-reliance, and the homespun movement were immediately concerned with their social projects.

The civic order that emerged was not identical in different places. The movement had greater success in putting together Hindu–Muslim unity in towns where a Hindu–Muslim cleavage had not already emerged in local politics. India's towns had been having elections for local governments since the 1880s. If local politics emphasized some other cleavages—for example, caste cleavage among the Hindus or Shia–Sunni divisions among the Muslims—then the Congress Party and Gandhian social workers found it easier to bring Hindus and Muslims together in the local civic life. If, however, Hindu–Muslim differences were the dominant axis of local politics, the national

[44] It should, however, be pointed out that in Calicut and the neighbouring areas, it is the left wing of the Congress Party, later splitting from the parent organization and becoming the Communist Party of India (CPI), that engaged in the most systematic association building.

movement could not build integrated organizations with the same success. Though originally a child of politics, these organizations, once firmly in place, acquired relative autonomy from politics. Depending on how integrated or communal they were, they began to create very different pressures in politics. To sum up, the role of intercommunal civic networks has been crucial for peace at a proximate level. In a historical sense, however, a space for them was created by forms of mass politics that emerged all over India in the 1920s.

For problems of endogeneity, this reasoning suggests a twofold conclusion. If a historical perspective is applied, it turns out that a transformative ideological shift in national politics, seeking to address social evils and to reorient the fight for independence, was the cause of a systematic organizational effort. In the short to medium run, however, the organizational civic order, instituted by the national movement, became a constraint on the behaviour of politicians. Given the thrust of the national movement, the civic constraint on politics was especially serious if building or destroying bridges between Hindus and Muslims was the object of politicians' strategies.

CONCLUDING OBSERVATIONS

Are the conclusions of this paper India-specific or have they resonance elsewhere? Two sets of concluding observations—one on civil society and one on ethnic conflict—are in order.

Putnam has used the term 'social capital' for civic networks.[45] My use of the term 'networks of engagement' differs from Putnam's in two ways. First, my focus is on inter-ethnic and intra-ethnic civic ties, not civic ties per se. Communal and ethnic organizations, focusing on a single religious or ethnic group only, can be shown to generate a great deal of trust among their members. If they are plentiful, such organizations, by Putnam's definition, can endow a place with a high degree of social capital. However, in my materials, these organizations not only are often incapable of preventing Hindu–Muslim riots but are also associated with the escalation of communal

45 Robert Putnam, *Making Democracy Work: Civic Traditions in Italy* (Princeton: Princeton University Press, 1993). It should be noted, however, that since writing *Making Democracy work*, Putnam has introduced the notions of bridging and non-bridging civic networks. Putnam acknowledges the distinction further in *Bowling Alone* (New York: Simon and Schuster, 2000).

violence. What matters for ethnic violence is not whether ethnic life or social capital exists but whether social and civic ties cut *across* ethnic groups. Stated differently, trust based on *inter-ethnic*, not *intra-ethnic* networks is critical.

Second, while civic engagement in Putnam's work rightly includes both formal and informal interactions between individuals and families, the difference between the two forms should also be noted. For ethnic peace, everyday engagement between ethnic groups may be better than no interaction at all, but it is also qualitatively different from the more formal, organized engagement. Everyday inter-ethnic engagement may be enough to maintain peace on a small scale (villages or small towns), but it is no substitute for inter-ethnic associations in larger settings (cities and metropolises). Size reduces the efficacy of informal interactions, privileging formal associations.[46]

My findings also have implications for the literature on ethnic conflict. Although disaggregated statistics on local or regional dispersions of ethnic violence have not been systematically collected for many countries, it should first be noted that the data that we do have—for example, for the United States or Northern Ireland[47]—show roughly the same large pattern that exists in India. On the whole, ethnic violence tends to be highly concentrated locally or regionally, not spread evenly geographically across the length and breadth of the country. A countrywide breakdown of ethnic relations, more characteristic of civil wars, is rare: we tend to form exaggerated impressions of ethnic violence, partly because violence and not the quiet continuation of routine life is what attracts the attention of media.

[46] This reasoning also suggests a third way in which this research differs from Putnam's *Making Democracy Work*. In Putnam's formulation, the existence of social capital differentiates good governance from bad. The relationship between social capital and communal violence, however, yields a different formulation. If my argument is right, civic networks determine the presence or absence of riots, but they are politically constructed in the long run. Putnam's study appears to emphasize the independent role of social capital in both the short run and the long run.

[47] For the US, see Stanley Lieberson and Arnold Silverman, 'The Precipitants and Underlying Conditions of Race Riots,' *American Sociological Review* 30 (December 1965); and for Northern Ireland, see Michael Poole, 'Geographical Location of Political Violence in Northern Ireland,' in John Darby, Nicholas Dodge, and A. C. Hepburn, eds, *Political Violence: Ireland in Comparative Perspective* (Belfast: Appletree Press, 1990).

It is more common to have pockets of violence coexisting with large stretches of peace.

If we systematically investigate the links between civil society and ethnic conflict, there is a good chance we can get a good theory that can explain these local or regional variations. The reason for this intuition is quite simple. Though networks of communities can be built nationally, internationally, and, in this electronic era, also 'virtually,' the fact remains that most people experience civic or community life locally. Business associations or trade unions may well be confederated across local units and business or labour leaders may also have national arenas of operation, but most of the time most businessmen and workers who are members of such organizations experience associational life locally. The type and depth of these local networks—whether they bring ethnic communities together or pull them apart, whether the interactions between communities are associational or informal—are the variables that have the potential for explaining the observable patterns of ethnic violence and peace.

Though such research has not been done, some potentially powerful indications are available. A few existing studies of post-1969 Catholic–Protestant violence have dealt with intranational variance in violence. John Darby, for example, has studied three local communities in Greater Belfast—Kileen/Banduff, the Upper Ashbourne Estates, and Dunville.[48] All three communities have mixed populations, but the first two have seen a lot of violence since the late 1960s, whereas the third has been quiet. Darby found that churches, schools, and political parties were segregated in all three communities, but Dunville had some distinctive features not shared by the other two. In contrast to the segregated voluntary groups in the first two communities. Dunville had mixed Rotary and Lions clubs, soccer clubs, and bowling clubs, as well as clubs for cricket, athletics, boxing , field hockey, swimming, table tennis, and golf. There was also a vigorous and mixed single parents club. These results are quite consistent with my Indian findings.

Studies of racial violence in the United States are also of interest, but in a different and potentially highly challenging way. There is—to the best of my knowledge—no good theory emerging from these studies that can explain city-level variance in racial violence in the

[48] John Darby, *Intimidation and the Control of Conflict in Northern Ireland* (Dublin: Gill and MacMillan, 1986).

1960s. Why were Newark (New Jersey), Detroit (Michigan), Los Angeles (California), which together accounted for a very large proportion of all deaths in the 1960s riots, so violent? And why did Southern cities, though politically engaged, not have riots?[49] The studies show that economic inequalities between African-Americans and white Americans neither explained the *timing* nor the *location* of riots, but no firm alternative explanations have been provided. Lieberson and Silverman's work comes reasonably close to what I am arguing for India: they emphasize local integration, especially African-American participation in the local government structures.[50] But to my knowledge no scholar has investigated whether civic associations—labour unions, churches, PTAs, and so on—were on the whole racially better integrated in the peaceful cities.[51]

If they were not—and here lies the innovative potential of American race relations in a comparative sense—we might need an initial distinction in our theory between (1) multi-ethnic societies that have a history of segregated civic sites (unions, churches, schools, business associations, and so no)—for example, the United States and South Africa—and (2) multi-ethnic societies where ethnic groups have led an intermixed civic life—for instance, India and Sri Lanka. Interracial or intercommunal civic engagement may be a key vehicle of peace in the latter, but, given the relative absence of common black-white civic sites in countries like the United States, there may not have been any space historically for inter-racial associational engagement, leading to puzzles about the precise nature of mechanisms that led to peace in a different historical and social setting.

If we think about the above distinction further, it may actually be more accurate to say that *groups*, not *societies* as a whole, have a history of segregation. In India, where political parties, unions, business associations, film clubs, and voluntary agencies are by and large ethnically quite mixed, segregation has marked relations between the scheduled castes, who were 'untouchable' for centuries, and the 'upper castes.' Historically, there have been no civic or associational

[49] Donald Horowitz, 'Racial Violence in the United States,' in Nathan Glazer and Ken Young, eds, *Ethnic Pluralism and Public Policy* (Lexington, Mass.: Lexington Books, 1983).

[50] Lieberson and Silverman (fn. 55).

[51] The Kerner Commission Report had an excellent chance to give us an explanation. It missed the chance because it studied the riot-afflicted cities only, not the peaceful ones.

sites where the upper castes and the former untouchables could come together. Similarly, Protestants, Catholics, and Jews could eventually find common civic sites in the United States, but blacks and whites on the whole could not.[52]

'Self-policing', a mechanism of peace proposed recently by Fearon and Laitin, may well be relevant to such segregated settings.[53] In the terminology developed in this paper, it means intra-ethnic, or intra-communal, policing. If exercised by elders, by an ethnic association, or by civic organizations such as black churches, intra-ethnic policing may lead to the same result as inter-ethnic engagement does in India. Cross-country research must take such alternative possibilities seriously. Much remains to be learned.

---

[52] Nathan Glazer, *We Are All Multiculturalists Now* (Cambridge: Harvard University Press, 1996).

[53] James Fearon and David Laitin, 'Explaining Interethnic Cooperation', *American Political Science Review*, 90 (December 1996).

BIBLIOGRAPHY

Acomb, E. M. (1967), *The French Laic Laws 1879–1889*, New York: Octagon Books.

Alba, V. (1968), *Politics and the Labour Movement in Latin America*, Stanford, CA: Stanford University Press, 67–96.

Alberti, Giorgio (1968), '"Movimentismo" and Democracy: An Analytical Framework and the Peruvian Case Study', mimeo, Bologna, CESDE.

Alexander, Jeffrey (1997), 'The Paradoxes of Civil Society,' *International Sociology*, 12(2).

Almond, Gabriel and Sidney Verba (1963), *The Civic Culture: Political Attitudes and Democracy in Five Nations*, Princeton, NJ: Princeton University Press.

al-Naqeeb, K. H. (1990), *Society and State in the Gulf and Arab Peninsula*, London: Routledge.

———— (1991), 'Social Origins of the Authoritarian State in the Arab East', in E. Davis and N. Gavrielides (eds.), *Statecraft in the Middle East: Oil, Historical Memory, and Popular Culture*, Miami: Florida International University Press, 6–24.

al-Sayyid, M. K. (1995a), 'A Civil Society in Egypt?' in A. R. Norton (ed.), *Civil Society in the Middle East*, 1, Leiden: E. F. Brill.

———— (1995b), 'The Concept of Civil Society and the Arab World,' in R. Brynen, B. Korany and P. Noble (eds.), *Political Liberalization and Democratization in the Arab World*, 1, Boulder CO: Lynne Rienner.

Althusius, Johannes (1995), *Politica*, edited and translated by Frederick S. Carney, Indianapolis, IN: Liberty Fund.

Amin, Shahid (1996), *Event, Metaphor, Memory: Chauri Chaura, 1922–92*, Delhi: Oxford University Press.

Amirahmadi, H. (1990), *Revolution and Economic Transition: The Iranian Experience*, Albany, NY: SUNY Press.

Andersen, Walter K. and Shridhar D. Damle (1980), *The Brotherhood in Saffron, The Rashtriya Swayamsevak Sangh and Hindu Revivalism*, Boulder, CO: Westview Press.

Anderson, C. (1967), *Politics and Economic Change in Latin America*, Princeton, NJ: Van Nostrand.

Anderson, Perry (1976–7), 'The Antimonies of Antonio Gramsci,' *New Left Review*, 100.

Anek, Loathamatos (1972), *Business Associations and the New Political Economy of Thailand: From Bureaucratic Polity to Liberal Corporation*, Singapore: Institute of Southeast Asia Studies.

Anzaldua, Gloria (1989), *Borderlands: La Frontera*, San Francisco, CA: Aunt Lute Books.

Appadurai, Arjun (1996), *Modernity at Large: Cultural Dimensions of Globalisation*, Minneapolis, MN: University of Minnesota Press.

Arendt, Hannah (1958), *The Human Condition*, Chicago, IL: University of Chicago Press.

———— (1970), *On Violence*, New York: Harcourt Brace and World.

Aron, Raymond (1965), *Main Currents in Sociological Thought*, London: Weidenfeld and Nicholson, 1.

Audi, Robert (1989), 'The Separation of Church and State and the Obligations of Citizenship,' *Philosophy and Public Affairs*, 18 (Summer), 269–96.

Avineri, Shlomo (1972), *Hegel's Theory of Modern State*, Cambridge, UK: Cambridge University Press.

Bagdikian, Ben H. (1983), *The Media Monopoly*, Boston, MA: Beacon Press.

———— (1989), 'Lords of the Global Village,' *The Nation*, 12 June.

Bailey, F. G. (1966), *The Civility of Indifference*, Ithaca NY: Cornell University Press.

Baloyra, E. (ed.) (1987), *Comparing New Democracies: Transition and Consolidation in Mediterranean Europe and the Southern Cone*, Boulder, CO: Westview Press.

Barber, Benjamin (1984), *Strong Democracy*, Berkeley, CA: University of California Press.

———— (1996), 'Three Challenges to Reinventing Democracy', in P. Hirst and S. Khilnani (eds.), *Reinventing Democracy*, Oxford: Blackwell Publishers.

Barkey, H. (1995), 'Can the Middle East Compete?', in L. Diamond and M. Plattner (eds.), *Economic Reform and Democracy*, Baltimore, MD: Johns Hopkins University Press.

Barnett, Anthony (1996), 'The Creation of Democracy,' in P. Hirst and S. Khilnani (eds.), *Reinventing Democracy*, Oxford: Blackwell Publishers.

Basu, Tapan, Pradip Dutta, Sumit Sarkar, Tanika Sarkar and Sambuddha Sen (eds.) (1993), *Khaki Shorts and Saffron Flags: A Critique of the Hindu Right*, Delhi: Orient Longman.

Bayart, Jean-Francois (1986), 'Civil Society in Africa,' in Patrick Chabal (ed.), *Political Domination in Africa*, Cambridge, UK: Cambridge University Press.

Bayly, C. A. (1999), 'The Indian Ecumene: An Indigenous Public Sphere,' in *Empire and Information: Intelligence Gathering and Social Communication in India, 1780–1870*, Cambridge, UK: Cambridge University Press, 180–211.

Bayly, Susan (2001), *Caste, Society and Politics in India from the Eighteenth Century to the Modern Age*, Cambridge, UK: Cambridge University Press.

Beetham David (ed.) (1994), *Defining and Measuring Democracy*, London: Sage.

Bellah, Robert, Richard Madsen, William Sullivan, Ann Swidler, and Steve Tipton (1985), *Habits of the Heart*, Berkeley, CA: University of California Press.

Bellin, E. (1995), 'Civil Society in Tunisia', in A. R. Norton (ed.), *Civil Society in the Middle East*, 1 & 2, Leiden: E. F. Brill.

Bendix, Reinhard (1990–1), 'State, Legitimation, and "Civil Society",' *Telos* 86 (Winter), 143–52.

Benhabib, Seyla (1992), 'Models of Public Space: Hannah Arendt, the Liberal Tradition and Jürgen Habermas,' in Craig Calhoun (ed.), *Habermas and the Public Sphere*, Cambridge, MA: MIT Press.

Berger, Peter and Hsin-huang Hsiao (eds.) (1990), *In Search of an East Asian Development Model*, New Brunswick, NJ: Transaction Books.

Berger, Peter L. and Neuhaus, Richard John (1977), *To Empower People: The Role of Mediating Structures in Public Policy*, Washington, DC: The American Enterprise Institute.

Berman, Sheri (1997a), 'Civil Society and the Collapse of the Weimar Republic,' *World Politics*, 49 (April), 401–29.

——— (1997b), 'Civil Society and Political Institutionalization,' *American Behavioral Scientist*, 40(5), 62–74.

Bernhard, Michael (1993), 'Civil Society and Democratic Transition in East Central Europe,' *Political Science Quarterly*, 108(2), 307–26.

Béteille, André (1994), 'Equality and Universality', *Cambridge Anthropology*, 17(1), 1–12.

——— (1995), 'Universities as Institutions,' *Economic and Political Weekly*, 30(11).

——— (1996), 'Civil Society and its Institutions,' First Fulbright Memorial Lecture, United States Educational Foundation in India, Kolkata.

Bianchi, Robert (1989), *Unruly Corporatism: Associational Life in Twentieth Century Egypt*, Oxford: Oxford University Press.

Bill, J. A. (1996), 'The Study of Middle East Politics, 1946–1996: A Stocktaking', *Middle East Journal*, 50(4).

Birnbaum, Pierre (1988), *State and Collective Action: The European Experience*, Cambridge, UK: Cambridge University Press.

Blaney, David and Mustapha Kamal Pasha (1993), 'Civil Society and Democracy in the Third World,' *Studies in Comparative International Development*, 28(1).

Blecher, Marc J. (1991), 'Developmental State, Entrepreneurial State: The Political Economy of Reform in Xinji Municipality and Guanghan County,' in Gordon White (ed.), *The Chinese State in the Era of Economic Reform: The Road to Crisis*, London: Macmillan.

Blomkvist Hans and Ashok Swain (2001), 'Investigating Democracy and Social Capital in India,' *Economic and Political Weekly*, 36(8), 639–45.

Bloodworth, Dennis (1986), *The Tiger and the Trojan Horse*, Singapore: Times Books International.

Bobbio, Norberto (1989), *Democracy and Dictatorship: The Nature and Limits of State Power*, trans. Peter Kennealy, Cambridge, UK: Polity Press.

Bollen, Kenneth (1993), 'Liberal Democracy: Validity and Method Factors in Cross-National Measures', *American Journal of Political Science*, 37, 1207–30.

Bondurant, Joan (1965), *The Conquest of Violence: The Gandhian Philosophy of Conflict*, Berkeley, CA: University of California Press.

Bonnin, Michel and Yvres Chevrier (1991), 'The Intellectual and the State: Social Dynamics of Intellectual Autonomy during the Post-Mao Era,' *China Quarterly*, 127 (September), 569–93.

Bourdieu, Pierre (1984), *Distinction: A Social Critique of the Judgment of Taste*, Cambridge, MA: Harvard University Press.

Boyte, Harry (1992), 'The Pragmatic Ends of Popular Politics,' in Craig Calhoun (ed.), *Habermas and the Public Sphere*, Cambridge, MA: MIT Press.

Brand, L. (1995), 'In the Beginning was the State...the Quest for Civil Society in Jordan', in A. R. Norton (ed.), *Civil Society in the Middle East*, 1 & 2, Leiden: E. F. Brill, 148–85.

Brass, Paul (1997), *Theft of an Idol*, Princeton, NJ: Princeton University Press.

Brass, T. (1995), *New Farmers' Movements in India*, Ilford: Frank Cass.

Bratton, M. (1994), 'Civil Society and Political Transitions in Africa', in J. B. Harbeson, D. Rothchild and N. Chazan (eds.), *Civil Society and the State in Africa*, Boulder, CO: Lynne Rienner, 64–71.

Brodsgaard, Kjeld Erik (1993), 'State and Society in Hainan: Liao Xun's Ideas on "Little Government, Big Society"' mimeo, University of Copenhagen.

Bruneau, T. (1982), *The Church in Brazil: The Politics of Religion*, Austin, TX: University of Texas Press.

Bryant, C. (1995), 'Civic Nation, Civil Society, Civil Religion', in John Hall (ed.), *Civil Society: Theory, History, Comparison*, Cambridge, UK: Polity Press (1995), 136–57.

Brynen, Rex, Bahgat Korany and Paul Noble (eds.) (1995), *Political Liberalization and Democratization in the Arab World*, 1, Boulder, CO: Lynne Rienner.

Budge, I. and D. McKay (eds.) (1994), *Developing Democracy*, London: Sage.

Bulmer-Thomas, V. (1987), *The Political Economy of Central America since 1920*, Cambridge, UK: Cambridge University Press.

Burdick, J. (1992), 'Rethinking the Study of Social Movements: The Case of Urban Christian Base Communities in Urban Brazil', in A. Escobar and S. Alvarez (eds.), *The Making of Social Movements in Latin America*, Boulder CO: Westview Press, 171–84.

Calhoun, Craig (ed.) (1992), *Habermas and the Public Sphere*, Cambridge, MA: MIT Press.

————(1993), 'Civil Society and the Public Sphere,' *Public Culture*, 5, 267–80.

Callahan, William A. (1994), 'Local Alternatives to "Asian Democracy".' *The Nation* (24 December).

Cantori, L. (1997), 'Civil Society, Liberalism and the Corporatist Alternative in the Middle East', *Middle East Studies Association Bulletin*, 31(1).

Carrithers, Michael, Steven Collins and Steven Lukes (eds.) (1985), *The Category of the Person: Anthropology, Philosophy and History*, Cambridge, UK: Cambridge University Press.

Castaneda, J. (1993), *Utopia Unarmed: The Latin American Left after the Cold War*, New York: Knopf.

Cava, R. D. (1989), 'The "People's Church", the Vatican, and Abertura', in Alfred Stepan (ed.), *Democratizing Brazil: Problems of Transition*, New York: Oxford University Press.

Chan, Anita (1993), 'Revolution or Corporatism'? Workers and Trade Unions in Post-Mao China', *Australian Journal of Chinese Affairs*, 29 (January), 31–61.

Chandhoke, Neera (1995), *State and Civil Society: Explorations in Political Theory*, Delhi: Sage.

———— (1998), 'The Assertion of Civil Society against the State,' in M. Mohanty, P.N. Mukherjee and O. Tornquist (eds.), *People's Rights: Social Movements and the State in the Third World*, Delhi: Sage.

———— (2000), 'Languages of Civil Society: Translations, Slippages, and Domination', paper presented to conference on Voluntary Action and Civil Society, Hyderabad, 1998.

———— (2001), 'The "Civil" and the "Political" in Civil Society,' *Democratization*, 8(2).

Chandra, B. (1984), *Communalism in Modern India*, New Delhi: Vikas.

Chatterjee, Partha (1986), *Nationalist Thought and the Colonial World: A Derivative Discourse?* Delhi: Oxford University Press.

———— (1993), *The Nation and its Fragments: Colonial and Postcolonial Histories*, Princeton, NJ: Princeton University Press.

———— (1997), 'Beyond the Nation? or Within?' *Economic and Political Weekly*, 32(1–2), (4–11 January).

———— (1998), 'Community in the East,' *Economic and Political Weekly*, 33(6).

———— (2000), 'Two Poets and Death,' in Timothy Mitchell (ed.), *Questions of Modernity*, Minneapolis, MN: University of Minnesota Press.

Chaudhury, Nirad C. (1951), *The Autobiography of an Unknown Indian*, London: Macmillan.

Chhibber, Pradeep (1990), *Democracy without Associations*, Ann Arbor, MI: The University of Michigan Press.

Chibber, Pradeep and Samuel Eldersveld (2000), 'Local Elites and Popular Support for Economic Reform in China and India', *Comparative Political Studies*, 33, 350–73.

Clark, John (1991), *Democratising Development. The Role of Voluntary Organizations*, London: Earthscan Publications.

Clark, Kenneth (1982), *Ruskin Today*, Harmondsworth, UK: Penguin.

Clayton, Andrew (ed.) (1996), *NGOs, Civil Society and the State: Building Democracy in Transitional Societies*, Oxford: Intrac.

Cohen, Jean L. and Andrew Arato (1992), *Civil Society and Political Theory*, Cambridge, MA: MIT Press.

Cohen, Joshua (1990), 'Comments on Nancy Fraser's "Rethinking the Public Sphere" paper presented to the American Philosophical Association,' Central Division, New Orleans.

Cohen, Joshua and Rogers, Joel (1992), 'Secondary Associations and Democratic Governance,' *Politics and Society*, 20 (December), 393–472.

Colas, Dominique (1997), *Civil Society and Fanaticism: Conjoined Histories*, Stanford CA: Stanford University Press.

Coleman, James (1988), 'Social Capital in the Creation of Human Capital', *American Journal of Sociology*, 94 Supplement S95–S120.

———— (1990), *Foundations of Social Theory*, Cambridge, MA: Harvard University Press.

Collier, Ruth Berins (1999), *Paths Toward Democracy: The Working Class and Elites in Western Europe and South America*, Cambridge, UK: Cambridge University Press.

Collingwood, R. G. (1992), *The New Leviathan: On Man, Society, Civilization and Barbarism*, Oxford: Clarendon Press.

Comaroff, John L. and Jean Comaroff (1999), *Civil Society and the Political Imagination in Africa: Critical Perspectives*, Chicago, IL: University of Chicago Press.

Commission for a New Asia (1994), *Towards A New Asia*, Kuala Lumpur.

The Compact Edition of the Oxford English Dictionary (1982), Oxford: Oxford University Press.

Conde, R. C. (1974), *The First Stages of Modernization in Spanish America*, New York: Harper and Row.

Constituent Assembly Debates (1989), *Official Report*, New Delhi: Lok Sabha Secretariat, 2nd reprint, Book 1.

Corradi, J., P. W. Fagen, and M. A. Garreton (eds.) (1992), *Fear at the Edge: State Terror and Resistance in Latin America*, Berkeley, CA: University of California Press.

Dahl, Robert (1971), *Polyarchy*, New Haven, CT: Yale University Press.

Dalal, C. B. (1971), *Gandhi: 1915–1948: A Detailed Chronology*, New Delhi: Bharatiya Vidya Bhavan.

Darby, John (1986), *Intimidation and the Control of Conflict in Northern Ireland*, Dublin: Gill and Macmillan.

de Tocqueville, Alexis (1969), *Democracy in America 2*, New York: Harper and Row.

————— (1981), *De la Democratie en Amerique 2*, Paris: Flammarian

Diamond, L. (1994), 'Rethinking Civil Society: Toward Democratic Consolidation', *Journal of Democracy*, 5(3), 4–17.

Ding X. L. (1994) 'Institutional Amphibiousness and the Transition from Communism: The Case of China,' *British Journal of Political Science*, 24, 293–318.

Drake, P. (1996), *Labour Movements and Dictatorships: The Southern Cone in Comparative Perspective*, Baltimore, MD: Johns Hopkins University Press.

Dreze, Jean and Sen, Amartya (1995), *India: Economic Development and Social Opportunity*, Delhi: Oxford University Press.

Duncan, R. (1976), *Latin American Politics: A Developmental Approach*, New York: Praeger.

Dwivedi, R. (1998), 'Resisting Dams and "Development": Contemporary Significance of the Campaign Against Narmada Projects in India,' *European Journal of Development Research*, 10(3), 135–83.

Eckstein, H. (1961), *The Theory of Stable Democracy*, Princeton, NJ: Princeton University Press.

Eckstein, S. (ed.) (1989), *Power and Popular Protest: Latin American Social Movements*, Berkeley, CA: University of California Press.

Edwards, Bob and Michael Foley (1998), 'Civil Society and Social Capital Beyond Putnam,' *American Behavioral Scientist*, 42(1).

Edwards, Bob, Michael Foley and Mario Diani (eds.) (2001), *Beyond Tocqueville*, Hanover: University Press of New England.

Edwards, Michael (2002), 'Enthusiasts, Tacticians and Sceptics: The World Bank, Civil Society and Social Capital,' http://www.worldbank.org/poverty/scapital/library/Edwards.pdf.

Ekiert, G. (1991), 'Democratization Processes in East Central Europe: A Theoretical Reconsideration', *British Journal of Political Science*, 21, 26–55.

Eldridge, Philip J. (1995), *Non-Government Organizations and Democratic Participation in Indonesia*, London: Oxford University Press.

Eley, Geoff (1992), 'Nations, Publics, and Political Cultures: Placing Habermas in the Nineteenth Century,' in Craig Calhoun (ed.), *Habermas and the Public Sphere*, Cambridge, MA: MIT Press (1992).

Elshtain, Jean (1995), *Democracy on Trial*, New York: Basic Books.

Encarnacion, Omar (2000), 'Tocqueville's Missionaries,' *World Policy Journal*, 17.

Erickson, K. (1977), *The Brazilian Corporative State and Working Class Politics*, Berkeley, CA: University of California Press.

Escobar, Arturo and Sonia Alvarez (eds.) (1992), *The Making of Social Movements in Latin America*, Boulder, CO: Westview Press.

Esposito, J. and J. Voll (1996), *Islam and Democracy*, Oxford: Oxford University Press.

Evans, Peter (1996), 'Government Action, Social Capital and Development: Reviewing the Evidence on Synergy,' *World Development*, 24(6).

Evans-Pritchard, E. E. (1951), *Social Anthropology*, London: Cohen and West.

Fatton, Robert (1992), *Predatory Rule: State and Civil Society in Africa*, Boulder, CO: Lynne Rienner.

Fearon, James and David Laitin (1996), 'Explaining Interethnic Cooperation,' *American Political Science Review*, 90 (December).

Feldman, Shelly (1997), 'NGO's and Civil Society: (Un)stated Contradictions, *Annals of the American Academy of Political and Social Science*, 554, 46–55.

Felski, Rita (1989), *Beyond Feminist Aesthetics*, Cambridge, MA: Harvard University Press.

Ferguson, Adam. (1986), *An Essay on the History of Civil Society*, New Brunswick: Transaction Publishers.

Feyerabend, Paul (1993), *Against Method*, New York: Verso.

Field, M. (1985), *The Merchant: The Big Business Families of Saudi Arabia and the Gulf States*, Woodstock, NY: Overlook Press.

Finkle, Jason L. and Richard W. Gable (eds.) (1996), *Political Development and Social Change*, New York: Wiley and Sons.

Foley, Michael and Bob Edwards (1996), 'The Paradox of Civil Society,' *Journal of Democracy*, 7(3), 38–53.

Forbes, H. D. (1997), *Ethnic Conflict*, New Haven, CT: Yale University Press.

Forment, Carlos. A. (1995), 'Civil Society and the Invention of Democracy in Nineteenth Century Cuba', mimeo, Princeton (September).

Foucault, Michel (1980), 'Body/Power', in Colin Gordon (ed.), *Foucault on Power/Knowledge: Selected Interviews and Other Writings 1972–1977*, trans. Colin Gordon, Leo Marshall, John Mepham and Kate Soper, Brighton, UK: Harvester.

Foweraker, Joe and Roman Krznaric (2000), Measuring Liberal Democratic Performance, *Political Studies*, 48, 759–87.

Fraser, Nancy (1986), 'Toward a Discourse Ethic of Solidarity,' *Praxis International*, 5(4) (January).

——— (1989), *Unruly Practices: Power Discourse and Gender in Contemporary Social Theory*, Minneapolis, MN: University of Minnesota Press.

——— (1990), 'The Uses and Abuses of French Discourse Theories for Feminist Politics,' *Boundary 2*, 17(2), 82–101.

Freeman, Michael (1995), 'Human Rights: Asia and the West,' in James T.H. Tang (ed.), *Human Rights and International Relations in the Asia-Pacific Region*, London: Pinter.

Fruhling, H. (1984), 'Repressive Policies and Legal Dissent in Authoritarian Regimes: Chile 1973–1981', *International Journal of Sociology of Law*, 12, 351–74.

Fukuyama, Francis (1995), *Trust: the Social Virtues and the Creation of Prosperity*, London: Penguin.

Fuller, C. J. (ed.) (1996), *Caste Today*, Delhi: Oxford University Press.

Galston, William (1992), *Liberal Purpose*, Cambridge, UK: Cambridge University Press.

Gandhi M. K. (1972), *Satyagraha in South Africa*, Ahmedabad: Navajivan Press.

——— (1993), *An Autobiography: The Story of My Experiments With Truth*, Boston, MA: Beacon Press.

Garreton, M. (1989a), *The Chilean Political Process*, Boston, MA: Allen and Unwin.

——— (1989b), 'Popular Mobilization and the Military Regime in Chile: The Complexities of the Invisible Transition', in S. Eckstein (ed.), *Power and Popular Protest: Latin American Social Movement*, Berkeloy, CA: University of California Press.

Gause, F. G. (1994), *Oil Monarchies: Domestic and Security Challenges in the Arab Gulf States*, New York: Council on Foreign Relations Press.

Geddes, Barbara (1991), 'Paradigms and Sand Castles in Comparative Politics of Developing Areas', in P. Crotty (ed.), *Political Science: Looking to the Future*, Evanston IL: Northwestern University Press.

Gellner, E. (1994), *Conditions of Liberty: Civil Society and Its Rivals*, New York: Penguin Press.

———— (1995), 'The Importance of Being Modular,' in John Hall (ed.), *Civil Society: Theory, History, Comparison*, Cambridge, UK: Polity Press (1992).

Gereffi G. and D. Wyman (eds.) (1990), *Manufacturing Miracles: Paths of Industrialization in Latin America and East Asia*, Princeton, NJ: Princeton University Press.

Geremak, B. (1992), 'Civil Society Then and Now,' *Journal of Democracy*, 3(2), 3–12.

Germani, G. (1981), *The Sociology of Modernization: Studies on Its Historical and Theoretical Aspects in Latin America*, New Brunswick, NJ: Transactions Book.

Gerth, H. H. and C. Wright Mills (eds.) (1946), *From Max Weber*, New York: Oxford University Press.

Ghai, Yash (1995), 'Asian Perspectives on Human Rights,' in James T. H. Tang (ed.), *Human Rights and International Relations in the Asia-Pacific Region*, London: Pinter.

Glazer, Nathan (1996), *We Are All Multiculturalists Now*, Cambridge, MA: Harvard University Press.

Goh Chok Tong (1994), 'Moral Values: The Foundations of a Vibrant State' Address delivered at a National Day Rally 21 August 1994, in 'Social Values, Singapore-Style,' *Current History*, 93(587), 417–22.

Gold, Thomas B. (1985), 'After Comradeship: Personal Relations in China after the Cultural Revolution,' *China Quarterly* 104, 657–75.

Goody, Jack (1996), *The East in the West*, Cambridge, UK: Cambridge University Press.

Gough, Kathleen (1955), 'The Social Structure of a Tanjore Village', in McKim Marriott (ed.), *Village India*: Chicago IL: University of Chicago Press.

Graham, B. D. (1990), *Hindu Nationalism and Indian Politics: The Origins and Development of the Bharatiya Jana Sangh*, Cambridge, UK: Cambridge University Press.

Gramsci, Antonio (1973), *Selections from the Prison Notebooks*, London: Lawrence and Wishart.

Gray, John (1993), *Post Liberalism: Studies in Political Thought*, London: Routledge.

Green, Martin (ed.) (1987), *Gandhi in India: In His Own Words*, Hanover, NH: University Press of New England.

Guha, Ranajit (1982), *Subaltern Studies I*, Delhi: Oxford University Press.

———— (1997), *Dominance without Hegemony*, Cambridge, MA: Harvard University Press.

Gunther, R., P. N. Diamandorous and H. J. Puhle (eds.) (1995), *The Politics of Democratic Consolidation: Southern Europe in Comparative Perspective*, Baltimore, MD: Johns Hopkins University Press.

Gupta, Dipankar (1997), 'Civil Society in the Indian Context,' *Contemporary Sociology*, 26(3).

———— (1999), 'Civil Society or the State: What Happened to Citizenship?' in Ramachandra Guha and Jonathan Parry (eds.), *Institutions and Inequalities*, New Delhi: Oxford University Press.

Gyimah-Boadi, E. (1996), 'Civil Society in Africa', *Journal of Democracy*, 7(2).

Habermas Jürgen (1962), *Strukturwandel der Öffentlichkeit*, Berlin: Luchterhand.

———— (1987), *The Theory of Communicative Action*, 2, *Lifeworld and System: A Critique of Functionalist Reason*, trans. Thomas McCarthy, Boston, MA: Beacon Press.

———— (1989), *The Structural Transformation of the Public Sphere: An Inquiry into a Category of Bourgeois Society*, trans. Thomas Burger with Frederick Lawrence, Cambridge, MA: MIT Press.

———— (1992), 'Further Reflections on the Public Sphere,' in Craig Calhoun (ed.), *Habermas and the Public Sphere*, Cambridge, MA: MIT Press.

Hadenius, Axel (1992), *Democracy and Development*, Cambridge, UK: Cambridge University Press.

Hadenius, Axel and Fredrik Uggla (1996), 'Making Civil Society Work, Promoting Democratic Development: What Can States and Donors Do?' *World Development*, 24(10).

Haggard, S. and R. Kaufman (1995), *The Political Economy of Democratic Transitions*, Princeton, NJ: Princeton University Press.

Halebsky, Sandor (1976), *Mass Society and Political Conflict*, Cambridge, UK: Cambridge University Press.

Hall, John (1985), *Power and Liberties: The Causes and Consequences of the Rise of the West*, Berkeley, CA: University of California Press.

———— (1995), *Civil Society: Theory, History, Comparison*, Cambridge, UK: Polity Press.

———— (1998), 'The Nature of Civil Society,' *Society*, 35(4), 32–41.

Hann, C. and E. Dunn (eds.) (1996), *Civil Society: Challenging Western Models*, London: Routledge.

Hansen, T. B. (1999), *The Saffron Wave: Democracy and Hindu Nationalism in Modern India*, New Delhi: Oxford University Press.

Hansen, T. B. and C. Jaffrelot (eds.) (1998), *The BJP and the Compulsions of Politics in India*, New Delhi: Oxford University Press.

Harik, I. (1992), 'Privatization: The Issue, the Prospects, and the Fears', in I. Harik and D. Sullivan (eds.), *Privatization and Liberalization in the Middle East*, Bloomington, IN: Indiana University Press.

Harriss John (2001), *Depoliticizing Development: The World Bank and Social Capital*, London: LeftWord Books.

Havel, Vaclav, Vaclav Klaus and Petr Pithart (1996), 'Rival Visions', *Journal of Democracy*, 7(1).

Hawthorne, Geoffrey (2001), 'The Promise of "Civil Society" in the South,' in S. Kaviraj and S. Khilnani (eds.), *Civil Society: History and Possibilities*, Cambridge UK: Cambridge University Press.

He Baogang (1993), 'The Dual Roles of Semi-Civil Society in Chinese Democracy,' Discussion Paper 327, Institute of Development Studies, University of Sussex, Brighton, UK.

He Qinglian (1993), 'Dangdai Zhongguo Nongcun Zongfa Zuzhide Fuxing' (The Revival of Clan Organisations in Contemporary China's Countryside), *Ershiyi Shiji* (*Twenty-First Century*), 16 (April), Hong Kong, 141–8.

Hedstrom, Peter and Richard Swedberg (eds.) (1998), *Social Mechansims: An Analytical Approach to Social Theory*, Cambridge, UK: Cambridge University Press.

Hefner, Robert (ed.) (1998), *Democratic Civility*, New Brunswick NJ: Transaction Publisher.

Hegel G. W. F. (1942), *Philosophy of Right*, T. M. Knox (trans.) Oxford: Clarendon Press.

Held David (1987) *Models of Democracy*, Cambridge, UK: Polity Press.

————— (1989), *Political Theory and the Modern State: Essays on State, Power and Democracy*, Cambridge, UK: Polity Press.

————— (1993), 'Democracy: from City-States to a Cosmopolitan Order?' in *Prospects for Democracy North South East West*, Cambridge, UK: Polity Press.

Heller, Patrick (2000), 'Degrees of Democracy: Some Comparative Lessons from India', *World Politics*, 52, 484–519.

Hewison, Kevin (1993), 'Nongovernmental Organizations and the Cultural Development Perspective: A Comment on Rigg (1991),' *World Development*, 21(10), 1699–1708.

Hewison, Kevin and Garry Rodan (1994), 'The Decline of the Left in Southeast Asia,' in Ralph Miliband and Leo Panitch (eds.), *Between Globalism and Nationalism: Socialist Register*, London: Merlin Press.

Hicks, N. and G. al-Najjar (1995), 'The Utility of Tradition: Civil Society in Kuwait', in A. R. Norton (ed.), *Civil Society in the Middle East*, 1 & 2, Leiden: E. F. Brill, 186–213.

Hingorani, A. T. (1998), *Gandhi for 21st Century: The Village Reconstruction*, Mumbai: Bharatiya Vidya Bhavan, Manibhavan Gandhi Sangrahalaya.

Hinnebusch, R. (1995), 'State, Civil Society, and Political Change in Syria', in A. R. Norton (ed.) *Civil Society in the Middle East*, 1 & 2, Leiden: E. F. Brill, 214–42.

Hirst, Paul (1994), *Associative Democracy: New Forms of Economic and Social Governance*, Massachusetts: University of Massachusetts Press.

Ho Wing Meng (1977), 'Asian Values and Modernization,' in Seah Chee-Meow (ed.), *Asian Values and Modernization*, Singapore: Singapore University Press.

Hofheinz Jr., Roy and Kent E. Calder (1982), *The Eastasia Edge*, New York: Harper and Row.

Holston, James and Arjun Appadurai (1996), 'Cities and Citizenship,' *Public Culture* 8 (Winter), 187–204.

Horowitz, Donald (1983), 'Racial Violence in the United States,' in Nathan Glazer and Ken Young (eds.), *Ethnic Pluralism and Public Policy*, Lexington, MA: Lexington Books.

———— (1985), *Ethnic Groups in Conflict*, Berkeley CA: University of California Press.

Howe, Stephen (1992), 'The New Xenophobes,' *New Statesman Society*, 4(149), 12.

Howell, David (1995) 'Europe Must Prepare for Easternisation,' *The Independent* (21 August).

Howell, Jude (1994), 'Interest Groups in Post-Mao China: Civil Society or Corporatism?' paper presented at 16th World Congress of IPSA, Berlin (21–5 August).

Howell, Jude and Jenny Pearce (eds.) (2001), *Civil Society and Development*, Boulder CO: Lynn Rienner.

Huang, Philip (ed.) (1993), '"Public Sphere/Civil Society" in China: Paradigmatic Issues in Chinese Studies III' *Modern China*, 19(2) (April).

Huntington, Samuel (1968), *Political Order in Changing Societies*, New Haven CT: Yale University Press.

———— (1991), *The Third Wave: Democratization in the Late Twentieth Century*, London: University of Oklahoma Press.

———— (1996), *The Clash of Civilizations and the Remaking of the World Order*, New York: Simon and Schuster.

Ibrahim, Saad Eddin (1995), 'Civil Society and Prospects for Democratization in the Arab World', in A. R. Norton (ed.) *Civil Society in the Middle East*, 1 & 2, Leiden: E. F. Brill, 27–54.

———— (1998), 'Religion and Democracy: The Case of Islam, Civil Society and Democracy,' Inogushi, Newman and Keane (eds.), *Changing Nature of Democracy*, Tokyo: UN Press.

———— (1998), 'The Troubled Triangle: Populism, Islam and Civil Society in the Arab World,' *International Political Science Review*, 19(4).

Inglehart, Ronald (1997), *Modernization and Postmodernization*, Princeton NJ: Princeton University Press.

Isaac, K. A. (1994), 'Library Movement and Bibliographic Control in Kerala: An Overview,' Paper presented at International Congress of Kerala Studies, Trivandrum (August).

Ismael, J. (1993), *Kuwait: Dependency and Class in a Rentier State*, Gainesville, FL: University Press of Florida.

Jaffrelot, C. (1996), *The Hindu Nationalist Movement in Indian Politics*, New York: Columbia University Press.

Jenkins, Rob (1999), *Democratic Politics and Economic Reform in India*, Cambridge, UK: Cambridge University Press.

——— (2001), 'Mistaking "Governance" for "Politics": Foreign Aid, Democracy, and the Construction of Civil Society' in S. Kaviraj and S. Khilnani (eds.), *Civil Society: History and Possibilities*, Cambridge, UK: Cambridge University Press.

Jesudason, Savarirayan (1937), *Ashrams, Ancient and Modern: Their Aims and Ideals*, Vellore: Sri Ramachandra Press.

Johnson, J. (1958), *Political Change in Latin America: The Emergence of the Middle Sectors*, Stanford, CA: Stanford University Press.

Joshi, Ishan (1999a), 'Mob Rule', *Outlook*, 8 February, 12–18.

——— (1999b), 'A Wee Swing to the Right', *Outlook*, 16 August, 28–9.

Kalelkar, Kaka (1956), *Report of the Backward Classes Commission*, New Delhi: Government of India.

Kamrava, M. (1998), 'Frozen Political Liberalization in Jordan: The Consequences for Democracy', *Democratization*, 5(1), 138–57.

Karl, Terry Lynn (1990), 'Dilemmas of Democratization in Latin America,' *Comparative Politics*, 23(1), 1–2.

Katzenstein, Mary, Smitu Kothari, and Uday Mehta (2001), 'Social Movement Politics in India; Institutions, Interests and Identities,' in Atul Kohli (ed.), *The State and Poverty in India*, Cambridge, UK: Cambridge University Press (2001).

Kaviraj, Sudipta and Sunil Khilnani (eds.) (2001), *Civil Society: History and Possibilities*, Cambridge, UK: Cambridge University Press.

Keane, John (1988), *Democracy and Civil Society: On the Predicaments of European Socialism, The Prospects for Democracy, and the Problem of Controlling Social and Political Power*, London: Verso.

——— (1998), *Civil Society: Old Images, New Visions*, Stanford, CA: Stanford University Press.

Keck, Margaret E. and Kathryn Sikkink (1998), *Activists Beyond Borders: Advocacy Networks in International Politics*, Ithaca, NY: Cornell University Press.

Kelly, David and He Baogang (1992), 'Emergent Civil Society and the Intellectuals in China,' in Robert Miller (ed.), *The Development of Civil Society in Communist Systems*, Sydney: Allen and Unwin.

Kim Dae Jung (1994), 'Is Culture Destiny? The Myth of Asia's Anti-Democratic Values,' *Foreign Affairs*, 73(6), 189–94.

King, Gary, Robert Keohane, and Sidney Verba (1993), *Designing Social Inquiry*, Princeton, NJ: Princeton University Press.

Knack, Stephen and Philip Keefer (1997), 'Does Social Capital have an Economic Pay-off?' *Quarterly Journal of Economics*, 112(4) (November).

Knox, T. M. (1953), 'Introduction' in G. W. F. Hegel, *Philosophy of Right*, Oxford: Clarendon.

Koh, Tommy Thong-Bee (1993), 'The 10 Values That Undergird East Asian Strength and Success,' *International Herald Tribune* (11 December).

Kohli, Atul (1987), *The State and Poverty in India*, Cambridge, UK: Cambridge University Press.

——— (1990), *Democracy and Discontent*, Cambridge, UK: Cambridge University Press.

——— (ed.) (2001), *The Success of India's Democracy*, Cambridge, UK: Cambridge University Press.

Kothari, Rajni (1988), *State Against Democracy: In Search of Humane Governance*, Delhi: Ajanta Publishers.

——— (1989), 'The NGOs, the State and World Capitalism,' *New Asian Visions*, 6(1), 404–58.

Krishna, Anirudh, 'Moving from the Stock of Social Capital to the Flow of Benefits: The Role of Agency,' *World Development*, 29(6).

Krugman, Paul (1995), 'Asia's Growth: Miracle or Myth?,' *Foreign Affairs*, 73(6), 170–7.

Kukathas, Chandran and David W. Lovell (1991), 'The Significance of Civil Society,' in Chandran Kukathas, David W. Lovell and William Maley (eds.), *The Transition from Socialism: State and Civil Society in the USSR*, London: Longman Cheshire.

Kumar, Krishan (1993), 'Civil Society: An Inquiry into the Usefulness of an Historical Term,' *British Journal of Sociology*, 44.

Landim, L. (1996), 'Nongovernmental Organizations in Latin America', in R. Camp (ed.), *Democracy in Latin America: Patterns and Cycles*, Wilmington, DE: Scholarly Resources, 207–22.

Lee, Ben (1992), 'Textuality, Mediation, and Public Discourse,' in Craig Calhoun (ed.), *Habermas and the Public Sphere*, Cambridge, MA: MIT Press.

Levine, D. (1986), *Religion and Political Conflict in Latin America*, Chapel Hill, NC: University of North Carolina Press.

Li Quiang (1993), *Shehui Fenceng and Liudong (Social Stratification and Dynamics)*, Beijing: Chinese Economy Publishing House.

Lieberson, Stanley and Arnold Silverman (1965), 'The Precipitants and Underlying Conditions of Race Riots,' *American Sociological Review*, 30 (December).

Lijphart, A. and C. Waisman (eds.) (1996), *Institutional Design in New Democracies: Eastern Europe and Latin America*, Boulder, CO: Westview Press.

Linz, J. and A. Stepan (1996), *Problems of Democratic Transition and Consolidation: Southern Europe, South America, and Post-Communism Europe*, Baltimore, MD: Johns Hopkins University Press.

Lionnet, Francoise (1989), *Autobiographical Voices: Race, Gender, Self-Portraiture*, Ithaca, NY: Cornell University Press.

Locke, John (1967), *'The Second Treatise of Civil Government'* in Peter Laslett (ed.) *Two Treatises of Civil Government*, 2nd edition, Cambridge, UK: University Press.

Lockwood, David (1992), *Solidarity and Schism*, Oxford, UK: Clarendon Press.

Loh, Christine (1993), 'The Rights Stuff,' *Far Eastern Review* (8 July) 15.

Lukes, Steven (1973), *Emile Durkheim: An Historical and Critical Study*, London: Allen Lane.

Lundwall, Jonna (2002), 'Same but Different: A Comparative Case Study of Two Indian Districts in Search for Mechanisms Linking Social Capital to Democratic Performance', Department of Government, Uppsala University.

MacIntyre, Andrew (1991), *Business and Politics in Indonesia*, Sydney: Allen and Unwin.

——— (ed.) (1995), *Business and Government in Industrialising East and Southeast Asia*, Sydney: Allen and Unwin.

Mahajan, Gurpreet (1998), *Identities and Rights: Aspects of Liberal Democracy in India*, Delhi: Oxford University Press.

——— (1999), 'Civil Society and its Avtars: What Happened to Freedom and Democracy?' *Economic and Political Weekly*, 34(20) (15–21 May), 1188–96.

Mahathir Mohamad and Shintaro Ishihara (1995), *The Voice of Asia* (translated by Frank Baldwin) Tokyo: Kodansa International.

Mahbubani, Kishore (1995), 'The Pacific Way,' *Foreign Affairs*, 74(1), 100–11.

Mainwaring, S. (1986a), *The Catholic Church and Politics in Brazil, 1916–1985*, Stanford, CA: Stanford University Press.

——— (1986b), 'The Transition to Democracy in Brazil', *Journal of Interamerican Studies and World Affairs*, 28.

——— (1989), 'Grassroots Popular Movements and the Struggle for

Democracy: Nova Iguaçu', in A. Stepan (ed.), *Democratizing Brazil: Problems of Transition*, New York: Oxford University Press, 168–204.

Mainwaring, S., G. O'Donnell, and J. S. Valenzuela (eds.) (1992), *Issues in Democratic Consolidation: The New South American Democracies in Comparative Perspective*, South Bend, IN: University of Notre Dame Press.

Mallet, Victor (1994), 'Confucius or Convenience?,' *Financial Times* (5 March).

Mamdani, M. (1996), *Citizen and Subject: Contemporary Africa and the Legacy of Late Colonialism*, Princeton, NJ: Princeton University Press.

Mann, Elizabeth A. (1992), *Boundaries and Identities: Muslims, Work and Status in Aligarh*, Delhi: Sage Publications.

Manor, James and Richard C. Crook (1998), *Democracy and Decentralization in South Asia and West Africa*, Cambridge, UK: Cambridge University Press.

Mansbridge, Jane (1993), 'Feminism and Democratic Community,' in J. Chapman and I. Shapiro (eds.) *Democratic Community: NOMOS XXXV*, New York: New York University Press.

Maravall, J. M., C. Bresser-Pereira, and A. Przeworski (1991), *Economic Reforms in New Democracies*, Cambridge, UK: Cambridge University Press, 77–131.

Marriott, McKim (ed.) (1955), *Village India*, Chicago IL: University of Chicago Press.

Marshall, T. H. (1977), *Class, Citizenship and Development*, Chicago, IL: University of Chicago Press.

Marx, Karl (n.d.), 'The Eighteenth Brumaire of Louis Napoleon,' *Selected Works*, New York, 2, 415.

——— (1977), *Critique of Hegel's Philosophy of Right*, Joseph O'Malley (ed.), Cambridge, UK: Cambridge University Press.

Mayer, Peter (2001), 'Human Development and Civic Community in India: Making Democracy Perform,' *Economic and Political Weekly*, 36(8), (24 February) 684–92.

McConnell, Michael (1992), 'Accommodation of Religion: An Update and a Response to the Critics,' *George Washington Law Review*, 60 (March) 685–742.

Menon, Dileep (1995), *Caste, Community and the Nation: Malabar, 1900–1948*, Cambridge, UK: Cambridge University Press.

Michelman, Frank (1988), 'Law's Republic,' *Yale Law Journal* 97, 1493.

Miller, J. (1996), *God Has Ninety-Nine Names: Reporting From a Militant Middle East*, New York: Simon and Schuster.

Mirsky, Yehudah (1993), 'Democratic Politics, Democratic Culture,' *Orbis*, 37(4), 567–80.

Mohanty, Monoranjan (1998), 'Social Movements in Creative Society: Of

Autonomy and Interconnection,' in Mohanty, Mukherjee and Tornquist (eds.), *People's Rights: Social Movements and the State in the Third World*, Delhi: Sage.

Mohapatra, Bishnu (1999), 'Social Connectedness, Civility and Democracy: A View from an Orissan Village,' paper presented at 'Democracy and Social Capital in Segmented Societies: The Third International Conference,' Sweden: Vasasalen, Uppsala University.

Montesquieu, Baron du. (1964), *De l'Esprit des Lois*, Paris: Seuil.

Morris, Matthew (1998), *Social Capital and Poverty in India*, IDS Working Paper 61, University of Sussex, Brighton, UK.

Mouffe, Chantal (1992), *Dimensions of Radical Democracy*, London: Verso.

Muntarbhorn, Vital (1993), *Human Rights in Southeast Asia. A Challenge for the 21ˢᵗ Century*, Bangkok: Chaiyong Limthongkul Foundation.

Murthy, Srinivasan B. (ed.) (1987), *Mahatma Gandhi and Leo Tolstoy Letters*, Long Beach, CA: Long Beach Publications.

Muslih, M. (1995), 'Palestinian Civil Society', in A. R. Norton (ed.), *Civil Society in the Middle East*, Leiden: E. F. Brill, 1, 243–68.

Mutchler, D. (1971), *The Church as a Political Force in Latin America*, New York: Praeger.

Narayan, Deepa and Michael Woolcock (2000), 'Social Capital: Implications for Development Theory, Research and Policy,' *World Bank Research Observer*, 15 (August).

Norton, A. R. (ed.) (1995–6), *Civil Society in the Middle East*, 1 & 2, Leiden: E. F. Brill.

O'Donnell, Guillermo (1973), *Modernization and Bureaucratic-Authoritarianism*, Berkeley, CA: Institute of International Studies, University of California.

———— (1993), 'On the State, Democratization and Some Conceptual Problems: A Latin American View with Glances at Some Postcommunist Countries', *World Development*, 21(8), 1355–69.

O'Donnell, G. and P. C. Schmitter (1986), *Transitions from Authoritarian Rule: Tentative Conclusions about Uncertain Democracies*, Baltimore, MD: Johns Hopkins University Press.

Offe, Claus (1985), 'New Social Movements: Challenging the Boundaries of Institutional Politics,' *Social Research* 52 (4) (Winter), 817–68.

———— (2000), 'Civil Society and Social Order: Demarcating and Combining Market, State and Community', *Archives Europeennes de Sociologie*, 41, 71–94.

Oi, Jean (1992), 'Fiscal Reform and the Economic Foundations of Local State Corporatism in China', *World Politics*, 45(1), (October), 99–126.

Okin, Susan (1989), *Justice, Gender, and the Family*, New York: Basic Books.

Olson, Mancur (1982), *The Rise and Decline of Nations: Economic Growth, Stagflation and Social Rigidities*, New Haven, CT: Yale University Press.

Omvedt, G. (ed.) (1982), *Land, Caste and Politics in Indian States*, New Delhi: Authors Guild.

Ostrom, Elinor (1998), 'A Behavioral Approach to the Rational Choice Theory of Collective Action', *American Political Science Review*, 92, 1–22.

Owen, R. (1985), *Migrant Workers in the Gulf*, London: Minority Rights Group.

Oxhorn, Philip (1995a), *Organizing Civil Society: The Popular Sectors and the Struggle for Democracy*, University Park, PA: Pennsylvania State University Press.

———— (1995b), 'From Controlled Inclusion to Coerced Marginalization: The Struggle for Civil Society in Latin America,' in John Hall (ed.), *Civil Society: Theory, History, Comparison*, Cambridge UK: Polity Press.

Palmer, M., A. Leila, and E. S. Yassin (1988), *The Egyptian Bureaucracy*, Cairo: The American University of Cairo Press.

Pandey, G. (1990), *The Construction of Communalism in North India*, New Delhi: Oxford University Press.

Parekh, Bikhu (1993), 'The Cultural Particularity of Liberal Democracy,' in David Held (ed.), *Prospects for Democracy North South East West*, Cambridge: Polity Press, 1993.

Parsons, Talcott (1965), 'Full Citizenship for the Negro American?', *Daedalus*, 94(4), 1009–54.

Paul, S. (2002), *Holding the State to Account: Citizen Monitoring in Action*, Bangalore: Books for Change.

Pelczynki, Z. A. (1971), 'The Hegelian Conception of the State' in *Hegel's Political Philosophy: Problems and Perspectives*, Cambridge, UK: Cambridge University Press.

———— (1984), 'Nation, Civil Society, State: Hegelian Sources of the Marxian Non-Theory of Nationality,' *The State and Civil Society: Studies in Hegel's Political Philosophy*, Cambridge, UK: Cambridge University Press.

Poole, Michael (1990), 'Geographical Location of Political Violence in Northern Ireland,' in John Darby, Nicholas Dodge, and A. C. Hepburn (eds.) *Political Violence: Ireland in Comparative Perspective*, Belfast: Appletree Press.

Portes, A. and Kincaid (1985), 'The Crisis of Authoritarianism: State and Civil Society in Argentina, Chile, and Uruguay', *Research in Political Sociology*, 1.

Portney, Kent and Jeffrey Barry (2001), 'Social Capital and the City,' Edwards, Foley and Diani (eds.), *Beyond Tocqueville*, Hanover: University Press of England.

Prabhu, R. K. and U. R. Rao (1967), *The Mind of Mahatma Gandhi*, Ahmedabad: Navajivan Press.

Prasad, Rajendra (1956), 'Gandhi in Bihar,' in Homer Jack (ed.), *The Gandhi Reader*, Bloomington, IN: University of Indiana Press, 149–59.

Przeworski, A. (1991), *Democracy and the Market: Political and Economic Reforms in Eastern Europe and Latin America*, Cambridge, UK: Cambridge University Press.

Putnam, Robert D. (1993), *Making Democracy Work: Civic Traditions in Italy*, Princeton, NJ: Princeton University Press.

———— (1995), 'Bowling Alone: America's Declining Social Capital,' *Journal of Democracy*, 6 (1).

———— (1996), 'The Strange Disappearance of Civic America,' *American Prospect*, 8 (Winter).

———— (2000), *Bowling Alone*, New York: Simon and Schuster.

Raeff, Marc (1983), *The Well-Ordered Police State*, New Haven, CT: Yale University Press.

Rahnema, Majid (1989), 'Shifting [sic] the Wheat from the Chaff,' *New Asian Visions*, 6(1), 5–13.

Ramanujan, A. K. (1991), 'Introduction,' *Folktales from India: A Selection of Oral Tales from Twenty-two Languages*, New York: Pantheon.

Rawls, John (1971), *A Theory of Justice*, Cambridge, MA: Harvard University Press.

Reintges, Claudia M. (1990), 'Urban Movements in South African Black Townships: A Case Study,' *International Journal of Urban and Regional Research*, 14(1), 1990, 109–34.

Reitzes, Maxine (1994), 'Civil Society, the Public Sphere and the State: Reflections on Classical and Contemporary Discourse,' *Theoria*, 83/84, 95–121.

Remmer, K. (1991), *Military Rule in Latin America*, Boulder, CO: Westview Press.

Retzlaf, Ralph (1962), *Village Government in India*, Bombay: Asia Publishing House.

Richards, A. and J. Waterbury (1990), *A Political Economy of the Middle East*, Boulder, CO: Westview Press.

Richards, G. (1986), 'Stablization Crises and the Breakdown of Military Authoritarianism in Latin America', *Comparative Political Studies*, 18(4), 449–85.

Robison, Richard (1993), 'Mahathir Paints False Picture of Asian Region,' *The Australian* (14 December).

Rodan, Garry (1992), 'Singapore's Leadership Transition: Erosion or Refinement of Authoritarian Rule?,' *Bulletin of Concerned Asian Studies*, 24(1), 3–17.

————— (1995), *Ideological Convergences Across 'East' and 'West': The New Conservative Offensive*, Department of Development and Planning, Aalborg University Denmark.

————— (1996a), 'Theorising Political Opposition in East and Southeast Asia,' in *Political Oppositions in Industrialising Asia*, London: Routledge.

————— (1996b), 'The Internationalisation of Ideological Conflict: Asia's New Significance,' *The Pacific Review*, 9(3), 328–51.

————— (1996c), 'The Prospects for Civil Society in Southeast Asia,' University of Toronto-York University Joint Centre for Asia-Pacific Studies.

————— (1997), 'Civil Society and Other Political Possibilities in Southeast Asia,' *Journal of Contemporary Asia*, 27(2).

Rodan, Garry and Kevin Hewison (1996), 'A "Clash of Cultures" or the Convergence of Political Ideology?' in Richard Robison (ed.), *Pathways to Asia: The Politics of Engagement*, Sydney: Allen and Unwin.

Rogowski, Robert (1995), 'Symposium on *Designing Social Inquiry*,' *American Political Science Review*, 89 (June).

Rosenblum, Nancy L. (1987), 'Studying Authority: Keeping Pluralism in Mind,' in J. Roland Pennock and John W. Chapman (eds.), *Nomos XXIX: Authority Revisited*, New York: New York University Press, 102–30.

————— (1989), *Liberalism and the Moral Life*, Cambridge, MA: Harvard University Press.

————— (1993a), 'The Moral Uses of Pluralism: Freedom of Association and Liberal Virtue Illustrated with Cases on Religious Exemption and Accommodation,' The University Center for Human Values, Princeton University.

————— (1993b), 'The Moral Uses of Civil Society,' *PEGS: The Newsletter of the Committee on the Political Economy of the Good Society*, 3 (Summer), 5–6.

————— (1994), 'Democratic Character and Community: The Logic of Congruence,' *Journal of Political Philosophy*, 2, 67–97.

Rothstein, Bo (ed.) (1995), *Demokrati som Dialog (Democracy as dialogue)*, Stockholm: SNS Forlag.

Rousseau, Jean Jacques (1968), *The Social Contract*, Harmondsworth: Penguin Books.

Rowe, William T. (1993), 'The Problem of "Civil Society" in Late Imperial China,' *Modern China*, 19/2 (April), 139–57.

Rudolph, Lloyd I. (1956), 'The Origin of Party: From the Politics of Status to the Politics of Opinion in Eighteenth Century England and America,' Ph.D. Dissertation, Department of Government, Harvard University, Cambridge: MA.

Rudolph, Lloyd I. and Susanne Hoeber Rudolph (1967), *The Modernity of Tradition; Political Development in India*, Chicago, IL: University of Chicago Press.

———— (1987), *In Pursuit of Lakshmi*, Chicago, IL: University of Chicago Press.

Rudolph, Susanne Hoeber (1971), 'Gandhi's Lieutenants–Varieties of Followership,' in Paul Powers (ed.), *The Meaning of Gandhi*, Hawai, HI: Hawai University Press, 41–58.

———— (2000), 'Civil Society and the Realm of Freedom,' *Economic and Political Weekly*, 35(20), 17(62–9)

Rudolph, Susanne Hoeber and James Piscatori (eds.) (1997), *Transnational Religion and Fading States*, Boulder, CO: Westview Press.

Rudolph, Susanne Hoeber and Lloyd Rudolph (2000), *Reversing the Gaze: The Amar Singh Diary, A Native Subject's Narrative of Imperial India*, New Delhi: Oxford University Press.

Rueschmeyer, D., E. H. Stephens, and J. D. Stephens (eds.) (1992), *Capitalist Development and Democracy*, Chicago, IL: University of Chicago Press.

Ryan, Mary (1992), 'Gender and Public Access: Women's Politics in Nineteenth Century', Craig Calhoun (ed.), *Habermas and the Public Sphere*, Cambridge, MA: MIT Press.

Sachs, J., A. Varshney, and N. Bajpai (eds.) (1999), *India in the Era of Economic Reforms*, New Delhi: Oxford University Press.

Sadowski, Yahya (1993), 'The New Orientalism and the Democracy Debate,' *Middle East Report*, 23(4), 14–20.

Salect, Renata (1992), 'Nationalism, Anti-Semitism, and Anti-Feminism in Eastern Europe,' *New German Critique*, 57, 51–65.

Sasono, Adi (1989), 'NGOs [sic] Roles and Social Movement in Developing Democracy: The Southeast Asian Experiences,' *New Asian Visions*, 6(1), 14–26.

Savarkar, V. D. (1969), *Hindutva! Who is a Hindu?*, Bombay: Veer Savarkar Prakashan, first published 1923.

Schneider, C. (1995), *Shantytown Protest in Pinochet's Chile*, Philadelphia, PA: Temple University Press.

Scott, James (1978), *Moral Economy of the Peasant*, New Haven, CT: Yale University Press.

Seidman, Steven (ed.) (1989), *Jurgen Habermas on Society and Politics: A Reader*, Boston, MA: Beacon Press.

Seizer, Susan (1997), 'Dramatic License: Negotiating Stigma on and off the Tamil Popular Stage (India)', PhD dissertation in the Department of Anthropology, University of Chicago, Chicago, IL.

Seligman, Adam (1992), *The Idea of Civil Society*, Princeton NJ: Princeton University Press.

Sharp, Gene (1973), *The Politics of Non-violent Action, Part I: Power and Struggle*, Boston MA: Peter Sargent.

Shils, Edward (1991), 'The Virtue of Civil Society,' *Government and Opposition* 26(1), 3–20.

———— (1997), *The Virtue of Civility*, Indianapolis, IN: Liberty Fund.

Shklar, Judith (1991), *American Citizenship: The Quest for Inclusion*, Cambridge, MA: Harvard University Press.

Shubane, Khehla (1992), 'Civil Society in Apartheid and Post-Apartheid South Africa, *Theoria*, 79, 33–42.

Shue, Vivienne (1989), 'Emerging State-Society Relations in Rural China', mimeo, European Conference on Agricultural and Rural Development in China, Sandbjerg Castle, Denmark.

———— (1994) 'State Power and Social Organization in China,' in J. Migdal, A. Kohli and V. Shue (eds.), *State Power and Social Forces: Domination and Transformation in the Third World*, Cambridge: UK: Cambridge University Press, 65–88.

Suu Kyi, Aung San (1994), 'Empowerment for a Culture of Peace and Development,' address to World Commission on Culture and Development, 21 November 1994 (presented on behalf of the author by Corazon Aquino).

Skilling, H. Gordon (1988), 'Parallel Polis, or An Independent Society in Central and Eastern Europe: An Inquiry,' *Social Research*, 55: 1–2 (Spring/Summer), 211–46.

Smith, B. (1982), *The Church and Politics in Chile*, Princeton, NJ: Princeton University Press.

Smith, P. (1995), 'The Changing Agenda for Social Science Research on Latin America', in *Latin America in Comparative Perspective: New Approaches to Methods and Analysis*, Boulder, CO: Westview Press.

Solinger, Dorothy J. (1992), 'Urban Entrepreneurs and the State: The Merger of State and Society' in A. L. Rosenbaum (ed.), *State and Society in China: The Consequencs of Reform*, Oxford: Westview Press.

Spalding, R. (1981), 'The Mexican Variant of Corporatism', *Comparative Political Studies*, 14, 139–61.

Spivak, Gayatri (1998), 'Can the Subaltern Speak?' in Cary Nelson and Larry Grossberg (eds.), *Marxism and the Interpretation of Culture*, Chicago, IL: University of Illinois Press, 271–313.

Spulbeck, S. (1996), 'Anti-Semitism and the Fear of the Public Sphere in Post-Totalitarian Societies: East Germany,' in C. Hann and E. Dunn (eds.), *Civil Society: Challenging Western Models*, London: Routledge.

Srinivas, M. N. (1955), 'The Social System of a Mysore Village' in McKim Marriott (ed.), *Village India*, Chicago IL: University of Chicago Press.

————— (1979), *Remembered Village*, Berkeley, CA: University of California Press.

Steadman, John(1969), *The Myth of Asia*, London: Macmillan

Stepan, Alfred (1978), *The State and Society: Peru in Comparative Perspective*, Princeton NJ: Princeton University Press.

————— (1985), 'State Power and the Strength of Civil Society in the Southern Cone of Latin America', in P. Evans, D. Rueschemeyer and T. Skocpol (eds.), *Bringing the State Back In*, New York: Cambridge University Press.

————— (1988), *Rethinking Military Politics: Brazil and the Southern Cone*, Princeton: NJ: Princeton University Press.

Steward, John (1996), 'Democracy and Local Government' in P. Hirst and S. Khilnani (eds.), *Reivueating Democracy*, Oxford: Blackwell.

Stolle, Dietlind (2000), Communities, Citizens, and Local Government. Paper for LOS workshop 'Investigating Social Capital', Solstrand (18–21 May).

Strand, David (1993), 'Calling the Chinese People to Order: Images of State and Society in the *Sanmin zhuyi* of Sun Yat-sen,' paper presented to conference on 'State and Society in East Asia' at University of Copenhagen, 29 April–2 May.

Sullivan, D. (1992), 'Extra-state Actors and Privatization in Egypt', in I. Harik and D. Sullivan (eds.), *Privatization and Liberalization in the Middle East*, Bloomington, IN: Indiana University Press.

Sullivan, Kathleen (1988), 'Rainbow Republicanism,' *Yale Law Journal*, 97, 1713.

Sunstein, Cass (1988), 'Beyond the Republican Revival,' *Yale Law Journal*, 97, 1593.

Tandon, R. and R. Mohanty (2002), *Civil Society and Governance*, New Delhi: Samskriti.

Tapper, R. (1990), 'Anthropologists, Historians, and Tribes People on Tribe and State Formation in the Middle East', in A. R. Norton (ed.), *Tribes and State Formation in the Middle East*, Berkeley, CA: University of California Press.

Tarrow, Sidney (1996), 'Making Social Science Work Across Space and Time: A Critical Reflection on Robert Putnam's Making Democracy Work,' *American Political Science Review*, 90(2), 389–97.

Taylor, Charles (1990), 'Modes of Civil Society,' *Public Culture*, 3(1), 59–118.

Taylor, Richard W. (1986), 'Modern Indian Ashrams,' *Religion and Society*, 33 (September).

Tester, K. (1992), *Civil Society*, London: Routledge.

Thompson, E. P. (1968), *The Making of the English Working Class*, Harmondworth: Penguin Press.

Tripp, Aili Mari (2000), 'Political Reform in Tanzania: The Struggle for Associational Autonomy,' *Comparative Politics*, 32(2), 191–215.

Unia, P. (1991), 'Social Action Group Strategies in the Indian Subcontinent,' *Development in Practice*, 1(2), 84–96.

Valenzuela, J. and A. Valenzuela (eds.) (1986), *Military Rule in Chile: Dictatorship and Opposition*, Baltimore, MD: Johns Hopkins University Press.

van der Veer, P. (1994), *Religious Nationalism: Hindus and Muslims in India*, Berkeley, CA: University of California Press.

Van Rooy, A. (ed.) (1998), *Civil Society and the Aid Industry*, London: Earthscan, 6–30.

Vanourek, Gregg, Scott Hamilton and Chester Finn (1996), *Is There Life after Big Government? The Potential of Civil Society*, Indianapolis, IN: Hudson Institute.

Varshney, Ashutosh (2000), 'Is India Becoming More Democratic?' *Journal of Asian Studies*, 59, 3–25.

———— (2002), *Ethnic Conflict and Civic Life: Hindus and Muslims in India*, New Delhi: Oxford University Press.

Veliz, C. (1976), *The Politics of Conformity in Latin America*, London: Oxford University Press.

Verba, Sidney, Norman Nie, and Jae-on Kim (1978), *Participation and Political Equality: A Seven Nation Comparison*, Cambridge: Cambridge University Press.

Vilas, Carlos M. (1996), 'Prospects for Democratization in a Post-Revolutionary Setting: Central America, *Journal of Latin American Studies*, 28 (2), 461–503.

Violante, Luciano (ed.) (1996), *Mafie e antimafia: Rapporto '96*, Rome: Laterza.

Vogel, Ezra (1989), *One Step Ahead: Guangdong Under Reform*, Cambridge, MA: Harvard University Press.

Wadley, Susan (1994), *Struggling With Destiny in Karimpur; 1925–1984*, Berkeley, CA: University of California Press.

Wagley, C. (1968), 'The Dilemma of the Latin America Middle Class', in *The Latin American Tradition*, New York: Columbia University Press, 194–212.

Wakeman, Frederic Jun (1993), 'The Civil Society and Public Sphere Debate: Western Reflections on Chinese Political Culture,' *Modern China*, 19/2 (April).

Walder, Andrew G. (n.d.), 'Popular Protest in the 1989 Democracy Movement: The Pattern of Grassroots Organisation,' Seminar Series of the Universities Service Centre, Chinese University of Hong Kong.

Walzer, Michael (1983), *Spheres of Justice: A Defense of Pluralism and Equality*, New York: Basic Books.

———— (1991), 'The Idea of Civil Society,' *Dissent* 38 (Spring).

———— (1992), *What It Means to Be American?*, New York: Marsilio.

Wank, David (1992), 'Symbiotic Alliance of Entrepreneurs and Officials,' paper presented to conference, Arden House, Harriman, New York, (25–30 August).

———— (1995), 'Private Business, Bureaucracy and Political Alliance in a Chinese City,' *Australian Journal of Chinese Affairs*, 33 (January), 55–71.

Warner, Michael (1990), *The Letters of the Republic: Publication and the Public Sphere in Eighteenth Century America*, Cambridge, MA: Harvard University Press.

Weber, Max (1958), *The Religion of India: Hinduism and Buddhism*. New York: The Free Press.

Weffort, F. (1992), *Qual Democracia?* São Paulo: Companhia Das Letras, 42–69.

Weiner, Myron (1978), *Sons of the Soil*, Princeton NJ: Princeton University Press.

Weller, Robert (1998), 'Horizontal Ties and Civil Institutions in Chinese Societies,' Robert Hefner (ed.), *Democratic Civility*, New Brunswick NJ: Transaction Publisher.

White, Gordon (1978), 'Politics and Social Status in China', *Pacific Affairs*, 51/4 (Winter), 561–84.

———— (1987), 'The Impact of Economic Reforms in the Chinese Countryside: Toward the Politics of Social Capitalism', *Modern China*, 13/1 (October), 411–40.

———— (1991), 'Basic Level Government and Economic Reform in Urban China,' in *The Chinese State in the Era of Economic Reform: The Road to Crisis*, London: Macmillan.

———— (1993), *Riding the Tiger: The Politics of Economic Reform in Post-Mao China* London: Macmillan.

———— (1994), 'Civil Society, Democratization and Development (I)', *Democratization*, 1(3), (Autumn).

———— (1995), 'Civil Society, Democratization and Development (II)' *Democratization* 2(2), (Summer).

White, Gordon, Jude Howell and Shang Xiaoyuan (1996), *In Search of Civil Society*, Oxford: Clarendon Press.

Wilmer, Clive (2000), 'Go to Nature,' *Times Literary Supplement* (7 April), 3–4.

Wilson, P. and D. Graham (1994), *Saudi Arabia: The Coming Storm*, Armonk, NY: ME Sharpe.

Whyte, M. K. and W. L. Parish (1984), *Urban Life in Contemporary China*, Chicago, IL: University of Chicago Press.

Wood, Ellen Meiksins (1990), 'The Uses and Abuses of "Civil Society",' *Socialist Register*, London: The Merlin Press, 60–84.

Xu Dingxin and Qian Xiaochuan (1991), *A History of Shanghai General Chamber of Commerce (Shanghai Zongshanghui Shi)*, Shanghai: Social Science Press.

Yamagishi, Toshio and Yamagishi, Midori (1994), Trust and Commitment in the United States and Japan, *Motivation and Emotion*, 18, 129–66

Young, W. Crawford (1976), *The Politics of Pluralism*, Madison, WI: University of Wisconsin Press.

Young, Iris (1987), 'Impartiality and the Civic Public: Some Implications of Feminist Critiques of Moral and Political Theory' in Seyla Benhabib and Drucilla Cornell (eds.), *Feminism as Critique*, Minneapolis MN: University of Minnesota Press, 56–76.

———— (1989), 'The Ideal of Community and the Politics of Difference,' in Linda J. Nicholson (ed.), *Feminism and Postmodernism*, New York: Routledge, Chapman and Hall, 300–23.

———— (1990), *Justice and the Politics of Difference*, Princeton, NJ: Princeton University Press.

Zakaria, Fareed (1994), 'Culture is Destiny: A Conversation with Lee Kuan Yew,' *Foreign Affairs*, 73(2), 109–26.

Zavos, J. (1999), 'Searching for Hindu Nationalism in Modern Indian History: Analysis of Some Early Ideological Developments', *Economic and Political Weekly*, 34(32) (7 August), 2069–76.

AUTHOR INDEX

SUBJECT INDEX

ACWF, 295
Absolute monarchies, 47–8
Abstract rights, 172–3, 174
Academics, 152
Accountability, 104
Age of Consent Act, 401
Agora Project, 405
Agrarian society, 431
Agricultural-export economies, 336
Agriculture, decollectivization of, 274
Alienation, theory of, 58
Aliran, 321
All China Federation of Trade Unions (ACFTU), 283
All-China Qigong Association, 290
All China Women's Federation (ACWF), 283
All India Backward Classes Commission, 199
All India Spinners Association, 377
All India Village Industries Association, 377
American liberalism, 107
American society, 12
Anglo-American civil society, 391
Anti-capitalist ideologies, 359
Anti-democratic elites, 336, 359, 368

Anti-government movements, 268
Anti-Muslim sentiment, 364
Anti-Politics, 77
Anti-poverty programme, 422
Arab Socialist Union, 346
Arya Samaj, 363
Ascriptive identities, 180, 186, 219, 427, 431
Ascriptive markers, 147
Ashram as,
    coffee house and, 399–404
    exemplar of imagined society, 395–9
    public sphere, 390–3
    training academy for non-violent cadres, 393–5
Asia, elite culture in, 311–15
Asian alternative, 306, 312, 315, 323
Asian Century, 311
Asian culture, 310–11, 316
Asian renaissance, 311
Asian values, 306–12, 315–17
    revival of, 306–11
    western support for, 315–17
Association, freedom of, 154
Association of Democratic Women, Chile, 332